ISTANBUL

Also by Bettany Hughes

The Hemlock Cup: Socrates, Athens and the Search for the Good Life

Helen of Troy: Goddess, Princess, Whore

ISTANBUL

A Tale of Three Cities

BETTANY HUGHES

DA CAPO PRESS

Cataloging-in-Publication data for this book is available from the Library of Congress.

First Da Capo Press edition 2017
Reprinted by arrangement with Weidenfeld & Nicolson, an imprint of
The Orion Publishing Group Ltd., an Hachette UK Company
ISBN: 978-0-306-82584-2 (hardcover)
ISBN: 978-0-306-82585-9 (e-book)

Published by Da Capo Press
www.dacapopress.com

Da Capo Press books are available at special discounts for bulk purchases in the U.S. by corporations, institutions, and other organizations. For more information, please contact the Special Markets Department at Perseus Books, 2300 Chestnut Street, Suite 200, Philadelphia, PA 19103, or call (800) 810-4145, ext. 5000, or e-mail special.markets@perseusbooks.com.

10 9 8 7 6 5 4 3 2 1

For Jane and Karl – who sustain me body and soul.
For Robin Lane Fox who gave me hope.
And for those who can no longer walk the streets of Istanbul.

CONTENTS

✤

LIST OF ILLUSTRATIONS AND MAPS   xiii

PROLOGUE   xix

NOTE ON NAMES   xxv

INTRODUCTION   I

PART ONE: Byzantion, Byzas' City, 800,000 BC – AD 311   7

1. Bones, Stones and Mud   15
2. City of the Blind   19
3. City of Light   26
4. Persian Fire   31
5. City of Siege   41
6. Wine and Witches   49
7. All Roads Lead from Rome: The Egnatian Way   59
8. The Enemy Within   71
9. Persecution   76
10. The Meek Shall Inherit the Earth   80

PART TWO: Constantinople, City of God, AD 311–475   87

11. The Battle of Milvian Bridge   95
12. City of Gold   99
13. In the Name of Christ's Blood   106
14. Queen of Cities   111
15. Faith, Hope, Charity and the Nicene Creed   116
16. Helena   123

17. Births and Deaths   128
18. Pagans and Pretenders   133
19. The Problem with Goths   141
20. A Dove of Peace or a Fist of Iron: Theodosios   146
21. Battles in Heaven and on Earth: Gaza and Alexandria   154
22. Christian Particles in a Pagan Atmosphere: Nova Roma   162
23. Statues in the Sky: Ascetics   168
24. Sex and the City: Eunuchs   172
25. The Sack of Old Rome: The Problem with Goths,
    Part Two   177
26. Vandals, Wisdom and Attila the Hun   182

PART THREE: The New Rome, AD 476–565   191

27. City of the Mother of God   197
28. The Golden Age   205
29. Earthquakes and Fires   216
30. The Phoenix City   222
31. Spectacular, Spectacular   230
32. Law and Order   234
33. The Jewish City   239
34. The Classical City   243
35. All Is Vanity   248

PART FOUR: The World's Desire, AD 565–1050   257

36. The Silkworm's Journey   265
37. Al-Qustantiniyya   274
38. A Bone in the Throat of Allah   279
39. Monks by Night, Lions by Day   287
40. Byzantium and Britannia   291
41. Icons and Iconoclasm   299
42. Viking Foe-Friends and the Birth of Russia   306
43. Within the Walls   315
44. The Varangian Guard   321

PART FIVE: City of War, AD 1050–1320   327

45. A Great Schism?   335
46. 1071, 1081 and All That   339
47. The City of Crusades   346
48. Negotiating Monks and Homicidal Usurpers   352
49. Venetian Peril, Chivalric Kingdoms   358

PART SIX: Allah's City, AD 1320–AD 1575 (Islamic Calendar 720–983)   369

50. Yıldırım: The Thunderbolt   377
51. No Country for Old Men   387
52. Twilight City   393
53. The Abode of Felicity   398
54. One God in Heaven, One Empire on Earth   406
55. Renaissance City   416
56. A Garden of Mixed Fruit   423
57. A Diamond between Two Sapphires   432
58. The Muslim Millennium   441

PART SEVEN: Imperial City, AD 1550–1800 (Islamic Calendar 957–1215)   449

59. Gunpowder Empires and Gunning Personalities: Dragomans and Eunuchs   455
60. The Sultanate of Women   461
61. The Janissaries   468
62. The Great Siege of Vienna   474
63. The White Slave Trade and the White Plague   482
64. White Caucasians   488
65. Soap and Smallpox   493
66. Tulips and Textiles   499

PART EIGHT: City of Revolt and Opportunity, AD 1800 (Islamic Calendar 1215) onwards   507

67. O Love! Young Love!   513
68. Massacre   518

69. Revolution   524
70. Tsargrad   532
71. Scutari   538
72. One-Way Traffic   546
73. A Sick Man in the Rose Garden   552
74. Gallipoli: The End of an Empire   559
75. The Red Apple   576
76. The Catastrophe   582
77. The Last Caliph   587
78. Global Futures   592

Coda   601

Acknowledgements   603
Timeline   605
Appendix: The Other Roman Empires   634
Notes   638
Bibliography   705
Index   763

A diamond mounted between two sapphires and two emeralds ... the precious stone in the ring of a vast dominion which embraced the entire world. THE DREAM OF OSMAN, C. AD 1280[1]

Those who had never seen Constantinople before gazed very intently at the city, never having imagined there could be such a place in the world. GEOFFREY DE VILLEHARDOUIN, FOURTH CRUSADE, AD 1204[2]

If one had but a single glance to give the world, one should gaze on Istanbul. ALPHONSE DE LAMARTINE, POET, WRITER AND STATESMAN AD 1790–1869[3]

O, my God! Let this town flourish to the end of time. SULTAN MURAD IV, AD 1638[4]

ILLUSTRATIONS AND MAPS

❖

PAGE

21 Jug from Fenerbahçe Yacht Harbour *(Courtesy of Şevket Dönmez)*

35 Engraving of Pausanias, c. 1880 *(Alamy)*

37 *Top:* the Serpent Column, c. 1752 *(American School of Classical Studies at Athens, Gennadius Library)*; *bottom:* remains of the Serpent Column *(Mary Evans)*

54 Byzantine coin, c. first century AD *(Classical Numismatic Group Inc., www.cngcoins.com)*

67 Reconstruction of the Milion *(Greek Strategos/Creative Commons)*

82 The Arras medallion *(British Museum)*

97 Symbols used on the shields of northern European tribes c. AD 300 *(Private collection)*

126 Bronze medallion of Helena *(Alamy)*

127 Constantine crowned by Tyche, fourth century AD *(Hermitage Museum)*

138 Relief showing investiture of Ardashir II *(Alamy)*

149 Boats from the Theodosian harbour excavation *(top: Institute of Nautical Archaeology; bottom: Istanbul University)*

156 Bronze steelyard weight in the form of a bust *(Met Museum)*

170 Relief of a Stylite saint *(Alamy)*

199 Anatolian sun goddess *(Getty)*

207 Mosaic of Empress Theodora *(Alamy)*

224 Woodcut of the Haghia Sophia *(Alamy)*

226 Reconstruction of the Column of Justinian *(Antoine Helbert)*

228 The imperial district of Byzantine Constantinople *(Cplakidas/Creative Commons)*

232 Ivory diptych, AD 517 *(Alamy)*

270 Imitation Byzantine coins from Xinjiang, China *(British Museum)*

271 Engraving of the Nestorian Stele, 1887 *(Alamy)*

295 Byzantine copper coinage from Rendlesham, Suffolk *(Suffolk County Council)*

313 The Piraeus Lion *(Private collection)*

325 A Byzantine woman spearing a Varangian guardsman *(Biblioteca Nacional de España)*

363 Engraving of hippodrome and Christian monuments of Constantinople *(Alamy)*

381 Map of Constantinople from the *Liber Insularum Archipelagi (Bridgeman)*

389 Urban cannon in the Istanbul military museum *(Alamy)*

396 Gennadius II and Sultan Mehmed II *(Getty)*

401 Map of Topkapı Palace by Antoine Ignace Melling *(Courtesy of the University of St Andrews Library, rfx DR724.M4)*

410 The Sürre travelling through Damascus, c. 1895 *(University of California/ HathiTrust)*

414 Funeral procession of Joachim III, 1912 *(Alamy)*

418 Sketches for Galata bridge by Leonardo da Vinci *(RMN/Bibliothèque de l'Institut de France)*

425 Greek, Syrian and Ottoman women, engraving, 1581 *(Bibliothèque nationale de France)*

435 Boats on the waterways of Istanbul *(Alamy)*

439 Süleyman the Lawgiver's procession through the Atmeidan *(British Museum)*

444 The Great Comet over Istanbul *(Topkapı Palace Museum Library)*

471 Janissary soldiers *(Getty Images)*

485 *The Slave Market, Constantinople* by William Allan *(Getty)*

492 Photo card of 'Zumiya the Egyptian', c. 1870. *(Greg French Early Photography)*

497 Regency fashions, 1805 *(Mary Evans/Alamy)*

501 Tulip-patterned tiles *(Alamy)*

503 View of Constantinople by Antoine Ignace Melling *(Courtesy of the University of St Andrews Library, rfx DR724.M4)*

522 *The Massacre at Chios* by Eugene Delacroix *(Getty)*

526 Nusretiye Mosque, c. 1900 *(Getty)*

528 Galata Bridge, late nineteenth century *(Library of Congress)*

530 *Top: Fishermen's houses on the Bosphorus* by Edward Lear *(Bridgeman)*; bottom: Daguerrotype *(Bibliothèque nationale de France)*

534 Cartoon of Catherine the Great *(Royal Collection)*

543 Royal Navy ratings at the top of Galata Tower *(Imperial War Museum)*

547 The future Edward VII near the Sea of Galilee *(Royal Collection)*

554 Submarines in Taşkizak dockyards *(Smithsonian Museum)*

562 German cruisers *Breslau* and *Goeben* in the bay at Constantinople, c. 1915 *(Getty)*

567 Anzac Beach, Gallipoli, by Charles Snodgrass Ryan *(Australian War Memorial)*

571 War orphans sheltering in a mosque *(SALT Research)*

573 Mustafa Kemal Atatürk, c. 1915 *(Alamy)*

575 Map of the Sykes-Picot agreement *(The National Archives)*

578 Hunger map of Europe, 1918 *(Library of Congress)*

584 Greek refugees leaving Istanbul, 1922 *(Getty)*

590 The Princess of Berar *(Imperial War Museum)*

596 A master working on the dome of Süleymaniye Mosque *(SALT Research, Ali Saim Ülgen Archive)*

599 Graffiti on a shop window *(Author's collection)*

PLATE SECTIONS

✦

SECTION ONE

Neolithic footprint from Yenikapı excavations *(Istanbul Archaeological Museum)*
The fishermen of Constantinople, Codex Matritensis of Skylitzes *(Alamy)*
Tondo portrait of Septimius Severus *(Bridgeman)*
Christ depicted as the sun god Helios *(Alamy)*
Constantinople as Tyche *(British Museum)*
Illumination said to show Julian the Apostate's flayed body *(British Library)*
The Peutinger map *(Bridgeman)*
Mosaic portrait of Emperor Justinian *(Getty)*
The Desborough necklace *(British Museum)*
Mosaics from the Great Palace *(Alamy)*
Illustration of the interior of a synagogue in Constantinople *(Alamy)*

SECTION TWO

Greek Fire, Codex Matritensis of Skylitzes *(Bridgeman)*
The burial shroud of Charlemagne *(Bridgeman)*
A panel commemorating the end of iconoclasm in Constantinople *(Bridgeman)*
A philosophy school in Constantinople, Codex Matritensis of Skylitzes *(Alamy)*
Siege of Constantinople from a chronicle by Jean Chartier *(Bibliothèque nationale de France)*
Seated Scribe by Giovanni Bellini *(Bridgeman)*
Miniature of Istanbul by Matrakci Nasuh *(Alamy)*
Ottoman troops laying siege to Vienna *(Getty)*
Ali Pasha depicted in a German newspaper *(V&A)*
Feast for the Valide Sultan, Ottoman watercolour *(Bridgeman)*

Parade of Confectioner's Guild and the Parade of Road-Sweepers, from the
Surname i-Vehbi *(Topkapı Palace Museum Library)*

SECTION THREE

Western visitors to Constantinople *(Walters Art Museum)*
Hilye by Yahya Hilmi *(Sakıp Sabancı Museum)*
Panorama of Constantinople by Henry Aston Barker *(Alamy)*
Le Bain Turc by Jean-Auguste-Dominique Ingres *(Alamy)*
Women in an ox-drawn cart *(Gülhan Benli)*
Ortaköy Mosque *(Alamy)*
Battalion divers at the Imperial Naval Arsenal *(Library of Congress)*
Trackside simit sellers *(Alamy)*
The Golden Horn *(National Geographic)*
The Theodosian Walls in modern Istanbul *(Alamy)*

MAPS

✤

Designed by Jamie Whyte

PAGE

8 Prehistoric sites around the Bosphorus, Sea of Marmara and Black Sea

11 Early Greek settlements along the Bosphorus

13 The Classical City, c. fifth century BC to third century AD

58 The Via Egnatia

88 Constantine's Constantinople, c. AD 337

90 Theodosios' Constantinople, c. AD 450

92 'Barbarian' tribes, c. AD 350–450

192 Golden Age Constantinople, c. AD 565

194 The Byzantine Empire at its greatest extent

258 Trade routes to Constantinople, c. seventh to eleventh century AD

260 Conflict with Constantinople, c. seventh to eleventh century AD

262 Eleventh-century Constantinople

328 The Crusades

331 The Byzantine Empire, c. AD 1050 and 1204

332 Constantinople after the Crusades

370 Ottoman and Byzantine territory in the east Mediterranean, c. AD 1451

372 Sixteenth-century Istanbul

374 Expansion of the Ottoman Empire, AD 1300–1683

450 Attacks and blockades, AD 1624–c. 1900

452 The Ottoman Empire, AD 1566–1923

509 Ottoman involvement in the Crimean War

510 The First World War

512 Expansion of Istanbul, AD 1807–2000

PROLOGUE

AD 632–718
(10–100 IN THE ISLAMIC CALENDAR)

Verily you shall conquer Constantinople. What a wonderful leader will he be, and what a wonderful army shall that army be!

TRADITIONAL HADITH ASSERTING THE PROPHET MUHAMMAD'S
DESIRE TO CONQUER CONSTANTINOPLE[1]

The wind of death grabbed them . . . The Romans were besieged, but the Arabs were no better than them. The hunger oppressed them so much that they were eating the corpses of the dead, each other's faeces and filth. They were forced to exterminate themselves, so they could eat. One modius of wheat was worth then ten denarii. They were looking for small rocks, they were eating them to satisfy their hunger. They ate rubbish from their ships.

MICHAEL THE SYRIAN, SIEGE OF CONSTANTINOPLE, AD 717[2]

We do not know the name of the messenger – but we live with the fallout of his message.

The Byzantine Emperor Constans II was a twenty-five-year-old ruler in his capital city of Constantinople in the high summer of the seventh century AD.[3] News arrived that a ferocious force of Arabs, many of whom called themselves Muslims – 'the ones who submit'[4] – with a pine-fresh navy of 200-odd ships, had attacked the islands of Cyprus, Kos, Crete and Rhodes. Constans and his Christian court knew that these Muslims, adherents of a religion not yet a generation old, were a desert people – men so ginger about the sea that a popular Arabic street phrase whimpered, 'The flatulence of camels is more pleasing than the prayers of the fishes.'[5] With his superior numbers and a maritime tradition stretching back at least to the city's celebrated foundation by sailors from mainland Greece 1,400 years before, Constans sailed out from his glittering, gold-domed city, praying that this would be a ritual humiliation for his Muslim foe.

Yet within just a day of fighting Constans would be the one degraded – jumping overboard dressed as a common sailor and crouching on the deck of a regular boat, desperately fleeing the slaughter between modern-day Cyprus and Turkey.[6] The casualties in this Arab–Byzantine, Muslim– Christian conflict were so great it was said that all around the sea was stained red, flushed with human blood. Muslim sources called this the Battle of the Masts; new models of boat, the dromons and *shalandiyyāt*,[7] forced hand-to-hand fighting as Byzantine and Arab vessels were roped together. And, disconcertingly for Christian Constantinople, against all the odds, it was the followers of Muhammad that won.

For a fat half-century the city of Constantinople, credited as God's earthly home, would find herself both physically and psychologically besieged. This was a city that believed she was divinely favoured and that she would remain unconquered until the end of the world. Just a century before this New Rome, the wealthiest city on earth, had been the Christian capital of an empire of a million square miles. The people of Constantinople had such faith in their protector the Virgin Mary that the Mother of God would come to be called the city's 'commander in chief'.

Fleeing the scene of the battle, the Byzantine Emperor Constans had returned first to Constantinople, but eventually travelled on to the security of Sicily, leaving his mother city exposed. Those abandoned in the historic centre of the city itself, above what had once been an ancient Greek acropolis looking out over the Sea of Marmara, or sitting scattered along the shores of the Bosphorus and the Golden Horn, offered nothing like a united front. To some, Arab conquest seemed a certainty. Within just a few years of the Prophet Muhammad's death in AD 632 (year 10/11 in the Islamic calendar), Muslims had looked set to rule much of the known world. In 632 Arab forces had conquered Byzantine Syria, in 636 a Byzantine army was beaten back in Yarmuk, in 640 the capture of Heliopolis had allowed for progress into Byzantine Egypt, in 641 Alexandria had fallen, in 642/3 Tripoli was captured, and now this advance nudging north. If events had followed what seemed to be their natural course, Istanbul would have become the seat of caliphs fifteen centuries ago.

But immediately after the Battle of the Masts there was a lull. The fledgling Muslim community was weakened by a succession crisis and by internecine strife – eventually resulting, from AD 661, in the world-shaping split between Shia and Sunnis that still endures.[8] In Constantinople life continued, if a little anxiously. Many left the city, unsure whether she could feed or protect them. The imperial dynasty had recently introduced a mutilating form of punishment – rhinotomy – when the noses of disgraced emperors would be split (and the tongues of their wives). The golden nose-cover would become a feature of the Byzantine imperial palace and of places of exile. In outlying territories Byzantine populations hunkered down in fortified settlements such as Monemvasia in the Peloponnese, or physically buried themselves, their homes, their churches and their granaries into the soft rock in Cappadocia, Asia Minor. Emperor Constans had even tried to move the capital to Syracuse in Sicily.

The anxiety was justified: first in AD 667[9] and again in 668 and 669, the Arabs would be back, bringing an army right up to Constantinople's Golden Gate. Still using the Greco-Roman boats and those Greco-Egyptian boatmen whom they had pressed into service after conquering the port-city of Alexandria in 642; lowering at the settlement of Chalcedon, just one thousand metres from Constantinople across the Bosphorus straits and within clear sight of the city, the Muslim Arabs teased and threatened those who were trapped within the 'World's Desire'.[10] There was now, indisputably, a new maritime power on the block. Each spring from Cyzicus on the coast of Asia Minor the Arabs attacked. All that would hold them back was Greek Fire, Constantinople's diabolic secret weapon made from a combination of Caucasian crude oil, sulphur, pitch and quicklime, with an effect similar to napalm; along with the firepower of a 500-ship navy built by Constans while absent in Sicily.[11] Fresh analysis of the Syriac and Muslim sources suggests that we should think of these early Arab aggressions as nagging incursions, rather than as a full-blown and consistent strategy of besiegement.

In AD 717 all that would change.

Defeated by Constantinople's walls and by her cutting-edge weapons, but never taking their eyes off the prize, in AD 717 (year 98–99 in the Islamic calendar) Muslim armies returned. The Arabs had secured a base on Gibraltar in 711, footfall to much of the Iberian peninsula. Swathes of the Middle East and North Africa, and the edge of Europe, were theirs. Now it was time to secure the city of God. In 717, the besieging forces, led by the brother of the Syrian-based Umayyad Caliph Süleyman, attacked by both land and sea. Byzantine control of the Caucasus and Armenia had already evaporated. A Muslim fleet of 1,800 supported a vast army. Constantinople's leaders were so fearful that all inhabitants were instructed to prove that they had the wherewithal to fight and a larder plump enough to survive a full year; those who did not make the mark were expelled. That year the city planted wheat in the gaps between her famous walls.[12] Meanwhile, buoyed up by an eschatological vision – that a ruler bearing the name of a prophet (Süleyman is the Arabic equivalent of Solomon) would take the city – the attacking army made up predominantly of Arabs and Berbers stockpiled vast resources and arms, including naphtha, and jerry-built their own siege walls of mud around Constantinople, isolating those within from their allies.

Yet the Arab plan had an Achilles heel: the seaward sides of the city could not be blockaded by their fleet. First that preposterous Greek Fire – its use directed from the walls of Constantinople by the Emperor himself – and then the convenient defection of a number of Christian Coptic Egyptians on the Muslim ships meant that supplies, men and morale could keep scuttling into the city under the cover of darkness from that squid-black sea. The treacherous currents in the Bosphorus snared Muslim relief ships sailing up from the Sea of Marmara. The Arabs' own destruction of the surrounding countryside had left the invaders with no food of their own; famine, fear and disease worked its way systematically through their camps. A severe winter, when the earth was white with snow, saw not besieged but besiegers eating pack-animals, possibly even turning to cannibalism.[13]

Finally on the Feast of Dormition, 15 August AD 718, the Arab commander ordered the retreat. Constantinople's protector, Mary the Mother of God, whose image had been paraded around the walls, was credited with victory.[14] Realising that they had the upper hand, the exhausted Constantinopolitans rallied to attack the retreating enemy one last time – many Muslims drowned, others were harassed by Bulgars. The troops that survived limped their way back to allied territories and then home.

These events became legends before they were history. The onslaughts and heroism and desperate escapes introduce us to a recurring theme in

Istanbul's history, that this is a city that lives a double life – as a real place and as a story.

The songs of Constantinople's sieges and ocean-borne battles would be sung around the campfires of both sides in the conflict for generations to come. Medieval chroniclers and later sources paint-boxed up the narratives: it was said that the Byzantine Emperor Leo III had sunk the Muslim fleet by touching the Bosphorus with his cross. Many declared that Constans had flown a cross while his soldiers sang psalms and that the Muslim commander Muawiyah had displayed a crescent with his men reciting the Qur'an in Arabic beneath. Memorialisers ignored the fact that both armies probably spoke Greek, that soldiers and civilians would have been able to understand one another perfectly – as they yelled insults and threats and muttered their prayers.

In Christian and Muslim households alike AD 717 became an episode of epic history and of deferred victory. Ottomans would later make pilgrimage to the mosques and shrines they believed had been founded within the city at the time of the siege.[15] Much Arabic literature declared that the Muslims had in fact won – and looked to a further and full vanquishing of Constantinople and her territories at the end of days.[16] It was said that the Arab commander Yazid I had scaled Constantinople's stubbornly resilient walls before the 674 siege and thus was known hereafter as *fata al-'arab*, 'the young champion of the Arabs'; that Arab commandos had entered the city and had hanged a Byzantine emperor within Haghia Sophia in revenge for the slaughter of Muslims. In the West, tales of Constantinople's tribulations are, in fact, still sung; in Tolkien's *The Lord of the Rings* the Battle of the Pelennor Fields, a fight for the city of Minas Tirith by land and over waterways,[17] draws inspiration from these attacks. And each year on 15 August populations across the Christian world still thank Mary for her miraculous powers of protection. That Constantinople had not fallen increased her allure. In the minds of many, the city took on fantastical proportions.

Along with the tales of triumph we are firmly informed by Byzantine sources that around the time of the sieges of Constantinople Arabs occupied Rhodes, breaking up and then selling off to a Jewish merchant one of the wonders of the ancient world, the Colossus (which some said had been toppled by an earthquake in 228 BC, others that it had been restored by various Roman emperors or indeed thrown into the sea). This beast of antiquity was then dragged by 900 camels (3,000 according to a few excitable chroniclers) to be sold off as scrap metal. This particular event, although enthusiastically retold in a number of medieval texts and in many reputable modern histories, appears in no Arab sources. Perhaps it is an embarrassed denial – or perhaps this 'history' is simply a story with all the hallmark tropes of vandalism and philistinism expected of both Jews and 'Saracens', spiced with a tinge of eschatological anxiety.[18]

Cultural memory, the hope of history, is often as potent as historical fact.

This is Istanbul incarnate. A place where stories and histories collide and crackle; a city that fosters ideas and information to spin her own memorial. A prize that meant as much as an abstraction, as a dream, as it did as a reality. A city that has long sustained a timeless tradition as old as the birth of the modern mind – where past narratives are nourished that tell us who we are in the present. In hard historical terms the Arab failures did indeed mark a change of ambition. The drive now was not to 'cut off the head' of Byzantium's empire, but to focus on the territories all around – east, south, south-west. The result was 700 years of an uneasy parallel existence between the new monotheists, one that witnessed collaboration as well as conflict. But no one forgot that the 'bone in the throat of Allah' had not been taken.

For men of many faiths and for East and West alike, Istanbul is not just a city but a metaphor and an idea – a possibility describing where we want our imagination to take us and our souls to sit. A city that encourages abstractions and armies, gods and goods, heart and body, and mind and spirit to travel.

NOTE ON NAMES

✦

Not only is Istanbul the city of many names, but there are many ways to transliterate, configure and spell the names of her rulers, inhabitants, protagonists, territories, enemies and allies. In general I have opted for the Greek forms of, for example, Eastern emperors – but I have also used popular forms such as Constantine and Michael where appropriate. Absolute consistency is almost unachievable and arguably a little self-congratulatory – in a city that was often described as 'luminous' my hope has been to illuminate rather than to obfuscate. Turkish phonetics have been employed with the kind help of Robin Madden, Lauren Hales and my splendid copyeditor Peter James and proof-reader Anthony Hippisley.[1]

The classical Greek name **Byzantion** (**Byzantium** in Latin) almost certainly derives from the Proto-Indo-European *bhugo* – a buck. It possibly has a local Thracian root **Buz** connected to waters and fountains. Either way, greater Istanbul's naturally rich flora, fauna and geology are recognised in the city's first historical label Byzantion. **Constantinople** comes from the Latin name Constantinus – the nomination of Constantine the Great, the Roman emperor who refounded the city in AD 324, giving rise to a civilisation that was called **Byzantine** only in the sixteenth century (by the historian Hieronymus Wolf in 1557). The city was referred to as the **New Rome** from AD 330, the standard Persian and Middle Eastern name for the Byzantine Empire was and is **Rum**. **Istanbul** is either Turkic patois of the Greek phrase *eis ten* (or *tin*) *polin* – into or towards the city, or of Islam-bol, Islam abounds. The Greeks themselves referred to the place as **Stinpolin**, **Stanbulin**, **Polin** or **Bulin** from at least the tenth century AD. After the Ottoman conquest there was a convenient similarity between the Turkish form of Stanbulin, **Stambol**

and **Islam-bol**. As well as enjoying the religious ring of Islam-bol, until
the twentieth century Ottomans also called the city **Kostantiniyye** or
Kostantiniye, a version of the Arabic **al-Qustantiniyya**. The name
Constantinople/Kostantiniyye was formally dropped only when the
Turkish Postal Service Law of 28 March 1930 insisted that mail no longer
be addressed to Constantinople. The city was now officially Istanbul. For
over 1,500 years in speech and in texts this metropolis was referred to
simply as **He Polis** – The City – or **Ten Polin** – To the City; the Chinese
name for the Byzantine Empire, **Fulin**, is a corruption of Polin.[2]

The settlement in its earliest historical iteration as Byzantion gets not
even a passing reference in the Hebrew Bible and Greek New Testament
(a mention of the Bosphorus has now been shown to be a mistranslation).[3]
Although Istanbul would come to have a thriving Jewish population, in
the biblical Judaic tradition this place was always 'other', a misty presence
– neither a city of sin nor a promised land. Byzantium is also absent from
the *Iliad*. For the early Greeks too the curve of earth that broke from the
Bosphorus into the Sea of Marmara was a liminal, forested territory that
kept its mystery, a spirit at the edge of civilisation. Tradition has it that
the devil showed Jesus a view of the Bosphorus, the Golden Horn and the
Byzantine acropolis from Çamlıca in Asia to demonstrate 'all the glory of
the world and the kingdoms therein'. This was a settlement that came to
be portrayed as perfection, and therefore as temptation incarnate.

On the ground in the cultural jumble of the city there were Romans
who stopped speaking Latin in the seventh century AD along with Greek-
speaking Muslims who were present until the ninth. While Latin invaders of AD 1204 described the inhabitants as **Graikoi** (Niketas Choniates,
History), the Christian men and women of the city avoided the ancient
Greek **Hellen** because of its pagan associations, instead preferring **Ro-
maios**. Greeks in the twenty-first century across all continents still call
themselves **Romaioi** – Romans, children of the New or Second Rome.
Ethnic Greeks from Istanbul are still called **Romoi** or **Rumlar**.

Although it is an important psycholinguistic choice, to write of the
natives of this city from 700 BC to AD 1450 as Romans is a little confusing. So in this book the ancient Romans are called **Romans** and those
that lived in what was once Byzantion and then Byzantium, and then
Constantinople, I refer to as **Byzantines**. **Byzantium** refers to either the
city or the idea of the empire of the Byzantines. The name of the city

itself was certainly used both to exalt and to limit the urban entity. For centuries in the medieval West, Constantinople's civilisation was called **Constantinopolitan**. But just before the city's fall to the Ottoman Turks in 1453, Constantinople was predominantly a walled ruin with scant lands attached.[4]

The Ottomans in Istanbul originally used the name **Turc** to designate someone rather rough, from hicksville. A **Turk** is used today in urban slang on the west coast of the United States to describe a boy who is super-spunky – an inversion of a popular, stereotypical anxiety that had endured for centuries and has recently been revived in political rhetoric as Turkey seeks membership of the European Union.[5] In AD 1578 John Lyly asked if there 'was never any Impe so wicked & Barbarous, any Turke so vile and brutish';[6] while dictionaries in 1699 defined a Turk as any cruel-hearted man. As well as denoting a squat, armless piece of bedroom furniture, the term **Ottoman** was more frequently heard in the parlours of the West in reference to the Ottoman peril that threatened Christian civilisation.[7]

The **Bosporus** (Cow Strait) came to be known as the **Bosphorus** in medieval Latin and Greek and the name has stuck – I tend to use the later, popular rather than the pure form. When describing a general, non-time-specific aspect of the city I use the name **Istanbul** or, if the sources encourage it, Byzantium, Constantinople or Kostantiniyye. Sometimes this may be chronologically inappropriate, but I think the long-dead inhabitants of Byzantion, Byzantium, Constantinople and Istanbul will understand and, I hope, forgive me.

INTRODUCTION

✦

> Though all other cities have their periods of government and are subject to the decays of time, Constantinople alone seems to claim a kind of immortality and will continue to be a city as long as humanity shall live either to inhabit or rebuild it. PIERRE GILLES, AD 1550[1]

On 4 February 1939 the BBC transmitted an audio-recording of W. B. Yeats's poem 'Sailing to Byzantium'. This was the broadcaster's tribute to the firebrand Irishman who had died seven days before. Crackling and hissing, the clipped, RP Queen's English hangs somewhere between the sublime and the sinister, the recording itself a broken reminder of what the great city of Byzantium had and has become. A sonorous male voice intones Yeats's lines, telling of a place that lived in the poet's head and lives still in our imagination: carnal, splendid and ineffable – charismatic in the true Greek sense of the word, full of an otherworldly grace which ignites an earthly desire.

> And therefore I have sailed the seas and come
> To the holy city of Byzantium.
>
> O sages standing in God's holy fire
> As in the gold mosaic of a wall
> Come from the holy fire, perne in a gyre,
> And be the singing-masters of my soul.
> Consume my heart away; sick with desire
> And fastened to a dying animal
> It knows not what it is; and gather me

Into the artifice of eternity.
Once out of nature I shall never take
My bodily form from any natural thing,
But such a form as Grecian goldsmiths make
Of hammered gold and gold enamelling
To keep a drowsy Emperor awake;
Or set upon a golden bough to sing
To lords and ladies of Byzantium
Of what is past, or passing, or to come.

It is Istanbul's multi-dimensional nature, past, passing, to come, that fanned my own love affair with the city, a relationship that has endured over four decades. The history of this place with three names – Byzantion or Byzantium (c. 670 BC to AD 330), Constantinople, al-Qustantiniyye then Kostantiniyye (c. AD 330 to 1930), Istanbul or Stimboli (c. AD 1453 onwards) – is often isolated into discrete blocks: ancient, Byzantine, Ottoman, Turkish. But, for me, Istanbul's cultural, political and emotional strength comes from the fact that the city's narrative is not confined by lines in time. It is a place where people are connected across time by place, which is why I embarked on the Heraklean, sometimes Augean, task of using clues in the landscape to tell a story of this city from prehistory to the present.

Chance historical survivals around the modern metropolis – the bases of late antique columns in shopping streets, springs next to mosques (ancient pagan shrines that would become Christian churches and then Muslim sanctuaries) – endure today as touchstones for the city's variegated populations. Istanbul often lives outside time; for this reason this settlement was also called the New Rome, the New Jerusalem, Allah's Eternal City. Over 8,000 years, over 320 generations' worth of humanity have lived, worked and played here. It is a continuum that has left behind some frustrating gaps, but also a rich trove of archaeological and literary evidence, much of which is emerging only now from the earth and from the archives, and around which I have centred this book. Istanbul has been a host to grandstanding historical characters, but in addition to focusing on others with overt power, on these pages I have tried to appreciate the lived experience of those who may not have realised they were history-makers. Etymologically, aspirationally and philosophically, a city is the people who live within it. So in this book you will find women as well as men. You will find the poor as well as the rich, and the weak as well as the strong.

What follows is not a catch-all catalogue of Istanbul's past. It is a personal, physical journey – an investigation of what it takes to make a city: in particular an examination of the new evidence on offer that speaks of the global nature of Istanbul's backstory – a means, perhaps, to comprehend both the city and ourselves. Istanbul has always been a critical station in a temporal and a neural network. A city is an entity that is not self-sufficient – it survives and indeed thrives both on specialisation and on the connections it enjoys beyond its boundaries. So I have focused on game-changing events or ideas which shaped Istanbul or thanks to which she won influence elsewhere. I have tried to understand in what ways the settlement (and its population) has had to adapt and evolve to endure across the millennia, and how that crucible of fervent activity has then sparked out to fire the wider world.

Byzantion comes into focus in the lines of Herodotus in the fifth century BC when the Father of History commemorates a pontoon bridge built by one of the most powerful men on earth to link Asia to Europe.[2] As I was working on this book, 2,500 years on, the first underwater tunnels between continents, championed by Turkey's President Erdoğan, were completed in Istanbul. An attempted coup by factions of the military to overthrow Erdoğan and his government on 15 July 2016 saw tanks parked on the Bosphorus Bridge connecting the Asian and European sides of the modern city. Istanbul's Taksim Square and Atatürk Airport were occupied and the cross-continental Fatih Sultan Mehmet Bridge was also blocked. During the night, citizen-protesters on the Bosphorus Bridge – since renamed the 15 July Martyrs Bridge – were grazed by gunfire. By dawn young rebel soldiers, hands raised, surrendered above the waterway that breaches Eurasia; some were then lynched. Istanbul is a protean, pyretic place whose mood and *modus operandi* could determine the future security of East and West.

Because Istanbul is uniquely well served by both land and sea, she has long satisfied our philosophical and physiological drive as a species to travel, to explore, to connect and to control. A rhino-horn of land that juts into the Sea of Marmara, 1,700 miles east of Paris and 1,400 miles north of Baghdad, Stamboul proper, which was founded at the very edge of Europe and within eyeshot of Asia, comes into her own in the classical age when boat technology developed to allow more people, trade goods, armed troops and novel ideas to travel. She flourished when men and women acted on a prehistoric word-idea that, I would argue, kick-starts civilisation. This Proto-Indo-European term *ghosti* (from which we get the words guest, host and ghost) referred to a kind of unspoken etiquette, a notion that on seeing strangers on the horizon, rather than choose to fell them with spears or sling-shots, instead we should take the risk of welcoming them across our threshold – on the chance that they might bring new notions, new goods, fresh blood with them. Over time this word-idea evolved into the Greek *xenia* – ritualised guest–host friend-ship, an understanding that stitched together the ancient Mediterranean and Near Eastern worlds. Thanks to new DNA skeletal evidence we now realise that ancient peoples travelled far greater distances and more systematically than we once thought.[3] If civilisation is about reaching out beyond the horizon to embrace the unknown, about making connections, about working out how to live with ourselves and with others, then for both East and West alike Istanbul is perfectly placed to satisfy that urge. And today the need to understand the narrative of what one Byzantine called 'the city of the world's desire' is ever more urgent.

Istanbul's story is racing up the modern political agenda. As well as the recent drama of civil strife and terror attack, her influence goes a long way to explain the geopolitical shape of all our lives. The city has supported the world's most tenacious theocracies, she sustained the domination of Christianity as a world religion, she frustrated caliphs and then embraced the longest-lasting Caliphate in history. Next to Mecca, Medina and Jerusalem, Istanbul is considered by many to be Sunni Islam's holiest place. Middle Eastern identities, Balkan conflict, the split of Croatia and Serbia, the role of Turkey in the European Union, an expansionist Russia, conflict in the Holy Land, holy conflicts in the US and Europe, the contested borders of the states of Iraq and Syria (and Israel) and the stateless refugees who flee them: all have their roots in the history of the city of three names. If you like, Istanbul is a Rosetta Stone for inter-national affairs. Her rulers' hotspots across time – Damascus, Libya, Baghdad, Belgrade, Sarajevo, Cairo, the Caucasus and Crimea – are our own. Many of our ancestors in Europe, the Near East, the Middle East, the Far East and North Africa were allies or subjects or citizens or slaves of either the Greek, the Roman, the Byzantine or the Ottoman master. Currants and cotton, bathmats and ballistics, as well as human traffic

– travellers, captives and refugees – have long been traded from the ports and highways of the 'Queen of Cities'.

Istanbul's topography might have moulded her history, and her story the landscape of our lives, yet the physical scale of the city has rarely seemed to deserve the magnitude of the fabled enemies and heroes that she has attracted: Constantine I, Attila the Hun, Genghis Khan, the new army of Islam, Tamerlane, Ivan the Terrible, Catherine the Great, the British Empire, Islamic State (IS). But of course the idea of Istanbul is exponentially bigger than her footprint. As a metaphor and a location the city appears in Greek drama, in the Qur'an,[4] in Shakespeare;[5] there are Turks in Molière and Ottomans in Machiavelli. Istanbul is there in the 007 film franchise – the ultimate Bond backdrop in the inter-continental mind's eye. The Turks use a special tense when describing the legends of their city – 'as was remembered'.[6] Istanbul is a place of business and pleasure, a place where stories match their weight to histories. In ways both great and small we owe more to this city and to the culture that she sponsored than we might know: the term lingua franca, the Adoration of the Virgin Mary, the Nicene Creed, the name of the Roma, passports, the fork, jingoism, the fact that some call themselves White Caucasian, the basis of modern Western law – all were forged in Istanbul's furnace. Greek dramas, Roman philosophy, Christian texts, Islamic poetry – many world-class examples were preserved only thanks to the work of the men (and sometimes the women) in the city's scriptoria (workshops established for the copying, translating and analysis of manuscripts) and libraries, madrasas and monasteries; Istanbul has done much to furnish civilisation's shared memory bank.

Today, rag-and-bone men in their horse-drawn carts overtake Ferraris stuck in the city's grinding traffic-jams. Super-tankers carrying oil from Russia and giant cargo ships taking luxury goods from the Sea of Marmara to the Black Sea menace local fishermen. Trains and growling buses bursting with passengers deliver 10 million Istanbullus a day into and out of the centre – even more in greater Istanbul, a sprawling area that still supports primary, secondary and tertiary industries and an unofficial population of 16 million or so. The modern city stretches 100 miles across. Seagulls wheel around the minaret of the Blue Mosque as they once did around Constantinople's church domes. Yes, this is a fantastical city – a city of the soul – but it is born from the earth it inhabits; it is anchored.

Istanbul is the longest-lived political entity in Europe. It is a conurbation that over the last 8,000 years has grouted together a mosaic of settlements and micro-cities to form the grand, messy picture that is the modern metropolis. Many districts in the city were once their own cityettes: Chalcedon, Chrysopolis, Sultanhamet, Psamathion, Cosmidion and Sycae/Pera/Galata on the Golden Horn – all now coalescing like a drop of mercury into greater Istanbul. At the latest count archaeologists have identified pre-Chalcolithic remains in Stamboul itself under the ancient hippodrome – reaching back deeper than the forty-two human-habitation layers measured at the site of Troy. Phoenicians, Greeks, Romans, Genoese, Venetians, Jews, Arabs, Vikings, Azeris, Armenians, Turks all have called a patch of this earth between East and West their home. We feel at the centre of the globe here, because we are indeed connected to many worlds.

So what follows is an organic examination – an archaeology of both place and culture that tries to understand a city which affects our lives in ways that we have forgotten or are yet to realise. In writing this book I have had to travel to the very edges of empire: to Georgia to find Dmanisi, where now all that is left is a lone monk and a wisp of smoke on a dew-heavy hill, but where Byzantine, Persian and Armenian caravan routes once converged on the Silk Roads' axis alongside the (recently discovered) remains of the oldest hominids in Europe, four foot high, who were probably killed by sabre-toothed tigers;[7] to the porous border between Turkey and Syria; and through the heat of Arabia and the chill of the Dolomites. I have climbed into ancient Chinese tombs and have had to negotiate the fault lines that followed the fall of Istanbul's territories after the Great War of 1914–18, as well as snipers on the Armenian–Azeri border, terrorist threats in the Arab Emirates and different ways of being Muslim in the world separated just by the barbed wire of the Anatolian–Iraqi interface. I have eaten in the Topkapı Palace while protesters were arrested outside and then joined those protesters, and the tear gas, in Taksim Square. I have watched as a sea of Turkish flags, waved by 5 million rallying together to defy the July 2016 coup near the site of one of the city's oldest ports has rouged the city – a blush visible from space. The research for this book has taken me to many places. But truly to understand the story of Istanbul we first have to go to the edge of historical time, to prehistory, and look beyond.

PART ONE

✦

BYZANTION

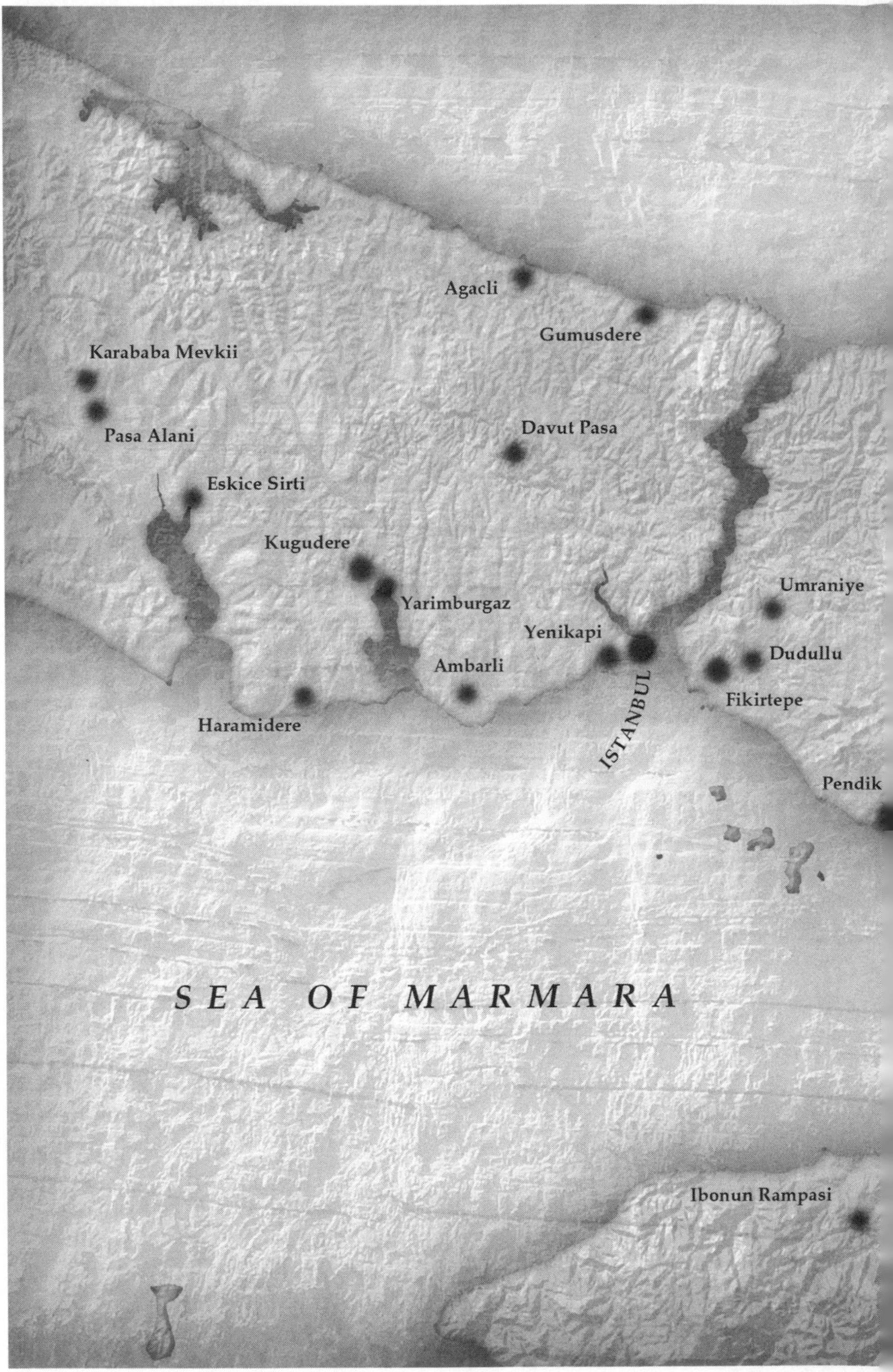

Agacli

Gumusdere

Karababa Mevkii

Pasa Alani

Davut Pasa

Eskice Sirti

Kugudere

Umraniye

Yarimburgaz

Dudullu

Yenikapi

Ambarli

Fikirtepe

ISTANBUL

Haramidere

Pendik

SEA OF MARMARA

Ibonun Rampasi

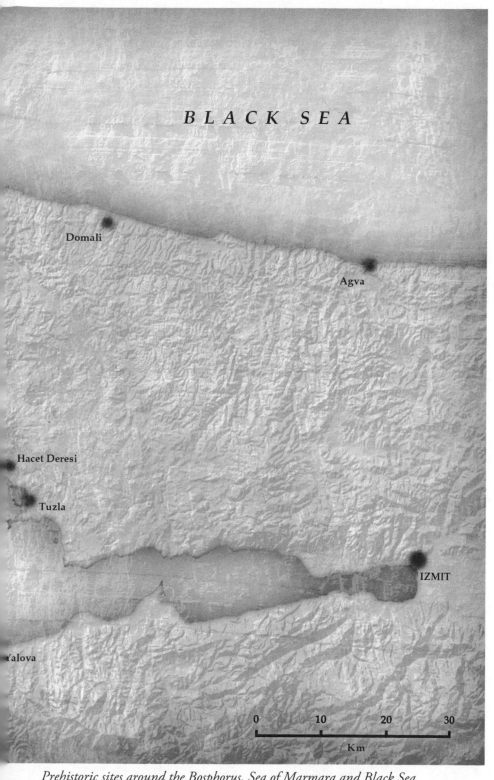

Prehistoric sites around the Bosphorus, Sea of Marmara and Black Sea

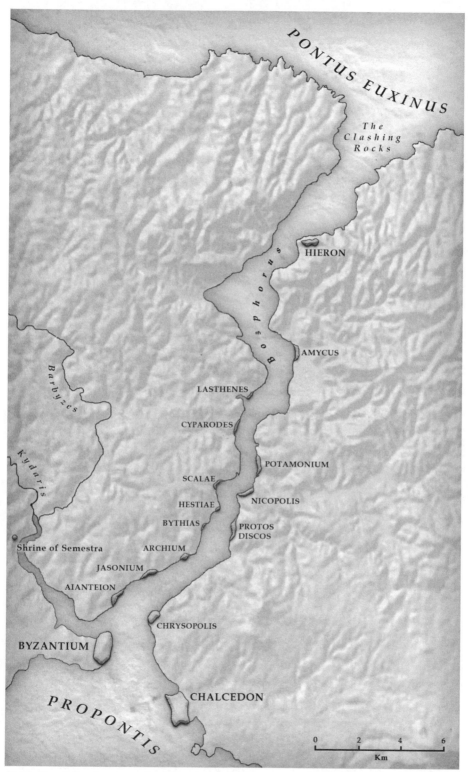

Early Greek Settlements along the Bosphorus

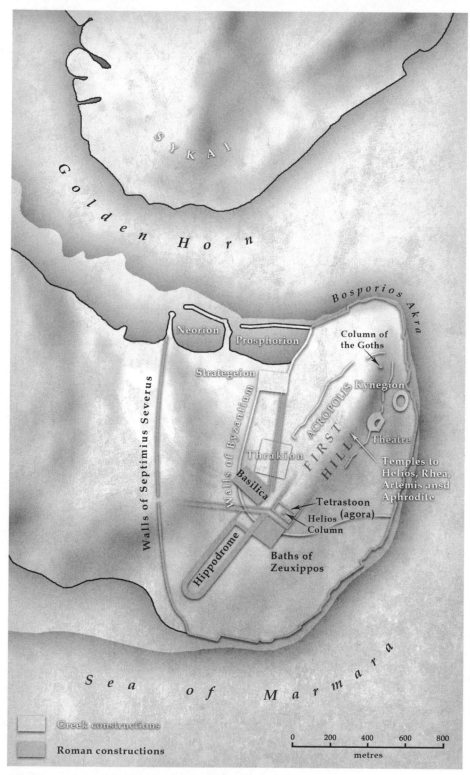

The Classical City, c. fifth century BC to third century AD

CHAPTER 1

BONES, STONES AND MUD

800,000–5500 BC

Suddenly a huge wave rose up before them, arched, like a steep rock; and
at the sight they bowed with bended heads . . . Then a vaulted billow
rushed upon them, and the ship like a cylinder ran on the furious wave,
plunging through the hollow sea. And the eddying current held her between the clashing rocks; and on each side they shook and thundered; and
the ship's timbers were held fast. Then Athena with her left hand thrust
back one mighty rock and with her right pushed the ship through . . .

APOLLONIUS RHODIUS DESCRIBING JASON'S JOURNEY THROUGH

THE BOSPHORUS, *THE ARGONAUTICA*[1]

A coffin might seem an odd place to start. In 2011, tucked up under
the new Yenikapı metro station in the centre of modern-day Istanbul,
opposite shops selling dusters and plastic buckets, a body was found.
Curled into a foetal position, orientated south-west–north-east, cradled
within a lattice of wood beneath and a single piece of wood above, surrounded by wattle-and-daub neolithic houses with funerary urns near
by, this Stone Age woman was buried in what is, to date, the world's
oldest wooden coffin.[2] The 8,000-year old remains are either a unique
find, unusually well preserved in the anaerobic conditions of Istanbul's
mud, or instead a unique insight into the burial practices of our neolithic
Anatolian ancestors. Dating to the period 6300–5800 BC (close in time to
the world's earliest-known formal 'town', Çatalhöyük in central Turkey),
the young woman lying here was clearly attempting a good life for herself.
In the same excavation archaeologists have found, in an oily layer beneath
the seabed itself, the tools – including a wooden shovel, seeds and burnt
organic remains – that belonged to her social group. Some think the

shovel was in fact a canoe oar, making it the earliest ever found, again, 8,000 years old. Remarkably too, well over a thousand human footprints from this prehistoric hamlet have survived. Some of these Stone Age Istanbullus travelled barefoot, others used delicately made leather shoes, possibly even wooden clogs – similar to those worn in the modern city's hammams.[3]

This was a location that was well worth walking to – a patch of earth that gave life. A total of 236 natural springs have been charted in the wider Thracian peninsula[4] – the region between the Black Sea and the Aegean Sea on whose eastern edge Istanbul is found – streams, springs, rivers, lakes and lagoons, all set within oak, chestnut and pistachio forests. That young woman in the coffin had joined many generations – reaching back to the paleolithic age – who appreciated the charms of what is now greater Istanbul. Her earlier mesolithic neighbours were found nearby, alongside the giant bears of the Pleistocene in the Yarımburgaz Cave which overlooks the edges of the modern city. The pale limestone rock,[5] reached by an old road that runs past factories promoting tea services and pens of sheep waiting for slaughter at the Festival of Eid, offers a natural home. Extending more than half a mile into the rock face and fifty feet high in places, under earth and manure in the Yarımburgaz Cave, traces of greater Istanbul's very first human inhabitants – their spearheads, bone fragments and other stone tools of quartz, quartzite and flint – have been uncovered in what are still ongoing excavations. The view from the cave-complex today is of the modern city stretching like a phagocyte around a lagoon or *gölü* called Küçükçekmece; in the Stone Age it would have been of dense woods and water. In the winter bears hibernated here, in the spring human communities moved in. Some remains in the cave reach back 800,000 years – 600,000 years before the advent of *Homo sapiens* – making this site in greater Istanbul one of the oldest inhabited locations in the Near East. Archaeologists and a number of the city's officials are rather perturbed that recent human activity in this prehistoric treasure trove has included film-making, drug-taking, mushroom-farming and prostitution.

The early hominids and their Stone Age descendants would have lived in an evolving landscape very different to the one we see today: the Sea of Marmara was originally a brackish inland lake, as yet unidentified

pachyderms roamed the valleys, panthers the hills, and over 9,000 identified species of flower bloomed. Giant deer, mammoth, spotted hyenas
were all here, luxuriating in a climate that would come to be two degrees
warmer than our own.

That wooden coffin was uncovered when $4 billion worth of sub-aqua
tunnel was being constructed to join the Asian and European sides of the
modern city. In addition, four human burials and four cremations dating
to around 6000 BC have been found. The area is revealing itself as an
archaeological theme park: when a drought in 2007 forced local farmers
to cut new irrigation channels 17 miles away from the city centre, archaeologists swooped in and rescued modest little finds that are proving to
be historic gold. Because here, at the edges of Küçükçekmece Gölü and
on Istanbul's Black Sea shore, is the earliest evidence of the meat and veg
of human civilisation in Europe – naviform core (boat-shaped, worked
stone) and pressure-worked flint. There are also meat-cleavers, flint knives,
bone-scrapers.[6] Were these the locations of a prehistoric hunting lodge? A
rest-stop for men and women who sometimes hunted, sometimes farmed?
Excavations at the upper end of the Golden Horn are expected to yield
further evidence.[7] Greater Istanbul, almost certainly, has been hiding
evidence of farming in Europe a full millennium before it was originally
thought to have arrived.[8] The neolithic community which lived in and
around Istanbul was winning out in the struggle to survive on earth. But
then the earth fought back.

Around 5500 BC in an earth-shattering, epoch-forming intervention that
would determine the city's character and ensuing life-story, the topography of greater Istanbul was created.[9] Following a dramatic rise in sea
level after the melting of ice-sheets, sea floodwaters tore inland to scour out
the Bosphorus. The Black Sea was transformed from a shallow, freshwater lake into a maritime opportunity as saltwater shellfish replaced fresh.
The waters here could have risen by as much as 238 feet over a period of
300 days. The Golden Horn formed as an estuary with natural harbours,
fed by two springs known as the Sweet Waters of Europe, Kydaris and
Barbyzes. In the creation of this new world many lives were destroyed;
signs of human habitation, drowned buildings and worked timbers are
now emerging from the Black Sea bed. Some estimate that 10 cubic miles'
worth of water hurtled over the land-sill within one year, flooding more

than 600 square miles of land. It was an event that destroyed one world but also made a world-class city a possiblity.

Where a number of civilisations such as Egypt could have a somewhat ginger relationship with the oceans, in Istanbul water is so ever present that her inhabitants are forced to make it friend rather than foe. 'Garlanded by waters'[10] is how one chronicler described the city.[11] Istanbul today is lapped by the Golden Horn, the Bosphorus and the Sea of Marmara; to the north is the Euxine or Black Sea, and to the south, through the Hellespont or Dardanelles, the Mediterranean. This 'Liquid Continent' – also called through time the White Sea, the Faithful Sea, the Bitter Sea, the Great Green and Mare Nostrum – offered opportunity and obliteration in equal measure. In a world of oar and sail, of inlets and natural harbours, the creation of two continents with the advent of the Bosphorus meant that Istanbul's land became possibility incarnate.

So when we spend time in the company of Istanbul we must remember that this is a story of a city and also a story of the sea.

CHAPTER 2

CITY OF THE BLIND

c. 682 BC

Megabazus . . . made a comment that the people of the Hellespont have never forgotten, nor ever will. He happened to be in Byzantium, and learned that the region of Chalcedon had been settled seventeen years earlier than Byzantium. This information prompted him to declare that the Chalcedonians, during that period, must have been blind. 'Why otherwise, when there was such a perfect spot available for a new city, did they choose one far inferior? They could only have been blind!'

HERODOTUS, *HISTORIES*[1]

In May 2016, news was released of another remarkable archaeological find in Istanbul. Under jaunty summer homes along the coast of the Sea of Marmara at Silivri, a 4,000-year-old round tomb, like the kurgans of Central Asia, protecting a warrior whose body had also been bent into a foetal position, was revealed. The Turkish authorities announced that the burial shows there was Central Asian influence right back at Istanbul's prehistoric birth. It is a significant claim. The ancient Greeks had long declared that the settlement where the body was discovered, Selymbria (today's Silivri), had in fact been founded by them.

The stories that swirled around the ancient city of Byzantion and its hinterland were as important as its histories. And the legends that explain the myth of how the Greeks came to ignite what is now Istanbul are predictably vivid. Zeus, the king of the gods, was, as usual, having an affair with a mortal – this time a priestess of his wife Hera called Io. Io was turned into a cow by a furious Hera (in some accounts Zeus himself turns Io into a cow to protect her); Hera then sent a gadfly to torment the tempting young woman. The Bos-porus – the Ox-Ford – was said to take its name from the passage Io made through the strait. Io then gave birth to a daughter, Keroessa, who was brought up by a nymph called Semestra on the banks of the Golden Horn (the waterway known as the Keras in antiquity), where the young woman continued the family tradition of entanglement with the Olympian gods and slept with the sea god Poseidon. Keroessa and Poseidon's son Byzas went on to found Byzantion. Another version of the city's foundation myth – which perhaps edges closer to a Bronze or Iron Age truth – remembers that the Thracian King Byzas, ethnarch of the Megarians, son of that self-same nymph Semestra, married a local princess Phidaleia who brought as her dowry the land that became Istanbul.

Thracian pottery dating back to 4500 BC and a fragment of a gorgeous, greenstone macehead has indeed been found deep under Istanbul's historic centre. Those neolithic communities with their wooden coffins knew that this was a good spot to put down roots – and that knowledge did not mysteriously vanish in the Chalcolithic, Bronze and Early Iron Ages. The wedge of land that sits between the Golden Horn, the Bosphorus and the Sea of Marmara (in antiquity the Propontis) which is now called the Sarayburnu, or Palace Point (for the ancient Greeks the Acropolis and for Latin speakers the Promentorium Bosporium) was a particularly welcoming place for human inhabitants. There are seven hills all around, high enough for protection, low enough for habitation. This would indeed have been a good place to set up home.

Excavated near the Byzantine hippodrome in the 1920s and 1942 were large Thracian pots – one, rather brilliantly, with its side moulded into the shape of a human face. So forget the Hellenic myths: local people were here long before the Greeks came from the west. Native habitation around the area now occupied by Topkapı Palace, by men and women who traded and farmed, is continuous until at least 1100 BC; as modern Istanbul is an historical mille-feuille, excavations in the centre are tricky, but one can be sure that further evidence will emerge for the early life of the city. Tantalisingly unpublished accounts of explorations by underwater archaeologists in 1989 at the Fenerbahçe Yacht Harbour near Kalamış Bay describe divers being able to feel architectural structures beneath the thick seaweed – buildings which could well once have housed an Early Bronze Age population, as their 4,000 year-old pots have been discovered nearby.[2] The waters here both make history and hide it.

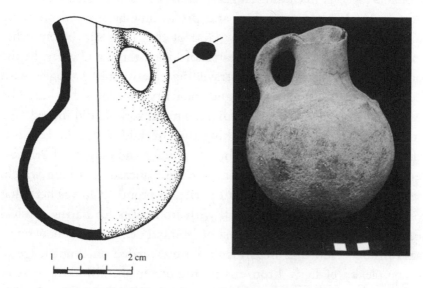

A jug from Fenerbahçe Yacht Harbour. These discoveries point to an as yet unexcavated prehistoric settlement on the Asian side of the Bosphorus.

So the very first Istanbullus, the native locals, speak to us quietly; their story has to be teased out of the earth and the dark waters of the Bosphorus. It is Istanbul's immigrant Hellenic population who trumpet their presence. The Greeks – who invented the notion of history and so were very adept at writing themselves into it, asserted that the ancient settlement of Byzantion was their own.

While Zeus, Hera and Io were sorting out their bitter love triangle, the epic poets tell us that Jason and his Argonauts (Herakles, Orpheus, King Nestor and the rest – a veritable rollcall of legendary Greek power) would have sailed past the site of Byzantion on their adventures in the Black Sea. The detailed and delicately painted marine frescoes on the Greek island of Thera (Santorini) – miraculously preserved in pumice in c. 1615 BC when the island erupted in one of the biggest geophysical events of the human experience – tell us that these early Greeks did indeed pioneer sailing technology. Uniquely they would have been able to chart their way not just around the Mediterranean coasts, but through deep ocean waters too.

The stories abounded, both recounting these cross-continental journeys and perhaps inspiring them – how Hellenic Jason gathered his

Argonauts together (including Augeas, whose vast stables Herakles would be forced to clean) for adventure and profit, how he stopped off along the Bosphorus and discovered the land of the rising sun before other Greek heroes headed to Asia in search of Helen, Troy and glory. In the Homeric epics we hear of Jason travelling east where he tangles with Medea of Colchis, her aunt Circe and the feisty Amazon tribe. Lured by the promise of gold (early and prodigious metalworking did indeed take place in the region – perhaps sparking the Greek idea that the East was 'rich in gold')[3] and then detained by the potions and poisons of Princess Medea, Jason succeeded in penetrating the Caucasus – a land which, in the Greek mind, wept with both peril and promise.[4] It was here that Prometheus was chained to a rock with iron rivets for daring to steal fire from the gods. Archaeology east of Istanbul demonstrates how myth grazes history. New digs in Armenia have extended our knowledge of the complexity of Early Bronze Age, fire-driven metalworking east of the Bosphorus.[5] When a Royal Navy party were digging on the island of Imbros in 1917, just to the south of Istanbul, in order to erect an obelisk to commemorate comrades who had fallen at Gallipoli, they came across a lustrous gold cup dating to c. 2500 BC. This Imbros Cup was a real version of the golden cups utilised by Homer's gods. Istanbul's hinterland has gained its mythic reputation with good reason.

On his journey Jason was said to have had to deal with giant clashing rocks (almost certainly a description of the Bosphoran entry to the Black Sea), but then rendered them passable for all who followed. Little surprise that we hear from the Boeotian poet Pindar that the East was the place that both seduced and made heroes.

Fresh evidence from the Caucasus shows that Bronze and Iron Age Greeks did indeed make the journey from the Aegean through the compelling channel of the Hellespont, now the Dardanelles, across the Sea of Marmara, up the slim Bosphorus – only 700 yards across in places, although up to 400 feet deep in its central channel – and then past sandy shores and across the Black Sea. Close to Batumi on the Black Sea coast of modern-day Georgia, behind a freshly excavated fifth-century BC necropolis where scores of Greek graves are emerging from the sand and scrub as tightly packed as any municipal cemetery, there are Bronze Age mounds. The newly discovered Greek artefacts and remains here in Asia speak not just of trade relations but of boots on the ground. Heroes of the imagination, such as Jason, are matched by hard evidence of hero-adventurers in the flesh.[6]

Istanbul still remembers Jason. The little fishing village of Tarabya, now a haunt of the city's glitterati, was originally the Greek Therapeia (the name means cure or healing, and Therapeia became a favourite summer location for foreign ambassadors in the later Ottoman period). Therapeia had been renamed in the fifth century AD as part of the Christianisation of the region by the patriarch Attikos, who disapproved of its pagan name Pharmakeus. Now, *pharmaka* from the Bronze Age onwards can mean drugs, or useful herbal things – hence today's pharmacies. But the *pharmaka* referred to here at Pharmakeus, from an age before history had been invented, were said to be the lethal poisons of Princess Medea – thrown, the story went, into the bay halfway down the Bosphorus on the European shore, when the spurned royal beauty from Colchis, psychotic with grief and rage, was in hot pursuit of her duplicitous lover.

So we know that the Greeks travelled to Istanbul and beyond.[7] The exact form of boat and the exact length of journey are fiercely contested. From the Greek mainland, give or take a week, sailing in daylight and putting in to sleep and eat ashore in the evenings, to reach the Bosphorus would have been a month's journey.[8] The elegant, long and narrow boats, fast under oars with a large rowing crew, could have managed 6 knots with the wind abaft the beam. But heavy seas were a problem, sailing upwind an impossibility and both known and unknown dangers a certainty. There were perilous pressure points, not least the Sounion cape, the south end of Euboea, the northerly wind and the south-going current of the Dardanelles.

Tentatively leaving the open sea to steer a course between two continents, past wooded hills and grimly barren rocks, Greek adventurers would have sailed blind up the Hellespont not sure where that tricky, inviting channel might lead. And (a little ironically given their claim to have had the brilliance to spot Byzantion's potential) where they originally landed was, arguably, the wrong place. On the Asian side of the entrance to the Bosphorus settlers developed the site of Chalcedon in a natural bay on the eastern shore of the Sea of Marmara. Chalcedon sits, a thousand metres or so across the channel, from the site of Byzantion. Around campfires, in city squares and at royal courts and in classical texts, for centuries it was thus Chalcedon, 'the city of the blind', that was acclaimed as the first European landfall in an area now firmly subsumed within modern-day Istanbul at her Asian edge.

The land here at Chalcedon was, in truth, not virgin. As with the archaeological discoveries across the water, neolithic cultures have left plenty of evidence of their tough, hopeful lives nearby at Fikirtepe. Hunters and fishermen survived here in rough mud huts – feasting from a land thick with fig trees, using spoons and ladles made of wild cow bone. In the Bronze Age commercial colonists from Phoenicia arrived too. Today ancient Chalcedon has become the busy little Asian suburb of Kadıköy. There is a demotic feel to the streets; this is where Istanbullus will take you to show that the city has a social history, not just a global future; there is a sense of the domestic here, as hazelnut merchants wait for you to come to them and housekeepers make the trip across the water from European Istanbul in search of the finest fresh mountain cheeses. Clerics of all colours sell their wares; in the Armenian church the caretaker sits for hour after hour in the hope of visitors to whom he can offer a welcome. One of the city's oldest synagogues is in Kadıköy, so too Roman Catholic and Serbian shrines. Veiled local girls nip in and out of sixteenth-century mosques built by the early Ottomans as a statement both of piety and of the city's new Muslim aesthetic. And today the area is dominated by transport hubs: the Haydarpaşa railway station, like a European castle with the Marmara as its moat, built in 1908 to service the lines to Baghdad, Damascus and Medina; and bus and minibus terminals too. From antiquity through the medieval and early modern worlds, Chalcedon was a critical transit point.

Chalcedon, less easy to protect than Byzantion, might not have been an obvious colonial choice, but there may well have been method in those early Greeks' madness. The graves and human-faced pots and mace-head fragments on the high hill of old Stamboul tell us that the spot the Greeks would call Byzantion was already occupied. New settlers, rather than a full-scale invading army, do not have the resources to mount a ten-year siege – whatever tales they bullishly told about the exploits of their ancestors further down the Asian coast at Troy. Chalcedon was the city perhaps of the blind-sided rather than the blind. Today we casually nip from Asia to Europe for the equivalent of less than a pound sterling, the cost of a ferry-ride. Twenty-seven centuries ago there was more at stake. In Byzantion someone, nameless as yet in history, had got there first.

But in the first half of the seventh century BC it was said that the gods themselves, through the babbling riddle of an oracle, instructed the inhabitants of a city on the Greek mainland, the Megarians, to push the boat out (literally) and found another city 'opposite the city of the blind'.

If Chalcedon was the city of the blind, what greater chances for a city of clear sight.

CHAPTER 3

CITY OF LIGHT

c. 680–c. 540 BC

That dolphin-torn, that gong-tormented sea.

W. B. YEATS, 'BYZANTIUM'

For Byzantium has a fruitful soil and productive seas, as immense shoals of fish pour out of the Pontus and are driven by the sloping surface of the rocks under water to quit the windings of the Asiatic shore and take refuge in these harbours. Consequently the inhabitants were at first money-making and wealthy traders . . .

TACITUS, *ANNALS*[1]

Megara, a mid-size coastal town on the Greek mainland, is not immediately inspirational. Today one is greeted on the access road just off the Athens-to-Sparta highway by a display of outsize tractor-tyres and exhaust pipes. The town is split in two by a railway line complete with a rusting brown locomotive, abandoned half a century ago. Modest, workaday and self-contained are adjectives that spring to mind. Megara is a city so resolutely agricultural that during the regime of the Colonels (1967–74) some of her inhabitants made their way to Athens to protest against the Junta on tractors, only to be turned back by tanks. It is a region, said the conservative pamphleteer of the fourth century BC, Isocrates, disparagingly, where men farm rocks. Well, rocks and wool and horses and salt. Salt was of course one of the alchemical minerals of antiquity, offering – thanks to its preservative properties – a choice between survival and starvation. Keeping their salt safe became a priority; Megara's port was eventually connected by long walls to the city proper. And perhaps it was that gift from the sea, the gift that kept on giving, which encouraged the

Archaic Greeks here to turn their gaze seawards and then to stretch their imagination east beyond their immediate horizon.

We are told that it was the Megarian Greeks who 'founded' Byzantion. The Greeks said that the god Apollo, in an oracle from sacred Delphi, had guided them to this spot. Doubtless the leaders of the city did make their way inland to receive Apollo's blessing, but one suspects they already had their expansionist plan in mind. The generous nub of land on the edge of the Sea of Marmara might not have been virgin territory (the Megarians probably developed the pre-existing Thracian trading post, attested to by those pots and that macehead); but this splendidly strategic settlement offered the kind of life that sparked a longing to set sail and to plough through the swelling seas eastwards. We should imagine the hopeful, winner-takes-all adventurers leaving Megara and heading out towards the rising sun. Watching as the seashore landscapes that they passed changed from yellow limestone to marble white and volcanic black, how they seemed comfortingly familiar, and then changed once more as Europe threatened to become Asia.

The attractions of the patch of earth and coast that they would call Byzantion are self-evident. It is brilliantly situated for trade and defence: the wedge of land protected by the Sea of Marmara, by the Bosphorus and by its estuary the Golden Horn forms a natural toll-gate. The ease of fishing here, later commented on by the Roman historian Tacitus, allowed for both self-sufficiency and profit. Tuna swimming with dolphins from the Black Sea into the warmer waters of the Sea of Marmara were diverted into a natural harbour created by the Golden Horn; the name is said to come from the number of glistening fish and marine mammals that could be caught here when they made their annual migration south. Local fishermen who worked in Istanbul before the mass pollution of the 1960s talk of the surface of the water diamond-bright with scales. There are still dolphins – it is easiest to catch sight of them early morning and evening; they are in ever-diminishing pods now, but there were once vast schools. The ancients wrote of sea-mackerel, swordfish,[2] sea turtles and monk seals too.[3] Early Byzantine coins were decorated with the image of a dolphin leaping under an ox.[4] Greek fables declared that Agamemnon tried to bribe Achilles out of his sulk on the battlefields of Troy with the promise of Bosphoran fishing rights. It would have been self-evident to pioneers that this was a prize worth fighting for, jealously guarded by the spirits both above and below the water. The rich geological past offered the archaic Byzantines a plump future.[5]

And so the Greeks (almost certainly bit by bit, expanding that pre-existing Thracian trading settlement over a period of time) arrived in the place that they would call Byzantion – and whether with bloodshed or peaceably, they pump-primed what would become one of the greatest cities on earth.

The Greeks arrived during a remarkable chapter in the human story. In Europe and Asia in the seventh to fifth centuries BC a new phenomenon – the citizens' city – was slowly being born. This was a different kind of place where ordinary people could become economic actors; where merchants and traders succeeded thanks to nous and wit and chance and skill – not simply as a result of the accident of birth, the patronage of kings or the blessings of high priests. It was a time when advances in iron technology allowed for better tools and better harvests, so fatter bellies and more time to think. There were better ships and weapons too – conflicts escalated as a result of a kind of inter-city arms race. Cities were in many ways perturbing places, where millennia-old ties of kith and kin and ways of being were challenged. But the roads built to move those well-armed armies around allowed ideas to travel in their slipstream. As Byzantion was founded, urbane men had the chance to do more, to have more. And, as is attested by the ideas of thinkers such as Socrates, Confucius and the Buddha, ever more urgently, they understood the need to comprehend their world better and therefore to exploit their potential to be better in it. This was the moment in time when the city became humanity's future.

Byzantion, strategic, benefiting from the cultural, intellectual and economic fruits and drive of both East and West, was well placed to succeed.

Speaking Greek in their guttural Doric dialects, the Megarians (closer in culture to their Peloponnesian near-neighbours the Spartans than to the more experimental Athenians) set out to create in Byzantion a version of the world they knew. On that Thracian headland they built Greek baths, gymnasia, stoa (roofed colonnades) and water systems. They made sacred offerings in the Lykos River which once flowed around the city centre. Excavations under the Ottoman prison made infamous by the film *Midnight Express* (now a luxury hotel) have revealed a Phrygian cloak pin (exotic, central Anatolian accessories must have been desirable) and

Greek-style bowls, finely decorated, for mixing wine and pouring oil.

The Megarians brought with them to Byzantion their somewhat Doric attitude to life, as they took a delight in martial music, and pinned their calendar to the celebration of certain religious festivals such as the Hyacinthia and the Carneia. A sixth-century BC dedication from Byzantion at the whispering site of Olympia in mainland Greece has just been identified; the beta and epsilon letters used are indeed typically Megarian.[6] So early Byzantion was a predominantly Hellenic city culture of 20,000 or so citizens, with 'barbarians' all around. Although burial practices suggest that the Greeks fraternised with the native Thracians, they chose to tell stories about themselves that highlighted their Greekness, thus proving to the known world that Byzas' City was no mere roughneck frontier town. We might picture these colonisers at night with the sounds of the new around them, comforting one another with inflated tales of the greatness of their mother-city – reminding themselves that it was one of their own, Orsippos, who was said to have been the first to run naked in the Olympics and that Greece's answer to Robin Hood, the Megarian Theagenes, had secured the support of the poor by killing the cattle of the rich. (It is telling perhaps that Theagenes went on to become a tyrant.) These Megarians knew they needed to subdue their surroundings if they were to stay in charge. In bullish, supremacist, Spartan style, the local population were quickly proclaimed *prounikoi* – burden-bearers – by their new Greek rulers.[7]

We should imagine the intrepid Dorian Greeks on the Byzantine acropolis, watching as other Greek colonists anxiously powered past them up the Bosphorus to the Black Sea, perhaps allowing themselves a quiet moment of satisfaction – knowing that in possession of the city of the clear-sighted they had already struck gold. Through the seventh and sixth centuries BC Greek influence in the area escalated. Tentative Greek settlements, originally built of mud and then of stone, sprang up on the coastlines of Asia Minor. The Megarians' Byzantine colony was economically unique in that it was also the guardian of a channel between continents. Istanbul's sixth-century BC ancestor was a place where it was (indeed is) impossible not to be aware of the hopes and fears, plans and desires of others.

But within just a few generations, the desirable would become the desired. After the careful, optimistic, painstaking foundation of Byzantion as one of a starburst of Hellenic cities, in stormed the Greeks' nemesis in the form of the blistering zeal of Persia. Hurtling across the Bosphorus, Persians controlled the city from c. 546 BC, administering it from Dascylium (currently being excavated) with local Greek tyrants installed as apparatchiks of the new Achaemenid Persian Empire, established in around 550 BC. The Byzantines, it seemed, did not have a taste for Eastern rule – they shrugged off their Asian lords. But the Persians would return, spearheaded by Emperor Dareios and then by his son Xerxes, and backed by the manpower of the 50 million heads they commanded across their vast territories. That self-same Megabazus, a Persian general and the man who, according to Herodotus, had labelled Chalcedon the city of the blind, under the orders of his god-king emperor and in command of a force said to number 80,000 men, 'began the reduction of those communities that did not submit to Persia'.[8] Unfortunately for the inhabitants of Byzantion, Byzas' City was on the Persians' list.

CHAPTER 4

PERSIAN FIRE

c. 513–411 BC

> Having bridged by pontoon the fish-haunted seas of the Bosphorus,
> Mandrocles offered this gift to Hera in memory of his work.
> Having won a crown for himself, and glory for the Samians,
> Making flesh the will [the mind's-vision] of King Dareios.
>
> HERODOTUS, *HISTORIES*[1]

One of the blue 'sapphires' between which Istanbul was said to sit 'like a diamond' was the Bosphorus. The Bosphorus is not just a testing psychological boundary; it is a tricky physical one too. The mix of saltwater and freshwater here swirls and eddies. Satin-smooth shapes are quilted into the water, a mesmeric pattern masking ferocious tides. The flow of the channel across the 22-mile stretch changes nine times between the Black Sea and the Sea of Marmara. A newly discovered underwater river, a submarine channel, on the floor of the strait itself, helps to explain its fickle nature.[2] Water and sediment running through the massive, immersed drain generated by the Black Sea deluge twist in the opposite direction to the general water flow: here there is a 'double-sea'. Many have drowned in the waters or have died smashing into rocks masked by stealthy sea-fogs. But for the Persian Great King of Kings, Dareios the Great, all this was nothing. When you looked at the world from his point of view and from his power bases in Susa, Babylon, Memphis and Persepolis, the hinterland of Greek Chalcedon is conveniently flat; around the Meander plain gentle hills are now covered with folds of olive groves. The entry to Europe is inviting; it is the mountains of the Caucasus range or those ringing the Greek Peloponnese that could be perceived as barriers. Those choppy straits of the Hellespont and Bosphorus were just streams, those coast-hugging islands – Samos, Lesbos, Chios – simply stepping-stones to a new continental landmass, ripe for the plucking.

And so standing in Asia, looking out over the green hills of Europe, for the man who would join the Red Sea to the Mediterranean by gouging out a canal, and who would institute a universal currency to encourage trade across the known world, to collapse the small, wet gap between continents must have seemed like child's play – an act that has accumulated legendary proportions but that was, for the most powerful ruler on earth, practicable. And so it is that the textual life-story of Istanbul begins with a bridge. Herodotus' description of Dareios' massive, mile-long pontoon, one of the Emperor's eye-wateringly audacious projects, writes Byzantion into history. The motivation for this bridge was a spot of bother in the West.

Nebuchadnezzar III, a Babylonian client-king, had revolted and, delighted to hear this, the Scythians who ranged across the northern edge of the Black Sea and controlled the European territories that now stretch west from modern-day Istanbul had decided to play up. Determined to chase the Scythians back to their Thracian and Balkan homelands; sitting on the Greeks' sacred Black Sea temple, To Hieron, where Zeus of the Fair Winds was honoured to ensure the safe passage of boats, Dareios in around 513 BC commanded Mandrocles, an engineer from the island of Samos, to construct a pontoon of boats stretching from the Asian to the European Bosphoran shore. Dareios might have been about to conquer the known world, but he did not want to get his feet wet in the process.

At this stage it is not clear whether Byzantion was a reluctant subject or a compliant ally of Persia. It now seems likely that the Persians had set up a taxation-cum-extortion point on the site of Chrysopolis (today the neighbourhood of Üsküdar on the Asian shores of the Bosphorus in wider Istanbul, a location that will assume huge significance under Constantine the Great) – to squeeze money from ships as they were forced towards the headland by the Bosphorus' tricky currents.[3] For the next twenty-five centuries, milking passing ships for cash would be a popular pastime for those in control of the strait and the city. The Persians would not have wanted anyone to interrupt this lucrative operation: the inhabitants of Byzantion would find themselves on the wrong side of Persian ire.

There were many at this fringe of civilisation who did not want to become part of the Persians' sprawling, Aramaic-speaking, multi-ethnic empire. When Dareios' predecessor Cyrus the Great had first engaged with the Scythians he was killed by a Scythian Queen and his head carried around in a skin full of blood – the notion being that the thirst for power that had inspired him could now be quenched.[4] At the beginning of the fifth century BC a tinder-line of revolt had been lit along the coast of Asia Minor and in the islands off shore. In response Dareios' fire had a diabolic heat to it. Cities were razed, adults killed or enslaved, boys castrated and girls taken as concubines to the Great King's court. By 494/3 BC the uprisings had been crushed and Byzantion and Chalcedon had been torched. The Byzantines and Chalcedonians would have watched across the Bosphorus straits as black plumes in the sky smoke-signalled their compatriots' misfortune. Herodotus tells us that Byzantion's population, some freedom-fighters among them, fled for refuge to the sandy southern shores of the Black Sea, and then drifted back, eventually contributing a number of ships to the Persian war fleet.

Sailing the stretch of water between Asia and Europe, one senses that the grudge between Eastern tyrant and Western territory was personal. Yes, Persia desired land and human booty, but successful colonisation is all about quality not quantity. From now on power-players in Asia and Europe alike wanted the blessed and strategically acute stretch of coast around Byzantion with its wooded, easy-to-protect hills to smile back at them in submissive recognition.[5]

In 491 BC Dareios demanded the capitulation of all of Greece, insisting that those plucky Greek city-states, 700 or so in the Aegean region, offer up symbolic gifts of obeisance in the form of earth and water. The revolts might have been crushed but victory would not be quite so straightforward. Persian strategy did not factor in the unique sense of community that the Greeks seemed to possess. A tradition of decision by council, of joint identity through language and religion, of power by mythical association, furnished the Greek city-states with tremendous resilience. For the Persians the humiliation of their subsequent defeat at the Battle of Marathon in 490 BC was an unpleasant surprise.

But when Dareios died in 486 BC his ambition did not die with him. Dareios' son and successor Xerxes had no intention of letting territories like Byzantion revert to Greek ownership. In 480 BC the Battle of Thermopylae on land and the Battle of Artemisium at sea – critical engagements between the might of the Persian Empire and the city-states from across the Greek-speaking world – were the first in a series of blistering aggressions. Themistocles, that vocal Athenian champion of democracy, led the Greeks by sea. On the Persian side a prominent naval commander was – almost uniquely in all recorded history – a woman, Artemisia, Queen of Halicarnassus (modern-day Bodrum). The 'Father of History' Herodotus, himself from Halicarnassus, a child at the time of the conflict, tells us that Artemisia boasted high birth, five ships and 'a man's will'. Of all the 150,000 or so combatants on that watery battlefield, Artemisia would have been the only female. A crushing message was being delivered by Persia: the Greeks were so effeminate that the omnipotent Xerxes could afford to send a mere woman against them. The Battle of Artemisium was considered to field no clear winner and, in the wake of Persian success at Thermopylae, ten weeks or so later, Xerxes' men incinerated the Archaic temple on the Athenian Acropolis, killing the priests who guarded it. Backlit by flames, the Persian Emperor watched the dreadful realisation of his will. Inspecting the artefacts remaining from the firestorm, which were transferred to the New Acropolis Museum in Athens, I have touched the traumatised Archaic statues that were victims of this onslaught; blistered and buckled, one can still sense from their broken stone-skin the heat of Persian fires. Xerxes then sat on a high hill to watch what he believed would be the obliteration of the Greek allied forces in a naval engagement at Salamis.[6] Byzantion looked set to be just one of many settlements under continent-wide Persian control.

But, like Marathon in 490 BC, Salamis was a disaster for the Persians. Tempting their ships into a treacherous crosswind, the Greeks won with the application of brain rather than brawn. In the chaos Artemisia rammed her fellow Persian ships, apparently without disgrace: 'my men have become women and my women men', Xerxes spat. As the Persian troops limped back to the Middle East, this scrapping Queen was entrusted with the safe return of Xerxes' defeated sons to Asia Minor. After a further defeat at Plataea, Persia kept her attentions focused on the East.

And then, for Byzantion, came an interesting twist. The city would become a political pawn not just in the power-play between Persia and Greece, but among the Greeks themselves.

One Pausanias – lauded Spartan leader of the victorious Greek troops at Plataea, nephew of the heroic Spartan King Leonidas (who had fallen at Thermopylae defending Europe from Persian advance) – seems to have become enthralled by the city. By this stage a confident little settlement, Byzantion's strategic benefits and use to the newly formed allegiance of Greeks, the Hellenic League, was apparent. There was also work to do: some of those handsome Doric buildings had been burnt down by Phoenicians (reported Herodotus) after the Ionian revolt, so for the right man, Byzantion was a project. Back in Sparta, Pausanias had been ruling as regent for the dead Leonidas' young son.[7] Pausanias was in many ways a model Greek: after securing victory at Plataea he had ordered a number of Sparta's slave population of helots to put a simple meal on the table, in contrast to the engorged victory banquet readied in the defeated Persian commander's tent. He had led out an army of around 100,000 men and lost only ninety-one. His massive achievement was recognised with the

Pausanias was a golden Greek hero, as represented in this engraving of c. AD 1880. His entrapment by the delights of Byzantion resulted in his recall to Sparta and subsequent un-heroic end – holed up on the Spartan acropolis where he starved to death.

offer of a tenth of all booty from the Persian engagements – the loot
ranging from concubines to golden platters.

But sent as the head of the Hellenic League's navy to break the Persian
garrison in Byzantion and to keep a weather eye on the East, sailing out of
the diminutive little port of Hermione (still a stop-off for the smaller ferries and local sea taxis today), Pausanias liberated Cyprus and Byzantion
and then he went rogue, ending up, with unseemly haste, as Byzantine
dictator. In the words of the historian Thucydides, 'Pausanias treated this
more like a tyranny than a military command.' Byzantion seemed to turn
Pausanias' head and in so doing turned the tide of history.

For a man from the notoriously pleasure-denying city-state of Sparta,
Byzantion perhaps became Pausanias' own little corner of paradise. There
is a strong possibility that Pausanias built the city's first walls to safeguard
all that invigorating, lush loveliness – a revealing move,[8] especially as the
Spartans despised city walls, bragging that 'our young men are our walls
and our battlements the tips of their spears'.[9] Athens had completed their
own ring of steel in 478 BC, the very year Pausanias secured Byzantion –
his was a city for which the tyrant clearly had big plans. In every way his
triumphs seem to have intoxicated Pausanias. The Spartan commissioned
self-aggrandising poems and inscriptions – even adding his name, and
his name alone, to the base of the Serpent Column erected in Delphi by
the Greek allies to commemorate Persia's defeat. A surreal and splendid
object – a golden tripod for the god Apollo, supported by a serpentine
bronze column 18 feet tall in the form of entwined snakes – this was not
just a religious offering but a war memorial. The names of the thirty-one
Greek states that had combined to fight the Persians were engraved on
the serpentine coils. Embarrassed officials, once they realised Pausanias'
hubris, quickly scrubbed out the Spartan's flagrant self-promotion.

Eight hundred years later, the Serpent Column was moved to Byzantium's hippodrome. One cannot help but feel that Pausanias would be
secretly pleased to know that this monument – a rather etiolated creature
now – is one of the few remaining classical antiquities to survive back
in modern Istanbul in the public space next to the Blue Mosque, today
a favourite lunch-break stop for tourists and young Istanbullus. This remarkable artefact was described by Herodotus, and what remains of it
stands exactly where (according to the historian Eusebius in the fourth
century AD) it was placed by the Emperor Constantine. The original gold

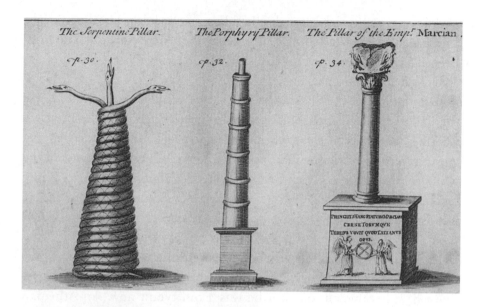

The Serpent Column still stands in a rather diminished state in the hippodrome in Istanbul, and was commemorated by visitors to the city, for example in the image above from the AD 1752 publication of 'The Travels of the late Charles Thompson, Esq. Containing his observations on France, Italy, Turkey in Europe, the Holy Land, Arabia and Egypt, and many other parts of the world'.

cauldron supported by the snakes had been melted down in the AD 350s, and just one snake head survives in the Istanbul Archaeological Museum. Even if unwittingly, right in its historic heart, the city still honours the Spartan man who so passionately loved her.

In antiquity however, Pausanias' glory days would be short-lived. Worse than all his maverick machinations, Pausanias flirted with the Persians, wearing Persian dress (some whispered), bedding Persian women, toying with the idea of a dynastic marriage with Xerxes' daughter[10] – and all the while commanding a Greek fleet from his Byzantion base. After being recalled by a somewhat embarrassed Spartan command, probably in 477 BC, for a yellow-card warning, Pausanias hastened back to his adopted town.

Even though Byzantion was now theoretically under Athenian protection, Athens flexing her muscles as a maritime power, Pausanias remained. It became all too clear he was a full tyrant now. An Athenian force led by Kimon sailed out to demonstrate the error of Pausanias' ways. Finally, in around 470 BC, the privateer-general was peremptorily recalled to Sparta. His passion for Byzantion had turned this poster-boy into an embarrassment. On arrival back in Sparta Pausanias was hounded to the city's acropolis, where he remained walled up in Athena's temple, starved to the point of death – and was dragged out only so that his corrupting corpse would not pollute the sanctuary.

Pausanias' end might have been ignominious, but it seems he left his adopted city with two gifts that would become defining features of the settlement: its protecting walls, and the enduring truth that Byzantion, Constantinople, Istanbul would be a place where individual reputations could be both made and broken, and where both dreams and nightmares might be realised.

This Spartiate's cock-suredness was in fact rather handy for Athens. Implying that the Spartans could not be trusted to marshal their own leaders, let alone spearhead a pan-Hellenic coalition, the Athenians manoeuvred to ensure that their own city-state took the lead in Hellenic protection. Keeping the peace in the Eastern Mediterranean with bespoke ships was an expensive business. The newfangled triremes that the city-state had been developing – following the Delphic oracle's instruction to the new democracy to 'put their trust in a wooden wall' – were killer whales on the Aegean: beautiful, deadly and expensive, and so Athens demanded tribute from those she protected. Travelling its own length in six seconds at speeds up to 8 knots (new research suggests possibly even 12 knots), the trireme boasted at the prow an Athlit-style battering ram,[11] and it was packed with free oarsmen in the hull. These boats were lithe and lethal. City-states and settlements across the Eastern Mediterranean had to sign up to the 'democratic project' to help keep these super-craft afloat. We can see Byzantion's name, along with many hundreds of others, marked up on a three-man-high stele still standing in Athens' Epigraphical Museum. Out of a total annual tribute of 400–600 talents, Byzantion's contribution was 15 a year, proportionately a huge amount, paid from tolls imposed on passing ships and all that rich tuna-fishing.

From this point on, with Pausanias' misbehaviour in Byzantion the perfect excuse for strong-armed, regional control, Athens was on course for its Golden Age.

With the story of Pausanias', and hence Sparta's, disgrace fresh in every-one's minds, the Athenians had struck home their advantage. Calling a meeting at the wind-lashed sacred island of Delos in the heart of the Cyclades, the Athenians were declared the hegemon of an offensive–defensive anti-Persian alliance of Greek city-states that we now call the Delian League, and ten citizens of Athens were declared *hellenotamiai*, 'treasurers of the Greeks'.

For close on thirty-five years Byzantion kept on delivering up loot to Athens' tribute collectors, Byzantine gold joining the other precious metals, cash and jewels from across the region. In 454 BC, work on the Delian League headquarters at Delos suddenly stopped. Slaves put down their chisels and the Hellenic Treasury was moved to Athens. Soon the loot would be stored in what suddenly looked less like a sanctuary and ever more like an imperial vault: the new Parthenon temple on the acrop-olis. Athens was now an imperial force with the big idea of *demos-kratia* – the power or grip of the people on its side. For fifty years, Athena's city became adept at exporting democracy across the Mediterranean at the point of a sword. It has been estimated that – in addition to the cultural gifts that the city gave to the world as the 'city-hall of wisdom' – some 50,000 refugees were displaced across the Eastern Mediterranean as a result of Athens' aggressive, imperialising tactics.

In 440 BC, along with the island of Samos – possibly prompted by political shifts around the Black Sea (Istanbul always turns her eyes north as well as glancing west and staring east and south) – the inhabitants of Byzantion revolted. Freedom lasted only a year – the Athenians were in full can-do mode at this time. The philosopher Socrates might have been one of those in the hoplite ranks who sailed out to suppress popular re-action against the 'violet-crowned',[12] 'oily'[13] politics of Athena's city-state. As soon as their chance came in 411 BC, with unrest fomented this time by the Spartans (by now Athens' arch-enemies, their adversaries in the Peloponnesian War), Byzantion rebelled once more. After she had been taken from Athens in 410 BC by the Spartan naval leader Mindaros with the help of Persian subsidies, her inhabitants – remembering perhaps their original Dorian foundation – welcomed in the Spartan general Clearchos, who had already been representing their interests back in his home town.

After a century as a trading chip in the power-play between Persia and Greece, thanks to her strategic position on the Bosphorus, useful for interests operating north to south as well as east to west, Byzantion was now a pawn in the game of chess between Athenian and Spartan ambition.[14] As such she would have a front-row seat for the desperate and debilitating final act of the pitiless Peloponnesian War, and would secure her place in history as a settlement attractive to agents who were confident that they could control those near and far with both maritime and martial force.

CHAPTER 5

✦

CITY OF SIEGE

c. 450–400 BC

The rest of the region is fair and extensive, and contains many inhabited villages; for the land produces barley, wheat, beans of all kinds, millet and sesame, a sufficient quantity of figs, an abundance of grapes which yield a good sweet wine, and in fact everything except olives.

XENOPHON, *ANABASIS*[1]

The Athenians were besieging Byzantion; they had built a stockade around the city, and were attacking its wall with missiles from a distance and by close assault. Now the Athenians, finding that they were unable to accomplish anything by force, persuaded some of the Byzantines to betray the city . . .

XENOPHON, *HELLENICA*[2]

Twenty-four centuries ago, Byzantion was afflicted by two persistent adversaries: besiegement, and a man from the West who wanted to make his name in the East.

The fifth century BC gave Byzantion copper-bottomed status as a prize-city. And because it had value and appeal and purpose, the settlement became a stage-set on and around which some of the greatest characters in ancient history played out their lives – the general and author Xenophon, the Carian vice-satrap Mausolos who gives his name to mausoleums (his own was one of the wonders of the ancient world), and the Athenian turncoat-general Alcibiades. Alcibiades is one of those characters so extreme he would have been too good to make up.[3]

Born an aristocrat, with a Spartan wet-nurse, Alcibiades tore a strip through the classical world as he has done through history. The mess-mate of the philosopher Socrates, his would-be lover, he was everything the Athenian thinker was not. Feckless, over-sexed, immoderate, dazzling, raffish, louche, Alcibiades would be described by ancient authors as 'the adored tyrant of Athens'.⁴ Aristophanes wrote that the people of Athens 'pine for him, they hate him, but they wish to have him back'.⁵ He was infuriatingly irresistible, and impossible to ignore – flouncing round Athena's city in a purple cloak, even though such undemocratic displays were frowned upon, refusing to play the *aulos* (a bit like our oboe) because it made his mouth pucker up in an unattractive way, espousing drink from first thing in the morning, and, according to the comic poet Eupolis, starting the trend of peeing into a pot while still at dinner. He had led Athenian troops on a disastrous campaign in Sicily in 415 BC and, thanks to the mysterious vandalism of the herms in Athens' streets, had been accused of sacrilege in his absence. After a sojourn with Athens' arch-enemies, the Spartans, making friends to the point of impregnating the Spartan King's wife, Alcibiades then fled east and ended up in Asia Minor, acting as a double agent for the Persian viceroy Tissaphernes. Alcibiades – look-at-me, lisping, love-locked – seems to have been in his element as he made Byzantion and her environs his playground, and he could soon be found burning up and down the waters between Asia and Europe.

By the end of the fifth century BC Athens was gasping. Twenty years into a debilitating war with the Spartans, her coffers and optimism were running dry; the city had lost around a third of her population to plague and was now starting to haemorrhage allies and territories. The treatment of prisoners of war by both sides broke all codes of Hellenic honour – fellow Hellenes were branded, starved and stoned to death. Sniffing the Greek-on-Greek wastage, power-mongers in the East turned their sights west once more. Two generations after their defeat at Salamis, the Persians were again ready to flex their imperial muscles. Alcibiades, a political operator of Machiavellian skill, who always managed to keep his options open, made use of the network of spies, diplomats and messengers that stitched the Mediterranean together and suggested to Athens that she should give up the democratic experiment and take Persia as an ally against the Spartans. Athens ignored his spicy advice and instead floundered around in a hideous ideological civil war, voting the democracy out of existence and watching helplessly as Alcibiades – their one-time golden boy – commandeered ships at Samos into what was, in effect, a private navy, while Sparta picked off key cities such as Byzantion.[6] There was a febrile wind blowing across the Eastern Mediterranean – no one's future was certain.

Xenophon's vivid accounts of the machinations along the Bosphorus, of the men who were fighting over the spoils of land and sea, make for thrilling reading; he is a performative author. We hear of Persian generals plunging into the waves on their horses, the water rising neck-high on the terrified animals; of operators like Alcibiades slipping along the waterways, negotiating here, threatening there. It is easy to appreciate why the ancients acted around Byzantion with such vigour. Whether it be on the Sea of Marmara, the Bosphorus or the Golden Horn, any craft within sight of the city breaks the choppy, petrol-blue water here and makes it froth white with purpose. Landfalls are tantalisingly close. For pumped-up sailor-soldiers, Byzantion's turf must have seemed like a giant, status-enhancing adventure playground.

At this point Alcibiades could simply have 'Medised' – gone over to the Persians. The Persians were clearly as charmed by him as both Athenians and Spartans had been, putting him on a retainer and naming pleasure gardens after him. But of course this attention-seeker of monstrous proportions had friends and family and a reputation to recover in Athens. The challenging stretch of water between Europe and Asia was one he now knew well. Acting like quicksilver, twisting and turning, after success leading an Athenian fleet at the Battle of Cyzicus on the Asian side of the Marmara Sea in 410 BC (where incidentally, through antiquity, the anchor-stone of Jason's Argo was said to be displayed), he helped to set up (or to revive) a customs house mid-stream, close to Byzantion and to what is now called Leander's Tower – demanding 10 per cent of transportable wealth from all passing traffic.[7] Administered from Chrysopolis, which the Athenians had retaken,[8] the levy was impossible to escape; and Alcibiades started to deliver substantial treasures back to his mother-city.[9] Soon he would have the opportunity to offer up an even greater prize.

It had become clear that unless Athens retook from Sparta the city of the blind – Chalcedon – and Byzantion too, her essential, umbilical link to grain supplies via the Black Sea would be cut. Control of the strait, of the boats that transported food around the Eastern Mediterranean and of the settlements at the waters' edge had become a tool of empire. Troops were sent to besiege Chalcedon first. Although not present from the outset, Alcibiades made an appearance, mid-campaign, supporting his co-general Thrasyllos and then tearing off to the Hellespont, commandeering resources, making strategically important friends and hell-raising. Returning to the Athenian fort of Chrysopolis, regrouping, using his considerable charm to persuade settlements such as Selymbria on the Marmara coast over to his side, Alcibiades joined his Athenian messmates determined to retake Byzantion itself.

Byzantion had been lost to the regular Spartan forces, and was now controlled by a combination of Sparta's ex-helot slaves freed after a period of service in the army, Spartan non-citizens, Megarians, Boeotians and Byzantines – all under the purview of the mildly psychotic Spartan Clearchos, who had been sent out two years before specifically to prevent recapture by Athens. In late 408 BC, a winter blasted by ferocious weather, with a force of 5,000 or so men, Alcibiades surrounded the city. A siege wall was built, similar to that constructed around Chalcedon a few months before, snipers were positioned strategically and ladders were prepared to assault the walls; in the harbour Peloponnesian boats were harried. Clearchos meanwhile had sailed out from Byzantion to try to obtain Persian help and, conveniently, a vocal faction within the walls seemed eager to negotiate with the legendary warrior at their gates. There had been resentments brewing during the siege: heavy-handed Clearchos was it seems preserving the best – and later the bulk – of rations for his Peloponnesian compatriots. The occupying Spartan garrison was well provisioned but locals were going hungry. Somehow word got out to Alcibiades, a man with friends in all the right places, and immediately he smelt an opportunity.

The accounts then diverge. Xenophon tells us simply that Alcibiades sweet-talked his way into the city, agents within the walls opening up the gates at night and letting in their one-time enemies. Diodoros Siculus suggests a more complex series of events, reporting that the Athenian fleet pretended to leave, but then attacked Byzantion's harbour to draw attention away from the betrayal that was taking place on the landward side. By the time the Byzantine garrison realised their mistake, pro-Athenians within the city had let Alcibiades and his men in – the Athenian operator promising emollient terms to those who did not resist.

Whichever account is true, Alcibiades, through trickery rather than brute force, took a city that would, over the centuries, thwart many attackers. The lady's-man, man's-man maverick had charmed his way into one of the region's most strategic settlements – another notch to add to his tally of conquests.

Lionising his own wily manipulation of the Persian powers that were still visibly operating in the region, Alcibiades made it clear that the Athenians had him to thank for their success. It had required a hero of his now legendary proportions to give Athens control of the most important junction on the Bosphorus. In the process Alcibiades had, conveniently, secured Chrysopolis as a tax-collection point, earning a healthy income as his countrymen charged boats for the right to venture up and down between the Sea of Marmara and the Black Sea. Back in Athens playwrights such as Euripides memorialised Alcibiades as a returning hero, giving one in the eye to the Spartans.[10]

Whether or not Alcibiades can claim the full credit, the salvation of Byzantion and Chalcedon and the liberation of the grain supply back to Piraeus and into Athenian bellies was enough to earn this prodigal son adulation on his return home. As he was tentatively approaching the port of Piraeus, it was soon clear that bad-boy Alcibiades would indeed be welcomed back as a hero once more. We are told that after a speech in the Boule in the Agora and then to the Assembly up on the Pnyx, the massed Athenians started to shout and to cheer at his homecoming. It was quickly agreed that Alcibiades' confiscated property should be returned and that the stele marking out his charges should be upended and thrown into the sea.[11]

Yet within just four months Alcibiades would be back in the East once again. The Athenian mother city was in no mood for mercy; at the tail end of the debilitating Peloponnesian War her own great statues, including the decorations on the glittering Athena in the Parthenon temple, had been melted down for coin. In 405 BC at the Battle of Aegospotami – 150 miles or so down the coast from Byzantion, and half a dozen miles from the future conflict of Gallipoli – Lysander, the triumphant Spartan admiral, and his men truly found their sea-legs. By this point Alcibiades was to all intents and purposes a Thracian warlord. He barrelled in with good advice that the Athenian naval officers ignored; in the bald, cover-free landscape, he said, it was ridiculous to leave Athenian triremes so exposed. The Athenians blanked their troubled anti-hero and instead set out to forage for supplies. The Spartans attacked. All but two boats were taken captive. All Athenian citizens on board – possibly as many as 3,000 – were lined up and summarily executed.[12]

Clearchos – by all accounts a bloodthirsty authoritarian – became tyrant of Byzantion once more. The local population, with the Athenians the losers in the war, had apparently asked Sparta back in to keep control – perhaps conveniently recalling the Dorian profile of their founding fathers, the Megarians. In the fallout many of the city's aristocrats were executed by grimly inclement Clearchos. A few who could be proved to be pro-Athenian managed to slip away at night, ending up back in Athena's city.[13]

Meanwhile, opposite Byzantion, the settlement of Chrysopolis which the Athenians had used as a base during the Peloponnesian War saw a final whirlwind of activity. With the populations of Sparta, Athens and their allies traumatised – or dead – many Greeks decided to cut their losses and sell their services as mercenaries to the Persians.[14] Included in one of those mongrel forces – the Ten Thousand – was a follower of Socrates, the general and historian Xenophon.

In 399 BC, the year that Socrates was being poisoned in Athens with hemlock for crimes against the state, the Ten Thousand after a grindingly difficult campaign dragged themselves back to Chrysopolis to sell their 'booty' (largely engraved vessels of precious metal produced in Anatolia along with livestock and slaves). The agreed plan had been that the campaign-jaded hordes would then be ferried to Byzantion across the Bosphorus and assured safe passage home. Thankfully on the European mainland, the smell of the mother-country in the air, Xenophon and his fellow mercenaries eagerly massed on a patch of open ground near the Byzantine Gate of Thrakion. But instead of water for their horses, lint for wounds, money for the road, there was a curt head count and an enforced disbandment – you can imagine the rumble of disbelief and then the rage. Furious, the troops turned on Byzantion itself and drove out the Spartan senior command. There was even a wild suggestion in the weary war tents that Xenophon should step up to the mark to take the city of Byzantion as a tyrant – that he could found a virtuous new civilisation here based on the principles of the philosopher Socrates that he so loved, establishing Socratic-flavoured kingship as rehearsed in Xenophon's own writings. But Xenophon, like Socrates attuned to Laconic (Spartan-esque, from the Spartan's land of Laconia) ideas and sometimes branded a La-conophile, pointed out that Byzantion was a Doric-leaning city, ruled by Spartans in a Spartan-dominated world. If the mercenaries took over the city it would be the focus of rage and firepower within weeks. Xenophon persuaded his men not to mount a full attack.

Originally planning to sail back to Gytheion, the little Spartan port from which Paris was said to have eloped with his stolen Helen centuries before in the Age of Heroes, Xenophon was double-crossed once again and ended up in Spartan employ fighting a Perso-Spartan game in Asia Minor.

The messy regime-changes, the half-cocked attempts at self-determination, the fluctuating allegiances all suggest that at this time Byzantion – and her satellites Chalcedon and Chrysopolis – enjoyed only staging-post, way-station status. They were strategic locations, but lacked their own strategists, sites that were geopolitically too useful for their own good, the focus primarily of other men's ambition. In this historical slice of time, Byzantion suffered one siege after another and a rash of interventions.

It is no coincidence perhaps that one of the most comprehensive an-cient works on engineering, *Mechanike Syntaxis*, was produced by Philo Mechanicus, born in Byzantion around 280 BC. Much space in this compendium is devoted to the best preparation for sieges, the design of siege craft, harbour building and missile construction, including a re-peating crossbow. Interestingly, two of Philo's recommendations in times of siege are to ensure there are sufficient doctors on hand to deal with the inevitable trauma and enough men versed in cryptography to pass messages across the barricades. Byzantion's geographical blessings must have sometimes seemed a curse to those who lived there.

Close on 6,000 miles to the east, a new archaeological dig indicates what would be Byzantion's future, and arguably her salvation.

Beneath the main square in Luoyang in central China – where elderly couples learn to waltz and Maoists protest under the Red Flag – an ex-traordinary burial was uncovered in 2002. Twenty-four horses had been slaughtered and laid in front of the showy war-chariots of their king around the time of Alcibiades' siege of Byzantion. These dead animals were the ultimate status symbol. Imported from the steppes, and often

described as Tianma, celestial horses, they were said to be sired by dragons and to sweat blood. The hunger for these creatures across the East
would stimulate a chain of trade that would end up running along the
routes we now name Silk Roads – all the way from Xian in China to
the far reaches of the Roman Empire, with the city of Byzantion as its
western nodal point. The Luoyang burial is a ghostly pre-echo of times
to come in beleaguered Byzantion. Stimulated by desire for status goods
from distant lands, international trade would secure Byzantion's character, status and standing. A city that connected the Far East to a wild
West. This would become a city worth fighting for and protecting; rather
than just a well-placed military prize, thanks to her position at the edge
of continents, emotionally people wanted to be here and economically
she would realise her massive potential.

But first Byzantion needed to earn her reputation as a city of spirit and
pleasure and sin.

CHAPTER 6

❖

WINE AND WITCHES

c. 400–c. 200 BC

Byzantion makes all of her merchants drunkards. The whole night through for your sake we were drinking, and frankly, it was darn strong wine too. At any rate I rose this morning with a head for four.

MENANDER, FOURTH CENTURY BC[1]

Cluster [of grapes], full of the drops of Dionysus, you rest indeed under cover of Aphrodite's golden chambers. No longer will your mother vine, throwing the beloved vine-twig around you, spring forth the divine leaf over your head.

MOERO (POETESS OF BYZANTION), *ARAI*, THIRD CENTURY BC[2]

Was it simply jealousy? Amplified travellers' tales? Easy access to the fruits of three continents? The peril of a trading town where what goes abroad stays abroad? Whatever the reason, there were manifold reports of the Byzantines' love of the bottle. The historian Theopompus of Chios, 'lover of truth',[3] wrote of Byzantion's ways in the latter half of the fourth century BC:

this city was situated at a trading place, and the entire population spent their time in the market-place and by the water side; hence they had accustomed themselves to amours and drinking in the taverns. As for the Chalcedonians before they all came to have a share with the Byzantines in the government, they devoted themselves unceasingly to the better pursuits of life; but after they had once tasted of the democratic liberties of the Byzantines they sank utterly into corrupt luxury, and in their daily lives, from having been the most sober and restrained, they became wine-bibbers and spendthrifts.[4]

The supply of inebriates in Byzantion was obviously good. After all, this city was on the edge of a continent that had been producing wine since at least 6000 BC.

In the back rooms of the Archaeological Institute in Yerevan in Armenia are stacked mounds of milk crates and plastic bags. Inside there are so many archaeological artefacts that the finds spill over into the corridors and up the stairs. Here there are treasures indeed: delicately woven, multi-colour matting and a straw skirt, both graphically designed, vast, dark pots for storing food, the world's oldest leather shoe – all found within the Areni Cave in southern Armenia and dating from c. 4100 BC. And here too, prised from beneath layers of preserving sheep dung, in 2007 emerged what is claimed to be the world's oldest winery. Within the musty dark of the cave, protected by the fast-flowing Arpa River that rushes through Armenia and Azerbaijan, there were found large fermentation vats and wine presses, along with terracotta drinking cups and skeletal remains, suggesting perhaps that the alcohol consumption here – from vats that each contained 14 or so gallons of red wine – was part of a mass, collective ritual to send off the dead. In some versions of the story of Dionysos – avidly worshipped in Byzantion – this god of wine was said to have come from either the Near East or Thrace. The Hebrew Bible relates that Noah's Ark came to rest on Mount Ararat (it was in the thirteenth century AD that Marco Polo popularised the idea that this was the Ararat in the southern Caucasus) and that he came down to cultivate the land and to plant vines – from which he 'became drunken'.

New archaeological evidence in Istanbul buttresses the literary hyperbole: wine was vigorously imported, exported and enjoyed here. From the metro excavations in the city centre at Sirkeci from 2004 onwards, an amphora handle fragment from Thassos (a Greek island famous for its honeyed wine) has been retrieved – the mark of ownership distinctive – a satyr dancing, back arched, head thrown back. There are other tantalising fragments of a full life: the wild curls of a maenadic woman tumble on a broken pot; there is a sleek black lamp to light the way for those Athenians who manned that piratical military customs base at Chrysopolis – pottery of the kind that turns up back home in the Athenian Agora; there are amphorae too from Chios, Sinope, Knidos, Rhodes, North Africa, for warming brews to keep out the chill on coastal lookouts. All of these are now, for the first time in 2,400 years, seeing the light of day.

Some drank while others worked – the skeletons of the men and women who lived at the Bosphorus' edge from the fifth and fourth centuries BC point to a life expectancy of between thirty and forty years and suggest that they endured tough conditions while alive. Remains of a temple of Poseidon, again unearthed in 2004, demonstrate that the sea god was expected to protect that trade in wine-filled amphorae from across the known world and to look after the men who guarded its entry points.

And despite Byzantion's appearance in written history in the classical period predominantly as a military and an economic prize, the archaeology reminds us that when she was not being besieged or attacked or the focus of trade between the power-players of the moment, the day-to-day experience of the city revolved, quite naturally, around making life as enjoyable as possible. Stroll through Gülhane Park in the Eminönü district of modern Istanbul and you will walk among the ghosts of the ancient Byzantines. Where tourists meander, where families play and lovers kiss, the original Eastern Mediterranean inhabitants here lived their lives and buried their dead – they are memorialised on the headstones that survive. So we can meet Byzantion's early street entertainers, astronomers, sailors and doctors. We hear (from a fourth-century BC author, possibly Aristotle) that 'wonder-workers' (jugglers, musicians, soothsayers, charm-pedlars) were heavily taxed in the city:[5] these must have been itinerant entertainers who enjoyed a roaring trade in this port-pleasure town.

Priests and priestesses are also commemorated on the headstones. The other great comfort for the ordinary men and women of Byzantion would have been their habitual religious experiences, rushing around to as many as eight shrines or sanctuaries a day, sending up invocations or leaving little offerings, fervently trying to keep the gods of sea, sky and earth onside. The ancient Greeks had no separate word for religion. Gods, goddesses, demi-gods and spirits were simply everywhere and in everything – and as a 'blessed' and an ethnically mongrel place, Byzantion was thought to be an earthly home to more spirits than most.

Byzantion had a Greek timbre, but the Eastern nature of the settlement could not be Doric-columned out. It was always clear that this was a foundation on the edge of Asia. Along with the Greek deities that you would expect to be honoured here with temples and shrines – Aphrodite and Dionysos (both vigorously worshipped), Apollo, Hera, Athena, Artemis and Rhea – not to mention the establishment of Spartan-style festivals such as the Hyacinthia and Carneia, the local Thracian deity Zeuxippos was also venerated, and the goddess Bendis. From the mid-fourth century onwards, the Egyptian deities Serapis and Isis were worshipped, as was the mystical mistress of nature, Kybele. Typically flanked by big cats, possibly tracing a 9,000-year-old ancestry to the pre-goddess fertility figurines of Çatalhöyük in southern Turkey, Kybele is a strange and unforgiving creature. Her rock-cut gateways in central Anatolia led, it was thought, to another dimension. Today they are still extraordinary, otherworldly. Stumbling through the frost, avoiding hostile shepherds' dogs with anti-wolf collars, intrepid visitors can still find them in what was once the kingdom of the man with the fatally golden touch, Midas. The blind openings, solid rock doorways through which Kybele was thought to control passage between life and death, watch the world as they have done for close on three millennia, staring blankly from cliff faces.

Word spread about the power of this creature. Greeks sometimes call her Meter Oreia, mountain mother, or Kubileya, the Hellenised version of the Phrygian word for mountain.[6] At Byzantion she came to be worshipped as Rhea-Kybele – the Great Mother of Nature. Kybele would go on to command a new sanctuary in the Athenian Agora, and then, according to Ovid, she travelled from the landscapes of Pessinus in Asia Minor, in the foothills of Mount Ida, via the Aegean island of Tenedos to Rome to provide support against Hannibal and Carthage.[7] Kybele's black stone was carried from the Palatine every year to the Almo (a tributary of the Tiber) to be bathed. The Taurobolium, one of her shrines in Rome, where Roman priests stood under a deluge of blood as bulls were sacrificed for the goddess above, is hidden beneath Christian buildings under St Peter's Square. Kybele even survived the Christianisation of Roman Byzantium and was honoured every year in a grand procession through the city centre. So we should think of the men and women of Byzantion worshipping Kybele and other diverse divinities – passionately, piously, perennially.

Recognising the debt that the colonisers owed to the power of the waterways here, sanctuaries were set up overlooking the Bosphorus and at the entrance of the Black Sea a toll-gate was swiftly established post-colonisation. The tremendous value of this access point was glorified in a religious complex on the Asian side of the straits known simply as To

Hieron, the Shrine, a crucial sacred space and a refuge, now concealed under the Byzantine fortress on Yoros Tepesi, a small headland that narrows the entrance to the Black Sea mouth. Across the Bosphorus those early settlers developed another temple which came to be of less importance, the 'European' or 'Byzantine' temple – the earthly home of the god Serapis and possibly of the goddess Kybele before him. To Hieron was said to have been founded by Jason, no less, before he left for his adventures on the Black Sea; or alternatively by Phrixos, son of the King of Boeotia, who brought the Golden Fleece to Medea's father King Aeetes. The great and the good donated gifts here, King Dareios sat 'surveying the Pontus' at To Hieron before he invaded Scythia. A deep harbour below (Macar Bay today, the Harbour of Phrixos in antiquity), supplied with natural spring water, made this an essential stop-off point before longer voyages. If one passed the Harbour of Phrixos sailing towards the Aegean from late September, the interest rate on loans to traders went up, a rise justified by the increase in danger from both pirates and bad weather.[8]

The city's calendar also tells us of the power of the waterways that edged Byzantion. The month of June was called Bosporios, when a festival known as the Bosporia was mounted. One intriguing inscription tells us that games at the mid-summer festival included races between naked young boys carrying torches.[9] Other months hint at the lush nature of the city: February was the month of Dionysos; September of Malaphorios, the 'Apple-bearer'. In the religious artefacts, fragments of offerings and inscriptions and shrines, that have survived in the centre of the city and in what is now greater Istanbul, along the Bosphorus and up the Golden Horn we get a sense of the recognised value of this budding city in a widening world – value believed to be god-given.

With geopolitical threats all around (for a time Byzantion became a plaything of King Mausolos, who controlled much of the western Anatolian seaboard – the pumping-veined, soft-ripple-necked power of the surviving stone warhorse from this Carian ruler's mausoleum leaves one in no doubt as to the scale of his ambition), in the fourth century BC Byzantion started to put her trust in a particular kind of supernatural force-field – that of the sorceress Hecate. Hecate almost certainly originated in the Near East, probably in Caria. A potent, respected goddess-witch, she was thought to have been the protector of liminal places, and perhaps that is why she was honoured in sacrifice with the gift of the guardians of earthly gates and crossings – dogs. Dogs were both sacrificed to Hecate and dedicated at her shrines. The small temples to Hecate that studded Byzantion, situated all around the city's perimeter close to the gates, must have been loud with the sound of dogs barking, yapping and howling. Hecate was honoured with a statue overlooking the Bosphorus known as Lampadephoros (Torch-Bearer) in gratitude for her care of the city and her people. She also appeared on the city's coins and is, a little unexpectedly, still a ghost in Istanbul today – it is a Hecate-style star and moon that adorn the blood-red Turkish flag. In times of trouble Hecate's symbol is everywhere – draped on public buildings, from bridges, across offices and over metro stations.

Coin of Byzantion, c. first century BC–first century AD. The goddess Hecate was thought to be a protectress of the city. Her symbol was a moon and a star, a design echoed on the Turkish flag today.

In the fourth century BC it was believed that Hecate had shown her true colours and had come to the city's aid against a new enemy, the Macedonians.[10]

You often need those you push away. Philip of Macedon, a one-time ally of Byzantion, was a force of nature with a keen appetite for territorial expansion who in 356 BC had conquered Thrace and founded Philippi, a city that would go on to be the site of the game-changing battle between Octavian, Antony, Cassius and Brutus, and of St Paul's first European Christian community. Having unified his kingdom in what is now northern Greece and having acquired a power that allowed for the stockpiling of exquisite goods (discovered in his tomb were protective Medusa heads, a gilded leather cuirass, elegant silver wine jugs, a golden diadem so delicate that the oak leaves and acorns still shiver in the breeze, and armour decorated ominously with images of the siege of Troy), Philip II of Macedon made it clear that his was a name to be reckoned with.

In 340 BC he headed for Byzantion. There he made use of the expertise of his newly created mechanical engineering corps, employing diabolically effective new siege machines including a torsion catapult where firepower was physically twisted in to the engineering – to try to subdue the benighted city.

Philip attacked and besieged Byzantion for a scant year. In real terms this was a failure: we are told that barking dogs (sent, it was insisted, by the walls' protectress Hecate, who had also magically illuminated torches and lit up the sky to reveal the city's danger) betrayed the Macedonians' attempted breach of the city's defences.[11] But in all likelihood Philip always knew that he would never take the Greeks' convenient staging post, the city with serious economic heft, given its control of the straits. This was instead a provocative exercise to tempt Athens into a war.[12] Athens duly came to Byzantion's aid, fearful that her vital supply of grain via the Black Sea (from the Danube basin, eastern Crimea and the Azov coasts) and down the Bosphorus was to be interrupted. Athenian nerves were justified. Philip proceeded to capture the entire Athenian grain fleet later that year, 230 Athenian and allied boats in total, near the sanctuary of To Hieron, thought to radiate a sacred force-field over the waters below, a sacrilege described as the Macedonian king's most 'unlawful act'.[13] Philip scuppered all the Athenian vessels, 180 of them, selling off the contents and reusing the wood for his siege engines, and returned only those belonging to Rhodes, Chios and Byzantion.

And it is here once again that we find that events in Byzantion become a happenstance motivator of history. During Philip's absence on the Bosphorus, his son Alexander, aged only sixteen, had been made regent and quickly got busy – campaigning against the Thracian Maedi and founding, for example, the city of Alexandropoulis. Yet although Alexander is credited (surely falsely) with the establishment of the Strategion, the military training ground, in Byzantion itself, all extant sources tell us that in fact this brilliant, history-disrupter crossed into Asia not via the

Bosphorus but via the Hellespont. There is a sense that the prodigiously driven young man wanted new fields to fight in, not those already scent-marked by his father. Byzantion would not feature in Alexander's blitz-krieg. A battle fleet that Alexander had left to defend the Hellespont did not claim any victories, so he ordered his men to row up the Bosphorus and then march inland to the Danube. During Alexander's lifetime the musician and wit Stratonicos referred to Byzantion dismissively as 'the armpit of Greece'.[14]

Alexander then stormed on to Babylon – Mesopotamia was where real riches were to be found. When Babylon submitted to the conqueror, silver altars were piled with frankincense and perfume. Caged lions and leopards were brought as gifts, and the streets were spread with flowers. In northern Egypt Alexander ordered the foundation of his namesake metropolis, Alexandria, a settlement that would boast one of the greatest libraries on earth – and that would, in time, come to be subject to Christian Constantinople.

Alexander may have bypassed Byzantion, but he gave the city a gift. The legacy of the exploits of the man we remember as Alexander the Great lived on in the expansive Seleucid Empire named for Alexander's favoured officer Seleucus – an empire that at its height stretched across the Near and Middle East and the northern Indian subcontinent. And so the West came East. Delphic aphorisms were carved into stone in northern Afghanistan. The Emperor of the Indian subcontinent Ashoka issued edicts in parallel translation – in Mauryan and in Greek. Describing the Greeks as barbarians, the *Garga Samhita* (a Sanskrit astrological treatise that only survives as fragments) grudgingly praised their skills in astrology; the Buddhas in the Gandhara region famously smile out from the features of a Greek face. In many ways it was the back-blast of Alexander's Greekness that would nurture Byzantion – propelling Hellenic influence beyond Asia Minor and the Caucasus into the Indian subcontinent and the Middle East. Alexander would ensure that the Greeks and their cities did not look alien in Eastern eyes. He might have bypassed Byzantion but he catalysed the city's relevance to the Far East.

There is no little irony in the dismissive attitude Alexander seems to have demonstrated towards Byzantion. Centuries later, pagan Alexander would be reincarnated as the city's Christian saviour. John Chrysostom, one of the patriarchs of the settlement that was by then called

Constantinople, recorded that gold medallions featuring Alexander's head were worn as amulets by those Byzantine citizens who could afford them. Alexander is linked to the city as the mysterious 'Great Philip' in the *Apocalypse of Pseudo-Daniel* written in Byzantium some time before the ninth century AD:

> [he] will rise up and gather his troops in the Seven-Hilled City [Constantinople] and make war such as there has never been, and rivers of blood will run in the streets of the Seven-Hilled City . . . Four Angels will bear him to Haghia Sophia and crown him king . . . and he, accepting the orb from the angels, will trample the Ishmaelites, Ethiopians, Franks, Tartars and every nation . . . Then his four sons will rule, one in Rome, one in Alexandria, one in the Seven-Hilled City and the fourth in Thessalonika.[15]

Yet despite the triumphalist tone of these visions from the future, in historical reality during the Hellenistic period the city walls of Byzantion were steadily dismantled. 'Liberated' from her Persian allegiance in 334 BC by Alexander's campaign against Dareios III but then harried by Gauls, Goths and Persians, Byzantion was attacked by Rhodes for charging increased tolls on boats in and out of the Bosphorus in order to pay tribute demanded by her Gaulish harassers. The city managed to stay afloat financially, minting her own coins, controlling other sites such as modern-day Yalova (which boasts efficacious hot springs) on the Asia Minor coast and caretaking the Bosphorus as a kind of free international trade zone. Supported economically by the inheritors of a portion of Alexander the Great's territories, the Ptolemies – operating out of the city of Alexandria and keen to keep supplies including myrrh, chickpeas and salted fish[16] flowing through the straits – Byzantion thrived because so many needed her. Even so, for the next five generations or so we hear of Byzantion/Byzantium mainly in relation to other men's ambitions. And then the Greek city was put to the service of one of the greatest history-makers of all time. Although Byzantion would indeed come to call herself proudly the New Rome – a city, like her alma mater, built on seven hills – her initial fate was to be the feeble plaything of the might, and the idea, of the newly confident Mediterranean power, Rome.

Yet it was Roman drive and nous that would also give Byzantion a new kind of future. In the second century BC a super-highway – starting in Dyrrachium (today Durrës, Albania's second-largest city) on the Adriatic and known as the Via Egnatia – was constructed as the first paved highway to cross the Balkan peninsula and for over 2,000 years remained the principal thoroughfare from Rome to the city we now call Istanbul. Originally commissioned to help subdue the potentially troubling new province of Macedonia and masterminded by one Gnaeus Egnatius, the province's proconsul in c. 146 BC, this crucial infrastructure, driven through central Europe as an instrument of control, would prove transformative for all three iterations of Byzas' legendary foundation, Byzantium, Constantinople and Istanbul – a road that joined the Ionian Sea to those Bosphoran straits, a fairy godmother to the fortune of this seaside settlement. Byzantion was no longer just a way-station. Thanks to the wit and will of Rome and of her pet project, the Via Egnatia or Egnatian Way, Byzantion was about to become vitally connected.

The Via Egnatia

CHAPTER 7

❖

ALL ROADS LEAD FROM ROME:
THE EGNATIAN WAY

c. 146 BC ONWARDS

via illa nostra, quae per Macedoniam est usque ad Hellespontum militaris . . . (That military road of ours, which goes through Macedonia
right up to the Hellespont)

CICERO, *DE PROVINCIIS CONSULARIBUS*[1]

Beyond a table laden with cherries in the summer and an elderly stove
that pumps out fuggy heat in the winter months in a quiet storeroom in
northern Greece sits a fabulous enigma. The shape and size of a grave-
stone, the ancient, expensive, carefully carved marble storyboard seems
to commemorate both the world's first recorded traffic accident and a pig
which had become a man's best friend.

Erected at the side of the Egnatian Way and then later built in to
the wall of Roman fortifications at Edessa, the stele tells a tragicomic
tale. A pig, it seems, was being driven along the Via Egnatia by a man
called Choiros for sacrifice at a religious festival. A thundering carriage
is portrayed: four horses with raised, prancing hoofs dramatically realised in stone appear to crush the pig, which is now shown prostrate on
the ground beneath them. The owner (presumably), a man in a sensible
hooded cloak, perches on his wagon looking bereft. The pig's story is
carefully inscribed around the pictures: 'all the road I crossed on foot,
steadily . . . But by the force of the wheel I have now lost the light . . .
Here I lie, owing nothing to death any more.'[2]

Whether this is a Roman spoof, an expensive joke (*choiros* means pig in
Greek, or in this context, pig-face) or a heartfelt memorial to a sacrificial
animal who met a sticky end on the road between Italy and Istanbul some
time in the late second century AD, it is a wonderfully vivid postcard from

what was one of the ancient world's most crucial arteries, a super-highway that would transform Istanbul's fortunes.[3]

Built by Roman engineers who travelled out in flat-bottomed boats from Brindisi to Dyrrachium, the Via Egnatia irrevocably turned Byzantion from a staging post into a destination. A city of promise now had the chance to establish herself. There had been a pathway on this route before – the western section of the road, initially called the Candavia Road, followed the course of the River Shkumbin in Albania. An author known as Pseudo-Aristotle gives a further clue: 'There is a spot in the middle in which, when a common market is held, Lesbian, Chian and Thasian goods are bought from the merchants who come up from Pontus [the Black Sea], and Corcyraean amphorae [from Corfu] from those who come from the Adriatic.'[4] Philip and Alexander's palace at Pella in Macedonia was built beside the forerunner of the Egnatian Way; Hellenistic bones and high, circular burial tumuli flank the route – private signs of devotion for public consumption. Alexander the Great would have marched out past these temples of the dead on his mission to conquer the world.

These desire-paths, the shortest and most effective route between two significant points, can prove remarkably tenacious – and indeed if we travel through the Balkans on motorways or B roads, some of which are still called Egnatia Odos in Greece or the Rruga Egnatia in Albania, we are following directly in the footsteps of our classical ancestors. Under the Romans, access to the route of the Via Egnatia and to its facilities was restricted. In theory only those with an official pass or diploma could use the amenities of this highway. Imperial business sent missives and diplomats and loot and soldiers in both directions, but there could well have been locals who dared to trudge tentatively up and down the mule path that sat alongside the main drag. Although this road would shape global culture in all manner of ways – political, religious, social – initially it had a stark purpose: to move men in one direction and money in the other. The Egnatian Way facilitated both military control and the collection of the *portorium*, a tax on those revenues from shipping and trade and fish that proved to be both Byzantion's blessing and its curse.[5]

Initially terminating at the natural boundary of the River Maritsa (also known as the River Evros) close to the modern Greek–Turkish border, the Via Egnatia eventually ran all the way from Dyrrachium, across modern-day Albania, Macedonia and northern Greece through to Byzantion. By linking up with the Via Appia, which joined Rome to Brindisi (just across the Adriatic from Dyrrachium), the Via Egnatia extended the reach of the Eternal City further east as far as Nicopolis (Purk) in Armenia Minor thanks to the Via Ponticas, which began in Byzantium and led to the Eastern Silk Roads. The Egnatian Way would nourish the Roman desire to enjoy an 'empire without limits'.

This Roman road was an evolutionary creature, adapting to its environment – its width ranging from 13 feet in some of its remotest regions to 65 in the cities. An edging of large stone blocks stopped carts slipping off, and a central stone spine in places allowed for two-way traffic. In the mountainous areas gravel was a more practical surface; some sections were waterproofed with packed clay. Brilliantly engineered, even neglected, largely abandoned stretches of the road are often still in use: when I last travelled it in 2015, many refugees from Syria were, inadvertently, shadowing ancient Romans as they used the Via Egnatia to move west. A number of halfway hotels have sprung up along the route, offering hot water, currency, passports, the signage written in both English and Arabic.

In true ancient Roman style, when the Egnatian Way was constructed there was a rigid format and vigorous branding: inns were located every 30–40 miles, mileage distance markers (still cropping up – one was recently discovered on a river bed in Albania) stood at every thousand paces, while signage, camps, stations with animals or supplies were to be found every 7 to 14 miles (a Roman mile is about 1.5 km). Whether the traveller was from Britannia, Gaul, Spain, Illyria or Thrace, she or he would know that this could be none other than a Roman project.

Up until this point in the early Roman period, the literature of the ancient world has made it very clear that roads are perilous places. Think of the bad things that happen along them: Oedipus kills his father, Theseus engages with the psychotic serial killer Procrustes, who tempts travellers into his home, then straps them to a bed and either chops or stretches them until they seem a snug fit, before murdering them. And indeed in reality the Via Egnatia would be haunted by the notorious mugger-pirates, the Cravarites. But in many ways, both psychologically and topographically, with the establishment of this international highway it was roads that were linking mankind. In one sense the Via Egnatia marks a beginning of the modern way of being. Arriving right up to the walls of Byzantion and then continuing through its gates to the city's ancient centre, Byzas' City would now be connected not just by three seas, but by the world's largest trunk road.

In the Roman psyche the East had long been a place of danger, but also a place of plenty. The first Emperor Augustus famously said of Rome that he found a city built in brick but left it in marble – all that money had to come from somewhere. India was repeatedly described in Roman sources as a land of unimaginable wealth. Pliny the Elder complained that the Roman taste for exotic silks, perfumes and pearls consumed the city. 'India and China [and Arabia] together drain our Empire. That is the price that our luxuries and our womankind cost us.'[6] It was the construction of the Via Egnatia and attendant road-systems that physically allowed Rome to expand eastwards, while the capture of Egypt intensified this magnetic pull. Rome had got the oriental bug, and Byzantium, entering into a truce with the Romans in 129 BC following the Roman victory in the Macedonian Wars that kick-started Gnaeus Egnatius' construction of the Via Egnatia, was a critical and vital destination before all longer Asian journeys began.

For the next three generations the city furnished supplies as Roman forces engaged in disastrous battles with adversaries from the East such as the king and poisoner Mithridates VI of Pontus; the Byzantines watched in 74/73 BC as 30,000 Roman troops were slaughtered around Chalcedon. Chrysopolis was renamed Scutari (remembered in the modern name for the area, Üsküdar) possibly after the leather shields, the *scuta*, of the Roman garrison based there, scraps of which are now turning up in the digs to build Istanbul's new metro system. The much-discussed war waged by the powerful consul Pompey 'on the pirates' – as has been pointed out, a PR campaign with a similar vigour to our 'war on terror'[7] – allowed him and subsequent power players from 67 BC to keep a white-hot focus on the commercial potential of the East. It was engaging with the son of Mithradates in Anatolia in 47 BC that inspired Caesar to write to a friend in Rome, 'veni, vidi, vici'. Meanwhile, when Byzantium was cited in Roman texts, it seems to appear as a put-upon plaintiff; witness the Roman historian Tacitus' *Annals*:

the Byzantines, who had been granted an audience and were protesting in the senate against the oppressiveness of their burdens . . . mentioned their offers of help at various times to Sulla [general and statesman], Lucullus [Roman consul and victor over Mithradates and at the Siege of Cyzicus] and Pompey; then their recent services to the Caesars – services possible because they occupied a district conveniently placed for the transit of generals and armies by land or sea, and equally so for the conveyance of supplies.[8]

And again Pliny the Younger – nephew of Pliny the Elder and imperial magistrate – in his correspondence with the Emperor Trajan would plead for the mitigation of 'the expenditures of the city of Byzantium – which are abnormally high'.[9]

Back in 42 BC, the would-be leaders of Rome, Antony and Octavian, in hot pursuit of Julius Caesar's assassins, Brutus (who had secured Macedonia) and Cassius (who operated from Syria), had met their opponents in this escalating civil war to fight on the Egnatian Way, at the Battle of Philippi. Nineteen legions were involved, and the lyric poet Horace was an officer on the losing side, one of the 'Liberators'. This was a battle for the West-East road-system and for the gold and silver mines all around, as well as for the republic and the idea of *Romanitas*. The victorious agents of imperial power raised a vast triumphal arch across the Egnatian Way just outside Philippi – now a tumble of blackened blocks, abandoned in the middle of a maize field. Local farmers frequently turn up arrowheads, broken swords and the smashed remains of helmets on the battle-plain that advanced the story of Old and New Rome. Virgil who wrote stirringly of Philippi in his *Georgics* has turned out to be not just poet but prophet:

> the plains . . . grew twice fat with
> the blood of our men.
> To be sure, a time will come
> when a farmer in those lands
> as he works the ground with his curved plough,
> will find javelins corroded with rough rust
> or with heavy hoes will strike against empty helmets
> and will be astonished by great
> bones when graves have been dug up.[10]

Travelling to Byzantium, merchants and diplomats could stop off at the bathhouses built at regular intervals along the Via Egnatia. One splendid, neglected example, the Ad Quintum in Albania, sits quietly at the edge of the arterial highway that now covers the old Roman road. Its walls still a pale, Roman red, the site is protected only by nettles, goat droppings, clouds of mosquitoes and barking dogs. But what is now a collapsing ruin, overshadowed by the giant, toxic steelworks built opposite in the 1970s by Mao's China, was once proof that an uninterrupted line of Romanness extended from the Eternal City right through to the city of Byzas.

In AD 73 Byzantium was formally incorporated as a province into the Roman Empire by Vespasian, who then founded a mint on its ancient acropolis.[11] Hadrian's engineers also set to, starting an aqueduct some time after AD 117[12] (the philhellenic Hadrian himself may have visited the city in AD 123, sparking a cultural revival in the city),[13] tapping a spring in the Belgrade Forest to feed the lower town. The walls of the city were maintained and repaired. The historian Cassius Dio reported on their plangent presence: '. . . I had also seen them [the walls] standing and had even heard them "talk" . . . the sound would continue from one [of the seven towers] to another through the whole seven . . . as each received the sound from the one before it, took up the echo, the voice and sent it on. Such were the walls of Byzantium.'[14]

Now, 800 years after her Greek foundation, Byzantium was starting to sound, to taste and to smell as other Roman towns did; she was also part of something bigger than herself, part of the idea that was Rome. Yet in AD 193 the city found herself on the wrong side of a political power struggle, and felt the white heat of a wronged emperor's wrath.

A man of action and Roman emperor for a month and a year in AD 193–4, Pescennius Niger had been favoured by his predecessors Marcus Aurelius and Commodus. Recognising Byzantium's strategic and material wealth – 'rich in men and money' as Herodian put it in his *History of the Roman Empire*[15] (all those fish still nudging towards the Byzantine shore and ignoring Chalcedon, the city of the blind) – Niger chose Byzas' City as his centre of operations, not least because it was 'surrounded by a huge, strong wall of millstones . . . fitted so skilfully . . . the entire wall appeared to be a single block of stone'.[16] From Byzantium Niger declared himself the true emperor and a rival to Septimius Severus in Rome – a man whom he branded a charlatan.

Severus hurled himself after the pretender who had slandered him. Realising that he was outnumbered and outmanoeuvred, Niger fled to nearby Nicaea, but still Severus surrounded Byzantium. What followed was a brutal, three-year siege. Cassius Dio gives a vivid account of the wily Byzantine inhabitants snaring enemy boats (by sending divers to cut their anchors and attach chains that could then be retracted from within the city walls) and pulling them in for supplies, using women's hair to braid as ropes, hurling masonry from the theatre and bronze statues on to their assailants.[17] A desperate few escaped when rough weather and storms ensured that no one would be foolhardy enough to pursue the fugitives. Those left behind ended up soaking leather to eat and finally 'devouring one another'. The situation in Byzantium was beyond desperate.

Zigzagging through Asia as his support melted away and as Severus bullied his way into favour, the usurper found himself quickly running out of options. Niger was eventually caught and beheaded in Antioch – his rotting skull delivered to the walls of Byzantium to persuade them to finally open their gates. The city refused to capitulate and Severus gave the order to pulverise both the walls and the proud, disloyal populace inside. Hubris would not be tolerated. A number tried to escape in boats built of joists, planks and rafters from their homes. Many were wrecked and the fugitives' bloated and bloodied bodies floated to the shore. Within Byzantium there were 'groans and lamentations'. Severus put to death her soldiers and magistrates and turned the city into a shell. 'Stripped of its theatres and baths and, indeed, of all adornments, the city, now like a village, was given to the Perinthians [a neighbouring city] to be subject to them.'[18] Niger's gamey head, which had been displayed on a spike, was then sent on to Rome.

This could have been the beginning of the end for the city, but following his triumph Septimius Severus decided, together with his son Caracalla, charmed by the place as Alcibiades and Pausanias had been before him, to rebuild Byzantium, bigger and better, with a new circuit of walls. Two ports on the Golden Horn were included in the plans (both filled in in the nineteenth century) and the walls now enclosed two hills (much would come to be made of the fact that Byzantium, like Rome, was blessed with seven hills). The Baths of Zeuxippos, open to the public, were constructed. The military training ground, the Strategion – today underneath the modern-day Sirkeci station – and the state prison were perked up.[19] The Strategion had direct access to one of Byzantium's ports – this was a city where military might had to relate to waterways as well as land. A colonnaded avenue between the two hills, the Portico of Severus, extended the Via Egnatia into the city itself and formed the basis of the Byzantine processional route of the Mese and of today's procession of shops and trams along the Divanyolu. The Emperor briefly called the city Augusta Antonina, in honour of his son (Caracalla was a nickname; his given name was Lucius Septimius Bassianus and his imperial name was Marcus Aurelius Severus Antoninus Augustus).

Severus also laid the foundation for the hippodrome for chariot races and the Kynegion, a combination of a zoo and animal extermination arena, later used for public punishments and (up until the Christian era) for public executions.[20] Amphitheatres for wild-animal shows, a kind of interactive animal park – as could be found in the most aspirational cities of the day – and a new theatre were also erected.[21] So when we think of Byzantium in its ancient Roman lifespan we should conjur the cityscape punctuated by the yowl of big cats, the thrum of ostriches and the screech of distressed elephants (the bone remains of all these have appeared in the recent Yenikapı excavations) – animals imported to satisfy a gruesome, voguishly Roman pleasure in live-action death.[22]

Severus did not just beautify the city, he manufactured its importance. In the centre of Byzantium the Emperor erected a showy monument that came to be called the Milion, a marker from which all distances across the Roman Empire, no less, would now be measured. The Milion was the mother of all milestones.

Despite this significant incarnation of a fabricated idea – that this city (rather than other settlements on the Bosphorus) is the very point where Europe ends and Asia begins, and vice versa, and from which all significant distances can be physically measured, mile upon Roman mile – today the Milion is notably unprepossessing. All that remains of the monument, once a stone canopy decorated with the finest statuary, is a pockmarked, amorphous, meagre lump in the heart of the modern city. The remains of the Milion sit at an intersection of the tramlines that circle around the hippodrome – now the Sultanahmet Meydanı – and in front of the Ayasofya. A few tourists stop to notice the antiquity, wounded cats use the hedges around it for shelter, sweet wrappers and cigarette butts gather at its base. But neglected though it is, this stump of rock was, and

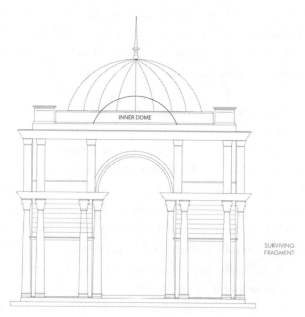

A reconstruction of the Milion monument erected by Septimius Severus in Byzantium, from which all distances in the Roman Empire would be measured

is, truly totemic. Through time, the Milion would be considered a kind of ground zero for civilisation: a point at which all spatial perceptions of the non-barbarian world should begin. The Milion marks out distance, and it marks the moment when Byzantium truly becomes a topographical and cultural reference point shared by East and West.

The Emperor Severus went on to conquer Mesopotamia and to elaborate his homeland town of Lepcis Magna in today's Libya, rebuilding the Forum and port (from which lions were shipped to Rome and to Byzantium to be tormented in the Colosseum and amphitheatres). Septimius' purpose was to prove to the world that the axis of power had shifted and that this North African settlement had always been fit for a mighty emperor. Archaeological discoveries in the sands here include an exquisite series of Roman-period mosaics, in which warriors hound animals and a spent gladiator lords it over the corpse of his sparring partner. If we are to try to revive second-century Byzantium in our minds, the extant remains at Lepcis are a useful guide. At the inception of the 2011 uprisings in Libya, Colonel Gaddafi had turned Severus' palatial remains into an arsenal, parking tanks and weaponry within the ancient stones. Lepcis is an incarnation of this region's high-octane, personality-driven ancient history. In Severus' life-story, and in the establishment of the Milion at Byzantium, we are starting to see a geopolitical body whose beating heart lies, once again, in the East.[23]

In AD 212 Severus' son Caracalla had instituted universal Roman citizenship for the freeborn – over 30 million men and women from Syria to Scunthorpe, including the inhabitants of Byzantium, now believed that they were stakeholders in the Roman project. Yet Caracalla's reform came at a difficult time. Within two generations, in AD 257 the Goths, travelling down from the Black Sea, attacked Byzantium, but were repulsed by the city's new Severan walls, although they did manage to occupy Chalcedon, dangerously close. The Gothic forces had a burning desire to take the city; a decade later they returned and eventually gave up the fight only after the Emperor of the moment, Claudius II – now triumphantly known by the name of those he vanquished, Claudius Gothicus – had left 50,000 barbarians dead.

Urban memory (urban myth probably) maintains that in the city today there is a stubborn reminder of Claudius' triumph, the Column of the Goths. This unique, ancient Roman remain stands neglected in Gülhane Park at the end of a dusty path in what was once the city's zoo, a stone's throw from the locus of the great animal displays of antiquity.[24] It is still visible at the back of the Topkapı Palace. The 18.5-metre-high column – once topped, we are told by Nikephoros Gregoras, by a statue of the city's legendary founder Byzas – declared to the world that 'Roman' cities such as Byzantium would not be harried by barbarian enemies. The column is in fact built on an older shrine described by the local geographer Dionysios of Byzantium as being dedicated to Athena Ekbasios, 'Disembarkation Athena'.[25] This was just one of the many sanctuaries and place-names in Byzantium proper and up and down the Bosphorus that remembered the early journeys of adventuring Greeks – both real and legendary. The Goths' Column is almost certainly a giant 'X marks the spot' where Iron Age Greeks first set up shop in the city they would call Byzantion. Today it is ignored by the many tourists who prefer the delights of the Topkapı Palace behind them, its appeal hardly enhanced by a red Fiat (manufactured in Turkey by Tofaş) that was for years permanently parked at its foot.

Meanwhile, to the south-east of Byzantium, Queen Zenobia from her base at Palmyra – an oasis on the Silk Roads – was giving Rome's rulers a real run for their money. By AD 271, with the exception of Anatolia, Zenobia controlled most of the ex-Roman East. The Roman Emperor Aurelian gathered his forces in Byzantium in the winter of 271/2 to attempt the recapture of imperial territories. The Romans knew only too well that they should fear the firepower of greater Syria. In 260 Emperor Valerian had been captured by Persians, forced to bend over and then been used as a mounting block by their ruler, before being flayed and stuffed as a warning to future Roman ambassadors: 'his skin, stripped from the flesh, was dyed with vermilion, and placed in the temple of the gods of the barbarians, that the remembrance of a victory so signal might be perpetuated, and that this spectacle might always be exhibited for our ambassadors'.[26]

Zenobia – no less sure of herself – chose to be portrayed on coins from her mints in Antioch as a full-blown Roman empress – Septimia Zenobia Augusta – with a fashionable Roman hairstyle to match. Sailing out to Asia Minor from Byzantium probably in April AD 272, Aurelian defeated this recalcitrant Queen, who was then frogmarched back along the Egnatian Way to Rome. The ancient sources contradict one another, some saying that Zenobia was so sickened by defeat that she died before she left Asia and that it was her corpse that was carried across the straits, others that she travelled through Byzantium and along the Via Egnatia a captive in disgrace.[27]

Palmyra, considered too beautiful even then – where archaeo-botany has now shown that the desert city supported 220 different species of flora – was not put to the sword and flame. Zenobia's city survived until it was, in part, destroyed by the soldiers of Islamic State in the year of this book's completion.

The Goths and upstart monarchs that ringed Byzantium might have been temporarily defeated, but clearly there was trouble brewing on all sides. If Rome was to control citizens across the Middle East she needed an Eastern base. To spread Roman muscle the Tetrarchy – the Rule of Four – was established in AD 293. Diocletian now ruled from Nicomedia and Maximian from Milan as senior emperors (Augusti), while Galerius in Sirmium (modern-day Sremska Mitrovica) – the 'glorious mother of cities' according to one author, Ammianus Marcellinus – and Constantius

Chlorus in Trier were junior emperors (Caesars) with responsibility for Gaul, Britannia and the Rhine.

The idea that was Rome might be shoring itself up with new structures and new layers of management, but the cultural climate within which the Tetrarchy ruled had been irrevocably changed. A century and a half after the Egnatian Way had been created by the Roman machine, 700-plus miles south in Bethlehem a boy had been born whose philosophies and lived example would determine the fate of this highway and the city that it led to – indeed the fate of the world. Old Rome had built a communications system to facilitate military control, but these roads would become a medium by which men could connect, and deliver new ways of considering what it was to be human.

While the hard evidence in the ground can lead us to think that it is predominantly trade or raw ambition that motivates our desire to build roads, settlements and systems, increasingly historians and neuroscientists alike believe that we create infrastructural links driven by our fundamental desire to share ideas. And now, across the Hellespont, over the Bosphorus and the Mediterranean and along the Via Egnatia would travel one of the biggest ideas of all, an idea that would grow into the most powerful of world religions and that would determine the future, form and function of Byzantium and of Christendom – the notion that man has power over death itself.

CHAPTER 8

THE ENEMY WITHIN

c. AD 41–c. 311

Pliny to Trajan:

I placed two women, called 'deaconesses', under torture, but I found only a debased superstition carried to great lengths, so I postponed my examination, and immediately consulted you. This seems a matter worthy of your prompt consideration, especially as so many people are endangered. Many of all ages and both sexes are put in peril of their lives by their accusers; and the process will go on, for the contagion of this superstition has spread not merely through the free towns, but into the villages and farms. Still I think it can be halted and things set right. Beyond any doubt, the temples – which were nigh deserted – are beginning again to be thronged with worshippers; the sacred rites, which long have lapsed, are now being renewed, and the food for the sacrificial victims is again finding a sale – though up to recently it had almost no market. So one can safely infer how vast numbers could be reclaimed, if only there were a chance given for repentance.

ON CHRISTIANS, PLINY IN BITHYNIA[1]

In Philippi, halfway between Rome and Byzantium, along the Via Egnatia, the splash of Serbian girls being baptised in the icy, sacred Angitis stream under wind-whisked, shuddering white poplars competes with a christening of Greek-Philippine twins in the neighbouring church. These faithful families join many thousands every year who make the journey to this remote stretch of northern Greece because, in around AD 50, it was at Philippi that the New Testament claims the very first conversion of a community to Christianity took place. Travelling along the Egnatian Way (still visible, running next to the handsome Forum in this abandoned Macedonian-Roman town), the apostle Paul, following his Damascene conversion, chose this route to spread the word of a new cult – the cult of Christ. Arriving here (if we follow Luke in the Acts of the Apostles),[2] the urgent traveller came across a group of women, among them a businesswoman, Lydia of Thyateira. Lydia seems to have been one of the many traders in this, the 'major city of the district'; she is described as God-fearing – so not Jewish, but friendly towards Judaism. There is a possibility that Lydia was invented by Luke, but Thyateira to the south of Byzantium was indeed a renowned centre for purple-dye production; traders would have used the Egnatian Way to generate new business and to oversee their supply chain; and women at this time were frequently in charge of textile businesses. So whether she is fact or fantasy, Lydia's story rings true. In that buzzing little place – overlooking the battlefields where Octavian and Antony had defeated Caesar's assassins Brutus and Cassius (the shift from republic to empire now commemorated only by that ne-glected, collapsed triumphal arch that once spanned the Egnatian Way) – Lydia listened to what Paul had to say about social justice, about freedom from sin and the promise of everlasting life, and then promptly converted along with 'everyone in her household'. Ever since, the traditional site of Lydia's baptism has become a place of pilgrimage and the words that – according to the New Testament – Paul uttered here, 'Believe in the Lord Jesus and you will be saved,' are familiar across the globe. The road to Istanbul is a neglected player in the inner lives of millions.[3]

A rather nebulous figure, Andrew the Apostle, who appears in the New Testament as both a fisherman elder brother of Simon Peter and as a follower of John the Baptist, was said – after being instructed to become a fisher of men – to have founded, in AD 38, a see in Byzantium which would then expand to become Constantinople's patriarchate. But Chris-tianity's historical beginnings in Byzas' City would, in truth, have been rather more humble and ad hoc. The very first Christians in Istanbul would have met in homes; the house-church, often managed by women, was the distinguishing feature of the early Christ-cult. Meetings were small, secretive. Once the Gospels started to be written down at the end of the first century AD these would have been read out by one or two respected members of the group, as most Christians could neither read nor write. It is with good reason the earliest Christian texts sound like stories. At the end of the session there might have been a communal meal of thanksgiving and then visitors would slip away. A trading city such as Byzantium, which had always had to apply the unwritten rule of *xenia*, of hospitality, was well placed to network ideas and support visiting teachers. The city's proud Christian character, a character that would spark a new world order, would have taken its initial faltering steps in first- and second-century AD Byzantium not perfumed by incense or holy wine, but by the smell of freshly baked bread and olive-oil lamps, with the sound of babies mewling in disturbed sleep, dogs stirring outside kitchen doors and Greek slaves teaching a few lucky infants their ABCs. And all the while Kybele would have been worshipped at her rock shrines, Hecate at the city's walls and Dionysos praised at the city's ports.

In the mosaic of belief that was the Roman Empire, Christianity was, by the third century AD, still just one of many sects jostling for space – as is illustrated by an articulate little letter sent to the Emperor Marcus Aurelius. Written in AD 176 by a Christian called Athenagoras, the letter's plea that the Romans should stop persecuting Christians is supported by the list the writer cites of the other eccentric faiths that were practised across the empire. Along with a rollcall of a number of 'minor' cults, such as the worship of Helen Adrasteia (Helen the Inescapable or the Destroyer) at Troy, the Christian puts his case: we are of only minimal concern, he says, the implication being – it is not as though we Christians are going to form a world-religion or anything.[4]

But with Christian populations steadily increasing in cities such as Byzantium, the Romans undoubtedly had a problem: in a world of many cults, many gods, how pluralist should they be?

Discovered purely by chance in 1996 as a highway was being widened, just 9 miles from Tel Aviv on the edge of Israel's Ben Gurion Airport and kept out of sight for thirteen years after its excavation, a mosaic dating from c. AD 300 vividly illustrates the problem.[5] Concealed under a mere 5 feet of dirt for eighteen centuries at the town of Lod, ancient Lydda, also famous for its trade in purple (Lydia would certainly have known of the place), 55 feet long and 30 feet wide, this superb – and intriguing – example of Late Roman-period mosaic work has been painstakingly restored.[6] The skill of ancient craftsmen has conjured sea monsters, leaping fish (bream, mullet, snapper) and wild animals from three continents (rhino, giraffe, an elephant, dolphins) out of tens of thousands of coloured stone cubes. The artisans, almost certainly themselves shipped in to do the work, have inadvertently made their own mark. Beneath the mosaic itself one worker, wearing a typical Roman sandal, has left a distinct footprint next to the design sketches that he was mapping out. A dog, possibly a cat, has unhelpfully wandered across the delicate outlines here too, leaving a line of paw-prints behind.

But what at first looks like a nature-worshipping pastoral scene – all leaping stags and charming rabbits – has a darker message. It is only at second glance that the blood comes into focus. The mosaic's idyll is spiked with gore. A wild-eyed deer strains away from the claws of a lioness; an ox bellows in fear, a tiger in slavering pursuit; a leopard rips into a gazelle; a hunting dog lies in wait for that plump rabbit. The mosaic blood is perfectly rendered, dripping and then pooling on the ground.

So who sponsored this grisly scene? Well, with all those exotic animals – and a merchant ship – there is an interesting possibility that the owner was a games-maker, a man perhaps who garnered his fabulous wealth by feeding the voracious late Roman appetite for slaughter at the gladiatorial games in cities such as Byzantium. The bone evidence from the hippodrome tells us that tigers, antelopes and rhinos were indeed imported to the killing grounds in Byzas' City for just such a purpose.

In the third and fourth centuries AD – the timeframe within which our mosaic was built – Lydda was party to a struggle for temporal and spiritual power. The region had long been home to pagans, Greeks, Romans and Jews but now too to members of this emerging Christ-cult.[7] The Lod mosaic would have been witness to an age of Christian persecutions. Another of Byzantium's local saints, Mocius, was said to have been beheaded in the city after the lions that he was thrown to refused to devour him. It is estimated that the Emperors ordered the massacre of perhaps as many as 20,000 Christian men and women over the space of a few years. The death rate in the East was particularly high. Christianity, radical and undeniably popular, was flourishing and then being repressed in a ring around its littoral Middle Eastern birthplace.[8] The men in control were rattled by Christianity's message of moderation, of everlasting life and of social justice. This merchant of Lydda's choice of interior decoration is perhaps a reflection of the brutality of the age.[9] The house had been mothballed, all treasures and household items carefully removed. Its owner was clearly fleeing something – what, we do not yet know. But what is certain is that from the Balkans to Baku, Christians and Jews were being persecuted – and those in the city of Byzantium were no exception.[10]

CHAPTER 9

PERSECUTION

c. AD 240–304

> And wild beasts and dogs and birds of prey scattered the human limbs here and there, and the whole city was strewed with the entrails and bones of men, so that nothing had ever appeared more dreadful and horrible, even to those who formerly hated us; though they bewailed not so much the calamity of those against whom these things were done, as the outrage against themselves and the common nature of man.
>
> EUSEBIUS OF CAESAREA, *ON THE MARTYRS OF PALESTINE*[1]

Around AD 273 an old man called Lucillian, still honoured every June by the Orthodox Church as St Lucillian, was said to have converted to Christianity late in life in the town of Nicomedia, where he was beaten, imprisoned and tortured. He was, the hagiographer's account goes, then dragged to Byzantium where, refusing to deny his faith, he was crucified in the centre of the city along with four other men who were beheaded. A virgin who watched these ghastly deaths and then tended to the victims was also decapitated.

Lucillian – whether he was fact or fabricated – was not alone.

St Euphemia – a woman who will come to take a central role in the story of Byzantine Christianity – was so brutally murdered in September AD 303 across the water at Chalcedon that she was said to haunt populations on both sides of the Bosphorus. The manner of her death was vividly described by one Asterios of Amaseia, who, taking a walk to clear his head one day, was struck by the sight of a series of ultra-realistic paintings showing Euphemia's gruesome martyrdom – her teeth 'like pearls' extracted, her lonely imprisonment in a grey shift, her agonising death as she was burnt alive. (Frescoes depicting Euphemia's death were uncovered close to the Byzantine hippodrome in 1939. The remains of the church they animated can still just about be made out at the edge of a car park serving the law courts.) Others told the story that Euphemia had been broken on the wheel on Diocletian's orders for refusing to sacrifice to the god Ares and was then mauled to death by a bear in Byzantium's amphitheatre for the pleasure of a paying audience. Some accounts and paintings depict the young woman being beheaded.

A church was erected at Chalcedon in St Euphemia's honour (where the critically influential Fourth Ecumenical Council of AD 451 would later be held). The palace of a prominent Persian eunuch, Antiochos, from the fifth century was in the seventh converted into a martyrion or shrine for the martyr Euphemia. Today city-dwellers pass by the remains close to the hippodrome without so much as a second glance. Euphemia's miracle-working relics, allegedly oozing uncorrupted blood from time to time, preserved in a silver casket and today still kept in St George's Church in the Greek Orthodox patriarchate in the Fener district of Istanbul, were a totem for the city across two millennia.

Christian-hunting, cruel but sporadic under Nero – though much less sustained and less systematic than historical accounts would have us believe – was formalised by Decius in AD 249–50. But the Emperor Valerian in 257–8, followed by Diocletian and Galerius, had taken these interventions to new levels. Asia Minor had been a vital seedbed for the emerging faith group and it felt the clinical blows particularly keenly. It was said that a consultation with the oracle of Apollo at Didyma offered the chance to take action against the 'just on earth'. The original advice stipulated this should happen without bloodshed, but Maximinus Daia (Galerius' nephew) oversaw burnings, tortures, exiles and the systematic downgrading of Christians who were now no longer allowed reddress to law, or to hold formal positions in imperial or civil society. We should picture the Christians of Byzantium being checked in and out at the gates set in Severus' walls and at the public baths. Goods in the market were sprinkled with the blood of sacrificed animals, to pollute them and to offend Christian sensibilities; tax exemptions were offered to those willing to persecute Christian women and men.

Diocletian and his fellow tetrarchs had stabilised the empire – Persia was briefly humiliated, Egypt and the Danube subdued, Britain had been recovered and now Rome needed to tidy up that loose end of belief. The tetrarchs' conviction was that the *pax deorum*, the peace of the gods, doing old things in old ways, would ensure stability. These were men who dressed in purple and gold as if they were kings; we can see from a votive offering found in Albania how a widespread belief in the one true God would be more than a little tiresome: 'To our Lords Diocletian and Maximian, the unconquered Augusti, born from gods and creators of gods'.[2] Christianity was a threat. The Church Fathers might have wildly exaggerated the scale of the abuses but there were enough for anti-Christian outrages to become a gruesome theme of the city's narrative in late antiquity.

And yet, despite the efforts of the men who controlled Byzantium, the Great Persecution failed. Being Christian was steadily becoming part of the fabric of the Roman world. From Nicomedia in AD 303 it was ordered that all churches and scriptures should be destroyed or handed over to the authorities and all religious meetings banned.[3] On the ground many found it convenient to mislay these orders; but there were still knocks on the door at the dead of night, men and women were disappeared, and homes and meeting places were torched. The Berber author Lactantius (a Christian, so not an unbiased source) describes one such episode: 'still twilight . . . they forced open the doors . . . the scene was one of plunder, panic and confusion . . . Then the Praetorians [soldiers who could act as the emperor's bodyguard or as a kind of secret police] came in formation, bringing axes and other iron tools . . . they levelled the lofty edifice to the ground within a few hours.'[4]

In AD 303 to 304, in an intimidating display of pagan power, Diocletian demanded that the entire population of the Roman Empire adhere to traditional religious practice while he targeted the legal rights of Christians. The message to the inhabitants of Byzantium and other Roman cities in Europe, Asia and Africa was clear: you were either 'with us' or 'against us'.[5] Particularly worrying for the imperial machine was the appeal that this vogueish new faith exercised in army barracks. Rome's soldiers, the grout that kept the Roman mosaic together, were converting in increasing numbers – they who potentially faced mortality every day attracted, partly, by a notion of life after death.[6]

An example had to be made of the Christians.[7] Diocletian's palace in Split – it was more of a town within a town – was said to have witnessed many executions in its barrel-vaulted cellars. Images of Christians with a rope around their neck attached to a vast weight suggest a water-based method of persecution. What is clear is that from his limestone and Egyptian granite retirement home, covering 9 acres and fed by mineral springs, Diocletian personally ordered the death of 3,000 to 3,500 Christians.[8]

One young man aged thirty or so, who had been taught and trained in Diocletian's court, must have witnessed much of this suffering first hand. He would eventually react in a way that would reconfigure the political and spiritual landscapes of Europe, Asia and Africa. Global history would shift, powered by the desire of the new ruler of Byzantium to burn his way through the scrub of life, making a mark, clearing a path – an unorthodox saviour of the idea that was Rome. And the most loyal and inspirational partner in his epoch-shaping endeavours would be the city that he would come to call Constantinople.

CHAPTER 10

✤

THE MEEK SHALL INHERIT THE EARTH

c. AD 272–311

Beginning from Britain in the far west where it is decreed by Heaven itself that the sun should set, I have repelled and scattered those horrors which held everything in subjection, so that the human race, taught by my obedient service, might restore the religion of the most dread Law . . . I could never fail to acknowledge the gratitude I owe, believing that this is the best of tasks . . . Indeed, my whole soul and whatever breath I draw, and whatever goes on in the depths of my mind, that, I am firmly convinced, is owed by us wholly to the greatest God.

FRAGMENT OF PAPYRUS, FOURTH CENTURY AD,
NOW STORED IN THE BRITISH LIBRARY[1]

Before we investigate the Christian conversion of Byzantium, we have to visit the mizzling, hilly city of York.

A young soldier was soon to claim dominion of the known world. In the years between AD 235 and 284, the Roman Empire had seen change and churn, no fewer than fifty men had been proclaimed Roman emperor. The kingmakers and the people were proving fickle, but eventually a combination of clout, nous, chance and charisma would win the day.

It was a strange set of circumstances that had got this illegitimate boy to such a threshold of power. Deep in the vaults of the British Museum in London is a heavy silver coin, minted by a soldier called Carausius. Holding this glinting disc, which sits year in year out on a velvet rag in a small wooden box, is an electrically exciting experience. It is part of a tremendous metal trail, a survivor from a time of extreme ambition and of megalomaniac delusion.

Carausius had been the commander of the fleet patrolling the

Britannicus Oceanus (the British channel). Those back in Rome suspected that he was withholding captured treasure and taking bribes from pirates to boot, thus allowing them to continue their plunder. Rome passed the death penalty. Carausius reacted by declaring himself emperor of northern Gaul and the whole of Britannia. He announced that all he wanted was to rescue Britannia from imperial neglect, and to prove his point he minted coins in silver once more – unheard of since Diocletian had debased the empire's coinage. His subtext was audacious: 'Forget those cheapskates back in the mother city. I am your best-chance champion now.' With the fervour of a man newly empowered, Carausius stated that he was Rome's true saviour. The medallions and coins that come tumbling out of wooden boxes in the Museum's stores blare out, '*EXPEC-TATE VENI*' (Come the Awaited One), '*RESTITUTOR BRITANNIAE*' (Saviour of Britain). On one bronze medallion there is a coded message, '*RSR*'. One scholar recently decrypted the acronym – they are the first letters of a phrase from Virgil's *Eclogues*: '*REDEUNT SATURNIA REGNA*' (The Golden Age returns).[2]

A single hoard of 760 personalised Carausian coins among a total of 53,000 found in Frome in 2010 by a metal detectorist gives us a sense of the scale of Carausius' unorthodox and wildly ambitious enterprise.

Constantius Chlorus, who had started his career as a bodyguard to Emperor Aurelian and was elevated to the rank of Caesar in AD 293, was sent to deal with this edge-of-empire outrage, harrying Carausius from the other side of the channel. Constantius Chlorus' job in Britannia was in fact completed by Carausius' fair-weather finance minister Allectus, who murdered his master and then went on to run his own Britannic Empire for the next three years. Rome's soldiers hunted down Allectus' men in waters off the Isle of Wight and at Silchester in Southern England. Once the job had been completed, Constantius judged it a timely moment to arrive in Britain. We are told that, sailing up the Thames with his invasion fleet, he was met with cheers and flowers from the citizens of Londinium – realists, perhaps, accepting the inevitable. Constantius now had his own gold medallion made, declaring him '*REDDITOR LUCIS AETERNAE*' (The restorer of light everlasting).[3]

*

The Arras medallion, struck to commemorate Constantius' arrival in Britain.
London is depicted as a kneeling woman.

Thirty years before, in c. AD 272, Constantius, according to some sources, had had a love-child, Flavius Valerius Constantinus, by a humble woman, an innkeeper's daughter, *vilissima* (extremely lowly) as the author of the *Origo Constantini* put it. This mother was called Helena; the boy would become Constantine the Great.[4]

Extraordinary what influence one Greek stable-maid can have. As Bishop Ambrose so memorably summarised Helena's life story, she travelled '*de stercore ad regnum*' (from the dung heap to a kingdom). Impregnated by a passing soldier, giving birth near the Moesian city of Naissus (in present-day Serbia), Helena's rags-to-riches narrative might be exaggerated but the lifelong devotion of her firstborn son Constantine, who had been named for his father, was marked. Byzantines would later tell the story that exhibits typically hybrid pagan–Christian elements – that Constantine was conceived in an inn where his soon-to-be-emperor father had managed to find a room; here Constantius was told by Apollo in a dream that the innkeeper's daughter he'd enjoyed was now carrying his son. The soldier left her a purple chiton and golden necklace; this was to be no conveniently forgotten bastard. Helena's historical circumstances almost certainly form the basis of the Cinderella story – a humble beginning that would become a globally significant fairy-tale.

When Constantius Chlorus was elevated to the rank of Caesar within the Tetrarchy (Constantius would become Augustus of the Western Empire in AD 305), his first-born bastard found himself summoned to court in Nicomedia and offered an appropriately rigorous education.[5]

Latin was his native tongue, but the young lad became well versed in Greek, philosophy and, inevitably, the arts of war. Constantine was farmed out to give direct military service to Diocletian in the East, campaigning through Palestine and the Middle East. He must have shown promise – the implication is that he was hot-housed – but perhaps his mistake was to make it clear just how much he had benefited from his early education in Diocletian's capital. Because Constantine's potential was a little worrying. Chroniclers would later delight in tales of how the savvy young lad had saved himself from the lethal tasks set him by one of the other tetrarchs, Galerius, who had worked his way up from being a herdsman and clearly wanted Constantine out of his way so that his own chosen heir (and nephew) Maximinus Daia could succeed to power.

Back in Britannia, as full emperor from AD 305, Constantine's father Constantius acquitted himself honourably – he repaired Hadrian's Wall (decades before the furthest barrier to the north, the Antonine Wall, had been quietly dismantled). The tone of the Romans' engagement with those troublesome natives, the so-called Picts, was by this time characterised by spear-rattling displays of aggression and by neat bribery. Vast hordes of Roman silver have been discovered since the year 2000 by both archaeologists and metal detectorists in Pict territory. Much is hacksilver – coin hacked up to use in barter – the sheer quantities an indication of how much Roman coin was paid to keep the natives quiet.[6] On the way back from dealing with the Picts, Constantius decided to break his journey at the Roman fortress in Eboracum (modern-day York), where he set to repairing the facilities of the site, the remnants of which are now visible in the undercroft of York Minster. The military headquarters here, along with toppled pillars, furnaces for bathhouses and barracks, is slowly emerging as archaeologists dig. If one climbs down into the once-dank undercroft of the cathedral, it is possible to make out the edge of the Roman basilica and a newly revealed section of Roman road – pagan foundations for the towering monument to Christianity above. A section of the fortress wall still stands proud in the gardens of the Yorkshire Museum.

But little did Constantius know that when he authorised Eboracum's building programme he was refurbishing his deathbed.

Constantine had managed to get himself a commission to help to sort out those pesky northerners with his father. Later chroniclers elaborate on this development, describing how the young man escaped the evil, pagan grip of low-born Galerius, surviving against the odds despite being sent to battle lions and to cross the swamps of the central Danube, and then sneaking out at dead of night to head north-west to join his father. The truth probably lies somewhere between high drama and humdrum imperial policy. After the long journey towards the edge of empire Constantine arrived at Boulogne – the site of his father's victory over rebellious Gauls – and made the crossing that now transports alcohol-laden day-trippers back to England. He sped from the Kentish coast up to York but arrived to the news that his father was dying. We are told that just before Constantius passed away on 25 July he whispered that this illegitimate boy was his heir.[7]

Immediately Constantine, not just a dusty, road-worn fighter but a cultured man, was proclaimed emperor – illegally. Having received the command to take his father's mantle, he emerged from the imperial quarters at Eboracum draped in imperial purple. We should imagine the roar of the soldiers' approval, drummed in from their compact barracks in this chilly corner of empire to greet as their future a man who had already crossed the length of the Roman Empire from Babylon to Britannia. The panegyrics were composed in Greek and Latin to welcome in this next phase in Rome's long history: 'O Britain, fortunate and happier now than all lands to have been the first to have seen Constantine Caesar.'[8]

The wily, square-jawed, illegitimate soldier was declared Caesar Constantine I, or as he would soon be known, Constantine the Great. This was a usurpation, and decades of civil war would follow. In that flat northern light – on a hill pretty now with tearooms and shoe shops – a decision was to be made that would impact on a million square miles-worth of human experience.

But first Constantine had to share power with six others. A conference of AD 308 declared Galerius' childhood friend and military companion Licinius as senior Emperor in the West with Constantine only as Caesar – his junior.[9] In the first decade of his reign Constantine's backdrop was western Europe. Initially he based himself at a gorgeous new palace in Trier (in present-day Germany) surrounded by the finest frescoes and other works of art – a sumptuousness that would come to typify an age described as 'jewelled'.[10] This had been his father's headquarters and the two-storey red-brick basilica still dominates the splendidly fertile Mosel valley. Following Napoleon's clean-up campaign in the nineteenth century and restoration of the town's imperial landmarks, Constantine is still remembered fondly here. Taxi drivers proudly point out the ruins of his baths, and across the handsome Roman Bridge is the Hotel Constantine. But Trier is a location on the Rhine frontier – the kind of place that demands steady control and consolidation, not a springboard to nourish adventure. We know that Constantine covered much ground at this stage in his life. He revisited York and Trier and travelled to Cologne, Beauvais, Autun, Châlons, Vienne, Arles, Aqua Viva, Sirmio (near Brescia), Milan and Rome, taking measure of his turf.

This man on the move had no intention of frittering away his career in liminal territories that supported trouble, weeks of rain and failed pretenders. In AD 310 Constantine engaged with Maximian in Gaul. The story went that Maximian planned to execute Constantius' scrapping-boy, but Constantine was warned of the plot and a eunuch was substituted in his place. Maximian, having duly killed the eunuch, was then 'encouraged' by Constantine to commit suicide. To shore up his own claims to power, Constantine now linked himself by adoption back to the triumphant, genocidal Claudius Gothicus, the Emperor who had shown the world that Byzantium belonged not to the barbarians but to Rome. This was going to be a Caesar who played Rome's power game on the front foot. In 311 Galerius died and Licinius and Constantine allied themselves against the joint forces of Maximinus Daia and Maxentius. Constantine had been told that after his acclamation as Caesar, followed by the delivery of his portrait to Rome, Maxentius (Maximian's son) had mocked the image of Constantine, declaring him 'the son of a harlot'. On Maxentius' orders Constantine's statues were torn down across Rome. Conflict was inevitable. Constantine marched south and then along the Via Flaminia towards Rome itself. Years later, this struggle among the tetrarchs would be given a religious gloss. Whatever its political or personal motivation, Constantine must have known that this fight for territory and for control of the idea that was Rome would also be a fight to the death.[11]

PART TWO

❖

CONSTANTINOPLE

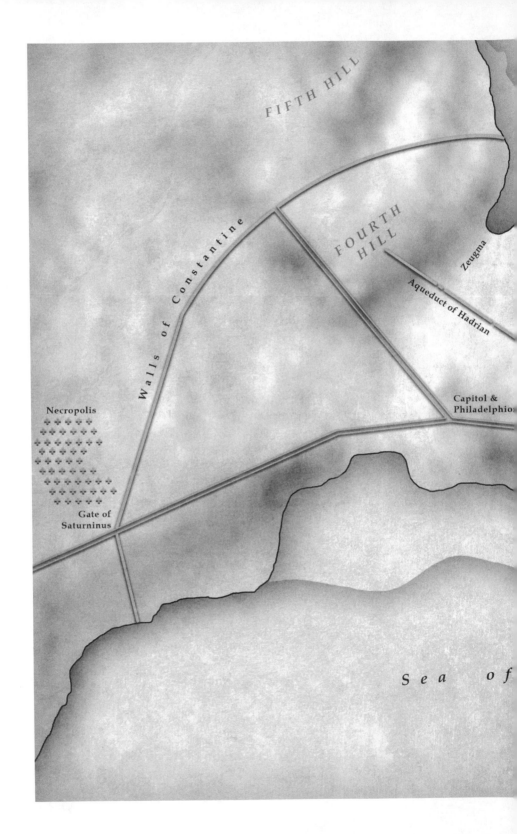

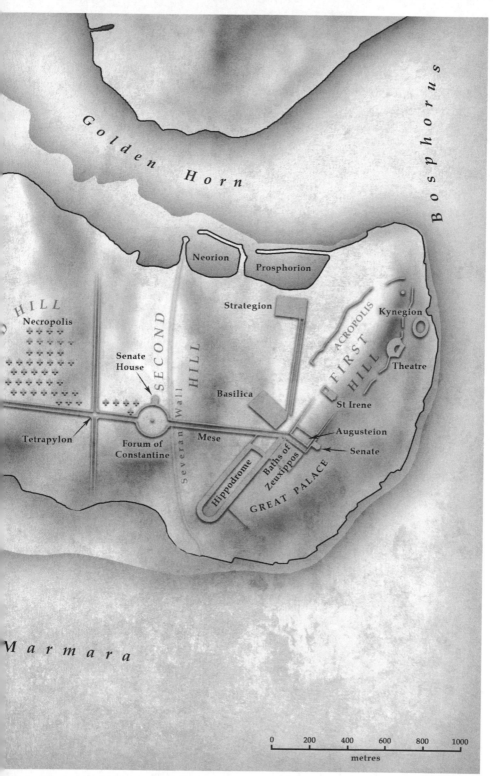

Constantine's Constantinople, c. AD 337

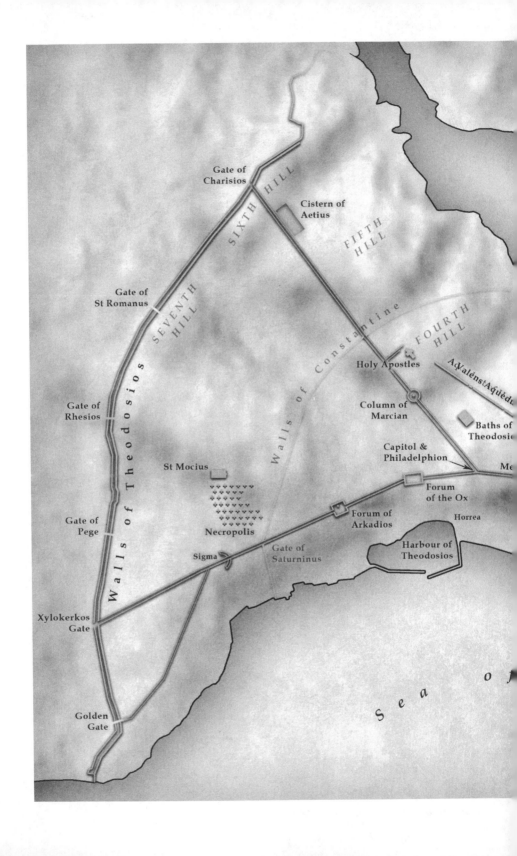

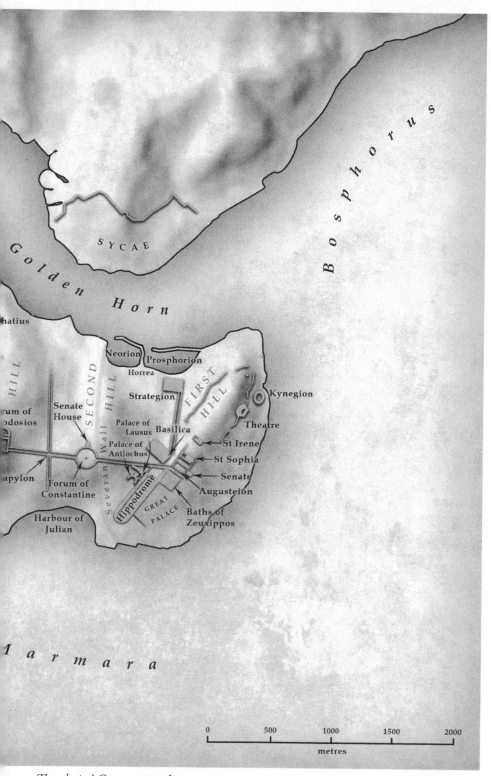

Bosphorus

Golden Horn

SYCAE

hatius

Neorion   Prosphorion

Horrea

Strategion

SECOND   FIRST
HILL   HILL   Kynegion

HILL

rum of   Senate
odosios   House   Theatre

Palace of
Lausus   Basilica
apylon   Palace of   St Irene
          Forum of Antiochus
          Constantine   St Sophia

Harbour of   Hippodrome   Senate
Julian   GREAT   Augusteion
                      PALACE
                             Baths of
                             Zeuxippos

Marmara

| 0 | 500 | 1000 | 1500 | 2000 |

metres

Theodosios' Constantinople, c. AD 450

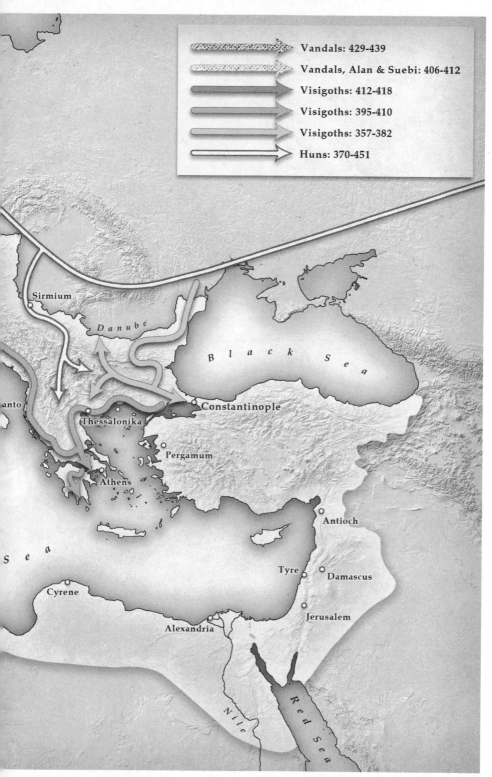

Legend

- Vandals: 429-439
- Vandals, Alan & Suebi: 406-412
- Visigoths: 412-418
- Visigoths: 395-410
- Visigoths: 357-382
- Huns: 370-451

Sirmium

Danube

B l a c k   S e a

Constantinople

Thessalonika

Pergamum

Athens

Antioch

Tyre

Damascus

Cyrene

Jerusalem

Alexandria

Nile

Red Sea

'Barbarian' tribes, c. AD 350–450

CHAPTER 11

✥

THE BATTLE OF MILVIAN BRIDGE

AD 312

He said that about noon, when the day was already beginning to decline, he saw with his own eyes the trophy of a cross of light in the heavens, above the sun, and bearing the inscription, CONQUER BY THIS. At this sight he himself was struck with amazement, and his whole army also, which followed him on this expedition, and witnessed the miracle.

EUSEBIUS, *LIFE OF CONSTANTINE*[1]

A handsome, solid farmhouse called the Villa Malborghetto, just beyond the northern outskirts of Rome, is not perhaps the most obvious location for a game-changing dream. But archaeological excavations have shown that this was, indisputably, where Constantine camped before his attack on his arch-rival Maxentius – and where, a later ancient source declares, at the end of October AD 312 the future ruler of Byzantium dreamt that he had been chosen to save mankind. Whether the dream was real or contrived, the significance of this metaphysical moment, a mythical and spiritual justification for the foundation of Constantinople, cannot be overstated.

The official strategy for the idea that was Rome had disintegrated into the worst kind of power-play. After his acclamation at York, Constantine had been married off to Maxentius' sister Fausta when she was little more than a child. For a few years there was an uneasy peace between the two brothers-in-law; Constantine focused on securing the frontiers while Maxentius bedded in at Rome. But relations soon broke down. Constantine defeated Maxentius' army at Turin and Verona and then set his compass for Rome. A siege by Constantine of the mother city, which was walled and well supplied, would have been fruitless, but inexplicably choleric Maxentius made the catastrophic decision to leave the security of Rome and meet Constantine and his forces beyond the city, on a field abutting the Via Flaminia and the River Tiber. Was this hubris or superstition or simply folly? The Sybilline oracles had declared that on this day an enemy of Rome would be defeated. Commentators coolly critique Maxentius' move as poor strategy; in reality it was probably desperation. Recent archaeology has revealed in the territory controlled by Maxentius walls raised and moats half built; metaphorically as well as physically this feels like the work of a man who was fully aware of the capabilities of his enemy, and who was operating with his back against the wall.[2]

An alternative version of the story goes that as Constantine was travelling south preparing for hostilities to begin, the Caesar and would-be Emperor was visited by a miracle. A vision suddenly appeared to him in the sky – a bright, blinding sun with a blazing cross throbbing above it. We are told that forthwith Constantine's troops were rebranded, instructed to sport a new kind of logo, a 'divine sign', on their shields and banners. An interesting possibility here is that a Christian gloss has been conveniently sealed over pagan historical fact. A number of the fiercest fighters in Constantine's *auxilia* (originally non-citizens but by this time a rag-bag of citizens and 'barbarians') were Germanic. The 'barbarisation' of the Roman army was well developed at this stage and Constantine had of course been operating in the 'barbaric' lands of the West for the last decade. Some of these crack squads carried shields bearing runes or the image of a double-headed snake described by one source as resembling a slightly skewed X. Both symbols appear very like the Christian Chi Rho logo – the first two letters in Greek of Christ's name. Describing the shields as bearing a sign of Christ could well be an expedient conflation.

So is Constantine's divine vision all just fabrication? In astro-geological terms could Constantine's experience have been of a solar halo above the Alpine passes, or even a meteorite that created the Sirente impact crater in Abruzzo? This would have hit the earth with almost a thousand tons' worth of force – the equivalent of a small nuclear bomb. With shockwaves and a mushroom cloud, it would have been an impressive spectacle – but then that would have been a phenomenon witnessed by Maxentius too and we do not hear a squeak of this earth-shattering event from his side. Was Constantine's vision perhaps an unusual alignment of planets – what is known as a syzygy? Persuasive research in 2014 demonstrated that at

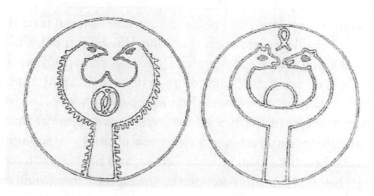

Symbols used on the shields of northern European tribes, including the Cornuti. Constantine may have conflated these with a Chi Rho symbol. Heaven-sent writing was also said to have appeared to the emperor: In hoc signo vinces – *'In this sign you will conquer'.*

the end of October the night sky in this part of Italy is particularly bright. The constellation of the Swan sweeps up over the Eagle with Venus, Jupiter, Saturn and Mars in alignment. Constantine's Christogram – as depicted in frescoes and on coins – is often featured against stars.[3]

Eusebius, Bishop of Caesarea, who lived from c. AD 265 to 340, describes Constantine's vision at Milvian Bridge in terms notably similar to those used for St Paul's conversion. But in truth, would Constantine have seen a pagan – that is, Apolline – or a Christian Chi Rho vision in the sky? Constantine's lusty, globe-trotting father had certainly been a fervent acolyte of the unconquerable sun god Apollo, and Apollo remained a favourite of the emperor's even after his Christianisation programme. Was this some meteorological phenomenon that reminded the fighters of the Sol Invictus – the Roman god of the Unconquered Sun, particularly popular in the Roman army – later being repurposed as Jesus Christ?

Whatever the physical or spiritual truth of the fantastical sign, the historical story is a dramatic one. Maxentius' troops numbered over 180,000 according to antique sources, though it was probably more like 30,000– but still a substantial figure: this was an empire fighting for its life. Maxentius had made that fatal mistake of crossing the Tiber and almost certainly disabling the Milvian Bridge in preparation for a siege, so as Constantine advanced his own troops were now crossing back over a wooden pontoon, which had become a point of weakness at their backs. Early photos of the site show a peaceful stretch of water. But on that late autumn day the Tiber became a thrashing, drowning pool, thick with sick and shit and blood. Constantine – fired up perhaps by whatever it was that he had seen – forced his troops to drive their countrymen back, until they were knee, waist, neck deep in the river's water. The pontoon of boats that they had constructed for access broke up under the weight of the struggling men. Just such a clever row of ships – a pop-up bridge – across the Bosphorus had brought Dareios and his Persian forces west 900 years before. Now this pontoon's failure on the Tiber would smooth Constantine's passage east.

Constantine marked his victory at Milvian Bridge by carrying Maxentius' drowned, decapitated head forward to Rome on a spike.[4] A commemorative arch was raised, probably within twenty-four months, on the very spot of Constantine's victory. Originally traversing the Via Flaminia, this four-sided structure – embodying in stone the successful coup of this illegitimate pretender – today holds up that modest farmhouse Malborghetto. Roman flagstones, part of the very highway that had brought Constantine and his army to their triumph, have been revealed beneath the villa's medieval flooring.

A quiet spot now, for centuries this villa was recognised by travellers as the landmark that announced that the visitor had arrived in Old Rome. But the Battle of Milvian Bridge was for Constantine, emotionally, strategically and spiritually, arguably the moment that he fled from it.

CHAPTER 12

✣

CITY OF GOLD

AD 311–24

The people cried with one voice, 'Constantine cannot be overcome!'

LACTANTIUS, *DE MORTIBUS PERSECUTORUM*[1]

The Emperor [Constantine] always intent on the advancement of religion erected splendid Christian temples to God in every place – especially in great cities such as Nicomedia in Bithynia, Antioch on the Orontes, and Byzantium. He greatly improved this latter city, and made it equal to Rome in power and influence . . .

SOZOMEN, *ECCLESIASTICAL HISTORY*[2]

Constantine was not yet in full control of Rome's territories. There were other rivals still to deal with. One operated out of the city of Thessalonika (modern day Thessaloniki or Salonica), an important commercial hub along the Egnatian Way in what is now northern Greece.

In AD 311, battling an agonising death from either gangrene or bowel cancer, and realising that his grand project of religious persecution had achieved little apart from sorrow and suffering, the Emperor Galerius had granted Christians freedom of worship. He died, leaving his temple (possibly his mausoleum)[3], the rotunda in Thessalonika, empty. This bullishly beautiful building, with walls 6 feet thick, originally designed with an oculus (an opening in the dome) like the Pantheon in Rome and converted down the years into a church and then into a mosque, is now empty once again. Bordered by lavender bushes and the remains of Galerius' palace, its visitors are tourists, a local cat and the Orthodox priests who hold rites here on festival days. It is quiet now, but as this audacious, self-aggrandising statement was being constructed, elsewhere in

Thessalonika there would have been the sound of death and fear. Nearby, St Demetrios' Church commemorates the Roman soldier Demetrios, a second-generation Christian who was run through by spears and martyred on Galerius' orders. Christian eradication looked to be the tenor of times to come.

Yet astonishingly, just ten years after the empire-wide edict of persecution and death, all Christians would be protected. In AD 313, building on Galerius' initiative, Constantine together with his co-Emperor Licinius (an old ally of Galerius) issued a further Edict of Toleration. Constantine's language in this edict, proclaimed in Milan, seems heartfelt: 'no one whatsoever should be denied the opportunity to give his heart to the observance of the Christian cult or to such religion as he deems best suited for himself'.[4]

Once he was established in Rome, Constantine blasted through pagan burial grounds (including those that had previously been the resting place of Maxentius' troops of crack squads) and decapitated pagan statues to replace them with Christian heroes, many of them representing himself and his mother Helena.[5] While still celebrating pagan games and banning business on a Sunday in honour of Sol Invictus, he also fostered the global church-going experience by overseeing the construction of churches with both a nave and aisles – replicas of that vast, red-brick basilica in Trier from which he had first tasted power. It was Constantine who built Rome's gold-standard churches, the Lateran and the Vatican. Architecture took a new form – now there were more curves and colours. Constantine's victory arch, dedicated in AD 315 and patched together with ancient spolia from architectural-salvage warehouses across the city, still stands by the Colosseum. The images of Constantine that were produced became absurdly outsize, perhaps to mirror the scale of the one true God whom the Emperor now claimed to represent.

Within months of his victory, the mints of Rome, Ostia and Ticinum (modern Pavia) were in Constantine's possession. As the acclaimed Emperor of the West he started to mint coins in his image[6] – no longer the bearded military man-of-the-road, but instead a leader who was clean shaven, aquiline, a ghost perhaps of Augustus or Alexander. As the years went on, the coins would amplify Constantine's spiritual nature, wide eyes staring heavenward, a mysterious, beatific smile curling on his lips, sometimes he was haloed. Gold from pagan temples was melted down to be turned into the new currency of choice – the *solidus*, the coin which officially replaced the Roman *aureus* and would continue to circulate until the eleventh century (it survives today in diminutive form in the French *sou*, meaning a little bit of money, and in the Italian *soldi* and the word soldier – one who serves the army for pay).[7]

In Rome Constantine built a fabulous palace complex for his loyal, wronged mother. The irony cannot have been lost on Helena, who was styled Augusta c. AD 324, that her husband Constantius had, thirty or so years before, 'put her away', favouring as his wife instead Theodora, a woman of nobler birth and better connections (Theodora was the stepdaughter of the Emperor Maximian). But Helena had the last laugh. Rome's new Emperor left his mother in charge of the Eternal City as a kind of lieutenant and moved on. There was a sense that Constantine's heart was never really in this one-time Caput Mundi; for him Rome was a battleground. Six years after Maxentius' defeat he would describe Rome as full of superstition, its cults 'leftovers from the tyranny of Maxentius', while the day of Constantine's triumph, 28 October, was celebrated as 'Expulsion of the Tyrant Day'. A young man who had spent much of his life patrolling the limits of empire remembered, perhaps, the possibilities of the East. But first Constantine had to clear out all those others with claims to power.

In AD 313 Constantine arranged for his half-sister Constantia to marry Licinius – now Emperor of the East – in Milan to seal their power-share. Yet within three years the fragile alliance was showing strain, and we find Constantine increasingly encroaching on Licinius' new Eastern territories. By 317 he had advanced towards Byzantium. The situation was steadily deteriorating and come 321 the two refused to recognise one another's consuls (the highest political office in the gift of the emperor), while Constantine seemed increasingly inclined to favour a Christian way of organising things. By 323 the 25 December birthday of Sol Invictus, the 'Unconquered Sun', the patron god of many soldiers, had become the birthday of Christ. Constantine, in pursuit of the Goths, was very clearly stepping on Licinius' turf and on his toes. And then, in 324 in Thessalonika (today Greece's second city), where Galerius had died that gruesome death, leaving an empty tomb and an arch, still standing, which marked the beginning of the end for Old Roman unity, Constantine prepared to attack his rival.

Constantine and Licinius met at Adrianople – modern-day Edirne at the western edge of Turkey – a city whose history-making significance in relation to Istanbul and the wider world is often overlooked. Crossing the wide and treacherous Maritsa River, marching through the flatlands where today gypsies farm roses and gladioli, on 3 July the two forces, armies in excess of 100,000 men, clashed in a firestorm. Although wounded, Constantine would days later chase Licinius down the Via Militaris, a northerly alternative to the Egnatian Way and joined to it by connecting roads, towards Byzantium, where he besieged his rival for a further three months. Using a fleet prepared on the wide bay of Thessalonika, with Constantine's son Crispus in command, he engaged with Licinius' navy all the way down the Dardanelles to what is now Gallipoli. Despite being outnumbered by more than two to one, Crispus' slimmer fleet found it easier to manipulate the straits and scored a decisive victory – smashing all but four of Licinius' ships. As history had already proved, a siege of Byzantium can devour resources, so the smart barmaid's son forced Licinius to meet him instead in pitched battle across the Bosphorus at Chrysopolis – the 'City of Gold'.[8]

As with Byzantium itself, Chrysopolis, known, you will recall, from late antiquity as Scutari and today as Üsküdar, is one of those zones of the sprawling modern city that has recently been excavated during construction of the metro system and has, appropriately enough, yielded archaeological gold. The borers, earth-shifters and sump pumps that made their way down here on the busy roads covering the lost rivers of Bulbul and Cavus Creek to Üsküdar Square have uncovered the stories of many past lives. A neat strip of grey concrete and paint covers over what, for an excavating season of forty-eight months, revealed so much.

Combs, shoes, sandals, wine glasses, all had been lost in the mud here. So too jetties and harbours, the fired and bituminised wooden structures still, unexpectedly, surviving intact in the straitside clay.[9] A curious burial of eighty men and women – the average age of death thirty to thirty-five – has appeared. The women have their arms crossed over their chests, the men over their abdomens. The number of oyster shells nearby, with pierced holes to allow them to be worn as decorations on a thread around the neck, suggests perhaps that these were worshippers of Aphrodite or of Artemis.[10] As you would expect in the harbour at the end of a caravan route across Anatolia, a number of goods commemorating trade have been found: pots decorated with ships, figurines of that traveller from the East, the goddess Kybele; and badges from a later date inscribed in Arabic script describing a chamber of commerce based here.[11] Fetid water, itself seemingly alive as it bubbles away quietly, gave a number of these amphibious treasures a strange new half-life in the city's Archaeological Museum when they were displayed after excavation. In the Ottoman era it will be from Chrysopolis-Scutari-Üsküdar that camel-trains will set out each year on pilgrimage to Mecca.

As ever the ancients (and remember, Constantine was well versed in the classics) had to understand the site of Chrysopolis by telling a story about it.

The ancient Greek myth of Chrysopolis marked both an end and a beginning. The 'golden' son Chrysos, child of Agamemnon and his Trojan-prize Chryseis, it was said, had been escaping the wrath of Clytemnestra, Agamemnon's first wife and her new husband Aigisthos, desperately seeking out his ill-fated half-sister Iphigenia who was at the time a priestess of Artemis in Tauris (present-day Crimea). Euripides explains Iphigenia's purpose in his drama *Iphigenia in Tauris*. It is a barbaric tale: having narrowly escaped sacrifice at the hands of her father, Iphigenia had been whisked off to Artemis' sanctuary where she, in turn, ritually sacrificed foreigners who landed on the local King's shores. (New discoveries in Armenia suggest to us that around 1100 BC in the Bronze Age there was indeed ritual sacrifice of young girls. The remains of a number of them have been found in a sanctuary in the Sevan region; they had been decapitated, with their hands tied together, but there is no sign of struggle, suggesting that this was some kind of ritual act.[12]) Good, golden, Greek Chrysos was attempting to save Iphigenia from this barbarity. But the boy-hero caught a fever, died and was buried on the banks of the Bosphorus before he could travel the final stretch north to fulfil his brotherly duty. Chrysopolis was founded where Chrysos lay. The ancient Greeks who chose to believe this backstory as the origins of one of their foundations were, none too subtly, reminding the Hellenic world of the oddness of barbarians and of the dangers of the unknown North and East, while underlining the frontier nature of this place which they had broken to their will and were now calling home.

Both Greeks and Romans had since succeeded in subduing 'barbarian' lands, and in turning Chrysopolis in particular into a battleground. With his good, imperial education, Constantine would probably have been aware of the mythical charge of his chosen arena. In AD 324 Licinius was hiding out at Chalcedon, but with reports that Constantine and his men had made it across the Bosphorus on specially prepared transport skiffs, he had no choice but to meet his nemesis. With both sides flaunting divine protection – Licinius images of Roman gods and Constantine his *labarum* – a new military standard boasting that enigmatic twisted cruciform symbol, possibly the Chi Rho, hanging from a cross – the historians of the day described this as a religious war. It was certainly blood-soaked. We hear that there was 'great slaughter at Chrysopolis'[13] and as many as 25,000 of Licinius' troops – a large proportion of them Goth mercenaries – were killed. On 18 September, under the strange yellow light that both the setting sun and the rising moon bring at this time of year, at Chrysopolis – the settlement where Alcibiades had raged and where Xenophon had counted out his booty before limping back to Europe via Byzantion – Constantine became Rome's sole Emperor.

Constantine was an individual of clear sight – not just a man who had visions but a visionary. So where now to establish the headquarters of his new empire? Chrysopolis, the city of his triumph? Chalcedon, the city of the blind? Unlikely. Nicomedia where he had been educated under Diocletian's watchful eye? Rome? Trier? Troy? We are told by Suetonius that Julius Caesar had once considered relocating Rome to either Troy or Alexandria, and now, three centuries on, Constantine would indeed head to the ancient city from which all Romans, thanks to the paternity of the Trojan hero Aeneas, believed they were descended.

The newly victorious Emperor made the two-day pilgrimage south, across the Propontis and down the Hellespont, to the location of the Greek camp and the tomb of Ajax[14] connected by a road to the plains below Troy. We are told that, in the region now farmed by itinerant workers from eastern Anatolia and Iraq growing tomatoes and cotton, Constantine 'went to the plain at the foot of Troy on the Hellespont . . . and here he laid out the plan of a large and beautiful city, and built gates on a high spot of ground . . . visible from the sea to sailors.'[15]

Constantine had a number of precedents. Other great leaders of the ancient world had also visited Troy: Xerxes in 480 BC and Alexander the Great in 334 BC – Alexander, sleeping with a dagger and a copy of Homer's works under his pillow, and styling himself a second Achilles. For Constantine this excursion was clearly a symbolic gesture, a neat way for an unorthodox ruler to attach himself to the might of the old. Troy was after all a city for heroes, a city remembered for resisting its enemies for ten long years and only then succumbing to a Greek trick. The noble Trojans were the ancestors of the Romans after all; they had defended their city with dignity; its name had travelled across both time and space.

But then, chroniclers tell us, the One True God intervened: 'when he [Constantine] had proceeded thus far, God appeared to him by night and bade him seek another site for his city. Led by the hand of God, he came to Byzantium in Thrace, beyond Chalcedon in Bithynia . . .'[16] This divine intervention was helpful, as the currents in and out of Beşik Bay on the Hellespont, where the sea once extended inland to make Troy a quasi-port, are in fact treacherous. Between May and October strong undertows power from the Sea of Marmara to the Aegean while a north-easterly wind blows head on as boats try to enter the straits. This would have been an ill-fated spot on which to found a world-class city. It is for good reason that there is none there today.

Byzantium does not have this trouble. It was within sight of Byzantium that Constantine had defeated his single-standing enemy, it was at Byzantium that his adopted ancestor Claudius Gothicus was said to have killed 50,000 Goths, and it was of Byzantium that Constantine had dreamt. Byzantium promised both good associations and a fresh start. The city had been sidelined by Diocletian, who preferred Nicomedia, and we have no official record of Constantine having visited Byzas' City before his attack on Licinius. So there have to be two possibilities here: either Constantine had broken off from Diocletian's tour itinerary as a young man and had been impressed by the place, or, more likely, this was a city whose reputation preceded it. Constantine also now knew, thanks to his three-month siege of Licinius – from the outside in – that Byzantium boasted walls that were near impossible to breach.

And so Byzantium would be Constantine's choice as the centre of operations for a new empire. Overlooking the field of slaughter at Chrys-opolis, this was always a city destined to observe not just her own battles – but because of those straits, because of those cheek-by-jowl continents, because of those critical roadways and waterways – to have a ringside seat at grander theatres, international, domestic, ideological, political, of war. But before Constantine could continue to found his new city at well-placed Byzantium, more blood had to be shed.

CHAPTER 13

✦

IN THE NAME OF CHRIST'S BLOOD

c. AD 326–30

Who would now want the golden age of Saturn?
Ours is a diamond age – of Nero's pattern.
SIDONIUS APOLLINARIS, A BISHOP IN GAUL C. 471–87,
IN A POEM ALLEGEDLY POSTED IN SECRET ON
THE DOORS OF THE PALACE[1]

There was already a vivid classical canvas in Byzantium, and now the new regime was going to colour it up. What followed was a family drama of tabloid proportions.

Bloody sacrifice might be increasingly out of favour but Constantine, allegedly, would now shed the blood of his own family. Hearing tell of an affair (so the majority of sources have it) between his wife Fausta and his son from his first wife Crispus (some said Fausta had polluted her husband's mind against her stepson), Constantine had his boy poisoned. Fausta claimed that Crispus had forced himself on her. Two or three months later, realising that he had been duped, the Emperor arranged for his wife to be sealed in an overheated bath – or bathroom – where she was burnt, scalded or suffocated to death.

What was going on here? A dangerous affair between a young lad and his hot stepmother? Power turning Constantine's head? Slander from later pagan authors furious at Constantine's rejection of the old gods and of Old Rome? Simply a myth (its similarities to the legendary, transgressive Greeks Phaedra and Hippolytus are striking)? Or a cool, strategic move, Constantine eliminating his eldest (but illegitimate) son in favour of his three legitimate heirs? And yet his beloved mother, the matriarch Helena, had brought up her grandson Crispus, as had

Constantine's favoured educator the Christian Lactantius. Constantine himself was probably illegitimate; what could possibly be the reason for such vile bloodshed?

With the extant evidence it is unlikely we can ever know the cause, the motivation or the truth of this tale because – and this is possibly the most telling detail of all – Fausta and her stepson Crispus have been erased from the monumental and primary source records. Apart from their sad story they have left not a single, contemporary, textual trace.

Whatever the motivation for this homicide, regret was said to have quickly stepped in. Just as the Emperor Ashoka had famously turned to Buddhism in the third century BC after realising the pain and suffering his genocidal ambition had caused, the (somewhat excitable) author Zosimus tells us that Constantine was consumed by the need, unequivocally, to sign up to a faith that might cleanse his soul. Impelled by grief, remorse or a newfound liberty, the wrong-side-of-the-bedcovers son of a soldier was on the move. In AD 325 Constantine outlawed crucifixions and gladiator shows. Horror at the double murder was said to be the driving force that sent his mother Helena to Jerusalem in search of sublimely potent relics and Constantine to found his new city, Constantinoupolis.

The truth is probably a little more quotidian. Constantine had been interested in Christianity before he started to bump off his family. And the city of Constantinople was, above all, an expression of imperial might – albeit one with a pulsing religious bass note. With an army swollen to at least 450,000, the new defender of both the idea of Rome and a fresh faith was well placed.[2] Having defeated the Tetrarchy, the message was now very clear. Constantine, from his base at Byzantium, the city marked out by Septimius Severus as the spot from which all distances in the Roman Empire could be measured, was one leader in charge of one territory as the servant of one God – and conveniently as a man who therefore held all the power of the pagan world in his purview. His adopted city, which was divinely favoured in terms of topography by the old gods, was now to see the favour of the One True God too.

On the face of it, this is theologically not an obvious move. Accepted as god-men, Roman emperors were themselves sublime, so why make yourself the follower of a forgiving God and of his impoverished, peace-preaching failure of a son? Why modify a spiritual landscape in which the emperor is a godhead to one where the emperor is merely a servant of the Divine?

We should consider the mood of the moment. Constantine was taking his turn with a religious brush that was creating a sfumato sketch across the continents of Europe and Asia. In Armenia, looking out over the dry plains of Anatolia towards Iran, from AD 305 onwards Armenian kings had been converting to Christianity. At rocky Khor Virap, in the long shadow of Mount Ararat, the Christian Gregory the Illuminator was said to have been held captive by King Tiridates III in a snake-infested dungeon for refusing to make pagan sacrifice. I have climbed down into this subterranean hole. The deeper one clambers, the danker and hotter the atmosphere becomes. The air is close, and the only sound comes courtesy of the whining flies that happily breed here 50 feet or so beneath the earth. From the fifth century onwards crosses were carved into the black basalt walls to commemorate Gregory's ordeal. It was said that his miraculous survival in this stifling, grisly pit encouraged King Tiridates' sister to ask for the Christian's aid when her royal brother was tormented by a demon. Once cured, Tiridates converted to Christianity and built a church over the evidence of Gregory's shameful incarceration. King and religious activist then travelled to Rome together where the story went that they inspired none other than Constantine with their accounts of the liberating truth of Christ's word.

In Georgia too, above the magnificent confluence of the Rivers Aragvi and Kura at Mtskheta, a half-hour drive from modern-day Tbilisi, a church was reportedly founded in the fourth century AD.[3] Today the faithful celebrate both their Christian faith and its pagan roots by tying coloured ribbons to the line of trees that leads up to this ancient foundation. By 337, Constantine undertook regular missions to this part of the Caucasus to help buttress his fledgling imperial religion. Even in mist-wrapped Britain, at sites such as the Roman villa of Lullingstone in Kent, men were decorating their homes with images of Christians; in Lullingstone we see them with their arms outstretched in prayer, above a room beautified by pagan river goddess-nymphs, whose nipples flow with life-giving water. The coming of the Lord was not just hoped for; it was known to be a fact of the near future. Those with temporal power, who listened to what was being said by priests and proselytisers, did not want to find themselves without a port in an eschatological storm. Rather than a threat, Christianity was looking increasingly like a means to unify and indeed to consolidate power. Who needs democracy or a republic if every man is equal in the eyes of God?

But as well as adopting symbols of Christ, Constantine still wrapped himself in Apollo's mantle – and so the Sabbath became Sun-day. Coins and inscriptions show the Christian Emperor continuing to honour Sol Invictus up until the time of his death.

As much ink as has been spilt debating the physical nature of Constantine's Christian vision needs to flow to address his psychological motivation. Perhaps his move to Christianity was a genuine revelation, a sense that the combination of ideas of universal peace with the *pax Romana*, the most robust peace the world had ever known, would be an irresistible one. Perhaps Constantine felt he was a god-man who had beaten death, Christ-like. With Christ on the throne there was no need for the goddess Kybele with her lions and her mysterious blind, rock doorways out in the wilderness offering a route between two worlds, the living and the dead. Now each and every Christian could open the door to another life – perhaps Constantine was making sure that he held the key. Whatever the origins of his faith, was it genuinely inspirational to see women and men with lowly backgrounds like his own mother's, sharing prayers that did not just allay fears, but that gave them hope? All that said, Constantine's Christian forgiveness needed a little work, as it did not extend to Licinius. In AD 325 the one-time Caesar, husband of Constantine's own sister, was executed on suspicion of treason; the following year Licinius' son suffered the same fate.

And so the city of Constantinople was founded on dreams, faith and hope but also on ambition and blood.

Up until now for any Christian there had been two great overlords – God/Christ and Caesar/King – with a default conflict between the two. Constantine could now be all things to all men, and he needed a headquarters to match. Byzantium would be transformed to make real an ambitious idea. The city he chose now felt robustly Roman. Even though Septimius Severus and his son Caracalla had never quite finished their grandstanding projects, the hippodrome and the Baths of Zeuxippos, the layout of the streets and public spaces and the grand forum surrounded by stoas and colonnades called the Tetrastoon just to the south of the ancient acropolis gave Byzantium tantalising potential.

Christian chroniclers reported that Constantine paced doggedly around Byzantium on foot, lance in hand, making it wider, bigger, larger and larger. 'When will you stop?' someone cried out. 'When He in front of me does!' came Constantine's reply.[4] Meanwhile, presumably to keep his options open, a pagan priest ploughed a furrow behind the emperor to bring good fortune. Most major cities and civilisations have argued that they were god-given. Because of its triumphant topography, this is something that Istanbul has never had to try too hard to believe.

The woody promontory between the Bosphorus and the Propontis was now singing to the purposeful sound of the carpenter's hammer and the stonemason's chisel. Constantine founded a new palace tumbling down the hillside to the sea, he extended the hippodrome, introduced a grid-system of streets, a circular forum, a Senate house, at least two churches, a new mint, a series of splendid private homes, inviting in high-ranking Romans from across the empire to occupy them, and the semi-pagan Capitolum to maintain the imperial cult – boasting statues of himself and his father in porphyry. From across the Empire Constantine imported bragging pagan statuary, including that triumphal Serpent Column from Delphi scent-marked by Pausanias. And protecting all this he reinforced the city walls. St John might have described Old Rome as 'Babylon', but this New Rome was a vigorous start for a new kind of Christian metropolis. There was, at last, the very real chance of paradise on earth for God and for his earthly stewards. This city that Constantine would name Constantinoupolis was, simply, God-given – or, as the Emperor put it, 'given to him by the command of God'.[5]

CHAPTER 14

✤

QUEEN OF CITIES

AD 324 ONWARDS

> He considerably enlarged it, surrounded it with superb walls, adorned it with various edifices, made it equal to the queen of cities, Rome, called it Constantinople, and made a new law commanding it should be called New or Second Rome; which law he caused to be engraved upon a stone pillar near his equestrian statue in a public square.
>
> SOCRATES SCHOLASTICUS, *ECCLESIASTICAL HISTORY*[1]

It is an epoch-defining monument that your eyes are not immediately drawn to. The stumpy remains of Constantine's porphyry column (now rising 115 feet but once a full 160 feet tall), from which the Emperor – in the guise of Apollo – declared to the world that he was the caretaker of God's home on earth, now fight to be noticed against the cheap mobile phone and tawdry lantern shops that guide visitors to Istanbul's Grand Bazaar.

But here, in many ways, we can understand the mind and the mountainous vision of the man who gave the world this city as a global power. Bringing in the raw materials to erect this look-at-me monument, a finger jabbing heavenwards, the focal point of the city's new Forum of Constantine, was itself an international operation. The distinctive purple stone comes from Mons Porphyrites in Egypt. A scrap of Byzantine graffiti on the tomb of the Egyptian Pharaoh Ramses VI in Egypt's Valley of the Kings gives us a clue to who was tasked by Constantine with sourcing adornments for his new city: the vandal, a certain Nicagoras, has scribbled his thanks for the all-expenses-paid trip to 'the most pious emperor Constantine, who has granted me this'. Constantine's excitable envoy was a torch-bearer in the Eleusinian Mysteries (an orgiastic ritual that had been taking place at Eleusis since the Bronze Age) – a pagan through and through. His quest was to source obelisks (which were ordered, but did not arrive till after Constantine's death) and the purple stone for the Emperor's column.[2] Once the sky-scraping blocks had been raised (successfully at first, but we know that by AD 416 the column drums had to be held together with iron hoops), they were topped with a curious statue – an anthropomorphic figure with distinct identity issues.

Made of bronze, crowned with a seven-rayed crown – each ray, it was said, containing a shard of the nails used to crucify Christ – with a spear in one hand and a globe in the other (imported, Constantinople's chroniclers wrote, from Ilium in Phrygia and then remodelled), the statue has been the source of gossip and conjecture from the moment it was erected. Was this Constantine declaring himself a combination of Christ, the Greek Apollo, a Trojan hero and the Eastern Sol Invictus? On his early coins the Emperor was shown in similar form with the sun's rays around him, while statues elsewhere in the empire were dedicated to 'Constantine Augustus the all-seeing Sun'. Every year on Constantine's birthday an image of Tyche, goddess of good fortune (significantly, remodelled from a statue of that Eastern Mother of Nature Kybele) was whizzed around Constantinople's hippodrome on a gilded chariot of Helios. Constantine I might be a Christian emperor, but he wore the clothes of the pagan world.

And what was concealed directly under the Column of Constantine was even more intriguing. A wooden image of Pallas Athena, known as the Palladium and believed to be a survivor of the Trojan War itself, was buried here. Smuggled out from Troy by Aeneas, so antiquity's poets tell us, this was an object that linked the might of Rome with her Hellenic taproots and with the wiliness of the first Romans (the Trojans) operating in the East. No need for Constantine to found his new city at Troy, Troy could come to him. Here too – it was claimed – was the very adze used by Noah to build the ark and the actual panniers from which Jesus distributed loaves and fish to feed the 5,000. It is all clever, magpie symbolism fusing together at a stroke the power of the Greeks and the Romans, of East and West, of monotheistic and polytheistic gods – a combination in a single column of the greatest stories on earth.

The scale of the soldier-Emperor's project was immediately apparent. Work on the ground could have begun as early as AD 324 – the same year as the Battle of Chrysopolis and six years before Constantinople was officially founded and renamed. By marking out an area for the city of nearly 3 square miles and extending the walls over a mile to the west, the Emperor had laid down a new perimeter which ensured that Constantinople was three times the size of classical Byzantium. One of Constantine's very first tasks, perhaps with the Troy model still in his mind, had been to encircle his newly-favoured city with new walls.³ Punctuated by gates – reputedly built by tens of thousands of Gothic prisoners of war – this distinctive, snaking line, visible from land and sea, would buttress the character of the city from then until now. Tracing the walls of various emperors through the history of Istanbul is like tracing the growth rings of an ancient oak. Thrillingly for archaeologists, Constantine's stone blocks (making up walls 174 feet high and over 13 feet wide) have just emerged from the earth, uncovered in those digs at Yenikapı that have also revealed the world's first wooden coffin. Stand next to these massive stones and you can virtually smell Constantine's ambition.⁴

Official dedication ceremonies for the city in AD 330 began with a bloodless sacrifice (no sacrificial animals officially allowed in New Rome) and lasted a full forty days and nights, starting on 2 April and culminating on 11 May, a biblically significant duration.⁵ The population of the city (many of the citizens were newly imported), were comforted to learn that some Roman traditions – such as the distribution of free bread, and in Constantinople's case oil and wine too – continued. The Forum from which Constantine's Column rose was built from scratch. Round, rimmed by a two-storey, semi-circular colonnade, punctuated by triumphal arches and edged by the Senate House (a mini-Pantheon in style, fronted by a porphyry pediment and four columns) to the north, the Nymphaeum to the south – where weddings were sometimes held – and the Praetorium (a courthouse, overseen by the prefect of the East) and prison to the south-east, this urban planning was both familiar and experimental.⁶ Similarly the establishment of a Capitol was what one might expect (honouring Jupiter, Juno and Minerva, Rome's 'state' gods), as was Constantine's building of temples to Rhea–Kybele and Tyche–Fortuna, but what stood out was the inclusion of a grand mausoleum within the city walls – the kind of thing only Augustus had erected and that Christians were now tending to do – as did the construction in premier position on the acropolis of two Christian churches. So we have to imagine the scene

in 330 when Constantinople as an emerging super-power was presented
to the known world.

Until the fall of Constantinople to Mehmet the Conqueror's soldiers in
AD 1453, the culmination date of 11 May would be celebrated in the city,
with the emperors of what would soon be the capital of the Byzantine
Empire cavalcading the processional way on silk carpets, travelling along
what was called the Mese, the Middle Road, an extension of the Via
Egnatia and a grand development of Severus' colonnade; while feasting
was arranged for rich and poor alike – entertainments as lavish as the
current regime could afford. Today 11 May is promoted via an online
seven-point plan (International Byzantine Plan) suggesting ways that the
global community can celebrate all things Byzantine, even if Christians
no longer run the city.

Although Constantine's dedication ceremonies had begun in the new
Church of Peace, Haghia Eirene (a later version of which still stands
within the grounds of the Topkapı Palace, built by Constantine close to
the pagan temples of Apollo and Aphrodite and possibly the development
of a house church), the triumphant foundation procession, bearing gifts
from the mother city of Rome, would have made its way to the Forum of
Constantine past the pagan temples of Rhea and Tyche and the temple
of Fortuna Redux – whose deity was responsible for bringing men and
women home safely.[7] The ceremonial way, the Mese, was punctuated by
colossal canopies in stone and bronze – four-pillared structures (known as
tetrapyla) sheltering statues of the Emperor and, as time went on, Christian relics. If one walks down the Mese's ghost today, Divanyolu Street,
at the intersection with the market street Uzunçarşı it is still possible to
enjoy a mental image of these grand constructions – although the kebab
joints, Irish pubs and key-ring vendors do not quite capture the spirit of
the original road. In Constantine's day the Mese was planted either side
with flowers and crops. Christ's first city must have looked very like a
splendidly appointed allotment.

Under Constantine the hippodrome of Byzantion was refurbished and
completed with a *cavea*, or tiered seating. The Milion erected by Septimius Severus – marking distances across the empire to all other cities
– was modified to become a modern version of Augustus' Milliarium
Aureum – his Golden Milestone. Severus' pagan Milion was now topped
with a pious group featuring Constantine, his mother Helena and that

fragment of the True Cross that she was (later) said to have found in Jerusalem. This enhancement of the Milion positioned Constantinople squarely as the beating heart of a communication network that reached even beyond empire. Splendid bronze gates to the imperial palace were approached via a Portico of Achilles. The Tetrastoon was renamed the Augusteion in honour of Constantine's mother, Augusta Helena. A silver statue of this second Helen towered above the space at this second Troy. For the next 1,000 years, as a walled city that many longed to put to siege, Constantinople's inhabitants – who could have been living in Troy itself if Constantine had gone with what, we are told, was his original plan – would tell one another the stories of the Trojan War, they would commission or reclaim statues of Trojan War heroes and preserve versions of the legend in their libraries and scriptoria.

Much is made of the fact that, like the Old Rome, the New Rome had been built on seven hills, and new myths were invented about the city's ancient past. It was not the old families of Rome but newcomers who were shipped in to administer a metropolis now four to five times bigger than the city left by Byzantium's last urban planner, Septimius Severus. This New Rome had a kind of inbuilt generosity – both accepting the power of her urbane ancestor and asking permission to play with exciting, fresh ideas about how to live in the world.

This was a grand experiment then; yet, paradoxically, in some ways none of this was new. Roman emperors had frequently founded cities in their own name – Constantine's behaviour is barely remarked upon by a number of contemporary chroniclers. Cities, shrines, sanctuaries were long thought to have been physically inhabited by spirits, nymphs, gods and goddesses. Christ might be a new kind of demi-god, but he was by no means the first to be honoured in this way. Yet what seems clear is that Constantinople, shaking off the Greco-Thracian name by which it had been known for at least 1,000 years, had an extraordinary sense of itself. Because Constantinople, women and men truly believed, was the city from which the single, all-creating, all-seeing and almighty God would rule the world.

Now the point of the Roman Empire – and of the men who represented it – was not just to colonise territory, but also to sit in sympathy with the spirit, to colonise the mind.

CHAPTER 15

✤

FAITH, HOPE, CHARITY AND THE NICENE CREED

AD 324 ONWARDS

He razed to their foundations those of them which had been the chief objects of superstitious reverence.

EUSEBIUS OF CAESAREA, *CHURCH HISTORY, LIFE OF CONSTANTINE*[1]

In Dyrrachium, modern-day Dürres, on the coast of Albania, where the Egnatian Way begins, there is a dilapidated amphitheatre. A few home-owners refused to move when the site was first excavated in the 1960s and 1980s and so now live on as twenty-first-century squatters right above and within this impressive remnant from antiquity. The Albanians hang out their washing and watch their satellite TVs above the Roman stones. But the site lives and breathes in more ways than one. Once the scene of the blood-soaked human and animal sacrifices on which late antiquity was so keen, with the advent of Christianity in the time of Constantine the games here were stopped. 'Bloody spectacles displease us,' we hear from Constantine in an edict of AD 325 and again, the sources tell us, he enlightened King Shapur of Persia thus: 'I . . . recoil with horror from the blood of sacrifices, from their foul and detestable odours . . .'[2]

Once Constantine had made it clear that Christianity would be toler-ated across his empire, a church was swiftly built within the amphitheatre itself and Christians were buried here following their timely, natural deaths where once they had been slaughtered for entertainment. Locals today defiantly light candles in the church's roofless ruins (Christianity was outlawed by the twentieth-century communist dictator Enver Hoxha, a ban not lifted until 1991), just as the inhabitants of Constantinople did 1,700 years before in their little clay lamps. Those Constantinopo-litan lamplights suddenly bore new images: no longer Helen of Troy's

Spartan mother, Leda, being raped by Zeus in the form of a swan, or Eros fluttering with his darts of pain, but fishes and crosses – turning up in their dozens throughout digs in greater Istanbul. The number of new, Christian-themed lamps points to the degree to which Christian belief was becoming normalised in Constantinople and nearby Chalcedon and Chrysopolis.[3]

For five and a half years Constantine had based himself in Nicomedia, now one of the uglier cities in modern-day Turkey (Izmit), strategising and administering. At the old palace of Diocletian, where he had once been taught to be a good Roman, and from which the persecution of Christians had been authorised, he walked with the ghosts of the past. In AD 325 he then changed the world in what is one of its prettiest settlements.

Nicaea, 100 miles south of Constantinople in Anatolia, is one of those places where it feels possible to be in two eras at once. Today called Iznik – producer of Ottoman Istanbul's finest tiles – Nicaea had long been a comfortable, flourishing, lakeside settlement. It is still a gated city; the rings of sturdy stone and late Roman brick walls once protected inhab-itants such as the historian Cassius Dio, who would tell the world, for example, that Boudicca was 'flame-haired', and the Greek astronomer Hipparchos, whose theories on the centrality of the earth to the universe endured until they were dismissed by Copernicus. Septimius Severus and Pescennius Niger had fought outside Nicaea's walls, and in 1204 it would be to Nicaea that Constantinople's leaders and population fled following the disaster of the Fourth Crusade when Constantinople was occupied by Franks from the West.

In AD 325 it was to this busy little hub, from the hot, sandy, sparkling settlements of North Africa, from damp Britain, from the Middle East and from the southern Caucasus that Christian men, eagerly, came. The son of the Gregory who had suffered long in that Armenian pit was one of them. Their destination was a place where lake waters, teeming with stork and salmon, promised resolution and balm for their troubled souls. At least 250 bishops made the journey – their prime purpose to debate a theological idea popularised by one man. A Libyan of Berber descent named Arius had been drawn to the heady intellectual hotbed that was Alexandria – the city founded in 330 BC as a centre of knowledge by Alexander the Great. Here Arius declared that the Son, Christ, was a

lesser divinity than the Father, God. Arius, and his outspoken opponent
Patriarch Alexander of Alexandria, had all been called to Nicaea by Constantine to thrash out what Christianity should look, sound and feel like.

The council called in Nicaea in AD 325 ran from 20 May to 19 June, the
most exquisite time of the year to be in Anatolia; one can just imagine the
sense of intellectual purpose, verve and theological excitement felt by the
participants as they conferred, their debates accompanied by the rustle of
oak trees grown for their gall-ink and the sound of entertainment in the
theatre – a theatre now abandoned to stray dogs and dog-brave archaeologists. The council itself convened in the Emperor's luxurious summer
palace by the lakeside. Constantine played a vigorous part. The debate
might be theological – were God and Christ of one essence (*homoousios*)
or were they divided? – but this vital question was not left just to men
of the cloth. The rejection of Arianism would colour the development of
European and Near Eastern civilisation from that point on and Nicaea
would rubber-stamp the religious power of temporal rulers. We hear that,
in advance of Constantine's entry into the conference, everyone fell silent,
rising at a signal as their Emperor-Lord walked between them, 'like some
heavenly angel of God, his bright mantle shedding lustre like beams of
light'.[4] At Nicaea, Constantine was celebrated as 'bishop to those without'.[5] The conversations between the men present were highly emotional.
It was rumoured that at one point Nicholas of Myra (the St Nicholas said
to be the ancestor of Santa Claus) struck Arius in the face, and Arius'
supporter Eusebius of Nicomedia responded by urinating on Nicholas'
gown. When the vote went against him, Arius was exiled along the Via
Egnatia to Illyria, modern-day Albania, and Constantine ordered that all
his works be burnt.

The decisions taken here in AD 325 would have real impact, settling not
just the relationship between God and his son, but also the possibility of
an ecumenical law, the date of Easter – now separated from the Jewish
Passover – and a number of canons, for example forbidding self-castration
and usury. The name of Constantine would be exalted by many billions
of worshippers, for thousands of years.

Following the debates at Nicaea, great feasts were enjoyed in the imperial palace, rooms which survive now as shadow-lines of stone in the
waters at the edge of the lake. But one of Constantine's concessions here
would not, for Constantinople, be a cause for celebration. Almost as an

afterthought, the Emperor agreed that Rome's Senate should still have precedence over Constantinople's own. Half a millennium later, this would cause Constantinople and her people much distress.

The fierce debates at Nicaea were forerunners of a characteristic that Constantinople would soon acquire – a reputation for robust theological conversation and quixotic discourse. The city was acquiring a kind of irradiated glow of piety. It was announced that Constantinople would gather together the relics of all the apostles; Constantine's new imperial mausoleum of the Holy Apostles was where the remains of the Sts Luke, Timothy and Andrew were to be buried. After his death Constantine was described as *isapostolos* – equal to the apostles. Constantinople was rebranding herself as a city that crackled with spiritual possibilities. Ancient Greek and Roman religion had always been a little leery about the possibilities of an afterlife, to say nothing of paradise, but now, for ordinary people, this was truly a viable option. Both raw, codified belief and the physical make-up of the streets of Constantinople, her churches, shrines and relic-caskets would help them to get there.

How would it have felt to live in this emerging Christian world? Now that those lights were being lit in Christian-logo lamps, to illuminate a different spiritual landscape, did the cityscape change to match? Constantinople certainly boasted a new skyline. A Byzantine church building has recently been uncovered in the centre of the city; this could be the renowned imperial monastery built in honour of the Virgin Mary. It seems that in Constantinople there was now a conscious elaboration of the *pax Romana*. *Pax* in Latin means literally a pact, an arrangement; indeed the Roman Empire's employment of peace often seemed more like pacification. The Greek word for peace, *eirene* (a state of peace in contrast to war, and then, following the Stoics, an inner tranquillity) and the Middle Eastern *shul, shalom, salaam* have a more holistic and elastic feel. Christian peace is an aspiration rather than an arrangement. In the construction of Haghia Eirene, the Church of the Peace of God, both a spiritual and a public relations statement was being made. The *pax Romana* which physically made the dissemination of Christianity possible was supported by the new, exciting notion of internal *eirene* – a kind of peace that was not just a practical but a philosophical possibility.

Near to the Church of Peace on what was the original ancient Greek acropolis an orphanage of St Paul and an associated medical centre were also soon established. Poorhouses and additional orphanages were to follow. Constantine supplied rations of bread in the city for 80,000 people every day. Nine hundred and fifty workshops were selected to help fund the free burial of the indigent poor of the city. As Constantinople grew, one of her trademarks was provision for the sick – hospitals specialising in hospice service, infectious diseases and maternal care would come to decorate the city. Steadily the number of slaves on the land that serviced the city started to decline. Instead there were more small-time farmers tied to the land; these were known as *coloni*, the equivalent of western Europe's bonded serfs.[6] Constantine's reforming motivations might have been complex, and they may have benefited from the hagiographers' gloss, but the success of his city was said to be due to 'the piety of the builder and of the inhabitants, and their compassion and liberality towards the poor. The zeal they manifested for the Christian faith was so great that many of the Jewish inhabitants and most of the Greeks were converted.'[7] Pagan commentators remarked on the apparent lunacy of redemptive forgiveness – the fact that in Constantinople even murderers could be cleansed of their sins. The premier murderer of the day was of course Constantine, but we must not be too cynical. The Emperor himself became actively involved in 'good works'. Virtue, as Aristotle so neatly put it, really can be its own reward. We hear from one textual fragment that Constantine encouraged his citizens – including women – to come to him to resolve troubles in a way that chimed with Jesus' message of social justice.[8]

Perhaps with Caracalla's donation of universal citizenship back in AD 212, inhabitants of the New Roman Empire now needed to feel an enhanced kind of belonging. In a Christian system your status could bleed beyond the old divisions of *humiliores* (of low status) or *honestiores* (privileged). Spiritual access was no longer dominated by dynasties of high priests. An emerging elite of bishops appeared. By the end of Constantine's reign some estimate there were over 6 million Christians across the empire ministered to by many thousands of clerics, including new men, not just the politically successful families of old.

Constantine repealed the punitive Augustan legislation against childlessness that must have blighted the lives of a number of women in the old Roman Empire. It was now all right to be infertile; all right to be childless; all right to be a virgin; all right to abstain from sex. Constantinople must have witnessed a huge release of energy, particularly from the female of the species. Women were ordained as deaconesses, initially anointing and baptising other adult women (this was done in the nude, hence the need for a female to officiate), a ceremony completed by a bishop's prayer. They were allocated a special section of the great Church of Haghia Sophia, and we should think of these brides of Christ dressed in their liturgical robes, some chanting and singing hymns in the all-female choirs. Up until AD 390 these were women of any age, but thereafter were typically over the age of sixty (there were more restrictions on female than on male deacons and harsher punishments if they stepped out of line).[9] In Constantinople there was a sacred role for the menopausal woman. One area of the city indeed came to be known as that of 'the Deaconess'.[10]

Beyond Constantinople's walls, Constantine started to appropriate key sites for Christianity. There was now a church in Bethlehem at the site of Christ's birth and Hadrian's pagan temple[11] was pulled down on the hill of Golgotha. On the busy south coast of Asia Minor near Tarsus, the Temple of Aegeae was demolished. Sanctuaries were destroyed at Afqa and Baalbek in the Lebanon too, an agricultural region where today hashish and opium are grown alongside the watermelons chilling in the river.[12] In Syria the temple of Zeus Apameus (at Apamea) would soon come crashing down.[13]

The Bishop of Aelia Capitolina – the Roman name for Jerusalem when it was rebuilt after its destruction in AD 70 – a visitor to Nicaea, helped Constantine to embark on an empire-wide new building programme. In Jerusalem the sanctuary of 'that impure demon called Aphrodite, a dark shrine of lifeless idols', was razed to locate the exact spot of Jesus' crucifixion. As the ultimate martyrion – the Church of the Holy Sepulchre – was built on the spot, it was said that Constantine had an opinion on minute details, down to the decoration scheme of the ceiling. Optimistically Constantine established a church, the Golden Octagon, in Antioch dedicated to the *homonoia*, or concordance. But in Nicomedia he built a church for his Saviour to commemorate victory against his enemies and God's foes. By the time of his death he had founded churches in Rome, Ostia, Albano, Naples, Capua, Jerusalem, Bethlehem, Hebron, Nicomedia, Antioch, Heliopolis and of course Constantinople. The idea and ideals of Christianity were physically mortared into the environment.

And in Thessalonika, Constantine ordered Galerius' show-off temple–
mausoleum to be turned into a church.

The majority of the empire's inhabitants were pagan. Did a kind of
solar monotheism, a neat adaptation of Apolline imagery, give them
comfort? The ancient gods were always shape-shifting, so did this new
church really just make yet another god-man bigger, shinier, even more
formidable? In the back rooms of the Byzantine Museum in Athens the
inch-by-inch restoration of one mosaic from Byzantine Thebes offers an
answer. Belonging to one of the well-to-do Roman nobles who were increasingly converting (by the end of the fourth century Christianity was
no longer a grass-roots, minority movement), the artwork is a splendid
hybrid. What strikes one immediately is that this is a hunting scene – the
kind displayed so vividly on the Lod mosaic. As the tesserae were slowly
reassembled it became clear that two Christian monks had been put in
the picture too.[14] So just as gods and spirits and demi-gods – made of
wood and clay, hippopotamus ivory and gold, were being smashed up, or
re-purposed, a new kind of religious creature was being grouted into the
New Roman landscape. As a species our minds crave disturbance. We
might seem to be creatures of habit, but we also delight in the unexpected
and the new.

So we have to ask what in practical terms motivated this grand, empire-
wide volte-face? Was it all Constantine's doing, the cool tactician at work?
Or should the filliping work of that feisty mother of his be accorded some
of the credit?

CHAPTER 16

✢

HELENA

AD 248–328

He did no public business without her consent, although she lived like a
harlot and practised all manner of lewdness all over the palace.

AELIUS LAMPRIDIUS, *THE LIFE OF ELAGABALUS*[1]

All politics are personal. All history too – and there is the curious chance
that many billions of lives have been shaped by the inclinations of one
woman.

We have to remember that Constantine's mother Helena was in
many ways the very incarnation of Christ's preaching. Starting life as an
innkeeper's daughter east of Byzantium in Bithynia, and ending up as
mother to the son of an upwardly mobile soldier, then cast aside when
that man, Constantius Chlorus, as number two to the Roman Emperor,
was made Caesar, Helena was an exemplar of the poor, the unclean, the
outcasts that Christ's teaching raised up. She had survived the chaos surrounding Diocletian and Maximian's Great Persecution of AD 303–11; she
was perhaps even converted by a family fleeing the Emperor Diocletian's
steel.

A later bogus, satirical history, *The Life of Elagabalus* in the *Historia
Augusta*, purportedly written to describe the wild lifestyle of the Roman
Emperor Elagabalus (who reigned AD 218–22), almost certainly takes
many a dig at Constantine, and suggests that this was a boy unabashed
by the strength of his mother's apron-strings. Later stories circulated that
the former good-time girl had been horrified to hear that her son was
considering becoming a Christian and insisted that he take up Judaism
instead. In a public faith-off in August 315, it was said that rabbis killed a
bull by whispering the name 'Jehovah' in its ear – only for it to be revived

when Pope Sylvester whispered 'Jesus Christ'. Helena was mightily impressed and her son had free rein to take the faith of his choice.[2]

Helena's traditional birthplace, Drepanum near modern-day Yalova on the Asian coast of the Sea of Marmara – now a spa town, much favoured as a weekend retreat by well-to-do Istanbullus – was a gentle boat ride from Byzantium and had been one of the ancient city's outposts. Once in power, Constantine's administration renamed the place Helenopolis and ensured it was lovingly refurbished. The Emperor's daughter was also given his mother's name – Helena. But apart from the riproaring tales and biographical potboilers of social climbing, concrete evidence of Helena's life in the Eastern Mediterranean is scant.[3]

In Constantinople itself it was recorded that Helena authorised the construction on the Seventh Hill of a martyrion and monastery dedicated to Sts Karpos and Papylos, both killed in AD 251 by the Emperor Decius at the foot of the south-western face of the Xerolophos – a busy, messy district today, populated by the few gypsies who have survived the city's clear-up programme. What remains of the martyrion can be accessed only via a car-wash and garage, but it seems it was one of a number of martyria dedicated to Christian martyrs in a zone that was originally just outside the city walls.

Around AD 327 Helena chose to make pilgrimage to Jerusalem. And this is where the stories really started to take flight: the Eastern Mediterranean, Asia Minor and the Middle East all claim to host hard evidence of this journey. On the island of Paros, Helena was said to have founded the Church of a Hundred Doors, a wonderfully atmospheric building. Locals, sipping their frappés, will still tell you that when the hundredth door is located and opened, Constantinople will return to Christian control. In Jerusalem, Helena oversaw the construction of the Church of the Holy Sepulchre, as well as a church to Mary Theotokos (that is, Bearer or Mother of God) over the site of Jesus' birth in Bethlehem and another at the precise place, it was claimed, on the Mount of Olives where Christ ascended to heaven.

Helena returned from the Middle East with shards of wood from the True Cross and a nail from Christ's crucifixion. The nail was made into a bridle for Constantine's horse, so Constantine-Christ could now lead his faithful subjects to victory. Constantinople had an urgent need for hallowed gewgaws such as these, objects with a kind of radioactive spirituality that would mutate and heat up the city's narrative. Without a headline-grabbing religio-historical past, the city had to manufacture her own significance. And so they started to flood in, the knucklebones of martyrs, the hair of saints, the thorns from Christ's crown, and in AD 614 the holy lance that speared Christ's side, which was put on display in Haghia Sophia the week after it arrived – for the men of the city to venerate on Tuesdays and Wednesdays and for the women on Thursdays and Fridays. Tradition has it that Helena's fourth-century relic-collecting fervour is still witnessed in the city. In the southern corner of the quiet, shuttered nave of the Church of St George can be found what is said to be the very column at which Jesus was whipped.

Imperial workshops sprang up in the city mass-producing the reliquaries in which these sacred remains were kept. Beautiful objects in themselves, few of those produced within Constantinople have survived. One, the size of a large matchbox but designed to be worn as a pendant, was recovered in 2006. It features delicately wrought figures of the archangels Michael and Gabriel; St Andrew, Byzantium's favoured apostle, is there as you might expect, and Jesus, barefoot, has one foot grasped by the donor – from his beardless state almost certainly a eunuch – who directs his prayers to Christ and to the Virgin Mary. Helena's relic-collecting work would be remembered across Europe. In the eleventh and twelfth centuries, during their own explosions of piety, Frankish craftsmen produced reliquaries telling Helena's story. In blazing enamel Constantine's mother is shown travelling to Jerusalem, questioning Jews, holding their feet to the fire to get the information she wants about the whereabouts of sacred remains and then testing out the efficacy of her dubiously acquired relics of the True Cross on the dead. By popularising relic-collection Helena introduced on to Constantinople's streets the sickly-sweet smell of enamel being burnished and of gems being bone-glue stuck to reliquaries, and the crack of rock-crystal being cut and polished so that the holy remains could be seen within – she offered the people of the city the chance to find beauty and inspiration and wonder in the body parts of the dead.

Helena's diadems, canopies and accessories – such as the orb – afforded her visible power. On coinage she is described as 'the security of the state'. The Empress Dowager is shown holding an apple, a symbol of both knowledge and fertility. She was also represented cradling a child on her lap sporting a huge halo behind – not just recalling the potent

A bronze medallion of Helena from the fourth century AD

Egyptian Goddess Isis holding her son Horus, as has so often been re-marked upon, but vividly mimicking the native Anatolian goddess of the sun – a supremely powerful creature. Bishop Ambrose of Milan declared that just as Mary had redeemed Eve, so Helena redeemed the sins of Roman emperors past. She was no mere consort but a partner in power – temporal and divine. Mother and son are still celebrated together on their feast day of 21 May and her skull has become a relic itself, sitting high on a wall in Trier Cathedral.

In Constantinople there was no escaping Constantine's mother, im-mortalised in ivory, porphyry and bronze, and on coins, personified as 'PAX', an olive branch and a sceptre in her hands. Helena's image ap-peared right across the city. This is not to say that Helena's standing and influence ensured that life for all Christian women in Constantinople was in any way a bed of roses. Women in the city were still fed half-rations, as they had been throughout classical antiquity. They were still the daughters of Eve.[4]

On a medieval copy of the Peutinger Map – a road map featuring the Via Egnatia in snaking red right down the middle, which was commis-sioned around AD 500 and based on an earlier Augustan version – Rome, Antioch and Constantinople are singled out for special attention. At Constantinoupolis a martial female figure points to a column – probably Constantine's. Constantinople would not officially be called the New Rome for fifty years after Constantine's founding of the city, but clearly this was an idea on the streets and in the popular imagination. We hear from the church historian Socrates Scholasticus in the mid-fifth century that an inscription on the Strategion called the city a 'second Rome'; and that is how it is referred to in a poem by Publilius Optatianus Porphyrius that predates 326 and Constantine's bold declaration '*aeterno nomine iubente deo donavimus*' (this is a city to which I have given an eternal name at God's bidding). Quickly too it would come to be known as the New or a Second Jerusalem.[5] That serpentine monument that had been brought from its pride of place before the imposing Temple of Apollo at Delphi was here to decorate a new omphalos – a new centre of the earth around which cosmological ceremonies revolved.

Each year Constantine commemorated his accession day (26 July) with feasts and parades, wild-animal shows and foundations, styling himself at once an Augustus and an Alexander and a Christian Apollo. Towards the end of his reign this must all have felt a long way from the husky shouts of soldiers on a July day in York.

Now the Emperor of New Rome just had to secure the unity of his colonising, Christian experiment, and the survival of his grand new Christian capital.

Constantine is crowned by Tyche, the goddess of fortune, on this intaglio from the fourth century AD. Tyche in Constantinople was often adapted from statues of the Eastern goddess Kybele and represented the city herself.

CHAPTER 17

✧

BIRTHS AND DEATHS

AD 336–7

> Then, as though their purpose had been effectually accomplished, they
> prepare on this foundation a truly dreadful sepulchre of souls, by building
> a gloomy shrine of lifeless idols to the impure spirit whom they call Venus,
> and offering detestable oblations therein on profane and accursed altars.
> For they supposed that their object could not otherwise be fully attained,
> than by thus burying the sacred cave beneath these foul pollutions.
>
> EUSEBIUS, *VITA CONSTANTINI*[1]

In Thessaloniki in northern Greece, a surprise is hidden behind aluminium
barricades and chicken-wire fencing. As they dug for a new metro system
beneath the modern Egnatia Odos, which runs straight through the
centre of town, the workmen making their way down through the earth
also went back in time. After wending one's way past hooting mopeds,
women placating toddlers with ice-creams and students on their way to
protest, if invited, one can duck under a tarpaulin and carefully descend
flights of wooden steps and a rickety ladder to find, 30 feet beneath the
modern road surface, a long, wide, marble-paved street. In the cool of the
earth this is a remarkable survival. Alongside rusting metal and concrete
piles as far as the eye can see the ancient road continues its subterranean
journey. Visible on the stone slabs there are the grooves made by centuries'
worth of chariots; in the pavements there are holes into which shopkeepers
would plant their sunshade canopies; and outside one of the rows of shops
(a goldsmith's, as we can tell from the finds here, and 20 feet above in the
twenty-first century it is still goldsmiths who ply their trade at this exact
spot) a young child has sat, sulking perhaps, while his parents shopped,
and has scratched a board-game into the street surface.

Constantine the Great was well aware that he needed to keep such lines of communication open if he was to hold his temporal position and spread his new religious blueprint. And so the Egnatian Way and its offshoots were vigorously refurbished. Constantine's city would be increasingly characterised by the ideas and goods – both sacred and secular – that were moved in and out along Byzantium's global arteries. The splendid marble road the Via Publica, Roman Thessalonica's high street, buried for centuries, is an incarnation of Constantine's ambition.

In AD 336, somewhat surprisingly, the heretic Arius, who had been exiled along the Via Egnatia, was allowed back into the city on the orders of Constantine, and it was on Constantinople's streets that the priest died what seems to have been a ghastly death. Vivid detail is supplied by Socrates Scholasticus, who drew his account from Arius' contemporary Athanasios:

> As he approached the place called Constantine's Forum, where the column of porphyry is erected, a terror arising from the remorse of conscience seized Arius, and with the terror a violent relaxation of the bowels: he therefore enquired whether there was a convenient place near, and being directed to the back of Constantine's Forum, he hastened thither. Soon after a faintness came over him, and together with the evacuations his bowels protruded, followed by a copious haemorrhage, and the descent of the smaller intestines: moreover portions of his spleen and liver were brought off in the effusion of blood, so that he almost immediately died. The scene of this catastrophe still is shown at Constantinople, as I have said, behind the shambles in the colonnade: and by persons going by pointing the finger at the place, there is a perpetual remembrance preserved of this extraordinary kind of death.[2]

This dramatic account, which quickly became part of the folk-legend of the city, might well be exaggerated, but if it is accurate there could have been many causes of such an end. Early life as an ascetic might have inflicted long-term damage on Arius, although some whispered that he had been poisoned. The Arius affair left Constantinople with the knowledge that it was a hotbed of religious controversy and with a sense that it should be a bastion of orthodoxy. As Arius excreted his life on the streets of Constantinople, Constantine was just getting into his stride. Yet within one year the Emperor too would be dead.

In AD 337 another ruler in the east, this time from Georgia, converted to Christianity; for Shapur II, King of the Sassanids (the inheritors of the Parthian and Persian Empires and a super-power in the region), enough was enough. Shapur II launched an attack on the Caucasus and drew fire from Constantine even though the Sassanid was operating beyond Byzantine territories. Absent patrolling the Danube, Constantine galvanised troops, declaring that he would bring a firestorm of Christian fury to the East and that he himself would be baptised in the River Jordan; he commissioned a replica of the tabernacle for the purpose. But death was on the horizon.

On 22 May AD 337, Constantine died where he had started his Constantinopolitan adventure – at Nicomedia. It seems he ended up there by accident, originally trying to cure a mystery ailment in the hot baths of Constantinople and then, when these failed, making his way across to natural springs in Asia. Constantine was baptised not a moment too soon by Eusebius of Nicomedia, an act that had not yet become associated with infants but was typically left late as it ensured that the dying had no opportunity to commit any more sins before they passed on to the next life.

The precise circumstances and location of Constantine's death have been left as a provoking historical puzzle for us to try to resolve.[3] The sources mangle one another. Some say Constantine died in the city of Nicomedia itself, others on the road heading towards it, in a *villa publica* (a state-owned building, literally a 'house of the people'). Some sources give the name of his place of death as Achyrona – was this what the *villa publica* was called? Was it in fact a community villa built on the site of an old chaff-house (an *achuron* being a chaff-house)? If indeed it was the latter, Constantine may have passed while surrounded by the dance of wheat germ floating in spring light. Are the chroniclers purposely vague because they do not want to admit that Constantine the Great died, clawing for comfort in a pub, a postal house or an agricultural building? That he was baptised with no pomp but with unseemly haste?[4]

For those in the region Constantine's unfulfilled religious grandstanding was disastrous. The reprisals against Christians that followed were gruesome. Across swathes of Anatolia and the Middle East, it was said that Shapur 'thirsted for blood'. Constantine's visible support of all Christians, not just those within Roman territory, resulted in their mass persecution beyond his borders.⁵ Exactly seven years after the inauguration of Constantinople as Christ's new temporal home, its champion was gone. It seemed as though the Christian experiment, master-minded from the Second Rome, might fail.

Constantine's coffin was taken back by boat from Nicomedia to Constantinople – a journey I last made in 2013 when news of the Taksim Square riots was starting to filter through and when central Istanbul was suddenly on fire. On his death Constantine was declared a god in Rome. The Emperor's body was laid out for over three months in a golden coffin in the Great Palace that he had built on the shores of the Sea of Marmara – the delay probably caused by his family and advisers squabbling over succession rights. This pioneering Emperor-High Priest had already built his temple-tomb – the Church of the Holy Apostles in the centre of the city – just as the Church of the Holy Sepulchre stood at the centre of Roman Jerusalem. This is where the world's first Christian Emperor was laid to rest.

Mystery surrounds the whereabouts of Constantine's remains today – the Church of the Holy Apostles was itself demolished by the Ottomans in AD 1461 (865/6 in the Islamic calendar). But sitting quietly in the weed-blasted ruins of the Haghia Eirene, the Church of Peace, there is a grand porphyry tomb, bearing the Chi Rho symbol and punched with holes, suggesting that it was once covered in some kind of material – 'shrouded in gold', as Constantine's tomb was said to have been. If this is indeed Constantine's missing resting place, scholars argue that the Christian symbolism does not simply declare a devotion to Christ, nor does it just confirm that Constantine was styling himself the thirteenth apostle – Constantine had of course built the Church of the Holy Apostles with the intention of gathering in relics of the other twelve men – it proclaims, perhaps, that this illegitimate Emperor-soldier saw himself as the very reincarnation of Christ.

After Constantine had died, there was such ecclesiastical outrage that this Christian ruler had been buried seemingly as though he was Christ among his Apostles that his own son removed Constantine's body to an adjoining mausoleum.[6] But what strength of character to put himself there in the first place, at the heart of the city now to be proclaimed the earthly home of God: staring at that blazing-eyed, eagle-like face, who would doubt it? We talk of the decline and fall of the Roman Empire, but here was a man who had a strategy for its survival. Constantine was a warrior. His priorities had been to protect and to preserve the territories that he fought for so ferociously – and to dress his empire in new spiritual clothes. Constantine had taken power with 10 per cent of the empire Christian and left it with, at our best estimates, perhaps as many as 50 per cent now believing in Christ as their Saviour.

Constantine had founded Constantinople in AD 330, praising God with bloodless sacrifice, and yet his own porphyry column was still honoured by eager devotees with incense, sacrifices and glowing flame. In truth, what kind of creature was this city that he had created – pagan or Christian? Because despite Constantine's visions, despite his deathbed baptism, his relic-collecting fetish, his establishment of Christian institutions and his destruction of shrines to the old gods, there were many in Constantinople who chose still to see, and to love, the pagan in the world around them.

CHAPTER 18

PAGANS AND PRETENDERS

AD 361–3

As for Constantine, he could not discover among the gods the model of his own career but when he caught sight of Pleasure, who was not far off, he ran to her. She received him tenderly and embraced him, then after dressing him in raiment of many colours and otherwise making him beautiful she led him away to incontinence. There too he found Jesus, who had taken up his abode with her and cried aloud to all comers: 'He that is a seducer, he that is a murderer, he that is sacrilegious and infamous, let him approach without fear! For with this water will I wash him and will straight way make him clean. And though he should be guilty of those same sins a second time, let him but smite his breast and beat his head and I will make him clean again.' To him Constantine came gladly, when he had conducted his sons forth from the assembly of the gods.

EMPEROR JULIAN ON CONSTANTINE I[1]

On Constantine's death his three sons – Constantine, Constantius and Constans – became co-emperors and carved up Constantinople's territories between them.[2] Constans, the youngest of the three brothers, was only seventeen when he inherited. With so much at stake, inevitably perhaps there was some infighting, but then executions and persecution followed hot on the heels of dynastic disagreements. Constans defeated and killed Constantine II, and eventually only the middle brother Constantius II was left standing, having united the empire after Constans' death in AD 350. Constantius ruled from Constantinople while, hostile sources reported, his favoured eunuch Eusebius to all intents and purposes managed military, state and religious affairs. Eusebius' influence matters. Constantine I (following Domitian's earlier law) had decreed that castrations could not take place within the Roman Empire, but this did nothing to interrupt the steady inflow of castrati to Constantinople from outside New Rome's borders – particularly from the Lazi region of the Black Sea.[3] In this early chapter of Constantinopolitan history it became clear just how much sway neutered men could wield. In fact, as we shall see, Constantinople institutionalises the power of the eunuch.

Despite Constantius' power-hungry machinations (supported, perhaps, by the old Emperor while he was alive) it would be Constantine's half-nephew (the son of his half-brother) and son-in-law who would in fact end up triumphant and in charge of Constantinople, a man whom we now call Julian the Apostate. A son-in-law gone bad is what every father dreads.

Julian had been born and brought up between Constantinople, Bithynia, Cappadocia and the southern shore of the Sea of Marmara, tossed around on the currents of court intrigue and shifting political alliances. Because he and his brother represented a potential rival dynasty, kingmaker Helena made her son's feelings clear by effectively keeping them under house arrest. The young, out-of-favour lad spent early summers away from the city's heat, with Constantinople in the distance, on a patch of land owned by his maternal grandmother. Julian later penned that here 'you will stand on the smilax, thyme and fragrant grasses. It is extremely peaceful to lie down there and gaze into some book and then while resting one's eyes it is very agreeable to look at the ships and the sea.'[4] His writings show a sensitive, you could say a callow, delight in the natural world around him: 'the first glimpse of spring is here, the trees are in bud and the swallows, which are expected imminently . . . remind us that we ought to be over the border'.[5]

Julian could be forgiven for latching on to the therapeutic value of tree buds given the trauma of his life story. Of nine male descendants in his direct family, only the two boys survived, and his mother had died when he was young. Lie as he might on fragrant hillsides he would soon be pulled back into the realpolitik of the great walled city of Constantinople that he could see on the horizon. As he grew up, imperial informers kept their tabs on him.

Though he was originally Christian, Julian was clearly transfixed by the power of pagan philosophy. He was educated by, among others, a pagan Spartan called Nicocles, the Christian Hecebolios and the eunuch

Mardonios. Sent on late antiquity's equivalent of the Grand Tour, Julian's travels took him to Athens. The sense one gets is of a sparky young man whose solace was to learn. He studied the works of Plato with such intensity that he came to believe that their philosophical explorations should be made manifest in political systems and in everyday life. Pythagoras too was an inspiration – Julian seemed to conceive of the world as a mystical, mathematically wonderful place, one that could be bettered through logic and the love of the good. This theurgy or theosophy supported and facilitated both an intellectual and an ecstatic passion. With pine-torches flaming, gongs clanging and thousands of devotees chanting around him, Julian was initiated into the Eleusinian Mysteries in the sacred site of Eleusis in Greece 15 miles south-west of Athens, where ideas of the afterlife had been honed 500 years before Christ was born. After twenty years as a Christian, the deep pull of paganism had demonstrably become harder and harder for Julian to resist.

Dragged back into the dirty business of territorial subjugation, in AD 355 Julian was, without much choice, forcibly declared Caesar of the West. Happiest among his books, this philosopher seems nonetheless to have had military nous and quickly to have become popular with his men. One of his soldiers and an invaluable eyewitness to this age, Ammianus Marcellinus – a fabulous ally for the historian – wrote extensively about Julian, describing his life and times. Frank and observant, Ammianus offers us gems, for example that Julian despised soldiers who slept on mattresses rather than on cold stone. We also hear that, back in Constantinople, Constantius had made himself wildly unpopular by setting imperial troops on religious dissenters; 3,000 Christians were killed in one day. Julian thought that Christianity was corroding the steel of the New Roman Empire and its people. In charge of Gaul, although he was ruler of a nominally Christian empire he rebelliously sacrificed to the goddess of war, Bellona.

When Constantius ordered Julian's troops – over his head – to leave for the East, Julian's soldiers revolted; one elite group, the brilliantly named Petulantes, defiantly held a crown above the philosopher-king's head. And so in AD 360 at the camp of Lutetia, modern-day Paris, Julian was declared Augustus.[6] Immediately the scholar-soldier was at odds with the rest of his extended imperial family. Constantius was enraged and declared the suspiciously pagan-leaning pretender a public enemy. The following year, not seeking a civil war but now having to defend himself, Julian marched against his in-law and one-time ally. Rushing from the East to meet him, Constantius succumbed to a fever, dying as he made his way towards the capital Constantinople, his courtiers managing to arrange a hasty baptism with minutes to spare.

As soon as Julian heard of his cousin's death and learnt that the armies of the East had declared their allegiance to him he continued to march through central Europe, along the Via Militaris, entering Constantinople through the Charisios Gate (the gate through which, a thousand years later, the triumphant Ottoman Mehmed the Conqueror would also ride). Julian was welcomed in by the people and, landed, as a child of Constantinople, a rightful leader of the city.

> When he [Julian] had approached Byzantium all welcomed him with songs of praise, hailing him as their fellow citizen and foster child inasmuch as he had been born and reared in this city. In other respects as well they made their obeisances as though he would be the author of the greatest blessings for mankind. Thereat he took charge of the city and the armies simultaneously.[7]

With this grassroots declaration, not just the value of the man, but of the city and her citizens was being trumpeted. Emperor Julian's first act was to give Constantius a Christian burial in the Church of the Apostles. Later he was credited with building Santa Costanza in Rome as a mausoleum for his wife (Constantius' sister) and his sister-in-law.[8] And now a new kind of Roman ruler was being sold to the world. Julian grew his beard to demonstrate that he was a philosopher; he dressed in simple clothing, a coarse mantle, for the same reason.[9]

Once in power, Julian was palpably confident. Sacrifices were restored – he described being 'told' by the gods that this was the path he should take. The Christ-cult – fledgling Christianity – was looking decidedly like a New Age flash in the pan.

The imperial court in Constantinople was purged. Eunuchs, spies, barbers – all were sacked. The pagan Emperor sometimes sat in among Constantinople's senators, trying through example and sheer willpower to force a return to a kind of ideal republican purity. Public buildings were extended in the city; the Harbour of Kontoskalion, now Kumkapı,

was built – still used by the city's fishermen; the completion of a new
library was rushed through and an edict went out that those temples that
had been damaged or destroyed by Constantine's crazy Christian experiment were to be rebuilt, stone by stone, brick by brick. Julian composed
a hymn to Kybele, the mother of nature,[10] his School Edict cauterised
the influence of Christian clerics in education (no longer allowing the
Iliad to be used as a teaching tool), and his Edict of Equality of Religion
of AD 362 returned Christianity to what it had originally been for Rome
– one of many curious Eastern cults. The scholar-Emperor-philosopher-
king seems to have followed segments of Plato's *Timaeus* to the letter
(did he believe therefore, one wonders, in the lost continent of Atlantis?),
following the view that mankind was ethnically diverse because it was
generated by the random sprays and spatters of the blood of Zeus.

Meanwhile, across the waters of the Bosphorus there was more clearing
up to do. In the trials of Chalcedon Julian purged the regime of his old
enemies. Particularly troublesome rivals such as the eunuch Eusebius,
who had arranged the beheading of Julian's brother Gallus (eunuchs were
described at this time as being 'more [in number] than flies around cattle
in springtime, and a multitude of drones of every sort and kind'),[11] were
burnt alive. The preservation of the details of these atrocities perhaps
says more about the outrage of later church clerics than about Julian's
unusual cruelty. A number of Julian's actions seem to suggest that he
was predominantly interested in reducing the power of Constantinople's
newly emerging Christian aristocracy.[12]

Brainy, brave and bullish, Julian was in many ways out of step, because
Christianity was no longer an exotic, plucky outsider but the future. Even
the fringes of empire were now dancing to the Christian tune. The fourth-
century landowner of Hinton St Mary in Dorset decorated his mosaic
floor with an image of a beardless Christ in front of the Chi Rho symbol
and flanked by pomegranates – a portrait, perhaps, of Constantine. The
hermit revolution begun by St Anthony in Egypt in AD 305 was rising in
popularity; the new Christian mystery of transubstantiation, promoted
by a spreading priestly class, seemed ever more appealing. In the plains
and hills of the southern Caucasus, that isthmus of land between the
Caspian and Black Seas, Christianity was steadily gaining ground. Still
sold as a religion of social justice and of gender equality, the ferociously
loyal 'brides of Christ' had no intention of returning to what were often

misogynistic pagan ways. The Christ-cult genie was out of the bottle.

History is, naturally, full of a bewildering complement of what-ifs, but if Julian had survived to complete his de-Christianising project he would have left the world a different place. All that pagan belief with, in some cases, a pedigree that stretched back many millennia, and still (despite the best efforts of IS) survives as an unbroken ancient tradition in some quarters of the world (Zoroastrians in Iran, Ezidis and Mandaeans in Iraq) might well have taken root again.[13]

Investiture of Ardashir II. The Persian King receives the Ring of Power, at his feet lies Julian the Apostate – the last pagan Emperor of Byzantium.

But it was not to be. In AD 363, just five months after his re-entry into the city, Julian was mortally wounded in battle against Constantinople's old enemies the Persians. We are told that as he died the Emperor – Socratic-like – encouraged those around him not to lament as 'he would become one with the sky and the stars' – positive, mystical words. The Delphic oracle though – as it so often did – may have better encapsulated the mood of the moment: 'Tell the king the fair wrought hall is fallen to the ground. No longer has Phoebus a hut, nor a prophetic laurel, nor a spring that speaks. The water of speech even is quenched.'[14] The sources tell us that it was a Constantinopolitan – a doctor at the bidding of Julian – who heard pagan Delphi's final, mournful pronouncement. Just a few years later, the sanctuary, the protector of the *omphalos*, the navel of the earth, to which ancient Megarians had travelled to receive the gods' blessing for their expedition to found Byzantion, and from which Constantine had brought that twisting serpent monument, was no longer offially named *hiera*, sacred; within a generation it would be closed down.

The staff officer Jovian, who had brought Constantius' body to the Great Harbour of Constantinople – where it had been met by Julian, who then led the funeral procession to the Church of the Holy Apostles – was declared emperor. Jovian swiftly reinstated Christianity as the state religion. But while travelling to the capital, and still 100 miles east of Ankara, he died of asphyxiation on the road.

A sequence of squabbling, potential successors then threatened to turn Constantinople and its territory back into a tatter of fragments controlled by warlords. This was an empire that did not quite yet know what it was, how it should operate. Eventually, a lieutenant of Jovian's named Valentinian took the reins of power, and made his brother Valens co-Emperor in the East. Almost immediately, while Valens was away on campaign, a coup was attempted from within Constantinople, led by a cousin of Julian's called Procopius.

Today the few dogs who have escaped the rabies cleanup in modern Istanbul, scavenging for scraps around rubbish-strewn old stones, lead you to Valens' fury. After almost being captured near Chalcedon himself, Valens managed to trap Procopius and to send the pretender's head back to his brother Valentinian in Trier. Legend has it that Chalcedon's city walls were torn down and reused to build a towering aqueduct. The aqueduct's arches still doggedly withstand car fumes above one of Istanbul's arterial roads. Part of a massive water system, the largest of all antiquity, the network of aqueducts that snaked through the Thracian countryside would eventually run a full 368 miles, delivering water from the Forest of Belgrade to the Imperial Great Palace and to the Baths of Zeuxippos. The city's provision of free water was a badge of honour. Academics eagerly go aqueduct-hunting in the summer to find the source of Constantinople's life-blood, the ghosts they seek still visible in the Thracian landscape, sinuously hugging hillsides on a gentle gradient. In time Constantinople could boast a network of reservoirs to keep the city watered – the three main reservoirs on their own held 130 million gallons.

Despite changes on the imperial throne, Constantinople was building momentum as she became a new-look Christian-Greco-Roman city. Towards the end of the fourth century there were almost 2,000 men of senatorial rank here; the Great Palace begun by Constantine the Great continued slowly to grow; and that grand aqueduct proudly spanned the third and fourth hills. As an entity, the city now had a sense of civocratic pride. But then a pernicious opponent appeared; Ammianus Marcellinus tells us they were men 'like savage beasts that have broken free from their cages . . .' men capable of bringing to the city 'the foul chaos of robbery, murder, slaughter and fire'.[15]

Constantinople was about to meet the Goths.

CHAPTER 19

THE PROBLEM WITH GOTHS

AD 376–8

A nobler man, a braver warrior,
Lives not this day within the city walls:
He by the senate is accit'd home
From weary wars against the barbarous Goths . . .

SHAKESPEARE, *TITUS ANDRONICUS*[1]

The last quarter of the fourth century AD saw a Gothic crisis, and the acceleration of global disruption that would percolate from Afghanistan in the East to the western edge of the Danube River with direct impact on Constantinople. The chain of events was almost certainly triggered by a significant environmental shift: malaria was recorded in the North Sea; new vegetation appeared on the steppes and in China glaciers advanced.[2] Chinese merchants wrote detailed accounts describing famine, death and, crucially, the rise of an apocalyptic force – men they called the Xwn. Persia too felt the pressure and built a protecting wall 100 miles long between the Caspian and Black Seas. Manned by 30,000 troops, some of them Roman, this separated a 'civilised north from a chaotic south'.[3] Persia and New Rome, long-standing enemies, were forced to become allies; the Shah was even invited to become the guardian of a Byzantine emperor's son.[4]

From AD 376 reports had begun to circulate that hordes of refugees and displaced peoples were cramming the 'barbarian bank' of the Rhine, pushed south and west by bloodthirsty Huns – those Xwn of the Chinese texts. We are told that 'the eruption of armed men from barbarian lands was like lava from Mount Etna'.[5] Huns were in some respects the Spartans of late antiquity. Training their young warriors to endure great hardship, they were described by anxious observers as wolves, as the seedbed of evil, as inhuman. All kinds of rumours circulated about these monster-men, myths systematically dismissed by sober historians. But recent skeletal analysis has shown that the heads of young Hunnish men were indeed bound in tight straps, forcing their skulls into a curious cone-shape.[6] Travel to the steppes of Central Asia and you can understand where that raw, do-or-die Hunnic drive comes from. You have to have a degree of ambition to match those endless horizons and that limitless sky. This was a land after all that would in time nourish more of Constantinople's enemies – Avars, Turks, Mongols, all of them adversaries of daunting proportions.

So in AD 376, beneath the epic drama of the Transdanubian hills, frantically fleeing this abominable force, women wailing, children clasping at skirts in fear and exhaustion, Gothic communities were harried to the edge of the Danube, the great line of water that delineated the history of both Old and New Rome.

The second-longest river in Europe[7] and the only major one that flows eastwards, the Danube joins a series of dots in the story of humanity. Rivers have long moulded the human experience. Many of our greatest conurbations arose because of them; they have transported armies, religions, treasures, epoch-changing ideas, along with the raw materials of civilisation. These ribbons of liquid history form geographical and cultural boundaries and have hidden – indeed still hide – some of the most exquisite artefacts ever made by human hand. Just think of the jewel-studded Battersea Shield recovered from the Thames at Battersea Bridge, and the entire Roman barge, complete with captain's kitchen, bed and cupboard contents discovered in the mud at the edge of the Rhine. Sometimes lost by chance, more often these treasures have been left as gifts to the great gods of the water. Rivers cherish history and they make it. And the Danube both saw and made more history than most.

Hadrian's Wall might have offered some local comfort and a symbolic line at the edge of the province of Britannia, but the Danube's *Limes Germanicus* was the serious north-eastern frontier for Rome's appetite-busting power. Through the modern countries of Germany (Bavaria), Austria, Slovakia, Hungary, Croatia, Bulgaria, Serbia and Romania, the ghosts of Roman fortifications still remain at the edge of the river, along 1,250 miles: bridgeheads next to car parks in Budapest, watchtowers in the woods of Austria, a legionary fortress dictating the layout of the street system of Regensburg; the new Roman Museum at Passau built on the site of an excavated Roman camp.[8]

And somewhere in the mud of the Danube close to Silistra in north-east Bulgaria, there is evidence of a humanitarian disaster whose impact would be felt by the people of Constantinople. In AD 376 many were slaughtered here. Weapons, coins, favourite bracelets have all been dropped in the riverine mud in a panicked dash for survival. Those who were left alive, washed up on the bank as a result of the Hunnic attack, human detritus, were Goths and Visigoths, peoples who had sometimes been allies of the Romans, and often converts to Christianity. Valens, Emperor in the East, eventually gave the order for these proud refugees to be allowed to cross the river. They swam, rafted, formed human chains – desperate to shelter within Rome's centuries-old security.

The men in power could swiftly have made these Goths a stake-holding part of their empire – because, despite lazy identifications as 'barbarians' (by ancient and modern authors alike), they were an organised, cultured people. There is no doubting the sophistication of Gothic and Visigothic society. In southern Spain (possibly called Andalusia by invading Muslim armies after the Arabic name for the Vandals, an east-Germanic tribe who will also feature in the story of Constantinople), the graves of the Vandals and Visigoths were found to be fat with fine, 'barbarian-made' gold jewellery. And consider this: in Rimini's central square, the Piazza Ferrari, there is a new discovery that helps us to appreciate what it really meant to be a Goth. Unearthed only in 1989 when the municipal gardens were being renovated, here, where the air is sweet with the scent of linden flowers, is a wonderful thing, good-naturedly ignored by the locals, men with Persil-white shirts who walk by chatting loudly about football scores. It is known as the Doctor's House, an archaeological site displacing the local council perennials, park benches and pushchairs. Enter the digs and at first your eye is drawn to the pretty, hectic patterning of the multi-coloured mosaic floor, and then the bones come into focus – human bodies carefully laid out, some simply covered with roof tiles. The mosaics are not Byzantine, Greek or Roman, but Gothic, and they cover a late Roman building (from the second century AD) where, according to the gruesome instruments also excavated, a surgeon once lived. These bodies probably belong to Christian men and women – many Goths at this time were Arian Christians buried within the walls, as was the Christian custom. The mosaic floor has been gouged and shattered to allow all those skeletons to fit inside. The body-sized bites in the mosaics give us a glimpse of the reality of the Byzantine world; its edges being gnawed by variegated forces, while corpses were laid out on mansion floors that were in turn built up over the ghosts of Old Rome.

Another corrective sits quietly in the Uppsala University Library in Sweden. The Codex Argenteus, one of the most splendid survivors from late antiquity, breath-stoppingly beautiful, reminds us to look at the end of antiquity with the eyes of its own age. Written in silver and gold ink on purple parchment, almost certainly made in Ravenna in the early sixth century for the Ostrogothic King Theodoric the Great, this is the earliest extant copy of the Bible in the Gothic language.[9] The translation of the scripture was completed in the fourth century by the Bishop Ulfilas, an Arian who actively evangelised the Goths, and the Codex Argenteus has made its way via various European peregrinations, escaping siege, bombardment and water damage, to end up in the University of Uppsala, the bible's home since 1669. Goths and Ostrogoths, some of whom spoke both Greek and Latin, found the association with Arianism a useful distinction – something that united them as they migrated through what were for them unknown lands, and which set them apart from the Western Romans and Orthodox Byzantines. Their unity certainly gave them strength.

But rather than dealing with the Goths like grown-ups, the Roman establishment derided them. The 150,000 men, women and children who had crossed the Danube expecting perhaps a welcome, at least the possibility of a loose, working relationship, now turned against the empire. They marched east to meet Valens' troops at Adrianople, modern-day Edirne, near the Greek–Turkish border. Valens, stopping at his vast palace on the lakes of Kuruçeşme – which in 2011 emerged from the toxic mud for the first time in 1,700 years – tore out from Constantinople to face the assembled Gothic army, 15,000 or so, in pitched battle. In August here the sunset is an unfeasible coral and the moon flames as it rises. The earth itself is hot. And it is not too fanciful to imagine the incandescent Gothic wrath on the battlefield here too, now overlooked by the tower blocks of Turkish social housing, where the chaos and carnage was so great that in AD 378 two-thirds of the Roman army was killed and the Emperor Valens' body was lost for days. Twenty thousand Romans died that day. The imperial court orator Themistius related that 'an entire army vanished like a shadow' in one summer afternoon.[10]

Theodosios, a Spanish general from a military family, was brought out of exile by Valentinian's son Gratian to help to deal with the crisis. Gothic troops had marched towards Constantinople itself, only to be repelled by Arabs employed in imperial service. Theodosios, de facto co-Emperor, pursued the Goths, then made a treaty. It is cowed, suppliant Goths we see crouching beneath New Rome's emperors in the hippodrome in Constantinople on the urgently commissioned stone base of the Egyptian obelisk originally ordered up by Constantine. Art not quite imitating life, but art telling the world what the natural order of life ideally should be.

Theodosios, a man used to travelling the seas to the edges of empire, who had seen what happened to this juvenile Christian experiment when the Christians within it did not present a united front, was determined to tidy up both the empire's porous boundaries and those loose ends of faith. After AD 392 he ruled as sole emperor from Constantinople. His conviction and religious drive would help to make Constantinople one of the greatest cities on earth, but would also shatter the lives of millions.

CHAPTER 20

❖

A DOVE OF PEACE OR A FIST OF IRON:
THEODOSIOS

AD 379–95

The whole city is full of it, the squares, the market places, the cross-roads, the alleyways; old-clothes men, money changers, food sellers: they are all busy arguing. If you ask someone to give you change, he philosophizes about the Begotten and the Unbegotten; if you inquire about the price of a loaf, you are told by way of reply that the Father is greater and the Son inferior; if you ask 'Is my bath ready?' the attendant answers that the Son was made out of nothing.

GREGORY OF NYSSA (FROM CAPPADOCIA), ATTENDANT
AT FIRST COUNCIL OF CONSTANTINOPLE AD 381[1]

Before I became a historian I had only a sketchy idea that every Sunday in church I was reciting a creed that a Spanish soldier had ratified in what is now Istanbul.[2] When one walks around Istanbul today, Theodosios I's hand is still brilliantly apparent. However impressive Constantine's foundation, this was not the summation but the beginning of something special. Themistius, court orator of Theodosios I (so we should be wary of the author's ebullience), describes how, under Theodosios, 'the beauty of the city is not, as heretofore, scattered over it in patches, but covers its whole area like a robe woven to the very fringe'.[3] The Forum of Theodosios, the largest in Constantinople, was built over the ancient Forum Tauri; fragments of the triumphal arch originally set up here still sit quietly next to the trams of Ordu Avenue. Constantine's towering obelisk, which had been languishing in the harbour, on which (it was believed) were written prophecies for the city, was erected in the hippodrome.

The obelisk's new base displayed both the power of Theodosios' court and the engineers' skill in its erection: 'A pillar with four sides, ever lying a burden on the earth, alone the Emperor Theodosios dares to upraise; Proclos was summoned to execute his order, and so this huge a pillar rose in two and thirty suns.' In truth, the obelisk had been broken en route from Egypt to the city and had arrived in the hippodrome only two-thirds its original size. Originally from Karnak, and initially set up there in a partyish atmosphere to the 'Lord of Jubilees' (the Egyptian deity Bennu, linked with the sun, creation and re-birth), the obelisk is a display of both religious and military might. The emperors of Constantinople might not have been able to read its hieroglyphs, but they would have liked what was there if they could. The marks lionised the combination of divine and secular power that had secured a Bronze Age victory for Pharaoh Tuthmosis III, one which 'fetters every land . . . making his border stretch to north and south . . . crossing the Great Circle of Naharina [the Euphrates] in valour and in victory . . . making great slaughter . . .'.[4]

Then there is the splendid Golden Gate, a triumphal archway astride the Via Egnatia, opened only for emperors being carried ceremonially into Constantinople in a carriage made of gold, or for those returning triumphant from battle. Decorated with chariots drawn by golden elephants, with fine statuary and with twelve reliefs showing scenes from Greek myth, as it rose glinting above the Marmaran plains of Thrace, the Golden Gate was for centuries a signal that travellers had arrived not just in the arms of civilisation but at the home of God. Built c. AD 386 (there is still speculation about which Theodosios commissioned the arch, Theodosios I or II), wide enough, it was trumpeted, for a ship to pass through, this wonderful piece of architectural showmanship still stands proud, even if it is a little dilapidated now and even if it was originally commissioned as a bravura distraction for the loss of face at Adrianople. Above the arch are written the words, 'Theodosios ornaments this gate after the downfall of the Tyrant. He who builds this Gate of Gold brings back the Golden Age.' A Victoria, together with the Tyche of Constantinople, is shown crowning the Emperor. Surrounded at the time of writing by allotments and market gardens, the entrance to the gate is blocked by plastic crates, and weeds, and piles of manure. A rusted ramp leads to a blank doorway.

Theodosios also supported the granaries that kept Constantinople's precious Egyptian grain dry and developed the water systems to ensure that fresh water flowed into the city. Themistius claimed that these waterways ran for 1,000 *stades*, or 115 miles. Dismissed as an exaggeration by modern historians, these measurements have now in fact been shown to be an underestimate; channels into Constantinople a full 140 miles long have been traced.[5] And Theodosios' harbour, or rather harbours, 2.5 miles' worth of quays, with piers that stretch between Gazi Mustafa Kemal Paşa Caddesi and Küçük Langa Caddesi in the modern city,[6] are testament to Constantinople's sense of purpose at this time. One of these, originally called Eleutherios (named after an official of Constantine's whose name means 'freedom') secured the city's position as a pushy player on the global trading stage.

Thrillingly, in 2004, the Theodosian *grand projet* came blinking back into the light. Freedom Harbour has been liberated. It is the excavations to build the Bosphorus' monstrous sub-aqua tunnel that have uncovered this archaeological miracle. It was in the southern Yenikapı district, 40 feet below street level, just behind humdrum shops, that the vast Theodosian harbour emerged. Three hundred yards inland from the current shoreline, and gradually obscured down the generations as the Lykos River silted up and made the harbour unusable, this was for centuries the powerhouse of both the fact of Constantinople and the idea of Byzantium. From beneath a layer of silt and sand first one, then another, then (to date) thirty-seven boats have emerged from the cappuccino-brown ooze. Into the boats' crevices have swirled seashells, bones, sand and pottery fragments. Many of the ships are all but complete and include designs of galleys unknown up until now. The very latest analysis has shown that the imported wood used to build this grand engineering project – large enough to serve what was becoming the busiest port in the Eastern Mediterranean – includes sweet chestnut, cypress and red and white oak.[7] As the harbour was built, the tang of sap and bitumen for waterproofing would have filled the streets and homes of Constantinople.

Slipping down 40 feet beneath the current sea level to visit these ghost-ships, as the timbers are lovingly sponged down and gently lifted from what was, for the early medieval inhabitants of the city, the seabed, is a remarkable experience. The remains here are not just wooden bones, but the flesh of late antique and early medieval life. Still resting in the boats' bellies there are pots of cherries, amphorae, fine glassware with scarcely a chip; there are even lengths of beautifully preserved ships' rope. In one boat, YK12, the captain's personal effects have survived intact – a mess

Excavation of the Theodosian harbour started in 2004. By 2016, 37 boats had been found. A number date from the fourth century AD and both the vessels themselves and their cargo are in a remarkable state of preservation.

kit and his own bespoke brazier. As workmen in high-vis jackets beetle around with wheelbarrows, the wooden piers emerge from the earth like teeth and the boats like giant cats' cradles; jackdaws pick over the digs as they once did over the food scraps from the working harbours themselves. Discovered here too are hundreds of horse carcasses (the Byzantines ate horses and, because they favoured a cruel kind of bit which shortened their lives, most of the animals were slaughtered when they were ten years old or so). The harbour digs have also yielded the remains of bears, donkeys and ostriches – all clearly butchered. There is even a dog whose broken foot has been tenderly reset by a devoted owner. Sprinklers keep the wood damp. Towers of milk crates – numbering close on 90,000, have been packed with what has been excavated so far. Originally piled high on the site under tarpaulins, these treasure-troves now line store-rooms across the city.

The digs here represent early medieval Istanbul as the linchpin be-tween three continents: Europe, Asia and Africa. As soon as the harbour discovery was made in 2004, mechanical diggers were banned, and so line upon line of local workers with picks and shovels made their way out to rescue the harbour and its contents as they had done 1,600 years before to create it.

Theodosios I solidified Constantinople's potential as a global economic player, but he also had a hand in how billions across the world today tune their spiritual lives. The council of AD 381 – called just a year after the Emperor had finally entered the city – amended the Nicene Creed, first developed in the imperial palace in Nicaea in 325.[8] This was a political moment when an item of belief became dogma – a requirement of faith. From spring to July 381 the First Council of Constantinople was held in Haghia Eirene, the Church of Peace, high up on the ancient acropolis of Byzantium. Although in hindsight officially termed an ecumenical coun-cil, at the time the participants referred to themselves simply as 'the holy synod of bishops from various provinces meeting in Constantinople'. The purpose was, explicitly, to coalesce orthodoxy, to unite the empire. The-odosios, it seems, was returning to the religious roots of his homeland in Spain where it was generally accepted that the Father, Son and Holy Spirit were of equal might and majesty – and where (conveniently once you had become God's temporal representative on earth) a Christ of full divinity was subjected to no dispute, debate or challenge. Whether emotional or political in origin, this new orthodoxy could be seen as a way of creating a 'them' and 'us' situation, distinguishing the pious inhabitants of the greater New Rome from all those barbarians beyond. But all was not serene in the Church of Peace. We are told that those attending 'screeched on every side, a flock of jackdaws all intent on one thing, a mob of wild young men, a new kind of gang, a whirlwind causing the dust to swirl as the winds went out of control, men with whom not even a ruler with the authority of fear or age would think it proper to reason, buzzing around as if they were in complete disorder like a swarm of wasps suddenly flying in your face'.[9]

And it was at this council, in a church now converted into a concert hall, that the wording of the Nicene-Constantinopolitan Creed, still re-cited in Christian churches across the world, was thrashed out.

It is at this council that Constantinople was first described as the New Rome in an official document.[10] But it was also on Theodosios' watch that a number of the most potent Greco-Roman traditions were, at a stroke, outlawed. In AD 381 the Great Goddess (Kybele to the Greeks, Magna Mater to the Romans) was defrocked: her cult was banned and her temples were closed. And there was more to come. Following the Theodosian Edicts of 391–2 pagan practice was deemed sinister, incense use was outlawed, private and public sacrifice was condemned. The year 393 saw the banning of the pagan rituals at Olympia (although ongoing archaeological analysis suggests that the games here continued); Theodosios dismissed the Vestal Virgins at Rome and made public, religious Roman holidays work days. The vast temples of Serapis in Alexandria and of Apollo in Delphi were brought crashing to the ground. The motivation for these root-and-branch changes might have been genuine piety, or megalomaniac drive, or possibly the result of the burden of rule – the Goths were increasingly the cause of nagging stress fractures across Constantinople's territory.

Theodosios I had partly dealt with the Gothic threat by absorbing Goths as key players in some areas of imperial administration. In strategically critical cities such as Thessalonika, he instituted a Gothic garrison. But there was a problem. Thessalonika was a settlement where passions ran high. Chariots and charioteers were still wildly popular in late antiquity, just as they had been in ancient Rome. Thessalonika boasted one of the largest hippodromes in the country. An insurrection in AD 390 when one popular charioteer was arrested for homosexual activity resulted in the murder of Butheric, the Gothic garrison commander, whose brutalised body was then dragged through Thessalonika's streets. Outraged, Theodosios put down this popular uprising with blinding ferocity. Some accounts record that close to the imperial palace in Thessalonika, whose remains are still visible, 7,000 were killed in one day, 'cut down like wheat'. A new mantra in the form of the Nicene Creed was now on the lips of the faithful: 'He will come again in glory to judge both the quick and the dead'. We should pause for a moment to think with what passion, hope and despair (including, perhaps, by the faithful dying in the hippodrome in the city nicknamed Symvasilevousa, 'Co-Reigning Capital with Constantinople') these words have been said over many centuries' worth of lifetimes.

The killing fields of Thessalonika have now been rescued from urban depression and corruption and turned, by the modern city's forward-looking mayor into a pleasant, seaside walk. Kids race one another; men play swing-ball; a hand-painted, outsize political banner flaps over the site which reads 'OXI' (NO) – a spirited answer to the European Union's request for Hellenic austerity.

Following Theodosios' trigger-happy response to the protest, Bishop Ambrose of Milan, the man who had baptised St Augustine and so secured a pivotal place in medieval history, excommunicated the Eastern Roman Emperor. As Theodosios had so much blood on his hands, Ambrose refused to let him back into the church until he had done penance for a number of months. We do not have the hard evidence of the rushed memos, the uncompromising messages, perhaps even the dark nights of the soul within the imperial palace in Constantinople, but it cannot be coincidence that soon imperial legislation ensured that there had to be a thirty-day lag before the decrees of the Emperor could be enacted. Within a few weeks of a Christmas meeting with Ambrose, Theodosios issued new laws. It could be the degree of soul-searching after the Thessalonika slaughter that then encouraged the Emperor to pass his draconian anti-pagan decrees of AD 392 that would change the experience of living in late antiquity and in the medieval age.

The immediate and cumulative effects of Theodosios' piety were – for many – pretty grim. Arians were ejected from churches 'with great disturbances'. Everyday people had everyday rituals demonised; 'hanging sacred fillets [strips of cloth] in trees, raising turf altars'[11] were, for instance, suddenly problematic. Punishments for pagan activity included confiscation of property and even death. And although these reforms did not take full effect overnight (the fact that subsequent emperors such as Arkadios had to publish rescripts of the legislation suggests the reforms had a light hold on many lives) and were often judgements or moralising suggestions rather than hard-edged law, they impacted on the ecology of civilisation across much of Africa, Asia and Europe.[12] Christianity was now the state religion of a new Roman Empire centred on Constantinople.

Theodosios I, the man who sorted out the physical priorities of Constantinople and the spiritual orthodoxy of the wider world, was the last Emperor of both East and West. He stayed in Milan to die, horribly, of oedema on 17 January AD 395, but his body was taken to Constantinople to be buried with great mourning and great pomp on 9 November the same year. One-upmanship from the New Rome over the Old: Rome might have housed the tombs of Peter and Paul, but Constantinople claimed to keep the empire of Christ Himself secure. Where else, as an emperor, would you want your body to lie?

CHAPTER 21

✦

BATTLES IN HEAVEN AND ON EARTH:
GAZA AND ALEXANDRIA

AD 395–415

during the celebration of the Communion, a child of about seven years, which was standing with his own mother, cried out suddenly, saying: 'Burn ye the inner temple unto the foundation; for many terrible things have been done in it, especially the sacrifices of human beings. And after this manner burn ye it: bring liquid pitch and sulphur and fat of swine, and mingle the three and anoint the brazen doors and set fire to them, and so shall all the temple be burned . . .

MARK THE DEACON, *LIFE OF PORPHYRY, BISHOP OF GAZA*[1]

On the banks of the River Ilissos in Athens (hidden under tarmac since 1956) where Socrates once dangled his toes while perturbing Athenian youth, there sits a little chink of gold that speaks volumes.[2] It is the coin minted in Constantinople by Emperor Arkadios in the year the Roman Empire was divided between Theodosios' sons Arkadios (aged twelve or so) who ruled the East from Constantinople and Honorius (aged around eight) in charge of the West. On the coin Arkadios is displayed as a Roman victor holding a standard; on the reverse a winged Nike tramples on a captive.[3] The symbolism is hybrid Greco-Roman, but it marks a moment when the world divided, when the East started to look east and the West west. A number of objects alongside this coin in the Byzantine Museum in central Athens were handed over as 'refugee heirlooms' after the exchange of populations across the ex-Ottoman Empire in 1923, when 1.3 million Greek Christians were forced to leave Asia Minor, and 500,000 Macedonian Turks and Muslims had to abandon their homes on the Greek mainland. The displaced, for the main part, had just the clothes they stood up in and the suitcases they could carry. Many walked, in both directions, along the Egnatian Way. This was a blunt, ideological and ethnic division whose seeds of a narrative describing an invisible line dividing East and West had been sown in antiquity. We still reap its unhappy harvest today. The provenance of the coin and its companions is therefore uncertain, but the broader narratives of the objects are rich.

Arkadios was very much his father's son; in charge of Constantinople at a time when pagan and Christian weather-fronts would collide.

Demonstrating the feeble hold that Theodosian Edicts had over the popular imagination, once again sacrifices, burning incense and the hanging of offerings on trees (though this continues across the Orthodox Christian world today) were banned. In the court of Constantinople there were mutterings. As a point of principle, as a sign of authority rather than religiosity, religious reform was a job that needed to be finished. It would have been too risky to start an inflammatory series of demolitions in Constantinople itself and the church-building programme had already swamped a number of pagan sanctuaries. The destruction of the Senate House in AD 404 by a militant Christian mob would be viewed by many with horror and disgust; but the dereliction continued in the provinces.

The heat of righteous, Orthodox Christian fury can be felt in particular in the story of the Temple of Marneion, Gaza in Palestine.[4] There was just one church here, presided over by a Bishop Porphyry – so unpopular, we are told, that one day his entry to the town had been blocked by thorn bushes and he had to escape from angry pagan crowds across the flat roofs of the city. Gaza had long been resistant to the idea of Christianity; a number of Christians had been enthusiastically martyred here under Diocletian, and even after the establishment of Christianity as a state religion bishops were allowed to hold territory only outside the city walls.

Zeus Marna, a Hellenistic incarnation of the prehistoric fertility god Dagon, was worshipped in Gaza in a temple originally built by the Emperor Hadrian. Bishop Porphyry had made a special visit to Constantinople to ask permission to close down Gaza's temples. His pleas fell on ears only too ready to hear them – those of Arkadios' educated, feisty, famously beautiful wife Eudoxia. And now in Constantinople's history we meet one of its most tenacious tropes, the potent and influential empress. Eudoxia had clout and bite. The pedestal of a silver statue the

Bronze steelyard weight in the form of a bust, dating to c. AD 400–450. It probably depicts one of Constantinople's premier Empresses, possibly Eudoxia.

Empress commissioned to glorify herself was discovered in 1847 during excavations in the city centre.[5]

Encouraged, we are told, by her personal eunuch Amantios, Empress Eudoxia was in agreement with Porphyry: an example should be made of Gaza. But the pagan locals had proved so resilient that special measures were called for. Soldiers, sent in AD 402 by direct command of the Empress, were ordered to surround the Temple of Marneion, armed with a new weapon to effect its annihilation. The temple's protectors barricaded themselves in; for ten days the Christian forces destroyed other sanctuaries in the city, and then returned to the Marneion. Inside worshippers and pagan priests were still trapped. A combination of crude oil, sulphur and pig fat was applied by the Empress's men to the temple's bronze doors.[6] Then someone threw on a blazing torch.

Now, bronze melts at a temperature of 1,742 degrees Fahrenheit. The average bonfire reaches only 800 degrees. On the face of it, the vivid early medieval description (by Mark the Deacon, that opened this chapter) of these events of AD 402 might fall into the category of excitable, eschatological myth-making. So with a team of chemists, in a deserted quarry in Wales, I attempted a reconstruction.[7] Within seconds of smearing our

pitch mixture on to bronze doors framed by stone and igniting the con-
coction, the metal doors discoloured and warped. The heat was ferocious.
Pig fat burns long and slow – after four hours the temperature in the
centre of the inferno measured 1,796 degrees. That day in Palestine in 402
the sky must have been red with flame, the air shimmering and distorting
in the heat, and the streets choked with a pungent black smoke. The men
trapped inside – presumably praying to their pagan gods to the very last
– would have been asphyxiated unless they were burnt alive.

In AD 407 a church was raised on the temple ruins, dedicated to the
Empress and cannibalising masonry that had survived the inferno; Palestine now had a new church named Eudoxiana. In the town itself the
pagan sanctuary's fine marble blocks, so exquisite and sacred that no one
had been allowed to walk on them, were used as common paving stones,
the ultimate gesture of disrespect.

Perhaps the Gaza genocide was retribution for the easy massacre of
Christians a century before. The horror stories of persecution became
so popular that ghoulish tales were told to children as a nightmarish
warning, tales such as that of Perpetua – martyred in the arena for the
governor of Africa Hilarianus' pleasure on his birthday in around AD
202/3, her companion Felicitas' breast still weeping milk for the child she
had just birthed.[8]

But we have to ask ourselves what space there was in New Rome's
empire for Christian mercy. Whatever one's faith, or lack of it, we should
imagine these terrible scenes and weep.

Counter-intuitively perhaps, the refugees from the first wave of attacks
against pagan shrines and institutions in the AD 390s frequently made
their way to Constantinople. Two such pagans on the run – who seemed
to be welcomed with open arms in the mother city – were the scholars
Helladios and Ammonios from Alexandria, now a settlement subject
to Constantinople. They went on to teach one Socrates Scholasticus of
Constantinople, who in turn would recount the detail of one of the most
abominable murders in the story of Christianity. The fact that men such
as Helladios and Ammonios survived in Constantinople demonstrates
that some pagans were tolerated, but there was real danger for those who
chose to swim against the new Christian tide.

Although the modern city of Alexandria preserves the ghost of the ancient streets in its grid system, to find the ancient city itself we have to go underground into its muggily close labyrinth of tombs, homes and warehouses – into a city of the dead. Here dog-headed Roman soldiers carved in stone protect graves, Greek architraves are surmounted by Egyptian designs and somewhere down here under the streets Alexander the Great himself is doubtless buried in a tomb that combines Greek, Macedonian and Egyptian elements. Once the Romans had taken over this city of hedonism and study after the vanquishing of Cleopatra, who died here in 30 BC, a strong Roman thread was woven through this bright cultural tapestry.[9]

Alexandria was a city where words and learning had greater currency than grain or gold. It was a place of many ideas, many gods; here knowledge really was power. Instead of coin, papyri texts were taken as port tax. A grand library – designed to contain all the ideas in the world – was built. At least half a million works were stored here, all carefully catalogued. From Alexandria, Eratosthenes measured the circumference of the earth, accurate to within 40 miles; Galen explored the potential of the human brain; and Aristarchos proposed that the earth moved around the sun rather than vice versa.[10] This was a city whose greatness depended on an open mind, a city which had seen much cultural diplomacy: first Alexander the Great embracing the Egyptian gods; followed by Ptolemy sponsoring the translation of the Bible from Hebrew to Greek;[11] then the creation of the *Didascalia*, which tried to reconcile reason and revelation, declaring that philosophy and theology were not only compatible but mutually beneficial – all this could have been a model for a variegated, tolerant form of political being.

It was grain from Egypt sent out from the port of Alexandria, carried by those boats now emerging from the harbour mud in Istanbul and into the granaries, mills and bakeries of Constantinople, that kept New Rome's citizens alive. When wealthy men commissioned household furniture they would decorate it with images of Tyche – good fortune – imagined as the four great cities of the day, Constantinople, Rome, Alexandria and Antioch, all typically personified as women. On one particularly splendid embellishment, made c. AD 330–70 and buried after the fall of Rome, Alexandria and Constantinople are dressed as twins, both with plumed helmets, and Constantinople is carrying a cornucopia and a dish for pouring sacred libations. The relationship between Constantinople and Alexandria was intimate and essential; the two cities were considered close family. But it was from the imperial capital of Constantinople that a blight would be sent back across the Sea of Marmara and the Mediterranean to mire Alexander's dream.

At the turn of the fourth century AD one woman operating in this city, the female mathematician, astronomer and philosopher Hypatia, produced ground-breaking works. The city's teaching rooms in the centre of the modern-day city are currently being excavated at Komm El Dikka. Protected by bland modern apartment blocks and evergreen cedars, the findings here are spectacular. Right next to the ancient road (the main street of Alexandria was 100 feet wide and artificially lit), twenty lecture rooms have so far been excavated. Here there are three rows of stone benches which accommodated thirty or so students at any one time. The professor sat on a throne-like stone seat, with a small podium up front on which we think students had to stand to present their ideas to the group. A canopy offered protection against the blistering Egyptian sun. Even with dogs lounging around in the dust and weeds colonising the one-time lecture halls, the atmosphere at Komm El Dikka is exciting and intimate, full of intellectual, practical and philosophical possibilities.

Hypatia was clearly an electrifying teacher. She redesigned the astrolabe and worked with her father on new mathematical formulae. We get a sense of her impact from the letters written to her by her pupils, including one Cynesius. In love with her, he proposed marriage – but Hypatia waved her menstrual rag at him, declaring that they were both better off focusing on things of the mind rather than of the body.

The broad-minded attitude in Alexandria seemed perfectly feasible when Christianity was just one of many streams of thought in the city. Christian thinkers in Alexandria even accepted that some pagan ideas could be religiously legitimate – 'science tinged with piety as long as they are righteous'. But in AD 389 following the harder religious line taken from the capital there had been clashes in Alexandria, when Alexander's great Temple of Serapis had been destroyed. The newly redoubtable Christian leaders started to fight among themselves and Hypatia was caught up in the civic and sacred power-struggle. One bishop, Cyril, had Hypatia in his line of sight, describing her as using her scientific instruments for the dark art of divination – to see the future. Hypatia's experiments were being billed as nothing less than black magic. Popular, respected, productive, Hypatia had little chance against the combined forces of a changing world and the ugly, poisoned darts of resentment and rumour.

We can trace Hypatia's fate down a nondescript backstreet in the north of Alexandria. Underneath the twenty-first-century surface lie the remains of the Caesareum – the monumental love-tomb designed by Cleopatra to mourn her dead paramour Julius Caesar, decorated with ancient Egyptian obelisks which have since ended up in New York's Central Park and on London's Embankment, now known as Cleopatra's needles. Completed by Augustus once he had wrested Alexandria from Cleopatra's control (and had sparked that double suicide of the Egyptian Queen and the love-sick general Mark Antony), and then turned into a place of imperial worship, from AD 412 the Caesareum had become Bishop Cyril's Christian headquarters.

Hypatia was caught in the crossfire between warring religious groups in the city. Frustrated and enraged, these were men who needed a scapegoat. In the spring of AD 415[12] Hypatia – about whom Cyril had so effectively muttered – was torn from her carriage. The philosopher was stripped naked and then dragged to the Caesareum's edge. The mob, its blood up, grabbed whatever lay close to them – *ostraka* (pottery fragments), we are told, probably broken roof tiles from a building site. What followed is hard to recount. The philosopher was flayed alive, then still breathing she was burnt and her dismembered body parts displayed around the city.[13]

Elsewhere in the city the library was ransacked. Already burnt once by Caesar's troops in 46 BC, it was put to the torch a second time by those loyal to the New Rome's religious cause. Hypatia's tragedy was also Alexandria's. Wandering through the streets, watching the horror, the closing of minds, the destruction all around him, the pagan poet Palladas was moved to verse at the plight of his home town:

> Is it true that we Greeks are really dead
> and only seem alive – in our fallen state?
> Where we imagine that a dream is life?
> Or are we truly alive and is life dead?[14]

After 350 years of wandering, striving, escaping intimidation and death, Christians were no longer the persecuted minority but the persecuting majority. Vast centres were opened across the Byzantine Empire where bread was distributed to the poor and needy. There were many reasons to be 'with us' not 'with them'.

Our contemporary source for Hypatia's life, Socrates Scholasticus, the chronicler-historian, born in Constantinople (taught, remember, by those two pagans who had fled earlier persecution in the city in AD 389–91 when the Temple of Serapis and its library were burnt to the ground) finishes his account of Hypatia's death with these words: 'Surely nothing can be further from the spirit of Christianity than the allowance of massacre . . .'[15]

CHAPTER 22

✤

CHRISTIAN PARTICLES IN A PAGAN ATMOSPHERE: NOVA ROMA

AD 381–465

> You should give up your childish festival,
> your laughable rites, your
> shrines unworthy of so great an empire.
> Oh noble Romans, wash your marble statues wet
> with dripping spatters of gore –
> let these statues, the works of great
> craftsmen, stand undefiled;
> let them become the most beautiful adornments
> of our native city – may no
> depraved purpose taint these works of art, no
> longer in the service of evil.
>
> PRUDENTIUS TO THE ROMAN SENATE,
>
> FIFTH CENTURY AD[1]

Non-believers might have been burning, but the overall landscape of Constantinople remained stubbornly pagan – or, at least, stubbornly classical.[2] In the early medieval period an ancient Roman or an ancient Greek would not have felt entirely out of place on Christian Constantinople's streets.

We need to pause for a moment to remember that, for the ancient and medieval populations, statues embodied all kinds of qualities and powers. They were thought to be psycho-physical parcels; an incarnation of both the rational and irrational. These images were painted, washed in softening milk-lotions, dressed in clothes, garlanded with flowers, perfumed with rose-oil. Their metal hair was so fine it lifted in the breeze and their rock-crystal eyes followed you as you walked past. Looking at those beautiful bodies and into those fine faces, the men and women of early medieval Constantinople would have expected to find a soul.[3]

Tellingly John of Ephesus, who lived for some of his life in Byzas' City, moaned that Constantinople's plebs mistook a Christian personification of the city for an image of Aphrodite. Even as late as AD 1204, when Latin Crusaders were harrying Constantinople, the city's people tore down a 30-foot high statue of Athena outside the Senate House in the Forum of Constantine because they thought she was actively welcoming in the unwanted Crusaders.[4] And on that wonderful Peutinger Map – a kind of Roman A to Z – that is indeed precisely how Constantinople is portrayed: as Aphrodite, the goddess of desire – a goddess the ancients understood to nourish both *eros* (passion) and *eris* (strife or war).

From Constantine onwards emperors made a point of collecting and displaying works – copies and originals – inspired by the old gods. A statue of Aphrodite, Artemis, Virgil, Romulus and Remus, and 'rosy-armed' Helen of Troy (fascinated by the story of the Trojan War, there were as many as 29 groups in Constantinople depicting the Fall of Troy), a giant Hermaphrodite, Julius Caesar and assorted philosophers or classical heroes could also be found in the city. Some were marble but most were bronze or silvered bronze. Gathered up from across the empire, 'stripping all other cities than Byzantion bare', as one contemporary put it, their shimmering presence made the city *kallos* – both good and great. Constantine (some argue his son Constantius II) surpassed himself with the acquisition of the red granite obelisk of Tuthmosis III (itself 1,800 years old when imported) erected by Theodosios I. The projects helped Constantinople to *look* like an imperial capital and enabled her inhabitants to swell with civic pride. Not that all this came without cost: inhabitants were taxed to pay for the complicated logistics, cities across Europe and Asia were strong-armed into delivering up their 'gifts' (the tradition of acquiring statues had started off as military plunder) and many were erected under duress by the city's criminals *damnatii ad opus publicum* – a kind of extreme community service.[5]

As a result of her grand, architectural salvage project Constantinople boasted many prime specimens, including the ivory statue of Zeus designed by Phidias and commissioned for the temple at Olympia; the gorgeous Knidian Aphrodite by Praxiteles; an exotic green stone from Lindos on Rhodes; and a splendid statue of Hera from Samos – collected by the grand chamberlain (and eunuch) Lausos. These three artworks, along with the basilica library containing 120,000 books, were tragically lost in a fire that swept through the city in AD 475.

The drive to collect pagan curiosities was not just motivated by dilettante interest; nor was it simply a means of grand self-glorification; it arose from the belief that these objects contained real and transferable power. Emperors from Constantine onwards gathered them in, partly to beautify their capital but also to remove such potent foci of sacrifice and worship from pagan temples all over the empire. Within the library of the Great Palace we are told there was an extraordinary version of the works of Homer: 'Among other Curiosities of this Place, was the Gut of a Dragon [probably a python], a hundred and twenty Foot long, on which were inscribed in Golden Characters the Iliads and Odysseys of Homer.'[6]

There are splendid tales of demonically possessed statues in Byzantine lands which had toppled, spitefully, on to prominent individuals, before being frantically buried to submerge their malign desires and designs. Bishop Porphyry – he with a penchant for religious arson in Gaza – physically harassed a statue of Aphrodite with the help of a cross-bearing mob. The brother of Emperor Leo VI became impotent and rushed to clothe the statues in the hippodrome and to burn incense in front of them in the belief that this gesture of respect would sort out his embarrassing medical issues.

The miraculous power of Christian icons is of course a natural progression of pagan ideas; in many cases earlier statues had the sign of the cross drawn on their foreheads, not just to purify them but to render them doubly potent. Facilitated by Theodosios' edicts a generation before there was, quite simply, a lot of classical material knocking around in redundant shrines and sanctuaries. Gathering it all together somehow proved that the new Christian administration had the upper hand. But surely it would have been so much easier to destroy such idolatry *in situ*? Materially and emotionally this was clearly very hard to do. So Byzantine officials preserved, appropriated and repurposed: the images of Isis from Egypt would be gathered in;[7] the shrine of Zeus Ammon in Libya was converted into a church of Mary Theotokos; the pawing-hoofed bronze triumphal quadriga of horses made with great skill by the metalworking islanders of Chios (the horses destined eventually to have their heads severed and to be unceremoniously shipped as loot to St Mark's in Venice after the Fourth Crusade of AD 1204, where they still sit on the upper floors of the Cathedral) were imported under Theodosios II and displayed in Constantinople's hippodrome. The Baths of Zeuxippos came to resemble a kind of steamy art gallery, the hippodrome an outdoor museum.

The vogue for the collection of pagan spolia encouraged the passing of laws not dissimilar to modern heritage regulations: in AD 383 a temple in Osrhoene in Mespotamia was ordered to be kept open so that the works inside could be enjoyed 'for the value of their art rather than their divinity';[8] and a *constitutio* of 399 passed by the Emperor Arkadios declared, 'If any person should attempt to destroy such work, he should not have the right to flatter himself as relying on any authority, if perchance he should produce any rescript or any law as his defence. Such documents shall be torn from his hands and referred to Our Wisdom.'[9] Here we have the Byzantine imperial administrative machine as the UNESCO of its day.

Naturally there was destruction and violence – newly converted Christians could prove their piety by smashing idols, and many pagans found conversion at the point of a sword highly convenient. In Corfu at Palaeopolis a church was jammed on to the site of a pagan temple, and improved archaeological methods[10] suggest that locals hyenaed-in, grabbing handy pagan building material to use for example as mortar.[11] But this was the exception rather than the rule. In general, temples, particularly those outside the walls of the city, were kept intact and were repurposed as public buildings or as handsome private homes. Recently excavated mosaics from the church of St Stephen at Um er-Rasas in Jordan show that as late as the second half of the eighth century, pagan temples were selected to signify certain Christian cities – a Temple of Zeus Hypsistos to represent the city of Neapolis and of Pan to mark a location in Egypt.

Along with physical, classical remains, the streets of Constantinople were saturated too with a classical, neo-pagan *modus operandi*.[12] The city's population, rich and poor alike, nourished and embraced the wonderfully named 'marvel literature'. Commonly, and right up until the Ottoman conquest in AD 1453, men and women in the city would trust all kinds of seers for activities as varied as undertaking merchant expeditions, hunting, starting a war and determining the right date to end breast-feeding or to start children on study-guides. *Seismologia* (earthquake guides), *selenodromia* (moon-phase books) and *vrontologia* (thunder guides) were wildly popular ways of predicting the future.[13] Occultists, magicians, alchemists, dream-diviners, interpreters of the voices of statues, bird-seers, geomancers, demonologists, masters of the apocryphal: a modern-day commentator could be forgiven for presuming that Byzantium was a hotbed of the dark arts.

Yet, although there were indeed numerous, vocal practitioners of these skills, the Byzantines themselves would have been surprised to learn of their colourful labels. Many of these men considered themselves to be 'philosophers'. They were individuals who delighted both in the purely intellectual pleasures of an enquiring mind and in the power of 'philosophy' to explain and predict the mysteries of the world. Some believed that it was the ascendance of Mercury in the sky that expedited the birth of these mercurial diviners, sacrificers, bird-seers, dream-interpreters, doctors, grammarians, lawyers, rhetors, military engineers.[14] Stars, plants, minerals, men – the activities of one were thought to direct the activities of another.

There is a kind of cosmopolitan energy to many of the pursuits of these Christian-occult philosophers. There were fierce debates about whether or not the biblical Abraham had been an astrologer. In miscellanies compiled from the twelfth century onwards, magic texts were represented along with biblical apocrypha, lapidaries, the liturgies of St James and St Basil, alchemical treatises and instructions for palm-reading, for geomancy, for divination. Many are brilliantly, vividly illustrated. There is an almost fevered sense that the truths of the troubling peculiarities of the world must be out there somewhere. The empire sponsored the work of astrologers from across its expanding territories – from Thebes, from the banks of the Lykos River in Phrygia, from Alexandria. Their ideas were not liminal but central to the lived Byzantine experience. Hephaistion of Thebes created an astrological compendium that would be employed for centuries, and Maximus Byzantius promulgated influential ideas on universal affinity – whereby every object in the world animate or inanimate was infused with a kind of divine spark that gave it direct, magical contact with the sun – which explained for example the miracle-working properties of the city's statues.

Astronomers were actively employed in Constantinople too – often all these starers-at-stars were grouped under one banner as 'mathematicians'. The stars above Istanbul, although veiled in pollution now, are particularly bright; their magnitude of less than six gives them the impression of brilliance. But there seems to be ambiguity over whether all this star-gazing was God's or Satan's work. Astrologers were by turns ostracised and embraced by the imperial court. The Church Fathers, understandably anxious about these magic-men with their traditions stretching back millennia, warned, 'Do not pay attention neither to astrologies, nor to bird omens, nor to other superstitions; do not even listen to the mythical oracles of the Greeks, the use of potions, the singing prophecies and the most unlawful things of the necromancers.'[15] There does in fact seem to be a shadily schizophrenic attitude to their work. Maximus Byzantius, after being in favour for decades, was suddenly executed in AD 371; there were book burnings and condemnations of his craft as sorcery.

But in the city there were many who wanted a focus for their hybrid Christian-pagan passion and come the fifth century, there were some extreme Christians – new kinds of cult follower – who offered an exciting alternative, returning to the desert roots of the Christian religion. The field of operations of these men was the demanding environment of sand and rock and drought; indeed their name derives from the Greek for desert, *eremos*. In Constantinople's landscape – spiritual and physical – the *eremos*, the hermit, became a new fixture. A number of these ascetics offered something truly radical in the place of all that quasi-possessed marble and rock crystal and gilding: statues that breathed.

CHAPTER 23

✛

STATUES IN THE SKY: ASCETICS

c. AD 420–95

The famous Symeon, the great wonder of the world . . . I am afraid that the narrative may seem to posterity to be a myth totally devoid of truth. For the facts surpass human nature . . .

THEODORET, *HISTORY OF THE MONKS OF SYRIA*[1]

Constantinople witnessed the popular power of ancient art – now not just in marble and bronze, but in mortal, carnal form.

The Stylites, human works of classical art perched on their columns, attempted to outdo the ferocity of the rock-crystal gaze of their lifeless pagan equivalents – and to praise the One True God with the extremity of their efforts. St Symeon (AD 389–459), the originator of the art, whose column near modern-day Aleppo once stood at 40 cubits (around 60 feet), lasted, we are told, in his stone pod for over thirty years while devotees and locals brought themselves and their animals to pace around the column seeking blessing and fertility. St Symeon's chosen form of devotion may have been inspired by the local tradition of raising phallic symbols on the top of columns, or by rituals for the Magna Mater Kybele, described in the second century AD by Lucian in his *De Dea Syria*,[2] or more simply imitating a statue seemed the best way to outdo their pagan, bronze and stone predecessors. St Symeon's column has, down the centuries, been whittled away by devotees and now resembles a giant snowball, a stubborn time-traveller. At the time of writing, the lump of stone in the grounds of the 'Fortress of Symeon' sixteen miles north-west of Aleppo, despite being hit in a mortar attack in May 2016, appears to be surviving the current Syrian crisis. Men have long believed that Symeon's column was protected by some kind of miraculous power.

One of the many who came to marvel at Symeon's piety was a man in his late thirties called Daniel. Daniel was clearly enraptured by the muscular Christian form of asceticism that he saw before him. The word ascetic comes from the Greek *askesis*, training – no surprise that these men were also described as athletes, individuals who through maximum carnal stamina and bodily stress would reach the *athlon*, the prize of immortality and of God. Christianity was of course in many ways an otherworldly religion – stateless Christians waiting in a form of limbo for the Second Coming. Now that the Roman emperors had acquired a territory to house this idea, and Christ was increasingly portrayed not as a humble revolutionary but as the crowned Pantokrator, the Ruler of All, ordinary people needed an intermediary, an intercessor who might punish his flesh in the way Jesus' flesh had been punished – a creature halfway between heaven and earth.

And it was to the Christian city of Constantinople that Daniel chose to take this new sensational religious performance art. Daniel's selection of Constantinople is critical. His biography tells us that having determined upon the life of the ascetic he was originally set on Antioch as his location, but a ragged man on the road advised him instead to head to Constantinople, 'and you will see a second Jerusalem, namely Constantinople; there you can enjoy the martyr's shrines and the great houses of prayer'.[3] Whether this is indeed what itinerants of the day truly felt or what chroniclers wanted to suggest to the world, the idea of Constantinople as a kind of super-holy, centrifugal force – where all that mattered in monotheism could be found – was being successfully promoted. Having spent most of his adult life in a monastery, and then nine years living in a decommissioned pagan temple, reputedly possessed by demons, the man who would be St Daniel the Stylite in AD 460 ascended a column 4 miles north of Constantinople in a place now called Kuruçeşme midway between Anaplous (now Arnavutköy) and Ortaköy on the European shore of the Bosphorus.[4]

In a detailed life written by one of his disciples in the fifth century, we are told that Daniel became a totem for the city; overlooking the Bosphorus, despite being tempted by 'harlots and travelling heretics',[5] he tended to the population's mental and physical needs. The men and women of Constantinople were keen for comfort in the wake of stresses such as the Great Fire in AD 475 (which had destroyed the Great Library and Lausos'

Relief of a Stylite saint, either Symeon the elder or younger, from Syria c. fifth or sixth century AD. *A monk on the ladder approaches with an incense burner.*

treasures, including premier artwork), and the Fall of Rome in 476 and Daniel assumed the role of the oracle. His opinion started to count, as he advised local power-brokers and visiting aristocracy, even royalty, on various matters, from how to deal with the invasions of Germanic armies to handling neighbours who appeared to be religious dissenters. When orthodoxy was threatened, Daniel descended to debate with bishops and emperors. A monastery was created at the column's base where St Symeon's relics were also preserved.

We are told that Daniel, after thirty-three years – his feet covered in sores, Thracian-wind-whipped as he ascended his pillar – asked for 'grace to end his life in holiness' and just before his death advised his followers to 'hold fast humility, practise obedience, exercise hospitality, never separate yourself from your Holy Mother, the Church, turn from heretics . . . When this had been done, and the brethren had heard the holy father's prayer and farewell they burst into such weeping and wailing that the noise of their lamentation sounded like unto a clap of thunder.'[6] Daniel died, in harness as it were, in his pod atop his column. His body was

immediately whisked away, before the faithful could start to cannibalise
and repurpose it as relics, and the corpse was then strapped to a plank
and displayed as an icon; eyewitnesses reported that above his body three
crosses appeared in the sky encircled by white doves.

Historians and neuroscientists are now working together on what the
implications of that sky-spectacle could have been. Fascinating research
from Harvard academics has suggested that if faith is strong enough we
can see what we want to see.[7] Religious involvement can activate extra-
personal brain systems. Before we dismiss the people of Constantinople
as gullible Dark Age hysterics, we should consider the fact that men and
women are still convinced by visions in the sky. Recently researching
in India, I was told by a very lucid ex-government official that his own
mother, after her death, was seen by many eyewitnesses ascending to
heaven in a flaming cloud. This woman, who drank only buffalo milk,
has since been deified and is now worshipped as a goddess in a busy little
temple on the outskirts of Jodhpur – just as goddesses have been since the
Bronze Age. The faithful here are called to prayer with conch shells and
praise the goddess with arms raised in the *orans* position.

Daniel's life is a helpful snapshot of a time when the public expression
of piety was in flux. We hear that Gelanios – the man whose land Daniel
had chosen to appropriate for his religious marathon – originally did not
want the stylite's column built here, where 'a white dove had fluttered and
then settled again'.[8] It is a 'before they were famous' moment: an ordinary
inhabitant of greater Constantinople had no interest in a desert ascetic
rocking up with his odd ideas and annoying column. We should spare a
moment to think of those habitual Istanbullus, pagan for millennia, who
were not necessarily delighted that their territory was being turned into a
New Age religious theme park.

CHAPTER 24

❖

SEX AND THE CITY: EUNUCHS

c. AD 350 ONWARDS

neither let the eunuch say, Behold, I am a dry tree. For thus saith the Lord unto the eunuchs that keep my Sabbaths, and choose the things that please me, and take hold of my covenant; Even unto them will I give in mine house and within my walls a place and a name better than of sons and of daughters: I will give them an everlasting name, that shall not be cut off.

ISAIAH 56: 3–5

Thou conquerest in beauty of soul as much as in beauty of face, for thou possessest everything that is worthy of thy name, and ever in the bedchamber, sending the emperor to sleep, thou dost sow all gentleness in his ears.

LEONTIOS SCHOLASTIKOS EPIGRAM, PRAISING KALLINIKOS

(A NAME THAT MEANS BEAUTY AND VICTORY)[1]

For there are some eunuchs, which were so born from their mother's womb: and there are some eunuchs, which were made eunuchs of men: and there be eunuchs, which have made themselves eunuchs for the kingdom of heaven's sake. He that is able to receive it, let him receive it.

MATTHEW 19: 12

By the fourth century AD, having a powerful third sex in the city of Constantinople had become a defining characteristic. Theoretically, the Greeks and Romans had always despised eunuchs, though we know from the Father of History Herodotus that Corinthians had sent eunuchs to Persia in the 580s BC. Men and boys were ritually castrated when captured as prisoners of war – Herodotus reports this as the fate of male children in the hands of Xerxes after the uprising of the islands off the coast of Asia Minor. Emasculated men transgressed popular Roman ideas of virility and virtue. Yet the cult of the Eastern goddess Kybele and her castrated son-lover-devotee Attis had been worryingly popular in the city of Rome. Followers of Kybele (a favourite deity, we should remember, of Byzantium) would slice off their genitals in a religious frenzy and then wear make-up and dresses to honour their goddess. Based in the East, at Nicomedia, the Emperor Diocletian appears to have started to appreciate the value of eunuchs. Galerius had captured the Persian Emperor's harem and held on to his eunuchs, starting, it seems, a late Roman craze for eunuchs at court. Eunuch slaves from Armenia, the Caucasus and Persia were brought in to service the tastes of Christian emperors and high-born women. With the rule of Constantine's sons the post of *cubicularius* – chamberlain (the grand chamberlain was *praepositus sacri cubiculi*) – was created, a uniquely privileged position and one available only to castrated men. The standing, influence and therefore the power of these staff of the sacred bedchamber grew exponentially.

As well as performing their formal roles – captain of the bodyguard, keeper of the privy purse, personal finance manager, dresser, secretary and grand chamberlain – and, it was whispered by the slander-merchants, providing sexual pleasure – high-ranking eunuchs were trusted strategists who were sent to quell mutinies, to resolve religious disputes. It was Amantios, Eudoxia's eunuch, who had petitioned on behalf of the bishop of Gaza to destroy the Marneion; Narses, sword-bearer to Justinian I, would glitter alongside him in military campaigns. Symeon the Sanctified was allowed on to Mount Athos – a eunuch who would then go on to found a monastery of eunuchs in Thessalonika. A sizeable number of patriarchs – the leaders of the Orthodox Church based in Constantinople – were eunuchs. The presence of this third sex – complicating the binary division of male and female – also, arguably, allowed women to enjoy an atypical degree of power in the city, a tradition that endured for 1,500 years, beyond the Ottoman conquest of the city in AD 1453.

Although polite translations of medieval sources have consistently rendered eunuch to mean celibate (and the word was indeed sometimes used in just this context), we hear of Assyrian nobles, of Arab prisoners of war, of Syrian nomads, of Black Sea farmers and of Italians working in Constantinople or her imperial territories who had all been desexed. A diplomat, Liudprand, presented four penisless carzimasians to the Byzantine court as a gift, while in the ninth century AD Basil I was gifted a hundred eunuchs by a rich Peloponnesian woman called Danelis. The accounts of doctors such as Paul of Aegina in the sixth century AD, describing castration by both compression and excision, and the reference in Justinian's legislation to the fact that only three out of ninety castrated boys survived one spate of geldings, give us an insight into the system and the scale of the castration process. It was thought preferable to create eunuchs pre-puberty. Initially ethnic outsiders, who brought the value of foreign experience and far-flung contacts to the beating heart of the capital, the eunuchs of Constantinople became increasingly popular. Ironically, as a result, the numbers of 'home-produced' eunuchs correspondingly grew; coming from Constantinople itself or its neighbouring territories, to some extent these unexotic, somewhat parochial, neutered men eventually lost their political bite.[2]

Eunuchs might have been slaves – and it has been argued that the ultimate imperial ruler needs the ultimate slave in the form of a castrated man – but in Constantinople many did exceptionally well for themselves. It was Lausos the eunuch, whose grand palace has recently been identified on Bab-ı Ali Street,[3] who gathered together one of the greatest collections of ancient art in antiquity: the Aphrodite of Knidos, the Zeus of Olympia, that strange Lindian stone and a Hera from the goddess's great temple at Samos. Displayed so that the people of the city could marvel at their potent, pagan debauchery, these works were high-end, exotic captives. Their presence in the city proved that high-ranking men in Constantinople were in charge of the classical pagan world rather than the classical pagan world being in charge of them. This collection was politically acute as well as an expression of refined, catholic taste. Characterised by contemporaries as generous, learned and wise, eunuchs were also typically appreciated as beautiful creatures whose fairness of form reflected the beauty of their soul; witness the poet Corippus exalting Narses, the Emperor Justinian's sword-bearer: 'He was in gold all over, yet modest in dress and appearance, and pleasing for his upright ways, venerable for his virtue, brilliant, careful, watchful night and day for the rulers of the world, shining with glorious light: as the morning star, glittering in the clear sky, outdoes the silvery constellations with its golden rays and announces the coming of the day with its clear flame.'[4]

Eunuchs were also depicted as angels, messengers on earth who enjoyed some kind of sublime hotline between heaven and earth. Standing between two worlds was their business. We hear about eunuch messengers in the popular stories of the saints of the day, men such as John the Almsgiver, a patriarch of Alexandria, who was summoned by the Emperor to Constantinople:

> The Saint whom God had called saw with his waking eyes a eunuch in gleaming apparel, a golden sceptre in his right hand, standing by him and saying: 'Come, I beg you, the King of Kings is asking for you!'

> Without delay he [John the Almsgiver] forthwith sent for the patrician, Nicetas, and said to him with many tears: 'You, my master, called me to go to our earthly King, but the heavenly King has anticipated you and has summoned to himself my humbleness.' He then related to him the vision which he had just seen of the eunuch, or rather of the angel.[5]

The attitude towards these de-sexed men in the city does seem to have been consistently mixed. Some early Christians – such as the church father Origen, self-castrated as a mark of his faith – were encouraged by the popular *Sentences of Sextus*: 'Cast aside every part of the body that does not lead you to self-control; for it is better to live continently without some body part than destructively with it.'[6] And again: 'You may see that people have saved the health of the rest of their body by chopping off and casting away parts. How much better to do this for continence?' Yet even Origen would go on to decry the process, his own self-castration it seems having taken place in a moment of youthful fervour. Eunuchs were often slurred; labelled devious or lustful. A wonderful tract, *In Defence of Eunuchs*, written by the archbishop of Ochrid (Ochrid being another station on the Egnatian Way in modern-day FYROM, the former Yugoslav Republic of Macedonia), stoutly defended their reputation. This was penned from a position of knowledge. Not only were many of the archbishop's friends eunuchs, his brother was one too.

Christian purity, career advancement, forced capture, a desire to be female, a desire to be 'other' – all these could explain the psychological comfort of being a eunuch. Did this state also subconsciously speak to those in a charged and fragile age of the likelihood of destruction and the possibilities of survival?[7]

The presence of eunuchs in Constantinople would damn the Byzantines in the eyes of many Western historians and chroniclers – both contemporary and with hindsight – but on many occasions it would be eunuchs, well connected, internationalist, undistracted by dynastic ambition, who would save the very city herself. And indeed it was a eunuch who, in one of Constantinople's greatest hours of need, would help to decide the city's fate: 'the eunuch ruled in the palace, and, like a very serpent, coiled his way round every office, throttling everything . . .'.[8]

CHAPTER 25

✤

THE SACK OF OLD ROME: THE PROBLEM WITH GOTHS, PART TWO

c. AD 395–410

We for love's clergy only are instruments,
When this book is made thus,
Should again the ravenous
Vandals and the Goths invade us,
Learning were safe; in this our universe
Schools might learn sciences, spheres music, angels verse.

JOHN DONNE, 'A VALEDICTION OF THE BOOK'

Informers were rife as never before, always fawning on the eunuchs of the court . . . the emperor was the worst kind of fool, and his wife, who was very headstrong, even for a woman, was devoted to those who controlled her, the omnipresent grasping eunuchs, and her ladies-in-waiting. She made life so unbearable for everyone that to the average person nothing was preferable to death.

ZOSIMUS, *NEW HISTORY*[1]

It was now that one of those outsiders within the city, a eunuch with great powers of persuasion and a strategic eye, came to prominence – a man whose place in history would colour the narrative that surrounded Byzantium. His role was key because while the sack of Rome in AD 410 is one of the few dates in world history popularly known, for operators on the ground now it was not Old Rome but New Rome, Constantinople, that was the critical prize. Arguably the departure of Rome's troops from Britain was a by-product of the vicissitudes of Constantinople.

Eunuch Eutropios had served under Theodosios I and immediately after the Emperor's death in AD 395 had persuaded his young son Arkadios to marry, not the daughter of another influential courtier Rufinus, but instead that unknown beauty Aelia Eudoxia. Rufinus was soon afterwards assassinated (some argue with Eutropios' help), while Eutropios in his turn would be executed four years later possibly at the behest of his own creature, Empress Eudoxia.

This was a time when the administration of Constantinople, and of Old Rome, needed strong leadership rather than internal discord. In Britain the army had rebelled, Magnus Maximus striking out for independence. Goths and Vandals were sometimes allies, sometimes enemies, of both New and Old Rome. It was Gothic troops, remember, who effected the slaughter of 7,000 ordered by Theodosios in Thessalonika. A half-Roman, half-Vandal named Stilicho (a protégé of Theodosios and married to his niece) held a protectorate and thus power in the West; while in the East Theodosios' young son Arkadios ruled with the help of Rufinus. The first King of the Visigoths, Alaric, who had learnt his warring craft from Rome under a Goth called Gainas and had originally led auxiliaries of Goths for Theodosios under Stilicho's command, swiftly became Stilicho's primary opponent. In AD 395 Alaric, who clearly felt undervalued by the imperial powers, broke his treaty with Rome and ravaged through Thrace. As leader of the Visigoths, he then decided to march against Constantinople.

Meanwhile Rufinus, from within the city, entered into secret negotiations as soon as Alaric's power became evident. He bestowed on Alaric the rank of a Roman general and gave his followers gold and grain. Alaric bypassed the Christian capital, his spies having already made it clear to him that a siege of this well-walled city would be pointless without specially designed weaponry, that the fortifications would otherwise be impossible to breach. Eutropios' dealings with Alaric in AD 397 were much praised in Constantinople. Although Stilicho's public-relations machine in Milan would spit, 'this time he [Alaric] comes as a friend . . . and hands down decisions in cases brought by those whose wives he has raped and children murdered . . .',[2] in Constantinople the eunuch and friend of the Goths was cheered through the streets, revelling in his own popularity parade. Meanwhile the Visigoth with an axe to grind stormed his way through Macedonia and Thessaly – turning up at Thermopylae, a latter-day Xerxes. But rather than fighting to the death as the Spartan King Leonidas (uncle to the aspiring tyrant Pausanias who had built

Byzantion's first walls) had done, the Greek garrison now preferred to open the gates and let their attackers in. Alaric was unstoppable; Corinth and Sparta swiftly fell. Stilicho was furious – a pathogenic people were being delivered direct to his turf. His priorities were to contain this threat and to stake a claim as the true protector of Rome – in both the West and the East.[3]

So Stilicho dispatched soldiers to Constantinople in AD 399 – in theory to reinforce the garrison. Stilicho's men met up with those of Eutropios, among them that ambitious Gothic opportunist Gainas. The polytheist historian Zosimus, who worked in the imperial treasury a century later, picks up the story: 'once Gainas and his men had prostrated themselves and received due welcome from the emperor, Gainas gave the signal. All at once they surrounded Rufinus, falling on him with their swords. One sliced off his right hand, another his left, while another cut off his head and ran off singing a victory song.'[4]

The assassin Gainas went on to install a military junta in Constantinople and – as a Byzantine general now – to hold on to power in the city for a number of months. Doubly unpopular both as an Arian and as a Goth, a man who deposed all anti-Goth officials in late AD 400, Gainas was not fit to rule – nor was he welcome. Spurred on by Eudoxia, Constantinople's inhabitants (and this is a population that may have reached as many as 400,000 at this time) rose up and slaughtered 7,000 auxiliary Goths stationed in the city. This is significant. Time and again in the city's history we find the people of Constantinople acting as a unit, remembering what the defining acronym of Roman culture – SPQR, *Senatus Populusque Romanus* – really means. The new Christian Empire of God frequently felt the sting of New Rome's populus – the men and women on the street who had a republican tendency to believe that their voice counted.

Back in the Senate at Constantinople three years before, Eutropios had branded Stilicho a public enemy. This allowed him to effect all kinds of legitimate punishments, for example diverting the grain supply for the West from Africa to Constantinople. In return, Stilicho called on the precedent of AD 330, when Constantine had conceded that Rome's Senate should have precedence over Constantinople's own. Yet one of Gainas' priority acts before he was hounded out of the city had been to have Eutropios exiled and then executed. Now on the run, Gainas managed to dodge a Roman fleet on the Hellespont and eventually fled north – where another ally of Constantinople's, Uldin, the King of the Huns, decapitated him and sent his head back to the city as a gruesome gift.

Eutropios had granted the Goth Alaric lands in present-day Albania. From AD 401 Alaric attempted to expand these and harried Roman territories. Stilicho was now dealing with unrest at all points of the compass. Enraged by the loss of troops, who had been withdrawn to defend Rome, the remaining soldiers in Britain had elected their own leader, Constantine III, who would oversee the final exit of troops from Britannia. Meanwhile it was rumoured that Stilicho planned to seize the Byzantine throne. Appalled, his soldiers rebelled. It would be another eunuch, Stilicho's own protégé Olympius, who masterminded the execution of the general in 408 – frustrated perhaps that Stilicho had, rather oddly, not acted on his own plan to slip over to the East and take control of Constantinople.

In the chaos that followed, the wives and children of barbarian *foederati* (not citizens of Rome but those who derived benefits from the empire in exchange for military service) – many Goths among them – were slaughtered; and Alaric's ranks swelled with those barbarian men, furious, bereaved, betrayed, who were left standing, perhaps as many as 30,000. The Goth with a grudge now had a force big enough to take Rome.

High-handed, ungrateful, double-crossing the Goths at every turn, Roman power-mongers could not see that Gothic muscle and nous could have been the city's future rather than her nemesis. Or rather the Romans ignored the ancient laws of the word nemesis – whose prehistoric, Proto-Indo-European root *nem* originally meant fair distribution, give and take, a just apportionment of resources. The Old Romans were maimed by a monster, in part, of their own making. Camped outside the walls of the city, Alaric was hoping to bully his way to a massive pay-out; the Senate in Rome attempted to meet his demands, but not fast enough. Many inside the city were starving and had already resorted to cannibalism. This was, after all, Alaric's third siege of the city. On 24 August AD 410, someone let the Goths in: 'Who could describe the horror of that night, and all its carnage? What tears are equal to such suffering? An ancient city, for so many years a queen, now falls in ruin, while throughout its streets lie countless corpses, motionless and still . . . death in ten thousand forms.'[5] Although storytelling has doubtless amplified the 410 incident, men and women in the city were still raped, axed, stabbed and starved.[6] To this day treasure hoards are being discovered where the wealth of centuries-old dynasties was frantically buried by those who could smell death in front of them. In the nearby city of Narni – pagan still in 410 – a number were convinced that their bloody sacrifices had saved them from Alaric's wrath. There is a palpable sense that many in the territories of Old Rome could see little strength in New Rome's religious experiment – and yet the sack of the Rome of Romulus and Remus was in many ways a side-effect of machinations within the Rome of Christ.

After the sack of Rome and the collapse of the machine whose constituent parts – the army, tax collectors, loyalty to an idea – had kept the *pax Romana* operative, the West fractured. Those who lived in the land the Romans had once sneeringly called Barbaricum now had the upper hand and the last laugh. The old Roman industrial mechanism was fissuring. Further afield, trading patterns were disrupted, and evidence from polar ice-caps shows that pollution levels dropped back to levels last seen at the time of Byzantion's foundation as smelting works across the empire were shut down. But what had been Old Rome's misfortune would open up new opportunities for her step-child, Constantinople. We should remember that what Constantinople witnessed in the dog days of the Western Roman Empire was not a clash of alien civilisations but a change in the dynamics of power. And key players, also Arians, also sometime allies of Rome, also on the run from the Huns, would help to shape the experience of the city for the next 150 years. It is time to meet another character on Constantinople's streets: the Vandals.

CHAPTER 26

✢

VANDALS, WISDOM AND ATTILA THE HUN

C. AD 429–76

And she [Sophia] brought a pall stitched with precious purple, where the whole vista of Justinian's achievements was picked out in woven gold and glittered with gems. On one side the artist had skilfully represented with his sharp needle barbarian phalanxes bending their necks, slaughtered kings and subject peoples in order. And he made the yellow gold stand out from the colours so everyone looking at it thought that they were real bodies. The faces were in gold, the blood in purple. And Justinian himself he had depicted as a victor amongst his courtiers, trampling on the brazen neck of the Vandal king, and Libya, applauding bearing fruit and laurel.

CORIPPUS, *IN LAUDEM IUSTINI AUGUSTI MINORIS*, SIXTH CENTURY AD[1]

Contemporaries say there were 80,000. For once, they may not have been wrong. A wandering people, who had crossed the Carpathian Mountains, the Vandals had their roving eyes on a premium prize. In many ways Old Rome was an irrelevance. Who needed a struggling city crammed with outdated architectural follies when an empire's bread-basket beckoned? And so Vandals in AD 429 packed on to boats, captured Roman dromons and skiffs, and headed across the Straits of Gibraltar straight for the fertile, grain-bearing lands of North Africa, some of which were controlled by Constantinople.[2]

Their confidence was immense, but these men were doubly divinely inspired. The Vandals had traditionally worshipped Castor and Pollux – thought, along with their sister Helen of Troy, to take the form of St Elmo's fire and thus to safeguard sailors in the open sea. While staying loyal to their pagan protectors, the Vandals had also recently converted to Arian Christianity. Perhaps the Vandals' pagan–Christian double-glazing and their certainty that they now espoused the 'correct' form of Christianity in a heretical world gave them just the psychological push they needed. Whatever the reason, in the attack on North Africa they brought with them their women and children: this was a mass migration. The Vandals had no intention of turning back.[3]

The Vandals had, like the Goths, been displaced by Hunnic advance. On the move since AD 406 (including in Andalucia from 409), they now turned to look across the Libyan Sea. The arrival of Vandals on the African continent set in motion a domino-line of activity. St Augustine, author of *The City of God* – the church father who promoted the notion of original sin so persuasively that it became the default position in Christian understanding – died as the Vandals were approaching to besiege his home town of Hippo in present-day Algeria in 430. Fellow monks fleeing the attack transported Augustine's radical ideas (the ultimate culpability of human pride) into the heart of the West. After the capture of Hippo the Vandals resettled Numidia in 435, and in 439 they sacked Carthage. On the sea Roman boats were hijacked, set alight and used as infernal battering rams, turned against their one-time brothers in arms. It seems the Vandals were maritime cuckoos inhabiting the vessels of whatever land they were harrying – the dromon in the region of Byzantium, the Viking knarr when in Germany. The desperate deployment of the Roman Danube river-defence force against their seemingly unstoppable progression opened up an opportunity for one Attila the Hun, who would go on to destroy vast swathes of Roman territory. To the north the Huns invaded while Vandals were gorging on African fruit.

If you walk through Bayswater in west London, like as not you will hear snatches of a heartfelt prayer. Bankers, their cleaners, kebab-shop owners and their student customers scurry past, not knowing that the muffled sounds they can just about hear escaping from the Orthodox cathedral here every day, the Trisagion, were once offered up to God as a plea for the salvation of civilisation in AD 447: 'Holy God, Holy Mighty One, Holy Immortal One, have mercy upon us.'

Sixty thousand Huns were said to have been employed as mercenaries by the Western Emperor against Constantinople and her Emperor Theodosios II. The Huns knew that they were feared; from the mid-430s they had consistently negotiated ever more expensive protection payments

from Constantinople. In AD 446 the Huns demanded both greater tribute
and a greater number of 'barbarians' who had left their tribes and were
resident in Constantinople, in effect asylum-seekers, to be offered up
from within the city. They were denied. Now there was a shift of attitude.
Later that year Hunnic forces captured the Roman forts at Ratiaria (the
headquarters of the Danube's protection fleet), and the Byzantine army
was defeated at Chersonesus on the Crimean peninsula. Taking territory
within 20 miles of the city the victorious leader, whom we know as Attila
the Hun, was determined to claim Constantinople for his own. In 447
Attila controlled the Balkans from the Black Sea to the Dardanelles – but
somehow, against all conceivable odds, Constantinople had not fallen.

Then, in AD 447, from the belly of the earth came a sign of divine
displeasure.

We are told that, while his subjects cried out their desperate prayer, the
Emperor Theodosios II walked, his feet bare and bleeding, and dressed
only in a white tunic – pacing the 7 miles across the city in late January
on stone-cold marble slabs. An earthquake had destroyed 57 of the 186
towers spaced along the city walls; entire sections of the 3.5-mile stretch
had crumbled. Those within the city knew that the line of limestone and
red-brick bands that Theodosios had so carefully constructed was the
only sure defence against their enemies – that is, an inner and outer wall
(with over ninety towers on each) and a dry moat, 60 feet wide. Pale imi-
tations of these defences would be built from Cairo to Caernarfon. Along
with their slaves, citizens from rival sporting factions (in particular the
city's egregiously competitive chariot-racing teams, the Blues and Greens)
set to work repairing the damage – a race against one another and against
time – desperate to make the city's fortifications whole once more; all
these men knew that their lives and those of their loved ones depended on
their success. The walls of Constantinople, we are told, were rebuilt, from
top to bottom, in sixty days. The vicarious efforts of the Praetorian prefect Flavius Constantinus, who oversaw the works, are proudly recorded
in a slab that still sits next to the Mevlevihane Gate where it was first
installed. 'By Theodosios' command, Constantinus triumphantly built
these strong walls in less than two months. Pallas [Athene – the pagan
goddess] could hardly have built such a secure citadel in so short a time.'

In early spring AD 447 – a time of the year when snow can cover the
city like a smog – it was only thanks to this frantic rebuilding that Attila,

advancing on Theodosios' city and getting as close as Athyras (modern day Büyükçekmece), decided to turn his attentions instead to the sunset edge of Rome's reach, making it as far west as Orléans in France. Constantinople was lucky. As Callinicus, who had witnessed the Huns' depredations in the Balkans, recorded in his *Life of St Hypatius*:

> The barbarian nation of the Huns, which was in *Thrace*, became so great that more than a hundred cities were captured and Constantinople almost came into danger and most men fled from it . . . And there were so many murders and blood-lettings that the dead could not be numbered. Ay, for they took captive the churches and monasteries and slew the monks and maidens in great numbers.[4]

Theodosios' protecting walls – sheltering a city that now occupied all of its seven hills – still greet the visitor to the historic centre of Istanbul.

But Old Rome would not be so fortunate. In AD 455, after they had broken down the surrounding aqueducts that brought water to her inhabitants, Vandals stormed what was left of the city.

The only scraps of Vandal language that survive are a joke in a Latin epigram and a brief allusion to a particular Arian ideology.[5][6] But we do have articulate archaeology from the new 'Vandal Kingdom' in North Africa. An olive press was set up in the Baths of Hadrian in the gymnasium of Lepcis Magna in Libya;[7] there are pottery kilns in the bath complex of Uthina in Zeugitana near Carthage; elsewhere we find metalworking and glass production; and lime-kilns were established, burning and breaking down Roman statuary to use as a fuel. There are some interesting continuities: olive-oil production still took place next to churches, just as it did within the pagan temple complexes. Poetry and panegyrics were enthusiastically composed in Latin, some have described the Vandal Kingdom as witnessing a cultural florescence.

But the Vandals have left grimmer remains too. In Rome, construction work close to the Trevi Fountain in 1999 shows a house, and probably its inhabitants, burnt to the ground when the Vandals sacked the city. Meanwhile in Constantinople and across the waterways that served her, the Vandals would rightly come to deserve the reputation that causes us still to call someone who destroys or pollutes a 'vandal', today.

Constantinople – divided into fourteen districts as the old Rome had been – was an ever more tempting prize. The *Notitia Urbis Constantino-politanae* written in the fourth century AD and then updated c. 447–50 describes Constantinople's wealth: 20 state bakeries; 120 private bakeries; 8 public and 153 private baths; 52 colonnaded avenues and 322 other streets – the list goes on. And increasingly, like the cities of Alexandria and Pergamon before her, Constantinople was seen as the greatest repository of knowledge in the world, because this was a city that collected, stored and enhanced the ideas of both men and women from three continents.

Sometimes what-if fantasies are useful. Imagine that the entirety of Western civilisation's coding for computer systems or prints of all films ever made or all copies of Shakespeare and the Bible and the Qur'an were encrypted and held on one tablet device. And if that tablet was lost, stolen, burnt or corrupted, then our knowledge, use and understanding of that content, those words and ideas, would be gone for ever – only, perhaps, lingering in the minds of a very few men of memory whose job it had been to keep ideas alive. This little thought-experiment can help us to comprehend the totemic power of manuscripts.

This is the great weight of responsibility for the past, the present and the future that the manuscripts of Constantinople carried. Much of our global cultural heritage – philosophies, dramas, epic poems – survive only because they were preserved in the city's libraries and scriptoria. Just as Alexandria and Pergamon too had amassed vast libraries, Constantinople understood that a physical accumulation of knowledge worked as a lodestone – drawing in respect, talent and sheer awe. These texts contained both the possibilities and the fact of empire and had a quasi-magical status. This was a time when the written word was considered so potent – and so precious – that documents were thought to be objects with spiritual significance. Think of the historical context: the Israelites had been commanded to take their sacred scrolls with them into battle, Egyptian scribes were exempt from military service and demanding physical jobs ('Be a scribe. It will save you from toil and protect you from every kind of work. It will spare you from bearing hoe and mattock, so that you will not have to carry a basket. It will keep you from plying the oar and spare you all manner of hardships');[8] in the Hebraic tradition, a woman accused of adultery can be made to consume 'the water of bitterness', including ink from a curse, where rinsed-off words were mixed with foul water.[9] In the Judaic tradition God *is* words, and from Plato we hear of a performance-enhancing mind drug: '"This invention, O king," said Theuth, "will make the Egyptians wiser and will improve their memories; for it is an elixir of memory and wisdom that I have discovered . . ."'[10]

To stimulate and secure the currency of words in Constantinople scriptoria sprang up around the city. One such, the St John Monastery, known as St John of Stoudios and founded in AD 453 or 462 in the Samatya district of modern Istanbul, is a sad ruin now; ivy, plastic bags and cat excrement decorate what was once a haven for the well-stocked mind. There are rumours of contentious plans to turn these tumbling bricks and stones into a functioning mosque. In its heyday there would have been a thousand monks here, styli scratching and fussing over their vellum and parchments. They catalogued and preserved, provided commentaries and censorship, work all made easier by the development of the more robust parchment codex in place of the roll. It was in Constantinople that the book review was invented. Scholars seem to have had access to books within a proto-lending-library system, and there were substantial libraries within the city walls. Thanks to Constantinople, we have the oldest complete manuscript of the *Iliad*, Aeschylus' dramas *Agamemnon* and *Eumenides*, and the works of Sophocles and Pindar. Fascinating scholia in the margins correct and improve: plucking work from the page 'useful for the reader . . . not just the learned',[11] as one Byzantine scholar put it. These were texts that were turned into manuals for contemporary living.

The children of Constantinople whose parents could afford it were given primary or secondary education. Lessons would take place in purpose-built schoolrooms in the city centre or in the courtyards of monasteries and churches. Constantinople was full of gardens – there are idyllic descriptions of lessons in the sylvan grounds of the Church of the Holy Apostles. Girls could be educated, but in the safety of their own homes. There were no fixed term-times – as ever in Constantinople, divination played a great part. We may picture keen parents walking through the city streets at night, anxiously scanning the stars to see if this was indeed an auspicious date for their beloved little Alexandros or Ioannis to start his schooling. Sometimes the church or state subsidised teachers who had been left out of pocket by families who had defaulted on their school fees. Teachers could occasionally be paid for their time in kind, in flour for example, or the cash equivalent of a modius of wheat. Children wrote on wax, or scratched out their lessons in mud dried over wood. With easy access to global resources the men and women of Constantinople had the opportunity to write on papyrus, then on parchment, then – accessing the latest technology developed first by China, then by the Arabs – on early forms of paper. But books were so expensive that generally texts had to be learnt by heart. The streets of Constantinople would have enjoyed the percussive sound of children's voices reciting plays, poetry and prayers out loud. Homer's *Iliad* and *Odyssey* were considered fundamental texts for both primary and secondary education. For the children who sat with the coast of Asia Minor in view, the tales of Troy were of course not legend but local history.[12]

Maintaining the totemic and tangible value of writing and ideas needed deliberate action. Towering thinkers and precocious talent were systematically imported to Constantinople because on 27 February AD 425, with great ambition and foresight, a school of higher education had been founded here. Building on the tradition for private higher education institutions in Athens, Alexandria, Antioch et al. (including the law school in Beirut, destroyed by earthquake), Theodosios II – later nicknamed Theodosios the Calligrapher because of his delight in manuscripts – established an institution that some call the University of Constantinople.[13] Theodosios II, born 'in the purple' in the Great Palace in the city (so an heir to the imperial throne physically birthed in a chamber decorated with porphyry marble and purple-draping silks) and proclaimed emperor within his first year, seems to have felt a passionate attachment to the city that raised him. He brought a love of learning to the heart of imperial power. Thirty-one professors were appointed to the university, each enjoying tax breaks and tasked with educating young men to do all that was necessary to help to run the complex Byzantine state bureaucracy. Some claim that the University of Constantinople was the first public higher-learning establishment in Europe. Here there were thirteen chairs in Latin and fifteen in Greek, with law, philosophy, medicine, arithmetic, geometry, astronomy, music, rhetoric all taught.[14] We recall the training young British boys were given in the classics in the nineteenth century to 'run an empire'. This was an approach pre-dated in Constantinople by close to 1,500 years.[15]

The possibilities of religious debate were energetically pursued on the city's streets, with Theodosios presiding over obdurate religious controversy. A commission was tasked with collecting from Byzantine territories legislation and edicts that postdated Constantine I's reign; these were then published in the *Codex Theodosianus* in AD 438. Inter-connecting vaulted chambers to store all this knowledge still exist under the hippodrome in present-day Istanbul. Where they were once tight with the smell of animal skin and ink, they are now empty – home to damp, to spiders and to rats.

Theodosios died in a riding accident while exercising his horse along one of his premier city's natural waterways, the banks of the River Lykos in AD 450. As a result, Vandal ambition only flourished.

In AD 468 Basiliskos of Constantinople was given command of a massive Roman force set up to expel the Vandals from North Africa. By the deadly use of fireships, the Vandals sank half the Roman fleet close to Cape Bon in modern Tunisia, causing the deaths or disappearance of 20,000 troops. This was one of the largest military operations in late antiquity and it had failed. Basiliskos fled back to Constantinople, licking his wounds, and hid out in Haghia Sophia. Disgraced, then banished, but refusing to give up, he eventually returned to Constantinople to rule for twenty-four months (it was on his watch that that disastrous fire ripped through the Great Palace and Library), only to find himself exiled once more by a rival, Zeno. Zeno wanted this pretender exterminated. Basiliskos begged that no blood should be shed and so he was abandoned, together with his wife and children, to die of thirst and exposure in a dry cistern in Cappadocia, 500 miles east of the city that he had wanted to control.

The same year, AD 476, when the last Roman Emperor of the West, Romulus Augustulus, was overturned by Odoacer, a Scirian, the imperial insignia were hastily evacuated under guard to Constantinople. After 800 years of success and influence Old Rome had simply run out of steam. Perhaps it was not just barbarians who were responsible for the fall of the Rome of Virgil, Nero and Caracalla, but in part the vigour, impact and psychological threat of her genetically modified child, Constantinople.

PART THREE

✤

THE NEW ROME

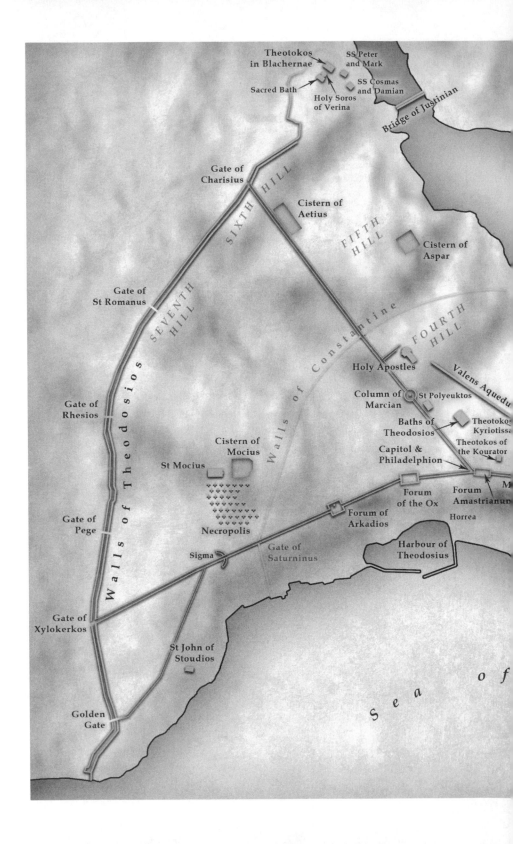

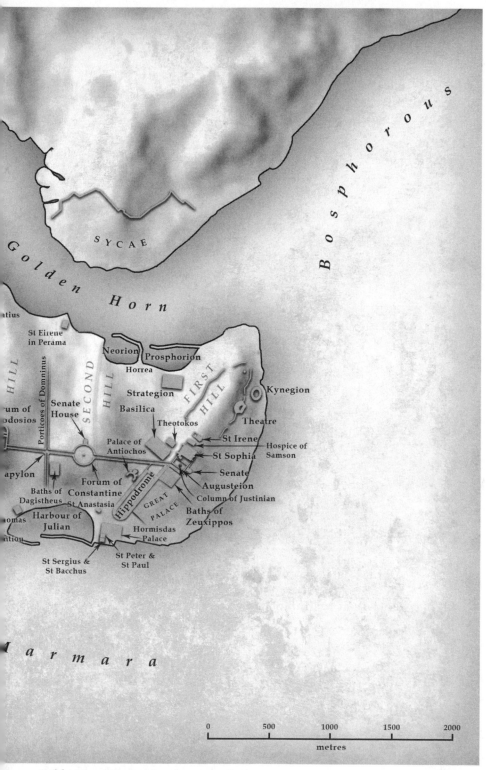

Golden Age Constantinople, c. AD 565

Within the map:

Bosphorous

Golden Horn

SYCAE

atius

St Eirene in Perama

HILL

Neorion
Prosphorion
Horrea

Porticoes of Domninus

um of
odosios

Senate House

SECOND HILL

FIRST HILL

Strategion

Basilica

Theotokos

Kynegion

Theatre

St Irene

Palace of Antiochos

St Sophia

Hospice of Samson

apylon

Senate

Augusteion

Forum of Constantine

Column of Justinian

Baths of Dagistheus

St Anastasia

Hippodrome

GREAT PALACE

Baths of Zeuxippos

Harbour of Julian

omas

Hormisdas Palace

ntiou

St Sergius & St Bacchus

St Peter & St Paul

Marmara

0   500   1000   1500   2000

metres

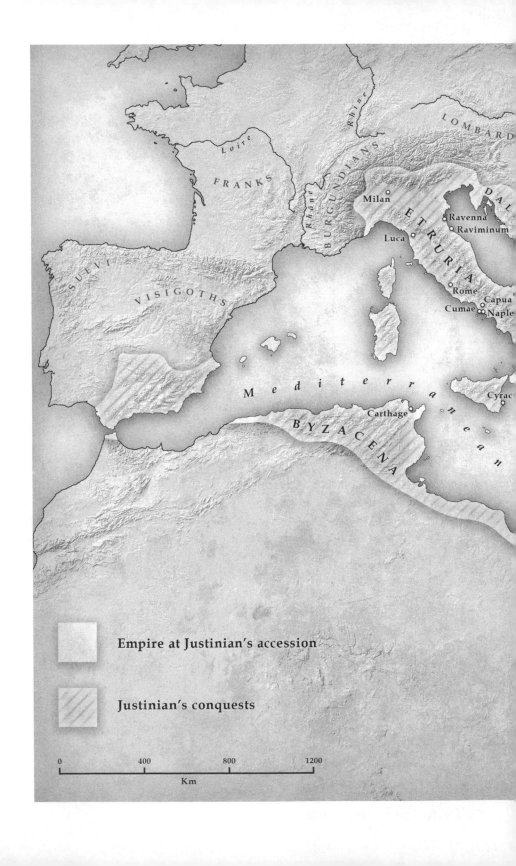

FRANKS

BURGUNDIANS

LOMBARD

Rhine

Rhône

Loire

SUEVI

VISIGOTHS

Milan

ETRURIA

Ravenna
Raviminum

DAL

Luca

Rome

Capua
Naples

Cumae

Mediterranean

Carthage

BYZACENA

Cyrac

Empire at Justinian's accession

Justinian's conquests

0   400   800   1200

Km

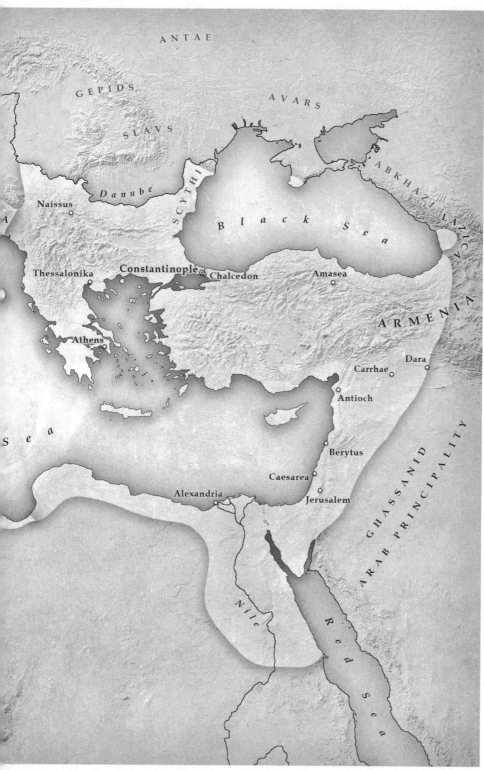

The Byzantine Empire at its greatest extent

CHAPTER 27

⊹

CITY OF THE MOTHER OF GOD

AD 431 ONWARDS

Mary the Theotokos, the holy ornament of all the universe, the un-
quenchable lamp, the crown of virginity, the sceptre, the container of the
uncontainable, mother and virgin.

ST CYRIL OF ALEXANDRIA, HOMILY AT THE COUNCIL OF EPHESUS[1]

The churches in the province of Asia send you greetings. Aquila and Priscilla greet you warmly in the Lord, and so does the church that meets at
their house.

I CORINTHIANS 16: 19 (NEW INTERNATIONAL VERSION)

On that little matchbox-sized reliquary – which was made in Constantinople close on a thousand years ago but was unknown to historians
until 2006 – along with sixteen men and a eunuch, there is one woman,
haloed with bright-blue enamel. The male figures pray to Christ and, as
she stands elegantly, her arms outstretched, also to her – to the Virgin
Mary.

There is a wonderful story concerning fifth-century Constantinople,
of a woman called Matrona. Matrona, we are told, was trapped in an
unhappy marriage. She resisted many temptations of the flesh and of
the spirit and instead expressed a kind of passionate desire for the city of
Constantinople – the city to which she would eventually travel in around
AD 472, disguised as a eunuch, to found a nunnery where she and her
sisters were allowed to wear the habits of male monks.[2] Matrona may be
flesh and blood or a literary conceit, but her existence on the page tells
us a great deal about the kudos of Constantinople for both women and
men in late antiquity. A few decades before, we also hear of one Melania,

an ascetic who became a wherry woman for sanctity – transporting holy relics across more than 1,000 miles to Constantinople and through Byzantine domains, territory ruled from 'The City' that was increasingly styling itself the true Holy Land.

In Melania's box of treasures we might have found the edge of a saint's cloak, the tears of Mary Magdalene, the thighbone of a martyr, perhaps even some drops of Christ's blood. From the fourth century onwards both the collection of relics and the journeys to wonder at them encouraged the phenomenon of pilgrimage – by all three sexes – in the Eastern Mediterranean and Middle East. The link between Jerusalem and Constantinople was strengthened by the press of footsteps pounding out a line between the city where Jesus flourished and the capital which understood itself to be the centre of his kingdom on earth.

Constantinople was a spiritual landscape where women were not invisible but evident. Following the Council of Nicaea in AD 325 and the first Council of Constantinople in 381 held in the Church of Haghia Eirene,³ two other Byzantine ports, Chalcedon and, a little further down the Asian coast, Ephesus, would host new debates – debates that would again determine the shape of men's and women's lives, not just then but now. Item one on the agenda in the fifth century was the nature of Jesus – was he mainly God, mainly man, or equally both? The discourses were precise, furious, divisive – an attempt to quantify the unquantifiable.⁴ An academic point around which these discussions flew was, logically, the nature of Jesus' mother. After bitter wrangling – which resulted in the expulsion from the city of the patriarch of Constantinople, Nestorios, and the triumph of Cyril of Alexandria (he who exacerbated hatred towards Hypatia in 415) – discourse dwindled to dogma. At Ephesus in 431 and then again in 449 and at Chalcedon in 451 it was declared that the Virgin Mary was not just the Mother of Christ – but Theotokos – the Bearer or the Mother of God.

In Christendom it would have been impossible for a woman to enjoy a greater role. Mary of Nazareth might get a mere sixteen mentions in the New Testament (thirty-two in the Qur'an), but soon her image would be inescapable, on icons, reliquaries and frescoes, and her name hymned in songs of praise across Constantinople and the vast territories that Constantinople was coming to control.

For the ancient, cosmopolitan trading city, the physical presence of a potent and quasi-divine woman was nothing new. In the Egyptian tradition of Isis, the goddess sits on a throne with her son Horus on her knee. There is certainly an Isis/Mary crossover. But in Anatolia there was more. There is a possibility that every time we appreciate an icon in an Orthodox church or a Marian statue in a Catholic church, we should imagine ourselves on the wind-buffeted hills above Hattusa, the ancient capital of the Hittite civilisation and today a fourteen-hour drive east of Constantinople. Since the Bronze Age, Anatolia had had a tradition of worshipping a sun goddess, the creator of all. This prehistoric deity, in four-millennia-old archaeological finds, is shown with a sun-burst behind her head and cradling a boy-child on her lap. Put these Early Bronze Age Anatolian images and icons of Mary and Jesus together and the iconography is startlingly similar. Mary is, in many different ways, a child of the East.

And now that Mary had been officially elevated to the position of Mother of the Divine, across the Byzantine Empire churches were being dedicated to Mary Theotokos. So it was that Mary was adored in the copper-making district of Constantinople, at a sanctuary over the spring of Blachernae, first built by Emperor Leo III in AD 473 to house the Holy Robe and the Maphorion – the Veil of the Mother of God – which

Anatolian sun goddess pendant, created c. 1400–1200 BC

he had brought to Constantinople; the church would later boast Mary's belt, supposedly added by Justinian I in the sixth century (the chapel was itself destroyed in 1434 in a fire said to have been started accidentally by noble children hunting pigeons).⁵ She was also adored in the shrine of the Virgin at the Zoodochos Pege, the Life-Holding or Life-Giving Spring – like Blachernae, still a place of Muslim worship today. Mary Theotokos was there too above Mount Sinai in Egypt's Sinai peninsula; and in Athens where the Parthenon Temple on the Acropolis was turned into Mary's Church. The names of two Byzantine bishops, Theodosios and Marinos, can still just be made out carved on the Parthenon's columns. Where the sun glares more harshly than it does in Istanbul, in Jerusalem, Mary's vast church of Nea was built to rival and to overshadow Solomon's Temple. The Byzantine Emperor Justin II established the feasts of Mary's Nativity and Dormition (her assumption into heaven). An image of Mary, believed to be *acheiropoietos* – not made by human hand, but taken from a portrait drawn by St Luke, was imported to Constantinople and copied again and again. An idea was becoming a cult.

The potency of Mary was entirely real to the people of Constantinople. Asking an inhabitant of the city from the fifth to the fifteenth century whether she or he believed in the might of Mary would have been like asking a Viking if he or she believed in the sea. And of course Mary's protecting power is still recognised across Greece. The Hodegetria football club based in the Piraeus was named for Mary when its leftist founders survived the Colonels' Junta of 1967–74, following, it was said, prayers to the Virgin. When a plague of grasshoppers scourged the island of Siphnos, all kinds of poisons and crop beatings were tried, but nothing could shift them. Then (the islanders eagerly relate), the icon of Mary from the Church of Chrysopigi – the Gold Spring – was carried around the fields, and the next morning a cloud appeared, a stain in the sky as the insects left en masse. On 15 August each year the Feast of the Dormition is observed, and the power of Mary the Mother of God is celebrated – whether in the form of an icon surrounded by song and carried by boat through the little harbour off the beach at Corfu, or the mass pilgrimage to Tinos, where, beseeching help for their loved ones, the faithful walk on their knees to kiss Mary's iconic face. Her icon is processed from the extraordinary church in Paros said to have been founded by Constantine the Great's mother Helena, and afterwards there is prodigious alcohol consumption; at the Panagia Erithiani in Chios the island delights in its unfeasibly lusty homemade fireworks. As one Eastern source put it, 'In place of that bitter fruit that Eve plucked from the tree, Mary gave mankind sweet fruit. And behold, the whole world enjoys the fruit of Mary. The virginal vine has borne a grape whose sweet wine has given comfort to those who mourn.'[6]

Meanwhile the role of women in Constantinople in physically support-ing and running house-churches – a phenomenon first attested by the New Testament stories of Priscilla – continued with a vengeance. When Gregory of Nazianzus, the future archbishop of Constantinople (whose remains were only returned to Istanbul from Rome in 2004, having been looted 800 years before by Latins during the AD 1204 Crusade), came into the city, his church was simply a villa owned by his cousin Theodosia. In the first 150 years of Christianity in Rome it has been estimated that half the city's churches were founded by women, and the tradition continued vigorously in New Rome.

While none of this tells us that there was female dominance in daily Byzantine life, it is perhaps no coincidence that the theological assertion that Mary was the Mother of God Himself, with the associated cultural landscape and attitudes on the streets, seems to have rubbed off on some women in the city – particularly the highest born. The exaltation of female potency was perhaps even engineered by them.[7] As will increas-ingly be seen, Byzantine empresses, their female courtiers and merchants' wives had defined, and in some cases unexpected, powers, influence and status.[8] In Constantinople there was a perfect storm of a pagan Eastern environment where female deities had real heft, combined with Roman legal attitudes to the rights of women and now this sublime role model in Orthodox Christian theology – of the Virgin Mary being the bearer of the Godhead. As the fourth-century Ephrem the Syrian put it, 'Through Eve, the beautiful and desirable glory of men was extinguished; but it has revived through Mary.'[9]

We must not be ahistorical, naturally there was still prejudice. One of Constantinople's favourite children, the archbishop John Chrysostom, would opine of visible women in the city that it would be better to cover oneself with filth than to watch them cavort in the theatre. Brought up by a pagan mother in Antioch but one of Constantine the Great's first-generation Christians, and set to become one of the most influential of

the Church Fathers, John Chrysostom espoused a simple, back-to-basics
kind of Christianity:

> Do not pay him homage in the temple clad in silk, only then to neglect
> him outside where he is cold and ill-clad. He who said: 'This is my
> body' is the same who said: 'You saw me hungry and you gave me no
> food,' and 'Whatever you did to the least of my brothers you did also
> to me' . . . What good is it if the Eucharistic table is overloaded with
> golden chalices when your brother is dying of hunger?[10]

Chrysostom (which means Golden Mouth) was thus named because
of his supreme ability to whip up a crowd. When that silver statue of
Empress Eudoxia was erected, he gave the people of the city a thorough
tongue-lashing for celebrating in a pagan manner, reminiscent (to him)
of Salome's wild dancing to secure the head of John the Baptist. What
chance could there be for real equity and equality in Constantinople
when women were discouraged from exercising their bodies and, in
many cases, their minds when they were still given half-rations as they
had been across much of the classical world; when Eve's sin hovered as a
cancer-shadow and when, in the middle of the fourth century AD, this
was the kind of opinion trumpeted from pulpits: 'What else is woman
but a foe to friendship, an inescapable punishment, a necessary evil – a
natural temptation, a desirable calamity, a domestic danger, a detestable
detriment, an evil nature painted with fair colours?'[11] John Chrysostom was so popular that, when he was exiled to Cappadocia and then
to the Caucasian edge of the Black Sea, the people of Constantinople
rioted. Bellowing their rage outside the Bronze Gates of the palace at
the loss of their clever cleric, they started a fire in the city that destroyed the Haghia Sophia and the Senate House. And at the very time
that Mary was being elevated to the status of the Mother of God in
Constantinople, in the West the ideas of St Augustine on original sin
would be twisted to imply that lust and its consequences were the fault
of woman, ensuring for the female of the species pain and suffering for
centuries.

Around this time we also hear of the first casual mention of a *monachos*
– a monk – an idea inspired by the Jewish (Essene) and Buddhist traditions that had spread along the Silk Roads. All-male monasteries

developed, and what has been called the study-hall syndrome crept into Christendom. Literate male clerics could now decide what was and what was not canonical, and slowly – possibly with unconscious bias – they wrote women out of scriptures, from other religious texts and increasingly from the religious experience. As a woman was being promoted theologically, on the ground deaconesses were less and less visible and male bishops were extending their territorial power.[12]

In a description by one bishop at the Third Ecumenical Council of the perfect Marian icon from Constantinople we can also perhaps read a tick-list of the attributes of the ideal, Constantinopolitan woman:

The Virgin, not casting her eyes to any inappropriate view, not dishonouring her natural beauty by covering colours, not sheathing her cheeks with the fake colour of the Phoenicians, not making conspicuous her honourable head by adding vain ornaments, not making her neck glitter by adding jewellery made of precious stones, not allowing her hands and her feet to be spoiled by golden chains . . . but full of the smell of the Holy Spirit, being dressed by the Holy Grace as with a garment, keeping the thought of God in her soul, having God as a wreath over her heart, her eyes shining of holiness . . . her lips dripping wax, beautiful in her way of walking, even more beautiful in her manners and so to speak, all good.[13]

So it would be entirely foolish to imagine the city as some kind of proto-feminist wonderland. But as a Christian woman living in the city, you were not living in the past. You are the past – living in the present.

Forty miles west of Istanbul there is a neglected monument. For 500 years, ever since Augustus defined the extent of empire, Rome's defensible natural boundary of the Danube had pretty much held; but then in AD 493, the Byzantine Emperor Anastasios, taking his cue perhaps from the ancient Athenians, built Constantinople's 'Long Walls', a massive fortification stretching from the Sea of Marmara to the Black Sea. Overgrown, collapsing stretches of these defences still stand in a 40-mile ring outside the city. Constantinople was, increasingly, resembling one of the epic cities, memorialised in ancient poetry and biblical texts – like Troy, Jericho, Babylon, cities protected by giant fortifications with a narrative and a reputation that had become legendary, whose stories the city's scribes so assiduously preserved.[14]

And now in Constantinople itself we will meet two of its most splendidly dramatic characters, who will both play the social, theological and political cards dealt to them to their very best advantage, and to the advantage of the city that was their home. One was a peasant turned emperor; the other was his wife, who in her own journey from prostitute to empress managed to combine the attributes of both angel and whore.

CHAPTER 28

THE GOLDEN AGE

AD 482–565

Carry my thought to that imperialism –
to those great honours that befell our race
in its illustrious Byzantinism.

C. P. CAVAFY, 'IN CHURCH'[1]

The future Byzantine Emperor Justinian I was born in AD 482 in Illyria in
the rolling hills around Tauresium,[2] which today sits quietly to the north
of the country whose name is for some FYROM, for some Macedonia.[3]
This is a part of the world where men still amble slowly down roads
carrying billhooks and scythes. The site of Tauresium is bucolic, deserted.
But 1,500 years ago this was a region with a reputation for birthing ferocious fighters. Justin, Justinian's uncle by marriage (to a slave girl whom
Justin bought and subsequently wed), had left behind his unpromising
career tending pigs and, fleeing rampaging barbarians, followed the call
to the capital Constantinople, where he made a good name for himself as
an upwardly mobile soldier, as a general and then as commander of the
imperial bodyguard, the *comes excubitorum* (literally an out-of-bed man).
He soon summoned his nephew Justinian to join him so that the rough
young man might better himself in the capital. The military training and
mind-training on offer in Constantinople paid off. Justinian's destiny did
not lie in the fields. In the twenty-first-century capital city of Skopje not
far from Justinian's birthplace, the peasant-turned-Roman Emperor has
recently been honoured with a monumental statue, 16 feet tall, enthroned,
the white marble creation costing north of a million euros. Alongside
Mother Teresa and Alexander the Great, Justinian ranks as one of the
region's greatest success stories.

Taught theology and law in the seminaries of Constantinople, Justinian was quickly embraced by the sentinels, the crack squad charged with guarding the Emperor. It was probably here that the young Justinian met another Illyrian in the city, a scrapping fighter called Belisarios. Together with Belisarios, Justinian would increase Constantinople's territories by 45 per cent to make his adopted city the centre of the greatest empire in the known world. It may be Belisarios that we see to the right of Justinian in the famous mosaic portraits in the north-eastern Italian city of Ravenna – the city that the pair reconquered in AD 540.[4] Justinian, his wife-to-be Theodora and Belisarios seemed to have matched talent with luck to enjoy real, lasting influence on both their age and our own.

Opportunity had come knocking. On the death of Emperor Anastasios, Uncle Justin, illiterate, nearing seventy, was acclaimed emperor. The ex-swineherd, who had already given his energetic, bright, capable nephew his own name, seems to have allowed his protégé a dry-run at power. In effect, from AD 520, the two ruled jointly; hints in the sources suggest that Justin became senile towards the end of his life and that it was Justinian who controlled Constantinople and her empire in all but name.

On 1 April AD 527 the Illyrian soldier was officially named Justin's successor. When Justinian was acclaimed emperor he made his way in through Constantinople's Golden Gate, down the processional route of the Mese, bordered originally with those wide vegetable gardens – the stuff of life of the city – and then with canopied walkways and sculptures (canopies and shops are still here, selling everything from apple tea to diamond-studded handguns). The shouts of acclamation for Constantinople's new ruler would have bounced off the marble colonnades and the bronze statuary lining the processional way. And one in the city in particular must have listened to this brouhaha with great pleasure. Three years before, a rather extraordinary woman had moved into Justinian's palace apartments to share his bed, and just three days after his investiture Justinian and his new wife, his showgirl-bride Theodora, were crowned together as joint emperor and empress.

Enjoying a flurry of revived interest in the twenty-first century, Empress Theodora deserves every moment of her late-found fame. Now honoured as a saint by the Greek Orthodox Church, this player in Constantinople's history has not been universally loved: 'This degenerate

The only surviving image of Empress Theodora (middle) can be found in the mosaics of Basilica San Vitale in Ravenna, completed c. AD 548

woman [Theodora] was another Eve who heeded the serpent. She was a denizen of the Abyss and mistress of Demons. It was she who, drawn by a satanic spirit and roused by diabolic rage, spitefully overthrew a peace redeemed by the blood of martyrs,' wrote Cardinal Baronius.[5] Our most detailed source for Theodora's life is a lascivious, spittle-flecked diatribe, a *Secret History* written by our key source for Justinian and Theodora's reign, Procopius (Procopius would write both hagiographies and damnations of the imperial couple and their works). Clearly gorged with literary and rhetorical tropes, Procopius' account has to be taken with a large amphora of salt – but many of the details ring true both for the age and as a backstory to the remarkable life of this girl from Constantinople.[6]

The Greek patriarch today talks of Theodora sympathetically, as one of the most influential characters in Orthodox Christianity's history and as having suffered a 'troubled childhood' in Constantinople. In truth, in her own lifetime, the young Theodora was both socially reviled – not even reaching the lowest rung of the social ladder – and lucky. Her mother was described as an 'actress-dancer' – a polite way of saying a prostitute – and her father was a bear-tamer and baiter. The street-performer pair seem to have been attached to one of the competitive factions of chariot-racers in the hippodrome, the Greens. Once her father had died and the family no longer enjoyed the Greens' protection, Theodora and her two sisters were wreathed in garlands by their mother, walked through the small lanes and subterranean corridors in the centre of the city and presented to the Blues. Without the Blues' say-so, this little family would have found it impossible to survive on Constantinople's streets.

It is hard to overstate how critically important these rival sporting factions were to the stability of Byzantium. It was the Greens and Blues, we should recall, who had competed to rebuild Theodosios' earthquake-wrecked walls. The hippodrome sat squarely by the corridors of power – imagine Wembley stadium sandwiched between 10 Downing Street and Buckingham Palace. The rival factions (Greens, Blues, Reds and Whites), the equivalent of tribes or gangs, would congregate here to roar their approval on the accession of a new ruler and parade out of the city to meet emperors returning from military campaigns. Byzantium's emperors had built an elaborate enclosed walkway which connected the palace to the hippodrome's southern side. The walkway exited at a protected viewing platform, the *kathisma*, and from this glorified balcony New Rome's Emperor, his family and his closest advisers would hear complaints or look out and hope that they inspired awe. When bread or water ran low, when an injustice was perceived, the factions took their complaint straight to the hippodrome. Sport, spectacle and a full belly were the glue that held this civic mass together – people with a raw, demotic power whose favour could carry or crush an emperor.

Coming as a kind of pleasure-package with her parents and sisters, as a girl Theodora performed acrobatic tricks and erotic dances in and around the hippodrome – part of the fringe of shows, spectacles and penny theatricals that accompanied the games. It was said by contemporary chroniclers that one of Theodora's most popular turns was a re-enactment of the story of Leda (the mother of Helen of Troy) and the Swan (Zeus in disguise). The Greek myth went that Zeus was so enraptured with Queen Leda when he espied her bathing by the banks of the River Euro-tas that he turned himself into a swan so that he could ravish the Spartan

Queen. Theodora, as Leda, would leave a trail of grain up on to (some said into) her body, which the 'swan' (in Constantinople in fact a goose) then eagerly consumed. The Empress's detractors delighted in memori-alising the fact that Theodora's services were eagerly sought out for anal intercourse, as both an active and a passive partner. As a child and as an adolescent woman Theodora would have been considered dirt, but she was, physically, right at the heart of human affairs in a burgeoning city in interesting times.

Theodora was also, obviously, wildly attractive. Born in either Cyprus or Syria, as a teenager – already the mother of a young girl and with a history of abortions – she left Constantinople as the companion of a Syrian official, the governor of Libya Pentapolis. The two travelled to North Africa, where, after four years of maltreatment, she found herself abandoned by the Byzantine official, her meal-ticket revoked. A dis-carded mistress, on the road, was as wretched as things could get in the sixth century. In the declarations of a number of the Church Fathers this was a creature to be cast out by Christendom. Theodora tried to find her way back to the mother city, making ends meet as a prostitute, and the only people to give the twenty-year-old reject shelter were a group of Christians in the city of Alexandria. That random act of kindness was epoch-forming.

Theodora had grown up in a city that was rapidly changing. Half a century before, we will recall, at the Christian Councils of Ephesus and then Chalcedon a remarkable thing had happened to another young girl. Bishops from across Christendom had been summoned to the buzzing Ephesian port (significantly, itself once sacred to Artemis, the virgin goddess of childbirth). They had walked along the wide marble streets, founded by Greeks, rebuilt by the Old Romans, and would have spent the nights cheek by jowl with the prosperous merchants who lived in Ephesus and crammed their homes with the high-end goods that are now turning up in digs – cluster-drop gold earrings, dazzling marble wall-coverings, delicate frescoes. After fierce theological debate it had been decided in this religiously freighted, premier city that Mary, a slip of a girl from Nazareth, was not just the Mother of Christ, but Theotokos, the very Mother of God. Spiritually, psychologically, socially, culturally, this was an extraordinary shift. Constantinople embraced Mary's promotion with gusto.

Theodora would have witnessed the birth of a new tradition in her home town; vast icons of Mary, in times of both trouble and triumph, were paraded around Constantinople. These were believed to project a kind of Christian force-field that could protect the city's walls and her inhabitants. Mosaic mounted on wood, each would have taken four men to carry. Whether it was that early impression – a sublime, glinting, golden girl rocking her way through the hilly streets of Constantinople, borne on the backs of sweating men – or the very real rhetoric of Christ welcoming in the weak and fallen women, or indeed the kindness of theologically engaged strangers in her hour of need, Theodora seems to have developed a ferocious Christian faith.

Not that this prevented her from sleeping with men for their secrets. Justinian was widening his power-base, and word was out that he wanted a web of informants across his vast territory. Falling in with a female spy called Macedonia in Antioch,[7] Theodora seemed to have accessed pillow talk of the most productive kind. She made her way back to her home town of Constantinople and, almost certainly by systematically bedding her way to the top as well as by gaining a reputation as the sharpest of information-merchants, she managed somehow to get the attention of Justinian. We can only imagine how Theodora, the showgirl, made her mark. Whatever her method, it must have been impressive.

Around AD 524 the chubby-faced, curly-haired, popular, effective and ever more powerful boy from Illyria had the laws of the land changed so that he could marry Theodora. With Justinian named as Justin's heir in 526, the prostitute could now become empress.

Justinian described Theodora as 'Our most reverend partner, granted Us by God'[8] (an opinion that would eventually earn him the bitterness of our two key sources for their marriage, Procopius and the Syriac John of Ephesus). We hear that 'neither did anything apart from the other to the end of their joint lives',[9] and we are told again of 'the extraordinary love which the Emperor felt for her'.[10] At a typical imperial wedding, officials, accompanied by an entire orchestra, would make their way through the corridors of Constantinople's Great Palace. Carrying perfumed towels they would prepare the Empress-to-be, offering her pomegranates and porphyry stone studded with jewels. Then flanked by senators the bride would be delivered into the arms of her Emperor. Justinian was writing Theodora into a collective urban myth that credited the Empress with sustaining the health and the fertility of the imperial office and thus of the city and the empire itself. This was no mere social elevation; by marrying Justinian, Theodora moved from being a mere mortal to a semi-sublime figure.

Justinian was invested in the Triclinium of the Nineteen Couches,[11] a Roman-style investiture hall.[12] Three days later on Easter Sunday, since Theodora had also been named as his successor, the two were acclaimed in a ceremony saturated with religious symbolism,[13] with the patriarch in attendance. The wording of the ceremony leaves one in no doubt as to the massive significance of this moment: 'You were selected by divine decree for the security and exaltation of the universe; you were joined to the purple by God's will. Almighty God has blessed you and crowned you with his own hand.'[14] Theodora, the guttersnipe, would now be Augusta, the ruler of an empire and of Christendom.

Thrumming with opportunity, the peasant farmer and the prostitute set about making their mark. In Egypt their names were carved into the wooden beams of the church on Mount Sinai, Justinian built a bridge across the Golden Horn joining the settlement of Sykai, modern-day Galata, to Constantinople,[15] and granaries were raised across the island of Tenedos (where it was said in epic works of poetry that Greek troops had hidden during the Trojan War to trick the Trojans into taking the wooden horse into their city). Ships carrying grain from Egypt needed a fair breeze to push them through the Hellespont to Constantinople. Now if a grain ship found itself waiting, becalmed in the Mediterranean, it would unload at Tenedos and make another trip back to Egypt: it was labour intensive, but guaranteed that an ill wind could not bring starvation to the city. A mirror city below street level was developed; 7,000 slaves worked to dig out cisterns underground, including the Basilica Cistern, an inverted cathedral supported by columns and sculptures stolen from monuments once in the sun, which alone held 22 million gallons of water to ensure that the city would not die of thirst, just as it would no longer die of hunger.

Justinian and Theodora delighted in their meritocratic luck and they indulged it with all the passion of the parvenu. Courtiers – even visiting ambassadors – could no longer just genuflect, but had to prostrate themselves fully in the imperial presence, pressing their foreheads to the floor in front of the husband-and-wife potentates. Senators were allowed the privilege of brushing the imperial feet with their lips.

Theodora frequently travelled across the Bosphorus or the Sea of Marmara to Asia. This young woman had once fled the continent, abused, rejected, a has-been whore. In AD 529 she returned at the head of an imperial train to Pythion (modern-day Yalova, an early colony of Byzantion and where Atatürk in more recent times revived the passion for bathing in the hot springs), with a retinue of 4,000; then she moved on to the high, green hills of Prousa (modern-day Bursa), where her own colourful bathhouse is still in use. A little ironically, Theodora's bath in Bursa now welcomes only men; as a woman one is allowed the merest glimpse of the empress's sixth-century bathing rooms before one enters a hammam in the later, rather splendid Ottoman additions. (Theodora's frequent visits to the baths might in fact have been an attempt to alleviate the symptoms of cancer that would kill her when she was only forty-eight.)[16] But still, it is remarkable to think of this eye-flashing upstart, bathing in the searingly hot natural mineral water here, her bodyguards and maids of honour all around, revelling in the knowledge that, with all the odds stacked against her, she had won.

And what a triumph to enjoy: Justinian's respect for Theodora was unshakeable. They had their religious differences: Theodora was a passionate monophysite (sometimes known as a miaphysite), believing that Jesus Christ was either wholly divine or that his nature was a total synthesis of the mortal and the divine – perhaps persuaded by her time with those salvational Christians in Alexandria and Antioch. She was opposed to a number of the assertions of the Council of Chalcedon of AD 451, while Justinian confirmed the Chalcedon doctrine. Although the rest of the world keenly felt this Chalcedonian split between Byzantine and Syriac orthodoxy, at home in their Great Palace overlooking the sea at Constantinople the two seemed to have rubbed along and positively enjoyed the sparks they created.[17]

Both exploited their role as God's earthly representatives with great seriousness. The Council which was held in Chalcedon in AD 451, the ancient 'City of the Blind', a short boat ride from the heart of Constantinople, concluded with its Chalcedonian Definition – an affirmation still accepted by the majority of the Catholic, Protestant and Greek and Russian Orthodox worlds but one which nourished divisions in Christianity that still play out today. Chalcedon declared that Christ was of

two natures, of equal substance, Godhead and manhood. Syrian, Armenian Apostolic, Coptic, Ethiopian, Eritrean and the Indian Orthodox
churches all rejected and still reject the doctrinal definition. The imperial
couple were as aware of the importance of the temperature prevailing in
theological debate in their time as we are now. It was said that Theodora
was 'fervent in zeal' and that Justinian too sent out messages about the
dispute with 'great zeal'. Justinian summoned bishops to Constantinople
to try to force them to recant what he deemed to be unorthodox thought.
Justinian is one of the first Roman emperors depicted on coins wielding a
cross (examples of which have turned up as far afield as India) and bishops
were sent out to proselytise in the Yemen, Syria, in Arabia to Ghassanid
Arabs, in Caria, Phrygia, Lydia and Lower Nubia.[18] Theodora sent out
her own missions too. There was a race between husband and wife to save
souls and to save them in the right way – Theodora's man for example
rushing to convert Silko, the King of the Nobatai, and his court.[19] Back at
home some theatres were closed down, eradicating the opportunities that
men and women had to get together for a shared, positive experience and
sparking a frustration that would soon come home to roost at Justinian
and Theodora's door.

The pretty little Church of Sts Sergios and Bacchos, also known as
Little Haghia Sophia, just south of the hippodrome built in honour of
two Syrian soldier-saint-heroes, was extended to become a monastery and
place of refuge for monophysites from AD 531.[20] It was not just Christ who
was adored here, but Theodora – witness the inscription on the entabla-
ture, still starkly visible above the heads of the muezzin and his faithful
congregation within what is now a mosque. This besought St Sergios 'in
all things [to] guard the rule of the sleepless sovereign and increase the
power of the God-crowned Theodora whose mind is adorned with piety,
whose constant toil lies in unsparing efforts to nourish the destitute'.
The Empress also garnered plaudits from others who were persecuted:
John of Ephesus refers to 'The Christ-loving Theodora, who was perhaps appointed queen by God to be a support for the persecuted against
the cruelty of the times . . . supplying them with provisions and liberal
allowances'.[21]

Once it became clear how much Justinian would allow her to do, it
seems there was no stopping Theodora. The palace became a seedbed
for the monophysite cause. In her palace quarters she protected one

recalcitrant patriarch for a full twelve years. Justinian's own apartments in the Palace of Hormisdas next to the Great Palace came to shelter 500 clergy and monks. There are accounts of state rooms being divided up into cells with curtains, matting and planks. Ascetics and religious men from Constantinople as well as from 'Syria and Armenia, Cappadocia and Cilicia, Isauria and Lycaonia, Asia and Alexandria' were all welcomed here. Women and children turned up for services in such numbers that on one occasion the floor gave way.[22]

Justinian and Theodora's time in power was also marked by the number of refugees they welcomed in to Constantinople. Struggling, homeless, stateless travellers came from East and West fleeing from the Persian and 'barbarian' troubles. Many arrived displaced from the Danubian and Gothic provinces by Huns and Goths; victims of Vandal atrocities had had their tongues cut out. The imperial pair built a hospice for refugees. The city was starting to build her reputation, which she still holds today, as a place of refuge. In AD 539 the holder of a new position, the *quaestor*, would ascertain from foreigners entering Constantinople their origins, identity and purpose. This refugee service seems to have worked better than the one operating in Istanbul at the time of writing this chapter in 2015, when out of my hotel window listless Syrian refugees can be seen lying as though dead on the sides of inner-city roads and trunk-route intersections.

Theodora also did more than most for her fellow women. Husbands now had to get the consent of their wives (twice) before taking on debt. Families had to return dowries to a widow. Men were charged more often with rape, their punishments increasingly severe. There were moves to stop girls as young as ten being tempted with the promise of food and clothes and then trafficked. Even in this, Theodora seems to have had Justinian's support. The Emperor enthusiastically quoted St Paul: 'in the service of God there is no male or female, nor freeman nor slave'.[23] And again: '[the previous law] did not take into account the weakness of women, nor that the husband enjoys their body, substance and entire life . . . who does not pity them for their services to their husbands, the danger of childbirth, and indeed the bringing into life of children. . .?'[24] Theodora founded a monastery for ex-prostitutes in a converted palace on the Asian shore where a military school (closed following the 2016 attempted coup) now stands, furnishing it with beautiful buildings that would be a 'consolation' to women and calling it Metanoia (Repentance).[25]

But even here Procopius managed to turn the enterprise against Theodora:

> But Theodora also concerned herself to devise punishments for sins against the body. Harlots, for instance, to the number of more than five hundred who plied their trade in the midst of the market-place at the rate of three obols – just enough to live on – she gathered together, and sending them over to the opposite mainland she confined them in the Convent of Repentance, as it is called, trying there to compel them to adopt a new manner of life. And some of them threw themselves down from a height at night and thus escaped the unwelcome transformation.[26]

Theodora and Justinian's (apparently joint) programme of social reform and justice must have been genuinely thrilling, erotic in the ancient Greek sense of the word, ambitious, zesty, rewarding.[27] A passing reference to Theodora turning serious issues into 'laughing matters'[28] has been used to imply that she never quite matched up to the opportunities in front of her – you can take the erotic dancer out of the hippodrome but you can't take the erotic out of the girl. But for me the arriviste seems intoxicated with possibility. This was going to be a partnership at once intensely carnal and intensely spiritual – a partnership that would, for good and for bad, have a material impact on the city of Constantinople.

CHAPTER 29

EARTHQUAKES AND FIRES

AD 532

The worthless voices of the people should not be listened to. Nor is it right
to give credence to their voices when they demand either that the guilty
should be acquitted or that the innocent should be condemned.

DIOCLETIAN, INJUNCTION CONTAINED WITHIN JUSTINIAN'S CODE,
PUBLISHED THREE YEARS BEFORE THE NIKA RIOTS[1]

uninhabitable because of dust, smoke and the stench of materials being
reduced to ashes, striking pathetic dread in those who beheld it.

JOHN THE LYDIAN, *ON OFFICES*, DESCRIBING THE SCENE
IN CONSTANTINOPLE AFTER THE RIOTS[2]

Istanbul is well designed for rioting. Roman squares and wide public
spaces encourage large gatherings; medieval street systems allow protesters to slip away if the mood of the authorities turns ugly. To me, caught
up in the Gezi Park/Taksim Square riots of 2013 in central Istanbul this
was glaringly apparent. Protesters poured in – and then the lucky ones
who could melted away down backstreets as the water cannon and tear
gas arrived. Overturned cars are horribly compelling, an incontrovertible
demonstration of the 'world turned upside down'. Above these inverted,
burnt-out carcasses, encircled by dogged dissentients and opportune glue-
sniffers every morning after the nights of conflict, someone had written
on a broken shop window a graffito: 'Byzantium – Constantinople – Istanbul – is ours!' The state clampdown, the destruction and the looting
here in 2013 left hanging in the air not just the acrid taste of carbon
but questions about social order and freedom of expression. Gezi Park
in 2013 echoed another epoch-defining event 1,500 years before. Even a

dispersing thunderstorm in the twenty-first century recalled this, one of the most impactful demonstrations of public action in the story of the city – the great Nika riots of AD 532.[3]

The passions of the racetrack in Constantinople had always run high. On the face of it the Nika riots were protests sparked by those charioteering factions, in particular the Blues and Greens, who massed together in the hippodrome and ferociously sustained their bonds across classes, rank and wealth, as urban tribes. Identified by their extravagantly billowing coloured sleeves these were the P – the *populus* – in the new SPQR. Typically these sporting teams worked against one another (at the beginning of the sixth century AD the Greens had killed 3,000 Blues in the theatre of Constantinople);[4] only on the rarest occasions had they worked as one. Beneath the curved end of the hippodrome – in through an ivy-covered metal door, past dripping steps and ghostly pigeons, with broken stone crunching underfoot – one can access the heady place where the chief charioteers met to plan tactics and to get their racing teams battle-fit.[5] A number of grievances and beliefs pushed people into one faction or another: loyalty to your *deme* (the base unit of the city), political frustration, theological anxiety, business networks.

The flashpoint for the Nika riots – on a day which should have seen the people celebrating Constantine's establishment of the New Rome – seems to have been taxation and unpopular legal reforms. Justinian had inherited a draining tussle with the Persians in the East and to pay for his military campaigns taxes had been raised. Initial success, victory under the command of Belisarios, was followed by humiliating, expensive defeat. From the Caucasus to the Danube, populations and soldiers were jumpy; news of trouble on both eastern and western borders galloped back to the city. A series of smaller riots had broken out. Seven men had been condemned to death but two of those, at the very point of hanging, had pretty miraculously escaped when the hangman's scaffold broke. Rushed away by the crowd and then scooped up by sympathetic monks – one loyal to the Greens and one to the Blues – the two malcontent protesters were then barricaded into the Church of St Laurentius in the Petrion (also know as Plateia)[6] district of the city.

Typically Constantinople's charioteering factions maintained a life-defining rivalry; quixotically, they now united, yelling for Christian mercy. Blues and Greens alike tore back to the hippodrome – the space where the Emperor and his people could meet, often at the summons of one or the other – belting out a new cry: 'Long Live the humane Greens and Blues!' Justinian failed to appear and, despite the biting chill of an Istanbul January, passions ran high. The first bout of serious rioting detonated.

From the willing plebeian consumers of the bread-and-circus affairs of the hippodrome right up to the senators, all were involved. We have to ask ourselves whether this was the raw courage of *hoi polloi*, or whether disgruntled senators saw an opportunity to fan the flames of discontent – less a revolution, more of an opportunistic coup. Constantinople's leaders were men who held ranks such as *clarissimus, spectabilis, illustris, gloriosus* and even *gloriosissimus*. Constantinople's leading families had efficiently climbed the social ladder after they were first brought in by Constantine as 'new men'. Justinian, do not forget, was demonstrably of peasant stock. Many in the Senate, we know, resented his demotic roots and his devotion to a dirty street-dancer. Ironically, at the time of the riots, a number of his fiercest aristocratic critics were taking shelter with him in the palace – including perhaps one of our greatest sources for the event, Procopius.

The rioters surrounded the Praetorium, burning it, almost certainly effecting the release of the prisoners within. Justinian then tried carrot rather than stick, choosing with imperial beneficence to continue with the games on the morning of Wednesday 14 January. The rioters were not to be so easily bought and – instead of lighting up the hippodrome with their pleasure – they put it to the torch. Belisarios was sent out to try to contain the discontent, and Justinian – in desperation, one suspects – made some concessions. His unpopular administrators – Tribonian who had been so influential in drawing up Justinian's Law Code, Eudaemon who had arrested the original malcontents and the wily cleric operator John the Cappadocian – were hung out to dry.[7]

On Friday 16 January, as the fires spread to the old Church of Haghia Sophia, the Emperor realised he was out of his depth and summoned to the city the equivalent of stormtroopers – a unit of Goths to suppress the violence. The following night he expelled two of the city's aristocrats, Hypatios and Pompey, from the palace. They promptly went on to rabble-rouse the crowd and to offer a viable alternative as men who could seize power. This expulsion was an odd move, and no historian has satisfyingly deconstructed the rationale. Was Justinian simply resentful? Hoping the posh-boys Hypatios and Pompey would be torn limb from limb? Was it a blind moment of fury and score-settling? Calculating double-think, offering up a focal point so that protesters could be corralled into one spot and then be massacred?

Whatever the motivation, the following morning Justinian's mood seems to have softened. The Emperor emerged once again above the hippodrome to address the murmuring crowds and swore on a copy of the Gospels that this time he would listen to the people's demands and pardon the rioters. Kind words – but they were having none of it.

The Greens and the Blues, together, proclaimed Hypatios – a nephew of Emperor Anastasios I – the true heir to the imperial throne. On 18 January, he was bedecked with a golden necklace at the *kathisma* and the crowd hailed him as emperor: multi-dimensional chaos ensued. Justinian sealed the *kathisma*'s exit into the palace and vanished.

Much of the city was by now in flames, and a hastily convened council of the uprisers debated whether or not to attack the palace itself. Justinian was prepared to take his money and to fly – just as Prime Minister Erdoğan hunkered down in Morocco while Gezi Park was burning in 2013. Perhaps, as with Erdoğan, absence appealed as it put a distance between Justinian and the violence which could then be claimed to be authorised by another. An escape route was easy to arrange, via the sea gate of the Palace of Bucoleon, whose lintel is just visible on the overgrown slopes that lead down to the Sea of Marmara, and which serviced the highest-ranking courtiers. Boats were ready and waiting. Then Theodora stepped up, showing, according to her biographer Procopius, both spectacular grit and an impressive knowledge of ancient rhetoric:

I consider that flight, even if it leads to safety, is especially wrong at this juncture. For just as it is impossible for a man who has come to the light not to die as well, it is intolerable for one who has been an emperor to be a fugitive. May I never be without this purple, and may I not live on that day when those who meet me do not address me as mistress. If you now want to save yourself, Emperor, there is no problem. For we have money, and the sea and the boats are here. But consider the possibility that after you've been saved you might not happily exchange that safety for death. A certain ancient saying appeals to me that royalty is a good funeral shroud.[8]

I have recited this extraordinary speech overlooking the current archaeological digs that are, with painstaking slowness, revealing Justinian and
Theodora's Great Palace just behind the Four Seasons Hotel in Sultanahmet. It is hard not to be roused by those big, bold words, to feel the
passion *in extremis*; but Procopius doubtless preserved them for history
as an insult. This full-blooded, unfeminine force, low-born Theodora,
like the riots themselves, was – he cleverly implies – an inversion of the
natural order. A good Greco-Roman woman was not meant to speak out
in public, and woe betide any man who listened to her if she did. Theodora cited the Athenian author Isokrates. Procopius retranslates the key
word as royalty, but the original passage, which would have been familiar
to a number of those well-educated Constantinopolitans, referred not
to a king but to a tyrant. Written up with hindsight, the messy end of
the riot, ordered by Emperor-cum-tyrant Justinian, was therefore being
memorialised as Theodora's fault.[9]

But what followed was a bloodbath. Justinian, apparently persuaded to
stay by his scrapping street-fighter wife, surrounded the charred hippodrome where the crowds were still massed and calling for a coup, ordered
his troops to attack. The protesters were in large part unarmed. Imperial
troops with the help of the Goth soldiers commanded by Belisarios and
Hunnish troops under Moundos, the grandson of Attila, killed some
30,000 to 50,000 on a single day. On Monday 19 January, ten days after
the initial unrest, Hypatios and Pompey had their hands and feet bound
and were thrown into the Sea of Marmara. Eighteen leading aristocratic
conspirators were exiled and their property was seized. The story is still
told in the city that many of the slaughtered protesters are buried in a
common grave under the hippodrome.[10] It was reported that at least a
tenth of the city's population had been cut down.

'He established a secure, orderly condition in every city of the Roman
state and dispatched sacred rescripts to every city so that rioters or murderers, no matter to what faction they belonged, were to be punished;
thus in future no one dared to cause any kind of disorder, since Justinian
had struck fear into all provinces.'[11]

From the outset Justinian had made it clear that he intended to rule
with the firmest of hands. The Nika riots were probably caused by a reservoir of resentment. In a fit of piety, Justinian and Theodora had happily

watched as theatres closed down – bringing entertainment and the need to connect on to the streets. Afterwards, propaganda poetry, *kontakia*, was quickly commissioned, praising the Emperor and pointing out that the riots were a warning from God to the Byzantines. Their sin had caused all this trouble: 'On Earthquakes and Fires' was its uncomforting title. It marked the advent of a liturgical form that is still characteristic of Orthodoxy today.

Following the Nika riots the appearance of Constantinople changed both above and below ground. One of the first instincts of the pumped-up mob had been to smash and to burn. Much of the old city was torched. But destruction can also offer opportunities. The space was cleared for Justinian to step in as saviour and as pious urban planner. Within forty days of the riot's end he set to building Constantinople high once again.

CHAPTER 30

THE PHOENIX CITY

AD 532

Solomon I have surpassed thee!

NARRATIVE OF HAGHIA SOPHIA, CONTAINING THIS QUOTE
ATTRIBUTED TO JUSTINIAN BUT IN FACT PART OF THE MYTH-MAKING
AROUND THE CONSTRUCTION OF THE HAGHIA SOPHIA,
AFTER THE NINTH CENTURY AD

So the church has become a spectacle of marvellous beauty, overwhelming to those who see it, but to those who know it by hearsay altogether incredible . . . And it exults in an indescribable beauty.

PROCOPIUS *DE AEDIFICIIS* 27

It was said that an angel had watched over the reconstruction of Haghia Sophia and that its structure was blessed because Justinian used within it wood from Noah's Ark. Originally built on the ancient Greek acropolis by Constantine the Great, then rebuilt by Theodosios, burnt down, repurposed by Justinian and built again after riot damage, the hallmark dome of this Church of Holy Wisdom – 180 feet above the ground – seemed to be suspended by a golden chain from heaven. Haghia Sophia was to be the largest religious building in the world for over a millennium. Today it sits like a species of megafauna that has survived some distant Ice Age. The descriptions of eyewitnesses and later visitors to the city make it clear that this was a cornucopia of craft, joined together in an expression of heartfelt piety and sheer will.

Just forty days after the riots, work started; within six years the project was complete. The architects Anthemios of Tralles and Isidorus of Miletus (the latter had been head of the Platonic Academy in Athens) oversaw design and construction. Bricks from Rhodes were used because of their distinctive pale colour. It was later said that each brick in the building was stamped with the words of Psalm 45: 'God is in the midst of her; she shall not be moved.' Paintings, pillars, architraves and ceilings were faced in silver. Sunlight bounced off the church's polished marble. The medieval gloom today is deceptive – Haghia Sophia would have been a light-show of reflected brilliance. Bronze and gold were imported as well as 'marble meadows'[1] from across the known world; green stone from Haemos in the Balkans, green again from Lakonia, blood-striped from the Iasian Peaks and yellow from Lydia, crocus-gold from Libya, Tyrian purple. This was a celebration of God's work in all its gaudy glory: columns from the Temple of Artemis in Ephesus decorated the interior, and there were doors from Zeus' temple at Pergamon.

The building might have had a pagan constitution but the treasures of the earth were harvested to honour God and, critically, God's relationship with both man and woman. Commemorated on the finials of the interior columns were the initials of Justinian and Theodora, entwined together. Here were the glory and grandeur of Greece and Rome combined with every Eastern excess once imagined by Athenian playwrights such as Euripides (who mocked Helen of Troy for being tempted to Anatolia by Paris and his 'golden houses of the East'). Greco-Roman fantasies of the East were now being made tangible by Greek-speaking Romans.

For Procopius, Haghia Sophia was an object of awe:

For it soars to a height to match the sky, and as if surging up from amongst the other buildings it stands on high and looks down upon the remainder of the city, adorning it, because it is a part of it, but glorying in its own beauty, because, though a part of the city and dominating it, it at the same time towers above it to such a height that the whole city is viewed from there as from a watch-tower. Both its breadth and its length have been so carefully proportioned, that it may not improperly be said to be exceedingly long and at the same time unusually broad. And it exults in an indescribable beauty. For it proudly reveals its mass and the harmony of its proportions, having neither excess nor deficiency, since it is both more pretentious than the buildings to which we are accustomed, and considerably more noble than those which are merely huge, and it abounds exceedingly in sun-light and in the reflection of the sun's rays from the marble.[2]

Even today, in crammed, neon-lit Istanbul, the unlit Haghia Sophia enjoys a glowering presence at night. In the gloaming it has the pull of a Black Hole, the polar opposite of its medieval phosphorescence, when a thousand lighted oil-lamps would guide in sailors and their boats from the Bosphorus and the Sea of Marmara. We focus on the visual qualities of this extraordinary building, but we sideline the phenomenal strength of its story in religious and psychological terms.

All creations – statues, shrines, buildings – were at this time considered to pulse with a kind of dynamic power, offering a comforting presence that was believed to contain and to cherish both metaphysical and phys-ical expressions of the business of being human. And this mother of all churches was dedicated to Sophia, Holy Wisdom. The word *sophia* in Greek originally meant a kind of practical skill. Characters in Homer were described as *sophos* – wise – if they could tame a horse, or build a boat. This sense continues into late antiquity, personified as Lady Wisdom. Not only does Lady Wisdom allow a mystical, distinctly sensuous ap-preciation of the world and its mysteries; she encourages a foot-forward, practical engagement with it. This is the wisdom of the streets and of

This French woodcut dating from the late nineteenth century imagines the appearance of the Haghia Sophia before the Ottoman conquest of AD 1453

women, not just of men in their study halls. Sophia appears as a fleeting character in the Hebrew Bible and Greek New Testament, as well as in numerous popular religious writings. Lady Wisdom is more frequently found in the Apocrypha – religious works that were often believed to contain inconvenient truths and so were exiled from canonical texts. For many Christians Sophia was understood to be a kind of sublime force which had birthed Jesus himself.

Sophia might not have ended up in the canon, but she was a popular and populist notion in both antiquity and the medieval world. Our word wisdom and Sophia share a common, prehistoric sense – the Proto-Indo-European root suggests a clear-sighted understanding of the world. The Sophia church was also dedicated to the Logos – the Word – the manifest and recondite Wisdom of God. So this great building was made up not just of bricks and mortar but of an idea – an imaginative understanding of the eternal power of both masculine and feminine ways of being wise, of the possibilities of negotiating the world with both mind and mystery. It is a remarkable statement from a building at the heart of the city that considered itself the heart of the world.[3]

In the Hebrew Bible Sophia's equivalent Hokhma is described in Proverbs 8 as being 'better than rubies, and all the things that may be desired . . . I am understanding . . . set up from everlasting, from the beginning . . . whoso findeth me findeth life'. The building of Haghia Sophia was not just a placatory offering to the divine; it was an answer.

The new Haghia Sophia was Justinian and Theodora's crowning glory. But elsewhere in the city there were other excitements. Following the debacle of the riots Justinian now needed to prove who was boss. The Emperor shored up his city; the palace itself was given a large granary, a bakery and a cistern, so any future issues of sedition would at least not mean famine. (Justinian's cistern was rediscovered only in the sixteenth century, when visitors noticed locals sinking wells in their homes and pulling out fresh fish.) The Baths of Zeuxippos and Great Palace were refurbished, water supplies were renewed.[4] A new palace was built at Blachernae near the Theodosian Walls. Justinian's ambition was, explicitly, to animate and to replicate the glories of Old Rome and he quickly commissioned a recognisably Roman monument. From AD 543, a massive column, with Justinian in bronze astride a mount, dressed as Achilles and staring east towards Persia, reaching as high as the dome of Haghia Sophia, towered above the reconfigured Augusteion (its height a snipe at Constantine's own column that now looked paltry in comparison). It stood there until at least AD 1493, initially surviving the Ottoman takeover of the city. Constantinople's urban disaster was turning to Justinian's advantage.

Herodotus, who had witnessed the formation of those early Greek foundations such as Byzantion, called civilisation itself *to hellenikon* – the Greek thing. Now Constantinople could better Herodotus' vision of civilisation – a city with both Greek and Near Eastern genetic coding, strengthened by Roman muscle and sinew and wrapped in a Christian skin. As Theodora and Justinian walked and thought through the brilliance of the city growing up around them – the parade ground, the Augusteion, the Senate, the oval Forum of Constantine ringed with a giant colonnade, the hippodrome 1,400 feet long and 400 wide (whose

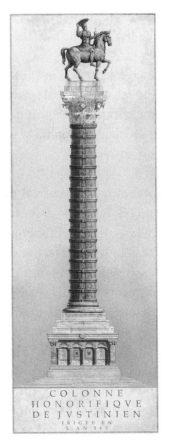

COLONNE
HONORIFIQVE
DE JVSTINIEN
ERIGEE EN
L AN 543

A modern reconstruction of the Column of Justinian by Antoine Helbert. The original was said to stand 70 metres tall and to be visible from the sea.

stone seats still turn up when there is building work, for example recently when extra toilet facilities were being installed in the gardens of the Blue Mosque), all set off by new churches, new monasteries, new safe-houses, new water-supplies – they would have recognised that Rome never fell, it simply moved 854 miles east; and that this was a Christian Rome, commanded by a High Caesar, now returning to Christ's Eastern roots.

Constantinople in its heyday was a colour-coded world: imperial potentates were buried in purple porphyry tombs; only certain ranks were allowed to wear red boots; the *scholai* guardsmen, all 5,000 of them, were dressed in white. And while a rooftop journey through Istanbul today offers a vista of lead, fifteen centuries ago roofs, walls and gates were wrapped in polished bronze. The city was a crown packed with jewels. It was not just poetic hyperbole that had encouraged Themistius to write, 'The city gleams with gold and porphyry . . . Were Constantine to see the city he founded . . . he would find it fair, not with apparent but with real beauty,'[5] and Procopius to exclaim, 'Indeed each [the churches of Sts Peter and Paul and of Sts Sergios and Bacchos] equally outshines the sun by the gleam of its stones, and each is equally adorned throughout with an abundance of gold and teems with offerings.'[6] Other Constantinopolitan features excited Procopius' lyrical powers:

> As one sails from the Propontis up toward the eastern side of the city, there is on the left a public bath. This is called Arcadianae, and it is an ornament to Constantinople, large as the city is . . . And the unruffled sea flows quietly about this court, encircling it with its stream, coming in from the Pontus like a river, so that those who are promenading can actually converse with those who are sailing by . . . Columns and marbles of surpassing beauty cover the whole of it, both the pavement and the parts above. And from these gleams an intensely brilliant white light as the rays of the sun are flashed back almost undimmed.[7]

The sad irony is that the centre of operations for Justinian and Theodora, the Great Palace and its adjunct the Palace of Bucoleon (the Palace of the Ox and Lion, described as being built to 'evoke the admiration both of strangers and of our own subjects'[8] and reminiscent in its heyday of a forbidden city),[9] now survives as a pile of bricks and rubble behind an

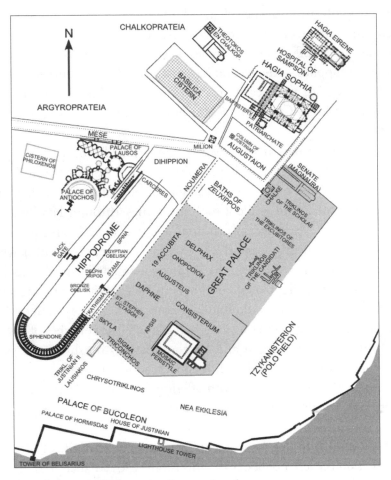

The imperial district of Byzantine Constantinople

aluminium fence.[10] Uncovered when developers started to build in Istanbul's Sultanahmet district, the battle over the use of the prime ground continues; the hope is to turn this rich space into an archaeological park. Here there were once great things: a towering entrance portico known as the Chalke Gate which showed, in golden mosaics, Justinian vanquishing the Vandals and Goths, with Theodora represented alongside her lover-Emperor. Giant equestrian statues welcomed visitors. Beyond the iron gates clad in bronze 'appropriate to imperial power' there was the Consistorium, the meeting hall, the Delphax (a court), the Tribunal of the Nineteen Couches, the Magnaura, the audience hall, and the Triklinos, the banqueting room. The rest of the palace, with many of the private and public rooms connected by porticoed walkways, cascaded down to the sea. Today, modest private homes squat in the palace's seaward walls, where the imperial monograms of Justinian can just about be made out on the remains of a column. Refugees from Syria, Iraq and Afghanistan camp in the shade of its broken walls. They cook supper on little braziers, the victims of the fallout of the vacillations of many imperial powers in the region, Roman, Persian, Byzantine, Ottoman and European.

Although the sea walls have, in places, survived through to the twenty-first century, the great treat of much of Justinian and Theodora's world was hidden for centuries beneath the ground. The amputated jaw from the Delphic Serpent Column in the hippodrome, Eudoxia's silvered pedestal – these had seemed to be the best the excavations could offer. But then came a gift from the past. Beneath the modern-day Arasta Bazaar, behind overpriced kilims and silk dressing gowns, an exquisite series of mosaics was excavated in the 1930s and again in the 1950s. The elaborate, exquisitely executed schemes, hidden from AD 1606 thanks to Ahmed I's ambitious construction of the Blue Mosque above them, were carefully laid on the floors of the Great Palace. On this wonderful artwork, created with both grace and brio, heroes spear big cats, a mother breastfeeds her baby, children ride on camels, play with hoops, an eagle – the image of Constantinople defeating its besiegers – grapples with a snake, and charioteering rivals are splendid in their blues and greens. With those fine mosaics in front of you, the raw ambition of this time and place is vibrantly clear. The mosaics sing out that there is nothing these imperial powers could not do – and there was the satisfaction that they were doing good.

The Greek delight in the theoretical allows for all kinds of experiments. And, post-riot, it seems that Justinian and Theodora were encouraged to make technology bend to the will of God. There were many ambitious projects across Constantinople's territories, but their greatest, the Haghia Sophia, was a wonder of Christendom and is still one of the marvels of the human experience.

CHAPTER 31

SPECTACULAR, SPECTACULAR

AD 521–c. 650

You seat yourself in the theatre and feast your eyes on naked women . . .
You would not choose to see a naked woman in the marketplace, yet you
eagerly attend the theatre. What difference does it make if the stripper is
a whore? . . . Indeed it would be better to smear our faces with mud than
to behold such spectacles.

JOHN CHRYSOSTOM, *8TH HOMILY*[1]

Of course we should not just picture the city as full of high art. Istanbul
enjoys an inherently dramatic landscape; throughout her history, the
city's inhabitants seem to have felt galvinised to generate their own drama
to match.

The bloody bullfights popular in Spain, France, Portugal and parts
of Latin America are a pale descendant of the exotic animal fights that
continued to be staged in Christian Constantinople. In this city which
preached sermons of peace and co-existence as well as of retribution, up
until the end of the sixth century criminals could be thrown *ad bestias*
– to be devoured as their punishment, and for the crowd's pleasure. The
remains at the amphitheatre of Aphrodisias in Anatolia suggest the means
by which audiences were protected: posts, ropes and nets (a bit like our
cricket nets) would have stopped them being mauled. When it became
too costly, and perhaps simply too dull, to ship in big cats and hyenas,
bulls and bears were bred for use in the local, lethal pleasure-palaces.
By the seventh century this particular form of inflicting death seems to
have stopped in Constantinople; the amphitheatre, the Kynegion rebuilt
by Severus, was now used only for the spectacle of man-on-man public
executions. In a cruel twist of its purpose as the venue where the Emperor

met his people, from time to time the hippodrome would become the place of choice to execute the imperial leader.[2]

So to avoid becoming the show themselves, Constantinople's emperors needed to keep their people on side. We know that when he was on his way up, still just a consul in the city in AD 521, Justinian had mounted lavish consular games – his eyes clearly already on the prize. The experience of living in Constantinople would have been a jangling, communal one. The inhabitants inherited a Greek obsession with religious festivals, a Roman delight in spectacle, and this in a city with an Eastern *mise-en-scène*. Add to that the fundamental belief in the power of competition – the Greek word for contest, *agon*, gives us our word agony – and you have a potent, public-performance mix. Interestingly, the word *agon* first appears in Homer's *Iliad* as a place to meet, and meeting itself soon becomes a competitive act. Constantinople's ancient roots meant that it was a stage set for struggle: the squares, racetracks, amphitheatres and processional ways were the perfect locations for playing out the martial business of living, competing and winning out.

Come the fourth century AD, physical prowess was demonstrated in theatrical acrobatics rather than in the traditional boxing, wrestling, running, jumping, discus and javelin of the ancient city's gymnasia – think Cirque du Soleil rather than the Olympics. And travelling through the centre of Constantinople, Justinian would have been exposed to one of the city's most vivid influences – live theatrical performance. For centuries the Romans had ensured that the Greek idea of theatre – a shared space in which to toss around ideas of what it is to be human, to examine and in some cases to bind the wounds of mankind's own making – had been perverted into an arena for political posturing and rank sensationalism. Pantomimes and mimes in Constantinople were devised to excite emotion or lust. Theatricals had become either spectacles or crude vignettes in between sporting fixtures – we could imagine a pubescent Theodora as one of the players here. The Blues, Greens, Reds and Whites sponsored theatrical competitions as fervently as they did chariot races.

Like charioteers, actors belonged to different teams and their portraits were displayed across the city. The performances in Constantinople, of all kinds, became notorious. Descriptions of half-naked actresses imitating the lifestyles of sea-nymphs in 'Mimes of Thetis' may possibly be apocryphal, but then a substantial number of spectators did indeed drown

Diptychs give us splendid detail of the performance culture of Constantinople. Here female musicians entertain. This beautiful ivory diptych was lovingly formed to commemorate consular games in AD 517. Images of the city's performers even appear on bone combs.

during the festival of Brytae in AD 499 or 500, when, after fights broke out between the Blues and the Greens, they fell into the city's flooded theatre.[3] The risqué, high-octane performances became a trademark of the city: when Constantinople's hippodrome was portrayed in a cathedral in Kiev, clowns were painted alongside the chariots.

In Constantinople it was clear that the events staged were considered precious because they offered a direct line of communication between the city's leaders and her people. We should remember that it had been the passions of men aroused by a sense of belonging, brought about by the entertainments of Constantinople, that almost brought the city to the ground during the Nika riots. Elsewhere in the empire 'snuff dramas' were enacted – performances where condemned criminals were executed within elaborate mythological plots.

John Chrysostom (author in the summer of AD 399 of *Against the Games and Theatres*), he who was so anxious about the visible presence of women on Constantinople's streets, had fretted that visitors from elsewhere in the empire would be tempted into the metropolis to meet their moral ruin while citizens were choosing to miss church in favour of one of the big shows. A fabulous exchange of letters between the bishop of Gaza and the ascetics Barsanuphios and John of Gaza ends in the ascetics' advice that theatres are 'the workshops of the devil'.[4] Jacob of Serugh (another bishop) spits out, 'Who can bathe in the mud without being soiled?'[5] But John of the Golden Mouth trumps them all: 'Once your head is filled with such sights and the songs that go with them, you think about them even in your dreams ... Why are such things permitted when we are gathered together and shameful when we are by ourselves?' Others were more coolly dismissive; the highly skilled pagan rhetorician Libanios, tutor to John Chrysostom, knowing that the city was populated not by old aristocracy but by 'new men', moaned that the audiences in Constantinople were just soldiers, 'rhetorically incompetent'.

Christianity has often been blamed for the death of local theatre and of spectacle, but I suspect that in New Rome this was not just a doctrinal but also a financial issue. As charity took on a different form in Constantinople and across the empire – gifts to the poor or for the building of churches, to soup kitchens and hospitals – fewer donations for games were available. So the demise of theatre in the city can be explained as the fallout not of a morality but a popularity, contest.

Eventually, as a result of a pincer movement of Christian anxiety within and Islamic invasions from without, by the end of the seventh century the glory days of Constantinople's public theatre scene were over. Recent work on an inscription has shown that when a new governor was acclaimed he was commanded to 'Enter!' – a stage direction. The business of being Byzantine itself had become a theatrical experience.[6] Yet the buskined, histrionic nature of Byzantine affairs would be a cause for criticism down time.

However what is clear is that – despite, or perhaps because of, their origins as a subsistence farmer and dancing girl – Justinian and Theodora had no intention of simply offering the people of Byzantine Christendom bread and circuses. Their reforming project was not just one of show, but one of judicial substance.

CHAPTER 32

❖

LAW AND ORDER

7 APRIL AD 529 ONWARDS

An elementary framework, a cradle of the law, not based on obscure old
stories but illuminated by the light of our imperial splendour . . . you
have been found worthy of the great honour and good fortune of . . .
following a course of education which from start to finish proceeds from
the Emperor's lips.

JUSTINIAN'S *INSTITUTES*[1]

In Europe, every day, our lives are directly shaped by Justinian's (and
perhaps too Theodora's) prodigious energy. Within six months of his
accession, Justinian stood in the Senate and announced that he was embarking on the massive, ethical, intellectual, political, economic and cultural task of collecting, unifying, sorting and codifying all edicts, laws,
letters and legal cases that had gone to make up Roman legal practice
over the previous four centuries. The project might have been interrupted
by the Nika riots, but it would be enthusiastically carried through over
forty years.[2] Law for the early medieval Christian was a confusing, noisy
space: local law, Judaic law, Roman law, Christ's teaching, all fighting to
be heard. The material gathered into Constantinople on Justinian's orders
and sent back out across Christendom and the empire – in the name of
Jesus Christ – did indeed point a way forward. The radical legal innova-
tions fostered in Constantinople still form the basis of European law. It
was Justinian's *Codex* that enshrined the principle that we are innocent
until proven guilty. What we now call the *Corpus Juris Civilis* – that is,
the entirety of Justinian's legal project – reformed and enshrined Western
jurisprudence. A number of us are, arguably, Justinian's children.[3]

At a stroke, with his grand legal project Justinian got the attention of his subjects, whether elite or lowborn. This was a smart move – to declare himself both a just ruler and one clearly in control. The detail of the laws that emerged from this gargantuan process suggests, though, that the exercise was not entirely calculating. In many ways what was being worked towards here was a rubric with social justice squarely at its heart. The opening three lines of the *Codex* defined life under law as living honestly, hurting no one and giving each their due. This is Justinian as the new Solomon. And although the enterprise was predominantly practical, a vast operation in the cataloguing and control of history, it is also (with some marked exceptions) remarkably progressive, both socially and intellectually.

In the majority of ancient civilisations, justice was believed to be in the purview of the gods – even if it was meted out by divine representatives, by kings, aristocrats, or a priestly class. The Greek word for justice, *dike*, derives from the Babylonian for finger (we have a trace of this root in our index finger, the decimal system and the word judge: a *iudex*, a judge, is someone who points out the right way for a society to behave by directing us to the *ius*, the law or sacred oath). Originally justice implied obedience to a system demonstrated by the gestures of the gods. Ancient Greek culture then develops ideas of justice; *dike* is described increasingly in democratic Athens as something remarkable, a quality doled out to all men; there is a notion that each individual man has an equal capacity for being just. And Justinian's code facilitates that instinct.

And so in Constantinople's law court or Praetorium, just off the Mese – whose remains today sit under cheap, municipal paving, where old women sell seed for the pigeons and the few remaining letter-writers in the city type out missives for the illiterate of Istanbul – on Justinian's watch, the origins of our legal system were enacted.

Theodora seems to have been at Justinian's side in this task. We hear in telling detail that she was involved in generating certain reforms such as the measures aimed at eradicating malpractice among provincial magistrates.[4] Unsure how to word this piece of legislation, we're told the Emperor sought his wife's advice: the law was to be read out in churches by bishops on feast days 'in order that all persons may regard magistrates as fathers, rather than as thieves and persons plotting to deprive them of their property'. As has been pointed out, a number of contemporaries emphasised the irony in play here: Justinian and Theodora were infamous for confiscating property at will, doing precisely that which they were now declaring illegal.⁵ In one case a high-ranking courtier had been exiled and his property confiscated for having 'insulted and slandered' the Empress. Following the compilation of the *Codex*, Theodora was actively involved in the passing of laws securing the rights of property for women, ensuring access to their children, outlawing infanticide, outlawing pandering and outlawing pimping, as well as providing safe houses for homeless women in the city and increased penalties for rape. It is worth speculating too perhaps that Theodora's personal, traumatic memories inspired the remarkably empathetic detail in the legislative provision known as Novel 134.9 (passed after her death by Justinian in May AD 556) which ensured that women on trial were not held in prisons but lodged, with other women, in convents.

We have to pause for a moment to think of the impact of this project within Constantinople itself. Messengers and scouts were sent to basilicas, churches, council chambers and private homes across a million square miles to collect documents – some of them office copies but often the sole surviving evidence of a particular legal idea. This team of eager civil servants Justinian called 'New Justinians' – fresh blood who could help him to recalibrate civilisation. The New Justinians rushed back to Constantinople from all outposts of the Roman Empire; there must have been a sense of urgency and of purpose, because this reworking of the law was not only the Emperor's work, not only the empire's, but God's. The new Law Code was to be produced in the name of Jesus Christ and was promoted as the best and most pious way to keep his flock safe.

As you might also expect, this wide-ranging exercise in legal theory, swiftly put into practice, provided a robust opportunity to bond church and state. Justinian's laws were physically put on display in churches and read out within them. He codified the symbolic act we are still familiar with today, of taking a Christian oath on a Bible before legal business could be transacted.⁶ With Gospels being broadcast in the Senate House, the business of ruling and orthodox believing were becoming ever more intricately and explicitly tied.

Initially the task of codification and empire-wide legal reform was given to a committee of ten beavering away behind closed doors, but during the second phase of the project a forceful character from southern Anatolia called Tribonian refined the details – to advance the work but also to ensure that the legal findings suited the imperial plan. Tribonian was one of Justinian's favourite kinds of men – an arriviste, hungry for power and influence. His teams were set up in rooms throughout the Great Palace, and Justinian would be formally involved in bi-monthly sessions where disputes would be resolved by imperial decree or he would stop by for regular progress reports from the working groups. The Emperor 'who never sleeps' seems to have taken a keen personal interest. The past was considered not so much a reservoir of truth as a source of raw material that could be moulded into a new shape. Where necessary, laws were adapted to suit the needs and desires of New Rome.

Latin was the official language of the Byzantine court until the mid-sixth century.[7] The grammarian Priscian worked from Constantinople, and like the Emperor Justinian with his Law Code, he promoted the use of Latin across the empire. But Justinian also collected Roman laws in Latin and then from AD 535 sent these 'New Laws' (Novellae, or Novels) back out again in Greek. So Latin in Constantinople increasingly became like the scent of an orchard – delightful, interesting, memorable, sometimes magical, always deep rooted, but one of life's additional rather than essential pleasures. Constantinople might have been inhabited by Romans, but these Romans spoke Greek, and it was now those in the West who were increasingly referred to as 'Latini' – the Latins.

So individuals would make their way to this Eastern, Second Rome to seek justice in the city's spruced-up legal system, or sometimes Constantinople would come to them.

A brilliantly portrayed murder-trial in Lakica (ancient Colchis and present-day Georgia), the land of Medea, gives us the publicity-brochure version of this new legal code in practice. An overworked lawyer from Constantinople called Agathias wrote the account in his *Histories* (apologising for not having enough time to be a true scholar because of all the cases he had to deal with in the city). We know that this is chronicle written as public relations, because this paragon trial was trumpeted as 'worthy of . . . Imperial Rome and Democratic Athens . . . set up in the foot of the Caucasus'. Yet Agathias was also producing an operational manual: many of the details must have rung true, otherwise his work would have failed at the outset. So what follows is perhaps a blueprint rather than a verbatim account of Constantinople's judicial system in action.

Agathias describes a train of men descending on Colchis: shorthand writers, ushers with whips, officials from Constantinople and the berobed judge, also from the capital. Arriving too were experts in torture who came ready with their racks, neck-irons and pliers (torture was allowed under Roman law until AD 866).[8] The trial was conducted in public view, the local Colchian audience apparently not understanding all that was said, but still following along, rapt, mouthing the words and imitating the gesticulations of the lawyers involved. Found guilty, the condemned murderers were then paraded through the streets on the backs of mules before they were publicly beheaded. Christian justice was duly considered done.[9] Justinian's work offered a motif to the city of Istanbul – that this was a settlement where justice, and in particular, divine justice, was available to all. But the devil is in the detail – and his was also an initiative that created underdogs. Justinian's Code was both reforming and unreformed. The *Codex Justinianus* denied pagans, homosexuals, heretics and Jews the right to imperial office or to inheritance. Constantinople had long been, in its very essence, a cosmopolitan city. There were now many on its streets who were, at a stroke, barred from justice under the law and who would struggle for centuries against their branding as the city's underdogs.

CHAPTER 33

✤

THE JEWISH CITY
ANTIQUITY ONWARDS

> Our majesty too has at all times investigated and scrutinized what was
> being composed and if any doubts or uncertainties were found has in-
> voked the heavenly spirit and altered or rendered the law in proper form.
>
> JUSTINIAN'S *DIGEST*[1]

If you feel brave enough, peel away from the main thoroughfares of
the Grand Bazaar in modern Istanbul and explore the medieval alleys
that still interconnect them. You will pass the dark floods created by
indigo-dyers, working under Romanesque columns. Here black-market
money-merchants loiter. One sub-district still supports the copper-
workers, as it has done for centuries. To meet any artisans here – drawn
by the clanking sound of their craft – you have to make your way up
twisting, grimy backstairs or through broken, open doorways. The
accoutrements (giant copper fireplaces, sculptures and massage beds)
of the city's new potentates – upwardly mobile financiers and five-star
hotels – are being crafted here by hand, just as 1,600 years before workers would have made copper wonders for the Great Palace. Here in the
district known as Chalkoprateia there was a synagogue, its construction
permitted by Theodosios I. Many copper-workers were Jews. But the
synagogue was then burnt down by enraged Christians, and official
sources recount that the daughter of the lovely Empress Eudoxia, Pulcheria, built a Church of Mary Theotokos (subsequently converted into
a mosque) over the synagogue's remains. This little corner of Istanbul is
a reminder of a moment in time when the Jewish presence in Constantinople was visible but under threat. Soon bricks and mortar would be the
least of the Jews' worries; the new Christian Law Code, drawn up in the

city, would ensure a fragile future for Jews in Europe and the Near East.

Up until AD 425 there had been a Jewish patriarchate within Constantinople.[2] Synagogue, meaning 'assembly', is, of course, a Greek word. Jewish prayer-houses (also called *proseuchai*) were scattered across the Hellenistic world, one of the very oldest being on the sacred, wind-stripped island of Delos in the Cyclades: the island from which Athens had originally filibustered in ancient Byzantion's affairs as leader of the Delian League. Often serving as mercenaries; cheerfully employing the Greek key design (latterly called the Meander, after Anatolia's famous meandering river), Jews had lived and worked alongside Greeks for centuries. The Hebrew Bible had been enthusiastically translated into Greek in the Hellenistic city of Alexandria. But Constantinople was meant to be a brave new beginning for Christian power. Constantine the Great had wanted the Jewish question to be answered. Christ was a Jew: but Jewish men had bayed for his blood. 'Let us have nothing in common with the Jews who are our enemies, let us studiously avoid all contact with their evil way,'[3] the founder of Constantinople reportedly thundered. And so, taking his cue from the Gospel of St John, 8: 44, John Chrysostom had stood up in the pulpits of Antioch – where it was said, the word Christians was first coined – and in his crisply titled homily 'Against the Jews' warned against the diabolic nature of Jews. The words of this persuasive teacher – who had been taught by the pagan Libanios – still appear in Christian prayer books.[4]

The falling-out between Jews and Christians has been described by one historian as 'a family quarrel. That of course did not prevent it from going lethal, early; perhaps it guaranteed it.'[5] And the excitable nature of the words of men such as John Chrysostom indicates the close-knit relations of Jews and Christians in the first 300 years of Christianity. As minority monotheists in a predominantly polytheist universe, of course Jewish and Christian men and women must have stuck together, debated scripture, partaken of the odd, clandestine sacrifice. We have to think of the cultural inheritance of these new Christians. Both Greeks and Jews had shared a fervent belief in the power of ritual and the cremation of whole animals – in Greek, a holocaust. When the temples to the old gods were finally closed down, how did the only recently converted Christian inhabitants feel about those bloody Jewish sacrifices? Disgust? Resentment? Temptation?

Then with Justinian's Code in AD 532 – phase two of the great Byzantine tidying up – Judaism was no longer *religio licita*, no longer an approved religion. In 535 a second edict followed: all synagogues were to be converted into churches. Come the seventh century and Emperor Herakleios would try to ban weekday Jewish services and the recitation of the *shema* ('Hear O Israel', the centrepiece of morning and evening prayers) at any time. He also encouraged mass, forced conversion.[6] But in Constantinople there was a practical problem. This was a city that supported a thriving Jewish community – Jews worked in the leather and silk trades and as money-merchants. This was a characteristic that would endure up to and beyond the Second World War when up to 100,000 Jewish refugees were welcomed to Istanbul from across Europe.

The testing experience of being Jewish in Byzantine lands is searingly communicated in a neat little letter only now being fully analysed. Written in Hebrew and dating from AD 961, it gives us a fresh perspective on Byzantium's chequered relationship with her Jewish community.[7] Carefully set out on a scrap of parchment by one Moshe Agura to his brother-in-law, the epistle is beautifully direct. Moshe had lost contact with his family and he was struggling. The islands of Rhodes and Crete had recently been recaptured by the Byzantines from Arab Muslims and this was not good news for Jewish families. Crete was in fact turned 'upside down' according to the letter's author. The Byzantine Emperor Romanos Lekapenos, originally a peasant from Armenia, had imposed punitive legislation on Jewish communities across his empire.

Moshe's letter is emotional and emotive. The isolated Jew says that he would love to know if his family is still well, if indeed they are still alive, and whether he might fare better with them in Muslim-occupied Cairo. He is desperate for news. His letter is both a cry for help and a hint at a world that is fractured but also full of possibilities. The intimate document, which has survived by chance, is one of many that show how, by the ninth and tenth centuries AD, under Arab rule in the region many Jews could have greater intellectual, legal, mercantile, textual and indeed textile freedom. The little letter is a rare personal insight into a minority and into a moment in historical time.

Within a century of Moshe writing his letter, the Emperor Constantine IX Monomachos declared in a chrysobull or imperial decree from Constantinople enacted in July AD 1049:

The mighty King and God rebuffed the old Israel and selected a new one, and by giving His preference to this one before the other, He called it the chosen people and His desired, own inheritance. In this respect, he at the same time subjected the Jewish people to the Christian people, and so arranged it, that the religious and well-intentioned race ruled over the unfaithful and ungrateful one.[8]

So in Constantinople Jews lived a paradox. While the Byzantine emperors increasingly drew on Old Testament parallels, describing themselves as priest-kings and Constantinople as a New Zion, with the Byzantine Christians the true 'Chosen Ones', real Jews had no legal status, were consistently discouraged from using Hebrew and were occasionally subjected to forced conversion. The everyday prejudice is on record. Jewish men might have their beards set alight or find mobs drumming and chanting outside their homes. There are reports of Christians offloading sewage-laden water in front of their cottage-industries. Constantinople was a pioneer in that it combined Semitic mysticism with classical influences. On the ground this allowed for both tolerance and for prejudice.

On Justinian's watch there were other losers too in Constantinople's Great Legal Game. Paganism as well as homosexuality was more vigorously suppressed at this time. Between AD 528 and 546 Justinian's agents attempted to winkle out crypto-pagans in the imperial court and in the provinces, but the city's love–hate relationship with its classical past endured.

CHAPTER 34

❖

THE CLASSICAL CITY

AD 529 ONWARDS

Even I, a god, have learnt to live with the times

PALLADAS, FOURTH CENTURY AD[1]

The sixth century both nourished the study of the classical, pagan world in the territories controlled from Constantinople and inflicted killer blows upon it. The closing of the pagan school of philosophy in Athens around AD 529 has long been lionised as an epoch-defining moment, an act by which the timbre of Western society was, symbolically, defined. The reality is probably a little more parochial. The chronicle of John Malalas is our only direct source for the event, and from it we get a macabrely colourful sense of the mood of the times: 'the emperor [Justinian] issued a decree and sent it to Athens ordering that no one should teach philosophy nor interpret astronomy nor in any city should there be lots cast using dice; for some who cast dice had been discovered in Byzantium indulging themselves in dreadful blasphemies. Their hands were cut off and they were paraded around on camels.'[2] The 'dreadful blasphemies' almost certainly refer to divinations. Dice – often twelve-sided[3] – were used to predict the future; one suspects, in the case of the men whose hands were amputated, that officials in the city had heard of predictions that were not overly flattering to the contemporary regime.

Many have suggested that the Athens philosophy school – hotbed perhaps of pagan opposition – was closed as a reaction to subversion within the capital. Yet this closure was not directly referenced in any other sources. The school was formally established – as a revival of Plato's original Academy – to teach pagan philosophy in the late fourth century AD by an Athenian, Plutarch. It had waxed and waned in influence and was clearly beginning to struggle as the Christian population in the city became more influential and support from prominent pagan aristocrats started to melt away.

A wider law in the *Codex Justinianus* (published some time between AD 529 and 534)[4] severely cauterised the possibilities of being a non-Christian. Pagans, it declared, had to be baptised and could neither teach nor receive a municipal salary; children of pagans were to be forcibly taught the faith; if baptism was taken merely for convenience the neo-converts were to be punished or fined; and recalcitrant pagans were to have their property con-fiscated. They were then to be exiled. We are told that Justinian watched as Manichaeans were drowned or burned to death in front of him.

Just beneath the ancient Areopagus rock in Athens where the pre-democratic council of elders sat from the Bronze Age until the fifth century BC, excavations have revealed vivid evidence of the harsh reality of these edicts. The remains are ignored by tourists, walked over occasionally by tortoises. A series of fine houses has been abandoned, pagan statuary has been hidden in a nearby well, with empty hope (as it turns out, treasure that was never collected), and the interiors have undergone major renovation, pagan images in the floor mosaics having been replaced by a cross. Think of the scene – valuable property owned by men who were once held in high regard being repurposed to become desirable residences for Christians.[5]

The story of the Platonic Academy at Athens was a sign of the times.

We must not forget that although we describe the men and women of Constantinople as Byzantines, they called themselves Rhomaioi – 'Romans'. Despite Empress Pulcheria's law of AD 415 stipulating that pagans could not take up military or official imperial office (the Empress seems to have been dedicated to chastity and the cultural education of her young brother Theodosios), both pagan and Christian scholars passed on their ideas in Constantinople. Byzantine education relied heavily on classical texts. Particularly popular in Constantinople were the works of Homer and his stories of the Trojan War. There should be little surprise in that perhaps, as this was a city that was defined by the sieges it had endured: by the Spartans in 478 BC, by Alcibiades in 408 BC, by a rebel group from Constantinople in AD 515, by the Kotrigur Huns in AD 559, with others, even more testing, on the horizon.

So, clearly, even though Justinian had closed down the Platonic Academy in AD 529, classical culture was still all around. The variegated nature of the minds of men in Constantinople is revealed in their deeds (John Mauropous, for example, openly prays for the souls of Plato and Plutarch as late as the eleventh century) and in art works across the city. The ancient world was a kind of base note for Constantinople's radical new experiment – never dominant, but stubbornly there, refusing to let the Christian population forget what lay underneath. Miracle-workers and soothsayers attended to the inhabitants of the city, checking the wind direction under the giant weathervane, topped with a female figure and a jamboree of classical imagery, mounted on a pyramid above a tetrapylon close to the old Forum Tauri. The fifth-century Christian author Nonnos wrote a lengthy poem, the *Dionysiaka*, celebrating the god Dionysos' conquest of India; and in digs around Byzantine monasteries *ostraka* – pottery sherds, handy raw material for scratching out lessons – have been found covered in the maxims of the Greek author Menander, who had written so vividly about the boozy culture of Byzantion. Mounted Amazons gallop across Byzantine silver plates; in a ninth-century Gospel book (including copies of originals that could well be from the sixth century) the Massacre of the Innocents is portrayed in a form that recalls the murder of Hector's son Astyanax as described in many versions of the Trojan War story. A courtier marvelling in the eleventh century at the beauty of Skleraina – mistress of Emperor Constantine IX Monomachos – quotes from Book 3 of the *Iliad*: 'It were no shame . . . that a man should fight for such as she.' In that same century Zeus is portrayed as a Byzantine emperor somewhat anachronistically pulling an embryonic Dionysos from his thigh, and of course memories of beautiful Helen and the Trojan heroes who sought her out were conspicuous by their presence.[6]

The writers of Constantinople frequently employed a kind of archaised (Atticised) Greek. The streets of the new city were suddenly inhabited by those who spoke as the great orators of Athens, Sicily and Olympia would have done. In late antiquity, the upper classes turned an interest in the culture of language into a cult. There was a notion that from those spoken words and inky lines the potency that helped to forge ancient empires – as described for example by Virgil – could be revived once again.[7]

The thoughtful philosopher Boethius (c. AD 480–524) was fascinated by the Hellenophilic projects of Constantinople (he devised a grand plan

to translate Aristotle and Plato into Latin). Working for the Ostrogothic
regime, his sympathies with the Greek culture of the East were seen as
potentially seditious, and as a result he was imprisoned and sentenced
to death. Boethius' perceived loyalty to Constantinople and its culture
might have cost the philosopher his life, but it left humanity with a
beguilingly beautiful work. Written, urgently, before his execution,
Boethius' *The Consolation of Philosophy* asserts that imprisonment cannot
fetter the mind. Here, Sophia – or Lady Wisdom – reminds the captive,
'The only way one man can exercise power over another is over his body,
and what is inferior to that, his possessions. You cannot impose anything
on a free mind, and you cannot move from its state of inner tranquillity
a mind at peace with itself and firmly founded on reason.'[8]

Boethius' work was translated by Chaucer and then printed in Britain
by William Caxton in AD 1478; translated again by Queen Elizabeth I,
no less, in 1593, it has allowed many to ponder how best to defend moral
values, how to deal with suffering and injustice and to ensure that one's
reputation is rehabilitated when untimely death means that this is all
that we can leave for posterity. For me, as I wander through the ruins
of St John of Stoudios, as chai sellers pass and political parties break the
peace with their bellowing megaphones, it is genuinely moving to think
of the words and ideas salvaged here in this monastery, which inspired
others and then saved men over centuries from despair. We should thank
medieval Istanbul for choosing to preserve wisdom from all points of the
compass.

But while Constantinople was diligently maintaining the works of the
ancient Greeks and Romans, indeed of the ancient East, she was also
boxing herself into a cultural stereotype. Byzantium might be of central
historical importance, but as time passed, the city and her inhabitants –
drawn from the Caucasus, Asia Minor and the Middle East, as well as
from Thrace and Europe – would increasingly come to be liminalised in
civilisation's story, categorised as 'exotic' 'oriental' and 'other'.

So we might imagine Theodora and Justinian, drunk with ideas and
adventure and lust, partners in both justice and crime. The Emperor was
proud of his young law student protégés – the men he had christened
New Justinians – a keen generation who could put his plans into action.
Both rulers must have looked over that energetic, theistic landscape laid

out under a legalistic sky – all bigger and better and brighter and shinier because it was part of God's own plan. And while under Old Rome the emperors may well, in their darkest moments, have admitted that they were not really part-divine, the Christian message said, with a comforting clarity, that each and every human was just that. That was a handy backstory when you also happened to be the most powerful human on earth.

CHAPTER 35

ALL IS VANITY

c. AD 515–65

during this year a most dread portent took place. For the sun gave forth its light without brightness . . . and it seemed exceedingly like the sun in eclipse, for the beams it shed were not clear.

PROCOPIUS, *HISTORY OF THE WARS*[1]

innumerable other calamities happened both by land and sea . . . The sea also cast up dead fish; many islands were submerged; and, again, ships were stranded by the retreat of the waters . . .

EVAGRIUS, *ECCLESIASTICAL HISTORY*[2]

However ardently Justinian pursued his religious project, Constantinople would be singled out for a revisitation by the wrath of God or the gods – unnatural activity of the earth, plagues of unwanted invaders and a terrifying pestilence. But first came a storm of human creation.

That defeat of Basiliskos by the Vandals in AD 468 – when Constantinople's enemies had sent fireboats in among the Roman fleet – had become a nagging insult. On the streets of the city men also muttered about the disgrace of the fall of Rome in 455 – again to Vandal forces. In 515, when Constantinople was ruled by Justin's predecessor Anastasios, the Byzantine general Vitalian (who was half Goth, the product of a mixed marriage) had rebelled, his forces threatening Constantinople from land and sea. The chronicler John Malalas reported that Vitalian's men were defeated only by the use of a sulphurous, flammable chemical weapon whose recipe had been smuggled in from Athens – the first extant recorded mention of Greek Fire.

With a messianic certainty that he had been saved from the disaster of the Nika riots by divine intervention, Emperor Justinian believed it was now his fate to reclaim Roman territories in God's name. In a display of flinty purpose (and with helpful intelligence from an ally that the Emperor had been nurturing in the Vandal court), he instructed his old companion Belisarios to take action. Barbarians needed to be shown who was now boss: the Vandals must be routed from their North African kingdom. Sailing out from the city in AD 533, with Procopius an eyewitness, Belisarios landed in what is now Tunisia with an estimated 15,000 men. Within just four weeks the Byzantine forces had taken Carthage.

In an edict of AD 534, Justinian described the Vandals as 'enemies of body and mind', and indeed the 'reclamation' of North African Roman lands was driven by commercial interests as well as by faith and pride. The accoutrements of empire had to be protected, the olive presses, murex pools and garum factories restored to Roman hands. Churches were taken from Arians and, some evidence suggests, were given back to adherents of the Nicene Creed. Handsome mansions were renovated at Lepcis, fortified monasteries were built in Carthage and in both cities churches were dedicated to Mary Theotokos.[3] Those who had died fighting against Vandals were honoured as martyrs. Vandals were killed or deported, with some being reabsorbed into the teeming city of Constantinople where they lost their identity as a cultural group. The defeat of the Vandals enhanced notions of Justinian's might. And the historians and myth-makers of New Rome made sure that, to this day, the modern world thinks of the Vandals as a destructive 'other'.

Stories circulated in Constantinople about Justinian's general, Belisarios. His wife Antonina – like Theodora a former street dancer – was said to have sailed from Constantinople with the fleet like a latter-day Artemisia and to have led the infantry troops. Meanwhile Belisarios was reported to have made an example of drunken 'barbarians' by impaling them.[4] Belisarios is one of a handful of characters from the early medieval world who has become a household name. And with notoriety comes the problem of historicity. Did he really fight a giant whale in the Bosphorus called Porphyry? Did he really end his days as a blind beggar, out of favour, unrecognised, disrespected, feeling his way through the streets of Constantinople? Of course not – but he did set a new narrative in notion: that the Roman Empire was here to stay, and that it was ready to rule the world once again.

Belisarios paraded captive Vandals through the streets of Constantinople in AD 534 – a conscious echo of the triumphs of Old Rome. And yet, Procopius tells us, this triumph 'was not in the ancient manner',[5] because there were nuanced differences: Belisarios travelled not in a chariot from his home to the hippodrome, but on foot, and this was a victory on behalf of an emperor. At the head of the procession were treasures from Rome – captured by the Vandals in 455 – including the menorah taken from the Jews of Jerusalem by Titus in AD 70.[6] The Vandal King Gelimer, draped in purple, was there with his family, all now prisoners of war. We are told that as he dragged himself through the jeering crowds and saw Justinian regal above the hippodrome the barbarian High King muttered over and over again words from the Hebrew Bible: 'Vanity of vanities, all is vanity.'[7]

So it was another low-born soldier – applauded by his callgirl-cum-informant spouse Antonina – processing to a sports ground to honour a peasant and his prostitute consort who enjoyed the last Roman triumph. This moment would be commemorated in mosaic form above the entrance to the Great Palace, and when he died, the Emperor Justinian would be buried in a storytelling shroud: surrounded by the fruits of victory and divine blessing he triumphantly presses his foot on the neck of a mighty Vandal king.

But Belisarios was not finished. Spurred on, he tried to drive the Ostrogoths out of Italy. In AD 535 he invaded Rome, which then changed hands several times; Sicily fell but elimination of Gothic control on the mainland was another twenty years of fighting away. Over a period of four years the administration of Rome flipped as many times – taken by the Ostrogoths in 546, conquered by the Byzantines in 547 and again by the Goths in 550. In 552 Justinian's Armenian eunuch-general Narses took Rome once more.[8] The Basilica Santi Dodici Apostoli may have been founded to celebrate the recovery of the city.[9]

With each victory there were celebrations in the streets of Constantinople. The popular image of the Byzantines as scheming, superstitious, hedonists is just wrong. It is a lazy fallacy disproved by the complexity of the foreign relationships that the Byzantines had to keep in play – with kingdoms in modern-day Ethiopia, Eritrea, Yemen, the Caucasus, the Berber heartlands, and with the emerging Slavs north of the Danube and of course Vandal Africa. At the beginning of the sixth century men from

Constantinople and her territories had to strategise the Persian incursions into Armenia; in the Caucasus the consul Justin managed to secure the allegiance of Lazica and Iberia; the Christian kingdom of Axum (modern Ethiopia and Eritrea) likewise paid fealty after Byzantines had offered help against persecution by the Himyarite (Judaic-monotheistic) kingdom in Yemen.

But this level of international engagement was complicated. The handsome but mildering, grey-stone Roman fortress of Gonio in present-day Georgia, now visited by spooning couples, just a quick hop from the Turkish border and the good-time port of Batumi, saw some dogged military action. Justinian had found himself at war with the Sassanid Persians, who controlled much of the Middle East across to the Caspian Sea. Over the next two decades the Sassanid Persians would invade Armenia and harass the Caucasus. At Gonio, a massive fortification with wooded hills behind, the Black Sea in front and the wide expanses of the West tempting beyond, it is easy to understand why Justinian was determined to keep Eastern powers very firmly in the East.

Theodora's potency had, apparently, made things worse. Following a peremptory note to a Persian official, the Persians declared themselves horrified that a woman might have such a sense of herself: 'no state worth the name could be run by a woman', not least because 'She could not ever sate her lust . . .' – mind you, this opinion comes to us courtesy of scabrous Procopius. Theodora's disrespect might just have cost Justinian dear – his 'Eternal Peace' with the Sassanid Empire, negotiated in AD 532, came at a price, 11,000 pounds in gold. And the agreement was broken a few years later by the Persian king on those wide, grass-gold reaches of the land where Anatolia melts into Iran and Iraq. Fighting and counter-agreement continued until 562 when lands taken by the Persians were abandoned and an annual tribute of 30,000 solidi was paid by the Romans as a bribe to ensure peace.

The Eternal Peace with Persia degenerated into Caucasian scrapping, while come the AD 540s the Slavs had crossed the Danube. The nomadic Avars were paid from Constantinople's coffers to guarantee their allegiance against spear-rattling Slavs, Lombards and Gepids.[10] Without a standing army, the maintenance of an expanding Byzantine empire was proving to be disturbingly pricey.

And now Constantinople would have to deal with not just man-made, but natural disasters.

Istanbul is cradled by a series of fault lines, the North Anatolian Fault Zone being particularly active. Earthquakes and tsunamis, in geological terms, are a feature of the settlement. Between AD 120 and the present, thirty tsunamis have ravaged the Mediterranean; over ninety have hit the Turkish coast in the last three millennia. Work from 2008 on the deposits found in the Theodosian harbour shows that the city was subjected to a series of particularly terrifying tsunami events and earthquakes in the city's so-called Golden Age (January 447, September 447, September 480, August 553). Towards the end of 557 and again in 558 massive earthquakes shook Constantinople's walls once more, allowing the Kotrigur Huns through in 559. The waves that pounded the city averaged 20 feet in height; water raged at least 200 yards inland. In sympathy with his people and their distress Justinian went crownless for forty days.[11]

Recall that post-riot Justinian had commissioned a propaganda poet called Romanos to produce his *kontakion* 'On Earthquakes and Fires' – proof that the city's distress was sent as punishment from God. We would be fools to miss the signs that they saw. Constantinople was indeed rocked by a fearsome and inexplicable force, one that seemed to be wrenched from the earth's very core.

In the new digs at Yenikapı chaotic deposit layers have been found in the mud – an unnatural mix of ceramics, horse and camel bones, seashells, marble blocks, trees, fragments of boats and their cargo – all representing the horror of lives, minds and beliefs shattered.[12] The ships discovered in the Theodosian harbour, hit by something hard and quick and preserved under a layer of silt and sand, are almost certainly victims of these petrifying tsunami events.[13] We also hear about the living nightmare from the historical record: 'the sea became very wild, rushed right in, engulfed a part of what had formerly been land, and destroyed several houses . . .'.[14]

In traditional chronologies the world, created in around 5500 BC, was approaching an eschatological age. And indeed it did seem to be turning upside down. An earthquake in Antioch was said to have claimed close on 300,000 lives, although this figure is almost certainly wildly exaggerated.[15] There were deaths, throughout the region, of biblical proportions.

The cultural impact of these inexplicable horrors should not be underestimated. Studies now argue that disproportionate environmental events can create religions – and it seems can modify them too.[16] Increasingly at this time we find the female role in Christianity being played down, perhaps a result of a cumulative eschatological anxiety, the impact of natural disasters, the increasing popularity of St Augustine's ideas on original sin, or indeed the power of the study hall to create an 'official', male-dominated narrative for the faith. There seems to have been a sense that God was somehow displeased by Christendom. Steadily, we find the power of women as mediators of the faith diminishing.

And then in the sixth century AD came a truly malign global phenomenon – the hardest hit that the northern hemisphere has been in the last 2,000 years. There were crop failures in Ulster and China, a 'dry fog' crept over the Middle East, and the city of Teotihuacán in today's Mexico was reported to have suffered a slow collapse. The cause of all this turmoil has been much debated: eruptions of Krakatoa and a meteor or comet strike are among the possibilities. Whatever the root cause, the environmental changes seem to have catalysed the spread of a new pathogen – one we call simply the plague.

The plague, travelling in from Asia via Egyptian ports, sped along established trading routes.[17] It reached Constantinople in the spring of AD 542 and lasted, initially, for four months (with further outbreaks across the century; the final, significant epidemics taking place in 687 and 697). Suffering in the city was truly dreadful. Famine followed. This was, naturally, believed to be an affliction sent by God. The number of dead was so great that mass graves, we are told, were dug in what is now Galata, where children today play in municipal gardens. Corpses were piled on to ships and then sent to drift out to sea. At a conservative estimate, the city was not just decimated: 20 per cent of the population were killed. You have to pause for a moment to think of the reality of this horror. Nine hundred a day dying in Constantinople in the mid-540s, Justinian's right-hand man Tribonian probably among them. Justinian – despite at one point developing telltale swellings in his groin – survived.[18] Such challenges would have broken a lesser man, but Justinian met Constantinople's challenges with counter-action. To the west in Durrës in Illyria (present-day Albania, the Roman province here was called Illyricum) where the Egnatian Way began, following the earthquakes and tsunamis that shattered his territories, Justinian ordered the broken walls of the city to be rebuilt. His hopeful symbol – a tree of life – can still be made out above the kids dropping fags and gypsies selling fluorescent underwear.

Despite Theodora's regular trips to her hot baths in Prousa, the Empress died young, in AD 548. For twenty years her body lay in a porphyry tomb in her own mausoleum next to the mausoleum of emperors adjoining the Church of the Holy Apostles. Justinian would divert triumphal processions here for ten years after her death just so that he could light candles for his Augusta. But on 14 November 565, after a reign of thirty-eight years, Justinian, dying in harness, joined his dead dancing girl. The two had been catnip to one another – reforming, innovating, building, colonising. Procopius' vicious depiction of Theodora as the partner who wore the trousers might just be right – Justinian's vacillating character is arguably echoed in his Law Code, a curious mixture of reforming and unreformed.

Our sources for the imperial pair are nothing if not vivid. What did Procopius see during these African campaigns, one wonders, that he nourished such a fierce hatred of his great leaders? Was he one of the crypto-pagans in the court who was horrified by the killing in the name of Christ's blood, and so quietly held on to information to turn against his employer – a medieval whistle-blower? Whatever the motivation, in his *On Buildings* we have a panegyric for Justinian and his work in Constantinople, while in his *Secret History* we read of Theodora and Justinian's damnation.

The dynamic between Theodora and Justinian and between those who followed in their perfumed, glittering footsteps as they strode through Constantinople, the city that now controlled over a million square miles, is brilliantly immortalised on the mosaics at Ravenna (the town, thanks to Justinian, reclaimed by Byzantium) in the Church of San Vitale – she with a halo, her cloak decorated with the wise men bringing gifts as if to the Mother of Heaven; he as the Thirteenth Apostle. In death as in life the two reign over the court of Constantinople as over the Court of Judgement in the heavenly kingdom. Theodora and Justinian knew the Gospel to be true because they lived it: the meek *shall* inherit the earth.

*

Just as the sea had brought trouble to Justinian's city, it also brought opportunity. By AD 500, the Byzantine navy was the most powerful in the world. Boats were vital to this ocean-edged civilisation. And as control of central seaports in the region came, for 'The World's Desire' and her rivals, to resemble an ever tightening net, with the trade of the sea its catch, and with the power-brokers of the day wanting the upper hand in whichever happened to be the most economically and politically acute nexus – whether that was Alexandria, Segesta, Lepcis Magna, Lepanto or Gallipoli – so the critical specialness of Byzantium, Constantinople, Istanbul could not be denied.

The city's inhabitants too seemed to appreciate the 'garland of waters' by which they were surrounded. Justinian had even passed a law preventing the view of the sea from being blocked: no buildings were allowed within 100 feet of the seafront. There was inevitably development-creep with cheeky individuals putting up awnings and within them buildings: 'In this our royal city one of the most pleasant amenities is the view of the sea . . . Anyone who offends in this way must be made to demolish the building he has put up and further pays a fine of ten pounds of gold.'[19] Meanwhile, those who had a view revelled in their good fortune. The poet Paul the Silentiary was lyrical: 'From three sides I view the pleasant expanses of the sea struck by the sunlight from all quarters. For when saffron-mantled Dawn envelops me, she is so pleased that she has no wish to go on to her setting.'[20] Agathias Scholasticus wrote: '"The gods set toil before virtue," said the poet of Ascra, speaking prophetically of this house. For after mounting the long flights of steps with exhausted feet, my hair was all soaked with sweat; but from the summit I looked on the fine view of the sea. Yea! Perhaps a good room is a surer possession than virtue.'[21]

Connected by land and by sea, seismic culturally and geologically, Constantinople as a port city was constitutionally not closed, but open. And in the East there were exciting developments – a thread of history that would define Constantinople's future. The story of the city is soon to become the story of silk.

PART FOUR

✤

THE WORLD'S DESIRE

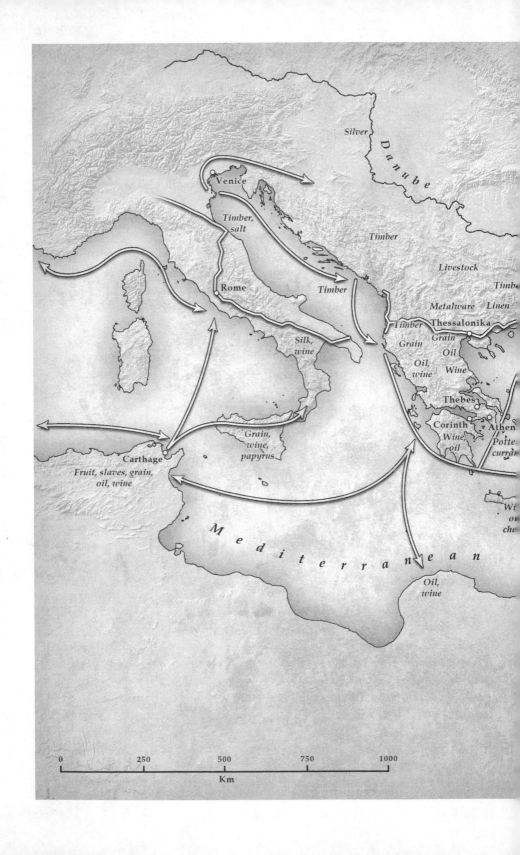

Silver

Danube

Venice

Timber, salt

Timber

Livestock

Timber

Rome

Metalware   Linen

Timber   Thessalonika

Timber

Grain   Grain

Oil,   Oil

Silk, wine

wine   Wine

Thebes

Corinth   Athen

Grain, wine, papyrus

Wine,   Potte

oil   curra

Carthage

Fruit, slaves, grain, oil, wine

Wi

or

che

M e d i t e r r a n e a n

Oil, wine

0   250   500   750   1000

Km

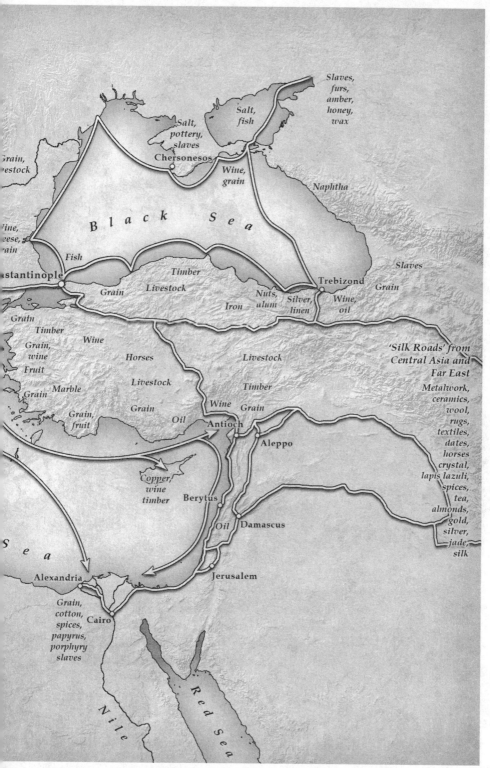

Trade routes to Constantinople, c. seventh to eleventh century AD

Venice

Rome

Carthage

Thessalonika

Ath

Mediterranean

	Caliphate Victories	Byzantine Victories	Bulgarian Victories	Sassanid Victories
7th Century	☾☆	☧	𝟙	✕
8th Century	☾☆	☧	𝟙	
9th Century	☾☆	☧	𝟙	
10th Century	☾★	☧	𝟙	
11th Century		☧	𝟙	

Caliphate possessions 717AD

Caliphate conquests to 1025AD

Byzantine possessions 717AD

Byzantine conquests to 1025AD

First Bulgarian Empire 681AD

First Bulgarian Empire 1017AD (before Byzantine annexation)

Black Sea

Pliska

Constantinople

Trebizond

Rus' raid against Constantinople and Bythnia 941 AD

2nd Abbasid Invasion 806 AD

First Abbasid Invasion 806 AD

Antioch

Aleppo

Jerusalem

Alexandria

Cairo

Sea

0   250   5

Km

Conflict with Constantinople, c. seventh to eleventh century AD

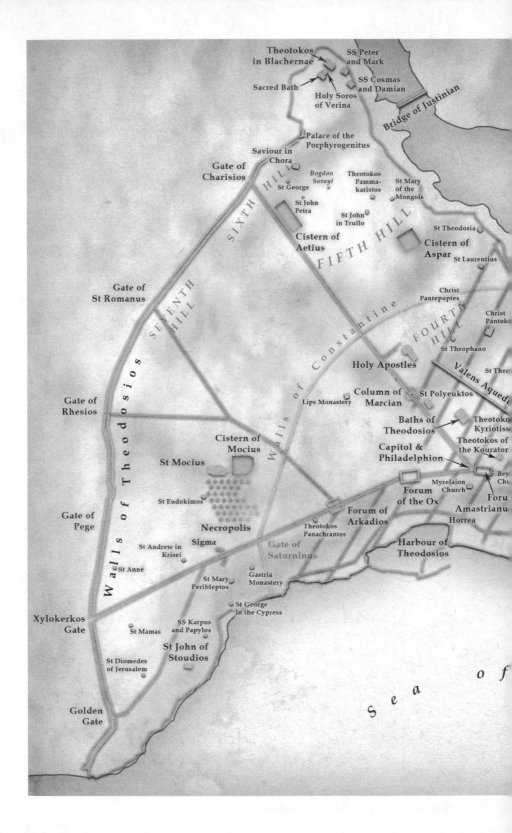

Theotokos
in Blachernae

SS Peter
and Mark

SS Cosmas
and Damian

Sacred Bath

Holy Soros
of Verina

Bridge of Justinian

Palace of the
Porphyrogenitus

Saviour in
Chora

Gate of
Charisios

*Bogdan
Sarayi*

Theotokos
Pamma-
karistos

St Mary
of the
Mongols

St George

St John
Petra

St John
in Trullo

St Theodosia

SIXTH HILL

Cistern of
Aetius

FIFTH HILL

Cistern of
Aspar

St Laurentius

Gate of
St Romanus

SEVENTH
HILL

Christ
Pantepoptes

FOURTH
HILL

Christ
Pantoks

St Theophano

St Thec

Holy Apostles

Walls of Constantine

Valens Aqued

Gate of
Rhesios

Column of
Marcian

Lips Monastery

St Polyeuktos

Baths of
Theodosios

Theotoko
Kyriotiss

Cistern of
Mocius

Capitol &
Philadelphion

Theotokos of
the Kourator

St Mocius

Bey
Chu

Walls of Theodosios

Forum
of the Ox

Myrelaion
Church

Foru

St Eudokimos

Gate of
Pege

Necropolis

Forum of
Arkadios

Amastrianu

Horrea

Theotokos
Panachrantos

Sigma

St Andrew in
Krisei

Gate of
Saturninus

Harbour of
Theodosios

St Anne

Gastria
Monastery

St Mary
Peribleptos

Xylokerkos
Gate

St George
in the Cypress

St Mamas

SS Karpos
and Papylos

St Diomedes
of Jerusalem

St John of
Stoudios

Golden
Gate

Sea o f

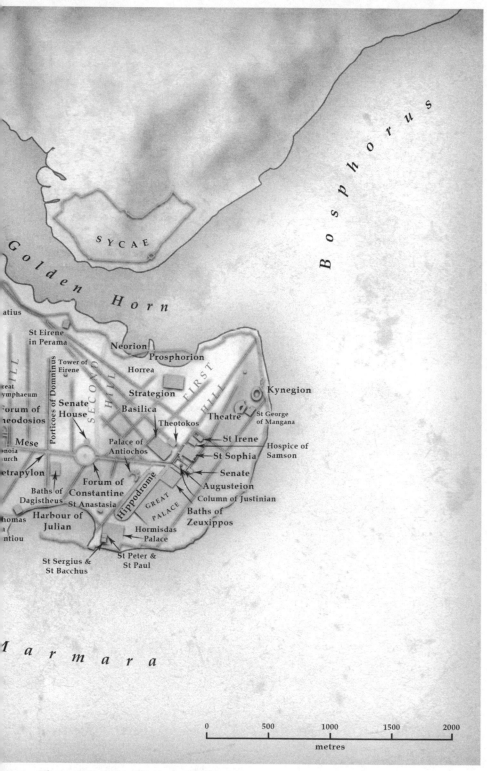

B o s p h o r u s

Golden

Horn

SYCAE

...atius

St Eirene
in Perama

Neorion

Prosphorion

Tower of
Eirene

Horrea

...reat
...ymphaeum

Portices of Domninus

SECOND HILL

FIRST HILL

Strategion

Kynegion

...orum of
...heodosios

Senate
House

Basilica

Theatre

St George
of Mangana

Theotokos

Mese

Palace of
Antiochos

St Irene

...noia
...urch

St Sophia

Hospice of
Samson

...etrapylon

Forum of
Constantine

Senate

Hippodrome

Augusteion

Baths of
Dagistheus

St Anastasia

GREAT PALACE

Column of Justinian

...homas
...a
...ntiou

Harbour of
Julian

Baths of
Zeuxippos

Hormisdas
Palace

St Sergius &
St Bacchus

St Peter &
St Paul

M a r m a r a

| 0 | 500 | 1000 | 1500 | 2000 |

metres

Eleventh-century Constantinople

CHAPTER 36

❧

THE SILKWORM'S JOURNEY

c. AD 552 ONWARDS

Those that are fit for you shall be marked with a leaden seal and left in your possession; those which are prohibited to all nations, except to us Romans, shall be taken away and their price returned ... As we surpass all other nations in wealth and wisdom, so it is right that we should surpass them in dress. Those who are unique in the grace of their virtue should also be unique in the virtue of their raiment.

BISHOP LIUTPRAND OF CREMONA, *THE EMBASSY TO CONSTANTINOPLE* (DESCRIPTION OF SILKS FOR TRADE IN THE BYZANTINE EMPIRE)[1]

The emperor Yang-ti of the Sui dynasty always wished to open intercourse with Fu-lin [Constantinople] ... In [AD 643], the king of Fu-lin Po-to-li [Constans II, Emperor 641–68] sent an embassy offering red glass, lu-chin-ching [green gold gems], and other articles. T'ai-tsung [the Tang emperor] favored them with a message under his imperial seal and graciously granted presents of silk. Since the Ta-shih [the Arabs] had conquered these countries they sent their commander-in-chief, Mo-i [Muawiya], to besiege their capital city; by means of an agreement they obtained friendly relations, and asked to be allowed to pay every year tribute of gold and silk ... their lord offered lions and ling-yang [antelopes] ...

FROM THE *CHIU-T'ANG-SHU* (OLD TANG HISTORY), WRITTEN MID-TENTH CENTURY AD, AND DESCRIBING EVENTS IN THE YEARS AD 618–906[2]

Roads exist to transport not just goods and armies and migrants but thoughts, yet around AD 552 two men of ideas travelled through the Byzantine Empire specifically to transport things. The story goes that two Christian monks – most likely 'Nestorians',[3] from the Church of the East – had, on their travels, observed silk-making in China (in some later versions these are Buddhist monks travelling from east to west). Up until this point, silk-production had been thought to be a craft of Indian origin. Using their contacts in Sogdiana (modern-day Tajikistan and Uzbekistan), medieval chroniclers excitably related that, hidden within bamboo canes, silk moths' eggs and larvae were smuggled out by the intrepid travellers – across the Caspian Sea, over the Caucasus via the Black Sea and into Constantinople.

Even though on the painted walls of Afrasiyab, ancient Samarkand, seventh-century AD Sogdian traders, carrying baskets of the silk cocoon, are indeed depicted enjoying animated, non-verbal, hand-gesture conversations with international merchants, the hard reality of this fabled, two-year journey is probably a little more nuanced. Silk import and manufacture preceded the monkish adventure: Chinese sources – which describe the products of pre-Justinianic Syria as being donkeys, mules, camels, hemp, grain, the mulberry tree and the mulberry silkworm – make it clear that there was some local silk production in Byzantine Syria before the arrival of those legendary Nestorians. But, however it got to the place that Emperor Justinian described as 'The Fortunate City', silk was to become synonymous with both the story and the standing of Byzantium.

Silk, particularly purple silk, had long been an almost mystically precious cloth in the Eastern Mediterranean. Back in the fourth century BC Aristotle had talked in his *Natural History* of silk fibre on the Hellenic island of Kos, and the 'Amorgian' cloth described in classical Greek literature may well be silk.[4] Bronze Age princesses almost certainly wore diaphanous raw-silk modesty cloths over their bare breasts and were definitely wrapped in the *porphyreos wanakteros* – the royal or kingly purple – which was produced in Syria and in coastal settlements such as Kommos, 2.5 miles from the modern-day town of Matala in southern Crete.

Both silk and purple production are stinking businesses. To extract purple dye a predatory sea-snail, the murex, must be factory-farmed, the stress turning the marine mollusc cannibal. The snails are then boiled, often in urine, to bleach out the dye – one estimate puts the ratio at 12,000 snails to colour the hem of a single garment. Silk production also generates an overwhelming stench as the silkworms defecate, and the cocoons are boiled to extract silk filaments. These were time- and labour-consuming industries. Medieval Constantinople must have been rank with the smell of them.

The Emperor Justinian avidly fostered the silk industry. In and around Constantinople spreading mulberry trees were planted to feed the silk moths. Imported silks from Persia had once been unravelled and worked on by women and children in the city. Now Constantinople owned the means of production. The Emperor ordered up beautiful specimens in rich colours, such as an altar cloth in Haghia Sophia embroidered with images of the hospitals and churches that he had founded with Theodora; elsewhere in the cathedral draping silks depicted Justinian and his Empress standing next to Christ and Mary. Procopius made it clear that Justinian's enthusiasm was political as well as artistic and monetary: 'He purposed that the Ethiopians, by purchasing silk from India and selling it among the Romans, might themselves gain much money, while causing the Romans to profit in only one way, namely, that they no longer be compelled to pay over their money to their enemy.'[5] Before the Nika riots destroyed so much of the historic city, well-to-do Constantinopolitan families would buy purple silks from an emporium called the 'House of Lamps'. There were purple-producing workshops close to the Baths of Zeuxippos. Cheaper versions of the 'imperial purple' were manufactured, coloured with madder. Tenth-century sources describe these export-quality goods as 'pseudo-purple'.

Every stage of the silk-making process was fiercely controlled by the Byzantine state, and both imperial and local workshops produced the cloth in Constantinople on a mass scale.[6] As a result both the city and the wider reaches of empire saw an exponential expansion in the silk industry. Land intensive as well as labour intensive (close on 7,000 mulberry trees were recorded on just one Byzantine estate in Reggio), the mulberry leaves had to be carefully diced into appropriate sizes according to the stage of the silkworm's development. The worms were fed at regular intervals day and night, the temperature kept constant and the humidity controlled. Leaf disease could blight an entire crop, so mulberry-caretakers armed with specialised ladders, knives and axes tended to the trees. Across Byzantine lands there was in fact a whole ecology of silk-workers, de-gumming, reeling, twisting and tailoring. Throughout the empire twelve different grades of silk were produced, from rough to spider-silk fine.

Bolts of the finest-quality silks could be used only by emperors them-selves, or were given as diplomatic gifts; factory-quality material was traded. The discovery of silks hidden in caves or tucked away in the lines of inventories from the sixth to the twelfth centuries shows that this un-feasibly sensuous and feather-light material was hoarded to be used as collateral in times of trouble. Silk was frequently employed as currency. Hard to break, light and lovely, Byzantine silk became an international object of desire and of inter-state commerce.

Once Byzantium started to lose land to Islamic forces, a hundred years after those stories of the silk-bearing monks had been told, silk produc-tion spread elsewhere in the Middle East – Islamic and Christian cultures sharing their aesthetic and their motifs: elephants, lions, mythical animals (part dogs, part birds) and inscriptions were woven through the silk in Greek, Latin, Arabic or Kufic Arabic. But even with regional production revving up in the Middle East, the 'made in Byzantium' label seems to have been the most desirable. Production intensified in Constantinople itself. Across Eurasia there were requests for 'Rumi' cloth (from the New Rome), and in Damascus a noted physician reputedly boasted of his own-ership of Byzantine silks and 300 gold brocades. Much of the silk was produced by Jews in the city. These Greek-speaking Jews would come to be known, in honour of the city in which they lived, as Romaniotes. By the tenth century Jewish workers could be involved in all stages of silk production, but not in the export of raw silk skeins. Benjamin of Tudela supplies us with a detailed description of the city's Jewish communities in the twelfth century: 'The numbers of Jews in Constantinople amounts to two thousand Rabbanites and five hundred Caraites [Jews who recognise the written Tanakh alone], who live in one spot, but divided by a wall . . . Many of them are manufacturers of silk cloth, many others are mer-chants, some being extremely rich, but no Jew is allowed to ride upon a horse, except Solomon Hamitsri, who is the king's physician . . .'[7]

From the late sixth century onwards, Constantinople would have sighed with the sound of silk, whether it was being manufactured or worn, spread across shrines and churches or draped over the dead.

The trade in silk tells us much about the internationalist experience of Constantinople and especially its early contacts with China. Known as

Fulin – an adulteration of the Greek *eis ten polin*, meaning to the city, Constantinople was clearly the subject of all kinds of tales in the Far East. The information ranged from the fantastical (a belief that lambs grew in the ground in Byzantium and had to be harvested with great care) to the precise (Constantinople's subject cities were measured, as were the lengths of the roads by which they were connected). As both fact and fantasy, Constantinople entranced China – witness for example this passage written in northern China around the middle of the tenth century AD after the fall of the Tang dynasty in a kind of encyclopaedia of global history compiled from Chinese documents:

> In the palaces [of Constantinople], pillars are made of se-se [lapis lazuli], the floors of yellow gold [probably bronze], the leaves of folding doors of ivory, beams of fragrant wood. They have no tiles, but powdered plaster is rammed down into a floor above the house [a ceiling-roof]. This floor is perfectly firm and of glossy appearance like jade-stone. When, during the height of summer, the inhabitants are oppressed by heat, they lead water up and make it flow over the platform, spreading it all over the roof by a secret contrivance so that one sees and knows not how it is done, but simply hears the noise of a well on the roof; suddenly you see streams of water rushing down from the four eaves like a cataract; the draught caused thereby produces a cooling wind, which is due to this skilful contrivance [a common device in the Near East].[8]

There are personal clues too that ambitious Chinese men and women wanted an association with what they knew to be a 'Fortunate City'. Imitation golden Byzantine solidi, first minted by Constantine the Great, have been found in the graves of a handful of the Chinese great and good from the fourth to the eighth centuries AD, and are also rather sweetly itemised in written burial lists. Even if the owner could not acquire the actual coins, the possession of phantom Byzantine coinage seems to have been a telling wish-before-death.[9] In similar Hellenophilic vein, the mid-sixth-century ruler Li Xian was buried together with a vase depicting the fall of Troy. Craftsmen and crafts alike travelled in both directions: in Istanbul, Chinese platters were used; the distinctive blue and white pattern that we have come to associate with China originated in the Arabian

Imitation Byzantine coins from sixth century Xinjiang, China

south, but was adopted by Chinese craftsmen and then sent out again along the Silk Roads.

Trade was clearly a great driver, but many journeys along the silk routes were made by men of the cloth, in particular Christians travelling from Constantinople. This was the reason those 'Nestorian' – Church of the East – monks were such prominent characters in the silk tale. In AD 482 the Henotikon, the Decree of Unity, confirmed the Council of Chalcedon's condemnation in 451 of the patriarch Nestorios and his 'heretical' ideas, which gave priority to the earthly nature of Christ (rather than the divine). The Nestorians of Constantinople therefore, in steady streams, started to leave, migrating to Persia (where the Church of the East established headquarters in Baghdad) and then on to India and China.[10] Spreading east, all along the Silk Roads, Christian communities had already hunkered down, and now the Byzantine influence gave the fledgling missions on the steppes and in India a shot in the arm.[11] Pictorial depictions of Church of the East Christians, Nestorians, have for example been located in the Turfan (Khocho/Gaochang) oasis in Xinjiang, north-western China. A lovely little wall fresco and the earliest manuscript evidence of Eastern Christian/Syriac texts,[12] only recently identified, are currently being studied by scholars. So when we think of that low-lying, remote landscape in northern China, we should imagine it spattered with something new: little pockets of Christianity.

Christianity is very portable – no shrines, no icons essential – just a message. Christian converts were already attested from the Yemen to

The Nestorian Stele, which was constructed c. AD 780 and erected near Singan, China. This engraving was made by an English visitor in 1887.

Sri Lanka. In AD 635 the first officially recorded 'Nestorian' missionaries would head to the Far East;[13] our evidence is a rather extraordinary object now known as the Nestorian stele.

The Nestorian stele, an 8-foot-high engraved block of stone, sits in Xian's Beilin Museum in dappled light, hymned by the dawn chorus every morning. This, the Memorial of the Propagation in China of the Luminous Religion from Daqin, was erected on 7 January AD 781, in a landscape where plateaus sit on plateaus and rock-faces seem to grow out of paddy-fields. It describes a century and a half of Christianity in China.[14] We read on the stele that one missionary, Alopen, who arrived in 635 from 'Roman lands', brought with him sacred books and images, written in Syriac, later translated into Chinese. Jesus Sutras (Christian scriptures in Chinese) from this year have also been uncovered.[15] The

Tang Emperor welcomed Christianity as a 'Luminous Religion', describing it as a source of mysterious, wonderful calm. In 710 a delegation came from Constantinople, bringing a Bible, icons and other 'sacred' objects. In Luoyang, right at the end of the Silk Roads, where market traders in the old town today still sell pearls in their bubbling oysters next to out-size calligraphy brushes (used by the elderly to paint Chinese characters in water on the streets as a form of art therapy), in 2006 another stele recording Byzantine Christian activity was uncovered. In the Far East Constantinople was coming to be known not just as a city where lambs grew in the ground, but as the protector and progenitor of a revolutionary idea.

The city that Justinian and Theodora had left behind in the second half of the sixth century was a vigorous hybrid, a place that sat between a number of worlds: Christian and pagan, conservative and reforming, East and West. Buried in a military-themed shroud in AD 565, Justinian went fighting to God – yet the style of his burial would prove not the climax of a chapter, but a prophecy of things to come. Because just as ideas and goods were moving out of Constantinople's territories, other forces were moving in. It was at this time (450–600) that a tribe occupying the steppes started to make its presence felt in China, attacking northern frontier garrisons. There are early, fluttering references to these warring bands in Chinese texts, and then the Turks – as the tribe came to be called – come into focus, acquiring a name that we can recognise: a kingdom called Tu-Küe is located on the Orkhon River south of Lake Baikal. Eventually Turkic raiders would become landowning warlords in the northern regions, and would work with the Chinese to control and to establish settlements along the Silk Routes. But their impact on Central Asia, and indeed on the city that the Chinese called Fulin, would be irreversible.

The relationship between the Turks and Constantinople had got off to a perilously bad start. Moving south, the Turks initially suggested an alliance with Justinian's successor Justin II; together the two would destroy Persia in a pincer movement. But New Rome's efforts failed pitiably, leaving the Turks exposed. The blunder would earn the city a new enemy. As the ambassador of the Turks commented frostily, jamming both hands in his mouth: 'As there are now ten fingers in my mouth, so you Romans have used many tongues.'[16] Justin II's antagonistic foreign policy continued. Avars, who had long been kept quiet by Justinian with tribute payments, were sent packing by the new Emperor. 'Never again shall you be loaded at the expense of this empire,' he was said to have sneered.[17] Justin II's barbs brought him no satisfaction; he ended his life a madman, wheeled around the palaces of Byzantium in a golden bathchair, biting the hands of those that he passed. Justinian's Golden Age – all its promises of universal peace and prosperity – was starting to have a rather tinny ring.

Within a hundred years the Turks would not just be turning up in the history books of others, but writing their own narratives,[18] and Constantinople would, for the rest of her lifespan as a Christian city, be under attack. The desirable was, once again, becoming the desired.

CHAPTER 37

❖

AL-QUSTANTINIYYA

AD 602–28

Peace unto thee, O Syria, and what an excellent country this is for the enemy!

EMPEROR HERAKLEIOS, ON RECEIVING NEWS OF THE BYZANTINE
DEFEAT AT THE BATTLE OF YARMUK (AD 636)[1]

Wander into an Orthodox church, the Church of St Panteleimon for example in the privet-proud suburb of Harrow, north-west London, and you might well hear the Akathistos, a prayer of salvation.

Once again in AD 626 the Virgin Mary, it was said, had come to the rescue of her favoured city. The Akathistos is still recited today in gratitude by Orthodox congregations – as it had been at the Virgin's shrine at Blachernae on the Golden Horn fourteen centuries before – for delivering Constantinople from her Sassanid Persian, Slav and Avar attackers. A ghostly Mary and her son Christ, eyewitnesses declared, had appeared from within the spring-protecting church – part of whose handsome adjoining palace is still standing – to ward off those enemies. The patriarch of Constantinople, Sergios, a relation of the Emperor Herakleios, had experience of active campaigning in Africa and had been left in charge of the city. Sergios is recorded as bellowing at Constantinople's besiegers: 'Lady Theotokos will put an end to your presumption and arrogance by her single command. For she is truly the mother of Him who immersed the Pharaoh and all his army in the middle of the Red Sea, and who will prove this daimonic horde listless and feeble.'[2]

The sacred robe – the Himation of the Virgin Mary – was processed around Constantinople's walls. Images of the Holy Mother and the Christ child were nailed to the city gates, and it was murmured from one street corner to another and even in the enemy camps that Mary, Queen of Heaven, had appeared in person, a veiled figure, to destroy Slavic boats in a violent, celestially powered tempest. In the eye of the storm on Istanbul's waterways the visibility is indeed zero, the sound deafening – it is not hard to imagine the Slavs' dread as they watched their compatriots drowning; nor is it hard to understand why, back in Constantinople, poetry was quickly penned, honouring Mary as the protector of Christ's earthly home.

But whether or not Jesus' mother was on their side, the blustering, brilliant reign of Justinian suddenly seemed a distant dream.

In the winter of AD 602 the subaltern officer Phokas had marched on Constantinople, stormed the city, taken the throne and then executed, in cold blood, the Emperor Maurice (himself a man who had obtained power after a bewildering series of imperial musical chairs), together with Maurice's sons. Until the stink of rotting flesh became unbearable, the heads of Phokas' victims were displayed outside the city in the Hebdomon, a parade ground adjoining a number of waterside palatial complexes, 7 Roman miles from the Milion. In what is now the upwardly mobile residential district of Bakırköy, the neat homeowners might not appreciate that their houses have such gruesome foundations. In 610 Phokas himself was murdered, by the incoming rebel Herakleios.[3] After he had been beheaded and desexed, Phokas' dismembered body parts were paraded through Constantinople's streets.

The chaos in the city had been exacerbated by a punishing campaign, in the winter of AD 602, against the Slavs, a 'new people' and a new enemy of Byzantium. The Slavs were a worryingly amorphous menace; they were described by contemporary chroniclers as having 'swamps and forests' rather than cities.[4] This was still an age in which unknown tribes could suddenly emerge from the miasma of unfamiliar lands. We need to appreciate how psychologically challenging all this would have been. Add to this the climatic changes that had pulsed through the region over the previous century and it becomes easier to appreciate that Constantinople's wider world was not sure, not charted, not settled, but rather a vale of tears full of sinister threats. Nothing could be taken for granted.

Herakleios was an emperor on the back foot from the very moment he came to power. The same year that Constantinople witnessed Phokas' messy death, the Persians captured Damascus and Caesarea; then came stomach-sinking news. In AD 614 Christian prisoners of war and the relic of the True Cross had been taken from Jerusalem and moved to the Persian capital of Ctesiphon. The following year the Persians were raiding just across the water from Constantinople, and in 617 they over-ran Palestine; that same year Avars were said to have carried away with them over a quarter of a million slaves from Constantinople's Thracian suburbs. Then Egypt, the city's bread-basket – indeed the empire's – was lost in 619. For the first time since Constantinople's establishment as the New Rome a scant 300 years before, the free distribution of bread on her streets suddenly stopped. Herakleios considered moving the imperial capital from Constantinople to Carthage. The carapace of this city of God was starting to look paper-thin.

Initially Herakleios tried to negotiate with the Persians, sending envoys to the Persian leader Khusraw to sue for peace. The Byzantine envoys were allowed their say and were then cut down. We are told that when news of their fate reached the city, panic paced through the streets. But Herakleios was not to be cowed: to help fund his anti-Persian campaigns, he would raise taxes and halve the pay of his officials; he even melted down the hanging lamps of Haghia Sophia. His coins were now reminted bearing the image of a cross on steps – resembling the crucifix on Golgo-tha Hill. The fight with the invaders of the south had become not just a matter of politics but of faith.

And indeed when the Persians then ranged within sight of the city at Chalcedon, supporting their new allies the Avar nomads from the north, with the Emperor away fighting elsewhere, it seemed that nothing less than a divine miracle could resolve Constantinople's predicament. We could, like the men and women of the city, believe it was indeed Mary's power, along with the removal of the remains of St Euphemia and St The-odore (the latter the son of an inn courtesan and hippodrome acrobatic performer – another of Constantinople's 'new men') from Chalcedon to Constantinople for safe-keeping. But in the end it was, in truth, a series of mundanities that saved Constantinople from destruction. The Avar tribes squabbled, the pasture wasn't good enough for their horses, and word came to the Persians that while their focus was in the West, in the East Turks were creeping into the Caucasus.[5]

Herakleios, stung perhaps by the sense that he had not been there to protect his city-child when she most needed his help, decided that valour was the better part of discretion. He went on the attack, meeting the Khagan of the Turks, offering him his own daughter's hand in marriage and the most luxurious gifts that Constantinople could rustle up: 'Taking off the crown from his head, he placed it on the Turk's and, after serving a banquet, presented to him all the utensils of the table as well as an imperial garment and earrings adorned with pearls. He likewise decorated with his own hand the noblemen of [the Turk's] suite with similar earrings.'[6] Herakleios then routed what remained of the Persian civilisation in Nineveh (present-day Mosul in Iraq) from AD 627 to 628. Khusraw was murdered and Herakleios, realising that he had the upper hand and appropriating the Persian title of 'King of Kings', swiftly negotiated favourable terms: the return of Byzantine territories and of those vital fragments of the True Cross, recovered by Helena, that had been snatched (it was said with the help of the Jews, who were then punished for their supposed collaboration) from Jerusalem. The relics were returned to the Church of the Holy Sepulchre after being processed in triumph through Constantinople.

But Herakleios had chosen a complicated ally. The fact that the Great Wall of China had been built higher, longer, stronger in part as a response to the raids of the Turks, 150 years before, should have worried the city of God on the edge of the Bosphorus. The Turks had been quietly getting stronger. Breeding the horses beloved of Indian and Chinese warrior leaders, never allowed to become irrelevant because of the Silk Road trade routes that abutted their territory and connected Constantinople in the West with Xian in the East across 4,000 miles, picking up some of the twenty or so languages spoken in the adjacent lands, exemplifying our desire as a species to communicate and to exchange, all forced this band of trader-warriors centre stage. Constantinople was nourishing a healthy trade between the Far East and the western reaches of Christendom, but in doing so she was also nourishing what would be a predatory enemy, an enemy who would eventually realise the nightmares of the Christian city.

Justinian's years in power had been very successful, but they had also been charged – these were thought to be the 'end of days', and there was an eschatological urgency to affairs. Herakleios' victory over the Avars was celebrated in epic verse that declared him not just a Roman emperor, *imperator*, but a biblical king, *basileus* – he now joined a long line of Old Testament kings, and the Greek title would continue until

Constantinople fell. Although the imagery, symbolism and iconography of this time was ever more proudly Christian – with coronations taking place within Haghia Sophia from AD 641, the paeans of praise penned by George of Pisidia, a deacon of Haghia Sophia, likened Herakleios not just to Noah and Moses but to Herakles and Perseus. These pagan allusions show that there was still a classical colour to much that went on in the city. Those who ruled from Constantinople had Greco-Roman culture in their hearts, minds and blood. The struggle between the Persians and the Byzantines, the 'Last Great War of Antiquity', had left both powers weakened. But this was not the time for Constantinople to leave her flanks exposed. Herakleios and the inhabitants of the 'Fortunate City' were about to tangle with a new force, a people of faith who believed that they were the pure, the cleansed, the prime representatives of the one true God.

In a sura – composed around AD 628,[7] before the Qur'an was compiled, there was approving mention in an Arabic hand of the Byzantine defeat of the pagan Sassanid empire. 'The Romans have been defeated in the lowest land, but after their defeat they will themselves be victorious in a few years' time. The affair is God's from beginning to end. On that day, the believers will rejoice.'[8]

Monotheists were, briefly, united.[9] But 'briefly' is here the watchword: because in a world of combative belief, of opportunity and flux, the region had thrown up a new challenger. Constantinople – al-Qustantiniyya in Arabic – would become what was said to be the bone that stuck in the throat of Allah.[10]

CHAPTER 38

❖

A BONE IN THE THROAT OF ALLAH

AD 622
(ISLAMIC YEAR ZERO)

In the jihad against Constantinople, one third of the Muslims will allow themselves to be defeated, which Allah cannot forgive; one third will be killed in battle, making them wondrous martyrs; and one third will be victorious.

TRADITIONAL HADITH OF MUHAMMAD, RECORDED 150 YEARS
OR SO AFTER THE PROPHET'S DEATH[1]

The Prophet Muhammad first appears on the historical stage in a glancing mention, as a walk-on character in one of the administrative themes of Constantinople. We are told that in c. AD 582, a boy aged eleven or twelve was travelling through Bosr (modern-day Bosra in southern Syria). Here there was a cathedral, a vigorous trading community and a monophysite monk called Bahira who spotted that there was something just a bit special about this orphan; a cloud was said to travel over him as he walked, shading him from the ferocity of the sun. And on inspecting the boy's back, the monk found certain prophesied signs. The monk then warned him to beware of – depending which version of the story you read – either the Jews or Byzantium.

It might be a while before such stories of Muhammad were told in Constantinople, but Bedouin travellers and traders already had a fixed and firm opinion of the lambent city to the north; their poets wrote about visits to the Byzantine Emperor and Byzantine artefacts have turned up in pre-Islamic caravanserais. One, 'Adi b. Zayd, is reported to have visited Constantinople where he was well received at court; on 'Adi's departure, the Emperor instructed the officials in charge of the post routes to provide his guest with horses and with every other assistance so that 'Adi might see the size and strength of his domains. An even more celebrated and elevated Bedouin poet, Imru' al-Qais, went to Constantinople to ask for help in regaining his lost kingdom. The Emperor Justinian was not unsympathetic to the plight of this visitor, but nothing more was heard of his request since Imru' al-Qais 'died on his way back to Arabia around the year AD 540.'[2]

And so while the Prophet Muhammad was for years of no account for the administrators of Byzantium, Constantinople would certainly have been on Muhammad's mind. The Rum, the Byzantine Empire and/or the Eastern Romans appear twenty-eight times in hadiths, Constantinople twelve times.[3]

The year AD 622 was world changing. The Emperor Herakleios had raised taxes for what was meant to be his decisive Middle Eastern campaign and now, as he set out from the palace at Constantinople, he would have performed certain religious rituals to ensure hallowed protection on the road. Later accounts describe the *profectio bellica* where the Emperor would pray for divine favour in Haghia Sophia and then at various shrines throughout the city in advance of battle.[4] This plucky fighter from Carthage had turned Constantinople's fortunes around. With the city disintegrating in strength and standing thanks to psychotic rulers and petty infighting, her citizens had seen raiding armies from Persia come as close as Chalcedon across the Bosphorus and Avar tribes within touching distance of her walls. But Herakleios had not caved in; instead he had taken Constantinople's fight to the East.

Meanwhile that fervent trader, the Prophet Muhammad, now a middle-aged man, was leaving Mecca to set up a new life in a town called Yathrib, that which today we call Medina.

Stories abound about Muhammad's early life, but the facts are sparser. It seems that he was probably born in around AD 570 to a trading family in the Banu Hashim, a branch of the Quraysh tribe, which had seen better times. Orphaned by the age of six and married to the successful businesswoman Khadija when he was about twenty-five, he travelled widely through Syria – where he would have been exposed to both Christian and Jewish ideas.[5] But then, we are told, aged fifty-two or so Muhammad embarked on a long and significant journey through the desert.

It would be from this journey, now called the Hijrah, that Istanbul after AD 1453 would take its clock and its calendar for close on 500 years – because, for Muslims, AD 622 was when time began.

A recent GIS and photographic account of the 210-mile Hijrah trek – a trek undertaken, we are told, by about seventy of his followers and then by Muhammad himself and his companion Abu Bakr – reveals both how punishing and how mesmerically handsome the landscape here is. Leaving Mecca in September the exiles would have passed the strange, stern grey rocks of Thawr, the lava tract of Dajnan, thorn bushes in the valley of Qudayd, the watercourses of Liqf and the ankle-twisting rocks around al-Khala'iq. At night camels and desert foxes slip by here without a sound. The land has been described by those who have walked it as 'a place where the wall between two worlds feels very thin'.⁶ Some kind of certainty seems to have been made manifest on that journey. But this was also a real expedition in real time; Muhammad was escaping the unpopularity of his radical, monotheist ideas in Mecca and would have had to defend himself along the way. There were almost certainly raids, or *ghazawat*, on locals – although this is played down by many Islamic chroniclers.

Once in Yathrib, we hear, a basic mosque was built with tree trunks to support its roof and one stone was set to denote the direction of prayer at Muhammad's home. Islamic sources relate that the Prophet stood on a tree trunk to preach here. Reconstruction of traditional homes from this time demonstrates that the rooms would have been sweet with the smell of dried palm leaves, beads of light dropping through gaps like sap. There was a feeling among this group of ready exiles that there was no aspect of life that was not holy. While the presence of the divine was the default position for many in medieval society, Islam and its followers had the advantage of the new. Their discussions about God emphasised his *tawhid*, his uniqueness and unity. The new Muslims won against the Quraysh in the Battle of Badr in AD 624. In 628 further revelation told them that they should face Mecca rather than Jerusalem to pray. Blood ties and civic precedent were now wiped clean and replaced with the supreme law of God, enacted following the word of Muhammad by a new kind of super-tribe.

The arrival in Yathrib – which came to be called simply al-Medina, 'the City', heralded Islam as a state-based, political and military force. The reorientation of this 'City' would eventually be felt in the other

'City', *He Polis*, 1,300 miles to the north. There are only a small number of settlements – Athens, Alexandria, Medina, Constantinople, Rome – whose reach in the imagination is so great that they need no proper noun: 'City' is simply enough.

The bleakly beautiful land that saw the birth of Islam seems to justify durability. The cool sand, the serpentine twists of that raw material of glass, induce big ideas about the possibilities of the world. And in his farewell address Prophet Muhammad apparently sanctified this predisposition: 'I was ordered to fight all men until they say, "There is no god but Allah."' The development of this fighting talk into something that smacks more of imperialism was justified by another seventh-century Muslim leader: 'Other men trampled us beneath their feet while we trampled no one. Then God sent a prophet from among us . . . and one of his promises was that we should conquer and overcome these lands.'7

The make-up of the Middle East in AD 622 was variegated: nomadic Arab tribes; large Jewish populations; Georgians; Armenians; Latin-speaking Europeans, with Greek-speakers dominating the cities. Monophysite communities mixed with Orthodox Christians; most men were loyal to the Byzantine Empire, a few not. The stakes in the religious game were being raised. In Constantinople, following his defeat of the Sassanid Persians, Herakleios was now, as mentioned earlier, *basileus*: king by divine right. But at the same time from Medina word was spreading that at last the Arabs had their own Prophet of God, with a similarly intimate connection to the divine – a Prophet who knew that God spoke to his people in their own tongue.

While the followers of Muhammad were enjoying a greater sense of themselves, the Byzantines, in tough times, treated these newcomers as a pipsqueak distraction. 'The Emperor can barely pay his soldiers their wages . . . much less [you] dogs,' they were reputedly told. One Roman envoy with a similarly dismissive attitude was then killed and sewn up into a camel.8 Someone should have taken heed of the warning signs because at Yarmuk just fourteen years later, astonishingly, the Byzantines would suffer a shaming defeat at the hands of these men whom, at first, they had considered simply an annoyance.

At the Battle of Yarmuk, blown by sandstorms, the once legendary tightness of the Roman army disintegrated.

Byzantines and Arab tribes had already clashed at Mu'ta in AD 629, but in theory there was little need for these two to tread on one another's toes. Herakleios' line of defence stretched from Ghazzah (Gaza) to the southern end of the Dead Sea, while Muslim Arabs operated further south. But Herakleios' defeat of the Sassanians had left a power vacuum in Arabia, with weapons from the defeated armies being traded and reused and mercenary soldiers ready to be bought by the nearest recruiting officer.

The Yarmuk battleground lay just inland from the ancient cities of Tyre and Sidon. Today it crosses the UN-controlled ceasefire line between Syria and the Israeli-occupied Golan Heights. The Muslims fielded around 25,000 men. the Byzantine numbers were greater, but there were problems. In the Byzantine army the less than entirely charismatic Theodore, Emperor Herakleios's brother, was in charge; Greek and Armenian leaders squabbled over strategy; all seemed to underestimate their opponents. The Byzantines, frankly, would not have started this battle if they had had any idea it would end in defeat. Crucially, over the six tightly fought days, the Islamic army's bite seemed keener. The Byzantines came with a menacing reputation – the heads and hands of their enemies were often paraded in public, captives tortured in town squares. But the spanking-new troops led by 'Umr ibn al-Khattab from Medina and Khalid ibn al-Walid (who was born in Mecca and died in Homs) seemed to have a sharp thirst for victory. It was said that these Muslims could fight in the midday heat without water, and the ferocity of the Arab women in the combat zone was reported on by chroniclers of both sides. By the end of the sixth day at Yarmuk, huge numbers of the Byzantine army had been annihilated or had fled. Herakleios, back in Constantinople, heard of the grim defeat only too soon.[9]

Descriptions of punishing clouds of dust were fielded as a mystical excuse for the humiliating obliteration. But the truth was clearer. From now on, Constantinople would be not the hunter but the hunted. This first significant engagement was in stark contrast to the storybook version of Byzantium's first encounter with Muhammad as a miraculous young man. On the dust-filled plains of Yarmuk, Constantinople's future was being redrawn. The Ghassanid ruler Jabala, fleeing from what was now Islamic-held territory into Byzantine lands, set down in Arabic an echoing sentiment:

Oh would that my mother no son ever bore
Nor my name had in history found place.
How I yearn for the land of my fathers of yore,
Damascus, the home of my race.

In AD 630 Herakleios had declared that all Jews must convert to Christianity – a reaction perhaps to reports that Muslim armies were spreading deep into Persia, having taken Mecca in the same year. The Persians too were converting to Islam; those that became Muslims were promised a percentage of all booty. In 638 the Arabs under Caliph Umar took Jerusalem (there is a slim possibility that Muhammad survived to lead his troops into the city)[10] with the help of Jewish forces who pointed the way and helped to clear up the Temple Mount; gratitude, some say, was expressed in the form of space for a new synagogue and for Galilean homes.[11] In the eyes of the Emperors of Constantinople, the Jews had demonstrably chosen the wrong friends.[12] In 640 Muslim Arabs took Caesarea, in 642 Alexandria fell, Armenia was formally under Arab control in 645 and Rhodes, Kos, Cyprus, Crete all succumbed. In 655 the Arabs also flexed their muscles on the seas in the emblematic Battle of the Masts, where the Byzantine Emperor Constans ended up curled on a boat's deck, desperate to escape. In 674 when the Arab fleet was stationed at Cyzicus (where Alcibiades had won that victory in 410 BC that then allowed him to retake Byzantion), the Greeks bombarded them with the lethal weapon which we call Greek Fire but which was then called Sea Fire, Sticking Fire or Roman Fire.[13] The heat and the smell of this chemical weapon were infamous, and its effects like those of napalm, but what recent experiments have shown are the unsettling screaming sounds that Greek Fire generates – the hiss of steam and flame, the screech and crack as timbers split. When it is deployed, the surface of the water appears to become one creeping blaze. The naval attacks by Muslims on Constantinople between 661 and 750, five signal attempts and failures, the 'shock and awe' of the city's response, were swiftly memorialised in the songs and poems of both East and West. Greek prose and poetry assumed a darker shade of purple, as can be seen in the lines of Theodore Grammaticus written after the failed Islamic attack of 674:

For behold just as you are, Lord of All, you saved your city from the crashing waves of the filthy and most evil Arabs, you stole away fear of them and the trembling and their returning shadows . . .

Where now, O cursed ones, are your shining bright ranks of arrows? Where now the melodious chords of the bow strings? Where is the glitter of your swords and spears, your breast plates and head-borne helmets, scimitars and darkened shields?[14]

Yet, within just fifty years of the 'start of time' in AD 622, year zero according to the Islamic system of dating, Byzantium had lost two-thirds of her territories. Within seven years the key cities of Damascus (635), Antioch (637) and Edessa (640) as well as Jerusalem had fallen away from Constantinople's control. Within a century Muslim armies had not only reached southern France but had raided in Afghanistan, occupied Central Asia, taken large swathes of the Indus Valley (equivalent to modern-day Pakistan) and even reached the western edge of Imperial China. Their leader came to be called called *khalifah* – Muhammad's successor, the deputy of God. The Persians would not return as a force to be reckoned with until the sixteenth century and, critically for the people of Constantinople, their grain would not come from Egypt again until the Ottomans joined the dots and, from their headquarters at what was by then the Islamic city of Kostantiniyye, take Egypt once again in 1517.

A sign of the extremity of the time was that Herakleios' grandson Constans II attempted to evacuate the capital to Syracuse in Sicily in the dog days of his reign (AD 663), although he was not followed by the bulk of Constantinople's inhabitants.[15]

The level of understanding and sympathy between Muslims, Christians and Jews at this time is much debated. Some Jewish texts praised the Muslim advance and saw these new monotheists as a relief from Roman tyranny; others described Muhammad as a false prophet, 'for prophets do not come armed with a sword'.[16] Churches continued to be founded in Islamic-occupied territories and Muslims helped with the rebuilding of the church of Edessa after an earthquake of AD 679.[17] Even in Jerusalem, current excavations are revealing just how extensively the Church of the Holy Sepulchre was expanded and refurbished up until the tenth century, including the construction of a brand-new church next door in the early Islamic period. Christian families and monks on and around Mount Sinai were protected by a written Achtiname (testament) said to be sealed with an imprint of the Prophet Muhammad's own hand in the second year of the Hijrah – a sacred document that ended up in Constantinople once the Ottomans had established control over Egypt in 1517. But any long-term Abrahamic, Christian and Marian solidarity was lost in the harsh realpolitik of the drive to acquire new land and new favour from God. Constantinople would be coveted by successive Muslim rulers, the perfect city and a perfection that needed to be enjoyed. In the collection of Middle Eastern and Persian folk-tales *One Thousand and One Nights*, Arab forces travelled to the city by boat but were thwarted in a siege. Jihad, 'striving in the path of God', a means of spiritualising the pre-Islamic *ghazawat* or raids, now became a divine order for the taking of the cosmopolitan settlement that was described by many as greater than Rome, 'The Queen of Cities'. Islam might have begun as a line of hoofprints in the sand – Allah's word carried on that warm, desert wind – but what it came to desire would be the control of a Greco-Roman city garlanded by waters: 'You will liberate Constantinople, blessed is the Amir who is its Amir, and blessed is the army, that army.'[18]

CHAPTER 39

✤

MONKS BY NIGHT, LIONS BY DAY

C. AD 692
(72/3 IN THE ISLAMIC CALENDAR)

Stay there [Constantinople] until you conquer it or I recall you.

SÜLEYMAN, THE UMAYYAD CALIPH IN CHARGE OF THE AD 717
SIEGE OF CONSTANTINOPLE, WRITING TO HIS BROTHER
MASLAMA (THE GENERAL LEADING THE ATTACK)[1]

Monks by night, lions by day.

DESCRIPTION OF A MUSLIM CAMP, SPIED UPON BY A CHRISTIAN
ASCETIC, AS TOLD BY AL-AZDI, IN HIS *TARIKH FUTUH AL-SHAM*[2]

Who in the East now owned the hotline to God? The leaders of Constantinople and of the ever increasing Muslim territories started to engage in wars of propaganda and faith. 'There is no God but God and Muhammad is the Messenger of God' were the declarations on coins issued in AD 692 by the Caliph Abd al-Malik; in the last few years scholars have even suggested that some coinage carried an image of Muhammad himself.[3] The Byzantine Emperor Justinian II responded in kind – his coins now showed Christ on one side and his own image as the 'Servant of God' on the other. Constantine the Great had always seemed less squeamish about using the image of Christ as a human (whereas before Jesus had typically been portrayed as a lamb), and Constantinople had long revelled in her religious art. Two-dimensional icons and mosaics were thought of as intercessors between the people and the divine as these could not be judged to be blasphemous graven images. Eastern Orthodox Christianity believed that God and man could meet and then unite through these lovingly prepared visual aids. The dome of Haghia Sophia was considered the dome of heaven, and it was religious art that led the eyes of the faithful to God.

But the purity of early Islam, which started to denounce the use of the human form in sacred representations, clearly had a troubling attraction. At the council known as the Quinisext, held in the imperial palace in Constantinople in AD 692, stubborn pagan practices were once again outlawed: masques in the streets, wild animal shows, priests at the hippodrome, women dancing in public, both sexes cross-dressing, invoking Dionysos and bonfire-leaping.[4] Byzantium needed to clean up her act.

Meanwhile the Muslim diaspora, which had of course emerged from a world dominated by classical influence, was cherry-picking the best of the Byzantine. Mosaics in the Friday Mosque, Damascus (rebuilt by the Umayyad Muslim rulers from a church of St John in AD 705–15) on which pearls hung down in doorways drew not only on themes in pre-Islamic, Arabic poetry but also on Byzantine example.[5] The mosque was decorated by Byzantine craftsmen with golden tesserae sent by Justinian II; and it has been suggested that the layout of Damascus itself was conceived as a mini-Constantinople, the Umayyads building their city in Syria as their version of the city to the north that they so yearned to take (a frustrated desire after the failed siege of Constantinople of 717–18).[6] The so-called Blue Qur'an, written in gold and silver Kufic script on indigo-dipped vellum, in part took its inspiration from Byzantine precedents where imperial and patriarchal administrators would write on purple-dyed folios.[7] Some argue that decorative ivory furniture panels from the Abbasid residence at al-Humayma recall those of the Byzantine 'Grado' chair, which is possibly from Constantinople.[8] Ivory carving was certainly one of the crafts enthusiastically pursued in the Christian city.[9] The maxims of Menander, scratched out so carefully on broken pottery sherds, turn up in Arabic (although they were attributed to Homer). Constantinople's passion for learning was further stimulated by scholars from the south – men who, patronised by the Abbasid Caliphate in the mid-eighth century, translated vast numbers of texts a century before the Qur'an was tentatively translated into Greek. Byzantine craftsmen were used to decorate the Dome of the Rock in Jerusalem.[10] So now it was not just 'the City' that attracted an immense expenditure of energy, but the newly invigorated cities in what was a newly Muslim world.[11]

The question started to be asked, in terms of belief, culture, divine favour and firepower, who was leading whom?

*

With Egypt lost, Sicily and Central Africa were now the only suppliers of Constantinople's grain, and those licit supply chains were perilous and expensive to maintain. The challenges of globalism were felt as keenly fifteen centuries ago as they are by many of us today. More and more Christian cities fell. Meanwhile, in what is now Italy, Lombard encroachment gradually squeezed Byzantine influence into a mere corridor of power from Rome to Ravenna.

Initially those living in former Byzantine lands under their new Muslim masters would have noticed much continuity, with vines still appearing on incense-burners and furniture decorations and bare-breasted Amazons still leaping across the luscious textiles used as showy dividing curtains in Egypt. But in practical terms Constantinople now had to focus her attentions north. It is from the seventh century onwards that we find the city involved in missions to convert her one-time enemies the Slavs.

Focus on the East had left the West exposed. There was a perceptible sense of Constantinople shrinking in towards herself as control became more centralised. As a consequence the contrast and colour dials at court were ratcheted up – the intrigues and power play in the World's Desire grew ever headier. And then came a pause. The Muslims suffered defeat at the hands of Charles Martel near Poitiers in AD 732, as they had done in 717–18 when their troops were decimated by disease and by lack of food outside the walls of Constantinople. There would be no further Muslim sieges of Constantinople until the fourteenth century.[12] With the solidification of Muslim control in al-Andalus (as Muslim Iberia was known) and the Abbasid Caliphate around Baghdad – which by the tenth century would became the largest city in the world – Islamic focus seemed now to be on development rather than colonisation. But the ambition to conquer Constantinople still gnawed. The city was now described in apocalyptic, eschatological terms as one of the four 'Cities of Hell'. She appeared in Islamic songs, paintings, sermons.

An archaeological find reminds us of the level of Constantinople's anxiety at this time. The coiling enormity of a sea-chain with links each the size of a man's arm and a full stretch of half a mile has been plucked during the writing of this book from the mud thanks to rescue-archaeology in modern Istanbul. A barrage almost certainly installed by Emperor Leo III (originally in the form of a floating wooden boom) c. AD 730, this desperate defence stretched from the western banks of the Golden Horn to the Megalos Pyrgos, or Great Tower, at Galata.[13] On the Northern shore the submerged foundations of its terminus are still just visible. The Golden Horn chain would thwart many attackers (although it would be circumvented by Kievan Rus in the tenth century and broken by a Venetian ram in 1204), but those Cyclopean coils feel like an admission of weakness rather than a statement of strength.

It is understandable that, around this time, we find Constantinople remembering that she had originally been the child of Rome – and considering that it might be politic to make a conscious effort to reach back out to the Far West for support and succour.

CHAPTER 40

✤

BYZANTIUM AND BRITANNIA
FIFTH, SIXTH AND SEVENTH CENTURIES AD

King Arthur said that he would take his fleet to Constantinople. He would fill a thousand ships with knights and three thousand with foot-soldiers, until no citadel, borough, town, or castle, no matter how high or mighty its walls, could withstand their assault.

CHRÉTIEN DE TROYES, *CLIGÈS*, C. AD 1176[1]

The Tintagel headland on the wild, windy north coast of Cornwall is a haunting place at the best of times. But in 1983 a scrub fire revealed something that had never before been charted: blocky stone homes and storehouses dating from the fifth and sixth centuries AD. The scale and provenance of the finds are breathtaking. Just 10 per cent of this site has been excavated and yet in that 10 per cent there are more Byzantine pottery fragments than have been uncovered anywhere else in western Europe. Some are stamped with crosses, an unambiguous connection to the city that believed herself to be the beating heart of Christendom. This is a monumental hoard a long way from home.

The pottery is now kept in the dusty Victorian calm of the storerooms of the Royal Cornwall Museum, Truro. Hold that carefully glazed, well-travelled slipware and immediately the nearby, rugged north Cornish coast takes on a rather exotic gloss. As Byzantium was reaching her Golden Age the natural harbours and coastal cliffs here must have witnessed a bustling scene – trans-oceanic sailors bartering luxury goods and raw materials (spices and incense, perfumed oils, fine dining ware) and locals lapping up the travellers' tales of the exotic lands the merchants and sailors had seen, populated by wild beasts, dark maidens and soldiers of Christ.

Tintagel's hidden treasure seems to show hard evidence of direct contact with Byzantine traders who sailed out from the Eastern Mediterranean to western Europe via North Africa. Amphorae here, identical to those found in a Byzantine shipwreck in the Mediterranean, are certainly Eastern and could well have started life in Syria, western Anatolia or Constantinople itself. The fierce sailing conditions on the return voyage of a round-the-world trading trip would have necessitated a stopover in Cornwall. Whichever tribal king had control over this nodal point of exchange – a jutting headland connected by a narrow rock bridge, a God-created castle at the edge of the sea – would have been the talk of the age. All these are circumstances which may have given rise to tales of a mighty, well-connected warrior king who entertained a high-octane court filled with stories of monsters and magic and foreign lands. The legend of King Arthur starts to emerge soon after those Tintagel storerooms were built. It could well be that trade with Constantinople formed, or fed, stories of a British, Christian king with exotic Eastern connections.

Utterly unhelpful for the historian but irresistible for the tourist guides, the digs here have also yielded from the late Roman period an inscribed stone – reused as the cover for a drain – on which a recalcitrant 'Dark Age' lad and his mates have scratched their names. One of those responsible for the graffito is called Artugno – a name that when Latinised becomes Arthur. This certainly is not a king, but an Arthur definitely 'was here'.

Why did traders from the East embark on this 4,000-mile journey from the heat of the Mediterranean to salt-sharp Cornwall? The critical clue here seems to be tin. Our single extant piece of written evidence for the Cornish tin trade at this time comes from the life of St John the Almsgiver of Alexandria. We have already met St John; he was the priest and patriarch who dreamt of angels in the form of eunuchs.[2] A feisty-sounding individual, he established almshouses (prefiguring a system of state welfare, they included provision and shelter for women who had given birth on their own) in North Africa in the sixth century: St John's piety offers us historical gold. We are told that he had been visited one night in a dream by Lady Compassion. He was inspired by this to make the world a better place, and his subsequent good deeds included furnishing a poor man with a boat so that he could travel to Britain. On his return the boat's cargo of tin miraculously turned to silver in the saint's hands. The popular story has as its purpose moral instruction but delivers us history by accident.

It could be that all this fine pottery was making its way west so that Cornish tin (a vital constituent of bronze) could come east; but tin could, by this time, be sourced in small quantities from Cappadocia in central Anatolia. It seems instead that Byzantium simply wanted to keep open the channels of communication with western Britain. A reference in Procopius tells us that Justinian established diplomatic relations with the British (sending subsidies to the barbarians of 'Brettania') – he had after all secured the international grain trade thanks to those granaries on Tenedos – and there is tantalising evidence that Constantinople may even have had a say in the appointment of religious and civic officials in the West.[3] Procopius also reported that Belisarios offered to 'give' Britain to the Goths (probably a quip since the Goths had offered to give Constantinople the island of Sicily). What seems certain, from the evidence continuing to emerge at Tintagel, is that Constantinople was a soft shadow in the minds of those Britons, a gilded child of a Rome whose own neglectful mother had left Britannia behind; and that distant Brettania was likewise an imprint on the mental map of the men and women of Constantinople.[4]

Evidence for life in Constantinople can be found elsewhere in Britain too – if we make the short journey to the eastern shore of the country.

Rowing up the River Deben in East Anglia from the North Sea towards Sutton Hoo is surprisingly choppy. Travelling in from the Near East, in the sixth and seventh centuries AD, to make contact with the gatekeepers of eastern Britain, this would have been one of the routes taken by merchants and emissaries from Constantinople and her territories. The women and men of Constantinople may have shared stories of barbarian Brettania, but visitors from the Fortunate City might well have been pleasantly surprised by what they found here. The buzzing, gold-rich Anglo-Saxon site nearby at Rendlesham (discovered only in 2008 and still being evaluated), where great kings and their courtiers once lived, has already yielded prolific but tantalising evidence of direct trade with Byzantium in the form of copper coins minted in Constantinople (there are also coin-weights marked to Byzantine standards).[5] The coins are scattered in such a way this seems very unlikely to be a hoard of foreign treasure – but instead ready money used or lost by visiting Byzantines, probably on their best behaviour, and probably under the protection of the local king.[6] To reach Rendlesham, visitors would have had to disembark at a landing place close to the Anglo-Saxon home of the dead, Sutton Hoo.

At Sutton Hoo the grave mounds make a bullish statement on the horizon. Standing proud enough to accommodate an entire tomb-boat that was manually pulled up from the river (probably by a combination of slaves and freeborn nobles as an act of respect) and buried, packed with treasure and a king's corpse, this necropolis declared to all who passed that the power of the Anglo-Saxon magnate buried deep within, and of his entourage buried round about, would even in death remain undimmed. And, critically for us, Sutton Hoo (the name recalling the Anglo-Saxon 'spur of the hill')[7] was where this nameless king chose to be buried, surrounded by splendid works from the Christian East.

The discovery of Sutton Hoo was in every way exciting. Grave-robbers had already attacked one mound (known as Mound Two) and then had a go at Mound One, missing the treasure store in the burial itself by just a few feet. The beautiful ghost of the lines of the boat still guide the visitor to the treasure that was once in its belly, including ten silver Byzantine bowls decorated with crosses and delicate rosettes. The rosettes, it has been suggested, were chosen because the floral iconography could be found in both Christian and pagan trees of life:[8] Anglo-Saxon kings and their courtiers here seem to have made efforts to keep all gods, old and new, onside; literary sources tell us that one of the kings of Sutton Hoo set up pagan and Christian altars next to one another. There was too a giant, flat silver dish (size clearly counted), a bit like a modern cake-stand, stamped with the mark of the Byzantine Emperor Anastasios I, who reigned AD 491–518. Two slightly crude seated figures on the dish's roundels may well represent Rome and Constantinople. In addition there were smaller bowls, a silver ladle and spoons – one clearly inscribed Paul, the other possibly Saul. There is even a bronze 'Coptic' bowl that could have been made in those central workshops in Constantinople and scraps of textiles from Syria. Here too there were over 4,000 garnets from the Indian subcontinent.

In another nearby mound (Mound Three), despite another attempted looting, archaeologists rescued the smashed remains of a limestone Victory plaque showing either a winged Nike or an angel, again from

Byzantine copper coinage from the site of the Anglo-Saxon royal settlement at Rendlesham, Suffolk, minted in Constantinople under Emperors Phokas, Justin II and Maurice Tiberius in the late sixth and early seventh centuries AD and uncovered between 2009 and 2015.

Constantinople, a bone box boasting a Christian Chi Rho inscription and the lid of another Eastern bronze bowl.[9]

And it wasn't just at Sutton Hoo and Tintagel that Constantinople enjoyed a vicarious presence, elsewhere in Britain at this time well-connected women wore the short bead necklaces sported by Empress Theodora in the Ravenna mosaics. Finger rings and brooches too – worn by both sexes – give a vigorous nod to Constantinople's high fashion.[10] Throughout Christendom, Byzantine plates and cloths became the status symbols *du jour*. In the French monastery of Chelles a full-length shift, the 'chemise' of the Frankish Queen St Bathildis (herself a fabulous character who started life as an Anglo-Saxon noble, was then sold into slavery and ended up the wife of Clovis II and the mother of kings), is a Byzantine rip-off. A wonderful gold seal matrix unearthed by a metal detectorist near Norwich in 1999 has the name 'BALDEHILDIS' on one side and on the other an image of a naked man and lush-haired woman locked in a passionate embrace beneath a giant cross. Across northern Europe the relics that travelled – a trend started, we should remember, by the Byzantine potentates Helena and Constantine – were wrapped, ideally, in silken cloths from the earthly headquarters of God overlooking the Bosphorus. Diplomatic gifts from Constantinople such as jewel-coloured silks were sent to territories that had neither the technologies nor the markets to reach such diaphanous heights.[11, 12]

Showy yes – but also perhaps an indication of Constantinople's careful cultural, trade and diplomatic relations with the West in general and with Brettania in particular.[13] There were admiring reports of clerics such as Tobias, bishop of Rochester from AD 693 to 706, 'who was as familiar with Greek as with his own tongue'. Benedict Biscop (who would go on to found the monasteries at Monkwearmouth and Jarrow) brought back Byzantine-produced silk cloaks from his travels which he then exchanged for land in Britain.[14] Whether or not there was a political sense of Eastern suzerainty at this time, it is clear there was a cultural one.

Children's textbooks tell us that St Augustine – a representative of the might of Christian Rome – came on a mission from Rome in AD 597 to convert the Anglo-Saxons to Christianity. But Augustine had been sent by Pope Gregory the Great, who had originally been papal legate in Constantinople. At this time the pope was the patriarch's equal, his secular representative in the duchy of Rome. Coins minted in Rome still carried the image of the Byzantine Emperor. An enticing collection of furled parchment letters, only now being translated in the Vatican Library, have made this pecking order crystal clear.[15] There appear to have been other strategic political and religious appointments too; in 668 Theodore from Tarsus in Cilicia – who had been educated at the university in Constantinople – was sent by the pope to be archbishop of Canterbury. There is a sense around this time that Britain has at last been regained as part of the *oikoumene* – a liminal land, a *ferox provincia*[16] but a territory that practically and emotionally was happy to be a part of something bigger than itself.

It is only after Old Rome's triumph at the Synod of Whitby in AD 664 – when it was decided that Easter would be calculated according to the Roman calendar and that monks would be tonsured – that Christianity in Britain looked, felt and sounded less Orthodox, less Eastern, more consistently Latin and Western; it was a downgrading of Eastern Christian influence that would go on to shape the history of the medieval and modern worlds. And while the fingerprints of the Byzantines could be found all over western Europe, our last stop is the far north of England.

Climbing the steep path from the River Wear up to Durham Cathedral, one can still feel that there is the chance here to get closer to God – a Western God found readily in the dynamic north-eastern skies. The columns of the cathedral at Durham are famously mischievous, barley-twisted and latticed – a modish, medieval joke. But the signs in dark stone on the ground around St Cuthbert's shrine within the cathedral have a perturbingly exotic feel. That is because for centuries, in the central tomb here, a bit of Byzantium lay buried.

St Cuthbert died in AD 687, but in the tenth century he was reburied as a Byzantine magnate. The rich purple silk that shrouded his body was almost certainly added to his tomb in 945, when the coffin was opened and the visiting King Edmund (of Wessex but with designs to be recognised as king of all England) placed on Cuthbert's body, wrapped in linen, two 'Graecian robes'. That was a great, and revealing, honour. Byzantine cloth clearly had a totemic quality – the finesse of the embroidery was breathtaking. The delicacy of the work is a reminder of the aesthetic pleasure that could surround those who were rich in Byzantium. Yet the images on Cuthbert's shroud are demonstrably pagan: one section is emblazoned with a representation of the fertility-bringing Nature Goddess. This 'Earth and Ocean' silk was of the very finest quality – large panels of the cloth still survive in the cathedral library's storeroom.[17]

But despite Byzantium's presence right at the edge of the known world, within Constantinople itself, a crippling self-doubt was creeping in. The city was experiencing a crisis of confidence and of belief.

CHAPTER 41

ICONS AND ICONOCLASM

AD 726

It is impossible for us to think without using physical images . . . by bodily sight we reach spiritual contemplation. For this reason Christ assumed both soul and body, since man is fashioned from both.

ST JOHN OF DAMASCUS C. AD 720[1]

Salvation lies not in the faithfulness to forms, but in liberation from them.

BORIS PASTERNAK, *DOCTOR ZHIVAGO*[2]

It is unnatural to climb on the guts of the earth. But at Palea Kameni, just off the Greek island of Thera, the obsidian-black volcanic extrusions and sulphurous hot springs offer that opportunity. The only inhabitants of this strange, volcano-made islet are a shy fisherman in a jauntily dec-orated Portakabin and his loyal, vociferous dog. Eager Chinese, Japanese and European tourists leave their mark here in high season – hundreds of rock-painted handprints, on the dark grey stone, pressed on with raw sulphur scooped from the volcanic mud beneath the sea.

But when the Theran volcano erupted here in AD 726, creating this sulphurous islet, the long-term impact of the massive geo-seismic event would have the unforseen consequence of diminishing the chances for man's opportunity to create art. Because Thera's eruption galvanised an iconoclastic crisis.

Only eight years before, the icon of the Virgin Mary (taken from that portrait said to be painted by none other than St Luke) was being paraded around Constantine's walls to help vanquish the marauding Arab forces ranged outside. Icons were believed to offer a kind of sublime force-field that protected those within. The explosion of 15 July AD 726 was the greatest eruption of the Cycladic volcano since the Bronze Age geo-seismic event of c. 1615 BC. Following the eruption in 726 Emperor Leo III seems to have developed a new religio-political policy that included the banning of icons. Often described by historians as an irrational, typically 'Dark Age' response, we have to pause for a moment to think of the horror of Thera's eruption. Ash clouds would have darkened the sun for weeks, electrical storms would have ripped through the sky and massive floating rafts of pumice 8 feet thick would have drifted across the Mediterranean and up through the Dardanelles. The sea would have seemed to boil; the magnitude of the 726 eruption was 4.1; the bulk deposit 4.5 billion cubic feet. The Eastern Mediterranean world was, physically, turned upside down.

The divine fury of such an event could not have been doubted, and thus was not ignored. Why this dreadful displeasure? the Byzantines must have asked themselves. Observing the Muslim Arabs who escaped the trauma – who worshipped the same God and prophets, but never in human form – naturally those in Constantinople must have started to think that perhaps idolatry was not their salvation but the source of their damnation.

So in c. AD 730[3] Leo III tore down the vast image of the Virgin above the Chalke Gate. A fracas broke out – the commander of the guards ended up dead and then Theodosia, a woman trying to protect the icon, was also killed. She is still remembered in the city, in the valley dividing the fourth and fifth hills, in what is now a mosque, Gül Camii – originally the church containing her relics where the last Byzantine Emperor would pray when it was 'garlanded with roses' before the fall of Constantinople to the Ottomans in 1453. For over 100 years following the eruption the city would ricochet between iconoclastic and iconophilic rulers. Leo was said to have removed the miraculously preserved body of St Euphemia and replaced the corpse with dry bones – to prove that the relics had no sublime power. Pope Gregory III reacted furiously, condemning iconoclasm and the city that was promoting it: these Christian cousins were starting to pull further and further apart. A churn of leaders maintained iconoclasm with varying degrees of intensity, but then Constantine V acted with particular force from AD 754 – executing, torturing or expelling monks and churchmen who refused to give up their icons or their craft. Many of the brightly painted rock churches in remote Cappadocia are the gaudy result of their exile. The simple, single black cross in the apse of Haghia Eirene is a rare, albeit severe, iconoclastic survivor.

The pervading impact of iconoclasm in Constantinople should not be underestimated. Since antiquity men and women had kept images of deities in their homes. The Queen of Cities was decorated, in the central public spaces, with giant images of Helena, of Christ, of Mary, of God and of his saints. If you could afford an icon, you owned one. Icon-veneration was how, as an ordinary person, you understood the closeness of your connection to the divine. There are stories of families rushing to hide icons in stables and in drains. A number were whitewashed. During the rise of Soviet power in the 1930s, Orthodox icons were not just taken out of churches, but laid down in front of firing squads. The pictures themselves were being executed. These bizarrely brutal images – captured on film – were widely circulated and go some way to explain the passionate re-embrace of the Orthodox Church in former Soviet countries today.[4] So we have to imagine the sense of loss and horror in Constantinople when images believed to be heavy with a kind of supernatural power were defaced, destroyed and denied.

No pre-iconoclastic images seemed to have survived in Constantinople. It was only in a mosque in the city, the Kalenderhane, behind a wall of brick, stone and earth, that a mosaic of the Presentation of the Christ Child in the Temple was found in 1969. Yet in the city today Muslims and Christians alike often have an icon in their home; many remember their grandmothers picking off little pieces of the surface paint to help cure mental or physical sickness. But 1,300 years ago, at a stroke, the tangible, direct line to God and to Christ was broken.

Then in AD 780 Empress Eirene, a young girl originally from Athens, as soon as she was widowed reversed state policy, although she had to wait seven years for the change to be formally implemented. At a council in Nicaea on 24 September AD 787 the veneration of images – the evidence cited being the number of 'miracles' effected by icons in the lives of the saints – was formally legalised once more. Icons were restored and icon-painters again picked up their paintbrushes.[5] The Church of Haghia Sophia in Nicaea which hosted this final Ecumenical Council – originally built by Justinian I as a baby sister to his cathedral in the capital – is today concealed behind a store selling watermelons and olive oil, close to a sacred spring and so a little dank. Following its conversion back to a mosque, it is not ideally maintained: early frescoes of Jesus here have started to bubble with damp and are in danger of being lost.

In Constantinople, equipment was brought out of storage and the icon-producing workshops began to hum once more. Wood was planed to provide backboards – lime, poplar, elder, birch, cypress, cedar and pine.[6] Animal bones and skins were boiled up to produce glue (in the summer the stench would have been ghastly). Pigments were mixed – cinnabar, malachite, verdigris. Once painted, the most luxurious icons were surrounded with precious stone, pearls and rubies. The icon-painters were the 'contemporary' artists of the day and they have become history's illustrators.

A decade after icons had been restored, Eirene consolidated her political power. On 15 August AD 797 – an auspicious day of course, the feast of the Assumption of the Virgin Mary – she imprisoned her own son within the Great Palace. Later that day her guards blinded her child and rowed the mutilated young man out to the Princes' Islands in the Sea of Marmara, where he later died. It was a gory act for a woman whose name means peace – particularly given that the blinding took place in the very bedchamber where she had given birth to her boy. Commentators of the day, an age red in tooth and claw, leave us in no doubt that even they were shocked: 'And the sun was darkened during seventeen days, and gave not his light, so that the ships ran off course, and all men said and confess that because the emperor was blinded, the sun had put away his rays. And in this way power came in to the hands of Eirene, his mother.'[7]

For places of such sea-swept brilliance and dappled light, which look from Istanbul's ferries like sunning otters, the Princes' Islands have a very dark history. Princes have been blinded, tortured and imprisoned here. What is an invigorating boat trip to the archipelago today would more typically have been one of pain in earlier centuries. Captives – if their eyes had been left intact – would have been able to see their lost city receding in the distance.

The Princes' Islands were also where on Christmas Day AD 820 the iconoclast (iconoclasm was instituted again from 815 to 842) Emperor Leo V's decapitated head and severed remains were taken by his widow Theodosia to be buried.[8] The Emperor had been beheaded by agents disguised as choristers in his own chapel; the assassins were allies of one Michael the Amorian, a man whom just the day before Leo himself had imprisoned in the palace. Michael was recognised as the next rightful Emperor while his hands were still manacled – a blacksmith had to be called in to cut through the irons.[9]

In Constantinople, within twenty-two years of Emperor Leo V's grisly end, icons would be back – championed by another Empress, Theodora, again after the death of her husband. This time, they were here to stay. Theodora marked the moment with a great celebratory mass in Haghia Sophia on 11 March AD 843. On Easter Sunday 867, a mosaic of the Virgin and Child was unveiled in that church. Its challenging confidence is astonishing; a thing that still inspires wonder in Istanbul today.

But we do not just have to examine the great monuments of Constantinople to find indications of the power of the icon. There are clues in the city's backstreets – and from the pen of one of the city's few recorded female poets, evidence that sheds a chink of light onto the experience of being an Orthodox Christian woman, in what some were increasingly, openly starting to call the Queen of Cities:

> A nun, a monk is a spiritual lyre
> an instrument harmoniously played . . .
> such a one is always rejoicing
> and celebrating a festival.
> A nun or a monk is a text-book,
> showing the pattern, and at the same time teaching;
> the life of a monk is a shining lamp for all.[10]
>
> I hate one who conforms himself to all ways
> I hate one who does everything for recognition
> I hate silence when it is time to speak.[11]

The impact of iconoclasm on one life at this time is brilliantly revealed in the life story of an inhabitant of Constantinople called Kassia. Also known as Kassiane, Eikasia or Ikasia, Kassia is now honoured as a saint. Born in the city around AD 810 to a noble family, Kassia was a prolific poet and hymn-writer. Her 'Hymn of Kassiani' is still sung in many churches on Holy Tuesday, when flocks of sex workers come to listen and to pray. This is no coincidence, as Kassia's hymn is highly sympathetic to 'fallen women' in particular and to the female condition in general. The lyrics, beautifully composed – 'Night is an ecstasy of excess . . . full of sinful desires . . . Do not disregard me . . . you whose mercy is boundless . . .' – talk of the problem of living with and dealing with sin.

Famously beautiful, Kassia had had her own brush with the issue of medieval female sexuality. It was said that as a young woman she had rejected the approaches of Emperor Theophilos when he offered her the 'golden apple' as part of a highly theatrical ceremony in which prospective (pulchritudinous or rich) brides were lined up for the Emperor to choose from. The golden apple was of course writ large in the classical memory. Greek myths told that Eris, the goddess of strife, had thrown down a golden apple during the wedding of Thetis and Peleus on which were inscribed the words 'for the fairest' – a clever little act of destabilisation. (Paris ends up giving the apple to Aphrodite, who offers him Helen of Troy in return.) Emperor Theophilos' chat-up line to Kassia was direct. 'From a woman come a flood of base things,' he was said to have leered. 'But also from a woman better things . . .' was Kassia's retort. She was referring to the salvational possibilities of Mary, but also, one feels, to her own capabilities.[12]

Kassia had had an early brush with Eris too. Accounts of her life tell us that as a child, refusing to relinquish icon worship and sneaking out to care for imprisoned monks, Kassia had been lashed. Others at the time suffered more severe punishments: monks who continued to paint icons had their hands mutilated so they could not continue their work; some were branded or tattooed on their foreheads.

Kassia next appears in the record as establishing a nunnery close to the renowned cultural centre of St John of Stoudios – that medieval seedbed of creativity that is, at the time of writing in 2016, a ruin in Istanbul's Samatya district. Social housing hems in the site which is now full of rubbish and protected only by chicken wire. Ivy clambers over what were once dormitories and workshops. As an abbess Kassia presided in this district over the cultural craft also practised by her male neighbours. She wrote prolifically, producing 49 known hymns and 261 non-liturgical verses. On the page Kassia's early schooling in Homer, poetry, philosophy, the Scriptures shines through. Some of the works are even reminiscent of Buddhist texts. Given the wealth of material stored in the archives and libraries of Constantinople and an attitude that high-born women could merit an education, some argue that women in Byzantium had greater degrees of literacy than their contemporaries in the West.

Although much of our evidence for the struggle of iconoclasm comes from later, iconophile authors, we still must ask, why did women fight for the preservation of these icons so vigorously? One thought is that they offered a genuine focus for private, spiritually nourishing devotion in a time when the public presence of women in churches had been sidelined. Even if women could not be centre stage in person, they could be there in painted form. Was there a subconscious sense that by destroying the images – often of the Virgin Mary – another female presence in the city was being physically attacked? Constantinople was unusual in sporting outsize statuary of empresses – singly and with their husbands. Perhaps iconoclasm felt like a dangerous step deeper into both physical and meta-physical misogyny.

The crisis of iconoclasm might have been resolved by AD 843, but for the people of the city it was soon to be matched by external threats. One was a new Holy Roman Emperor, taking the opportunity to rise in power while Byzantium was embroiled in her internal icon-angst (see Appendix); the other an adversary who hurtled to Constantinople's walls on the back of the north wind – the Vikings. One of the Viking escapades south was commemorated in stone within the ominous shape of a coiling dragon-snake on a runestone in Mariefred, Sweden:

> They journeyed boldly;
> Went far for gold,
> Fed the eagle
> Out in the east,
> And died in the south
> In Saracenland

GRIPSHOLM RUNESTONE

(C. AD 1050)

CHAPTER 42

VIKING FOE-FRIENDS AND THE BIRTH OF RUSSIA

AD 860–1040

Let's ride the Vakr [horse] of Ræfill [sea-king]!
Let's not drive the plough from the field!
Let's plough with a drenched prow out to Constantinople!
Let's receive the wages of the prince!
Let's move forward in the din of weapons!
Let's redden the gums of the wolf!
Let's create the honour for the powerful king!

ROGNVALDR JARL KALI KOLSSON, *LAUSAVÍSUR* [1]

Before the cold sea-curling blast
The cutter from the land flew past,
Her black yards swinging to and fro,
Her shield-hung gunwale dipping low.
The king saw glancing o'er the bow
Constantinople's metal glow
From tower and roof, and painted sails
Gliding past towns and wooded vales.

SNORRI STURLUSON, *THE SAGA OF HARALD HARDRADE* [2]

In the southern and western galleries of the great Church of Haghia Sophia, in 2010 and 2011 some remarkable, almost imperceptible, traces of graffiti were identified. Scratched into the marble surface with the end of a knife or with a cloak pin there are four tiny Viking ships. Once one's eyes have adjusted to the delicacy of the work, rather than the veins and general wear and tear of the marble, their shapes slide into focus – there is a galley, there a stern, and there a roaring dragon's prow. The sketches are a cryptic message. We have to ask what they are doing there and who made them.³

A clue is offered by the Vale of York hoard, buried in a hurry around AD 920 near modern-day Harrogate in the north of England and dug up in 2007 by keen metal detectorists, a local businessman and his son – the hoard weeps with silver coins and precious, sacred objects from Samarkand, Ireland, Afghanistan and Uzbekistan. It is a treasure in every sense. Concealed by an unpromising lead square, the hoard was itself buried in a gorgeous gilt vessel which was in turn lined with gold and decorated with vine leaves, lionesses, stags and a horse.⁴ Holding this cold, heavy gold pot is a charged privilege. Originally used to keep communion bread safe, the designer-container has itself been the victim of Viking attack. Snatched from the hands of a slaughtered cleric or, perhaps, offered up in tribute to Viking bully-boys – an enforced payment in return for a peremptory peace that operated across the medieval world – it is a beautiful, traumatised little thing that speaks of an age that was coloured by Viking longship diplomacy.⁵

Sixty years before that hoard was buried in the cold earth of England, Constantinople had suffered the attention of the Vikings. The Vikings called Constantinople, simply, Miklagard – the Great City. When they appeared on the horizon here in AD 860 across a still sea, the patriarch of the city Photios – a highly educated and well-travelled man – described their arrival as a 'thunderbolt'. Brandishing their swords as they hurtled around the walls, the attacking Norsemen found a breach. We are told that following the subsequent slaughter within, the city's water systems were heaped with bodies and ran crimson with blood. This horror felt worryingly like the punitive realisation of biblical drama – raids from the north as prophesied for the Israelites in Jeremiah: 'Behold, a people cometh from the north country, and a great nation shall be raised from the sides of the earth. They shall lay hold on bow and spear; they are cruel, and have no mercy; their voice roareth like the sea.'⁶ Once again it was said that the Virgin Mary's powers roused a storm that pushed the attackers back. Seven years later the city would give thanks for delivery from men those in Constantinople called Rus.

Today the wandering hordes of tourists in Haghia Sophia should pause for a moment to try to catch the echo of the fervent prayer for salvation first uttered here in AD 866 or 867 under the great mosaic of the Virgin and Child, fearfully recalling the events of 860. The Rus or Rhos were a people with whom the Byzantines would have a curious love–hate relationship, sometimes enemies, sometimes allies; their name in Old Norse was traditionally said to refer to the redness of their hair, but almost certainly meant men who rowed. These Rus were Vikings who had arrived from the country that we now call Russia in their honour. From the moment we first find them tangled in the historical record in the ninth century AD, the stories of Constantinople and of the inhabitants of Russia will be inextricably linked.

The Vikings make a modest historical entry in relation to the city when chroniclers recount that, in AD 839, envoys of the Byzantine Emperor Theophilos arrived at the court of Louis the Pious (the Holy Roman Emperor, son and successor of Charlemagne) on the banks of the Rhine at Ingelheim, together with a rather sorry bunch who had sailed down the Dnieper and then ended up in Constantinople, unable to get back to their homeland. It is a sympathetic picture, of stranded refugees being graciously cared for. But while Vikings have recently enjoyed something of a rehabilitation – historians clamouring that these were not just men who raped and pillaged, but communities who farmed and loved; who composed poetry and appreciated fine wines; who sat in saunas in the Shetlands amusing themselves with gaming boards made of fine walrus tusk; who wore striking eye make-up and organised dinner parties with ambassadors from Baghdad – we now appreciate that the Viking rehabilitation does not deserve to be absolute.

The very name Viking is critical evidence.[7] Viking could possibly come from the Latin for a trading town, *vicus*, or from the Scandinavian *vik*. *Vik* means a bay or inlet, which sounds harmless enough, until you learn that in Old Norse *vikingr* and *viking* were descriptions, specifically, of raiders and raids, particularly of a piratical nature – the *vik* being the bay from which, like a killer-whale, Viking boats with ill intent would slip. We cannot ignore the fact that the Vikings first entered England's historical record when they killed a royal official in Portland Bay, Dorset. Viking Beserrkers did indeed charge into battle semi-naked to prove their animal strength.[8] In AD 844 a historian from al-Andalus describes a brutal Viking raid on southern Spain by the relentless *majus* – the unbelievers. The bone evidence makes it clear that it was mainly teenage men in these smash-and-grab enterprises – 'gap years with attitude' as one expert has vividly put it.[9] These punkish warriors were often tattooed; many had their teeth striped with blue or sometimes filed to a tiger-sharp point. The sum total of evidence suggests that these were a people with a ravening, macho (in both the contemporary and the ancient Greek – battle-hungry – sense) ethos. The young girls they offered as human sacrifice to the gods were gang-raped by Viking nobility before they died. It is hard to imagine the horror. The thirty or so decapitated Vikings found in a mass grave near Weymouth in 2009 are an indication of the fury that many felt towards these 'pirate-raiders'.

And the Vikings came not just to loot and to burn, but to enslave. Slave trading was the Viking's *pièce de résistance*. Pens in towns such as Novgorod – previously thought to hold animals – we now realise were built to contain slaves.[10] Neck-chains and manacles have been found in Viking levels in Dublin and the female DNA in Iceland seems to come largely from captured Celts – Scottish and Irish women dragged to the new Viking settlement as 'comfort', human booty. In Byzantine territory the transfer and exchange of slaves would become a key factor in the balance of the economy.[11] We still recall Viking slavery every time we describe being 'in thrall' to someone, the Old Norse *þræll* meaning a slave.

Black and white slave trades ran in tandem in Constantinople. Turks were particularly prized for their courage, Nubians for their strength. The combined demand for slaves in the Byzantine and Islamic empires far exceeded that of Rome. It was an international racket that involved Venetians, Vikings, Jews (reportedly famous for their castration techniques), Muslims (in Arabic *saqlabi* means a slave, and came to mean a eunuch[12] or a concubine too). Slave is itself a version of Slav – peoples whom the Vikings enthusiastically harvested. Vast numbers of Islamic dirhams are being discovered, buried as hoards, in northern Europe and Scandinavia: southern cash to pay for captured humans. The Viking attitude to Constantinople indicates that they had little interest in acquiring this sacred, gold-roofed, sky-scraping, theatricalised cosmopolis – a city where visitors at the time breathlessly describe, in the Palace of the Magnaura (meaning fresh breezes), trees of gilded bronze, guarded by roaring, tail-twitching gilded lions, and an emperor's throne that elevated to the ceiling – as a city per se.[13] Rather, for the Vikings, Miklagard was a convenient spot full of fruit ripe for the plucking. Viking focus was not political gain but the opportunities offered for trafficking floods of silver and humanity to and from the Byzantine territories and the growing Abbasid Caliphate in Baghdad.

In one respect Vikings had something in common with the people of Constantinople. Like them, they were steeped in marine, maritime and riverine experience.[14] Vikings used sails only after the seventh century AD. Perhaps, as for the rowers of ancient Athens' triremes (built in the fifth century BC as part of the democratic experiment, propelled by free men and the vessels that had helped to take Byzantion), the sheer muscle-power involved gave the Scandinavian explorers a sense of shared, pumped-up purpose. Excavations in 1996–7 on the island of Zealand, a mere 20 miles from Copenhagen, have brought us closer to appreciating the visceral experience of being on – or being pursued by – one of those Viking boats. A royal warship has been teased out of the mud here. Some 120 feet long, possibly belonging to King Cnut, we should picture this on the sea – eighty men at the oars, sails billowing crimson and gold.[15]

So try to imagine the experience of being a Viking raider-adventurer. Making the 2,500-mile trip from Scandinavia to the Caspian Sea overland or in boats whose movement was compared to the flight of birds, with tribes such as the Pechenegs threatening to pick you off, proud to have contacts in every port, to bring back exotic trinkets, coal from the Caucasus, fierce-eyed hunting birds from Arabia, purple dye from Constantinople, nurturing lines of trade that connected your village back home to the Silk Routes and beyond, a sophisticated exchange network that explains the bronze Buddha found in Helgö, Sweden and possibly too the Norwegian penny that has recently turned up in Maine in the United States. These were men who had connections across four continents.[16]

And so the fact that Constantinople is best accessible from the sea helps us to understand why Vikings should become frequent visitors here – originally unwelcome, but then, curiously, as political and economic associates.

A century ago, when silk fragments were found in the Viking ship excavated in Oseberg in 1904–5, it was presumed that these had been looted from churches and monasteries in the British Isles. And yet it now seems that these silky souvenirs are evidence of a vigorous Viking fetish. The Vikings seemed to crave silk – that clever, class-ridden cloth that immediately indicated the rank and standing of those who wore it. Vikings could not get enough for sails and shrouds and splendours, transporting silks from Persia and Constantinople for their own pleasure. By the letter of the law around AD 1000 it was impossible to purchase more than a horse's worth of Byzantine silk on Byzantine lands. Nevertheless, flat-bottomed Viking boats, bulging with their sensuous, black-market cargo (in truth probably not the very finest Byzantine work), would ply up and down the Dnieper and the Volga to dress the great and the good of the Viking world.

In Viking settlements such as Kiev, whose docklands are covered with the log-built cabins of traders at the end of the ninth century, prizes from Byzantium have ended up in graves – axes, scramasaxes (single-edged knives), sabres and cavalry equipment. The Vikings used finely carved ivory flasks from Byzantine Italy and bore on their arms the proud, hooked-beak hunting birds of the Arabs. Silks were brought up to Constantinople by camel caravan and amber carried down by boat. But the Vikings didn't just acquire Constantinople's goods; they started to take on her ideas. Unexpectedly, a number started to Hellenise. Some flirted with Christianity, others converted. The self-same Photios who had watched Vikings harry his city sent out a 'bishop and pastor, with a flameproof book of gospels', no less. Whether the Vikings were trading or raiding, these were treacherous journeys, and perhaps that is why so many started to turn to the religion of Miklagard – which offered as flourishing an existence in the afterlife as it did in the here and now.

Perhaps it was also reports of that ferociously effective Greek Fire, the chemical-weapon calling-card of the Byzantine navy that can burn a boat to ash within twenty minutes, that weighed heavily on the Viking mind, encouraging allegiance rather than just violence. Theirs was a culture, after all, that was all about the power of wooden boats. And in the game of scissors, paper, stone, the New Romans had the ultimate weapon. So the two forces started to negotiate. To manage their uneasy stand-off, treaties of 'Peace and Friendship' were drawn up, personally vouched for by the power-players of the day. We have the names of some of these protagonists; Karl, Farulf, Vermund, Hrollaf and Steinvith in AD 907, 911, 944. On a promise of good behaviour, and on the understanding that only fifty Vikings at any one time entered through a particular gate of Constantinople the Norsemen were, initially, allowed free bed and board and unlimited baths in the Byzantine capital city – becoming B&B guests where once they had raped and maimed.

But after a brief honeymoon of uneasy diplomatic relations the Vikings regressed, turning instinctively perhaps to their traditional ways, ravaging their way along the Bosphorus in AD 941, torching churches and effectively nail-gunning the heads of priests. In no uncertain terms they were burnt off by Greek Fire and then bought off with gold and with Byzantine silks for their sails.

And the shift towards Viking Christianity was by no means absolute. Perhaps embarrassed by this dabbling with a cult of the meek, the following year, AD 942 the Viking leader Svyatoslav of Kiev styled himself a pirate of the steppes – sporting a single earring, a shaven head with just one strand of hair left, a horse-riding leader who reverted to paganism and to human sacrifice. The Byzantines paid him 1,500 pounds of gold to subdue the Bulgarians, taking note that he had just delivered a death blow to the Khazars on the steppes. The poacher turned gamekeeper turned poacher once more, and a Byzantine fleet armed with Greek Fire sailed up the Danube to push back Svyatoslav's encroaching forces. The Vikings' luck then seemed to start to bleed away. Outflanked, Svyatoslav had to press women into service (or so Byzantine sources tell us – delightedly recounting that when the corpses were stripped on the battlefield a number were mere girls). Soon after his engagement with Byzantine forces Svyatoslav was ambushed by Pechenegs and his skull was turned into a gold-lined drinking cup.

In a dynastic struggle that ended in death for two out of three, Vladimir, Svyatoslav's youngest son,[17] took the reins of power. Vladimir's rule would prove transformative both for Constantinople and for the wider world. Vlad began life as a good pagan, worshipping many gods, performing human sacrifice. But then, listening perhaps to the tales of his grandmother Olga who had been received in Constantinople and then converted, he decided which religion to favour (west European Christians he considered too run of the mill, Muslims too sorrowful – and, as one Viking put it, the Rus 'cannot exist without [the] pleasure of pork and drink'): the lucky recipient, in AD 988, of the vote for best mediator with the supernatural world was Byzantine Orthodoxy. And so we find a strange scenario – Vladimir married Emperor Basil's sister Anna in the most Christian of Christian ceremonies. The citizens of Kiev underwent a mass baptism; a church to Mary Theotokos was built by Byzantine craftsmen – along the lines of a similar church to the Mother of God in the Great Palace itself – on Starokievskaia Hill in Kiev. Come 1008 and a German missionary believed the Rus to be Christian.

Vladimir was, one suspects, tempted by marvels both material and spiritual. We know that emissaries sent by Grand Prince Vladimir from Kiev to Constantinople were dumbstruck by the sight of Haghia Sophia: 'We knew not whether we were on heaven or earth. For on earth there is no such splendour or such beauty, and we are at a loss how to describe it. We only know that God dwells there among men, and their service is fairer than the ceremonies of other nations. For we cannot forget that beauty.'[18]

So from now on Viking lands would steadily become Christian, while Viking traders would carefully itemise trade goods on birch-bark slips that included 'gold, silks, wine and various fruits from Greece, silver and horses from Hungary and Bohemia and from Rus, furs, wax, honey and slaves'.[19] Runestones across Scandinavia are inscribed commemorating

The Piraeus Lion – captured from the Piraeus port near Athens in AD 1687 by the Venetian general Francesco Morosini and erected in front of the Venice Arsenale – is covered in Viking runes, possibly carved by the Varangian Guard in the second half of the eleventh century AD.

expeditions 'to the Greeks'. And, having experienced their fighting prowess close up, the Byzantines now readily welcomed Vikings into their city as mercenaries. In AD 988–9 Vladimir sent his crack troop, the Varangian Guard (the name derives from the Norse *var*, a pledge of loyalty) – possibly 6,000 strong – to help Constantinople's rulers put down a rebellion. A spiky north–south alliance had been sealed.[20]

The Vikings made their mark both in Constantinople itself and in its hinterland: in the permanent Viking settlement only recently identified on the Arabian/Persian Gulf;[21] in the Viking-style wooden street and structures found in the Byzantine fortress at Nufăru in the Balkans;[22] in the runic inscriptions on the shoulders of the Piraeus lion sculpture that had stood on Piraeus harbour near Athens since the first century AD (looted during the Great Turkish War in the seventeenth century and now standing outside the Venice Arsenal); in additional graffiti on the marble balustrades of the Haghia Sophia where two dawdling Vikings have etched their names; and critically within the city itself as a new super-troop employed for protection by the imperial family. Soon we will meet these men, the Varangian Guard, but first we should picture the impressions of the imported heavies who almost certainly graiffitoed those Viking boats onto the walls of Haghia Sophia, and assess what they would have seen as they strode through the streets of their adopted hometown. Men such as one Bolli Bollason who came to Constantinople around AD 1020 to expand both his wallets and his mind; 'I have always wanted to travel to Southern Lands one day, for a man is thought to grow ignorant if he doesn't ever travel . . .'[23]

CHAPTER 43

✦

WITHIN THE WALLS

C. AD 1000–1100

Constantinople is a city larger than its renown proclaims. May God in his grace and generosity deign to make it the capital of Islam.

HASAN ALI AL-HARAWI, *INDICATIONS SUR LES LIEUX DE PÈLERINAGE*, TWELFTH-CENTURY ARAB WRITER[1]

The works of the Indians are rendered [into Arabic], the wisdom of the Greeks is translated, and the literature of the Persians has been transferred [to us] . . . as a result, some works have increased in beauty.

AL-JAHIZ, *KITAB AL-HAYAWAN*, BORN IN BASRA, ISLAMIC CALENDAR 159/60 (AD 776)[2]

In the heart of Athens, where tourists toy with Greek salads above the remains of the Agora and over the courtroom that hosted the trial of Socrates, archaeologists are working on the revelation of a splendid monument, the Painted Stoa – the colonnaded walkway that gave its name to Stoic philosophy. In order to reach this impressive classical limestone structure they have had to dig down beneath a Greek tavern, past the nineteenth-century and early modern city and under the period of Ottoman occupation in order to remove the honeycomb of Byzantine homes that squat on a piece of the glory that was Greece. Herein is one of Byzantium's problems. In the eighteenth and nineteenth centuries when the romance of classicism swept through Europe, Byzantine remains were often destroyed or neglected in order to reveal their classical foundations. Islamic-majority countries were typically underwhelmed by the remains of their Christian past. So Byzantium became the poor cousin of the archaeological world. As I picked through the Agora digs one hot

August afternoon, while large Byzantine food-storage jars were revealed alongside diminutive doorways and hearths (all destined to be carefully removed and stored), what came to my mind were the ordinary Byzantine lives lost from Constantinople over the years thanks to archaeological attrition. The domestic and cottage industry finds in Athens – once the 'violet-crowned', 'sleek' metropolis of Socrates and Plato, Xenophon and Alcibiades (but up until the eleventh century a regional Byzantine backwater which began to flourish once more from the twelfth as a centre of excellence for Byzantine art), are precious indeed.[3]

Yet despite the challenges of archaeology and of historical bias, from texts and from isolated finds we can start to piece together a picture of how the ordinary people of Constantinople lived. Inhabitants write contentedly of a city-home filled with olives and over which vines clambered, of the smell of the cypresses and in the morning the hum of bees in the city's market gardens. Constantinople must have been a pungent place: cedar oil, sandalwood, nutmeg, linseed, spikenard and smoked fish were all sold in the open markets, and there would too have been the ordure of a population of up to 800,000 souls. Moreover, come the eleventh century AD the city was the centre of an international perfume trade. Even one Empress, Zoe, who died in AD 1050, was said by the monk-historian Psellos to have delighted in the manufacture of scents and unguents in her chambers. Outside the gates of the Great Palace perfume-merchants were permitted to line their stalls so that the approach to the imperial quarters smelt ever sweet.

Arab visitors described the 'wonders' of Constantinople: date palms, honey, lavender-water flowing from the statues around the cistern. Dried meat and salted ham were very popular. As well as the fresh fish that you would expect from such a well-watered settlement, the city was infamous for holding on to the Roman delight in the (to us vile) fermented fish sauce *garum*, and for being among the first to introduce caviar in the twelfth century. Ship accounts show dried fruit from Syria, linen from Egypt, wax, olive oil, jewellery, books and hides all being traded through Constantinople's ports. When trade routes and military activity allowed, exotic produce from further east could also be found on the streets of Constantinople – oranges, lemons and eventually aubergines. The city's greatest industries were growing and harvesting food from the wheatfields and orchards found both within and outside the city walls

– Constantinople's officials were duty-bound to store enough food and drink for the city's population to survive a year.

Competing with the costers (traders were often women) was the hum of sung liturgy in the city's churches and monasteries. St Paul had asked Christians to 'pray without ceasing' and the monastics of Constantinople endeavoured to oblige. One extreme early example was the Office of the Sleepless Monks, where three choirs sang in eight-hour shifts across twenty-four hours. On the streets there were lutes, flutes and percussives. The scant examples of Byzantine melodies on record does not mean that this was a city without song; to the contrary, song and music were such a natural part of daily life that the melodies of Constantinople were simply carried in people's heads.[4] In all its guises the sonic landscape of the city was saturated with spirituality. Castrati dressed and sounded 'like angels'. A Muslim prisoner of war, Harun Ibn Yahya, described the theatrical displays on feast days – he was particularly struck by an organ being played at a banquet in the streets. Filled as the city was with both open and covered cisterns to ensure a sufficient water supply, the percussion of drips was a hazard of the many subterranean chambers. Rose beetles still fly now as they did then, bombarding the visitor with their low hum and petrol-green iridescence. The voices of Kurdish refugees drift through the abandoned monastery of St John of Stoudios today as they sing folk-tunes that would have been heard in the same streets a thousand years ago.

There was too a roaring trade in religious ephemera. Here Constantinople and Córdoba, Damascus and Baghdad shared a trait.[5] Pilgrims – Christian and Muslim alike – would physically ingest the dust or plaster from sacred images. They might buy these within the city or, better still, make pilgrimage to acquire sacred clay tokens; rehydrated, these were thought to be curative, to ward off snakes and other lethal annoyances. As the engine room of a monotheistic mega-state, Constantinople needed a steady supply of fuel for its population's belief. This came in the form of relics. A fragment of the True Cross for instance, decorated with pearls and gems, was inscribed on the back with the claim that the energies of life gushed forth from it and that 'Upon it Christ formerly smashed the gates of Hell, / giving new life to the dead; / And the crowned ones who have now adorned it / Crush with it the temerities of the barbarians.'[6] Eunuchs with their quasi-spiritual nature, often compared to angels in their 'garments of snow', with radiant complexions to match, were frequently the caretakers of relics (eunuchs' spiritual influence only added to the jibes that Byzantium was effeminate – the state's use of mercenaries an additional source of calumny). One splendid example was the covering for a fragment of the True Cross held in the Great Palace. Commissioned by a eunuch named Basil Lekapenos (illegitimate son of the banished usurper Romanos Lekapenos) some time around AD 950, its inscription declares sympathetically of Christ that 'God though he was, he suffered in a human body.' In this way the omnipresent geldings (a medieval inhabitant of Byzantium would be astonished to find that eunuchs are scarce on the streets of London, New York or Paris today) translated their own bodily suffering into a passionate, religious empathy.[7]

Where eunuchs wore silks and snow-white robes, on the backs of the ordinary city-dwellers would be found linen, felt, leather, wool, even cotton. In the imperial court eighteen different ranks were distinguished by eighteen different silk colourways. Some fashions endured pretty much unchanged from Roman times up until the fall of the city in AD 1453; in the imperial court a bejewelled silk scarf was worn whose purple recalled the death of Christ and whose gold commemorated his resurrection. Its design was pure Old Rome. Around the tenth century those women that could afford it seem to have swapped their plain headscarves for rather jaunty hats. Soldiers would wear the protective felt boiled up in the city's workshops. The city's poor would hope to pick up scraps – cast-off tunics and shoes were regularly handed out from monasteries such as Evergetis.

A number of religious establishments in the city were rule-bound to distribute food to the poor too (women were often discouraged from gathering at the gates in case they proved tempting to the monks within). At the poorhouse of Attaleiates, every day six men were taken into the refectory where they were given 'a piece of bread, and . . . either meat or fish or cheese, or dried or fresh vegetables which have been boiled'.[8] The extremely fortunate would find themselves at the table reserved for twelve in the Emperor's own dining room, the Triclinium. Included in the 228-strong guest-list, as well as those lucky poor of the city (usually on different nights), were international grandees, priests, Arab prisoners of war and even the barbarian tribesmen in imperial service entertained at the infamous 'hairy banquet'.

The excesses of the rich in the city would be remarked on still, centuries later, by Odo of Deuil, a chronicler of the Second Crusade in AD 1146 who made notes during a tour of Constantinople that had been offered by the Emperor to French visitors: 'as she surpasses other cities in wealth, so too she surpasses them in vice'.[9]

By the ninth, tenth and eleventh centuries the city had entered into a kind of culture-competition with her Muslim neighbours. One Caliph wrote to the Byzantine Emperor, 'The least of the territories ruled by the least of my subjects provides a revenue larger than your whole dominion.'[10] In the Muslim world it was rumoured that Constantinople's leaders funded their exploits through alchemy. The geographer Ibn al-Faqih solemnly described in his *Kitab al-Buldan* (Book of Lands) that Constantinople's emperors kept sacks of white powder which they turned through sorcery into gold. Muslim and Christian leaders kept a weather-eye on one another's scientific and artistic output. The Emperor Theophilos was asked by the Caliph to send the mathematician Leo to his court; in turn Arabic features could be found in Theophilos' garden. Spurred perhaps by accounts of the 'House of Learning' in Baghdad – in fact it was the Madinat al-Salam, the House of Peace – Theophilos promoted a building-and-arts programme. As he was an iconoclast, his Bryas Palace on the Asian shore was said to be an imitation of the Palace in Baghdad and his mechanical decorations a copy of the wonders produced by Harun al-Rashid (who for example sent a clock to Charlemagne – and around whom some of the *One Thousand and One Nights* fantasies are spun).[11]

So visitors might have commented on the extraordinary theatricality of Constantinople's imperial court – where the emperors sat on those hydraulically powered thrones, spangled with twittering birds, but these were the products of the invention-equivalent of an arms race. From AD 980, word was filtering through from al-Andalus of the sumptuous palace built by the Umayyad Caliph Abd-ar-Rahman III al-Nasir on the outskirts of Córdoba from 979. A series of splendid scorched ruins today, when it was new the Medina Azahara – the Shining Palace – would have scintillated. Made of white African marble and decorated with gold and silver tiles and with pools of mercury that sent the light shattering back out to dazzle visitors, the palace was described as 'a concubine in the arms of a black eunuch'. Here too there was a mechanical throne and automated birds. Wrecked by civil war within three generations of its construction, that beautiful white marble is now stained tobacco-brown where dripping lead from the roof joists melted in the inferno of its destruction.

The territorial range of Islam had become so vast that its conglomeration of income was staggering. One scholar has estimated that the material gains from the conquests of Muslim armies can be measured in the modern equivalent of many, many billions of dollars.[12] No wonder that local rulers received gifts and embassies from as far afield as Korea and India. Caliphs threw wedding parties where guests and decorations were physically encrusted with pearls and rubies, where purses full of silver and gold were offered as leaving presents.[13] The Arabs' silver dirham spread through the Middle East, North Africa and southern Europe, drawing all those lines of influence and wealth together.[14]

It was now Baghdad that was in the dreams of Byzantine men, rather than just Byzantium in the minds of Muslims. Constantinople would find herself challenged in body and spirit.

But a combination of Constantinople's market-culture, her polyphonic nature, her dependence on supplies from north, south, east and west and her unshaken belief in her God-given mission catalysed a sensibly accommodating self-confidence. In the tenth-century imperial document *De Administrando Imperio* commissioned by Emperor Constantine Porphyrogennetos the word *barbaroi* does not appear once and in the Emperor's handbook for imperial etiquette, the *De Ceremoniis*, the very best way to treat (and thus to get the best out of) foreign embassies was carefully set down. The men and women of Constantinople knew, from first-hand experience, of the conviction within the vast Muslim empire that thickly rimmed their lands. Hot-headed, unilateral aggression would only result in jihad. Constantinople, the City of God, was an entity that needed guarding, not squandering, that had to rely on displays of diplomacy and strength rather than on direct aggression. So to protect the protector, Constantinople invited in those men who had once stormed her gates – the Vikings.

CHAPTER 44

THE VARANGIAN GUARD

c. AD 1040–1341

And so the English groaned aloud for their lost liberty and plotted ceaselessly to find some way of shaking off a yoke that was so intolerable and unaccustomed . . . Some of them who were still in the flower of their youth travelled into remote lands and bravely offered their arms to Alexius, emperor of Constantinople, a man of great wisdom and nobility . . . This is the reason for the exodus of the English Saxons to Ionia; the emigrants and their heirs faithfully served the holy empire, and are still honoured among the Greeks by the Emperor, nobility, and people alike.

ORDERIC VITALIS, *ECCLESIASTICAL HISTORY* (TWELFTH-CENTURY

DESCRIPTION OF THE EXODUS OF ANGLO-SAXONS FROM

NORMAN-OCCUPIED BRITAIN TO CONSTANTINOPLE)[1]

These men come from the barbarian land next to the Ocean and are loyal to the Emperor of the Romans from the beginning; all carry a shield and on their shoulder a type of axe.

NIKEPHOROS BRYENNIOS THE YOUNGER, *HISTORY*

(DESCRIBING THE EVENTS OF AD 1071)[2]

As young men push second-hand mattresses past on wooden carts and kids sort through piles of redundant television aerials, behind a tyre shop on the Draman Caddesi, at what was the far north of the old city of Constantinople, hides one of the few scraps of evidence for one of the most remarkable phenomena of the medieval world. Here is the ruined oratory of St Nicholas' Church, originally the Church of St Nicholas and St Augustine, now known as the Boğdan Sarayı, just a stone's throw from Byzantium's Gate of Charisios, the Ottoman Edirnekapı, and from the restored Church of Chora. The contention is that St Nicholas' was founded by an Englishman escaping the Norman boot in the eleventh century. At the end of the nineteenth century, epitaphs from the church to '*Foederati, gardes-de-corps des empereurs*' were reused by the Ottoman authorities as building materials. The few scraps that the English ambassador at the time managed to rescue were then, sadly, destroyed in the great fire of Pera in AD 1870. The single survivor is an abbreviated inscription, 'INGVAR' – six letters commemorating foreign protectors of Constantinople. From the far West, the man remembered in the letters 'INGVAR' is an 'English Varangian'.[3]

For the rulers of Constantinople it had long been both a desire and a dilemma: to find a loyal group of bespoke strongmen to protect the Emperor – Constantinople's own equivalent of Old Rome's Praetorian Guard. An initial choice of Turks and Arabs and then Armenians (foreigners were thought to come free of conflicting, domestic loyalties) had backfired when these allies became enemies. For example, in AD 993–4, 'the great Roman nation went forth and with many troops came against Armenia. Bringing the sword and enslavement, the Romans mercilessly fell upon the Christian faithful and passed through the land, killing savagely like a poisonous serpent, in this manner being no different from the infidel peoples.'[4] Armenian bodyguards had suddenly become the enemy within, and back in Constantinople Armenians and locals fought in the streets to the death.[5] The issue of homeland security was becoming ever more urgent. In the West, Charlemagne had had himself crowned Holy Roman Emperor by Pope Leo III in 800, effecting his own cultural, political and military renaissance. The Byzantines were now surrounded by powerful rivals. To the south and east, from 762 the Abbasid Caliphate cemented its control from its new capital of Baghdad (it was said that Baghdad's founders had been advised by Nestorian monks; the new city was certainly based on the perfection of the circle as described in Euclid). Although this corrival 'centre of the universe' in fact drew firepower from Constantinople – the caliphs had their own civilisation to build – the developing confidence of Islamic culture would eventually see the downfall of the Queen of Cities. This was a time when the religious and political weather of both East and West was on the turn. Given her location, it was perhaps inevitable that Constantinople was caught in the eye of this cross-continental storm. The city would frequently find herself reacting to shifts in power at all points of the compass.

In AD 970, John I Tzimisces created the Athanatoi – the Immortals – a body of high-ranking Byzantines, a nodding reference to the 10,000 Immortals who, it was said, had protected the Persian emperors Xerxes and Dareios 1,500 years before. Mounted on horseback, adorned with gold, the Athanatoi completed successful campaigns against the Rus. But these local nobles had local scores to settle and vested interests to advance. So the Byzantine emperors, paradoxically, came to take as their most essential and privileged force of private protection first the Viking Rus and then those who fled the Norsemen – English noblemen. Six thousand Vikings went to Constantinople, sent over by boat in 988 by Vladimir of Kiev, now an ally. Established by the end of Basil II's reign, as a personal bodyguard to the Emperor, double-axes to the fore, the Varangian Guard must have been quite some sight on the streets of Constantinople. Processing with the Emperor during coronations, beating his path clear with jewelled whips in the streets, offering a glowering guard as he attended church, hurtling out to defend his person and his lands, this group made a mordant mark on the medieval mind.

One Varangian who arrived in Constantinople in around AD 1034 aged nineteen or so, with 500 men, was Harald Hardrada (more accurately Harald Hardradi – that is, Harold Hard-Ruler – though he was originally Haraldr Sigurdarson, and later King of Norway). Service in the Varangian Guard by this time was almost considered a rite of passage – an evolution of the 'gap year with attitude', the 400 years' worth of rape and looting, that had previously sent young Viking men out over land and sea. Harald's first impressions of Constantinople were later recorded by his court poet Bolverk Arnorsson: 'Iron-shielded our ships rowed lashed prows, hard along the shoreline. Iron-shielded our ships rode proud to harbour. Of Miklagard, our famous prince first saw the golden gables. Many a sea-ship fine arrayed swept toward the high-walled city.'[6]

Harald himself was elevated to the position of *spatharokandidatos*, a dignitary in the Imperial palace marked out by a distinctive gold chain around his chest. His exploits in the service of Byzantine imperial nobility over a period of nine years read like a latterday James Bond. It was said that Harald fought pirates on the Aegean and took eighty cities of the Moors. In service for over a decade he fell out of favour, then won his way back in again (blinding one captured emperor – 'The destroyer of the wolf's grid, had out both the eyes of the Great King', as we are told by his *skald* Thjodolf). Imprisoned in a dungeon in the city with a giant snake, he made a daring bid for freedom, riding over the chain stretched across the Golden Horn by dragging the ship's contents first to the stern to make the prow rise up and then ordering his men to rush to the bows. We find Harald back in Roskilde (the harbour from which that beautiful Viking boat has recently been pulled) and quite possibly, given his insider knowledge, advising fellow Vikings on their final raid on Constantinople in AD 1043 when Vladimir, the son of Yaroslav, powered up and down in the platinum light of the Bosphorus, and then watched as his fleet was destroyed by Greek Fire.[7] In the wake of his own disastrous expedition, Harald set to to plot his next adventure – the capture of England.

It is another great what-if. What if the ex-Varangian Harald Hardrada had succeeded in ruling Britannia, if he had not fallen to an arrow in the throat at the Battle of Stamford Bridge in AD 1066, the battle won by Harold Godwinson, who would then die with an arrow in the eye at Hastings? If Harald rather than his distant cousin William had conquered Britain, we would be living in a rather different world. Byzantium would not be an exotic, misunderstood 'other' but a kind of cultural fairy godmother, a training ground to England's new ruler.

But William came, Harald fell, and soon in Constantinople there would be new recruits in the Varangian camp close to the hippodrome. Displaced nobles and young bloods who would not, or could not, live under Norman rule set sail for the East, raiding and freebooting as they went. There are records of their rackety exploits in the Balearics, Morocco and Sardinia. These pugilistic opportunists arrived in Constantinople, probably around AD 1075 (though possibly as early as 1040), drawn, it was said, by news that 'heathens' were attacking 'the great city' Miklagard. Orderic Vitalis, the English chronicler and Benedictine monk, picks up the tale: 'the English exiles were warmly welcomed by the Greeks and were sent into battle against the Norman forces, which were too powerful for the Greeks alone'.[8]

We have an image of them now, shady, privileged, isolated – the perfect secret agents – distanced from their homeland, from kith and kin, warriors who were used to taking an oath of loyalty to their overlord. In

A Byzantine woman spearing a Varangian guardsman

Anglo-Saxon they would have been called the *hearthwerod* or hearth-troop, the king's bodyguard; here they were Varangians – pledging (now as high-end mercenaries) to defend their friends and to bring death to their enemies.

Clearly this was a situation not without its challenges. An intriguing illustration in the wonderful history of John Skylitzes shows a Byzantine woman from Anatolia in AD 1034 who has been badly handled by a Varangian guardsman. With knitted brows and direct aim, the harassed woman spears the soldier, and in the next frame of the medieval storyboard hangdog Varangians bring the woman her assailant's clothes as an apology. This private army could be headstrong – the Varangians themselves rioted against Emperor Michael V Kalaphates in 1041. It was probably Varangians who had scratched runes all over that Piraeus lion in the eleventh century.[9] But it seems that, overall, Varangian Guards were admired, and Varangian veterans were treated with great respect. We are told that Emperor Alexios I founded a small town for his English strongmen called Civitot,[10] although he swiftly called them back to the city 'to guard his chief palace and royal treasures'.[11]

We also hear that the Varangians were allowed to take land in what is modern-day Crimea, building a *nova anglia*; a Franciscan missionary records that in the thirteenth century the area was known as *terra Saxorum*. Catalan navigators over the next hundred or so years describe Varangian settlements around the Sea of Azov with names that recall their inhabitants' Western origins – Varangido, Susaco (Saxon or Sussex) and Londina.[12]

The arrangement certainly nourished a relationship between Constantinople and the English that had been hovering patiently in the wings since at least those early trading trips to Sutton Hoo and Tintagel. William of Malmesbury in his *De Gesta Regum Anglorum* says that Alexios I Komnenos 'venerated the fidelity of the English . . . and transmitted his esteem for them to his son'; in AD 1176 an embassy was sent from Constantinople to Henry II offering a marriage alliance between Prince John and Emperor Manuel's daughter (Henry sent back hunting hounds as a gift to the Emperor) – the suggestion being that the two heirs should take up residence in Constantinople. The 'special connection' almost paid off: in 1204, during the Fourth Crusade, it would be English soldiers who attempted to protect Constantinople's walls from the Frankish Christian attackers outside. The English might still be called 'barbarians' in Constantinopolitan sources, but they fought on the right side, as it were. Robert de Clari records that when Venetians managed to scale one section of the wall during the siege '. . . Englishmen . . . ran to them with swords and axes, and decapitated them all'.[13]

As time went on the Varangians came to hold a predominantly ceremonial role. We last hear of them in AD 1341, just 500 or so, disappearing from history at a moment when Byzantium most urgently needed help to survive.

The Varangians are provocative and captivating, and they remind us of the brilliantly variegated nature of the culture of Constantinople across time. Different faiths, cultures, races, all with a stake in the city, many on the make, trading, praying, politicking – ensured this was a hyper-connected place. But as the Varangians bedded in, Byzantium was about to be sorely tested by a treacherous foreigner and an old enemy: the covetous, ravening West.

PART FIVE

✦

CITY OF WAR

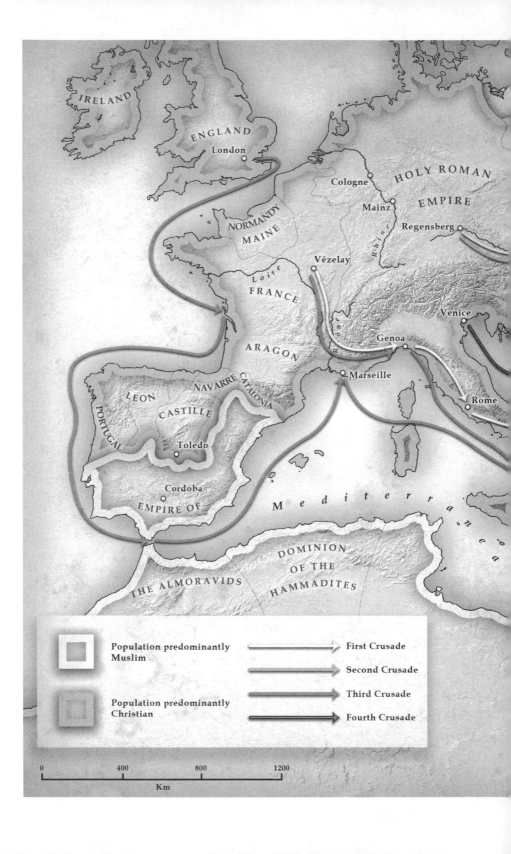

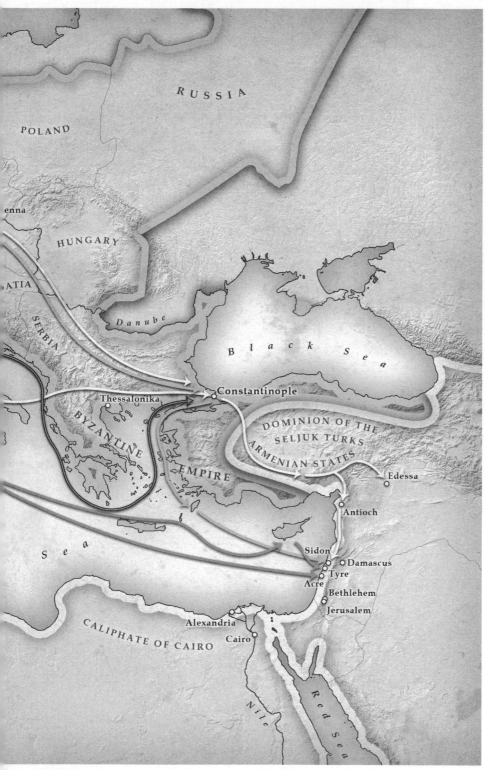

The Crusades

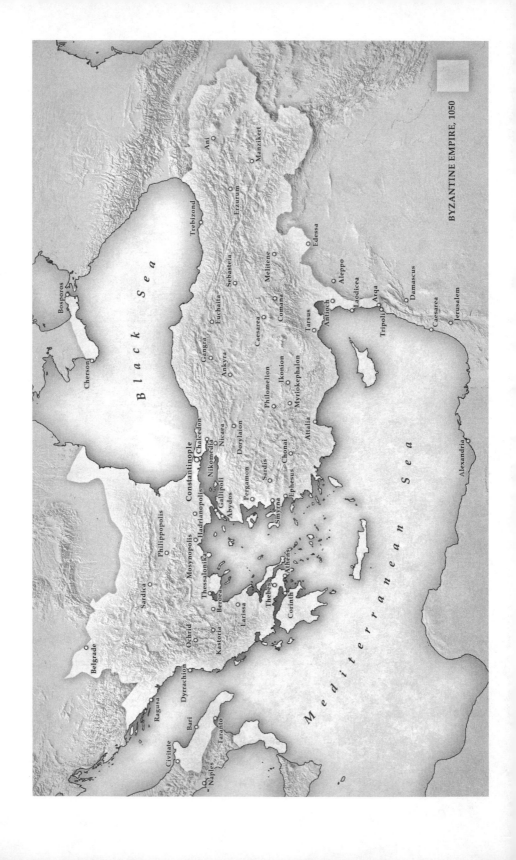

BYZANTINE EMPIRE, 1050

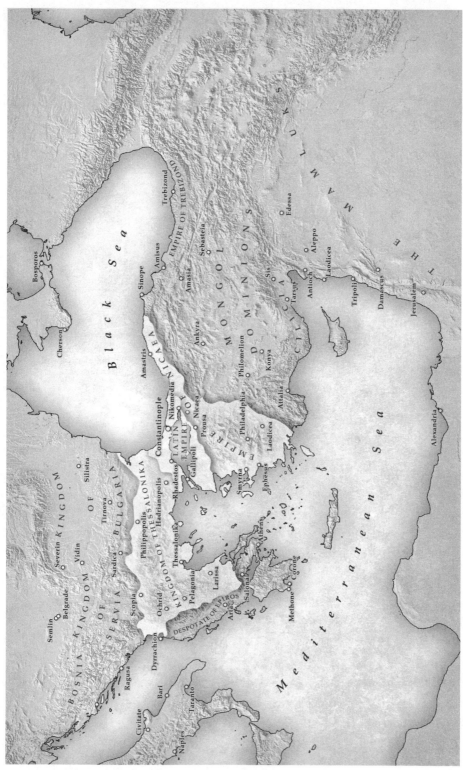

The Byzantine Empire, c. AD 1050 and in AD 1204

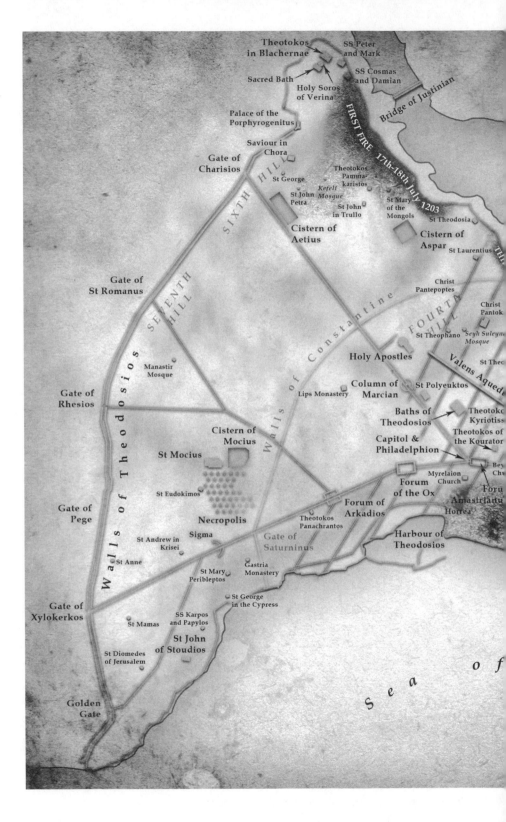

Theotokos
in Blachernae

SS Peter
and Mark

Sacred Bath

Holy Soros
of Verina

SS Cosmas
and Damian

Bridge of Justinian

Palace of the
Porphyrogenitus

FIRST FIRE 17th–18th July 1203

Saviour in
Chora

Gate of
Charisios

SIXTH HILL

St George

St John
Petra

Theotokos
Pamma-
karistos

Kefeli
Mosque

St John
in Trullo

St Mary
of the
Mongols

St Theodosia

Cistern of
Aetius

Cistern of
Aspar

St Laurentius

THE

SEVENTH HILL

Gate of
St Romanus

Christ
Pantepoptes

Christ
Pantok

FOURTH HILL

St Theophano

Seyh Suleyma
Mosque

Walls of Constantine

St Theo

Holy Apostles

Valens Aqued

Manastir
Mosque

Gate of
Rhesios

Walls of Theodosios

Column of
Marcian

St Polyeuktos

Lips Monastery

Baths of
Theodosios

Theotoko
Kyriotiss

Cistern of
Mocius

Theotokos of
the Kourator

Capitol &
Philadelphion

St Mocius

Myrelaion
Church

Bey
Chu

St Eudokimos

Forum
of the Ox

Foru
Amastrianu
Horrea

Gate of
Pege

Necropolis

Forum of
Arkadios

Sigma

Theotokos
Panachrantos

Gate of
Saturninus

Harbour of
Theodosios

St Andrew in
Krisei

St Anne

Gastria
Monastery

St Mary
Peribleptos

Gate of
Xylokerkos

St George
in the Cypress

St Mamas

SS Karpos
and Papylos

St John
of Stoudios

St Diomedes
of Jerusalem

Sea   o

Golden
Gate

Constantinople after the Crusades

CHAPTER 45

✤

A GREAT SCHISM?

AD 1054

A religious and national animosity still divides the two largest commun-
ions of the Christian world; and the schism of Constantinople, by alienating her most useful allies, and provoking her most dangerous enemies,
has precipitated the decline and fall of the Roman Empire in the East.

EDWARD GIBBON, *THE DECLINE AND FALL OF THE ROMAN EMPIRE*[1]

On 16 July AD 1054 in the high heat of summer, papal legates from Rome
led by Cardinal Humbert rode through Constantinople. They strode into
the cool of the Church of Haghia Sophia and slammed down on the altar
a bull of excommunication directed against the Orthodox patriarch Keroularios and others from Byzantium whom they judged to have offended
their church. In return, Keroularios promptly excommunicated the papal
legates. Thus began the so-called Great Schism. The impasse would not
be resolved until 910 years later in 1964.

The sense one gets is that this theo-political crisis, closely documented
on both sides, was prompted by a pernicious escalation of words; or rather
by men who did not heed the Greek philosopher Plato's warnings about
the dangers of the written word – that writing without conversation risks
becoming like an orphan: 'writing . . . when it is bandied about . . . ill-
treated or unjustly reviled always needs its father to help it; for it has no
power to protect or help itself'.[2] Furious rolls of parchment were dispatched post-haste between New and Old Rome, each more aggravating
than the last. The dispute was over both a thing and an idea. The headstrong Bishop Leo of Ohrid (whose brother was a eunuch and who had
been so fulsome in his praise of eunuchry) had written letters denounc-
ing the Latin practice of using unleavened bread in the Eucharist and

claiming that his church's ecclesiastical authority was ecumenical. The direct translation of ecumenical in Greek speaks of the whole Christian world – the *oikoumene* of Byzantium – but the touchy pope in Rome took this to mean that Byzantium was being said to enjoy universal power. As is often the way with rows, other subsidiary grievances were aired – that the Orthodox Church allowed priests to be married and that the rivals, each equally culpable in one another's eyes, misunderstood the truth of the Nicene Creed (the Latin church had amended it to assert that the Holy Spirit proceeded not only from the Father but also from the Son – the much-debated *filioque* clause).

Old Rome had just staggered through a grim catalogue of corruption. Three popes had been elected in one year. As part of their clean-up act standards were being raised and anomalies resolved. There was a right-eous, reforming fervour in the city. Constantinople just happened to have thrown oil on the flames. Constantine the Great had indeed agreed back in AD 325 that the Senate in Rome should have precedence over that in Constantinople; but this pecking order had been amplified down the centuries. Jesus' declaration that Peter was the rock on which his church was founded was slyly combined with fabricated texts. An extremely productive tract for the Roman cause was the so-called *Donation of Constantine* which had been forged some time in the late eighth or early ninth century. Declaring itself to be an account of historical goings-on around 320, it piously recorded that Pope Sylvester had baptised Constantine the Great, at the same time as curing him of leprosy. Naturally thankful, Constantine had offered an extraordinary catalogue of 'with gratitude' presents to Rome – control over vast swathes of territory including the cities of Alexandria, Antioch, Jerusalem and Constantinople (even though the city had not at that point been formally founded, a schoolboy error by the forger). Constantine's move to Byzantium from mainland Italy was itself said to have been in respectful recognition of Rome's ecclesiastical supremacy.[3] A dossier was being systematically sexed up, to the detriment of both parties.

But although sold down the centuries as the 'Great Schism', as a monu-mental, epoch-forming event, the truth is rather more pedestrian. The two Romes had in fact already excommunicated one another, in AD 864 on the watch of Patriarch Photios – he who had had to deal with that Viking threat and had sent out missionaries to convert the Rus. Despite this, both powers had continued to correspond and to debate and to support one another as political and military allies.

A sobering wind from Iceland might help to cool our desire for convenient divisions in world history. Icelandic and Norwegian Christians clearly felt a close connection to Constantinople. The Byzantine Emperor offered Christians in Iceland an alternative to the blustering Holy Roman Empire on their doorstep. Kings, aristocrats and pilgrims came to Constantinople to receive blessings and favours. In some documents the Byzantine Emperor and Jesus Christ were given the same title, *stólkonungr*. In return 'Kirjalax the king of the Greeks' (in this case Emperor Alexios IV) in AD 1203 asked for military help from the kings of Norway, Denmark and Sweden. In these accounts we hear casual mention of local political filibustering rather than an irrevocable split in the unity of the church.[4] The Great Schism suits our yen for boxes and lines in the sand, rather than the web of blurred lines that history in fact inhabits.

The issue between New and Old Rome was not so much the theology as the impact this theological squabble had on the political allegiances of the day. What happened in AD 1054 might not have been a schism, but it was a fracture, and one into which infection could creep.

The eleventh-century Byzantine historian Michael Attaleiates recorded the arrival in the skies of Halley's comet:

> During the course of the month of May of the fourth indiction, a bright comet appeared after the sun had set, which was as large as a moon when it is full, and it gave the impression that it was spewing forth smoke and mist. On the following day it began to send out tendrils and the longer they grew the smaller the comet became. These rays stretched towards the east, the direction towards which it was proceeding, and this lasted for forty days.[5]

We might be tickled by the sight of Halley's comet in the Bayeux Tapestry, but for those who lived in Constantinople the comet's appearance in AD 1066 presaged nothing but disaster. It was thought that these blazing passages across the sky brought mortal illness to emperors and bad luck to their people. A comet was said to have prophesied Constantine the

Great's death, and also the shedding of blood in the city that he had founded.[6] The superstitious were right to be fearful. The Norsemen were back – and this time not as friends but as foes. The Normans now had their sights set squarely on a new prize – the city of Constantinople.

CHAPTER 46

1071, 1081 AND ALL THAT

AD 1071–81

The bad condition of the Roman state at that time produced mortal plagues . . . Sometimes, though, it was Fate which introduced certain foreign pretenders from outside – an evil hard to combat, an incurable disease. One such was that braggart Robert, notorious for his lust for power, born in Normandy, but nursed and nourished by manifold wickedness.

ANNA KOMNENE, *THE ALEXIAD*[1]

The year AD 1081 was a busy time in a busy century. A new emperor, many muttered, a usurper, Alexios Komnenos, had stormed his way back into Constantinople with the help of a number of Turkish and Latin mercenaries. The looting, death and destruction that followed required that the pretender, now acclaimed as Alexios I, must endure a forty-day penance. So Alexios, aged twenty-four, founder of the Komnenos dynasty, whose lives would further flesh out the story of Constantinople, started his tenacious rule wearing a hair shirt and sleeping on a stone floor. Across the Balkans, Pechenegs, the Turkic tribe who were sometimes allies and often enemies of the Byzantines, were raiding and settling;[2] and in the West, having decided to excommunicate the religious leaders of Byzantium, Rome had also thought it expedient, in the short term, to ally with the Normans who were prowling southern Italy. Unfortunately for those in Constantinople, one of these bellicose nobles, Robert Guiscard, had particular designs on the Queen of Cities. And 1081 was the year in which he made his intentions clear.

Robert Guiscard was described in highly coloured terms by the chroniclers of the age:

This Robert was a Norman by birth, of obscure origin, with an over-bearing character and thoroughly villainous mind; he was a brave fighter, very cunning in his assaults on the wealth and power of great men; in achieving his aims absolutely inexorable, diverting criticism by incontrovertible argument. He was a man of immense stature, sur-passing even the most powerful of men; he had a ruddy complexion, fair hair, broad shoulders, eyes that all but shot out sparks of fire . . . Robert's bellow, so they say, put tens of thousands to flight. With such endowments of fortune and nature and soul, he was, as you would expect, no man's slave, owing obedience to nobody in all the world.[3]

His daughter having been offered the hand of the son of Constantin-ople's Emperor Michael VII Doukas (quickly withdrawn when Michael was deposed), Robert justified an invasion of the landmass that lay east across the Adriatic Sea. He was, he declared, simply seizing lands that should by rights already be his. He had been in possession of Bari on the heel of Italy since AD 1071 – having taken its impossibly sturdy fortifica-tions, overlooking a port that today tries to corral international migrants and refugees – and what remained of Byzantium was a tantalising three-day march following a nine-hour boat ride across the Adriatic. After powering over the sea to Dyrrachium, at the edge of what was once the ancient kingdom of Illyria and is now Albania, in the summer of 1081, Guiscard knew that the Via Egnatia would offer him an efficient route east. Constantinople's new Emperor Alexios also understood this only too well; he sent an army, 20,000 strong, jangling with Vikings, Anglo-Saxons and Turks to try to force the Norman back. But Guiscard had brought 30,000 men, and he was determined to win – Constantinople was a critical trophy.

Today the site where Norman and Byzantine forces met sits just off the Egnatian Way (the old road here now submerged beneath a three-lane highway) behind a sandwich bar and an exhaust-pipe dealer.

In among the 20,000 or so Byzantine soldiers, many mercenaries who had made their way west, there were a number of specialist fight-ers. As well as the *excubitores* and the Varangians, 500 or so would have belonged to the Kataphraktoi – the elite squadron typically mounted, their horses covered, like their riders, in full-face helmets and a protective chain mail. Contemporaries write with genuine awe about the discipline of these men, who would fight in a tight wedge formation. One source, the *Praecepta Militaria*, attributed to Nikephoros II Phokas,[4] eagerly lists their weapons: iron maces (many of them with spikes), daggers, lances, swords and iron rods. Alternatively named the Clibinarii (the name taken from a travelling oven, since both man and horse were encased in metal), the Kataphraktoi are thought to have originated as crack troops in the Persian army. Their reputation was legendary; it could well be a Kataphraktoi-style helmet that the Anglo-Saxon king was wearing in his ship-burial at Sutton Hoo. Kataphraktoi armour is certainly the model for many popular legends and fairy-tales.

The Kataphraktoi with their chain mail and spiked maces, the Varangians with their gem-encrusted tunics and double-edged axes, these men have become the stuff of fantasy. But the end for these particular crack-troops on the edge of Illyria was anything but. The Varangians surged forward but were isolated and then herded by the Normans into the nearby Church of the Archangel Michael. There they were surrounded by Guiscard's troops, the doors were barricaded from the outside, and the building and all inside were burnt to a cinder.

But, despite his gruesome successes on the Via Egnatia, Robert Guiscard could not quite drive home his advantage. Offensive was followed by counter-offensive, and it was finally in the Bay of Butrint that the Byzantine fleet showed Robert Guiscard its maritime nous, forcing the Norman back to Italy in AD 1084. On paper this was a failure – the only large-scale Norman invasion to have been successfully repulsed – but the Norman campaign brought Western forces into the Byzantine heartlands and worryingly close to Constantinople itself. Robert Guiscard's son Bohemond stayed on in the region to enjoy remarkable land-grabbing victories, and it was Guiscard, hymned in the *Gesta Roberti Wiscardi*, who ended up a hero of troubadours' tales.

In contrast Emperor Alexios I was slandered in the West. It was said that the Byzantine had defeated Guiscard only by trickery, promising marriage to Guiscard's wife Sichelgaita on condition that she poisoned her hero-husband. There was further elaboration – that the marriage took place and that Alexios then burnt his Norman queen alive.

But the truth is that Alexios managed all situations with a deft hand. Recognising that his territory – and indeed Orthodox land – was rapidly diminishing, he consolidated his rule, his army and his administration and strategised his way into the most stringent negotiating positions. The make-up of the Byzantine armies that went out to fight Guiscard tells us much. Those that died such a ghastly death, locked in that church, included English and Rus Varangians. Listening to their screams outside were 2,000 or so Turks, also fighting as Byzantine mercenaries. Although Western sources derided Alexios I for his choice of friends (the Muslim Turks were considered particularly offensive), Constantinople was the centre of a multi-ethnic and vigorously hybrid world. Just think back to the vacillating allegiances and deals that had been hatched, continuously, over the previous 1,600 years of the city's history. The Turks – some of whom it seems had converted to Christianity – were credible allies.

But further east a battle had in fact recalibrated ethnic and international relations. New Rome's Rubicon had been crossed; Constantinople simply had not noticed.

'The Byzantine emperor erected a marquee of red satin and a canopy like it and tents of silk brocades. He sat on a throne of gold; above him was a golden cross studded with priceless jewels and in front of him was a great throng of monks and priests reciting the Gospel.'

AL-HUSAYNI, WRITING IN THE LATE TWELFTH OR THIRTEENTH
CENTURY AD IN *AKHBĀR AL-DAWLA AL-SALJŪQIYYA*.[5]

A decade before, in AD 1071, while Guiscard was eating up Byzantine Italy in the West, worrying news had come to the Emperor Romanos IV Diogenes' private quarters in his palace overlooking the Bosphorus. Eastern Anatolia – flat, with wide horizons, remote and yet connected by some of the most ancient routes of antiquity, lends itself well to serving as a parade ground. And here were massing an old enemy who represented an immediate threat – the Turks. As Anna Komnene (daughter of Alexios I) recounted: 'the fortunes of the Roman Empire had sunk to their lowest ebb. For the armies of the East were dispersed in all directions, because the Turks had over-spread, and gained command of, countries between the Euxine Sea [Black Sea] and the Hellespont, and the Aegean Sea and Syrian Seas [Mediterranean Sea] . . .'[6]

Believing themselves descended from Noah, the Turks were now occupying the lands of ancient Urartu – from which Mount Ararat gets its name. With Lake Van in front and the shadow of Mount Ararat behind, there must have been some sense in their highly decorated, Edenic tents that these warrior-nomads were returning civilisation to its aboriginal roots. New cultures had been established by Turkic slave-soldiers such as the Ghaznavids, who ruled land from eastern Iran to northern India. The Ghaznavids were in turn defeated by the Seljuks, whose names – Moses, Jacob and so on – suggest that some of these men could have been of Christian or Jewish origin. As ever, the mosaic of the East was polychrome.

Answering anxious calls from his subjects, who feared the advance of this confident, alien force, Emperor Romanos went out from Constantinople to fight. In preparation the city's ruler would have celebrated the Eucharistic liturgy and recited other fervent invocations; soldiers of all ranks would have directed their prayers towards those saints who had died as martyrs and whom they would have considered particularly efficacious as protectors.[7] Before battle, if the army followed the tenth-century advice of the Emperor Nikephoros II, they would have fasted for three days and confessed their sins, to ready themselves and to purify their bodies and souls before the killing began.[8] We hear from impressed Arabic sources that:

> The Byzantines had assembled armies the like of which were seldom gathered for anyone after him. The total of their number was six hundred thousand warriors – self-contained battalions, successive troops and squadrons following one after the other, [so numerous] that the eye could not perceive them and their number could not be quantified. They had prepared an innumerable amount of animals, weapons and mangonels and pieces of equipment made ready for conquering citadels in war . . . What the Muslims saw of the great number, strength and equipment of the enemy terrified them.[9]

But, instead of returning in glory from the eastern Anatolian plains, the Byzantines were surprised by the Turkish combatants at the Battle of Manzikert and the Emperor's horse was cut from underneath him. Romanos had to fight for his life, in hand-to-hand combat, until he was eventually captured and brought mud-smirched to the tent of the Seljuk leader Alp Arslan – 'Hero Lion'. The Turk initially refused to believe that this could be the all-powerful ruler of the legendary city on the edge of two seas that his people called Rum.[10] Placing his foot on the Emperor's neck before he released him, Arslan sent a message back to Constantinople – the Byzantines needed to up their game.[11]

There were many in those sweeping, multiform territories, the Caucasus, the Middle East, Asia Minor, who were sick of Constantinople's taxes, who therefore found it easy to slide towards Islam – particularly when Muslim mystics spoke to them of saints and rituals and the prophet Christ in a way that was comfortingly familiar. Families quietly swapped the cross for the crescent. As the Turks advanced with their take-no-prisoners philosophy, resistance was, in many cases, futile. Within twenty years Turkish forces would reach the Mediterranean and within 150 years Anatolia would be called Turchia in Western sources.[12] After Manzikert Constantinople once again found herself accommodating stricken refugees. There were now new 'barbarians' at the gates – Seljuks who established the 'Sultanate of Rum' in Konya.

On what is now the Turkish border with Iraq, Seljuk ambition is in evidence in the town of Mardin which looks out over wide, flat, biblically appointed plains. Following the Manzikert victory, crossroad towns such as these fell to the Seljuk Turks. The Great Mosque, the Ulu Camii, almost certainly built in the eleventh century, rises above the tumble of the town down the hillside. Its splendid ribbed dome speaks of control of the land below which is rock-rich, dusty, watered by the Tigris River. At the same time in Baghdad, with its population of over a million and its devotion to the learning of Greek, Roman, Persian and Islamic authors in the House of Peace, the East had a thriving cultural centre. Constantinople was beginning to lose her moral claim to be the guardian of Sophia, of earthly and divine wisdom.

And what Constantinople could not realise was that, as well as a military embarrassment, Manzikert would be a narrative disaster too. Byzantine defeat would later be claimed as the triumphant birth of the Turkic polity and would be used as an excuse for a high-handed assertion by the West that the Christian East – and the city of Constantinople too – was no longer fit to look after its own affairs, let alone protect the Kingdom of God. Manzikert is a reminder that it is not systems but stories that motivate people; rumour and gossip that are often hard drivers of history.

So in the Eastern Mediterranean in general and in Byzas' City in particular around this time there seemed to be a certain jumpiness to things. There were a number of show-trials against heresy. In AD 1082, for example, a Platonist pupil of Psellos called Italos who believed in the transmigration of souls was condemned as a heretic. Basil, the leader of the Bogomils (a Balkan sect and possibly inheritors of the ideas of the Manichaeans or of the Paulicians from the eastern edge of Byzantine territories) in Constantinople, was publicly burnt to death in the hippo- drome in 1100.[13] From what was now their centre of operations, the Palace of Blachernae, or New Palace, on the northern slopes of the sixth hill (a building that showed Byzantium's preoccupations in its main rooms – the Hall of the Ocean, the Hall of the Danube, the Hall of Joseph) the imperial power-players of Constantinople actively tried to prevent conspiracies. Fittingly enough, the only section of the palace complex that survives today, the Prison of Anemas, ignored by locals who sell fresh fish and kebabs in the lanes round about and build car parks and lock-ups around the medieval stones, was said to have incarcerated political pris- oners. Religious hysteria is catching. Already in the West there had been a series of eschatological marches, flagellants, choreomaniacs – all extreme pilgrims suffering their way to salvation. Turmoil in Asia Minor and the Middle East had made it impossible for many to visit the Holy Lands in peace. With hindsight this was not the moment to invite the West to come in war to Byzantine lands; but Alexios I, as smart an operator as he was, was not acting with the benefit of hindsight. Constantinople's urban and military needs would spawn a new character in the story of the world, the Crusades.

CHAPTER 47

THE CITY OF CRUSADES

AD 1090–1203

Oh what a noble and beautiful city is Constantinople! How many monasteries and palaces it contains, constructed with wonderful skill! How many remarkable things may be seen in the principal avenues and even in the lesser streets! It would be very tedious to enumerate the wealth that is there of every kind, of gold, of silver, of robes of many kinds, of holy relics. Merchants constantly bring to the city by frequent voyages all necessities of man. About 20,000 eunuchs, I judge, are always living there.

FULCHER OF CHARTRES, *A HISTORY OF THE*
EXPEDITION TO JERUSALEM[1]

In the Altai Mountains that border Mongolia and Kazakhstan, at an altitude of 9,200 feet a remarkable discovery was made in 2014. Local herdsmen had alerted archaeologists to the burial of a young Turkic woman. Her feet poke out of her shroud in what look like leather ballet-pumps, she has been buried with a prettily embroidered felt travel bag, pillows, an iron kettle and the scraps of sheep and camel wool which have helped experts to date the burial to the sixth century AD. This woman was not rich, but she was laid to rest with a horse, presumably her own, which had been sacrificed. The presence of that mare, along with her twisted metal snaffle bit and sensible leather saddle, in this quiet little grave reminds us that the Turks were men and women who were compelled to migrate.

In the late summer heat of AD 1090, after thundering across Thrace with their rag-tag cavalry, Pecheneg Turks ravaged Constantinople's suburbs. The Turkic fleet, advancing from Smyrna under their leader Tzachas, also attacked her territories in the Aegean. Constantinople was, once again, suffering from her status as an object of desire.

Needing support against the Turks' dogged assault, Alexios had sent a well-worded message west to the pope. He implored 'his lordship and all the faithful of Christ to bring assistance against the heathen for the defence of this holy church, which has now been nearly annihilated in that region by the infidels who had conquered her as far as the walls of Constantinople'[2].

Pope Urban II responded in a speech delivered on the winter-hardened earth of a field in Clermont in central France on 27 November AD 1095:

> A foreign people and a people rejected by God, had invaded the lands belonging to Christians, destroying them and plundering the local population . . . Not I, but God exhorts you as heralds of Christ to repeatedly urge men of all ranks whatsoever, knights as well as foot soldiers, rich and poor, to hasten to exterminate this vile race from our lands and to aid the Christian inhabitants in time . . . May you deem it a beautiful thing to die for Christ in the city where He died for us.

And they followed his call. Crusaders headed for the buffeted brilliance of the Bosphorus en route to their ultimate goal, Jerusalem. These were not just soldiers. Ordinary men, women and children came too, the unarmed poor, a significant number walking as pilgrims. Many had 'taken the cross' – a crucifix daubed, stitched or tied on their left shoulders or across their chests. In the fields and lanes of Europe these travellers must have been an extraordinary sight. But they were not what Alexios was expecting. An offer of maybe 2,000 trained martial specialists would have been helpful, but a mongrel rabble of 30,000 eager, inexperienced souls? This was something unanticipated. Alexios must have kept in close touch with the ringleaders, masterminding the months of the Crusader-pilgrims' arrival, their overland routes and their quartering. After AD 1071, refugees had choked his city fleeing the disruption in Asia Minor. This clever usurper knew that he could not accommodate more newcomers, even if these were a levy united in faith and purpose, even if Byzantium was ten times the size of any city in the West. But he would have no choice, as his daughter Anna Komnene observed: 'Moreover, Alexios was not yet, or very slightly, rested from his labours when he heard rumours of the arrival of innumerable Frankish [Western European] armies. He feared the incursions of these people, for he had already experienced the savage fury of their attack, their fickleness of mind, and their readiness to approach anything with violence . . .'³ By AD 1097 over 10,000 Crusaders were massed outside Constantinople's walls. Truly, Alexios had started something.

Initially the city witnessed a personal crusade led by a man known to chroniclers as Peter the Hermit (his name in fact means Peter the Cuckoo). Anna Komnene elaborates:

> A certain Gaul, Peter by name, surnamed Kuku Peter, had set out from his home to adore the Holy Sepulchre. After suffering many dangers and wrongs from the Turks and Saracens, who were devastating all Asia, he returned to his own country most sorrowfully. He could not bear to see himself thus cut off from his proposed pilgrimage and intended to undertake the expedition a second time . . .

> After Peter had promoted the expedition, he, with 80,000 foot soldiers and 100,000 knights, was the first of all to cross the Lombard strait. Then passing through the territory of Hungary, he arrived at the queenly city. For, as anyone may conjecture from the outcome, the race of the Gauls is not only very passionate and impetuous in other ways, but, also, when urged on by an impulse, cannot thereafter be checked. Our Emperor, aware of what Peter had suffered from the Turks before, urged him to await the arrival of the other counts.⁴

Peter's paupers were not well behaved. A substantial number had died en route and, camped on the flat scrub outside Constantinople, in the internal, fantasy version of their wild project the survivors now believed that they should be given a hero's welcome. Alexios, as he looked out over this sea of hungry humanity, had no intention of finding the food for tens of thousands of extra mouths and, smartly, had the participants of Peter's Crusade transported to Anatolia, where many were swiftly dispatched by Turks. Peter returned to Constantinople, desperate for help, but Alexios was unmoved. We later hear of Peter the Hermit (his origins are in truth off the record) as a rallying voice, pumping up morale as Crusaders made their way down towards Jerusalem. Some credit Peter rather than Urban II with delivering the agit-prop that inspired the Crusading movement; others relate that Peter introduced rosary beads to the West.

Whatever his actual legacy, Peter represents a kind of ideological meddling that would serve few in the East, Christian, Turk or Muslim, well.

Ostensibly the purpose of this Latin–Orthodox collaboration (no sign of a Great Schism here), beyond the priority of retrieving Jerusalem, was to recapture – and to return to Constantinople – Byzantine lands. Alexios understandably took a managing role in the campaigns; but his allies did not play ball. In AD 1097 Frankish muscle saw Seljuk Turks relinquish Nicaea but high-walled Antioch would be trickier. Initially the Crusaders talked of the land they found being 'pregnant with produce', but after nine months men were sifting through the shit of their horses to find undigested seeds to eat. Having finally taken the city, Guiscard's son Bohemond, that other adventurer commemorated in troubadours' songs, refused to return his hard-won prize. Constantinople could do nothing; her leaders had been cuckolded. Antioch would remain an independent principality until 1268.

We must not underplay the millenarial anxiety at work here. Many truly believed that the end of days was upon them. Muslim sources for this period are telling; for Arab armies the Crusades were nothing much to write home about, just further examples of the run-of-the-mill, antagonistic engagements – Sunni and Shia, Bedouins or Arabs with Seljuk Turks – that had become a constant of the time. An anecdote from Baghdad neatly encapsulates the perceived apathy of Muslim rulers. A judge was said to have burst into the Caliph's court: 'How dare you slumber in the shade of complacent safety . . . leading lives as frivolous as garden flowers, while your brothers in Syria have no dwelling place save the saddles of camels and bellies of vultures!'[5] When, having continued their journey south, the Crusaders finally took Jerusalem in AD 1099, the bloodbath was unexpected and could never be forgotten. Success in Jerusalem was said to bring with it absolution from all sin. The Crusaders attacked the city with a frenzied ferocity.

Although a Muslim counter-Crusading fervour would ignite slowly (apparent from the mid-twelfth century), contact with the rough, stubble-chinned, pungent Crusaders started to generate folk-tales in the East describing Westerners as lubricious bogeymen. In the *Sirat al-Zabir*, a Portuguese anti-hero is pursued by an Arab hero through the streets of Constantinople, hiding in churches filled with snakes and pools of quicksilver and demonic automata.[6] Christian judges were said to act as panders and the children born as a result of fornication with prostitutes to be offered up to the church. The lack of washing by Westerners was much commented upon. When Saladin retook Jerusalem in AD 1187 he purged the Dome of the Rock with rose water.

We might wonder where the women of Constantinople and the surrounding Byzantine lands were in all of this. We do hear of a handful of high-born women who were involved in crusading campaigns: Eleanor of Aquitaine travelled to the Holy Land, Margaret of Beverley was said to have fought at Jerusalem with a cauldron for a helmet and Shajar al-Durr (originally a Turkish or an Armenian slave) was propelled by the chaos in the region to become ruler of Egypt for a few months in AD 1240. But generally women are absent from crusading narratives. However, the daughter of the Emperor Alexios, Anna Komnene is, somewhat unexpectedly, one of the finest chroniclers of the age, a splendidly direct communicator and a much-underrated source.[7] Producing a voluminous work from within the libraries and the women's quarters of the palaces in Constantinople, Anna talks of being tired, of writing late when the candles have burnt down; she is a very human companion through a sometimes bewildering medieval world.

Elsewhere we hear of the women of Constantinople waving their handkerchiefs from the windows of their high quarters, applauding the conflicts played out beneath them at the walls of Constantinople as if audiences at a civilised joust. It is Robert de Clari who will describe just such a scene in front of the land walls of Constantinople during the Fourth Crusade of AD 1203–4:

> the ladies and maidens of the palace were mounted to the windows, and the other people of the city, both ladies and maidens, were mounted on the walls of the city, and were watching this battle ride forward and the emperor on the other side. And they were saying to one another that our men seemed like angels, they were so beautiful, because they were so finely armed and their horses so finely accoutred.[8]

But we are then told by Robert that these self-same women, with great perspicacity, took the Frankish view and criticised Emperor Alexios IV for withdrawing behind the city walls. The whole account feels a bit made up. Imperial women and their courtiers would indeed have performed a ritual function as military engagement started but the sustained impact of the Crusading movement on women was in fact both more humdrum (some women were forced to postpone their marriages)[9] and more brutal.

The cold truth on the ground in this series of engagements was, as it has been through recorded history, one of rape and sexual violence. Even if the vast bulk of such atrocities have escaped the historical record, the legislation against them has not. As early as the tenth century the Pax Dei – the Peace and Truce of God, a move sponsored by the church to establish fixed times and places when and where fighting could be carried out – expressed a displeasure towards rape in war; the degree of Christian-on-Christian sexual violence in the Fourth Crusade would be condemned by Pope Innocent;[10] Richard II and Henry V both developed military codices that prohibited rape. But the European 'law of arms' – a kind of combat convention – allowed rape and torture if a conquering army had besieged a town. Rape proved ownership of both captives and territory and ensured dislocation and dystopia within local communities. Women and children were specifically targeted by Muslims and Christians alike from the First to the Fourth Crusades. Some accounts describe invasion at the time in terms of male penetration. Rape was not a by-product of war, it was a conscious military strategy. For the majority of women (and indeed men) living in this region at the time of the Crusades and had the misfortune to be in a town when it fell to crusaders, sexual violence in the name of God would have been not the exception but the rule.

CHAPTER 48

✤

NEGOTIATING MONKS AND HOMICIDAL USURPERS

AD 1106–87

> In every respect she [Constantinople] exceeds moderation; for, just as she
> surpasses other cities in wealth, so, too, does she surpass them in vice.
>
> ODO OF DEUIL, *DE PROFECTIONE LUDOVICI VII IN ORIENTEM*[1]

On 5 April AD 1106, a great storm destroyed the statue of Constantine
that had stood proud in the city for just short of 800 years. Many believed
that this was a sign that Constantinople would soon fall, but few could
have guessed from where the death-blow would come. The World's Desire
appeared to be flourishing: trade was booming, and spare cash was being
used to construct splendid complexes such as the monastery of Christ
Pantokrator. Attached to the Pantokrator church, in 1118 an asylum for
the insane and a hospital would be built which included beds for women
who could be attended to by a female doctor. The floor of the church was
laid with marble and one Emperor's son was buried here behind the very
slab on which it was said Christ had been laid when brought down from
the cross. The emperors had moved into new facilities too. Following the
example of Alexios I by and large, they lived in the upgraded Palace of
Blachernae on the Sixth Hill whose broken remains still stand above the
Golden Horn. Over time the palace came to be used as the Ottoman
Sultan's menagerie, as a brothel, a potter's workshop and a poor house,
but in the twelfth century the palace was splendidly appointed, and
visiting dignitaries – including the increasing number of Franks (also
known as Latins) in the city – would be proudly shown its mosaics and
great throne room and colonnades.[2] The walls of the city were carefully
guarded by those Varangians with their axes, archers and, *in extremis*, by
citizens who, confident that the Virgin Mary had their backs, used plates

or barrel-ends as shields. But as the thirteenth century approached, news came to Constantinople that the Byzantines were losing land in the West once more. One hundred years after Guiscard had locked men from Byzantium into a church and burnt it to the ground, the Normans were back on the Egnatian Way – and they did not come as Constantinople's allies.

In the purposeful little town of Kavala in northern Greece an inscribed stone stele – found in a graveyard – tells us that these new Normans burnt down not just a Byzantine church, but an entire city. The stele seems to be the only extant archaeological evidence of the total destruction there. Little surprise that the Latin Christian forces effecting this pernicious power-play were described by Byzantine sources as 'the wild beast of the west'.[3]

The Normans of Sicily had started their rampage in Thessalonika in AD 1185. Their aim was control of the vital artery of the Via Egnatia. And one of the characters caught up in the crossfire of these attacks was a man from Constantinople called Eustathios.

Homer had never lost his popularity as an author in Constantinople. Used as a teaching tool, and surviving censorship by the Church Fathers (in fact enjoying a renaissance as an allegorical study of Christian virtues), the *Iliad* and the *Odyssey* and the tales these epics inspired were circulated in both intellectual and popular circles. One of Homer's greatest champions was Eustathios. Born in Constantinople in AD 1110, Eustathios trained as a monk in the monastery of St Euphemia and subsequently at St Floros;[4] he was then employed in the patriarch's Department of Petitions and the patriarch's Treasury, and served as a deacon of Haghia Sophia and later as a professor of rhetoric. He was the epitome of the value that Constantinople placed on learning. He also wrote a splendid commentary on the *Iliad* and the *Odyssey*. One of his sources was the *Souda*, a brilliantly baggy encyclopaedia of 30,000 entries, alphabetically listing the main characters and narratives of the ancient world. In the *Souda* there are all kinds of treats, including a mini-biography of Homer, a physical description of Adam, the names of Helen of Troy's handmaids (and indeed the fact that one of them had composed the world's first sex manual). Described by medieval sources as one of the 'most learned men of the age',[5] Eustathios was laudably individual in his thinking; he decried slavery, and warned against military hubris as well as the self-serving lure of politics.

But once Eustathios became the archbishop of Thessalonika in the Church of St Demetrios – founded on the site of the old Roman baths where the Christian Demetrios was said to have been speared to death on the orders of Galerius and where students now gather to protest and to flirt – he would have to put all Constantinople's abstract education into practice. Imprisoned by the invading Norman forces, Eustathios would find himself employed as a negotiator. He was horrified by the 'babbling and shrieking' newcomers: for him they were 'demons', who 'have no acquaintance with anything good, because the vulgarity of their society has left them without any kind of experience of beauty'.[6]

In his work *On the Capture of Thessaloniki* we have an extraordinary eyewitness account of the Normans' brutality as they advanced towards Constantinople, with young girls being raped and the sick being stabbed in their hospital beds:

> we were led out through a mass of swords, raised up and quivering like a cornfield packed with ears of grain . . . a dagger waved from side to side as if it was about to be plunged into our vitals, and spears were pointed threateningly at our ribs from all sides . . . Alas what evil then followed! As if it had not been enough when I had previously made my way on foot through the corpses still steaming with warm blood, I was now conducted on horseback among others heaped in piles. The majority of them lay strewn before the city wall so close together that my little horse could either find no place to set his foot or had two or three bodies between his forefeet and his hindlegs . . .[7]

Eustathios was canonised by the Orthodox Church in 1988 – the only Homeric scholar, so far, to rise to such heights.

But Eustathios was not negotiating from a position of political strength; his alma mater was letting him down. Back in the capital, Constantinople had been behaving as her critics wanted her to. Alexios I had inadvertently seeded trouble for the city. As part of his economic-regeneration plan at the end of the eleventh century, the Emperor had welcomed in a number of Western traders who set up around the Golden Horn. Venetians who had come to the aid of Byzantium against Guiscard built a church, homes, and warehouses beyond the Golden Horn waterway, opposite the heart of Constantinople – the historic hub now also appearing in Arabic and Armenian sources as Stamboul. Elsewhere there were compounds for the Pisans and Genoese. Alexios realised that if the city wanted to protect herself against a wider world, she had to welcome that world in. His tactic paid off – Constantinople did indeed flourish. One Jewish visitor, commentating on the 'great stir and bustle' of merchants converging on the city, observed men 'who resort hither both by land and sea, from all parts of the world, for the purpose of trade . . . from Babylon and from Mesopotamia, from Media and Persia, from Egypt and Palestine, as well as from Russia, Hungary, Patzinakia, Budia, Lombardy and Spain . . .' [8] A poet resident in the city, John Tzetzes, remarked that 'those dwelling in Constantinople are not of one language or one race, but use a mixture of strange tongues. There are Cretans and Turks, Alans, Rhodians, and Chiots, notorious thieves.' [9]

But after Alexios came less far-sighted rulers. The Venetians had been granted generous privileges, not least control of the lucrative olive-oil export from Lakonia in southern Greece and dispensation from the 10 per cent tax normally levied on trade. Locals in Constantinople, understandably perhaps, were resentful. In AD 1171 the Emperor Manuel I Komnenos – possibly motivated by a needling, personal slight early in his reign in 1149 when Venetian sailors had mocked his imperial regalia during a joint Venetian–Byzantine campaign against Roger II of Sicily on Corfu [10] – had called in troops and, with much loss of life, forcibly expelled these merchants of Venice from the city, confiscating goods and demanding that the same be done in other Byzantine provinces – all to Venice's chagrin. [11]

Although this was a popular move in Constantinople, Manuel never strategically exploited the anti-Latin mood of the moment. Provokingly he had married his son, the future Alexios II, to the Princess of France (Agnes, later Anna). When Alexios, aged only eleven, came to the throne in AD 1180, his unpopular mother, the Frankish-Norman half-blood Maria of Antioch ruled as regent. Constantinople's people – always vocal – sent up a cry for a return to 'Hellenism'. Sniffing an opportunity, an imperial cousin named Andronikos, now an old man but with a highly colourful past that included extortion, embezzlement, prison escape, elopement and general dynastic skulduggery, was swept in through the gates on a tide of popular support as the new ruler of the city. Pumped up, the Constantinopolitan *hoi polloi* then charged to the 'Latin' quarter which they burnt and ravaged. On that May day, where fishermen now loudly sell their wares, the fishes' gills exposed like fields of bloody anenomes, there were many atrocities. A hospital run by the Military Order of St John (the Knights Hospitaller) was attacked, women and children were killed, so too the sick in their beds; a visiting papal legate was said to have had his head cut off and attached to the tail of a dog. Back in the palace the regent Maria was convicted of treason, held in a convent and then drowned at night. Andronikos declared himself co-regent; he had Alexios II, now age fourteen, strangled with a bow string, and the boy's body was thrown into the Bosphorus. Although he was fifty years her senior, Andronikos now married Alexios' thirteen-year-old bride.

There seems to have been something manic about Andronikos. Attempting to prove that he was a man of the people he had a vast image of himself, portrayed as a peasant carrying a scythe, painted onto the side of one of the churches in the city. The scythe was a warning to his enemies – Andronikos was said to have told his sons that he would cut down all giants so that they could rule over pygmies only. A man of his word, furious that they had tried to prevent him taking power, he impaled many of the men and women of Nicaea outside the gentle brick city walls that still stand. He promised 'to fall upon his family like a lion pouncing on a large prey.' But within three years of launching his campaign of terror, a counter-coup was mounted. Horrified by the accounts of Norman atrocities in Thessalonika and hearing that the Norman army was heading to Constantinople, in AD 1185 the citizens rose up against their tyrant. Andronikos tried to flee the city, but his boat was driven back by those tricky Eastern Mediterranean winds. Captured, he was ridden into the hippodrome slumped backwards on a camel and there he was lynched. Mutilated, suspended from the antique statuary gathered together so painstakingly by Byzantium's great and good, Andronikos' body was left to hang upside down. Eventually it was cut loose and then tossed into a nearby monastery garden. Not a glorious end for the Komnenos dynasty.

Now the inhabitants of Constantinople started to earn new epithets. No longer trumpeted in medieval chronicles as the citizens of the sacred Queen of Cities, they were 'the perfidious Greek nation', 'a brood of vipers', 'a serpent in the bosom'.[12] After a brief florescence, Byzantium was looking tired, degenerate, older, smaller, alone.

In AD 1187 Jerusalem was retaken by Saladin, a disaster of unparalleled proportion for the Christian Church; the West wanted someone to blame – and glared darkly at Constantinople. The fact that the Byzantines had recently enjoyed good relations with Muslim forces was seen as a betrayal, and a contributory factor in the calamity. Meanwhile Byzantium had also lost Bulgaria and Cyprus (in 1191 Cyprus had been sold to the deposed kings of Jerusalem by the English crusader Richard the Lionheart). And for a century now there had been trouble elsewhere, in al-Andalus, El Cid and his Muslim friends had established a very viable alternative to Christian courts. Castles here had been, in the last half of the eleventh century, the site of attacks and of a series of Christian losses. The cordial relations that Constantinople had once enjoyed with both Turkic and Islamic leaders meanwhile were collapsing. In Asia and in Europe it was beginning to seem impossible that the Byzantines could offer any kind of united front to their attackers – whoever they might be.

And then the ultimate insult: the earthly home of Christ, the capital of an empire that had established Christendom itself, the centre of the Christian cosmos, was about to come under attack from within, from soldiers of Christ whose political and religious allegiance lay in the West. Christendom was to witness a dirty civil war, catalysed by the rising power of Venice – its epicentre, Istanbul.

CHAPTER 49

VENETIAN PERIL, CHIVALRIC KINGDOMS

AD 1204–1320

The accursed Latins . . . lust after our possessions and would like to destroy our race . . . between them and us there is a wide gulf of hatred, our outlooks are completely different, and our paths go in opposite directions.

NIKETAS CHONIATES, *HISTORIA*[1]

'They gazed at its high walls, the great towers with which it was fortified all around, its great houses, its tall churches more numerous than anyone would believe who did not see for himself; they contemplated the length and breadth of the city that is sovereign over all others. Brave as they might be, every man shivered at the sight.'

EYEWITNESS TO THE ATTACK ON CONSTANTINOPLE AD 1204[2]

A bird's-eye view tells the truth about Venice, a strange, amphibious creature – one that cannot decide whether it is happiest on land or in the sea. It was only pain that had initially brought men to these marshes, as the local Veneti sought to escape persecution from Goths, Huns and Lombards as antiquity slipped into the Middle Ages. But this salty hideout was also proof of the resilience and imaginative brilliance of *Homo sapiens*. Rather than just a bolthole, an eccentricity, Venice became a crucible of world-class beauty and political and economic heft.

Venice is in so many ways a wild confection, but her bravura was a match for Constantinople's strategic straits and claims to the sublime. There was always something prickly about the relationship between these two cities. The tension perhaps started because Constantinople had an irksome habit of claiming to have founded Venice. The evidence is still there in the pink light that drifts into the abandoned Church of Santa

Maria Assunta in Torcello. Today only ten Italians and a priest live on the swampy islet at the northern edge of the Venetian lagoon, where once, at the height of its power in the tenth century, there would have been 10,000 – many more than Venice herself whose foundation Torcello had preceded.

A bishop of Ravenna – a servant of Constantinople – was said to have founded in Torcello what was originally a church to St Mary the Mother of God in AD 639. Peer through what looks like plastic-coated chicken wire in a dingy indentation in the church floor and you will see the remains of the local *magister militum*, a man called Maurice who completed the work. For centuries this region was under Byzantine authority. Constantine Porphyrogennetos described Torcello as the 'great trading station', and one of the lagoon's most valued commodities was salt – a trade that would have been intimately understood by Byzantium's ancient Megarian godfathers. Constantinople could pull rank over Venice, in terms of both military might and provenance. She had long been the stronger of the two cities and could legitimately claim a classical foundation. But Constantinople was about to feel the sting of Venice's resentment and lust.

The AD 1204 Crusade was originally directed against Muslims in Egypt with Jerusalem the ultimate prize. Mismanaged and under-resourced, the Crusading forces ended up on the Dalmatian coast, where they set up camp, working out how they could justify attacking the Christian city of Zara.

Meanwhile, Prince Alexios Angelos, the son of a deposed, blinded Emperor Isaac II of Constantinople who had sat under house arrest in a palace on the Bosphorus but kept his son alert to all opportunities for revenge, needed an army. When he heard of the Crusaders' dilemma, messages were swiftly sent. If this was a Crusade in search of a target, Alexios could offer the very best target of all. Promised 200,000 silver marks and Constantinople's submission to Rome in return for a seat on the throne, the Crusaders were persuaded. Following this silver-tongued, traitor prince eastwards, the Venetian prospectors honoured their end of the bargain, bringing Alexios to power in the Blachernae Palace in AD 1203. Then they sat and waited across the water in Chalcedon and outside the walls of Constantinople. But a year later the conniving prince had still not paid up.

Those Crusaders – Franks, Venetians, men from the Low Countries – had set out expecting to taste blood, glory and gold in exotic lands, but none had been forthcoming. Even if not motivated by riches they sought the redemption that Crusading promised. Hungry, cold, fearful and frustrated after a long winter outside Constantinople's walls, the malingerers were strung out and itching for action. At the end of March AD 1204, spurred on by clerics and leaders who suddenly remembered that Old and New Rome had been squabbling for a century or two over doctrinal differences, a justification was found. The Byzantines were said to be nothing less than the enemies of God.[3] Their accusers were Crusaders who had come armed with all the latest siege weaponry. The brilliance of Venetian mariners saw siege ladders mounted on the very masts of their ships, which were then sailed right to the sea-walls. Despite the Byzantines' best efforts the attackers gained footholds; elsewhere sappers set to work. Horrified, the people of Constantinople suddenly realised what was happening, but it was too late to escape. The Franks attacked for four days – then they scaled the walls and sacked for a further five.

When they broke in, guilt, perhaps, seemed to send the Crusaders wild: 'the sun witnessed what it should not'. There were rapes, burnings, impalings. Fully aware that Constantinople had kick-started the fetish for relic-collection, churches, shrines and palaces were ransacked to access their holy loot. In the pleasure gardens where city-workers stroll today between Haghia Sophia and the Blue Mosque there was carnage. History is usually written by the victors (and the Byzantines were horrified to realise that a number of their attackers could neither read nor write), but here we have a local eyewitness, whose house was close to the Haghia Sophia and who tells us in close and tortured detail exactly how dreadful these days were. Clergymen from the Latin forces made a beeline for the Church of Christ Pantokrator to raid the sacristy; they took treasure but also relics, including a thorn from the crown of thorns and a bone from what was believed to be the forearm of John the Baptist. Worse atrocities were in store for the living: 'tearing children from mothers and mothers from children, treating the virgin with wanton shame in holy chapels, viewing with fear neither the wrath of God nor the vengeance of men', the Crusaders, in the name of God, destroyed much of what they found in their path.[4]

In AD 1204 the city was defiled in every way. In among the spoils, the bronze wreaths concealing the joins in the porphyry Column of Constantine were taken to be melted down. The Megalos Pyrgos tower that held the protecting chain across the Golden Horn was toppled. The Christian city was being materially and morally torn apart.

It had been said hopefully by some when they had first seen the army massing that these were men 'who bore the cross of Christ on their shoulders'. The implication was that there would be a Christian understanding between those within and those without the city walls. It was an empty hope. The blind Doge of Venice, Enrico Dandolo – who was said by later Venetian sources to have lost his sight during those scuffles orchestrated by Manuel in Constantinople in AD 1171 – came to listen to the maulings and the massacres. He would have heard that a prostitute sat on the throne within Haghia Sophia; and that the donkeys brought into the church to carry off treasure skidded in the blood, filth and gore on the marble floors as they clattered off with their sacred spoil.

The Doge, a sightless, one-time guest of the city, seems a kind of negative image, an anti-hero to Constantinople's beloved Homer – the blind man who sang of the tragedy of greed and of cities that fall. Dandolo's conduct flew in the face of the ancient Greek ethic that stitched the Homeric epics and indeed Eastern Mediterranean society together – the power of *xenia*, of a respectful guest–host friendship. With intimate knowledge of what had been described throughout the medieval period as The Queen of Cities, it was the Doge who had told the Crusaders exactly where to attack, where the sea walls could be most easily breached. Dandolo died a year later, but his body was taken back to Constantinople, to be buried in Haghia Sophia itself. The spot is marked today by a nineteenth-century inscription; it is an appalling irony that this corrupting influence should be the first corpse ever to be buried within the Church of Holy Wisdom.

The body of Constantinople was dismembered and scattered. The four Chios-made horses in the hippodrome, brought to the Fortunate City by Theodosios II (although some argue it was Constantine the Great who had them shipped over from Old Rome), were taken to Venice. So too was a huddle of tetrarchs in purple stone, commissioned by Diocletian. Visit them now in Italy on the edge of St Mark's Square and you will notice one has half a foot missing. Wonderfully, this fragment of an appendage has since turned up in digs in Istanbul and is now on proud, somewhat pathetic, amputee display in the Istanbul Archaeological

Museum.⁵ A few items remain in Constantinople – that silvered statue-base of Eudoxia, the broken serpent's column from Delphi. But tons of bronze statuary were hacked down, smelted and then recast as coin. The Pantokrator Monastery became a centre for the trade of second-hand art and antiquities.

This desolation has sold the world a lie about what went before. To justify the attack, the native inhabitants of Constantinople had to be painted by the Western Crusaders as debauched, dissolute blasphemers. The palace, churches, shrines and libraries which had embodied their truth and their history were physically deleted, a scene of dreadful perdition. The shelf-loads of codices, parchment and vellum on which were stored the knowledge and ideas of both ancient and medieval worlds were plundered or put to the torch. The men and women whose families for generations had lived on the diamond between two sapphires could no longer speak for themselves. So Constantinople could now be described as a place of excess and foul corruption – rather than of fine beauty and profound scholarship – because the hard evidence had simply been destroyed.⁶

Following the carnage, the lucky few who could escaped to Nicaea, to Trebizond, and to Epirus in the west of Greece. Some made their way out through the Golden Gate, where eventually they settled, mocked, in Thrace. There was a desire to keep the dream of Constantinople alive. Nicaea became a spirited centre of learning, and Trebizond on the Black Sea, described as 'golden Trebizond', was developed with the help of Queen Tamar – a woman who adroitly controlled affairs from her acropolis in Tblisi and is remembered as 'the Holy Righteous King Tamar', the Christian Queen of Georgia.

The Byzantine Empire itself was split up. European powers lapped up their new territories – Venice appropriated western Greece from Dyrrachium to Lepanto (Naupactus); Baldwin of Flanders was given the empire of Constantinople to be ruled by his family (including his sister and mother of ten, Yolanda, for two years) – the list goes on.⁷ All was ratified in a treaty known as the Partitio Terrarum Imperii Romaniae – a forerunner of a notably similar division of Constantinople–Istanbul after the fall of the Ottoman Empire 720 years later, as Western forces partitioned up what was left of Istanbul's lands at the end of the First World War.

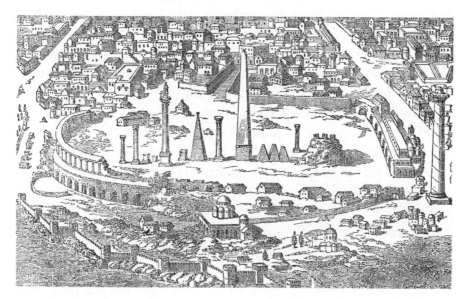

An eighteenth-century copy of a c. AD 1600 engraving of the hippodrome and Christian monuments of Constantinople, imagining what was left after the destruction of the Fourth Crusade

One former emperor of the city, Alexios V, was blinded by another, Alexios III. Sent out to feel his way around Thrace Alexios V was taken back into Constantinople and then thrown from the Column of Theodosios. Within the city the new rulers occupied the Bucoleon Palace, presiding over what they called a new Roman Empire. They converted some of the churches to Roman Catholic use. The Theotokos Kyriotissa, for example, which had been newly built just ten years before and still stands as Kalenderhane Camii close to the Valens aqueduct, was turned into a Dominican monastery. Covered with frescoes of St Francis, the monastery fielded a Patriarch who crowned a series of inopportune rulers in Haghia Sophia. Along with the loss of treasures and homes and books, the great fires started by the Crusaders had devoured much of the city's trade equipment. The silk industry for example would never recover, and many silk-workers fled to Asia Minor, where their great-grandchildren would end up producing silks for the Ottomans. Later authors described the city under the Latins as being neglected and enslaved.

*

But those in the old Byzantine territories talked and dreamt of the Fortunate City's recapture. In AD 1261 a high-ranking military commander
of Nicaea heard that the Venetian fleet was on exercise in the Black Sea.
Creeping into the city through a secret tunnel and reopening a gate in
the wall, he took possession of Latin-occupied Constantinople in the
name of Michael Palaiologos, protector of the boy-emperor John IV
Laskaris. Eventually, on 15 August 1261, the Feast of the Assumption,
Michael Palaiologos himself walked back in through the great Golden
Gate preceded by a copy of that miraculous icon of the Virgin said to
have been painted by the apostle Luke from life.

So while we think today of Greece as a quaint guardian of the idea of
Byzantium – all those icons and white churches – thanks to Constantinople's effective exile from herself, in real terms that is exactly what it
was. A diaspora developed, with many staying loyal to the religion, to the
name of the city and to the culture that Constantinople had nourished.
A thousand years cannot be shaken off overnight, so Byzantium lived on
in the territories that Constantinople had once controlled. And while in
some ways the returned Byzantines were more Latinised – they reduced
the power of eunuchs in the city, for example – iron had entered Constantinople's soul. From now on we find a great spike in the lists of Latin
religious errors being condemned. The people of Constantinople would
not forget that the first time their city had fallen to foreigners was to a
rival army fighting in the name of their own god. Christian unity would
seem to have become truly an impossibility.

But flowers can rise from the dust. In AD 1211, the Republic of Venice took
what had been the Byzantine island of Crete, which became a centre for
icon production, with works produced for both Byzantine and Venetian
patrons. The alchemy of Eastern and Western influence would nourish
Domenikos Theotokopoulos, known as El Greco – the artist from Crete
who, with his expressionist and dramatic style, some argue, gave birth
three centuries later to modern art. And when Constantinople was reconquered there was a modest but vigorous rejuvenation scheme. The
brilliance of the mosaics and frescoes in the church attached to the Chora
Monastery (those that survive date from c. 1315–21) and Pammakaristos
(which will become the home of the Greek Orthodox Patriarchate from
1456 to 1586), now Fethiye Camii, are testament to this grateful energy.

Pammakaristos' security guards might seem listless today, and local boys play football in the grounds, but the still and potent impact of the interior is unmistakable. In the bare brick monument, the visitor's eye is drawn up to the most breathtaking of images, Christ Pantokrator (c. AD 1310), in Chora to an an entirely charming scheme of the Virgin Mary's life.[8] Meanwhile in Venice, in terms of text, art and ideas, the East was coming to the West. Italian scholars brought back reports of the few surviving libraries and scriptoria – many of which had been attacked – still crammed with texts. They desired to devour that knowledge. There were other sources of inspiration. The Lion of St Mark is a hybrid of the cultures of the two cities. Originally a hollow-case bronze, dating to the seventh century BC and almost certainly from Anatolia, after its theft from Constantinople by Crusaders it was given wings, a Gospel book and an extended tail to become the representative of a Christian saint.[9] Stand by the gondolas and gelaterias in the piazzas and backstreets of La Serenissima and our minds should, in truth, turn east to Istanbul and beyond.

But do delicately detailed frescoes and mosaics embody a renaissance? Or was the artistic revival in Constantinople in the fourteenth century a last deep gasp, a recollection perhaps of what the city had been, before her imminent death? Because Constantinople would soon find that she had neither the will nor the wherewithal to defend herself.[10]

For Crusaders who arrived from the Netherlands, the English midlands and northern France, as they marched or sailed through Byzantium's territory, that glittering sea, those hot winds, the golden-stone castles that rose out of pale rocks must have themselves seemed like manifestations of a religious experience.[11]

Constantinople had invited the Latins here. She had used them as mercenaries and now had found that they were reluctant to leave. This dependence of Byzantium on guns-for-hire has long been used as a stick with which to beat the civilisation.[12] But the belief of Constantinople's rulers that they presided over God's plan might help to explain their unorthodox military policy. The Byzantine Empire, centred on Constantinople, existed to consolidate and defend rather than to attack. The Christian role of the men and women whose capital was Constantinople was to maintain a peace rather than to enforce an old Roman-style *pax*, so often a two-faced one as the Roman author Tacitus had famously opined; 'They [the Romans] make a desolation and they call it peace.'[13]

Unlike both the Muslims and the Latins, Byzantium did not indulge a particular penchant for holy war; in fact Byzantine authors use that phrase only when referring to battles for the possession of Delphi back in classical times. 'We must always preserve peace,' their chronicles say. The West on the other hand did not indulge in such squeamishness.

Repossession of Jerusalem might have been a religious reverie, but Constantinople offered more; this was a city of dreams in control of many thousands of square miles' worth of rich pickings. To Byzantium's horror, the Knights Hospitaller sensed the city's weakness and started to claim one Byzantine island after another. Rhodes was snatched after a two-year siege that began in AD 1306.[14] The fabulously Gothic fortified old town, from within which leading lights of England, France, Germany, Provence, Italy, Aragon and Castile in the guise of Knights Hospitaller would oversee medieval spy operations in Constantinople and Gallipoli, was a taste of things to come. Now Rhodes was part of a Western-facing, chivalric sea-girt kingdom of the Latins.

The Hospitaller castles started to form a necklace of fortifications across the Mediterranean. On the little island of Chalki, at Kolossi on Cyprus, at Bodrum,[15] if one climbs – pretty much vertically in places (the Greeks' perky disregard for health and safety is admirable) – past the ghost of an ancient acropolis to study the perilously fading 550-year-old frescoes commemorating St Nicholas' arrival on Chalki island, and if one gazes out towards Asia Minor and the wide waters all around, the strategic possibilities of this archipelago are startlingly clear. Passing birdlife – cormorant, albatross, Audouin's gull, Mediterranean shag, yelkouan shearwater and long-legged buzzard[16] – would have been able to tell the rulers of Constantinople that they were now almost completely encircled by hostile Christian forces.

Within the city itself Venetians and Genoese embarked on a proxy war, burning one another's warehouses and homes. There was trouble approaching from all points of the compass: from Genghis Khan in the East,[17] from those Knights on the Mediterranean fringes of empire, and now too from the south. The most potent legacy of the Crusaders had been, in the long term, to unite the Arab Near East against the Christian powers in the region and, in the short term, to expose the Christian world's Eastern bulwark to the ambitions of their sometimes friends and oft-times enemies, the Turks.

As Ramon Muntaner, a Catalan mercenary at the time, recounted:

The Turks had, in truth, conquered so much territory, that their armies arrived in battle array before Constantinople; and only an arm of sea, less than two miles wide separated them from the city as they brandished their swords and threatened the emperor, who could see it all. Imagine then the torment he must have felt, for they would have seized Constantinople itself had they possessed the means by which to cross that arm of sea.[18]

PART SIX

✤

ALLAH'S CITY

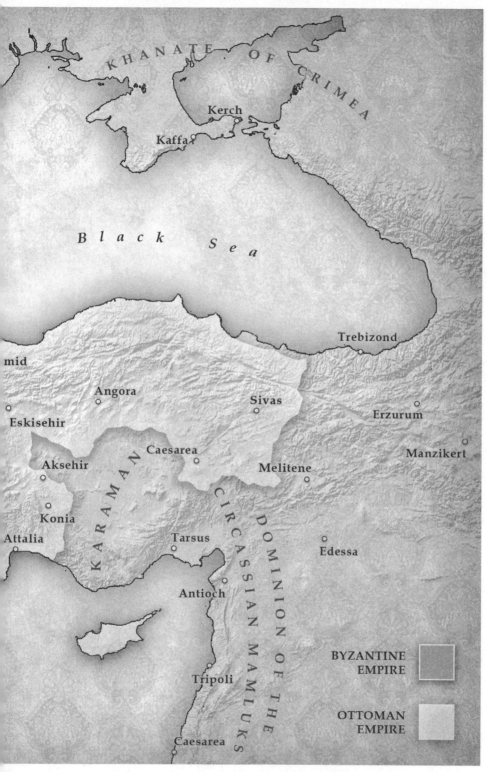

Ottoman and Byzantine territory in the east Mediterranean, c. AD 1451

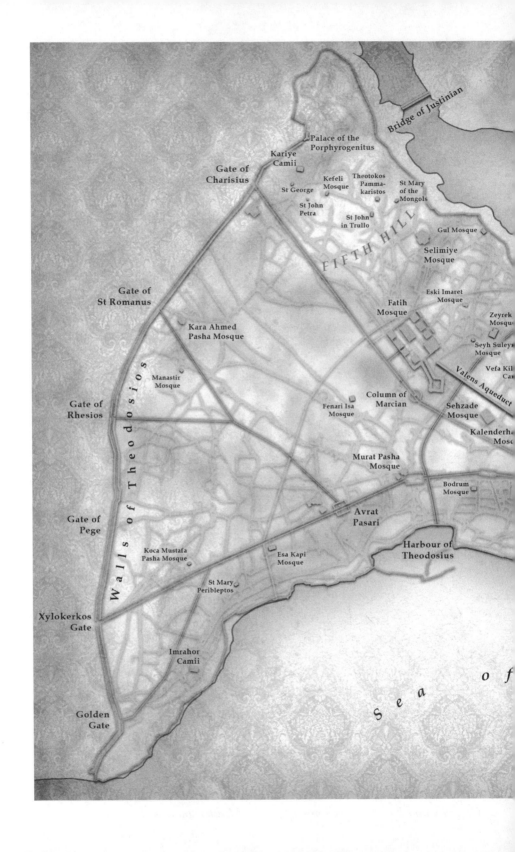

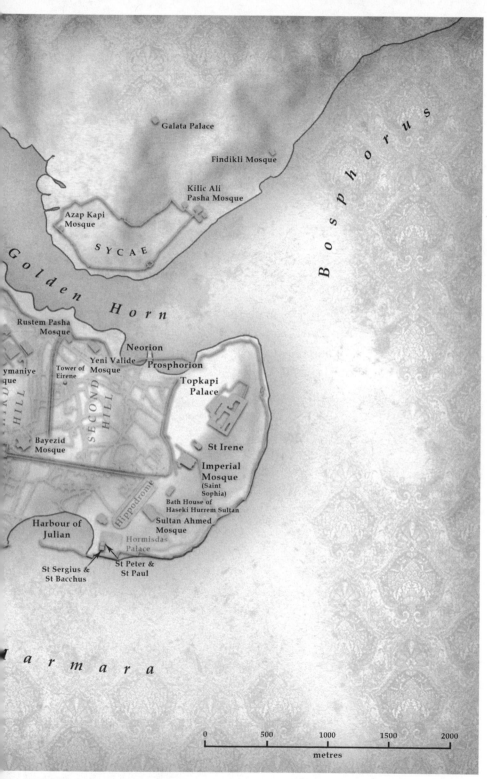

Galata Palace

Findikli Mosque

Kilic Ali
Pasha Mosque

Azap Kapi
Mosque

S Y C A E

B o s p h o r u s

G o l d e n

H o r n

Rustem Pasha
Mosque

Neorion

Yeni Valide
Mosque

...ymaniye
...que

Tower of
Eirene

Prosphorion

Topkapi
Palace

SECOND
HILL

Bayezid
Mosque

St Irene

Imperial
Mosque
(Saint
Sophia)

Bath House of
Haseki Hurrem Sultan

Hippodrome

Harbour of
Julian

Hormisdas
Palace

Sultan Ahmed
Mosque

St Sergius &
St Bacchus

St Peter &
St Paul

M a r m a r a

| 0 | 500 | 1000 | 1500 | 2000 |

metres

Sixteenth-century Istanbul

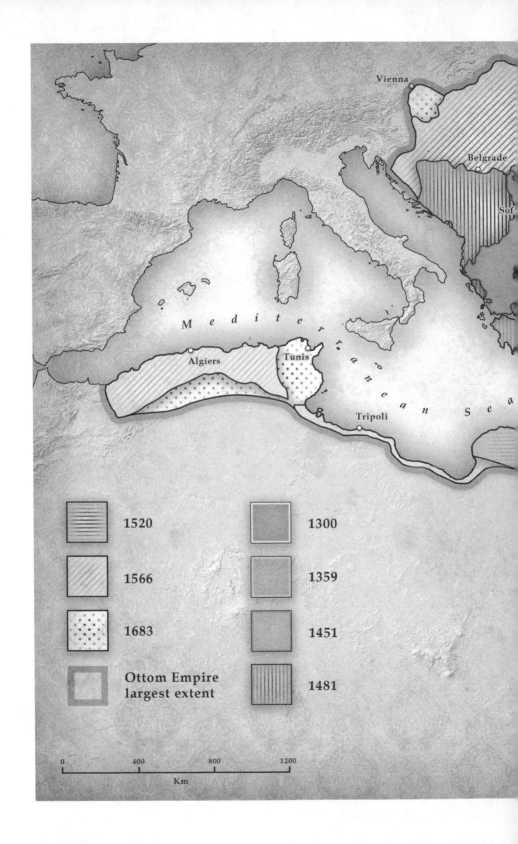

Vienna

Belgrade

Sof

Mediterranean Sea

Algiers   Tunis

Tripoli

1520	1300
1566	1359
1683	1451
Ottom Empire largest extent	1481

0   400   800   1200

Km

Expansion of the Ottoman Empire, AD *1300–1683*

CHAPTER 50

YILDIRIM: THE THUNDERBOLT

AD 1326–1453
(727–857 IN THE ISLAMIC CALENDAR)

In the valleys glittered stately cities, with domes and cupolas, with pyra-
mids and obelisks, with minarets and towers.

The Crescent shone on their summits: from their galleries sounded the
Muezzin's call to prayer.

That sound was mingled with the sweet voices of a thousand nightingales,
and with the prattling of countless parrots of every hue.

Every kind of singing bird was there.

The winged multitude warbled and flitted around beneath the fresh living
roof of the interlacing branches of the all-overarching tree; and every
leaf of that tree was in shape like unto a scymetar.

Suddenly there arose a mighty wind, and turned the points of the sword-
leaves towards the various cities of the world, but especially towards
Constantinople

That city, placed at the junction of two seas and two continents, seemed
like a diamond set between two sapphires and two emeralds, to form
the most precious stone in a ring of universal empire.

Osman thought that he was in the act of placing that visioned ring on his
finger, when he awoke. OSMAN'S DREAM, C. 1280[1]

Across the Sea of Marmara, in the city where Empress Theodora once
bathed, there was a sinister sound: the determined crunch and munch
of many hundreds of thousands of silkworms at work. The rank smell
of these silk workshops would have struck approaching visitors from a
good half-mile away. Then would come the thud and song of a thousand
looms and the hot tang of velvets, of silks and of damasks, newly made.

This home of the silkworms, which for centuries had been the Greek city of Prousa, was on the cusp of massive change. The Turks in the East had continued to consolidate their territorial gains. In AD 1326 one Orhan Gazi planted his standard on this high hill, a mere 100 miles south-east of Constantinople, and renamed the Byzantine town Brusa.

We are told it had all started with a dream. One night, Orhan's father, Osman (who also appears in the sources as Otman),[2] leader of the Otto-man Turks, dreamt that a great tree grew from his navel. The tree spread across the earth, and when a wind stirred its sword-shaped leaves these pointed towards the city of Constantinople.[3] The night before his vision, Osman had accepted that sorrow was inevitable, that his love for a beau-tiful girl in the city of Eskişehir, itself a strange, otherworldly, erotic place (from the Bronze Age onwards, a centre of the worship of that Eastern goddess of nature Kybele), would have to remain unrequited. It was this acceptance of grief and sorrow as a certainty of the human condition that liberated Osman to achieve greatness – the girl became his and so too would half of the known world. Osman's tribe was on the move.

Starting life in what is now north-west Turkey, the Ottomans had been just one of many semi-nomadic Turkic tribes originally from the Altai Mountains of Outer Mongolia. In the thirteenth century, while Con-stantinople was occupied by the Latins, Mongols had captured Baghdad in AD 1258 and the Seljuk Sultanate of Rum was on the wane – the axis of power was shifting. Osman's followers, who would come to be known as the Ottomans (or *Osmanlılar* – 'the people of Osman' in Turkish), were on hand to fill in the gap. Based in the valley of the River Sakarya – a waterway that has its source near a town called Black Castle (since 2004 renamed Afyonkarahisar, Opium-Black Castle) – they consolidated their power from what is now a quiet and respectable little conurbation, Söğüt. Seizing Söğüt in 1265, father, son and grandson then took one village, one valley, one town after another from a base at Yenişehir near Nicaea. In 1326 the Ottomans finally succeeded in capturing their first, major settlement, Prousa – the city that would become the first Ottoman capital – following a siege that lasted between six and nine years: 'A siege so tight that an infidel could not even extend a finger out of the castle.'[4]

A trip to present-day Bursa is illuminating. Although the town was aggressively developed as an industrial centre after the establishment of the Republic of Turkey in 1923, and the outskirts are now choked with car factories, a ghost of its early sylvan beauty survives. Halfway up the foothills of the Asian Mount Olympus to the south of the town, there must have been a sense here that raw nature still mattered – that this might be just another temporary vantage point from which travelling nomadic warriors could meet Christian armies on the plain below. The *rus* had long defined success for the Ottomans, not the *urbs*. Up in the old town of Bursa some trees have clung on among wooden *könak* mansions (the waterfront versions in Istanbul are known as *yalıs*). In the old town they still sell and eat goats' cheeses wrapped in goatskins, a method of preservation developed by those with a nomadic lifestyle. But Bursa does not feel like a glorified nomadic encampment. In among the high streets and parks and crumbling Byzantine fortifications are scattered a series of splendid early Ottoman tombs, the final resting place of the tribe's great leaders including Osman I. Here too is the impossibly beautiful Green Mosque, built within a hundred years of Orhan's arrival in the town. With these fine Islamic foundations a root was being consciously planted by people who had been peripatetic for millennia. Bursa's marvellous Turkic Renaissance buildings resound with Ottoman ambition. Osman and his children wanted to be not just masters in their own house, but masters of a subject empire. Soon the power-players of the region would be coming to the Ottoman interlopers with placatory offerings – livestock, metals, fine cloth.

The Ottomans in their newly built castle would have looked out over Bursa's plain – just beyond it the Sea of Marmara and in the direction of the city between two sapphires that would remain stubbornly unattainable for another fat century. But Orhan and his men had the patience to watch and to wait, because all around other cities had started to fall: Nicaea in AD 1331, Nicomedia in 1337, Chrysopolis in 1341 – not quite spitting distance from Constantinople but the breath of the Ottomans would have carried thus far. And on the European mainland there was more success from other members of the Ottoman family. Operating sometimes independently, Ottoman warlords made attacks on settlements along the Egnatian Way, and soon they would be in control of much of the Balkans.

While the Ottomans tasted one success after another, there were granular problems in Constantinople itself. In AD 1347 the eastern half of the Haghia Sophia dome collapsed, signalling, it was certain, divine displeasure. Then the Tower of Christ (the Galata Tower now), built in 1348 by the Genoese – traders newly favoured with the exile of Venetians following the Venetian disgrace of 1204 – pointed to a new threat from an old enemy. Genoese trading boats from Crimea had brought the Black Death into the city, and a third of Constantinople's population would be dead within the year.[5] Elsewhere others were declaring themselves to be the true emperors of the Romans: first was Stephen Uroš IV Dušan of Serbia in 1346, and his successors, for the next half-century, followed suit.

The future of Constantinople-Istanbul could have been a little different. There were attempts at reconciliation, to generate an Ottoman–Byzantine coalition. In AD 1346, Theodora, the daughter of the Emperor-in-waiting John VI Kantakouzenos, was married off to Orhan, the Ottoman leader. Greek sources were horrified; this was considered by many an 'abominable betrothal'.[6] Orhan was, as the fifteenth-century Doukas saw it, 'a bull which had been parched by the burning heat of summer, and was with mouth agape drinking at a hole filled with the coldest water but unable to get his fill'.[7] The Byzantines had in fact long negotiated with both Turks and Arabs, and their contact with Muslims was one of the reasons that Western sources declared them to be untrustworthy. But now this was all getting a bit desperate; rival claimants in Constantinople grabbed at Ottoman allies to ramp up their own firepower. Smelling their fear, the Ottomans coolly played the Byzantines off against one another. When John VI Kantakouzenos was crowned in 1347, the gold circlet on his head was mounted with coloured glass – all the real gemstones had been pawned to Venice.[8] And in 1326 in Bursa the first Ottoman coin had been struck; meanwhile, on the watch of the joint Byzantine rule of the two Johns (John V was a minor and so for a period ruled together with John VI), Constantinople ceased to issue gold coinage. More than a millennium's worth of tradition vanished with one signature at the old mint in a beleaguered city. Some time around 1357, John Kantakouzenos, who had now abdicated, wrote that the city's empire was a shadow of its former self. This was a tired civilisation, and something had to give.

Byzantine cities continued to fall, Didymoteichon by AD 1361, Plovdiv by 1364. The single successful military enterprise against the Ottomans was the recapture of Gallipoli, 'the Muslim throat that gulps down every Christian nation',[9] in 1366. Just a decade later the town was returned to

Map of Constantinople from the Liber Insularum Archipelagi, c. AD 1385–1430

the Ottomans as thanks for their help with an internecine coup inside Constantinople itself. Five hundred and fifty years on during the Great War and that settlement on the Dardanelles – the Kallipolis, the Beautiful City – would see a new horror when Muslim and Christian armies would meet once again to fight for vicarious honour and for virtuoso land. In 1367 a papal delegation was ushered into Constantinople, but the Byzantines recognised that they could expect no consolidated help from the West while the schism in the church stubbornly loomed. And then in 1369 – without so much as a murmur – for the sake of his city the Byzantine Emperor travelled to Rome to convert to Roman Catholicism.

By AD 1371 the new Ottoman ruler Murad I had taken Adrianople, overlooking the wide, misty Maritsa River, now a natural border between Greece and Turkey, surrounded by the flatlands where Valens had once been slaughtered by Goths. Murad then made this ancient settlement the new Ottoman capital of Edirne.[10] One Burgundian pilgrim Bertrandon de la Broquière would visit both Constantinople and Edirne in early

1433. He talked of jousts and celebrations in The Queen of Cities (both Western-style jousting and a local version of Persian polo were played here), but was clearly far more impressed by the scale of the welcome that he received in Edirne from the Ottoman Murad II in this glamorous, newly Islamic settlement, that had once been a bulwark against both Byzantion's and Constantinople's enemies. Many Christians joined the Ottoman forces in these shape-shifting years in hope of loot and of protection – it might be, retrospectively, why a Greek soldier features in the lines of the poetry of *Osman's Dream*. Others would find they had no choice in the matter.

It is now that we find the development of a cultural, military and religious phenomenon that would colour the experience of living in the city of Istanbul and of those who brushed with Ottoman might over the next 500 years. A proposal had been put to Orhan:

> The conquered are the responsibility of the conqueror, who is the lawful ruler of them, of their lands, of their goods, of their wives, and of their children. We have a right to do, what we do with our own; and the treatment which I propose is not only lawful, but benevolent. By enforcing their enrolment in the ranks of the army, we consult both their temporal and their eternal interests, as they will be educated and given better life conditions.[11]

The sons of the Christians newly under Ottoman control – those who were strong and aged between about six and fourteen – were repeatedly taken and pressed into service as administrators and as slave-soldiers. The process was called the *devşirme* (literally 'the collecting') and the result would be the Janissaries (the word derives from the Turkish *yeni çeri*, or new soldier), a martial group who were soon to become synonymous with Muslim Constantinople. They were super-troops with their own quarters, granted a salary and pension, trained, educated, lauded, so attachment to the Janissary Corps quickly became not a punishment in the Eastern Mediterranean and beyond, but a goal. The Janissaries developed a tight culture and nourished a religion of the road – Bektashi mysticism, a predominantly Sufi Islamic Dervish faith that incorporated elements of Christianity and Anatolian shamanism. All the way along the old Via

Egnatia – still a vital artery linking Europe to Asia – Bektashi lodges or *tekkes* started to spring up.

A few still survive: high above the Maritsa River, with the border of Greece and Turkey visible below, a Roman shrine has been repurposed. Water seems to run out of the earth magically here, 500 feet above sea level. For centuries this was part of a Bektashi lodge, now returned to Christianity as a chapel to St George. As the sun sets, the spring water in the shrine throws back dancing patterns of light. It is tempting to picture the Janissaries and their guests appreciating the day's end (all faiths were welcome in the lodges), worshipping within their wonderfully accommo-dating Turkic-Muslim-Sufi-Christian-shaman belief system. In robustly Orthodox Christian Greece, a few brave souls today still climb up here to leave ribbons and scarves as offerings on the thorn tree outside, gifts to the old spirits and to Allah, the scraps dancing beneath the noisy flapping of a giant blue and white Greek flag.

Now that the Ottomans circling Constantinople had their own stand-ing army – and as the silk trade in Bursa grew,[12] silks from the East typically being traded for woollen cloth from Europe – these determined Turks had both the economic and the military muscle with which to establish an empire.

Control of the Via Egnatia was key, and excavations in the town of Yiannitsa in northern Greece explain why. Next to what is now a Chinese supermarket, industrial-scale tanneries and stables for the refreshment of merchants' horses and camels have been discovered. Founded in AD 1383 as Yenice-i Vardar by Gazi Evrenos Bey, Yiannitsa (the name means 'new town of Vardar') would become one of a chain of settlements across what are now Albania, Macedonia and northern Greece. Access to this trade route would turn what the Ottoman invasion of Europe arguably was – a cacophony of competing land grabs by competing warriors – into an idea that could be sustained. Evrenos Bey (quite possibly a Byzantine convert), who set up soup kitchens along the old Egnatian Way, was buried in 1417 in an elegant mausoleum by the roadside in his new, Ottoman, city. A place of pilgrimage from the fifteenth until the early twentieth century but neglected after the fall of the Ottoman Empire, his resting place was briefly used as an agricultural store and has now been politely restored as a small art gallery.

In AD 1389 the Ottomans defeated a Christian coalition of Serbs,

Bosnians and Kosovians on the plain of Kosovo, a battle during which their leader, Murad I, was stabbed to death (some said by a Serbian deserter; an event celebrated by Slobodan Milošević during the horror of the Yugoslav wars). And then in 1391 the new Sultan Bayezid I started to tighten the net. He took Yoros Castle, on the site of Byzantion's old protecting sanctuary To Hieron. Sitting above an army outlook, protected by razor wire and malevolent dogs, the area still has a charged feel. In 1394 Constantinople itself had a Turkish quarter imposed where an Ottoman kadı (judge) enacted Islamic justice. The city was effectively under siege for a full seven years and all her lands were lost. In 1397 the fort of Anadolu Hisarı (the fortress of Anatolia) was built by Bayezid further down the Bosphorus towards the city, cutting Constantinople off from her Black Sea supplies. The fortress would soon become an Ottoman prison.

Bayezid I's progress was so fast, so ferocious, that he was nicknamed Yıldırım – Thunderbolt. Near Nicopolis on the Danube in AD 1396 a tentative European crusade against the Ottomans was annihilated. Christians were so desperate to flee the carnage they piled into overloaded boats and then chopped off the hands of their companions-in-arms who were desperately clutching at the sides. Constantinople's Emperor Manuel II (who as heir to the throne had already been forced to fight in the Ottoman army) was reduced to vassal status; he came to Henry IV of England in 1400 to beg for help – the only Byzantine Emperor ever to visit the country. Manuel, sleeping in the staterooms of Eltham Palace, while jousts were organised in his honour in the grounds, must have prayed that the old Byzantine trick of polished diplomacy would result in material salvation. But who wants to risk troops to save a distant, urban shell, trembling with a frightened and impoverished people? How the tables had turned since 1176, when an English king had been eager for the hand of a Byzantine princess.

For a few decades it was Mongol muscle rather than the Christian cross that gave New Rome reprieve. In AD 1402 Tamerlane's Mongol armies met the Ottomans near Ankara. New evidence beneath the countryside around Ankara airport indicates the ferocity of the engagement.[13] The Ottoman leader Bayezid was captured and later died in prison – the only Ottoman ruler ever to suffer this ignominy. In Anatolia, internecine strugle between the sons of Bayezid was followed by infighting between rival Ottoman warriors back in the Balkans. Yet though for a brief moment it looked as though there was to be some reprieve, in 1444 another crusade, called by some the Final Christian Crusade, suffered a crushing defeat near Varna on the Bulgarian Black Sea coast.

In AD 1422 the Ottoman leader, this time Murad II, had attacked Constantinople once again – punishment for the Byzantines' release of a pretender, the 'False Mustafa', whom Byzantine authorities had been charged with keeping prisoner on the island of Lemnos. Despairing wealthy Byzantines within Constantinople itself built houses with fortified towers to protect themselves. The ruins of Mermer Kule on the edge of the land walls might well be the broken remnants of one of these desperate domestic fortresses within the old walls.[14] Elsewhere – in what had been Byzantine territory – cities and villages in Hungary were left like a 'black field, black charcoal'.[15] In 1430, Thessalonika – already handed to the Venetians seven years before – fell, finally, to the Ottomans.[16] In 1448 the Russians chose to stop sending their monks to Constantinople for consecration.

There was a dreadful certainty to the Ottomans' momentum. They knew that if they stopped they would have to give up. So while Constantinople's rulers presided over a diminished and diminishing power – to all intents and purposes thirteen subsistence-economy villages jagged with ruins within a poorly repaired encircling wall (since AD 1235 Constantinople had been no longer a territory, but simply a reduced city) – the Ottomans were looking to the future and to the West to gather strength. Pisa, Genoa and Paris were on the rise now: the so-called Franks were no longer the slavering, vulgar barbarians observed by Eustathios during the siege of Thessalonika in 1185. The West was generating ideas and inventions to rival those that had been pouring from the East for millennia. There was word that in Hungary an engineer named Urban was developing gunpowder technology. Greek Fire had long been Constantinople's protection: now the lines of supply for the chemical weapon's essential ingredient, naphtha, which had once been imported from the Caucasus and the Middle East, had been cut. The Byzantines had used cannon against the Ottomans in 1396, but by the mid-fifteenth century they could afford neither gunpowder nor the gun-metal in which to pack it. For the Ottomans, money was not an issue.

And the vultures started to circle. As if it was an international charity-shop sale, Italians went to Constantinople to bring back manuscripts: one

Giovanni Aurispa collected 248 books during a single trip. Italy was now full of educated, Greek-speaking, poverty-stricken refugees, who could teach the classical language to Italians eager to improve themselves. Petrarch, with a little help from his friend Boccaccio, had already made contact with one Greek-speaker Leontios, in order to translate a copy of the *Iliad* that he had acquired. Hugging Homer's lines excitedly to his chest, even though he could not read a word, Petrarch was so thrilled by his project that he was moved to write a letter of thanks to Homer himself.[17] Venice would come to be called the New Athens because of her delight in Greek works. We are told that a lecture on Plato by George Gemistos (his nickname Plethon a homage to the Athenian philosopher) prompted the Medici family to sponsor the Platonic Academy in the city.[18] It has rightly been said that the Italian Renaissance owed much to Constantinople's sorrow.[19]

And all that was left to fall was Constantinople herself.

High-hilled Bursa had felt like an appropriate place for the incarnation of Osman's strange, pastoral dream which combined mystical, sexual, religious and topographical themes all in one. But its ultimate realisation would be bloodier. In AD 1452 a new Ottoman leader, Mehmed II, constructed his own fortress, Boğazkesen Castle, now known as Rumeli Hisarı, on the European shore of the Bosphorus. It was fitted with 'cannon like dragons'[20] whose cannonballs bounced on water. Mehmed's Janissary troops were instructed to use as target practice any ship that did not cough up customs duty. Constructed opposite To Hieron and the Anadolu Hisarı built by his great-grandfather in Asia, Rumeli Hisarı was a sure sign: the Ottoman invasion of Constantinople had started.

CHAPTER 51

NO COUNTRY FOR OLD MEN

AD 1453
(856/7 IN THE ISLAMIC CALENDAR)

Everyone who heard that the attack was to be against the City came running, both boys too young to march and old men bent double with age.

DOUKAS, *FRAGMENTA HISTORICORUM GRAECORUM*[1]

The spider is the curtain-holder in the Palace of the Caesars.
The owl hoots its night call on the Towers of Afrasiab

LINES SAID TO HAVE BEEN RECITED BY MEHMED THE
CONQUEROR AS HE WALKED THROUGH THE ABANDONED
BYZANTINE PALACE OF CONSTANTINOPLE[2]

God rings the bells, earth rings the bells, the sky itself is ringing.

LAMENT FOR THE FALL OF CONSTANTINOPLE STILL SUNG BY
ORTHODOX GREEK WOMEN AT FESTIVALS AND FUNERALS

On 29 May – the date of the Ottoman conquest of Constantinople in AD 1453 – modern Istanbul has recently been holding a new festival.[3] There are reminders of the event everywhere. Ottoman boats (as depicted on the sides of public buses) are dragged up from the Bosphorus and rolled over Constantinople's hills, recalling a wonderfully audacious move employed by Sultan Mehmed II when he requisitioned 3 miles of felled logs and olive oil supplied by the Genoese in order to enable his navy to force its way around the snagging chain in the Golden Horn. Chess-champ kids are bussed in from the regions to play en masse in the hippodrome. An Ottoman military band wanders around in the city. Locals – predominantly from the poorer districts such as the Fener, once a Greek quarter – flock to see a sound-and-light show recreating the moment Ottoman forces broke down the walls of Constantinople on the Golden Horn. The raising of the Islamic flag over the ramparts is met with a loud, and polite, cheer.

The Conquest Celebrations in the city are a political innovation. For many people, for many centuries, in many cultures, this date in May marked not a triumphant conquest but 'the fall'.

Mehmed's construction of the futuristic fortification of Rumeli Hisarı, with walls thick enough to withstand cannon fire, had been just the beginning. The young Ottoman leader was planning things carefully. He was the thirteenth Muslim ruler to attack the city – this adventure could not fail. It was said by contemporaries that his stratagem for taking Constantinople occupied his waking and sleeping thoughts. Eyewitnesses reported that 160,000 of Mehmed's men started to march down the Via Militaris from the imperial capital Edirne where the Ottoman ruler, aged only 12, had already been in charge as sultan between AD 1444 and 1446. Troops, tramping through a listless landscape, brought with them new, intimidating weapons, including that enormous cannon – with a 26-foot shaft and needing 200 souls to man it – named for its Hungarian engineer 'Urban'. Its blast was said to be deafening, and its formidable cannonballs, weighing up to 0.6 of a ton and able to travel almost a mile, still lie within the curtain wall at Yedikule Fortress (the name means Seven Towers), a phagocyte-like structure around the Byzantine Golden Gate built four years after the Ottomans took possession of Constantinople. The Ottoman army probably numbered closer to 80,000 men, but there were also a hundred Ottoman ships waiting, rocking in the Bosphorus. Mehmed's banners were erected all around the city, streaming strong in that Eastern Mediterranean breeze. By 5 April his men had Constantinople surrounded.

All that brilliant Byzantine technology was now failing: the chain across the Golden Horn was irrelevant now that the Ottomans were cutting down forests, oiling logs with olive oil and dragging boats overland; the walls, all five layers of them, which had withstood so many, had met their match – no one could beat the new generation of sky-scraping siege weaponry, paid for with all that income from silk, or the Ottomans' super-cannon which pounded the defences for a full month. Constantinople's long-term infrastructural enemy, the pontoon bridge, was built by Mehmed's engineers between Galata and the city. For those inside the

A Neolithic footprint from recent excavations at Yenikapı. To date well over one thousand prehistoric footprints have been found in central Istanbul and the surrounding area, which was once marshlands. Substantial communities lived here on the sides of rivers, before the creation of the Bosphorus.

The waterways that surround Istanbul are exceptionally well-stocked with fish. Throughout the history of the city, inhabitants have commented on this wealth. Istanbullus still fish each day from Galata Bridge and the banks of the Bosphorus. This image of the fishermen of Constantinople was produced in Sicily in the twelfth century in the Codex Matritensis of Skylitzes which covers the reigns of the Byzantine emperors from AD 811 to AD 1057.

A rare image of Emperor Septimius Severus – painted on wood. Shown here with his wife Julia Domna and their children Caracalla and Geta (Geta's face has been erased). Both Septimius and Caracalla commissioned extensive building works for Byzantium, including the erection of the Milion, from which all distances in the Roman Empire were measured.

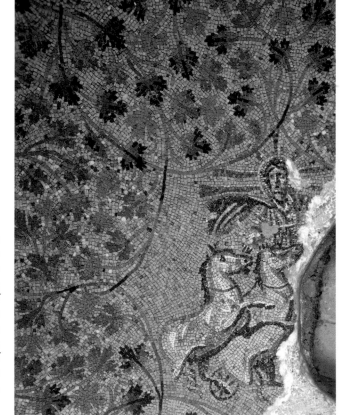

Christ depicted as the sun god Helios: an early Christian (late third century AD) mosaic from the ceiling vault of the mausoleum of the Julii located beneath St Peter's Basilica. Emperor Constantine appears to have encouraged the conflation of Christ with Sol Invictus – the Unconquerable Sun.

Constantinople was often portrayed as the goddess Aphrodite. On the Esquiline treasure, made c. AD 380 and discovered on Rome's Esquiline Hill, she joins the other major cities of the late Roman Empire (Rome, Antioch and Alexandria) as a 'Tyche', the tutelary deity of a city. Tyche was the daughter of Aphrodite and Zeus. Constantinople carries a cornucopia, an image of bounty.

the town of Milan

Illumination said to show Julian the Apostate's flayed body, from *The Fall of Princes* by John Lydgate. The author probably confused Julian with the Emperor Valerian, who did suffer such a fate – a reminder of the tangled web we have to unpick when studying medieval sources.

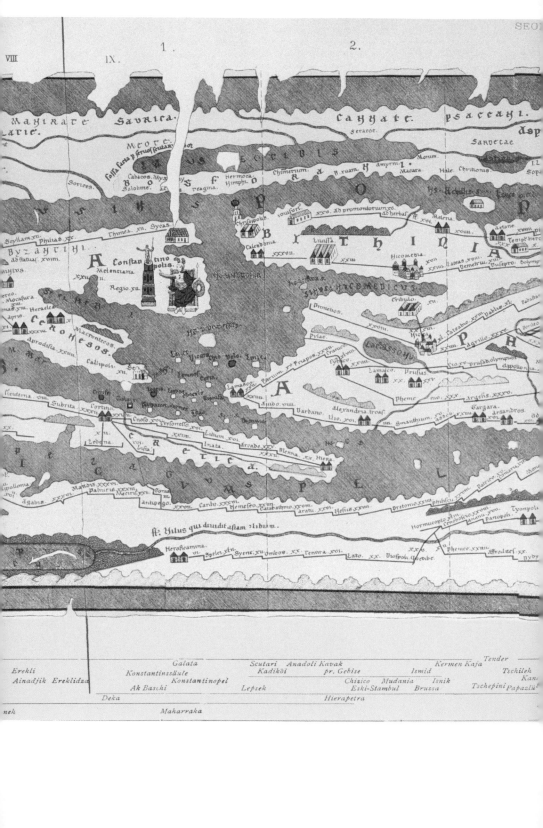

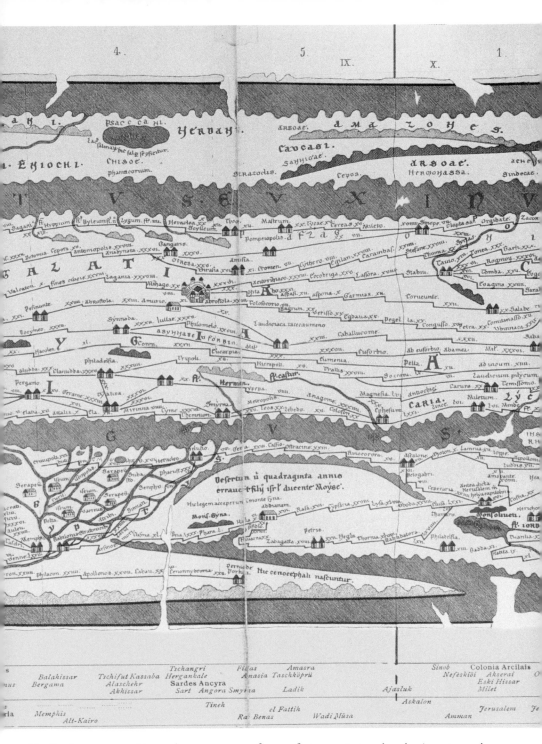

The Peutinger map, a thirteenth-century copy of a map first commissioned under Augustus and originally created c. AD 300–500 which describes the Roman road systems including the Via Egnatia or Egnatian Way that ran from the Albanian edge of the Adriatic Sea to Byzantium. Constantinople is represented as Aphrodite.

Mosaic image of Emperor Justinian in the Basilica of San Vitale, Ravenna. The church-building began when Ravenna was still under Gothic rule and the mosaic was completed in AD 548 when Justinian had recaptured many Roman lands.

The *Painting of the Six Kings*, an early Islamic fresco from the Qasr Amra, an Umayyad castle complex dating to the early eighth century AD. Four of the six kings can still be identified, including an unknown Byzantine Emperor (far left, in the blue patterned robe) whose face has been lost.

The Desborough necklace was the possession of a wealthy Anglo-Saxon woman in the seventh century AD and was strikingly similar to the jewellery worn by Theodora in the San Vitale mosaic (see page 207).

The mosaics from the Great Palace, hidden beneath the Blue Mosque from AD 1606 and rediscovered in the 1930s and 1950s, include the most exquisite detail. Here, children ride camels *(top)* and Constantinople is represented as an eagle under attack *(bottom)*.

Painting by Laura Lushington of a synagogue in Istanbul, based on an 1848 engraving. Jewish communities thrived in Istanbul for at least 1,600 years.

The Byzantines destroying Arab fleets with their secret weapon. Greek Fire – also known as Sea Fire, Sticking Fire or Roman Fire – has its first recorded use in AD 515. Illustration from the Codex Matritensis of Skylitzes.

The burial shroud of Charlemagne, who chose to be buried in purple-dyed cloth decorated with gold thread made in Constantinople. Charlemagne was crowned Holy Roman Emperor in AD 800 and died AD 814.

An icon from Crete, painted c. AD 1500, commemorating the celebrations that marked the end of Byzantine iconoclasm AD 843. Huge icons of Mary were regularly paraded around Constantinople. Note similarity in composition of the icon to the Hittite sun goddess and her child (see page 199).

The Monastery of St John at Studios founded in c. AD 462 sponsored philosophical debate and the preservation of texts in its scriptoria. This image from the Codex Matritensis of Skylitzes shows a philosophy school in Constantinople.

Detail from the Pala D'Oro, which now resides in the Basilica di San Marco in Venice, showing Christ Pantokrator. The altarpiece was constructed in Constantinople and Venice over four centuries from AD 976 to 1345, and is one of the most magnificent surviving examples of Byzantine enamelwork.

The siege of Constantinople by Ottoman forces in AD 1453, illustration from an account by Jean Chartier.

Giovanni Bellini's portrait of a 'Seated Scribe', possibly an image of the young Mehmed the Conqueror, created c. AD 1479–81.

A miniature of Istanbul by Matrakci Nasuh, a Bosnian polymath brought to Istanbul from Rumelia, which shows the zoning of the city in the sixteenth century and the hubbub of the waterways surrounding it. The artist ended up teaching at the Janissary Enderun School.

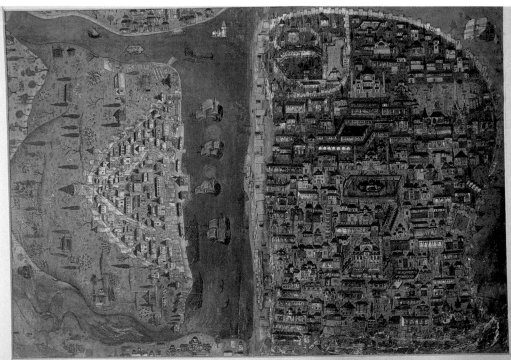

Ottoman troops laying siege to Vienna in AD 1529, from the Hünername, 'Book of Accomplishments', produced in Istanbul. An entire volume of the manuscript, which totals over 500 pages, is devoted to Ottoman military campaigns.

Ali Pasha depicted in an unknown German newspaper in AD 1571. He led the Turkish fleet at the Battle of Lepanto and was seized on the Ottoman flagship (shown in the background) and beheaded.

A seventeenth-century Ottoman watercolour illustrating a feast for the Valide Sultan with the presence of Madame Girardin from the French Embassy in Constantinople. The chief black eunuch stands on the left.

Left: Parade of Confectioner's Guild – an entire garden was made of sugar and paraded through the streets of Istanbul to celebrate the circumcision of Ahmed III's sons in AD 1720. *Below:* Parade of Road-Sweepers, from the same manuscript. Note Pausanias' Serpent Column is still featured.

Illustration by Heyrullah Heyri Çavuszade from an AD 1721 copy of the Hamse (Five Poems) by seventeenth-century Ottoman Turkish poet and scholar 'Ata'ullah bin Yahyá, showing a party with guests in European attire.

A nineteenth-century *hilye* calligraphy panel by Yahya Hilmi Efendi, describing the physical appearance of the Prophet Muhammad – a written portrait.

Panorama of Constantinople created by Henry Aston
Barker in AD 1799–1802 – son of John Barker who
invented the concept and the term 'panorama'.

Left: Le Bain Turc by Jean-Auguste-Dominique Ingres,
painted in AD 1862. For over 400 years composers, writers
and artists including Mozart, Edward Clarke and Matisse
found a rich seam in the subject of the enclosed rooms of
female pleasure-givers – particularly the richest of all, the
'seraglio', the harem of the Sultan in Istanbul. Ingres' *La
Baigneuse Valpinçon* was inspired by Lady Mary Wortley
Montagu's writings, but his subject became overlaid with
an erotic, sexual content that Montagu had explicitly
left unsaid, precisely because it was also unseen.

An ox-drawn cart transporting veiled Ottoman women to the promenade area, in a photograph by B. Kargopoulo, AD 1854.

Ortaköy Mosque – another of Istanbul's great monuments built by the Armenian family of Balyan, who also designed the Dolmabahçe Palace. Ortaköy Mosque was originally built in AD 1721 and then rebuilt in AD 1853–4 on the orders of Sultan Abdülmecid. This photograph was taken during the Sultan's procession to mosque, c. 1900.

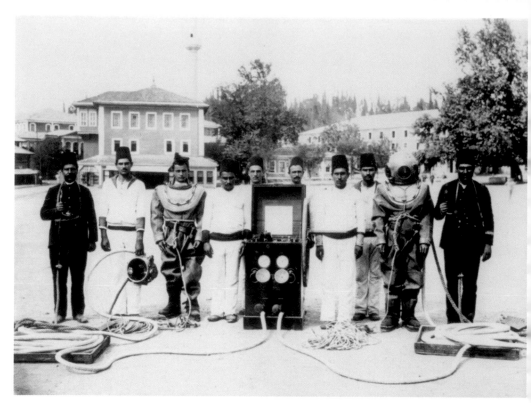

Battalion divers at the Imperial Naval Arsenal,
c. AD 1883–90. The Imperial Arsenal can still
be distinguished in Galata (it was originally
built on the site of Genoese docks) by the
decorations of cannons in the stonework.
By AD 1515 there were 160 docks along the
Golden Horn waterway. The imperial shipyards
are presently derelict – there are plans to turn
the site into luxury housing and hotels.

A colourised version of a postcard showing a
simit seller and a woman on the streets
of Istanbul, c. AD 1880.

The Golden Horn in 1923, the year the capital of Turkey moved from Istanbul to Ankara, by Jules Gervais-Courtellemont. This autochrome – the first colour photography process – has been tinted using potato starch. In 1922 Ernest Hemingway in the *Toronto Daily Star* wrote of the city: 'I stood on the dusty, rubbish-strewn hillside of Pera . . . and looked down at the harbour, forested with masts and grimy with smoky funnels . . . It all looked unreal and impossible.'

The Theodosian Walls foreground the modern city of Istanbul.

One of the titanic cannons designed by Urban (also known as Orban) for Mehmed II, now displayed in the Istanbul military museum

city walls who could not escape, this creeping intimidation, the singing of blades being sharpened and the drag of building materials to facilitate invasion, the screams as Byzantine ships were sunk at anchor in harbours, the sounds of an attack being methodically prepared, must have been petrifying. One contemporary historian wrote that the men and women inside Constantinople, watching the forces massed outside their walls, were 'half-dead, unable to breathe either in or out'.[4]

Yeats was right to describe this as 'No country for old men'; Mehmed, soon to be Mehmed the Conqueror, prefigured his assertion. We should imagine the man – not perhaps as we recall him, aquiline, regal, wrapped in squirrel-fur, from Bellini's famous portrait, which was painted after the artist's visit to the city in AD 1479 – but as he stood expectantly, still only twenty-one, outside Constantinople's walls. Mehmed the Conqueror – who had been the Ottoman Sultan for a decade – was determined that the Queen of Cities should fall. The early Ottoman armour in the Military Museum in Istanbul shows the degree of warrior sophistication in play on the flat Thracian lands that surrounded the city: helmets weighing 7.7 pounds; 100 feet of chain mail for protection. The attack lasted fifty-one days. Despite Emperor Constantine XI's assiduously desperate prepara- tions – stockpiling food, fixing walls – he was defending his city with only 7,000 men, perhaps as few as 5,000. The Ottomans sent a message to the imperial quarters in Constantinople overlooking the Golden Horn declaring that if the Emperor surrendered, there would be no destruction or massacre and Constantine XI could continue to live elsewhere, a vassal to the Sultan. The offer was refused.

In the forty-eight hours before Constantinople's final breach, the sacred relics of the city had been paraded behind icons of the Virgin Hodegetria ('She Who Shows The Way', pointing to Jesus as the source of mankind's salvation) and Virgin Blachernitissa (named after the shrine to the Virgin at Blachernae) – a last-ditch attempt to harness the power of the Mother of God to protect the metropolis she had once, apparently, blessed. Fighting was desperate. Byzantium had always relied on mercenaries, and the city's defenders in AD 1453 were primarily soldiers of fortune, among them men such as Giovanni Giustiniani Longo, the Genoese fighter who had brought 700 bounty-hunting men into the city. After seven weeks of besiegement, Constantinople's salvation really would take a miracle. The Emperor Constantine XI rushed to Haghia Sophia, where many had gathered inside. Prostrating himself silently on the floor he then celebrated mass and thanked those from the city (and beyond) who had come to fight with him. He had already said goodbye to his staff in the crumbling Blachernae Palace, where many had, it was said, 'cried and groaned'.[5]

On the final day of the siege fighting started at about 2.30 a.m. The wailing Ottoman soldiers with drums and bagpipes announced the attack. A breach was made in the wall, the Emperor and his men cutting down the first 300 or so Ottomans who made it through. But those cannon, outside the walls, which became so hot that they could only be fired every twelve hours, kept on pounding. The Ottomans made it through the inner walls to a small, open postern and once the star and crescent was flown from one tower, word spread that the city had been taken. The Byzantines faltered and the Ottomans surged in. Wounded in the assault, Giovanni Longo died three days later in a grand estate in the fertile, blossom-filled fields of Chios – the island that had been given to the Genoese in AD 1355 in the hope that they would rally against the Turks. The Emperor Constantine, we are told, had beseeched Giovanni to stay; the gun-for-hire must have known there was no hope of victory.

Once the Ottoman troops had squeezed their way in through the ever widening gaps in the walls, there was looting and rape – 'the warriors embraced the young beauties'[6] – after which around 4,000 souls were massacred with enslavement of those left standing. Western chroniclers talked of rivers of blood; of sacred relics plucked from their jewel-encrusted reliquaries to be crushed underfoot; of a Sultan who was crueller than

Nero or Caligula. Even Ottoman sources in later years confirmed that the Ottoman attack had become a byword for greed. Easy money in business was described as 'booty from Istanbul'.[7] The fall of Constantinople became a morality tale as quickly as it became history. The city's bejewelled, gilded, quasi-magical icon of Mary which had been paraded around the walls for succour in times of trouble past, now held in the monastery at Chora for protection, was broken up and her sublime decorations were traded on.

Mehmed entered the city not through the Golden Gate as all triumphal Byzantine rulers had previously done, but through the Gate of Charisios, what is now Edirne Gate. The Golden Gate, that Greco-Roman ragbag arch, gilded as it might once have been, and covered with images of the stories of Greece and of Rome, was irrelevant to the city's new rulers – useful perhaps only for architectural salvage. Edirne had been the imperial Ottoman capital for decades – this was where Mehmed had been born and the Via Militaris led straight from Edirne to this north-westerly point of New Rome. Today the Edirne Gate entrance to the city has been restored. The Golden Gate is choked with weeds.

It was said that when Mehmed the Conqueror rode in through the Gate of Charisios, he looked around him at the devastation, groaned deeply and wept: 'What a city we have given over to plunder and destruction.'[8] But quickly he dried his eyes and set to work.

A remarkable document in the closed stores at the British Library gives us an indication of the paperwork and planning that had preceded this epoch-defining moment. Unfurled across the length of a table it is beautifully executed, written in Greek in deep black oak-gall ink. The date marked is 1 June AD 1453 – just three days after Constantinople's walls had fallen. This particular document – a grant from Mehmed to the Genoese of Galata, which allowed the tight immigrant community here to continue their trade from what is present-day Karaköy, has just two neatly added little adjustments inserted into the margin. In all other respects this is a clean first draft. The whole regime-change had obviously been carefully worked out in advance, in minute detail. The document, signed by the local vizier Zaganos Pasha, has Sultan Mehmed II's monogram emblazoned at the top.[9] Galata was not taken by force, but all the inhabitants now had to serve the Sultan.[10]

The exact fate of the last Byzantine Emperor Constantine XI is unclear.

Some accounts declared that he was recognised by his silken stockings, which were embroidered with an eagle, and that his corpse was decapitated and processed around Constantinople. It was also reported that an angel had taken the dead Emperor's body, turned it into marble and buried it under the Golden Gate (an echo of the legend that from his resting place in the Church of Holy Apostles, Constantine the Great was taken to a cave from which he will arise again). A rumour started to circulate that the Golden Gate was blocked up by the Ottomans – just in case a vengeful Emperor rose from the dead.

And so Constantine XI – the namesake of Constantinople's founder Constantine I – had become not just the eleventh Emperor Constantine but the last Christian Emperor of The City. A chronologically vast, culturally ground-breaking metropolitan experiment was over. The strength of Rome – Old and New – had always been the security of its capital. If the city held, Rome lived. In its final half-century the civilisation of Byzantium consisted of just a few disparate city-states and one bedraggled and benighted town; and now that too had gone.

In Rome men cried out and beat their chests on hearing that Constantinople – the child of their own city – had fallen.[11] Contemporaries described this as 'the most grievous catastrophe known to history'[12] and as recompense for the fall of Troy. Meanwhile in Muslim territories men sent up prayers of thanks that another key prophecy of the Prophet Muhammad had been realised. Constantinople was now minted as Kostantiniye (a name that would appear on coins produced in the city until AD 1760, or 1174 in the Muslim calendar, when the nomination Islam-bol was decreed the preference of the Sultan). A theatrical response followed in Europe. Troubadours (a profession, which, with some irony, had developed under the influence of Islamic *ghazal* singers in al-Andalus) composed songs of lament and resistance. These were particularly popular with the chivalric order of the Golden Fleece – inspired by the Georgian kingdom of Colchis and the legendary exploits of the hero Jason beyond the Bosphorus. In AD 1454 Philip the Good of Burgundy staged a political masque, with banquet, to drum up support and relief funds for Byzantium. With the invention of printing there was a flurry of leafleting and blustering calls for crusades to take Constantinople back – but the religious and political bark here was fiercer than the bite.[13] Men beat their chests, and kept their swords in their scabbards.

CHAPTER 52

✧

TWILIGHT CITY

AD 1453–61
(856–66 IN THE ISLAMIC CALENDAR)

If only Turks had stood firm in the faith of Christ and Christendom, you
could not find stronger or braver or more skilful soldiers.

GESTA FRANCORUM ET ALIORUM HIEROSOLIMITANORUM[1]

It should be no surprise that the Ottomans' surveyors and pen-pushers
had been busy long before the great cannon Urban did his work. We must
remember that the Byzantine Emperor and Mehmed II, for years now, had
maintained a close correspondence. The 'False Mustafa', one of Mehmed's
uncles, had been traded between Byzantine and Ottoman leaders – the
Byzantine Emperor paid to do a jailer's job. Byzantine princesses had married the sons of emirs. Some Christians gave thanks for the protecting arm
that Ottoman armies could raise against the Catholic West. For the last
fifty-odd years the Turks had been in occupation of their own quarter[2] in
Constantinople, complete with mosque. From the moment they arrived
in the Western historical record, the Ottomans had liaised with Byzantine rulers. Osman gave local leaders gifts, fine carpets and clotted cream
from their seasonal herding of cows: conquering and cohabiting in equal
measure. In AD 1420 it was reported that Mehmed I and Manuel II had
sent one another tidbits of food while the Byzantine was on the Bosphorus
and the Ottoman was camped on her banks.[3] This could have been a city
where the two rulers, Christian and Muslim, collaborated.

For a decade after the fall, the hope of Constantinople survived in
a kind of half-life in the outposts of Trebizond, in Mystras and other
pockets in the Morea in the Peloponnese. Christian bishops and administrators hunkered down on these flotsams of Christianity, keeping the
reality of Byzantium going, just.

Mystras, in the foothills of Mount Taygetus just above Sparta, hosted scholars and artists, mirroring the final flowering of the Byzantine mother city under the Palaiologans. The last Byzantine Emperor, Constantine XI, was crowned here rather than in Constantinople in AD 1449. The settlement exists today as a ghost town. Frescoes appear out of the dusk, unlikely survivors among the ruins. At dawn the mist can be so thick that there is no other world; cold air falls off the mountain. Martins in the palm trees squabble over the news of the day. At night the mountain is lit only by starlight and glow-worms. Mystras is still a pilgrimage spot – visitors come to scatter petals in the abandoned Byzantine town.

For a decade or so after Constantinople's fall, Mystras must too have had an exciting intellectual purity to it. Its scholars continued to influence the Italian Renaissance. In Florence, the Platonic Academy had been founded in memory of Mystras' greatest child, Plethon. One can sit under mulberry trees here on the walls of the abandoned city-complex, the sun and scents of jasmine chase one another across the Eurotas plain below. Homer described this region as Sparte Kalligynaika – the land of beautiful women – and the Peloponnesian landscape here is heart-achingly beautiful too. Yet the reality after AD 1453 was that this was a small, isolated town clinging to a hillside, overlooking the ruins of another great city, Sparta – and now itself about to fade. The brothers of Emperor Constantine XI, Thomas and Demetrios, the last despots at Mystra, were tributaries of the Sultan, then vassals, before being forced into exile. In 1460 Mystra fell.

Trebizond on the Pontus too stayed an almost-empire, held together by the memory of what might have been. Men here must have talked often of Constantinople as they looked out over the cold comfort of the wide Black Sea. Trebizond in its turn fell in AD 1461.

On the *cassone* or marriage chest of a high-born young woman in Tuscany, made to protect her linen and chemises c. AD 1460, an item of furniture normally decorated with heroic scenes from Homer, Virgil or Ovid, we instead find depictions of the city of Constantinople and of Janissaries doing battle. But rather than a critique of the Ottomans, as was long assumed, the *cassone* (which ended up in the Palazzo Strozzi in Florence) had in fact been commissioned by canny Florentine patrons as a commemoration of Ottoman history and a reminder of the close trading relationship that the Italians enjoyed with the Ottoman Turks. Western players were very firmly keeping their options open with the new players in the East.

And scattered through the Orthodox diaspora, those New Romans, in their little churches, without a capital, a physical centre for their faith, now wanted to focus on the internal life – on an intimate relationship with their saints. In church halls and community centres, at funerals and festivals, to this day women in particular still lament the fall of Constantinople in song.

And yet there are no true caesuras in history: there is always some kind of continuum (a truth rather beautifully illustrated by the discovery in 2011 that in remote settlements around Trebizond villagers were speaking Turkish but with the grammar of the ancient Greeks).[4] In AD 1466 the bishop of Trebizond wrote a number of letters to Mehmed II, discussing the similarities between Islam and Christianity. Some were penned in Pera (the district of Beyoğlu today) and contain a suggestion that the two religions should still find a way to work together. Mehmed was, after all, said to worship an icon of Mary. Bishop George of Trebizond asserted, 'No one doubts you are emperor of the Romans. Whoever holds by right [of conquest?] the centre of the Empire is emperor as the centre of the Roman Empire is Constantinople.'[5] And in the bishop's treatise *On the Eternal Glory of the Autocrat and his World Empire* Mehmed is flatteringly said to possess '*Justitia, prudentia, peritia philosopiae peripateticae, doctrina in multis disciplinis*'. There is a forlornly hopeful sense that compromise and collaboration could, ultimately, be the best policy. Fascinating as these ecumenical proposals by the bishop were, they were never put into practice but stayed on parchment.

Two church communities in Constantinople itself remained fully operational. The patriarchate, originally based in Haghia Sophia, was offered the Church of the Holy Apostles by Mehmed and from there shuffled to the Church of Pammakaristos in AD 1456 after Holy Apostles had been demolished. Mehmed the Conqueror did not want a united Christendom on his doorstep and the Patriarchate was presided over by Gennadios II – a scholar-monk who was conveniently opposed to compromise or to collaboration with Latin Christianity. Mehmed allegedly came to Pammakaristos to debate and discuss Christian theology with his

appointee-clergyman. Some time around 1600 the patriarchate moved to
the Church of St George in the Fener district close to the Golden Horn,
where it still survives behind high walls and barbed wire and under the
watchful eye of guards armed with machine guns.

And on the hill above one can find an unexpectedly resilient traveller
from Byzantine Constantinople. The Church of St Mary of the Mongols
(dedicated to Theotokos Panaghiotissa), also known as Mouchliotissa ('of
the Mongols') or, after AD 1453 Kanlı Kilise ('Church of the Blood'), is a
guardian of stories across time. Founded in the 1260s when the Byzantines
retook Constantinople from the Latins, it was rebuilt in c. 1282 by the
illegitimate daughter of Emperor Michael VIII, Maria Palaiologina, who
had married a khan of the Mongols. St Mary of the Mongols remained
as a Christian building in Ottoman Istanbul – legend has it – because the
church was given to the mother of the renowned architect Christodoulos

Patriarch Gennadios II takes a warrant and imperial decree of religious freedom
from Sultan Mehmed II. Painting of the mosaic at the Patriarchate Church of
Ayias Yedryias.

in thanks for his help with the construction of Mehmed's great 'Victory' mosque, Fatih Camii.

Today, to find St Mary of the Mongols one has to tackle the labyrinth of streets above the old Greek district. The church might seem closed, but an Armenian Christian in the tenement block next door is on hand at his high window to offer the key to those who want to look inside. In the far right-hand corner of the cool, quiet interior there is a passage – an escape route – that the resident Orthodox priest will still animatedly tell you leads all the way to Haghia Sophia. The firman of Mehmed the Conqueror (or at least a copy), guaranteeing the survival of St Mary of the Mongols, is triumphantly displayed in the gloaming. This is the only Byzantine church in the city to cross the Byzantine–Ottoman divide.

The Emperor of the Roman domain was now a Muslim. The fact that both Roman and Byzantine Emperors had to control the city at their Empire's heart in order to rule had given the populace here real leverage. Despite the stubborn republican tendencies of Constantinople – the chronicler Niketas Choniates wrote of this 'populace of the market-place' that 'Their indifference to the rulers is preserved in them as if it were inborn . . .'⁶ – Mehmed, it seemed, had other plans. Istanbul, The City, was to be the centre of a new and glorious Islamic Empire, a reflection perhaps of Augustus' great vision and a homage to the dynamism of those Ottoman Turks who had travelled from the steppes and the Muslims who had first ridden out of the Middle East. Standing in the smouldering ruins, on an ancient acropolis that had already seen 8,000 years of evidenced history, the sharp smell of carbon and death in the air, ordering the construction of a new palace on the old Forum Theodosios, itself originally Constantine's Forum Tauri, Mehmed was clear: in conquered Constantinople there was much work to do both without and within.

CHAPTER 53

✣

THE ABODE OF FELICITY

AD 1453
(857/8 IN THE ISLAMIC CALENDAR) ONWARDS

A palace on the point of old Byzantium – a palace that should outshine
all and be more marvellous than the preceding palaces in looks, size, cost
and gracefulness.

KRITOBOULOS, DESCRIBING THE FUTURE TOPKAPI PALACE[1]

For a full 800 years this was where Muslim forces had wanted to be
– at home in Constantinople/Istanbul – and for others to be shunned
outsiders, excluded beyond the city walls. And now, after twelve failed
expeditions,[2] there was the time and the opportunity to make all those
dreams from before the invasion good.

This city would be the engine of a new Islamic empire, controlled by
a new Muslim Emperor. After the conquest Mehmed rapidly spring-
cleaned the Ottoman taxation system and seemed determined to make
the capture of Constantinople not just a strategic but a commercial win.
The control of the Bosphorus – 'greater than the Nile and mightier than
the Danube'[3] – had massive economic potential. But the Ottomans'
priority, in this devastated city, was to make it pure and physically to
mortar their sovereignty into the environment. In AD 1453 on the third
hill the new Ottoman palace, which would become Eski Saray, the Old
Palace, started to rise on the old Forum Tauri abutting the Forum of
Theodosios. Then in 1457 (861–2 in the Islamic calendar) serious building work started at the peak of the old Greek acropolis: this was the
Saray-ı Cedid-i Amire, now the New Imperial Palace. Only in the eighteenth century did this splendid series of structures become known as
the Topkapı Palace.[4] The New Imperial Palace would come to define
Istanbul. What we call Topkapı was a centre of political, social and

theatrical power. Initially an administrative centre, it was turned into a home by Mehmed's grandson, Sultan Süleyman the Lawgiver. Western sources were keen to emphasise that the Sultan was in sinister, lugubrious fashion shut away behind Topkapı's walls, but the New Imperial Palace was in fact the stage set for dramatic appearances as well as clandestine machinations, and it also provided a religious justification for dominance.

The Topkapı Palace was a complex built explicitly to impress, to buttress and to nourish a new, decidedly Islamic way of being. This was not just the home of a king. This was a fortified home of Allah, a four-point, sacred fortress whose traditions stretched across the Anatolian plains to Central Asia and back in time to the Bronze Age. This was where Allah's Grace – *kut* or *sa'ada* – was said to reside.

Topkapı was protected by 35-foot-high walls topped with guards. Sleek horses were groomed where tourists now assemble and Istanbul's enemies were executed where they now buy knick-knacks in the Topkapı tourist shop. Minutely cobbled pathways were constructed especially for the Sultan's use; he was the only man allowed to ride his horse into the inner courtyards. The areas around the Sultan's personal quarters were populated by mutes and by dwarves armed with scimitars. Many visitors spoke of an eerie silence within. The semi-shamanistic nature of the place (up until the eighteenth century no mirrors were used) transfixed travellers who entered.

There might be no mirrors but there were baubles aplenty. Barrels of emeralds, topazes and rubies came to be stored in Topkapı's treasury. Armenian craftsmen were imported by the boatload to work on the finest gold and silver fancies; the handiwork of eighty-four different cultures has been found to be represented in the treasure storerooms here. The early sultans played with chess sets made of rock crystal and decorated with rubies and gold. A single tankard, now on display in the Topkapı Museum, was crusted with emeralds, rubies, gold, onyx and marble. Solid gold candlesticks, 105 pounds' worth, are dressed with 666 diamonds; there are rock-crystal sherbet holders. The Ottomans pursued their love of glistening things by commissioning pottery decorated with fine gold lustre – in vast quantities. Songbirds sang in aviaries to create an impression of paradise. Eleven thousand slaves came to work in Topkapı's kitchens, to feed 6,000 mouths who in the early seventeenth century consumed 200 sheep, 100 kids, 40 calves, 60–100 geese and 100–200 chickens each day.⁵ Rather than a sign of indulgence in orientalist fancy, we would be churlish if we did not think this place a marvel.

The Topkapı Palace was laid out as if it were an Ottoman military camp, with the courtyards representing military zones. From the rule of Selim I (AD 1512) onwards all imperial administration also took place here. The Divan-ı Hümâyûn or Imperial Council of State, met in the Divan Square – the Square of Justice – four days a week. Ministers processed down the old Mese – the street now called the Divanyolu. Government was known in Western sources as the Porte, in other words the 'Gate' – because of a gate that gave access to state department buildings – and consisted of administrators and officials who organised, formalised and panoplied access to the Sultan's sphere. The term 'passport' first appears around 1540 and it has been suggested that it was inspired by movement in and out of the Sublime Porte. The most precious, the most highly guarded things were closest to the Sultan's marble-built tent. The state treasury was here – and so too his harem.

The ruling sultans of Istanbul, pump-priming a Renaissance economy in the East, quickly abandoned any pretence of distaste for grandeur. From AD 1458 (862–3 in the Islamic calendar) it was clear that Constantinople would be favoured as the capital over Edirne. As soon as the Topkapı Palace was completed, that popular Western painter, Gentile Bellini, was invited to immortalise Mehmed the Conqueror as a man who had arrived. This was a Renaissance prince who had compelling and formidable relevance in both the East and the West. Mehmed II built pavilions around the Topkapı, trumpeting the reach of his ambitions; the Byzantine and Italian-themed buildings were in ruins by 1891, but the Çinili Köşk, built by captured Karamanid craftsmen in 1472, still looks out over the Bosphorus with quiet confidence, a reminder of the Central Asian heritage of these medieval Turcomen. Some days, next to the Rose-House Park (Gülhane) where rose-scented sweets were prepared, the sultans would watch *cirit*, an exhilarating cross between polo and steppe horse-racing, a reminder of the beauty of the horses which had brought Mehmed's Ottoman ancestors so far.

A book of ceremonies, codified into dynastic law by Mehmed II, became a practical guide to the way the Sultan of Istanbul should behave.

*Late eighteenth-century map of Topkapı Palace by Antoine Ignace Melling –
much of the palace complex can be visited today*

The leader was customised to become a more mystical figure; he was
encouraged no longer to attend banquets or to take public audience –
instead receiving delegations in his private audience hall just four times
a week. The Sultan could watch the world from the Kiosk of Processions
and from a gold-domed gatehouse above the Court of Processions. Like
his Byzantine predecessors he was also glimpsed attending events at the
hippodrome – now called Atmeydanı. During private receptions, facing
his ceremonial window (from which he could observe gifts being processed or his enemies being executed), the Sultan was typically silent.
Ambassadors would approach with their arms pinioned to their sides
by royal guards; all others in the room stood with their hands crossed
and their eyes lowered. Although Sultan Süleyman I would experiment
with a kind of messianic, otherworldly charm, these new rulers of the
city were not thought to be supernatural; they might express themselves

predominantly in ecstatic poetry, but, using dynastic law codes, they also had to enact Sunni Islam rigorously and justly.[6]

But while the Sultan was a remote figure on paper, in practice his carefully staged visibility was paramount. His physical presence was important because of the complicated rules of Ottoman succession. In AD 1421 Mehmed I's dead body had been brought out and (at a sensible distance) played in front of a gullible crowd like a puppet to try to convince all he was still alive and thus prevent a succession crisis. Within Istanbul, procession to Friday prayer became an intently, self-consciously theatrical event. The Sultan wore kaftans decorated with carnations, the stitched flowers 2 feet wide. On occasions his horse was suspended in mid-air and given no food for a night so that man and mount would process with a dream-like grace.[7] All this show had a domestic as well as an international purpose. The early days of Ottoman expansion had not represented a coordinated attack, so the ruler of Istanbul had to use the city as a stage set from which to prove to rival *gazis* that his power was paramount.

Going to 'see the Caliph' (as the Ottoman Sultan would formally be recognised after AD 1517) became an itinerary point on the pilgrim's route from the West towards Mecca. It was to the Caliph that petitions and complaints were brought. There was even a popular tradition, vigorous up until the twentieth century, of the Sultan roaming around Istanbul at night in disguise. As late as the nineteenth century ambassadors sent fretful communiques reporting this clandestine behaviour, while the city's inhabitants whispered nervously of the Sultan's unsettling habit. At once politically and personally threatening, the Sultan, like a Greek god, might shape-shift and at any time appear at your elbow.

Where a sighting of the Sultan could be guaranteed was on one of his court's frequent trips to the city's many gardens. Gardens were fundamental in the culture of Muslim Constantinople. Constantinople has always maintained green space as a practical necessity in a city prone to siege, and now these urban lungs breathed faith. In imperial gardens gazelles were allowed to roam; elsewhere fruit trees were planted. In 2004, on the fifth hill in the Fatih district, a car park and sports facility took the place of Çukurbostan, the Sunken Garden, which itself was built on the Byzantine Cistern of Aspar and was, in the early twenty-first century, still heavy with fruit. Reports sent back by Western visitors from the sixteenth century onwards counted as many as 1,000 gardens in the city and 100 imperial gardens worked by 20,000 imperial gardeners. Many will know that the word paradise comes from the Ancient Avestan via the Old Persian word for 'walled enclosure' or 'surrounded by gardens'; but for the Ottomans the garden had particular significance. Turkic tribes had left arid lands in search of fertile soil further west. A Turkic aphorism advised that 'He who builds a house should plant a tree in front.' And the Ottomans quickly put down roots metaphorically and physically. Constantinople was filled with cherry, almond, pear, plum, quince, peach and apple trees. Even outside the poorest houses there were window boxes or a pot of herbs.

In Ottoman thought, the garden was an incarnation of the unified cosmology of Allah's creation. Unlike the more formal gardens that were being planted in Muslim al-Andalus (where the spectacular al-Hamra, the Red Fort, at Granada had been converted in AD 1333 into a royal palace built on Pythagorean principles of harmonious geometry), here horticulture was meant to represent God's bounty and the diversity of his creation. So fruit and vegetables, flowers, herbs and trees were all tumbled together. *Ghazel* poetry was recited often describing God's creation as one perfect garden, all part of a holistic, harmonising experience. There was much talk of long-necked lutes singing the language of the heart, of a garden of skies, of rivers of milk and streams of honey. The music played here was itself thought to be a religious experience, and for those beyond Istanbul's imperial heart there was frequent mention of the snatches of music from the city gardens, with the lyrics describing coal-black eyes and the dome of heaven, that would wind through the air.

Istanbul's gardens were not just pleasant planting schemes, but an outward sign of the harmony of justice, of the magnificence of the Ottoman dynasty. The city's gardens were thought to represent the imperial presence which was itself a representation of divine order. For the new, Muslim inhabitants of Constantinople, gardens had both hallowed and temporal potency.

But although these places were manifestations of the mystical they also offered an opportunity for larking about. Mehmed designed his garden complex for the New Imperial Palace specifically to bring 'beauty and pleasure, happiness and enjoyment'. There were later tales of dwarfs being thrown into the plunge pools in the Topkapı for imperial amusement. Western visitors described the Sultan stretching out and sunning himself like a cormorant during his garden sorties and in one case encouraging his harem to strip off their clothes and wade into the water so that they could be heroically rescued. As time went on, some of the public pleasure gardens in the city gained a rather louche reputation. Here moral and social codes were a little elastic. Wine was consumed and dancing girls encouraged corporeal rather than spiritual stimulation.

The green spaces doubled up as hunting grounds. Given Istanbul's actively nourished canopy it is little surprise that the city was increasingly rustling with wildlife. Roe deer were regular visitors; horned owls, golden orioles, greenfinches and nightingales were all recorded – and also killed. Approached by sea, Konstantiniye now seemed a forest dotted with woodmen's huts. The dome of the Ayasofya and the fingers of minarets emerging from the treetops – the oaks, cypresses and beeches – were the only sign that this was in fact one of the largest cities on earth. There were even orchards around the fortifications of Rumelia and Anadolu Hisarı, and the slopes down to the Bosphorus were described as tapestries of green, a mosaic of flora.

Frequent fires after the Ottoman arrival cleared areas which were then left to nature – the city's new inhabitants preferring to build beyond the city walls where the chances of escape were greater. In fact just six years before London's own Great Fire, 120 mansions, 40 baths, 360 mosques, more than a 100 madrasas and numerous houses (280,000 according to contemporary sources), churches and convents in Istanbul were destroyed by fire. The death toll in the city was thought to be as high as 40,000. The Divan-ı Hümâyûn tried to ban the construction of wooden homes, but in forest-filled Thrace this was an edict that was doomed to fail. And so the fear of fire became one of the cultural characteristics of the Ottoman city.

Istanbul's delight in flower power was commented on until the second half of the twentieth century. A visit to a friend in the city would be unusual with anything less than a single flower. Jonquils and geraniums, along with cucumbers, pumpkins and watermelons could all be found growing here. The inhabitants of the imperial court often wore flowers in their turbans; even the poorest ox-wagon was frequently garlanded. Since a hadith told that the Prophet Muhammad had stated, 'The space between my pulpit and tomb will also be included in the garden of Eden,' verdant cemeteries sprang up within the city walls and tombs were erected in gardens. As late as 1911 the Swiss architect Le Corbusier described the fruit gardens of Istanbul as 'heaven on earth', and during the First World War Western soldiers noted Turkish troops laying out little patches of turf and plant pots around their campaign tents.

With the city contoured by water and by hills, shaded by earthly gardens, it is possible to imagine this as a utopia, to believe that all this, and therefore perhaps too the world beyond, was yours. Kostantiniye was al-Mahmiyya or al-Mahrusa, the Well-Protected – protected from disaster by God and from injustice by the Sultan.[8] Whatever the faith of its ruler, pagan, Christian or Muslim, Istanbul has consistently encouraged whoever commanded it to believe that they had both earthly and sublime potential.

CHAPTER 54

ONE GOD IN HEAVEN, ONE EMPIRE ON EARTH

AD 1453
(856/7 IN THE ISLAMIC CALENDAR) ONWARDS

Now that the most atrocious Turk has captured Egypt and Alexandria
and the whole of the eastern Roman Empire . . . he will covet not just
Sicily but the whole world.

POPE LEO X, QUOTED IN CORRESPONDENCE AD 1517[1]

The world cannot any longer bear to have two suns in the sky.

ERASMUS, IN A LETTER TO A FRIEND[2]

We are told that when Mehmed II entered Constantinople and progressed
to the Haghia Sophia he carried the sword of the Prophet Muhammad in
front of him and took the city in the name of Allah. It was to the Church
of Holy Wisdom, Haghia Sophia, officially now described with an Arabic
transliteration, Ayasofya, that Mehmed first rode. Prayer carpets, said
to belong to the Prophet Muhammad himself, were brought into the
church, and the conquering army's first Friday prayers were recited under
those entwining initials of Justinian and Theodora. The journey to celebrate Friday prayers in Ayasofya and other premier mosques would come
to be one of the Muslim city's most splendid weekly events – a froth of
piety, of sacred showmanship, that continued across five centuries until
1935 (and which, controversially, may be revived). Mehmed had arrived in
Constantinople not just as a conqueror but as 'Lord of combatants for the
faith', the '*gazi* of *gazis*'.

So the burning question is this: how did Constantinople change once
her God had a new name? The Ottomans quickly treated Kostantiniyye
as a city – describing her, in the same terms, as a person – that had by
rights always belonged to Allah and was now simply being reclaimed.[3]

Western sources of the day might lament fallen Constantinople as 'desolate, lying dead, naked, soundless, having neither form nor beauty',[4] but others focused on Mehmed II's extraordinary energy and passion for his new urban project, 'for the City and its peopling, and for bringing it back to its former prosperity'.[5] Within a short time the Ottoman Tursun Bey, a bureaucrat and historian born in Bursa, who was with Mehmed during the siege, declared that Istanbul was 'prosperous, ornamented and well organised'.

And indeed the Ottomans quickly hit their stride. With the 'discovery' along the Golden Horn of the burial place of one of the companions of the Prophet, Abu Ayyub al-Ansari – killed in AD 669, it was claimed, in the first siege of Constantinople – the city had a new pilgrimage site. A mosque named after al-Ansari, the Eyüp Sultan Mosque, was built over the grave in 1458 just outside the old city walls (at Byzantine Kosmidion – where the Crusaders of 1096 had been allowed to camp and which had seen fighting between Byzantines and Franks in 1203–4). This would come to be the locus for the accession ceremony of Sultans – men who girded at their side what was said to be, and quite possibly was, Orhan Gazi's own sword. Circumcisions would also take place here. A natural spring rendered the spot extra-sacred. The fallen Ayyub, it was declared, had taken part in the migration with the Prophet Muhammad to Medina in 622, and ended up as his standard bearer. In what was originally a quarter associated with the martyred doctors Sts Cosmas and Damian, Christian miracle-working saints, he was now newly honoured. Gliding up the Golden Horn on their flat-bottomed boats, scores of the faithful would refresh themselves at the nearby well before they made their prayers at Ayyub's tomb, to the man whom they believed had been buried here for 800 years. Next to Mecca and Jerusalem the Eyüp shrine has become, for many, one of the most sacred in Islam.

The newly conquering inhabitants of Constantinople – also called Qustantiniyya in Arabic or Asitane, 'The Threshold' – claimed too that Abu Ayyub al-Ansari was not alone, but that seventy (an auspicious number) of the Prophet's companions had also fallen in the city that many were now calling 'Islam-bol – 'Islam Abounds'.[6] Minarets started to point to Allah's victory, and Arabic supplications were devised to keep the city safe. Prayers on the streets were said to rise to 'the courts of heaven'. Later visitors reported 700,000 Istanbullus at a time invoking

Allah together with prisoners released on the order of the Valide Sultan (the Sultan's mother) to pray for rain, for food, for victory in battle, or for release from plague.

And then the confidence of the Janissaries in the city, the bespoke army that had helped to deliver up Byzantium to Muslim control, led to a religious development that would permanently shape global geopolitics. Finding that one of their own had been tortured by the Sultan Bayezid II, who succeeded Mehmed the Conqueror in AD 1481, the Janissary slave-soldiers rampaged around the palace, demanding the Sultan's abdication, while he stared out at them nervously from behind his barred window. Bayezid II's unfavoured youngest son Selim had been sulking as governor of the tricky province of Trabzon (the former Trebizond) on the Black Sea, but he had long had his eyes on the capital. A devastating earthquake in 1509 had shaken confidence in Bayezid II as well as buildings in the city. Many were crushed by collapsing masonry and the event came to be known as 'Little Judgement Day'. The subsequent Janissary revolt offered Selim an opportunity, the king abdicated, and in 1512 Selim stormed the city, killed his brothers and nephews and claimed Istanbul as his own.

Immediately there was a problem. To the East, Shah Ismail of Persia had, two years before, conquered Iran, Azerbaijan, southern Dagestan, Mesopotamia, Armenia, parts of Central Asia and eastern Anatolia, and as the Black Sea regions of Georgia were his vassals this rival was looking perturbingly flush. Replicating the success of Constantinople's fall, Selim took gunpowder and artillery to Shah Ismail's door. Outnumbered, but winners in the region's arms race, at the Battle of Chaldiran in AD 1514, the Ottomans won.

The Mamluks in Egypt were Sunnis like the Ottomans, but it was said that they supported the Shia Safavids in Persia. Arguing that expeditions against fellow Muslims could be justified under the banner of holy war, Selim's troops stormed through North Africa and the Middle East, taking Islam's holiest places Mecca and Medina. One of Selim I's first acts was to publicly demand the keys of the Ka'ba a shrine which stands at the centre of The Sacred Mosque in Mecca.[7] Muhammad's bow and cloak and a number of his swords were delivered up from Cairo to Kostantiniyye – where they are still visited in the Topkapı Museum by quiet lines of the faithful. The Sultans would enjoy many titles but that of Khadim al-Haramayn, 'Servant of the Two Holy Cities', was of crucial personal and political significance. For the next four centuries Istanbul would control the Hajj route to Mecca; commercially, spiritually, strategically and emotionally, her influence was now writ large across the Middle East. And following the conquest of Mamluk Egypt the mufti of Islam became the Shaikh al-Islam – the Grand Mufti of the Ottoman Empire, a man responsible for religious advice to the Sultan and for devising an empire-wide educational policy. As a result, ideas and attitudes that were conceived in Istanbul played out in ordinary people's lives from the Caucasus to Crimea. A sequence of events that started with the need for a son to prove himself resulted in an epoch-forming shift. From 23 January AD 1517, Ottoman intellectuals could now argue that Istanbul was the new European base of the Islamic Caliphate and that its sultan was Islam's caliph.

And so the city started to witness new religious traditions. From now on every year the Sürre caravan, the custom of sending annual gifts (*sürre* meaning the gifts of the Sultan) to Mecca and Medina, was processed, with great pomp and circumstance, not from Cairo but from Kostantiniyye. White camels were perfumed and decorated; in the gardens of the Sultan's harem the long-lashed, bad-tempered beasts of burden (still a feature of the city up until the 1950s) were loaded with handmade gifts from his women before travelling on barges across the Bosphorus. There were devotional songs and chants. Packed into the litters were individual gifts of charity-money in leather pouches sealed with the words 'Come and go in safety'.[8] In Selim's reign alone 200,000 gold pieces were sent to Mecca and Medina. The Sürre then continued its journey from Üsküdar (medieval Scutari and ancient Chrysopolis), the caravan decorated with freshly minted gold coins and with pearls, accompanied by chandeliers, silk rugs, furs, handwritten copies of the Qur'an to the birthplace of Islam.

The covers for the Ka'ba were still delivered from Egypt as they had been before Selim's conquest (from AD 1798 after Napoleon's invasion, the sacred cloths were woven in the courtyard of the Sultan Ahmed Mosque and sent from Istanbul via Cairo to Mecca). After a year's use the Ka'ba's coverings were then gathered back into Kostantiniyye to be repurposed as coffin covers for the Sultan's family. Sections of the cloth were also cut off and sold to the faithful or were given to diplomats or to favoured politicians – the equivalent of Byzantium's relics. They were then

The Sürre travelling through Damascus on its way to Mecca from Istanbul,
c. AD 1895

reverently used as protective wrappings for the Qur'an, were mounted on
walls or were stored in generously jewelled boxes. Despite being a long
way from the bread-and-circus displays of the New Rome, bread, meat,
clothes and money were also all distributed during the jamboree to send
the Sürre on its way. Sultans could pay for 5,000 of the city's boys to
be circumcised at any one time in pious celebration of the Sürre's long
journey south.

At the heart of this newly configured Muslim power-base sat the
Sultan-Caliph. Talismanic shirts – stitched deep with pure gold and
silver thread – showing celestial spheres, astrological signs, magic squares
and lines from the Qur'an trumpeted the Sultan's untouchable nature.
Prepared with size, the stiff, glazed surface of the cotton, polished to
a high gloss (the material looked good and also acted like reinforced
armour), was a moving canvas. Sultanic talismanic shirts from India have
been decorated with the entire text of the Qur'an. We know that talismanic shirts made in the Topkapı Palace could take up to three years to

produce. The shirts were thought to protect the wearer from all kinds of disaster, natural and man-made.

Dressed in light, looking out over the Sea of Marmara and beyond to his gargantuan new empire, Selim I's global ambition was not in doubt. As he wrote himself in AD 1519:

> Flowed down a River Amu, from each foeman's every hair –
> Rolled the sweat of terror's fever – if I happed him to espy.
> Bishop-mated was the King of India, by my Queenly troops,
> When I played the Chess of empire on the board of sov'reignty.
> O SELIMI, in thy name was struck the coinage of the world,
> When in crucible of Love Divine, like gold, that melted I.[9]

By the end of Selim's reign in AD 1520, just eight years after he had stormed the city to establish what would be Europe's most tenacious Caliphate, Istanbul – already at least double the size of London – controlled around 15 million people in over a billion acres of land.[10] By the middle of the sixteenth century, the Flemish ambassador in the city, Ogier Ghiselin de Busbecq – the man who sent tulip bulbs back to the Lowlands – declared that Istanbul was now destined to be the centre of the world.

Unlike the Byzantines with their Greco-Roman heritage, Turkic Ottoman culture did not have a stem-cell sense of the *polis*, of the city-state, as the political and emotional heart of power. A project such as Istanbul was essentially another space which Allah could pervade. The critical psychological distinction for medieval Muslims was between the city (al-Madina) and the desert (al-Badiya).[11] Topography had long given Constantinople the feel of a series of encampments; the Ottomans' religious beliefs amplified that trend. Local religio-spiritual societies that practised in those lodges *tekke* or *zaviye* – each with a spiritual leader or şeyh – allowed for spiritual communion as well as discussions on science, music and literature. The energy of the city pulsed from local pods – *mahalle* – each with their own mosque. Above the *mahalle* was a tight system of governmental and state control at the pinnacle of which sat the Sultan. Viziers, the Sultan's right-hand men, were encouraged to found their own mosques, and the city was divided into thirteen districts – all but one named for the mosque at its heart. Privacy and respect for the private space, essential for nomad cultures and enshrined in Islamic cities, became a new priority. Across Kostantiniyye homes were being adapted to include their own courtyards and gardens so that women could spend time outside and uncovered.

Under Islamic law women possessed moveable and immoveable property rights. Often through agents (travel from the home was typically considered undesirable for the Muslim Ottoman woman) these home-worker businesswomen oversaw rental incomes, sales, bequests and property development and investment. Ongoing research suggests that women, particularly ordinary women, were more visible than stereotypes of the city might imply – gathering water at fountains, planting flowers, peddling goods. Typically, from the departure of the Ottoman fleet on campaign to royal marriages and births, women and girls were encouraged on to the streets to celebrate. In fact, so many started to appear at public occasions that the state banned women from saluting the arrival of the Iranian ambassador in AD 1574 in case they attracted unwelcome attention.[12] A millennia-long trope, beginning in history with Herodotus' comments on Egyptian women, of Western male observers believing that other cultures let their women run things, could carry some truth when applied to Ottoman culture. The Catholic priest Solomon Schweigger, travelling through Anatolia in the sixteenth century in order to translate the Qur'an, noted, 'The Turks govern the world and their wives govern them. In no other country do women enjoy themselves as much.'[13] Ottoman Istanbul echoed the earliest days of Islam when women had a religious as well as a social presence, being allowed to preach and teach in mosques from Jerusalem to Cairo.

Trade too became a religious affair. Before work, traders prayed for the Sultan, for Janissaries and for journeymen colleagues and purified themselves at the city's fountains during the day. One of the most vibrant areas of the conquered city was the Bazaar, built by Mehmed II in AD 1456–61, with close on 4,000 stalls, which spread out from the Bedestan (today the Old Bazaar). Rents from the Bedestan supported the Ayasofya Mosque. Smaller mosques had their own *bedestans*, the income from which supported the activities of the mosque itself, its imarets (soup-kitchens) and madrasas (schools). The whole zone from the Bazaar towards Edirne became a commercial centre. The conquest of Cairo in AD 1517 (922–3 in the Islamic calendar) meant that many master craftsmen – whose families had been in the city for generations thanks to the political stability of the Mamluks – now flooded into Istanbul to sell and to buy their wares. The endowment of Ayasofya included thirty millet-beer concessions. The beer's name, *boza*, was quickly bastardised by visiting English sailors to 'booze'.

While a number of the changes as Constantinople morphed into Kostantiniyye were organic, there was some deliberate destruction. Although originally offered to the Greek patriarchate, the Church of the Holy Apostles, built with such vision by Constantine and containing his tomb, as well as the bodies of a number of his successors, had been razed in AD 1461–2 to make way for the Fatih Mosque (which itself collapsed in an earthquake in 1766). Churches elsewhere were converted to mosques and the Haghia Eirene, the Church of Holy Peace – with no little irony – would become the arsenal of the Topkapı Palace.[14] The armoury collection here eventually formed the basis of the Istanbul Military Museum. In the new-build much Byzantine heritage was destroyed; Byzantine masonry can still be traced in the baths, hans (roadside inns or caravanserais), and mosques of the Ottoman city. One visitor from Albi in southern France, Pierre Gilles, reported in the sixteenth century on the dismantling and cannibalising of the statue of Justinian, the broken remains – a nose, an arm, a horse's fetlock – waiting on the ground to be melted down and repurposed as cannon metal.

But the Ottoman conquest does not feel like a complete cleft – neither the blood-crazed depravity nor the banner-unfurling triumph it is portrayed as being by many medieval and modern-day chroniclers of West and East. Christians were still allowed to participate in their processions and festivals, rescuing wooden crosses tossed into the Golden Horn at Epiphany (a practice that continues to this day) and dancing in the streets at Easter. Some of the Byzantine nobility were forced to convert (and to remain in the city as high-ranking pashas) but others kept their faith. Greeks who had been enslaved following the conquest were settled along the Golden Horn, and worked to rebuild their city before ransoming themselves out of their slavery. Mehmed's release of the anti-unionist monk Gennadios from slavery in Edirne and his re-establishment as the patriarch in Istanbul in AD 1454 ensured a focus of both Christian and Hellenising passion on the city that would endure through to the twentieth century. Many of the grand buildings in the centre of the city were indeed crumbling of their own accord – the Byzantine emperors had become squatters in those etiolated zones of their palatial quarters that were still inhabitable. And so what the Ottomans took on was a strategic location, an idea and a city that in physical terms was a husk of its former self.[15]

There was so very much that these two cultures, Muslim and Christian, shared – their ancient religious prophets, their myth stories, their God. Mehmed II had added Kaysar (Caesar) to his roll-call of titles. Süleyman I (who reigned AD 1520–66 and tried to insist that the city be called Istanbul) claimed to be the true heir to the Roman Empire. But the eagle had flown. In 1492 the Grand Prince of Muscovy married an heiress of Byzantium and started to sport on his courtly and military

Some Christian traditions continued in the city after the Ottoman conquest and still do to this day – here is the Greek Patriarch Joachim III's funeral procession in 1912.

furnishings the double-headed bird most avidly displayed in Byzas' City from around AD 1000 – to show that from Constantinople the power of this Christian Empire could look both East and West. The crescent was now displayed on the top of Ayasofya. And, with a Caliph-Sultan at its head, and the *qadis* (judges) communicating in Arabic, ensuring that the faithful followed the Qur'anic injunction to 'enjoin the good (*al-ma'ruf*) and forbid the evil',[16] Constantinople was, truly, at the start of a new chapter; a different kind of city.

The Ottomans, long a semi-nomadic, raiding people, needed others with deeper roots if this urban experiment was to work. They imported an administrative system and populations from across their newly consolidated territories – from Anatolia, from Trebizond/Trabzon on the Black Sea and from the Morea in the Peloponnese. Nobles, artisans, traders were particularly welcome. Prisoners who could pay their own ransom were given houses. The lag of a decade before any significant mosque-building was undertaken suggests that when the conquering forces first arrived they had neither the manpower nor the skill in town planning to remake the city in their own image. If this rebranded Constantinople was going to work it would have to succeed thanks to a mixture of pragmatism and PR.

CHAPTER 55

❖

RENAISSANCE CITY

AD 1453
(856/7 IN THE ISLAMIC CALENDAR) ONWARDS

Every corner a paradise, every garden an Eden
Every fountain a water of Paradise, every river, a river of honey.

TURSUN BEY, *HISTORY*[1]

In the backrooms of the Istanbul Archaeological Museum there is a series of letters originally written in Italian and translated into Turkish. The energetically inscribed scratches of ink are answers to a call for a bridge-building competition in the city. Sultan Bayezid II wanted access for people, horses, camels, water-buffalo, donkeys and mules over the Golden Horn and for boat traffic through it. Eager for a commission, many applied – including Leonardo da Vinci: 'I, your servant, heard that you intended to construct a bridge from Istanbul to Galata, but you could not because no expert could be found. I, your servant, know [how to make it]. I could raise an arch so high that nobody would want to pass over it because of its height ... I could construct it in such a way that even a sailing ship could pass under it.'[2]

New research sheds light on Leonardo's particular interest in Constantinople. His involvement stemmed partly from the fact that he had been working in Venice – that city umbilically linked to Constantinople for centuries. But the city's proximity to the Bosphorus also sparked a singular fascination. This was a stretch of water that in c. AD 1506 Leonardo would come to include in his 'Gaia Scheme' – a prescient theory about the danger of rising sea-levels and subsequent global, environmental destruction. The single-span bridge designs submitted by Leonardo – although never built – are elegant. A bird's-eye-view sketch (held at the National Library of France in Paris) shows a crossing with ends fanning out like a swallowtail. In homage to his charming designs one modern Norwegian artist, Vebjørn Sand, has followed the da Vinci Golden Bridge form in wood, so a little piece of a dream of Stamboul now sits in Oslo.

One suspects that, had he got the commission, Leonardo da Vinci would have appreciated the Muslim city's particular reverence for its water supplies. With Islam's emphasis on bodily purity, the movement of water around the city became a priority. All visitors subsequent to the conquest remarked on the proliferation of fountains and *taksim*, water systems; they noted the paradisiacal impression of running water and patches of green – fruit trees in the form of mulberry, fig and pomegranate. Stephen Gerlach, a priest in the Habsburg Embassy in AD 1573–6, memorialised the transportingly bucolic nature of Istanbul. Until the second half of the twentieth century whole swathes of the city remained verdant.[3]

Word quickly spread that the sultans were Renaissance princes with deep pockets. The artists Filarete (author of an expansive single-volume treatise on the imaginary ideal Renaissance city, Sforzinda) and Michelozzo (the Medicis' favourite architect) also advised on new buildings for Kostantiniyye. Arabic scientific knowledge was eagerly pounced on by Renaissance masters such as Albrecht Dürer, Ghiberti and Copernicus. Pietro Aretino, a humanist scholar, also contacted Süleyman the Magnificent seeking patronage.[4] Although Latin sources described the destruction of as many as 120,000 books and manuscripts during the Ottoman conquest, the early sultans were, demonstrably, promoters of knowledge and of the written word. One of Mehmed II's first acts in power was said to have been the foundation of eight schools for both primary and higher education; we know that he commissioned the creation of beautifully decorated books, lavishly bound in silk, leather and gilt, including translations of the *Iliad* and Alexander Romances – determinedly pursuing the Islamic tenet that to seek knowledge is Allah's will. Mehmed's forty prototype books would quickly become a style vogueish in western Europe.

Yet this was a Renaissance city with a twist. Nomadic and Islamic traditions, the remembrance from the desert of balm being a thing of the night, meant that much large-scale cultural activity now took place in Islamic Constantinople after dark. Since those Muslims who could afford it might take multiple wives, marriages and hence marriage celebrations were downgraded and the celebration of royal circumcisions started to

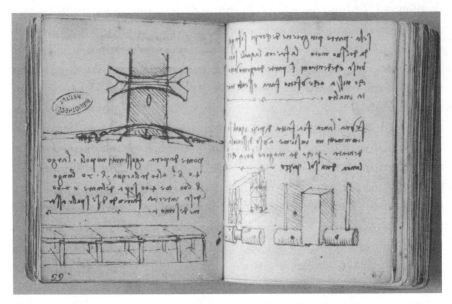

Sketches for a bridge across the Golden Horn by Leonardo da Vinci, c. AD 1502

outshine the gaudiest of Byzantine traditions. These nocturnal activities made for very good copy. Describing the fifty-two-day celebration of the circumcision of the future Mehmed III, son of Murad III, one French traveller noted that 'The midnight sports were passed away with burning of Fortresses, Holdes, Horses, Elephantes and other creatures made by arte . . .' In love with gunpowder – technology that had delivered the Ottomans city after city – the creatives in Istanbul pushed pyro-technology to the max. Fireworks that represented churches, unicorns and towns were produced (with the help of an English captive, Edward Webbe), and monumental *nahils* (decorative trees made of wire, wax, precious stones, mirrors and flowers – symbols of fertility and virility) were carried on floats around the city. Istanbul's firework displays could be mounted from land or water. Given that some festivities involved dancers and musicians performing on rafts lit with lanterns, with the people of the city crowding on to the water to watch, jostling so tightly together that oars could not move, accidents were inevitable.

Daytime displays were no less impressive. Selim II on his way to Friday prayers was jewel-studded from his white turban to his stirrups. As time went on, white sand would be laid in the Sultan's path. Murad

III's extravagant two-month-long celebration in AD 1582 to mark the circumcision of his son, and said to be a response to Catherine de' Medici's triumphs, threw everything at this opportunity for international PR. Visitors from East and West alike were sketched peering out at the spectaculars in the old Byzantine hippodrome where slaves carried intricate *trompe l'oeil* floats. Mountains exploded. The inmates of asylums were displayed in gold chains and women from the harem delivered menageries spun out of sugar. When princes travelled through the city, exquisitely woven fabrics, gleaming with silver and gold, were spread under the hooves of their horses. It was said of the heir apparent on the way to the palace of Ibrahim Pasha that as his horses passed, the marks of their hooves and nails on the priceless fabrics caused 'hundreds of stars and crescents to appear on the face of the beautiful *Dibas* (fabrics) as if the Heavens had honoured these satins'.

Some displays were so splendid, there were reports of Greeks and Armenians converting on the spot to Islam. Cannonfire marked the movement of the Sultan around Istanbul, as well as sounding out imperial births, deaths, circumcisions and the departure of the Ottoman fleet to war. When the cannon were in full voice it was said that in Kostantiniyye, 'The eyes and ears of the heavens became blind and deaf.'[5] One Sultan (Murad III) ordered that cannon should hold their fire until his pregnant concubine had given birth without mishap.

There is something else a little unexpected about Istanbul's Renaissance skyline. If you take a ferry trip across the Bosphorus and look either way, you will find that a large proportion of the historic, Islamic-period silhouettes were paid for by women. In the sixteenth century at least a third of all pious foundations in Istanbul had been erected by the female of the species. Customarily, upper-class Ottoman women might not be allowed out between sunrise and sunset, but they made sure they enjoyed an inventive urban presence.

Under Islamic law, women as well as men are guaranteed to inherit, so founding religious or charitable buildings became a sensible expression of piety. Building work in Istanbul was facilitated by the *vakıf* system of welfare (*waqf* in Arabic) which could protect a subject of the Sultan in the city from the cradle to the grave. Donors were often newly married women – the names on record range from the very grand to the very modest (we hear from the *vakıf* that one Sultan funded a full-time post for one man to go around the city removing graffiti and children's doodles from charitable foundations). Hospitals across the ex-Byzantine territories were established where both patients and doctors could be Muslim (or not), where music was played to those being treated for physical and mental sickness. In some institutions an outpatient, home-visit service was established.[6]

In Istanbul female charity was made permanent and incarnate. Süleyman's daughter Mihrimah founded the beautiful mosque on the peak of the sixth hill near Edirnekapı. The architect Sinan built the great complex of Atik Valide Mosque in AD 1580–9 for the mother of Murad III, Nurbanu Atik Valide Sultan,[7] boasting a mosque, convent, hospital, hospice, schools, public bath, caravanserai and public kitchen at Üsküdar. The hospital on the banks of the Bosphorus built for Nurbanu still operates today as a medical centre and has a calm, benign feel; pregnant cats wander in and are gently ushered out or are quietly tolerated.

When Turhan Hatice Sultan funded a fountain at Beşiktaş in AD 1663 she declared:

> The concubine Safiye's mosque still punctuates the banks of the Golden Horn.
> Hatice Sultan who is the crown of chastity of the well-guarded
> and the mother of Mehmed Khan, Sultan of the Sultans,
> the order of sovereignty and the community, pure of character,
> Caused this sublime fountain to flow freely
> so that the thirst of the whole universe might be slaked.

And Turhan Hatice in AD 1665, continuing the work of Safiye Sultan, cleared what had been a Jewish district to build the Yeni Valide mosque complex, the first imperial mosque built by a woman, and from whose ramparts she kept an eye on goings-on in Kostantiniyye.

So a sizeable proportion of the Ottoman city was planned in Topkapı's harem – where, from the mid-sixteenth century onwards the Sultan's favourite men and an ever burgeoning population of women were to be found. The harem – the name means sanctuary – had grown out of a combination of tradition and ambition. In traditional Turkic society, the root '*h-r-m*' was designated a sacred space designed, among other things, to protect the ultimate ruler. The Sultan's women were initially there by chance, simply because of their proximity to their lord. In this fabricated world strict taxonomy was necessary. The varieties of women within the harem had different nominations: Gedikıli Kadın – privileged or high-ranking; Gözde – 'In the Eye', so a favourite; Ikbal – those who stayed in favour with the Sultan after the first night; Haseki Sultan – the Sultan's special favourite. If a woman in the harem had a child who became the Sultan's eldest living son she was the Birinci Kadın, literally 'First Lady'. If that son succeeded to the throne the girl became the Valide Sultan – the Sultan's mother, a position of enormous importance. It was only the Valide's hand that Istanbul's sultans ever kissed.

Some of the less popular harem slaves could be manumitted after nine years. Free to leave, accomplished and with the smell of the Sultan on them they were considered a choice match. Travel around the northern edge of the Topkapı today, through a public park populated by families, weary backpackers and courting couples and the mountain-face walls of the harem, reminds one of the value of that which was being protected within.

When Süleyman the Lawgiver's Old Palace burnt down, his favoured concubine Hürrem had moved her apartments into the grand new impe-rial construction on the top of the old Byzantine acropolis. Advertising her nearness to her husband was a demonstration of Hürrem's power. We hear that the cypress-tanged, paint-fresh rooms here were 'exquisite, with prayer halls, baths, gardens and other comforts'.[8] In AD 1574 (the year that Murad III acceded) the Sultan moved his bedroom and privy chamber into the harem itself. After breakfast he would rejoin the men, who then helped him to run his empire. The harem was now its own world; along with domestic facilities the harem boasted a throne room and a prison. The sultans immortalised the appreciation of both their women and their city in poetry – attested by one *ghazel* written by the Sultan Süleyman I to Hürrem:

Throne of my lonely niche, my wealth, my love, my moonlight.
My most sincere friend, my confidante, my very existence, my Sultan
    [the chief consort of the Sultan was not called Sultana – a Western
    interpolation – but Sultan], my one and only love
The most beautiful among the beautiful . . .

My springtime, my merry-faced love, my daytime, my sweetheart,
   laughing leaf . . .
My plants, my sweet, my rose, the one only who does not distress me
   in this world . . .
My Istanbul, my Karaman [capital of the Karamanids north of the
   Taurus], the earth of my Anatolia
My Badakhshan [source of lapis lazuli on the Silk Roads], my Bagh-
   dad, my Khorasan ['land of the sunrise', a province of Persia]
My woman of the beautiful hair, my love of the slanted brow,
My love of eyes full of mischief . . .
I'll sing your praises always
I, lover of the tormented heart, Muhibbi [Süleyman I's nom de plume]
   of the eyes full of tears, I am happy.[9]

So the highest-ranking females in the city's imperial harems had some
leverage. Diplomatic marriage alliances were initially as critical politically
for the Ottomans as they were for those rival Islamic super-powers the
Safavids in Persia and the Mughals in India, but as time went on, the
Ottomans spurned these in favour of a vigorous, home-grown gene pool.
It was through the women of the harem that new dynasties, new power-
brokers, would be born. Not a cross-fertilisation of potency then, but an
Istanbul-centric concentration of diverse human talent. The slave population of the Sultan's inner city were now the mothers and sisters of kings.
These slaves – in particular his male pages and female companions – were
exalted as an artificial ruling elite. And the most influential seem to have
developed an attitude to match, operating as strategists and cultural patrons. Always cosmopolitan, Constantinople was becoming increasingly
multi-ethnic and a place of opportunity for some women and some men,
of diverse degrees.

CHAPTER 56

A GARDEN OF MIXED FRUIT

AD 330–c. 1930

I live in a place that very well represents the tower of Babel: in Pera they speak Turkish, Greek, Hebrew, Armenian, Arabic, Persian, Russian, Slavonian, Wallachian, German, Dutch, French, English, Italian, Hungarian . . . [The serving staff] learn all these languages at the same time and without knowing any of them well enough to read or write in it.

LADY MARY WORTLEY MONTAGU, WRITING TO A FRIEND
FROM CONSTANTINOPLE, AD 1717–18[1]

The harbour has been filled, vegetables have been planted in the wide fields and a few arbours have been planted. Fruits hang down from the trees, not sails as Fabios had told; the vegetable gardens are watered from inexhaustible fountains remaining from the ancient harbour.

PIERRE GILLES, *ISTANBUL* (DESCRIBING THE VLANGA GARDENS
WHERE MANY NON-MUSLIMS COULD BE FOUND)[2]

Travelling east through Europe, the last stop before Istanbul on the Via Egnatia is the Büyükçekmece Caravanserai. Reached by an audacious bridge designed by the architect Sinan, this long, low building – the size and shape of two tithe-barns – still shields lampblack soot from Ottoman-period candles in its niches. Next door is a madrasa and an ornate fountain. The caravanserai building, today used for community art projects, is a roomy, elegant workhorse. Typically founded by the Sultan himself or by local potentates, spaced along an imperial road-network where the Romans once built baths and rest-houses, these Ottoman equivalents of the Ad Quintum offered free lodging to travellers and merchants. Selim I initiated laws to check the goods held in the caravanserai each morning, and by the seventeenth century there were close on a thousand of these rest-stations in and around Kostantiniyye. Each night, in the grander institutions such as Büyükçekmece, travellers would be given wax and a taper for light and a bowl of soup, on Fridays the luxury of boiled meat and onions and saffron rice.

Animals (horses, donkeys, mules, camels, buffalo) and men bedded down together in the same sealed space which was locked up at night and opened again every dawn. Humans slept on raised stone benches – no windows for safety, so the odour each morning must have been rich. Western writers frequently commented on the 'filth' and 'stench' of the caravanserai. Fortunately, most of these medieval roadside motels – also known as *khans* – came with bathing facilities attached. But what a number of travellers mention is the caravanserai's value in terms not just of security and amenities, but of the potential for information exchange. Humming across the Ottoman Empire – and with particular vigour around Istanbul – could be heard the original lingua franca, a base of pidgin Italian with added Greek, Turkish, Arabic, Spanish and French elements. It was in this language of the road that merchants and peregrinators would communicate; news and advice was often shared late into the night. Whether you were from Illyria or from Babylon there was a reason to correspond, and the caravanserai offered a location.

The founders of Constantinople had been city-based soldiers; the founders of Istanbul were nomadic traders and warriors. The Ottomans understood the law of the road, and the absolutely essential nature of keeping those lines of communication serviced and open. Ottoman rule has been described as a dromocracy – a road-power, a road-based empire where the speed of trade, of warrior-movement and of information exchange was key. But the sultans, viziers and pashas, sitting in their ever more splendid quarters on Sarayburnu 'Palace Horn' (Seraglio Point in English), also needed to invite men in who could make a cosmopolitan city flourish.

And so they were summoned. Mehmed II, offering inducements – above all tax remissions – repopulated Constantinople. In some cases refugees were forced to return, but many powerful families clearly did well. The Ottomans did not make the mistake of some modern-day powers, who have attempted to reconfigure the Eastern Mediterranean and the Middle East; the Ottomans knew that a clean slate could only ever be a fantasy. Taking the multi-ethnic, multi-faith nature of their new experiment in empire as a given rather than as a surprise, they legislated intelligently. The old, Middle-Eastern millet system was warmly advanced by Mehmet II whereby each ethnic community in Istanbul could be tried and judged according to its own religious laws. The Arabic word *millah* means nation – and from the nineteenth-century onwards came to refer to those national communities living in Kostantiniyye. Each millet in Istanbul had their own detailed and binding charter. Whether Rûm (Greek Orthodox Christians), Syrian Orthodox, Armenian or Jewish, all enjoyed (at least to some degree) religious pluralism in Ottoman Istanbul. There were restrictions: non-Muslims could not open up businesses near mosques, and their houses had to be lower than 9 *dhira'* (22 feet) high.[3] But they were plangently present.

Constantinople had long been polyglot, but in AD 1492, close on 2,400 miles to the west, events in al-Andalus ensured that a new wave of migrants and refugees poured the city's way. The Sultan had already agreed to take some Jews into his empire from Spain in 1470 (although the city's resident Jewish community had in large part been enslaved or deported

Syrian, Greek and Ottoman women compared in AD 1581

at the time of conquest), but now there was mass immigration. When the Spanish monarchs Ferdinand II and Isabella I took Granada in al-Andalus, Muslims and Jews were killed or expelled. At the beginning of the sixteenth century many, perhaps 30,000, came directly to Istanbul.[4] There were now more than 8,070 Jewish households in what was once Constantine's capital. It was said that Sultan Bayezid II had recognised the opportunity which he had been offered: 'You call Ferdinand a wise ruler . . . [yet] he impoverishes his own country to enrich mine!'[5]

As a result, from AD 1492 onwards Istanbul supported the largest and most flourishing Jewish community in Europe. Arabs came too, converting St Paul's Church (briefly a Dominican monastery) in Galata into the Arap Camii, the Arab Mosque. The belfry of St Paul's became the minaret and a fountain was erected in the courtyard for purification. Where hipsters now hang out among the artisans' shops and pastel-painted homes, at night in their new city-home the Muslim refugees from al-Andalus sang of the tragedy of their expulsion from Spain.

Millenarial anxiety added to the influx. Traditional calendars – many produced in Istanbul – asserted that the world would end 7,000 years after it was created in 5508 BC. Christians started to proselytise, and to attack religious minorities. A number of the displaced ended up in Istanbul.

Many silk-makers came to live and work in the Vlanga area – the fertile zone of reclaimed land that covered what was once Theodosios' buzzing harbour. From the AD 1400s onwards, that busy port had silted over, and after the conquest it was set aside for non-Muslims. Excavators working on the site believe they have found pharmacy workshops here; it is a good place for growing herbs, with all that mineral-rich earth as soil, but it is low-lying, so often malodorous, and hard to defend. Jewish families also populated Sirkeci, and as time went on (often as the result of devastating fires that tore through the tightly packed Jewish quarters) communities sprang up in Balat and Hasköy on either side of the Golden Horn. One German, Hans Dernschwam, observed that by the sixteenth century the Jews in the city were as thick 'as ants', that there were twice as many Jews as Christians, and there were at least forty-two synagogues.[6]

There were, at a more conservative estimate, as many as 11,000 Jewish residents and eleven synagogues by around AD 1600, Sephardi Jews eventually joining the Greek-speaking Jewish inhabitants, the Romaniotes, and the Jews from al-Andalus. Running from newly Catholic Andalucia, these footsore travellers brought anxieties, ideas and technologies – including in AD 1493, fifty-odd years after it was invented, the city's first printing press. The Jewish printers physically carried their printing blocks and equipment with them. The fonts used in Istanbul could be neither Arabic nor Ottoman-Turkish (printing in Arabic script was legalised only in 1727).[7] So the Jewish community had hit an opportunity. Some also helped to expand Kostantiniyye's silk production in the city, a border-crossing industry which had, for centuries, been masterminded within the Jewish quarter. It wasn't just the Byzantines who profited from silk-making in the region.[8][9] The Medici had installed an agent in Ottoman Bursa to acquire the choicest pieces,[10] while in early nineteenth-century Thessalonika the British merchant and freeman in the Levant Company Bartholomew Edward Abbott traded internationally in silks from Constantinople, many still being produced by Jewish families.[11]

There is a sad irony that, although we have large quantities of silks exported from Constantinople, representing centuries' worth of global trade, the silken treasures themselves often wrapped in their own silk-shrouds, not one historic example has survived within the city itself thanks to natural decay in the damp conditions along with the depredations of the Rus, Latin Crusaders, invading Ottomans and all the rest. All Istanbul's own silks pre-1922 were smuggled out, looted, buried or burnt.

Istanbul's Jewish population after the Islamic conquest may have been welcomed in by Sultan Bayezid, but it suffered the same fluctuating fortunes as Jewish communities elsewhere. With the approach of the Muslim millennium there were sartorial restrictions imposed on Jews (and Christians) and alcohol was banned. When one of the key players in Sultan Murad III's harem, Safiye, planned her beautiful mosque which still stands overlooking the Bosphorus, synagogues and Jewish residencies were peremptorily cleared to make space. The great fire of AD 1660 was blamed on the Jews, and in retribution many were expelled from Eminönü. By the seventeenth century it was Armenians who largely managed the silk trade between Persia, Turkey and Italy, raking in huge profits as a result. After another fire in 1740, Jews were at first allowed to build without permits in Galata, Ortaköy and Üsküdar, but then the scale of immigration resulted in a new decree restricting Jewish construction in 1744.[12]

And yet Jewish families persevered to become amongst the most powerful in the city. Some of our very best descriptions of day-to-day life on the streets of Kostantiniyye come from one Rabbi Domenico Hierosolimitano, who worked as a court physician to Sultan Murad III (Domenico converted, but many of the sultans employed ethnically Jewish doctors). One of the Janissaries' responsibilities, both in the city and in the wider world, was to protect the interests of minorities in the Ottoman realm – Jews and Christians alike.

Yet there was one prominent group in Kostantiniyye herself who fell outside that jurisdiction: the Romani. Gypsies had too been long-established inhabitants of the city of Constantinople – it is their very connection with New Rome that probably gave the group the name Romani or Roma. But the Romani seem to have suffered renewed discrimination at the hands of their new Ottoman rulers. Although forced conversion was frowned upon, the mass conversion of many thousands of Armenian gypsies to Islam at Topkapı Palace was recorded approvingly by the city's chroniclers. Fleeing the invasions of Mahmud Ghazni, the first migrants from Rajasthan in northern India had arrived in Constantinople some time c. AD 1000–57. This had been a long, dusty journey north through Persia and Armenia (there are a number of Armenian loan words in the Romany language). Having settled briefly in the southern Caucasus, gypsy groups may have left Armenia pursued by Seljuk invaders. When they finally reached Constantinople, all Romani gypsies had to pay a special tax and were considered slaves of the state.

The Romani are first mentioned in the city in an eleventh-century source. It was recorded that the Emperor Constantine Monomachos needed help to rid his wildlife park of the wilder wildlife that kept on attacking and eating his show-stock. The Romani were called in. They struck down the hunters with 'charmed' meat. In fact throughout their urban history Romani families, particularly the women, are described as soothsayers and sorcerers, many offering to come into Istanbul's homes to alleviate the suffering of the sick. The practice became so popular that in the fifteenth century it was decreed that those in Constantinople who invited gypsies across their thresholds would not be allowed to take communion for five years.

A vivid description from the reign of Andronikos II describes one group of travellers in the Byzantine city – called Egyptians but almost certainly Romani – walking on tightropes, trick-riding, performing contortions.

The author confides that none of this was done with sorcery but all with 'adroitness'. A mirror-account from an Arabic source of the time also labels these performers 'gypsies'. In Constantinople Romani are recorded as working as bear-tamers and snake-charmers – and, deliciously, they were well known for making sieves, which a number of Romani families in the city still do.[13]

For close on a millennium Roma could be found in highest concentration just within the city walls at Sulukule. First officially recorded here in a census of AD 1477, Romani continued to dance at the henna parties of Muslim brides the day before a wedding up until the fall of the Ottoman Empire in the early twentieth century. A Lady Blunt in the 1870s described this cavorting as 'of the most unrestrained and immodest nature'.[14] In the late 1980s one could still dance all night in the little 'entertainment-houses' in the Romani quarter of Istanbul, the parties attracting Roma musicians from across Turkey (today Turkey has a population of some 4 million Roma, one of the largest in the world). When I visited Sulukule in 2008 there was a plan to move the 5,000-strong Romani population and to replace their gaudy one-storey homes with Ottoman-style villas for the city's new, upwardly mobile middle class. The demolitions started in 2011; many of Istanbul's Romani are now beggars, exiled to the roadsides.

To get a sense of the Romani encampments that once thrived in Istanbul, it is worth taking a trip to Edirne (the city that had started life as Adrianopole). Known by some as the 'gypsy city', there are villages here networked together with dirt tracks where gypsy dynasties still work as farmers, traders and musicians. In this Romani quarter I was treated to an afternoon of music from one band of brothers, cousins and sons-in-law all led by the patriarch called Faris Zurnacı, who promised me that his family could keep me dancing for three days straight. Chickens scratched, we drank Coca-cola from nine in the morning and ate home-made biscuits from ten and talked of the sad exodus of the Roma from Istanbul itself. While the old Ottoman millet system protected Rûm, Jews, Armenians, Assyrians – albeit as second-class citizens – the Romani were never afforded this benefit, a prejudice that seems to have prevailed.

Christian Constantinople had always been vividly colour-coded, but now the spectrum was expanded. Muslims wore yellow slippers with white or green turbans, Jews had yellow hats and blue slippers, Greeks were dressed in sky blue, Armenians favoured violet slippers. Muslims could paint their homes red as well as build them higher than Christians. While many still used the old names for their metropolis – Kostantin-iyye, Islam-bol or Stimboli, now there were new nominations too – the Jews called Istanbul *Kushta*, Armenians *Bolis*, Slavs *Tsargrad*.

When, in AD 1481, Mehmed the Conqueror died, the city's population was around 100,000. From the census of 1477 (which excluded military families and palace inhabitants) we can see that there were 8,951 Ottoman Turks in the heart of the city itself, 3,151 Greeks and 1,647 Jews with 1,067 other minorities; in Galata there were 535 Muslim, 572 Greek, 332 Frankish and 62 Armenian households. With fresh conquests the total population quickly expanded – one captive Spanish physician recorded that during his three-year stretch in Istanbul in the mid-sixteenth century as many as 29,000 slaves had been brought to the city and across the empire the overall population of Ottoman cities rose by 80 per cent.

If one had sailed up the Bosphorus from the Sea of Marmara 500 years ago, one would have been aware of two distinct cities – Muslim Istanbul emerging on the western shore and the infidel district, the land of the Gavur or Giaour (non-Muslims), across on the eastern side of the Golden Horn. While Istanbul itself grew more verdant, the home of the Giaour became ever more tightly packed with warehouses and houses crowding in on one another. And so just as Istanbul had begun its life as a collection of ancient settlements separated by water and opposite an acropolis, increasingly the city started to sunder once again, splitting like a drop of mercury.

An unintentional side-effect of having a multi-faith population was that in Istanbul there were many, and various, popular religious holidays. Throughout its history, visitors remarked on the number of inhabitants who could be seen in holiday dress; an implication followed that this was therefore an indolent and a pleasure-seeking city. In fact, with its religiously variegated population, it was in many ways extra-pious.

Considered as a series of fragments or as a whole, the Queen of Cities was beginning to deserve her nomination once more. Whether as refugees or as opportunists, whether invited or compelled, whether arriving as the desperate or as the inspired, thousands started to flood back to Istanbul. Foodstuff was delivered to Istanbul as a priority, while other outlying settlements were considered expendable. This was more than just a them-and-us situation: the *urbs* was the elite.

A city refounded by Muslim migrants was becoming a burgeoning cosmopolis that recognised that, in order to survive, it had to actively welcome in émigrés, refugees and adventurers.

CHAPTER 57

A DIAMOND BETWEEN TWO SAPPHIRES

AD 1502–65
(907–73 IN THE ISLAMIC CALENDAR)

The humble writer of these lines once himself saw ten Frankish infidels skilful in geometry and architecture, who, when the door-keeper had changed their shoes for slippers, and had introduced them into the mosque for the purpose of shewing it to them, laid their finger on their mouths, and each bit his finger from astonishment when they saw the minarets; but when they beheld the dome they tossed up their hats and cried Maria! Maria! And on observing the four arches which support the dome on which the date A.H. 944 [AD 1537] is inscribed, they could not find terms to express their admiration, and the ten, each laying his finger on his mouth, remained a full hour looking with astonishment on those arches ... I asked their interpreter how they liked it, and one of them who was able to give an answer said, that nowhere was so much beauty, external and internal, to be found united, and that in the whole of Frangistan [western Christendom] there was not a single edifice which could be compared to this.

EVLIYA ÇELEBI, *SEYAHATNAME*, DESCRIBING

THE SÜLEYMANIYE MOSQUE[1]

The waterways, the 'Sapphires' that cut through and enclose the city, have ensured that constitutionally Istanbul is a series of pods, pockets and neighbouring islands. And now the Ottomans, the men who originally came from plains ten days' wide, tasted the salt in the air and revelled in making boats their business.

The Ottomans knew that they could not have won Constantinople without maritime muscle, and Mehmed II imported Christian shipwrights to help to retain the city from Christian recapture. Bayezid II declared in AD 1502 that he wanted 'ships as agile as sea-serpents'², and promptly sequestered boat-builders and craftsmen from Chios to construct them. Competition with rival empires that had acquired access to the sea routes around Africa upped Kostantiniyye's maritime game. Ports, quays, piers, harbours were all extended and multiplied. The masted magnificence of Istanbul's growing navy was framed by the water-beetle scuttle of service boats and fishing vessels with their scimitar-curved bows. From 1516, when the Ottoman navy base moved from Gallipoli to Galata – just along from the stretch of the Bosphorus where resort-scale cruise ships dock today – 200 warships might be constructed in a single boathouse at the Kasımpaşa shipyards. The rich smell of wood being adzed and of hulls being caulked would have washed out from the yards as the full bellies of the city's new boats were smoothed, shaped and made seaworthy. Ships sailed out on patrol to deal with the pirates who raided grain ships across the Mediterranean and the Black Seas, but then themselves brought trouble home to roost. In the sixteenth century there were still plagues that swept through the city every twenty years or so (killing up to 20 per cent of the population with each assault). The large flea-market near the shipyards and the Imperial Arsenal exacerbated the situation, and the reuse of clothes and blankets plus the constant trundle of people and goods on and off the ships in ports brought both opportunity and pathogens to Istanbul's streets and quaysides.

By AD 1565 publicly funded *peremes* (rowing boats) plied up and down and across the Bosphorus, and soon there were 16,000 boatmen in the city. The sheer quantity of Ottoman boats on the high seas is witnessed by the number of wrecks originating in Istanbul and discovered by recent underwater archaeology. In 2014 after a three-month survey near Antalya, eight new Ottoman wrecks were discovered. Starting in 2004, investigations of the mud- and sand-covered remains of an Ottoman frigate, the *Ertuğrul*, which went down in a storm on its return journey to Istanbul in 1890 after leaving the Japanese port of Kushimoto, have revealed ships' nails the length of a forearm, glass perfume bottles and cooking pots. Earnings from trade in the Indian Ocean and through the ports of the Red Sea, the Persian Gulf and the Mediterranean funded handsome building projects in the city. Between 1592 and 1774 commerce on the Black Sea was reserved solely for Ottoman subjects. Raiding across the plains on horseback was a distant memory: the Turks and their allies were now masters of the waves.

As well as the burgeoning presence of merchant boats, military vessels and the Ottoman equivalent of the wherry, the Sultan travelled through Istanbul in fabulously ornate confections, carved *kayıks* – similar to Venetian gondolas. His harem were given their own vessels, the women's boats decorated with fruits and flowers. These domestic fleets were supervised and manned by a group who shared their name with the Sultan's gardeners. These men, the Bostancı, 5,000 or 6,000 at a time in any one administration, patrolled the port and the rims of the Bosphorus and Golden Horn – some maritime and riverine police by night, some rose-growers by day. The Bostancıbaşı was a powerful official. Mute Bostancıbaşı rowers were chosen, it was said, to babble and to howl on instruction so that the Sultan's conversations with guests on his waterways – for pleasure or business – could not be overheard.

The waterborne presence of the Sultan reminded Istanbul's people that he was in charge; the increasing presence of Ottoman ships in foreign waters reminded the world of his ambition. The truly exquisite series of early sixteenth-century maps created by the admiral and cartographer Hacı Ahmed Muhiddin Piri – known as Piri Reis – give an idea of just how intimately the Ottoman fleet was now able to view, to touch, to taste its prey. Piri Reis, born in Gallipoli, had spent his life at sea, initially off the coast of al-Andalus and then from AD 1492 in Ottoman service. He was present during the Ottoman conquest of Egypt in 1517 and he would go on to compile a world map series, his *Book of Navigation*, based on the works of other cartographers including those of Christopher Columbus. Many of his charts are an enchanting combination of texts and images; there are 5,704 extant copies across the world, with more being discovered regularly. Global powers were desperate to use Piri Reis' ground-breakingly accurate schemes, but the Ottoman court was always given first look. Süleyman the Lawgiver (known in the west as Süleyman the Magnificent, the Sultan from 1520), used his privileged knowledge to harry the coastlines of Europe, Asia and Africa.

It is significant that our earliest description of Süleyman I comes from a Venetian, Bartolomeo Contarini: 'All men hope for good from his rule.' No longer brigands from the East, the Ottomans were now part of the warp and woof of Renaissance Europe. Süleyman was a ruler who

Boats on the waterways of Istanbul from a late sixteenth- or early seventeeth-century Ottoman miniature

released rather than retarded the imagination. Roads were improved, castles restored, trading stations revived.

But Süleyman had desires as well as taste. His capture of Belgrade in AD 1521 and victory at the field of Mohács in 1526 had facilitated the Ottoman conquest of Hungary. A struggle with the Hapsburgs for central Europe ensued. In 1529, the Ottomans had been driven back from Vienna. As far as the West was concerned, there was a sense that they were just biding their time. They were right to be worried. The expulsion of Muslims from Spain in 1492 had pulsed a wave of resentment around the Mediterranean. So when one plucky privateer Hayreddin Pasha – remembered in history by his Western nickname Barbarossa (although it was in fact Hayreddin's dead brother who had the *rossa barba*, the red beard) – challenged the Christian army of the Holy Roman Emperor Charles V on the coast of Algeria, he found plenty of passionate Muslim supporters to sign up to the Ottoman project.

Barbarossa, it was chronicled, had paid his way to the position of commander of the Ottoman fleet with wild animals and with 200 of the finest female captives for the slave markets in Istanbul. The city certainly loved this man who had lavishly honoured her. For the next twenty years he would sail out from Istanbul's shipyards with sometimes 200 ships at any one time to capture more land, and more slaves for the Sultan. Barbarossa's drive was clearly exceptional: his landing at the ancient Roman port of Ostia prompted the ringing of alarm bells in the city. The windy islands of Andros, Serifos and Paros fell to the assault of his boats.

Lampedusa and Montecristo were raided. Ios, now known as Greece's party island, even Ischia, one of the first islands to be colonised by the Greeks before even those Megarians had set out for Byzantion (and the glamorous location of Richard Burton and Elizabeth Taylor's love affair on the set of *Cleopatra*), could not resist. Barbarossa swept them up like mullet in a net.

Süleyman himself attacked Rhodes. Today the gargantuan walls of the castle seem impossible to breach, but the Knights of St John finally surrendered on 20 December AD 1522 after a 145-day siege, eventually resettling on Malta and Gozo. The abandoned castle of the Knights' order in Bodrum – ancient Halicarnassus, built on an original Doric foundation by those adventuring Greeks and then cannibalising the construction of Mausolos of Caria's mausoleum – was handed over to Süleyman's forces. Winding, filled with nooks and crannies, the ruins of Bodrum castle still stand as testament to a medieval world and to a medieval balance of power that the Ottomans were steadily reconfiguring.

In AD 1537 Süleyman the Lawgiver moved his fleet to Butrint, on the coast of what was once Illyria and is now Albania, and conceived an audacious plan – to invade western Europe by creating a pontoon of boats from Albania to Corfu. The site of Butrint is redolent with history. The wetlands here protect the remnants of civilisations long dead. As well as the Ottoman, Venetian, Byzantine and classical stones, submerged in water, there are the ghosts of the wooden piers that the Ottoman fleet once used.[3] So outside the second-hand shoe-shops of Sarander and the Four Elements nightclub, just up the coast from Dürres, the starting point of the Romans' Via Egnatia, there is an opportunity to feel the aspiration and drive of this new, expansionist Ottoman force as she looked West.[4]

But, even though Süleyman imported thirty cannon, including the largest in the world, Corfu would not break. Many of the rural population were killed or enslaved, but thanks to the defence of a Venetian garrison, the island never fell, a fact rehearsed by patriotic guides in front of the mulish defence of Corfu's castle, which still stares out towards what was for 400 years Ottoman Albania, ruled by the Sultan-Caliph from Istanbul. Retreating, Süleyman's troops wrathfully torched Butrint and its surrounds.

Between them, Süleyman I and his right-hand man of the sea, Barbarossa, redrew the map. Every year Barbarossa's imperial victories are commemorated on the banks of the Bosphorus, and sailors who pass his high-domed tomb, built by Süleyman's architect Sinan, in Beşiktaş, still salute. On his death in AD 1546, he was eulogised in the city as the 'King of the Sea'. At modern-day Kuşadası, a little way down the Anatolian coast close to Mytilene (Barbarossa's birthplace), a floodlit fortified mansion, now a disco, is commemorated as his home. With Barbarossa Avenues and Barbarossa bars in the town behind and operatic sunsets over his fortress-lair at night, local Turks tell of their hero's bravery and brio. Through the seventeenth century the expansionist British might have comforted themselves with the maxim that God gave the sea to the Christians and the land to the Muslims, but this was increasingly nostalgic folk tale rather than hard fact.

Meanwhile the profile and the sonic landscape of the city of Istanbul itself was also being reconfigured. Sinan, a craftsman from Cappadocia who had worked his way up through the Janissary Corps, trained as a carpenter and died as the *mimar* or architect of one of the world's most memorable and impressive urban environments, would approach Istanbul as an exciting architectural canvas. Baths, mosques, markets, schools, hospitals were all designed by him half a millennium ago, and many of the 120 buildings that he created for the city are still standing. Sinan made Süleyman's metropolitan vision real, he was a lapidary for the city.[5] Given that he was vigorously acclaimed as a national treasure from the nineteenth century onwards, it has become a little irksome to Turkish patriots to accept that Sinan was almost certainly of Greek or Armenian origin. In 1935 a council assigned by the Turkish Historical Society went so far as to open up the designer's tomb to measure his skull to prove that he had the racial characteristics of a Turk.[6]

The tomb that the authorities raided is in the grounds of one of Istanbul's most glorious buildings, the Süleymaniye Mosque. Sinan built this house of Allah for his Sultan Süleyman I. Constructed of marble brought from both new quarries and architectural salvage across the empire as an act of religious adoration, the Süleymaniye still dominates Istanbul's skyline from the Third Hill, and is a treasure of Renaissance vim. Contemporary sources describe Sinan's work as 'glittering with light', 'joy-giving', 'heart-captivating'. Süleyman himself declared that this place of worship made him a Second Solomon. It was in fact in large part constructed by

Western prisoners of war, 'Franks', referred to by Ottoman sources as 'demons of Solomon'.

The Süleymaniye is not just an architectural wonder; research in 2008 showed that it was also constructed as a sound box in which to praise god.[7] Eighty-two per cent of the salaried workers employed here were used to keep the interior of the mosque, from dawn to dusk, singing with piety. Twenty worshippers each day would recite 'There is no God but God, and Muhammad is His Prophet', 3,500 times each – to ensure that the Sultan benefited from its recital 70,000 times. This was just the beginning. Others would sing prayers and eulogies. Every space in the mosque would have been filled for every waking second with music – the sound stealing out into the elegant courtyard, where cats now stroll nonchalantly and the city's workers wash themselves before prayer. The Süleymaniye soundscape must have been both mesmeric and motivating. The waves of sound were cleverly diffused and refracted by Sinan's design. Abutting half-domes, small lateral domes, windows and muqarnas (decorative vaulting) all ensured that the chants and melodies rolled evenly between the side wings and the central space. Construction accounts show that Sinan ordered up 255 clay jugs specifically to be set into the mosque's dome. These acoustic tools are now known as Helmholtz resonators. Absorbing infelicitous frequencies, these jugs would then have helped to reflect music and the human voice out into the mosque as a hemisphere of noise.

Sinan would go on to design the kitchens in the Topkapı Palace (the originals destroyed by a fire there in AD 1574), kitchens that still trumpet their presence with the chimneys that can be seen from across the Bosphorus. In the face of nineteenth-century Western critics who branded Istanbul as backward, Sinan was wheeled out as an example of the brilliance of early Muslim architecture. He was brilliant, but he was only latterly a Muslim, and he did not look back to indigenous Turkic culture, but rather forward to the Early Modern World.

In Edirne Sinan designed the Selimiye Mosque, stretching 230 feet into the air – a spectacle one English traveller, Lady Mary Wortley Montagu, would describe as 'the noblest thing I ever saw'. Sinan's Selimiye Mosque, still surrounded by a noisy, working bedestan as it would have been in the sixteenth century and whose dome was said to rival that of Ayasofya, was for many – who expressed their feelings with orientalist hyperbole – a new gateway to the East. In some sense it was the Selimiye Mosque in Edirne, commissioned by Süleyman but completed under his successor Selim II, that was Istanbul's new Golden Gate – a statement of power and intent to all Western travellers whose destination was the World's Desire.

What Süleyman presided over for a full forty-six years was a city that was changing in form and feeling. Eyewitnesses such as Pierre Gilles reported on the bulk of the seating in the hippodrome being demolished, its columns used for example in a new hospital commissioned by the Sultan.[8] Whereas it had long been those Great Walls that had defined Constantinople – the palisades that gave the original Greek *polis* its name – now the Ottomans developed a more fluid approach to their cityscape. The city's millennium-old enemy was within the walls, so the walls themselves became less significant. Foreign diplomats for whom the Golden Gate had once been a sign of welcome, and a symbolic entry to Christ's city within, now found that the entrance-way, newly developed as the Yedikule Fortress, was their cage. Yedikule endured as a high-end prison up until AD 1895. Given that the city's bone-stripping and glue-making factories were situated just outside the fortress, incarceration must have been exceptionally malodorous. New settlements bled along the edge of the Bosphorus and Golden Horn. Mosques were constructed along the seashore. Increasingly – and until the fall of the Ottoman empire in 1922 – married princesses were settled in showy shore-palaces, the *sahil sarayları* overlooking Istanbul's waterways.

And so towards the end of the sixteenth century the city was buzzing, polyglot. Trade from East to West was taxed in Kostantiniyye, and

Süleyman the Lawgiver's procession through the Atmeidan (the Byzantine hippodrome) from the frieze 'Customs and Fashions of the Turks', AD 1553

although this would eventually encourage western overseas expansion in search of more wealth and more land, in the short term Istanbul's revival as a global market represented floods of cash into the imperial coffers – all carefully accounted for by tax-farmers, many of whom were descendants of old Byzantine nobility. In AD 1529 Süleyman might have been driven back from Vienna, but in 1541 the Ottomans were victorious at the siege of Buda and then of Pest the following year, storming in where once Greek Orthodox ideas had successfully penetrated. Using the new dirty weapons of gunpowder and shot while some of their rivals such as the Mamluks still carried sabres on horseback, soon the Ottoman Empire would stretch from present-day Morocco to the Ukraine and from the edge of Iran to the Gates of Vienna.

A city of decay and dust when the Ottomans arrived, protecting a population of 60,000 at most, was now home to over 400,000. Istanbul was the greatest and most flourishing city in Europe and the Middle East – she could indeed be described as the diamond of Osman's dream.

CHAPTER 58

✢

THE MUSLIM MILLENNIUM

AD 1570
(977/8 IN THE ISLAMIC CALENDAR)

The . . . fear takes hold because of a prophecy the Turks have, that around
1000 years after the birth of Muhammad troubles will arise in that empire.

MATTEO ZANE, VENETIAN *BAILO* (BAILIFF) IN ISTANBUL[1]

Süleyman the Lawgiver, despite his achievements, died a down-at-heel
death. For decades he had continued to expand Istanbul's territories.
Campaigning in southern Hungary, exhausted and anxious, he fell
before his forces' narrow victory at the Battle of Szigetvár in AD 1566.
In 2015 archaeologists announced that they had discovered Süleyman's
tomb. A wide, muddy pit, crammed with monumental masonry, had
been exposed within modest smallholdings at the edge of a small apple
orchard. The tomb was robbed some time in the seventeenth century, but
it was here that the Sultan's heart and organs had been swiftly buried.
Süleyman's death was kept a secret to prevent a succession crisis and his
body was taken back to Istanbul. The powers behind the throne had to
be careful because the city was jumpy.

The impending advent of the first Muslim millennium had sparked all
kinds of eschatological visions.

In AD 1492, seventy-odd years before the auspicious dates of 1570–1
(a thousand solar years after Muhammad's birth) and a hundred before
1591–2 (a thousand lunar years after Muhammad's Hijrah),[2] a man whose
identity is lost to history had written to Jalal al-Din al-Suyuti, a leading
Egyptian scholar of religion, claiming that the world would end at the
Muslim millennium since the bones of the Prophet Muhammad could
not remain in the grave for over a thousand years. In response, al-Suyuti
composed *An Exposé that This Community Will Pass 1,000 Years (al-Kashf*

'an mujawazat hadhihi al-umma al-alf). In it al-Suyuti argues that God had given Muslims 500 years' respite because not everyone had had the opportunity to repent their sins.[3] The population of Istanbul remained jumpy.

Around AD 1571 anxiety heightened in the city. Burning crosses were said to have been seen in the sky. The Bektashi dervishes became an overtly central part of the Janissary experience. Genies were increasingly called on to protect Istanbul's inhabitants. Popular fantasies about the city, such as the significance of the Mosque of the Leaded Store (Kurşunlu Mahzen Camii) or Underground Mosque (Yeraltı Camii) – originally said to be the tombs of the Muslim fallen – 'reminded' Istanbul's faithful that Muslim monuments had existed here since the first Arab sieges of Constantinople in the seventh century AD. Many Arab sources, recall, had claimed the early sieges of Constantinople to have been victorious.

These recondite mosques and shrines were thought to have supernatural powers of all kinds; at the 'tomb' of Abu Sufyan ibn Harb (one of the original besiegers of the city said to be buried in Istanbul's soil) men came to pray for deliverance from the infidel, while Greek, Ottoman and Armenian women alike would come to lay their handkerchiefs at the sepulchre to ensure their luck in love.[4]

The enigmatic prophecy-cum-curse of the Red Apple – first publicised in AD 1545 by a Hungarian prisoner of war, one Bartholomaeus Georgievitz (who was kept captive in the city by the Ottomans for a number of years) and said to be written on Constantine's tomb – declared that the Christians would one day retake the 'Red Apple', which was variously interpreted as referring to dominion over Constantinople, Rome, Rhodes, Granada or of the entire globe:

> Our Emperor shall come, he shall take the realm of the Gentiles [Kiafir], he shall take the Red Apple and capture it: if unto the seventh year the sword of the Unbeliever [Giaour] shall not come forth, he shall have lordship over them unto twelve years: he shall build houses, plant vineyards, hedge gardens about, and beget children; after twelve years from the time that he hath captured the Red Apple the sword of the Infidel shall come forth and put the Turk to flight.[5]

Istanbul, we should remember, had long been not just a city that the world's powers coveted but a place in which dreams of becoming powerful enough to dominate the world were conceived. And in the sixteenth century, the men and women of Kostantiniyye whispered that the Red Apple was indeed Istanbul and that ghoulish Christian forces would soon be back to punish them.

Just as Justinian's orb had been thought to protect the Christian city's territories (hence the horror when the statue fell in the fourteenth century, at the very moment when the Ottoman Turks were circling Constantinople), this daimonic Red Apple was thought to have generated a kind of force-field around Istanbul. In AD 1571 – in the early months of the millennium itself by some calculations – the Ottomans would tell one another that the Red Apple's curse was being realised.[6] The inexorable advance of Ottoman might was about to be stalled.

Ottoman fears would be realised at a naval engagement (regularly pounced upon by Western sources as an excuse for triumphalist, anti-oriental propaganda). Witness G. K. Chesterton endeavouring to set the scene for the great naval battle of Lepanto:

> White founts falling in the courts of the sun,
> And the Soldan of Byzantium is smiling as they run;
> There is laughter like the fountains in that face of all men feared,
> It stirs the forest darkness, the darkness of his beard,
> It curls the blood-red crescent, the crescent of his lips,
> For the inmost sea of all the earth is shaken with his ships.
> The cold queen of England is looking in the glass;
> The shadow of the Valois is yawning at the Mass;
> From evening isles fantastical rings faint the Spanish gun,
> And the Lord upon the Golden Horn is laughing in the sun.[7]

The slate grey churn of the Thames in London offers us a piece of the jigsaw puzzle that is the Battle of Lepanto and a clue to the geopolitics of maritime engagement at this time. Among the most successful river operators in London today are the Turk family. The Turks' shipbuilding records appear to go back to the sixteenth century, and a Thomas Turk is mentioned providing a ship for the defence of the realm in AD 1295.

The Great Comet of AD 1577 over Istanbul: an astronomer in the city is using a quadrant to determine the comet's trajectory

On her accession, Queen Elizabeth I of England had taken advice and invested heavily in her Royal Navy; London now boasted new dockyards at Woolwich and Deptford and the country a new navy to match. The Turk family may have provided skill and know-how in the construction of the English fleet. But such specialist boat-building skill would soon be needed back on the Bosphorus.

In AD 1570, the Sultan Selim II had invaded Cyprus. The surrender of the island's Christian rulers at Famagusta in 1571 spurred, in the West, the formation of the Holy League. England was conspicuous by her absence. With the freezing out of Elizabeth I in Pope Pius V's *Regnans in Excelsis* bull of 1570 (which excommunicated anyone who obeyed her), the English monarch had free rein to ally herself with the Ottomans against Catholic Europe. It helped that the English also enjoyed trading with the Ottomans and their allies – saltpetre and sugar came in to English ports while cloth, iron and armaments went out. Indeed in 1596 Elizabeth's forces supported Muslims in an attack on Cadiz – an event commemorated in the opening scene of Shakespeare's *The Merchant of Venice*.[8]

The Sultan and his men knew that they were no longer fighting a united Western Christendom. An opportunity seemed to have presented itself. The Ottoman fleet set sail west from the docks of Istanbul.

The Ottomans were soon engaging the ships of the Holy League off the western coast of Greece at Lepanto (Naupactus in Greek), and it was clear that a victory for the Sultan would decisively disrupt European trading patterns. On this watery battlefield there was much invested – international allegiances, commercial interest, religious belief. The Virgin Mary, the soldiers of the Holy League chirruped, was now back where she belonged, in the West – no longer protecting the walls of Constantinople, but tempted into the castles and cathedrals of Catholic Europe by intercession and by rosary prayers. Throughout the battle, sailors twisted their rosary beads (an Arabic tradition that possibly made its way from the East via Constantinople) and called on the Virgin to remember them. There was good reason to cry out for succour. The naval engagement at Lepanto on 7 October AD 1571 was the last major battle fought entirely by galleys: planks were dropped between the boats and pumped up or petrified soldiers would crawl or balance along them to fight. The bloodshed was enormous – in effect this was an infantry engagement on the sea. For many at Lepanto, drowning must have been a mercy.

In the heat of the battle – already strung out by eschatological expectation – the Ottomans misread the situation. Taking galleasses to be merchant ships they attacked and were then pounded by the guns on board. The sea was calm so the European cannon could do their worst. When the Turkish commander Müezzinzade Ali Pasha, the Grand Admiral of the Ottoman Fleet who had been entrusted with the 'Banner of the Caliphs', a green banner with the name of Allah embroidered in gold 28,900 times, was captured, he was beheaded and his severed head displayed on a pike – a brutal act that punctured the Ottomans' morale. The 'Banner of the Caliph' too was in Christian hands. As the Ottomans believed this to be a religious battle, it was entirely relevant that God, it seemed, 'had turned another way'. The Ottoman line collapsed and after just four hours the Holy League, led by Don John of Austria, pressed home their advantage.

The poet and playwright Miguel de Cervantes, a combatant at Lepanto who lost his left hand in the fighting, later wrote of 'that day, which was so fortunate to Christendom, for all nations were then undeceived of their error, in believing that the Turks were invincible by sea'.⁹ In the West there were huge celebrations. Some of the spoils of war seemed to confirm the debauched stereotype of the Ottoman court. When Ali Pasha's flagship was captured, it was found to hold 150,000 sequins.¹⁰ It was said that the Venetians threw their rings into the waters, a 'marriage' with the sea that had delivered into their hands 200 Ottoman ships; while in Istanbul the Sultan, in disgust, bagged up European women from the harem and drowned them in the Bosphorus.

The mood in Istanbul after the battle was, initially, tense. Twenty thousand had been killed, including a number of skilled sailors, shipwrights, technicians, doctors. Fearing a Western invasion, some in the city prepared to escape to Asia Minor. It was said that, on hearing the news while in Edirne, the Sultan was unable to sleep for three days. But swiftly Selim II's naval commanders set to, building a new fleet in the dry docks of Istanbul.¹¹ A major renovation of the Imperial Arsenal (Tersâne-i âmire) on the Golden Horn followed. So while the West spilt a good deal of ink commemorating its triumph, the Ottomans buckled down and harvested the Thracian forests, not for paper but for wood. Eight months after Lepanto, Selim II had built 150 galleys and 8 of his own galleasses following the lead of Don John.

This was a huge enterprise, funded perhaps by that conquest of Cyprus. A pact was reached on 7 March AD 1573 between the Venetians and the Ottomans, one condition being that Venice would pay for the cost of war against Cyprus: 300,000 ducats were to be handed over in three years and the island was formally ceded to the Ottomans by Venice. The authorities in Istanbul populated the island by shipping out a number of petty criminals and 'undesirables' from the city to start a new life.

Far from licking their wounds, the rulers of Istanbul were now, demonstrably, in a position of strength.

A generation before Lepanto, King Henry VIII had begun to favour Ottoman fashions for both grand ceremonial occasions and 'fancy dress' parties. He posed for portraits on distinctive Ottoman carpets. 'Turkeywork' was bought in and imitated: the carpets with their distinctive cloud-band, Ushak birds and leaves in a swastika formation were textile treasures often displayed on tables as they were thought too fine for feet. *Ebru* – the distinctive marbled Ottoman paper that would later be so popular in Venice – which used a technique developed in Central Asia, became vogueish in Europe as early as AD 1575. As Western powers such as England started to acquire their own empires, as the importance of India rose in the conversations of traders and diplomats alike in the chilly corners of continental Europe and as the Ottoman Turks proved that they could fail as well as succeed, the exoticism of the Near East felt like a safer toy with which to play. And Istanbul would be the prime location for this double-edged rapprochement.

✤

PART SEVEN

IMPERIAL CITY

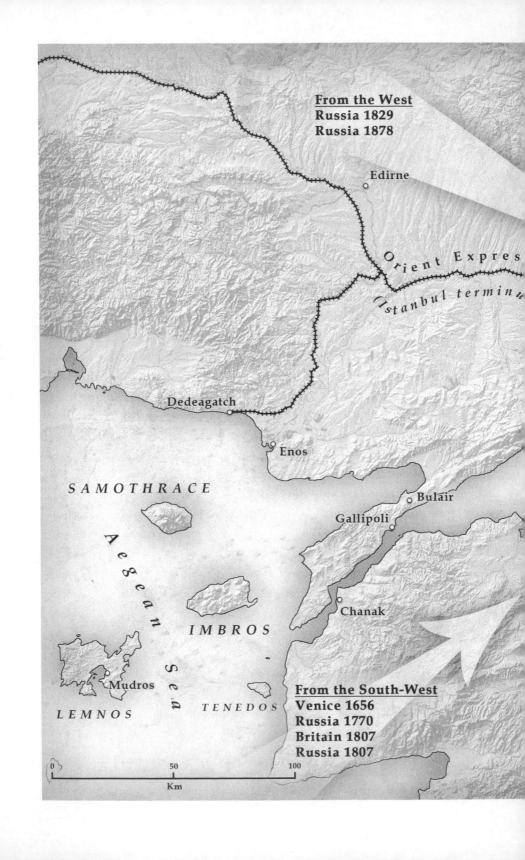

From the West
Russia 1829
Russia 1878

Edirne

O r i e n t   E x p r e s
(Istanbul terminu

Dedeagatch

Enos

S A M O T H R A C E

Bulair

Gallipoli

A e g e a n   S e a

Chanak

I M B R O S

Mudros

TENEDOS

LEMNOS

From the South-West
Venice 1656
Russia 1770
Britain 1807
Russia 1807

0   50   100

Km

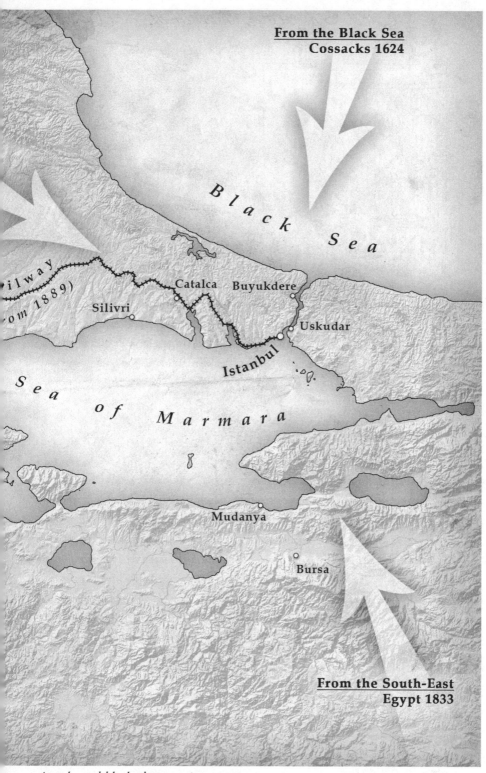

Attacks and blockades, AD 1624–c. 1900

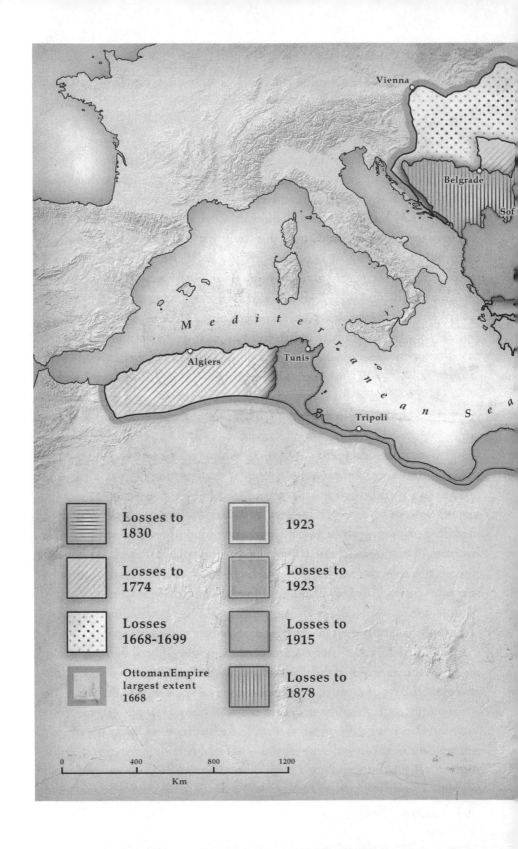

Vienna

Belgrade

Sof

M e d i t e r r a n e a n   S e a

Algiers   Tunis

Tripoli

	Losses to 1830		1923
	Losses to 1774		Losses to 1923
	Losses 1668-1699		Losses to 1915
	OttomanEmpire largest extent 1668		Losses to 1878

0   400   800   1200

Km

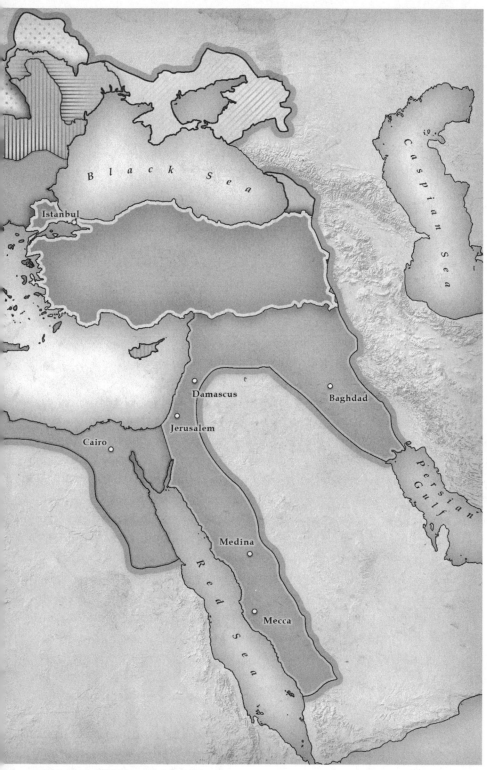

The Ottoman Empire, AD 1566–1923

CHAPTER 59

GUNPOWDER EMPIRES AND GUNNING PERSONALITIES: DRAGOMANS AND EUNUCHS

AD 1556
(963/4 IN THE ISLAMIC CALENDAR) ONWARDS

With this music and noisy crowds, this shah of the world
Made an excursion in Istanbul like the sun
He showed his beautiful countenance to all the people of Istanbul
He took their blessing and greeted them

GELIBOLULU MUSTAFA ALI, *SÛR*[1]

the city of Stamboul, the capital of the sultan of Rum, which is famous
for its largeness and extent, is not a tenth part of a tenth part of this city.

SUJAN RAI, *KHULASAT AL-TAWARIKH*[2]

On the banks of the River Ganges, above the holy city of Varanasi, there is a derelict palace. Staring mournfully south, it is one of Akbar the Great's summer homes, a link in a necklace of sandstone and brick that pulled together the lush Indian subcontinent in the name of Allah. One of the great Mughal emperors, Akbar (who reigned AD 1556–1605), was also one of its most open-minded – and most ambitious – earthly rulers.

A journey along the Grand Trunk Road today reveals the wells, lakes and mosques where Akbar stopped each year on his annual pilgrimage to Ajmer. But his grandest religious and territorial ambitions lay further south. By the end of Akbar's reign, Mughal territories spread from Gujarat on the west coast to the Bay of Bengal and from Lahore to central India. Mughal emperors would have themselves weighed on their birthdays: the gems, gold and silver on the other side of the balancing scale formed the present that they deemed appropriate to accept.[3] The pomegranates made of rubies and plates carved from solid jade that decorated the Emperor's dining tables in northern India were the Mughal equivalents of the

Ottoman's kilims and fine silk embroideries. The Mughal court was thick with opulence and self-belief.

The Ottoman acquisition of Jerusalem, Mecca and Medina, in AD 1517 would prove to be a thorn in Mughal flesh.[4] Both Mughal and Ottoman courts were Sunni. In close communication Mughal emperors and Ottoman sultans sent letters, embassies, gifts and spies to one another's palaces. The two cultures shared a Central Asian heritage (the Taj Mahal was inspired by the tomb of Tamerlane in Samarkand, built for the Turco-Mongol leader who had captured that Ottoman leader Bayezid I at the Battle of Ankara in AD 1402) and a devotion to Allah. Ottoman adventurers were respected in the subcontinent before the Mughals had arrived. Famed for their use of guns and muskets, Turkic dynasties ended up controlling Indian cities: one, Rajab Khan, was said to have built the castle at Surat in Turkic style. Some declared that a protégé of Sinan, Mimar Yusuf, helped to construct a number of the great Mughal structures at Agra and Delhi. The two courts sang the same elite songs, sharing the works of maestros such as the Persian poet Hafez Shirazi and the poet and musician 'Ali Sher Nava'i who wrote using the, now extinct, Central Asian language of Chagatai Turkic.[5] Travellers of the time reported being struck by familiar lines and melodies – the halls of Topkapı echoed the halls of Mughal Afghanistan. Given the propensity to tolerance of both imperial powers, this could have been a time of collaboration, an epoch of axis-shifting power when the Near East and Eastern Mediterranean might have united with the Indian subcontinent. Instead it was an age – with the Muslim millennium approaching – when these potent Islamic rulers needed to make their own marks in their own ways. The Mughal and Ottoman emperors circled one another like handsome, well-bred cats.

Akbar wanted to wrest control of Mecca from the Sultan. Brothers in God, their reigns coinciding in AD 1556–66, they were not brothers in arms. As Ottomans travelled from the salty brio of the Bosphorus to be with Allah at Mecca, Akbar's caravans came from the deserts – scattering monkeys along the road as Süleyman's men scattered starlings. Akbar's party stayed in Mecca for four years, from 1576 to 1580. The Mughal's caravan was said to include 600,000 gold and silver rupees and 12,000 kaftans, and included, at a respectful distance, the poor Muslims to whom the Emperor had given the funds to make the long pilgrimage.

Mughal nobility visited Istanbul. One prince set up home in Üsküdar, but blotted his copybook when he boasted that he was descended from the Ottoman's legendary enemy Tamerlane. Diplomatic channels were though firmly open: the Ottomans would come to petition the Mughals in Delhi. A precedent was set of sharing luscious, conversation-stopping gifts. From India to Istanbul came furniture inspired by the intricate Peacock Throne, and from Istanbul to Nadir Shah (an Afghan-Iranian insurgent, who briefly invaded India) a bespoke dagger decorated with emeralds and rubies.[6]

There was politic reason for public friendship. Both Delhi and Istanbul were aware of the ambition of a third 'gunpowder empire', the Shia Safavids who had come to control much of modern-day Iran and the Caucasus – and who, with the help of Ottoman munitions experts, had armed themselves with 500 cannons and 12,000 musketeers in response to a crushing defeat at the hands of Ottoman forces at the beginning of the sixteenth century. For 150 years Istanbul kept a weather-eye on the Safavids' ambition and on their allegiances. Both powers lost and re-captured Baghdad a number of times – a border finally being drawn in AD 1639, which still survives, in part, in north-west Iran and south-east Turkey. Istanbul, the Safavid capitals Tabriz and Isfahan and the Mughal strongholds of Agra, Delhi and Lahore benefited from an energising urban rivalry. The Mughal and Safavid rulers thrived on visible splendour: what would Akbar 'the Great' think today of the rubbish around the splendid Agra Fort, some of his palaces shabby and deserted, and the Safavid rulers of their bulldozed colonnades, where miniaturists once plied their art, while today Topkapı's gardens are daily manicured?

Economically, in the sixteenth and seventeenth centuries, India had the upper hand, but the Ottoman Sultan was still recognised as the great Caliph. A letter from the Mughal Emperor Humayun to the Sublime Porte at Istanbul declared, 'Gifts of sincere wishes to your exalted majesty the possessor of the dignity of Khilafat, the pole of the sky of greatness and fortune, the consolidator of the foundations of Islam. Your name is engraved on the seal of greatness and in your time the Khilafat has been carried to perfection . . .'[7]

Just as Constantinople had been a lodestone for Christians for 500 years, Kostantiniyye was now one such for Sunni Muslims.

*

The Ottomans cemented their enviable spiritual position with a mixture of display, diplomacy and firepower. Essential to their work was the dragoman. The word dragoman has prehistoric Hittite origins. A translator, fixer, ambassador rolled into one, the dragoman was a fundamentally Eastern creature. But with the vigorous operation of the *devşirme*, the 'harvesting' of the young men of subject nations for use as soldiers or imperial administrators, most dragomans in Istanbul had in fact started out in life as Christian boys from the West. They came from places as various as Birmingham, Venice and the Balkans, as well as from Egypt and Jerusalem. Part government official, part privateer, the dragomans might often have been self-serving, self-advancing and in service of their own country, but they represented a cosmopolitan skein of influence centred on Istanbul. The convert Ali Ufki (originally a Polish slave), who arrived in Istanbul in the second half of the seventeenth century, introduced tunes to the Sufic music of the court from the Genevan Psalter and one of the last dragomans in the city, Johannes Kolmodin, in residence 1917–31, originally came from Uppsala – that little Swedish town which had lovingly preserved the oldest Gothic Bible.

One of the critical attributes of the dragoman was a facility with language. Most dragomans were polylingual, with a command of Turkish, Persian, German, Armenian, Dutch, Italian, English – lists that would make today's Foreign Office recruiters salivate. Their skills would have been similar to those of Early Bronze Age traders and settlers who once heard as many as eight different languages at beach harbours along the Bosphorus and the Dardanelles. The Venetians set up a house in Istanbul, the *bailo*, where apprentice dragomans could be trained for up to fifteen years. These cadets were called *giovani di lingua*, language youths.[8] One, Giovanni Piron, was simply not adept enough linguistically and so at the age of seventy-five was still listed on the *bailo* payroll as an apprentice; and there were others like him. These trainee dragomans lived only with other men. The whole business of dragomanry was intensely competitive. Alliances were made and broken with alacrity, favours owed, information passed. Even if they started out as slaves – for example Giacomo Nores, captured when Cyprus was taken in AD 1573 (Giacomo's aunt, also seized on Cyprus, converted to Islam and her daughters ended up as sultanas to the Sultan Mehmed III) – the sons of the great dragoman dynasties could end up working for the Venetians, French, British, Dutch and Habsburgs and the Sultan all at the same time. In the 'Reigning City', as it was coming to be called, the dragomans both circulated news and made it.

Evidence for Istanbul's dragomans is slowly emerging from cardboard boxes in libraries and the backrooms of embassies across Asia and Europe. In the twenty-first century curators have turned up cartons of 'Old Turkish Documents', missives from Kostantiniyye that look set to contain historical gold.[9] From the sixteenth century onwards, Kostantiniyye had been the prized international posting (the *bailo* of Venice set up shop here in AD 1454, the French Embassy in 1535, the English in 1583, the Dutch in 1612, with Sweden, Poland and Russia following suit in the eighteenth century).[10] Originally based in Stamboul itself, embassies soon clustered across the Golden Horn while Galata became a crucible of a kind of vagabond national and personal advancement. Many Greek dragomans in particular (often known as Phanariots as many of them lived in the Phanar district) progressed to great heights, becoming the Sultan's Grand Dragoman or Grand Dragoman of the Fleet and, between 1716 and 1821, ruling as princes over Moldavia and Wallachia, modern-day Romania. Some dragomans converted to Islam; others such as an Englishman called Finch from Chorley suddenly appear in the city – their backstory and fate a mystery. Many dragomans communicated with shady individuals, of whom we hear in the official correspondence of the Sultan – men described as 'our unnamed servant', who are clearly secret agents. One of the hazards of being a Muslim spy or a dragoman double-agent operating beyond Ottoman borders was the real danger of being exposed if it came to light that you were circumcised. The fraught writings of 'Mahmut the Arabian' in Paris reveal this very particular kind of penis anxiety.[11] There were other hazards. As men who moved around Istanbul, many were exposed to the plague of 1573 (all pathogens led to the New Rome – epidemics were frequent in the city), and a number died in the Venetian *bailo*'s home. The life of the dragoman was perilous and exhilarating.

The dragomans were not the only immigrants to thrive: from the late sixteenth century the black African eunuch, typically from Ethiopia or elsewhere in East Africa, would come to have enormous influence in both domestic and international politics. After AD 1595 the chief black eunuch, Kızlar Ağası, had the right to administer the mosques of Medina, Mecca and Jerusalem – and the revenues that those holy destinations generated.

So, just as eunuchs had been a feature of the streets of Christian Constantinople, now they would be found, with equal mettle, in the Muslim city. By the end of Sultan Murad IV's reign in AD 1640 there were reported to be a thousand eunuchs in the imperial harem.

The eunuch in charge of the harem in Istanbul lived in a splendid series of interconnecting apartments, warmly lit with bronze lanterns and approached by a narrow court decorated with ornate tiles (the very flowers in honour of which the eunuchs were often named – hyacinth, narcissus). The doors were decorated with jewels, and over a gilded entrance to the harem were written words from the Qur'an: 'Do not enter the house of the Prophet except when you are allowed.'[12] Lesser eunuchs were crammed into windowless stalls above. The ruling eunuchs seem frequently to have chosen their own successors and had sufficient heft and influence to bring private armies of Mamluks into the city.

Many – particularly these dragomans and other foreign supplicants in Istanbul – muttered bitterly that because of their close access to the Sultan the eunuchs and women of the harem always enjoyed 'the last word'. A number of the Valide Sultan's closest ladies-in-waiting were Jewish and did indeed control access to her (extremely influential) ear. Edward Barton, representing both England and France at the end of the sixteenth century, moaned that his power of persuasion was diluted by the presence of one such woman, an accursed 'Mediatrix'.[13]

Thus it was to eunuchs and to female servants – using the information passed on to them by their chief dragoman – that the wilier heads of the state of the day would turn when they needed to do international business in early-modern Istanbul. Tongues started to wag that the 'Turk' women and their de-sexed guards had unnatural power. Come the seventeenth century and Istanbul would be described as a city ruled by a 'Sultanate of Women'.

CHAPTER 60

❖

THE SULTANATE OF WOMEN

AD 1546–c. 1650
(952–c. 1060 IN THE ISLAMIC CALENDAR)

> You are young
> And may be tempted, and these Turkish dames
> (Like English mastiffs that increase their fierceness
> By being chained up), from the restraint of freedom,
> If lust once fire their blood from a fair object,
> Will run a course the fiends themselves would shake at
> To enjoy their wanton ends.
>
> PHILIP MASSINGER, *THE RENEGADO* (AD 1624)[1][2]

Turn right past the chapel of New College, Oxford, into the chilly cloisters and at waist height there is a memorial plaque to Robert Dallam, who died in AD 1609 while installing the college's organ. Dallam's body is buried under the flagstones. If you know Dallam's family history you can understand why this craftsman died in harness.

Robert's father Thomas was a master organ-builder. His instruments were the toast of Europe, and in AD 1599 Thomas was sent by Elizabeth I, one of his organs tenderly packed in the hold of a galleon named *Hector*, to deliver the instrument as a gift to Sultan Mehmed III.[3] There was a horrible hitch when 'all glewinge failed' in Istanbul's heat and humidity. The (water) organ, which was prebuilt and then reconstructed on site, could be played by hand or by clockwork. Dallam accompanied the royal gift, overseeing its installation in the seraglio of the new, state-of-the-art Topkapı Palace. He wrote, slack-jawed, about what he witnessed on arrival: 'then they toulde me that yf I would staye the Grand Sinyor would give tow wyfes, either tow of his Concubines or els tow virgins of the beste I Could Chuse my selfe, in Cittie or contrie.' Elsewhere in *The*

Diary of Thomas Dallam we hear that there were among these women, by Dallam's own admission, 'verie prettie ones in deede . . . that sighte did please me wondrous well'.[4]

The contents of the harem might have been a surprise to Dallam, but one of the women he observed as exotic marvels had, in fact, already been in direct contact with his Queen. The story of the Sultan's harem is a reminder of how vigilant we should be when charting Istanbul's history: we must start by looking from the inside out rather than from the outside in.

A female operator in the highly decorated, heavily protected harem space was Nurbanu, the Valide Sultan, the mother of the Sultan – a position she held from AD 1574 until her death in 1583 – and hence a woman with unusual status and influence. Nurbanu almost certainly started life as Kale Kartanou, an Orthodox Christian from Cyprus. Described by ambassadors of the day as both exceptionally beautiful and exceptionally intelligent, she inspired gossip and rumour; it was claimed for years after her death that she was originally Cecilia Venier-Baffo, the illegitimate daughter of Nicolò Venier, Lord of Paros, and of Violante Baffo, a Venetian noblewoman. The confusion is understandable because Nurbanu was, in all likelihood, kidnapped by the Sultan's Grand Admiral Barbarossa around the age of twelve, as part of his package of fresh female meat destined to be presented to Selim II in the capital.[5][6]

Nurbanu appears to have accompanied Selim east to Konya with the royal household where she caught the Prince's eye. Soon she was bearing child after child; daughters at first and then finally one son, Murad III, in AD 1546. Clearly Selim's delight, Nurbanu was brought back to Topkapı and installed as his Haseki – his favourite. As the years went by her network increased, aided by those of her daughters who had free access outside the harem; married women who could operate as 'informants, couriers and political strategists'.[7]

Nurbanu seemed blatantly to promote the interests of Venice over the other players of the day in Istanbul, Pisa and Genoa. It was even rumoured that the Genoese had ordered her death by poisoning. The degree to which her favour was sought by the international community is clear from the thank-you notes that the Valide sent: for a bale of silk, for twenty-one robes made of two-coloured damask, for nineteen robes made of cloth of gold and for two dogs (unwelcome because of their size and coat-lengths).[8] She corresponds too with Catherine de' Medici. Hard and soft power was in play here: Catherine was so very taken by the embroidery skills on the gifts which she received from Istanbul that she proceeded to import a number of high-class Turkish seamstresses to decorate the soft furnishings of her own households in France. (Catherine's patronage of the arts, including those from the East, saw her described as the 'new Artemisia' after the Anatolian Queen Artemisia II – a dynastic descendant of the Artemisia I who had fought against Byzantine interests for the Persians, she who had built Caria's mausoleum for her brother-husband Mausolos back in the fourth century BC.)

Exploiting her rights to invest in property and to secure favour with Allah, Nurbanu installed the first library established by a woman in a splendid mosque in Istanbul – the mosque itself described by contemporaries as a 'mountain of light'.[9] The concubine built another mosque, the Atik Valide Cami, above Üsküdar. Although already the mark of high rank for women, building projects on quite this scale had rarely been seen before. Nurbanu's style has a tinge of that of a Theodora: in her establishments there were soup kitchens for the poor and homeless and hostels for travellers both wealthy and destitute.

The death of Sultan Selim II, in AD 1574, drunk, bathing in the harem, did not in any way clip Nurbanu's wings. She oversaw the construction of a series of baths across the city, including one with adjoining facilities for men and women close to her mosque.[10] Her baths at the entrance to the Grand Bazaar are still in use. Nurbanu ended her days in her private palace in the Yenikapı Quarter – close to the archaeological dig where Istanbul's first prehistoric inhabitant has recently been found. On her death, the Valide Sultan freed 150 of her female slaves, leaving each woman a thousand gold coins. Nurbanu is an exemplar of proximity to power bringing power. This harem girl was so respected that, atypically, the Sultan married her. The Valide Sultan is still buried with her consort in the *türbe* or tomb of Selim II in the garden to the south of the Ayasofya.

The involvement of harem women in international affairs did not stop after Nurbanu's death. Inspired perhaps by his father Selim II's adoration of Nurbanu, Murad III gave a pre-eminent position to his favourite, Safiye (meaning 'pure' or 'pleasing'), with whom he lived in the city of Manisa – long a training ground for Ottoman crown princes. Arriving at the age of thirteen from a village in the mountains of Albania and sold on as a concubine, Safiye quickly made her mark. It was rumoured, quite credibly it seems, that sick of her mother-in-law's oedipal interference (for example, filling the harem with the most beautiful and tempting women from the slave market, with some success as her son sired 103 children),[11] she was implicated in Nurbanu's inexplicably swift death. As with Nurbanu, a hot sexual relationship seems to have evolved into a strategic political one.

One Englishman in the city, John Sanderson, secretary at the English Embassy, sent back a report that Safiye had, while walking in the seraglio, 'espyed a number of boates upon the river hurrying together'. She then heard that it was the Vizier, bustling out to do 'justice upon certain chabies, that is, whoores. Shee, taking displeasure, sent word and advised the eunuch Bassa that her sonne [absent on campaign] had left him to govern the citie and not to devoure the women . . .'[12] In AD 1596 while her son Mehmed III was on campaign she released all the prisoners in Galata and Stamboul, holding on to only those who committed 'notorious' crimes.[13] Safiye donated her own money to the empire's war effort in 1597 – her contribution carved out for the refurbishment of cannon and the purchase of pack animals.

Safiye and Elizabeth I of England, the concubine and the Queen, struck up a relationship, ferrying gifts to one another. Elizabeth was said to have sent her Ottoman correspondent a large black English cat that stalked the harem until it died of natural causes. The items became increasingly ostentatious: Elizabeth shipped Safiye a beautiful gilded covered coach.

Safiye's patronage and protection really mattered. Having received a bejewelled portrait of Elizabeth I, she ordered a letter to be written to the English Queen in AD 1593, consolingly, conspiratorially: 'I can repeatedly mention Her Highness's gentility and praise at the footdust of His Majesty . . . the sovereign who has Alexander's place . . . and I shall endeavour for Her aims.'[14] Once her own son Mehmed III had been crowned, she wrote on his behalf to Elizabeth, who had petitioned for the freedom of Englishmen captured as slaves in North Africa: 'Your letter has arrived and reached [us] . . . God-willing, action will be taken according to what you said.' The chatty, intimate missive continues in a wonderfully mother-hen tone, assuring Elizabeth that Safiye, by then Valide Sultan, had admonished her son for forgetting the details of a treaty between the two maritime powers. Safiye adds, 'May you too always be firm in friendship. God-willing, may [our friendship] never die.'[15] Safiye sends clothes, two gold-embroidered bath towels, three handkerchiefs and a tiara with her note. Pearls, actual and of wisdom, were exchanged. On unpacking, the absence of the pearl and ruby tiara from this particular gift bequest was extremely irksome to a peevish Elizabeth; diplomats rushed, the item was recovered and the looming international crisis was averted.

And then comes a final, historic gem, revealing a surprisingly intimate connection and understanding. Safiye, via her Jewish maidservant Esperanza Malchi (who would end up out of favour and cut into myriad pieces, her cubes of flesh processed through the streets on dagger tips), asked Elizabeth for some make-up:

> On account of your majesty's being a woman ... [t]here are to be found in your kingdom rare distilled waters of every kind for the face and odiferous oils for the hands. Your majesty would favour me by sending some of them by my hand for this most serene Queen; by my hand as, being articles for ladies, she does not wish them to pass through other hands.[16]

The relationship between these women, across 4,000 miles of ocean, speaks of the relationship between Ottoman and European culture at this time. We should remember that while Ottoman fortunes were enjoying their golden age, Europe was both colonised and coloniser.

However close the relationship between the high-ranking inhabitants of cities such as Istanbul and London, the ferment of activity in the East sparked a counter-reaction in the West. Constantinople appears in both Shakespeare's *Henry V* and his *Timon of Athens* and the Ottomans throughout *Othello*. In popular plays the Turk appears again and again: in Thomas Kyd's *The Tragedie of Solimon and Perseda* (probably written by Kyd c. AD 1588), Fulke Grevilles's *The Tragedy of Mustapha* (1609), John Mason's *The Turke. A worthie tragedie* (1610) and Thomas Goffe's *The Raging or Couragious Turke, or Amurath the First* (performed by Oxford University students c. 1613–18). The Venetian Ottaviano Bon, who had served as the representative of Venetian interests in Istanbul, wrote a quasi-ethnographic work, *The Sultan's Seraglio: An Intimate Portrait of Life at the Ottoman Court*, which described among other things the women's preparation rituals for sex with the Sultan and was published to an eager audience in English in 1625. We hear from Bon that 'These virgins, immediately after their coming into the Seraglio, are made Turks: which is done by using this ceremony only; to hold up their forefinger, and say these words; law illawheh illaw Allawh, Muhammed resoul Allawh. That is, there is no God but God alone, and Mahomet is the messenger of God.'[17]

The sorties of Ottoman forces into the Western Mediterranean and Europe and the activity of pirates from the coast of North Africa to Cornwall (between seventy and eighty Christian vessels were taken by Barbary pirates each year from AD 1592 to 1609) nourished the idea of 'the Turk' as a libidinous bogeyman of the Western world. In pulpits throughout England, fervent prayers were raised to protect against 'the incursions and invasions of the said savage and most cruel enemies the Turks' and 'to repress the rage and violence of Infidels, who by all tyranny and cruelty labour utterly to root out not only true Religion, but also the very name and memory of Christ our only Saviour, and all Christianity; and if they should prevail against the Isle of Malta, it is uncertain what further peril might follow to the rest of Christendom'.[18]

Even King James VI in Scotland had been moved to write a poem celebrating the victory of the Holy League at Lepanto, that 'bloodie battell bolde',

> Which fought was in Lepantoes gulfe
> Betwixt the baptiz'd race,
> And circumcised Turband Turkes.[19]

But the irony of course was that Kılıç Ali Pasha – a commander at Lepanto who made it back to Kostantiniyye with a flag of the Maltese knights – was in fact an Italian from Bari. A lingua franca of the Ottoman court was, up until the late seventeenth century, Serbo-Croat.[20] Similarly, while some Englishmen were taken by force as prisoners of war, others seemed delighted to be transported to the East – and then to stay. The eunuch Hasan Ağa for example had started out life as one Samson Rowlie from Great Yarmouth. The Ingiliz Mustafa was originally a Mr Campbell from Inverary. When Charles II sent a Captain Hamilton to retrieve Englishmen enslaved off the North African coast they refused to come back. They were happy Muslim converts who had partaken 'of the prosperous Successe of the Turks'. Hamilton's own opinion was that they had changed the name of their God because of the kinds of women they were now meeting: 'Such ladies are generally very beautiful.'[21]

In the Anglophone world, 'to turn Turk' reeks of sex. As late as 1910, a year after the Imperial Harem in Topkapı had been officially disbanded, the designs for the illustrations of the Baedeker guide to Istanbul still showed the imperial seraglio as a blank. It seems there was long a misunderstanding or conflation of the Italian *serrare* – to lock up or enclose – and the Turco-Persian *saray* – palace. In the minds of the English and of continental Europeans the Grand Seraglio was a monumental, sexy, tantalising taboo.[22]

And here we meet a trope of Istanbul that will endure well into the twentieth century, a characteristic whose seeds were, arguably, sown when men looked east from ancient Megara, while others from Greece wrote of the heady, sensuous reputation of Byzantion. However muscular the actual political operations of the inhabitants of the Ottoman imperial palace, what the West chose to amplify – or to pursue – were its rapacious appetites and erotic promise.

CHAPTER 61

THE JANISSARIES

c. AD 1370–1826
(c. 769–1242 IN THE ISLAMIC CALENDAR)

We are the butterflies of the Divine Light . . . our spring is inexhaustible.

CEVAD PASHA[1]

[A] motley group of boys and old men, without any settled uniform except for [a] large, greasy, very awkward felt hat, or bonnet . . . It is so ungainly that it is continually falling off. The colonels are . . . distinguished by most extraordinary helmets which are so tall and top-heavy, that they are sometimes obliged to keep them on their heads with both hands . . .

REV. ROBERT WALSH, NARRATIVE OF A RESIDENCE
AT CONSTANTINOPLE (AD 1828)[2]

Lords of the day, they ruled with uncontrolled insolence in Constantinople, their appearance portraying the excess of libertinism; their foul language; their gross behaviour; their enormous turbans; their open vests; their bulky sashes filled with arms; their weighty sticks; rendering them objects of fear and disgust. Like moving columns, they thrust everybody from their path without any regard of age or sex, frequently bestowing durable marks of anger or contempt.

ADOLPHUS SLADE, RECORD OF TRAVELS IN TURKEY,
GREECE ETC. (AD 1833)[3]

What the gusset-plucking Western sources did not get wrong was the Ottoman lust for territory.[4]

Back in the fourteenth century, when Ottoman warriors found that they were acquiring more and more land, they realised that they needed not just intimidating, turf-grabbing warriors, but infantrymen to secure and to patrol territories. Since the clash between the Abbasids and the Umayyads, sultans had been allowed to claim one-fifth of war captives as their own. The system continued vigorously until the seventeenth century. Now recruited by means of the *devşirme*, these special soldiers of the Sultan had become a major force in the city. To understand Istanbul in the 350 years that followed its conquest by the Ottomans, we have to get to know the Janissaries and to appreciate that from Budapest to Baghdad, from Edirne to Crete, they were a domineering presence.

The arrival of new Janissary recruits in the city must have been an extraordinary sight. Divided into groups of 100, 150 or 200, these 'herds' of Christian boys, most aged around sixteen, were dressed in red and in a conical hat (to discourage escape) and were then marched towards the city from their villages and hamlets, typically from what is now Greece, Serbia, Bosnia or Albania. Many were brought into Istanbul along the Egnatian Way. Clothing and transportation costs were charged to their families.

The young men were chosen for strength and biddability. One physician recommended the selection of boys bearing scars, on the grounds that this was proof that they were happy to fight. This harvesting has been held up by Western commentators as symptomatic of the Ottomans' callous nature; it is still the subject of popular, disapproving TV programmes in ex-Ottoman countries such as Romania. Some in the *devşirme* were indeed physically torn from their mothers' arms. The villagers of Sis in the Caucasus mounted a raid on Istanbul to try to snatch their boys back, while in AD 1626 a total of 404 captives en route to Istanbul mysteriously 'vanished'; other villages bravely mounted both humanitarian and legal claims to prevent their sons being taken. Nonetheless, for many the *devşirme* was a fact of life that ensured, for at least one son in the family, training, survival and relief from the *jizya*, the tax that all non-Muslims in an Islamic state, the *dhimmi* (the Arabic means 'protected ones'), had to pay. Bosnian Muslims, for example, had actively requested permission to become Janissary stock.[5]

After the route march towards Istanbul, often policed by fellow Christians, the boys were allowed to rest for three days with a Christian family. They were then given a physical inspection, registered and circumcised. After seven to ten years' training – the brightest within the palace complex of Istanbul itself, but more likely with village families in Anatolia

– they were brought back into the city. Here they typically started on the bottom rung – hard labour in the mines, building ships, repairing buildings. When we look at the splendid architectural survivals of Ottoman architecture, we might imagine a Janissary's hands and the sweat of his brow. Some of these boys were trained in gun- and arrow-making, leatherwork, sewing, music, the preparation of the Sultan's sherbets.[6] Housed in wooden barracks – in time in both the Old Barracks and New Barracks – their quarters were their world. (The New Barracks, close to today's Grand Bazaar, could be found near the Orta (Ahmediye) Mosque and the so-called Meat Square, which had once been a Byzantine forum.) Here there were 'arbours' – even Janissaries were allowed gardens. Before major campaigns Janissary soldiers jostled en masse to perform prayers together close to the hippodrome. At the beginning of the seventeenth century there were as many as 35,000 to 40,000 Janissaries attached to Istanbul. So, excluding members of their households – common-law wives, children, servants – Janissaries and their affiliates represented a full 20 per cent of the city.

It had been the Janissaries camped out in Mehmed the Conqueror's fortress of Rumeli Hisarı – originally called Boğazkesen, the cut-throat or strait-cutter – who used passing ships as target practice on which to test the range of their cannon. Then, once they had helped to breach the walls of Constantinople, Janissary units were given control of Haghia Eirene, the Church of Peace, to use as an arsenal. One of the Janissaries' responsibilities was firefighting. Given the timber-built nature of Kostantiniyye (by the end of nineteenth century as many as eight fires per month ripped through the city, devouring homes and in particular warehouses where they could take hold undetected) as early as AD 1572 homeowners in Istanbul were told to keep a barrel of water for dousing flames. Where water failed, amulets were thought to be efficacious. In mosques, shrines, homes and streets, the city's population responded to these 'acts of God' with a combination of prayer, pagan practices and Islamic piety. The fires became so frequent that some started to suspect the Janissaries of starting blazes so that they could extort bribes before agreeing to put them out.

Originally contained strictly within their barracks, in the course of the seventeenth century 'the harvested' intermarried and grew in confidence, integrating with the rest of the city and becoming financially more independent as a result. It was Janissaries who had triggered the events

Janissary soldiers displaying their infamously elaborate headgear, sketched in the sixteenth century

that made Istanbul the headquarters of Europe's longest-lasting Caliphate in AD 1517, and in 1622 they forced Sultan Osman II to the prison at Yedikule Fortress where he was executed. After the so-called New Order army had been rehoused in new barracks in Üsküdar in 1799, Janissaries who opposed the New Order reforms burnt the structure to the ground.[7] Rebuilt by Abdülmecid I, this hospital complex was then used by Florence Nightingale during the Crimean War – the Scutari story with which we are familiar.

Not only would these captive slaves come to command enviable salaries and rations, but a number became Istanbul's entrepreneurs. It is easy to see how – well connected, well travelled, well trained, the Sultan's chosen ones – they were able to flourish. As well as their official roles, as guards of the woollen cloth, of the bakeries, of state sheep, as firemen, nightwatchmen and policemen, on the side Janissaries started to import grapes from Izmir, butter from Baghdad, rice from Anatolia, honey from the Balkans. Meat too. As logistics experts, the Janissaries organised the transport of livestock in to provision the city, and seemed to take quickly to the job of butchering. Starting at the slaughterhouses by Yedikule, the meat distribution acquired its own ritual. Those who suggest that killing desensitises to all loss of life would have a field day with Janissary psychology.

Each Janissary soldier was allowed a daily mutton ration of 60 dirhems, that's around 6.5 ounces.[8] So that would have meant 70,000 to 100,000 sheep brought into the streets of Istanbul every year, just to feed the Janissary Corps. On the packed-earth streets that ran through much of the city (frequently unpaved, the summer battle with street dust was a characteristic of Istanbul), flocks regularly had to be shooed away from drinking at sacred fountains. Fifteen tallow candles per soldier per week was a by-product of the regular animal slaughter (beeswax candles were reserved for the Sultan's enjoyment). From the windows of their barracks, soldiers could be heard practising their percussive music, using the cymbals, single kettledrums, triangles and tambourines that would eventually become all the rage and be adopted as 'Turkish' music in the works of Mozart, Haydn and Beethoven and within regular European orchestras. The Janissaries' ceremonial mace would be tossed in the air as they paraded through the city, a Muslim warrior practice that is the precursor of the routines of American drum majorettes. The Turks, before they converted to Islam, had a firm belief in the power of music. For them the cosmos itself was created by sound; music had the power to heal both distress and disease, which was why many Bektashi *tekkes* had rooms devoted to music therapy. Janissary soldiers added to the pulsingly rich soundscape of Istanbul.

The Janissaries helped to maintain the security, the smooth running and the chronicle-worthy theatricality of the Ottoman state. Boggle-eyed visitors to Istanbul often described the spectacle of Janissaries en masse, sashed and booted, ostrich plumes waving above their towering conical hats. By the end of the seventeenth century no longer only Christians (Muslim conscripts or volunteers found there were plenty of dead men's shoes to fill), those considered to be particularly sharp were trained up within the Enderun – a boarding and training school at Topkapı – which ran a 'talented and gifted' programme. But as well as servants of the Sultan the Janissaries were also a law unto themselves. In AD 1604 Galata's inhabitants complained that the Janissaries were kidnapping merchants.

And when there was revolt in Istanbul, the unrest spread like bracken-fire through the districts inhabited by the Janissary Corps. In AD 1622, 1632, 1648, 1651, 1655 and 1656 there were uprisings. The Janissaries (who when accused of wrongdoing were judged by their superiors rather than an outside court) were increasingly given unflattering collective labels – 'the mob', 'ravishers', 'extortioners'.

But typically the spilling of blood was officially sanctioned. Outside the Topkapı Palace was the Ibret Taşları – The Example Stone – on which were displayed the heads of those who had displeased the Sultan. Janissaries were the heavies charged with the beheadings. On the spikes of the walls of the Yedikule Fortress men could be left impaled until they died. The highly educated Janissaries were the Sultan's protection mob; in AD 1605 it was Janissaries who had destroyed the organ lovingly brought over by Thomas Dallam from England, the instrument considered inappropriately infidel for the sacred space of the Topkapı.

Whatever their civic and ceremonial function, the Janissary forces first and foremost had a job of work to do – to make real those dreams of global Ottoman control. By the second half of the seventeenth century the Ottoman Empire had reached its greatest extent. But it wanted more. In July AD 1683, 12,000 Janissaries marched, rode and ran towards Vienna.

CHAPTER 62

✧

THE GREAT SIEGE OF VIENNA

AD 1683
(1094/5 IN THE ISLAMIC CALENDAR)

... I will make myself your Master, pursue you from East to West, and extend my Majesty to the end of the Earth ... I have resolved without retarding of time, to ruin both you and your People, to take the German Empire according to my pleasure, and to leave in the Empire a Commemoration of my dreadful Sword, that it may appear to all, it will be a pleasure to me to give a publick establishment of my Religion, and to pursue your Crucified God, whose Wrath I fear not, nor his coming to your Assistance, to deliver you out of my hands. I will according to my pleasure put your Sacred Priests to the Plough, and expose the Brests of your Matrons to be Suckt by Dogs and other Beasts.

MEHMED IV, DECLARATION OF WAR ON EMPEROR LEOPOLD[1]

Veni, vidi, Deus vicit.

JAN SOBIESKI, LETTER TO POPE INNOCENT XI[2]

The walls of Vienna are disappointing. A scrubby section is just about identifiable[3] in between a travel agent and a post office. Most of the medieval and early modern remains can be glimpsed only when there is work on the city's sewerage system or when fibre-optic cables are laid.

But a discovery in the cellar of the nearby town of Tulln-on-Danube in early 2015 tells a more immediately vivid story. When land was being cleared to build a new shopping centre here from 2006, unexpected evidence came to light. Three feet or so beneath street level there was a complete camel skeleton – and not just any old quadruped but a Bactrian–dromedary hybrid, the first complete camel skeleton to be found in Europe. It had been squashed in with household rubbish – plates, pens, flagons – and the archaeologists' dating shows that this well-kept and rather splendid animal died soon after the AD 1683 Ottoman siege of Vienna.

So what was this camel's story? The bone evidence suggests that it would have been ridden into battle rather than used as a beast of burden. Had it run away from the Ottoman camp or battlefield? Been captured by locals? The fact that the animal has been buried rather respectfully, head back, bones uncut, shows that it was not butchered by a retreating Ottoman army – or by the hungry Viennese – but was allowed to live its natural life-span as a kind of curiosity, the most exotic of trophies.

It is a juicy archaeological find, but that camel is also an allegory for this moment in historical time. In AD 1683 the Ottomans, though still wildly fascinating and militarily impressive, were no longer the authors of their own story, no longer on an upward trajectory of invasion and cultural dominance.

The Ottoman assault on the West began in Istanbul with a bit of folk-theatre. Outside the Topkapı Palace was erected the *tuğ* – the Ottoman red and gold poled standard topped with a horse's tail. That horse-hair streaming in the salt of a Bosphoran breeze meant that the Sultan was calling his people to arms, as he would have done centuries before from the chill of his nomad's tent. In preparation the Ottomans had already built bridges, repaired roads, gathered in supplies of ammunition from across their empire.[4]

Collecting outside the city on a requisitioned meadow, the Ottoman forces were meticulously organised. Those great war percussives, kettle-drums stretched with camel-hide and big enough to fit five men inside, drummed up the fighting spirit. On some campaigns there were reports of so many candles being lit around Ottoman armies waiting to leave the city or on arrival at the battlefield that a rose garden of lights appeared. Confident in their use of gunpowder to destroy walls and to blow up ships and men, the Ottomans would also release coloured gunpowder before battle, the 'fireworks' used to celebrate the circumcision of princes back in the Topkapı Palace.[5] Western sources described the 'triumphant pompe unspeakable' that was associated with any departure on campaign. If the army returned victorious then horses were plumed, men, women and children were allowed to line the streets, wild animals were sometimes processed, even the poorest lit lanterns outside their homes. Hundreds of sheep (occasionally cattle too) were slaughtered, and brocades, velvets and damasks were hung from windows or shops or laid under the feet of the Sultan and his men. 'It is impossible for onely man to be exalted to a loftier degree of sublimation, then this Pagan when triumphal.'[6]

After the vigorous intercontinental expansion of the sixteenth century, Ottoman ambition had plateaued. Now the Sultan had his compass set firmly west. He wanted to take Vienna, a significant prize – which had escaped the Ottomans in AD 1529 when their attack was frustrated by appalling weather – and win control of the Danube too. Mastery of this natural border would open up what remained of Europe.

The Danube River commands attention. The name Danube itself almost certainly derives from the Proto-Indo-European *da* – waters that flow swiftly, rapidly, violently. Today the mechanical grinding up and down of concrete-fortress locks with monumental metal gates is a reminder that this is a wild river that has to be tamed. The very first pleasure cruise sailed from Vienna to Budapest in 1830, but for millennia this had been a watercourse with a serious job of work to do. Flatbed barges still power along the Danube's full stretch bringing piles of fresh-cut coal from the Black Sea, Crimean grain and cars fresh from the production line through central Europe.

The Danube formed the long edge of the Roman Empire – that border the Goths so memorably crossed back in the fourth century AD – and was the home of the Roman river fleet. The river was an artery along which supplies and armies could be transported. The vast ransom of a kidnapped Richard the Lionheart, brought home in disgrace along the Danube after a crusading foray, had originally paid for Vienna's high, brick-built city walls which, despite being mined and attacked with over 3,000 stone cannonballs, had famously withstood that first Ottoman siege of AD 1529. The sale of tax rights on the Danube would eventually allow for an influx of cash to the Ottoman court – which in turn would fund the so-called Tulip Age in the eighteenth century when Sultan Ahmed III filled his palaces with jewel-bright tulips, strapping nightlights to the backs of tortoises so that as they meandered they could illuminate the silky flower heads bobbing in the breeze from the Bosphorus. In the next century a tussle between the Russian and Ottoman powers on the Lower Danube sparked the First Crimean War. The Danube is a river that has shaped the lives of generations; its history is an essential component of the collective memory of both East and West.

But in AD 1683 the gods of the water were not on the Ottomans' side. Their army was 80,000 strong, and after crossing their Balkan territories there must have been a sense of optimism in the camps. Vienna, capital of the Habsburg Empire, controlled trade routes not only from the Black Sea via the Danube but from south to north. And yet since 1679 the city had been weakened as a result of a plague epidemic. Ottoman lands stretched as far west as Budapest and Sarajevo – surely Vienna would be next? Istanbul had within her sights dominion over western Europe – often referred to on the streets of Istanbul as Kafiristan (*kafir* meaning non-Muslim).

Surrounding Vienna the Janissaries and camp engineers quickly set to work, building siege engines and trenches through which Ottoman troops could approach the city's walls without being picked off as slowly moving targets. They camped here triumphantly, stubbornly, for three months. Waiting to attack, the Janissaries played their war songs long into the night: a jangling, aggressively joyful mêlée, the trumpets and cymbals, drums and reed pipes still have the ability to rouse spirits today. The spectacle from the ramparts of Vienna would have included phalanxes of multi-ethnic servicemen from the Middle East, North Africa and the Ukraine.

On the night before the first major battle, the Ottomans feasted – as if already enjoying the spoils of war. The Grand Vizier Kara Mustafa Pasha kissed a ceremonial sword and dagger and an imperial decree, while heralds cried out, 'May it be auspicious!' Banners and standards were waved and unfurled, an invasion of space before the invasion proper.[7]

The Sultan called the grand vizier and other leaders to his tent, commanding them to die fighting for the faith. As the Ottomans neared the walls, the cry of 'Allah! Allah! Allah!' was heard to ring out, cutting through the smoke and din.[8] Those within Vienna were already starving and diseased, Ottoman gunpowder was doing its work and the walls were pockmarked from the impact of cannonballs. On 8 September there was a fervent celebration of the Nativity of the Virgin Mary – she had been declared by Ferdinand II, the Viennese Emperor Leopold's grandfather, to be *generalissima sacrale* of the Habsburg armies. In September in this region the sunset is corn yellow and the moon a flaming blood orange; winds whip the dust up off the ground. But now it would be the pounding hoofs of horses, a titanic cavalry charge, that would raise the dust.

At the very last minute, Christian leaders had answered Vienna's urgent pleas for help. There were almost certainly 20,000 horses and riders here, and now with reinforcements a Christian infantry army 60,000 strong.[9] On 9 September, they attacked.

On good days the grey Danube has a serene majesty. Upstream there is a marble swirl as the River Inn brings its green minerals from the Alps. At night the startled bright eyes of woodland deer, muskrats and otters (mink too if you're lucky) reflect torches and flashlights; councils of cormorants are hunched on overhanging branches. All of this must have been experienced at first hand by the neolithic traders, the Roman colonisers, the customs-collectors, the missionary priests and river-bandits who have plied their trade along this stretch of water since prehistory. But in AD 1683 the river, outside Vienna, witnessed mass executions: first, it was said, 30,000 Christians who had been taken captive by the Ottomans and then 10,000 of the Sultan's men as, against all the odds, the Ottomans were overwhelmed in battle.[10] The bodies in the river were so thick that some Ottoman soldiers escaped by clambering over them as human stepping-stones.

Reports of the vanquishing of 'the Turk' and of the scenes on the banks of the Danube spread like wildfire through western Europe and were printed for popular consumption: '. . . the Emperour embarked on the Danube and landed above the Bridge before the Town and entered the city at the Stuben Gate . . . it [was] impossible to remove in so short a time such a number of Dead Bodies, both Turks, Christians and Horses, whereof the stench was so great on the Road it was enough to have caused an Infection'.[11]

It was widely, smugly, reported that plunder from the Ottoman camp produced enough lead to make 428,850 bullets. Ottomans captured after the failed siege of Vienna ended up serving in the courts of Western kings. One, who wrote *Some Memoirs of the Life of Lewis Maximilian Mahomet*, became George I of England's Keeper of the Privy Purse.

The gates and walls of Vienna have taken on symbolic significance. Hard-line political groups describe them as 'averting the original 9/11'. Yet although much vaunted as protectors of the West and of its idea of itself, it was not Vienna's walls themselves that made history, that turned Ottoman forces back. The fortifications had in fact been shattered by

Ottoman artillery and gunpowder. It was not monumental stone, but the unity of Christian Europe, the unity that Mehmed the Conqueror had first feared, which was now working against the rulers of Istanbul.

After the Viennese defeat, knowing how close he had come to opening up the West, the Sultan was enraged. On Christmas Day AD 1683 he decapitated his grand vizier Kara Mustafa Pasha in Belgrade.[12] Promotions in Ottoman service were prohibited as an austerity measure. The Russians, hearing reports of Ottoman distress, set off from Moscow with a million horses, 300,000 infantry and 100,000 cavalry. Their intention was to deliver a killer blow to Ottoman rule. In Istanbul, the Janissaries, still cocky with their plumed hats and brassy bands, revolted once more, killed their senior officers and the new grand vizier, invading his harem, mutilating his wife and sister and dragging them through the streets.[13] Official representations of the Viennese siege and of its fallout in song and illustration, back in Istanbul, pretended that none of this was a problem, that order had reigned on the battlefield and off.

The travel-writer Evliya Çelebi is one of the most observant and entrancing voices to have emerged from Istanbul.[14] Evliya had been told by the Prophet Muhammad in a dream (so he wrote) to explore his city on foot: '. . . I begin the account of my birthplace, the envy of kings and harbour of vessels, mighty fortress of the province of Macedon – Istanbul.'

Evliya is one of life's cup-half-full individuals. It was said of him that 'he cries the chant of every cart and sings the praises of every man who feeds him'.[15] Described by some as an Ottoman Herodotus, Çelebi wrote lovingly about the city's character, her taverns, her mosques and her smokers, and when he had moved on elsewhere (he travelled for forty years from the Crimea to Circassia, from Jerusalem to the Sudan) he also offers splendidly zesty texts describing Istanbul's wider territories, for instance: an annual convention of trapeze artists; tribes who had sex with the crocodiles of the Nile; and a disapproving account of the free conduct of Viennese women. Evliya Çelebi was pious and patriotic (if occasionally given to exaggeration); he had served with the Ottoman army and had, two decades before, visited Vienna. When he was dying in Cairo, one of his last entries concerns the AD 1683 siege. The tone is unusually ominous. At the time of his visit in 1665 Evliya had expressed his wish that Vienna should become Muslim, but a wild-eyed dervish in the delegation had cried out, oracular-like, 'In the year '94 [i.e. 1094 = 1683] may God not give this park and the walled city of Vienna into the hands of Islam, because they will destroy all of these buildings.'[16] The dervish proved prophet.

A lone, highly decorated and painted pavilion (the Amcazade), built by a grand vizier on the Asian shore of the Bosphorus in AD 1698, still – just about – stands today. Probably the oldest extant wooden building in the city, with just the reception rooms left, it clings on to the waterside with rotting piers a little like a Vietnamese fishing shack. This is where in 1699 the Treaty of Karlowitz was signed – codifying the loss of much of the Ottoman Empire to Austria, Venice, Poland and Russia. The terms of the treaty had been negotiated by one of the city's dragomans. Western nations were now allowed to restore and to build Christian churches in the capital. Thwarted in the West, the Ottomans had started to look east once more. In 1689 Süleyman II sent an envoy to the Mughal Emperor Aurangzeb, but it was too little too late. The Amcazade Pavilion seems to prefigure its own crumbling end.

The Ottomans were in trouble. New trade routes had opened up via Manila; China was making ever more effective use of the seaways (as demonstrated by the Selden Map, a detailed, seventeenth-century map of East Asia rediscovered in the archives of the Bodleian Library, Oxford, in 2008).[17] Power was steadily leaching from the capital to mini-dynasties in the provinces. The Ottoman court was represented in Western sources as a parody of itself. Ibrahim 'the Mad', who had been locked in the Kafes, the Princes' Cage (a kind of gilded purdah), since he was a toddler, was allegedly dosed up with aphrodisiacs; this voluptuary was then said to have assembled virgins and encouraged them to fight back as he ravished them. Those homes for the blinded, the Princes' Islands, were just the first in a network of islands scores-strong to the north, south and west, ready as places of exile. Some were little more than insular concentration camps; others were consolation prizes for those of the aristocracy or royal family who did not fit in with the current power-plays of court. A perfect storm of physical and political influences seemed to be converging to challenge Istanbul's security. Climatic change impacted on crops, Islamic inheritance rules negated the build-up of grand personal fortunes, and between AD 1500 and 1800 the number of Ottoman towns with popula-tions of 10,000 remained virtually static. Britain's increasing influence in

India stultified the traditional Asian trade routes. This was not the time to be embarking on pricey, foreign, failed campaigns.

They did not yet realise it, but the disintegration of the army as it retreated from Vienna also spelt the beginning of the Janissaries' end.

So could it be that at last the tide was turning – that those west of Vienna could now sleep easy in their beds, confident that their homes were safe and that daughters, sisters, wives were no longer at imminent risk of debauchment in a pasha's tent or in the harem of the sultan? For the last 200 years, the existence of a flourishing white slave trade centred on Istanbul and Cairo and spanning both Asia and Europe had been a fact that had dominated the collective imagination of West and East alike. From Thomas Dallam's excitable reports to Edward Barton's vivid description of a powerful woman of the Ottoman court as a *mediatrix*, a stereotype had been lodged. It was only in the seventeenth century that those in Istanbul were referred to by most Westerners as Muslims, followers of the religion of Islam. Up until then they had always been just 'Turks', 'Saracens' or 'Moors'.

The Ottomans might have been defeated in battle, but as the linchpin of an international trade in humans, and as an idea of what constituted 'the other', they would remain in rude health for the next 200 years. Throughout the West, male writers, artists and diplomats were disproportionately interested in what life was like in Istanbul for eunuchs and for the women they protected in the Sultan's household. The city of Istanbul had become synonymous with a phenomenon that was imagined as much as it was lived – the harem.

CHAPTER 63

THE WHITE SLAVE TRADE AND THE WHITE PLAGUE

AD 1348–1919
(748–1338 IN THE ISLAMIC CALENDAR)

> The. . . [children] go to pass a happy and splendid existence in Stamboul;
> and the price of their beauty probably rescues the family from starvation
> or procures them powder and shot to defend their independence.
>
> DR MORITZ WAGNER, *TRAVELS IN PERSIA, GEORGIA*
> *AND KOORDISTAN*[1]

> Live among diamonds and splendour as the wife of the Sultan.
>
> TRADITIONAL CAUCASIAN LULLABY[2]

A vigorous sex-slave trade had long been centred on Constantinople–
Istanbul. Following the massive loss of populations across Asia and
Europe in the wake of the Black Death (estimates vary from 75 to 200
million souls) in the fourteenth century, labour of all kinds had to come
from somewhere. Venetians and the Genoese, equipped with fast ocean-
worthy boats well-designed to keep precious cargo safe, had set their
compasses east. The lands beyond the Black Sea would prove particularly rich hunting grounds. With footholds established as the Crusades
disrupted Middle Eastern trade, the Italians were perfectly placed to
promote a business that, on parchment, was decried by the Papacy. That
pitiless plague might have originated on the Qinghai-Tibet plateau (experts currently think Yersinia bacteria were carried by the fleas of Asian
gerbils rather than black rats) and spread west along the Silk Roads, but
the solution would now come from the same direction as the problem.
Forget spices; humans were a newly modish commodity.

To understand the scale of this trafficking, we have to go to Poti, a harbour on the Georgian edge of the Black Sea coast, originally established

by Greeks at the time that Byzas was said to be founding Byzantion.[3]
Today Poti transports coal and grain in enormous containers which
haunt the Black Sea horizon. Stretching along the coast heading east are
the necropoleis of those immigrant Greeks who came here tentatively at
first and then in substantial numbers in the sixth and fifth centuries BC.
This was said to be the very landing spot of Jason and his Argonauts, who
then travelled inland up the Phasis River (today the Rioni) to retrieve
the Golden Fleece, to fight dragons and to bring ruin to Medea and her
family. Beyond Poti lies Batumi, a new Georgian pleasure-zone that lures
in Iranian and Turkish high- and low-rollers alike. There are neon-lit
casinos, penthouse swimming pools and swampy, unpaved backstreets.
The distant past feels very close here. Mosquitoes are a problem. One does
not have to try too hard to appreciate the double blight for those brought
to the ports, from antiquity onwards – the first station of an international
labour and sex trade. For centuries Poti was where men, women, boys
and girls were packed on to cramped wooden boats to start their loaded
journey west to the slave markets of Istanbul.

Invasion, battle, piratical raids were not necessary – the Black Sea trade
in humans was a flourishing and established business, enthusiastically
sponsored by local suppliers. Women were particularly active as dealers.
From North Africa we have evidence of one female slave-dealer who operated in a way remarkably similar to that of a number of the women who
work in trafficking rings today. It was reported, by St Augustine writing
about his homeland of Hippo in the fourth century AD, that she would
gain the trust of young girls from 'Mount Giddaba' by offering to buy
wood and then locking them up, intimidating and beating them before
selling them on to her contact traders.[4] Of all the slaves within Ottoman
territories, a number of the strongest specimens were sent to work in the
fields, harvesting sugar in particular, which was grown on Cyprus and
Crete. But a substantial proportion – particularly the prettiest of both
sexes – were destined for harem and household service. As many as 2,000
a year were transported across the Black Sea. In Istanbul in the seventeenth century 20 per cent of the population was unfree in comparison to
Venice, where the figure was closer to 3 per cent.

Yet for many local families, from the Ottoman period onwards (arguably as early as that fashion for the ancient Roman import of eunuchs from
the Caucasus), being traded for sex, servitude or for adornment was seen

as an essential opportunity. In Byzantium after the Crusades, slaving had for some time taken on an almost messianic quality, and the ensigns of slave ships were sometimes emblazoned with crosses. Under Ottoman rule, the tables were turned. Muslims could not be enslaved unless they were captured in battle or converted. Non-Muslim women from Georgia, Armenia, the Balkans, Greece and Russia could rise to become mothers of the Sultan, boys and young men to be grand viziers. We even hear of cases of free Stamboul Muslims who left for the Caucasus Mountains for a couple of years so that they could return as unrecognisable apostates, to be traded as slaves – with massively advanced career prospects. Many of the youngest would end up in halfway houses in Istanbul before they were sold on. Trained and tidied up, gentrified, girls would then become profitable marriage products for those who took them in. For thousands, and for generations, this was simply the way things were.

But we have to consider the day-to-day reality of this system. The girls could arrive at the transport ships at Poti harbour as young as three, brought in from the mountains or from the plains of Armenia. The territory around Poti is subtropical. The wetlands here support exotic birds and also insects, in particular those mosquitoes that are still such a bane. Malaria was frequently a problem. During their passage human cargo was kept below decks. The journey from Poti, across the Black Sea and down the Bosphorus, often with a stop-off at Trebizond (Trabzon under the Ottomans), would take around three weeks. On arrival in Istanbul this precious stock was sorted into spoiled or mint goods and would typically be taken to the slave market, the Süleyman Pasha Han, at the edge of the Grand Bazaar; men could also be sold naked in the Old Bazaar. The Istanbul authorities had already taken a levy at the city's gates on the arrival of each consignment (four gold ducats per capita in the sixteenth century) and then both buyers and sellers had to pay a tax.[5]

Today canaries, tortoises and leeches are sold in a pet market that has replaced the human pens. Protected by a large wooden gate, locked each day at midday, from at least the sixteenth century the living human produce was displayed either on the platforms between the wooden columns or – if especially valuable – within exclusive cubicles. The most desirable Circassian women could fetch up to 15,000 piastres. Here the boys, girls and young women were traded, while travellers, both Western and Eastern, watched the scene – slave-barter being a popular spectator sport. Some visitors became addicted to buying other humans; once they had run out of money they would come simply to watch the sales.

Once the girls had been bought by a household in Istanbul, they were given new Persian names which were pinned to their bodices like conference labels. If sold to the Sultan's household they would find themselves mixing closely with black eunuch jailer-companions – men who had also been rebranded and were now called those luscious-sounding names such as Hyacinth, Narcissus, Rose and Gillyflower.

Inside the harem buildings themselves the newly enslaved would be led through a series of dark and labyrinthine corridors, glimpsing perhaps some of those servants who kept the harem industry productive: the head stewardess, the head of the treasury, the chief laundress. In the Sultan's seraglio at Topkapı there were dining rooms, a library, a mosque. Through spy holes the girls might see the gaudy court beyond, where court officials were strictly colour-coded in those notorious rainbow hues of the city – ulemas (specialist Islamic scholars) in purple, mullahs (Islamic clerics) in pale blue, masters of the horse in bottle green, officers of the Sublime Porte wearing yellow shoes, court officers red, visiting

The Slave Market, Constantinople *by Sir William Allan who visited the city with diplomats negotiating Greek independence in* AD *1829–30. First exhibited in London in 1838.*

Greeks black, Armenians violet, while Jews might sport blue slippers. Janissaries at the Enderun School were also dressed in different colours according to their attainment levels. Even though some favoured girls could leave the harem decked in pearls, silks and tightly embroidered jackets, for most this must have been a safe but a dingy existence. With numbers here that could reach almost 4,000, many of the lowlier ranks ended up simply being the slaves of slaves.

The absence of nearby relatives in Istanbul was thought to make the imported girls less troublesome. If there were disputes, no family was close by to intervene, and since none were Muslim, they had no legal recourse to justice under the encompassing body of Islamic law, the *şeriat* (*Shari'a*.)

Although for many in the household, day-to-day life ran as it would have done in a number of royal courts of the day, sex in the Sultan's harem was likely until favoured girls fell pregnant, and then once a male child was produced sex typically stopped, to prevent infighting and to give these only sons passionate advocates within the palace. Ornate birthing chairs were trundled in and out of the quarters. Following Mehmed II's example back in the fifteenth century, fratricide had become permissible under Ottoman law: on his succession a new Sultan was expected to murder his brothers, a policy instituted to prevent dynastic struggles and palace coups. Many believe this harsh codification of the survival of the fittest did indeed give the Ottoman court some stability and strength, although it would eventually result in its etiolation. Diplomats sent back reports of the wailing processions when the fratricide laws were enforced and princes in the harem – on occassion as many as nineteen at a time – were garroted by a silken bowstring or a handkerchief, a job for those Bostancı whose namesake officials spent the bulk of their time tending roses and mimosas in the palace gardens or rowing the sultan in his gilded *kayik*. The doleful experience made it into some lines of Shakespeare, when Henry V chides his courtiers during his accession speech:

> Brothers, you mix your sadness with some fear.
> This is the English, not the Turkish court.[6]

The practice became less frequent after AD 1648 (only one prince on record was murdered between that year and 1808) and from 1603 extraneous princes were held in the Princes' Cage, or Kafes, within the harem, many from infancy onwards. This was a lifetime of luxurious incarceration, effectively a form of house arrest.[7] Once they reached puberty, education was no longer on offer and a number clearly developed psychological complications (two that we know of committed suicide). These inconvenient heirs were quietly murdered; it has been estimated that at least seventy-eight princes were strangled at Topkapı. There must have been an atmosphere of opportunity but also of tension and fear – where brothers and sons were frequently 'disappeared'.

In this enclosed environment pandemics were frequent. The piecing together of textual evidence now indicates that not only did large numbers of women and children in the harem (including sons and heirs of the Sultan) die of either cholera or tuberculosis, but the sultans with whom they had regular familial or sexual contact were also sufferers: Mahmud II, Abdülmecid I, Abdülhamid II and Mehmed VI all showed TB symptoms.[8] Indeed Mehmed VI Vahdeddin, whose mother died of TB and who was deposed in 1922 as the Ottoman Empire fell, showed, on autopsy, his left lung to be destroyed by the tuberculosis bacterium. New intakes – either via the slave markets or thanks to visitors on pilgrimage (infection carried back from Mecca and Medina and gatherings at festivals could claim 60,000 at any one time) – brought pathogens into the harem as if to a petri dish.[9]

One of the very last inhabitants of the sultan's harem, Princess Ayşe, who died only in 1960, recalled in her memoirs the horror of learning that her nurse had died of TB when a package containing her own baby clothes, her first spoon and pencil and a lock of her hair were brought to her: 'all kinds of things from my life spilled out before me. I began to weep.'[10]

CHAPTER 64

WHITE CAUCASIANS

AD 1453–1922
(856–1341 IN THE ISLAMIC CALENDAR)

The blood of Georgia is the best of the East, and perhaps in the world.
I have not observed a single ugly face in that country, in either sex; but
I have seen angelical ones. Nature has there lavished upon the women
beauties which are not to be seen elsewhere. I consider it to be impossible
to look at them without loving them. It would be impossible to paint
more charming visages, or better figures . . .

SIR JOHN CHARDIN, *TRAVELS*[1]

Strangers are not allowed to see the interior of the cage in which these
birds of paradise are confined.

WILLIAM MAKEPEACE THACKERAY, *NOTES ON A JOURNEY*

FROM CORNHILL TO GRAND CAIRO[2]

The exacting reality (for some) of the harem, did little to dampen external
fervour. Sexual fantasists and pseudo-scientists elevated Istanbul's captive women to legendary status. A potent, and pernicious, two-pronged
notion was born in the late eighteenth century – that the Sultan's concubines were perfectly white and that, in some way, they were also blessed.
Bizarrely, the perception of these companions and sex slaves – who were
traded widely across Ottoman territories – is one of the reasons that millions around the world still elect to describe themselves as being 'White
Caucasian'.

Just when the 'white gold' trade was really hotting up in the mid-
eighteenth century, a studious young German scholar was making his way
from his home town in Lower Saxony (now central Germany) through
high-hedged fields to the up-and-coming Göttingen University. In AD

1775 this eager craniologist, Johann Friedrich Blumenbach, published the first draft of a thesis, *De Generis Humani Varietate Nativa* (On the Natural Variety of Mankind), which would divide the world into five 'varieties': Mongolian, Ethiopian, Malay, American Indian and Caucasian.

Claimed by some as the father of physical anthropology, Blumenbach used as a research tool what he called his Golgotha, a collection of 245 skulls and mummified remains, among which were the remains of a young Georgian woman – the inspiration for his 'Caucasian' variety. He believed this particular skull to be 'perfect', and was moved by tales of the seventeenth-century Huguenot traveller-cum-jewellery merchant Sir John Chardin (born Jean-Baptiste Chardin) who, having travelled east from Constantinople by boat across the Black Sea, described Georgian women from the Caucasus as being simply the most beautiful in the world. Blumenbach concluded that the Caucasus was the locus for the origin of the human race, a veritable Garden of Eden. The complete edition of Blumenbach's *De Generis Humani* was finally published in 1795.

The Caucasus, a fat neck of land in the far north-east of the Ottoman territories between the Caspian and the Black Seas, already possessed a narrative claim, popularised by the account of the traveller Marco Polo in the thirteenth century, to be the birthplace of mankind. Marco Polo's tale proposed that the towering mountain here was the Mount Ararat of the Bible and that therefore the Caucasus was the physical location of the Garden of Eden and the final destination of Noah's Ark. Blumenbach's scientific research, by association, buttressed biblical certainty. Blumenbach wrote of his category 'Caucasian variety': 'I have taken the name of this variety from Mount Caucasus . . . because its neighbourhood, and especially its southern slope, produces the most beautiful race of men, I mean the Georgian.'3

Blumenbach's later work, *A Short System of Comparative Anatomy*, was translated and popularised by the well-regarded English surgeon William Lawrence in AD 1807. It is illustrated precisely in pen and ink, and the image of the Caucasian skull holds pole position. Although Blumenbach was not himself a white supremacist and was critical of the work of colleagues who were, his association of beauty with whiteness and with a biblical-origin myth easily slid into a value judgement. Race theorists at Göttingen would eagerly amplify the notion that white Caucasians came from a hallowed place – and that other 'varieties' of race were a corrupted version of the Caucasian paradigm. It was a dangerously neat fantasy but a nonsense that has prevailed; following Blumenbach, the existence of White Caucasians has been a non-fact that still surfaces in scientific and cultural taxonomy. The existence of Istanbul's harems served to perpetuate this perilously bad science.

So white people, it was twittered in scientific circles and polite society, as the age of enlightenment moved to the age of revolution, came from the Caucasus. This idea seems to have struck a particularly resounding chord in the collective Western imagination for a curious reason. The majority of the female concubines in the Sultan's harem – the most beautiful, it was murmured approvingly – were indeed Caucasians from the Caucasus, or as the West chose to call them, Circassians. As Leo Tolstoy wrote scathingly in AD 1855: 'They imagine the Caucasus to be something majestic: eternal virgin ice, rushing torrents, daggers, mantles, fair Circassians and an atmosphere of terror and romance. But in reality, there is nothing amusing about it.'[4]

The Circassians were in fact a tribal group from the north-western Caucasus, many of whom had been converted to Islam after the fall of Constantinople. A mystique surrounded these native men and women. Although Muslim, the women were typically, and excitingly, unveiled (unlike their Christian neighbours). Travellers were ostensibly horrified (yet clearly, secretly impressed) by the fact that they sometimes too wore make-up 'as an ornament'. Circassian men, famed for their valour, and fighting still in chain mail, were treated as the best kind of noble savage. As the mid-nineteenth-century traveller Edmund Spencer put it, 'No half-civilised people in the world display so pleasing an exterior.'[5] It is fantasy Circassians who gallop across the pages of many of our fairy-tales.

From the sixteenth century onwards, Circassian women were as close as the world got to international pin-ups. They were, quite frankly, hard to avoid. The French philosopher Montesquieu, the author of *Les Liaisons dangereuses* Choderlos de Laclos and the dramatist Racine had all written excitable harem narratives. Thomas Rowlandson's satirical sketch *Harem* caricatured the Sultan (with a pronounced erection), Circassian beauties draping themselves over him. Flushed, bare-breasted post-coital images of the imagined reality of Circassian harem life were conjured up by a number of the very best artistic talents of the day. Ingres' *Odalisque with Slave* was one of the most widely reproduced: soft porn masquerading as the popular genre painting of the modern age. Ingres, Edward Clarke, Emmanuel Kant, Frederic Leighton, all avidly described both Circassian homelands and the transport of their women to the Ottoman harems of Istanbul and Cairo. The very purpose of the Circassian race, it was said, was to beautify the ugliness of the Turks and Persians with whom they had to tangle.

The roots of this fabricated version of genealogy go deep. Witness the Venetian ambassador Jacopo Ragazzoni's description of that international operator Nurbanu in AD 1571: 'six months ago . . . the [Grand Signor], as a great token of his love, made a Chebin, which means that he took as legal wife [the prince's] mother, a Circassian woman, and bestowed upon her a dowry of 110,000 ducats, wishing to outdo his father, who had bestowed a dowry of only 100,000 ducats on the mother of Selim.'⁶ Nurbanu was in fact almost certainly from Cyprus.

In America too the idea of gorgeous, languorous women, available and yet exotic, from a remote Eastern land promised good box office. In the early 1860s Phineas T. Barnum 'imported' Caucasian women who, for a dime, would recount the tale of their capture and salaciously sensuous life in the Sultan's harem – and then their liberation by one of P. T. Barnum's agents. Ostensibly taught English by Barnum's heroes and exhibited as 'the purest example of the white race', these were in truth typically young Irish girls who had their hair coiffured into 'wild-woman' bouffant hair-styles.⁷ The reason for this untamed-hair choice seems to have been both a visual indicator of slavery and a cultural reference to the thick hair and sheepskin hats of native Caucasians. The hairdos were held in place with a combination of beer and egg white. Following Barnum's lead a 'Cir-cassian' could be found in most American sideshows. Beauty treatments such as 'The Bloom of Circassia' lotion were bestsellers in Europe and the US throughout the nineteenth and early twentieth centuries. Marketed as containing natural whitening ingredients from the Caucasus, these had the spurious claim to access a quasi-mythical land east of Constan-tinople where the women were preternaturally white 'Eves'. Whether in Istanbul's harems or on the streets of New York, the Circassian concubine was a potent mix of the known and the exotic.

And yet Blumenbach's Georgian skull, the original 'white Caucasian', of course belonged not to an imagined ideal but to a real captive human. She was a young woman, judging by the state of her teeth aged only

American photo card of a 'Circassian' woman known as 'Zumiya the Egyptian'
c. AD 1870

fifteen to seventeen, caught up in the advance of Catherine the Great into the Caucasus in the years AD 1787–91 who was then taken prisoner and brought to Moscow. While Catherine the Great was processing south from St Petersburg with her lover Grigory Potemkin arranging extreme *coups de théâtre* for the pleasure of his mistress – the evocation of an English garden, a recreation of the eruption of Mount Vesuvius, overnights in the Crimean Khan's palaces, displays by Circassian horsemen – our young girl was being flung from one soldier to another.[8] In a cover-letter sent in 1793, Blumenbach's benefactor and skull-dealer explained that this girl had died of venereal disease.[9] Blumenbach's source materials were the remnants of the harsh sexual realities of political ambition, and of the fantasies that can accompany imperialism.[10]

CHAPTER 65

✤

SOAP AND SMALLPOX

THE EIGHTEENTH CENTURY
(1111–1211 IN THE ISLAMIC CALENDAR)

Much unnaturall and filthy lust is said to be committed daily in the remote closets of these darksome Bannias [hammams], yea, women with women; a thing uncredible, if former times had not given thereunto both detection and punishment.

GEORGE SANDYS, *A RELATION OF A JOURNEY BEGUN AN: DOM: 1610*[1]

I have traversed great part of Turkey, and many other parts of Europe, and some of Asia; but I never beheld a work of nature or art which yielded an impression like the prospect on each side from the Seven Towers to the end of the Golden Horn.

LORD BYRON, LETTER TO HIS MOTHER (AD 1810)[2]

Orientalism was like a labyrinth: the more I advanced in it, the more entangled I became . . .

VAKA BROWN, *HAREMLIK: SOME PAGES FROM
THE LIFE OF TURKISH WOMEN* (AD 1909)[3]

The harem became symbolic of the Ottoman Empire itself – a wonderful place of promise, pleasure and confinement, an idea and a location that needed invading and then liberating.

So was Istanbul really now fulfilling her role as Aphrodite? Represented as the goddess of love and sexual desire throughout her recorded 2,000-year life, on maps and in marble and gilded statues, was laughter-loving Aphrodite now made flesh on the streets of Istanbul? Was this really a stew of steamy excess populated by glad-eyed women and willing young boys? This was what many wanted to believe, but material evidence and the record of the inhabitants of Istanbul themselves, and of one particularly feisty Western visitor, put us right. Lady Mary Wortley Montagu (having escaped engagement to an Honourable Clotworthy Skeffington) travelled via Philippi and Edirne to Istanbul from England as the ambassador's wife, with thirty wagons of luggage, and stayed from AD 1717 to 1718 in the city. The first woman to write first hand in English about Ottoman life and Constantinople, she described her experience of Ottoman hammams thus:

> The first sofas were covered with cushions and rich carpets, on which sat the ladies, and on the second their slaves behind 'em, but without any distinction of rank by their dress, all being in the state of nature, that is, in plain English, stark naked, without any beauty or defect concealed. Yet there was not the least wanton smile or immodest gesture amongst them. They walked and moved with the same majestic grace which Milton describes our general mother. There were many amongst them as exactly proportioned as ever any goddess was drawn by the pencil of Guido or Titian, and most of their skins shiningly white, only adorned by their beautiful hair divided into many tresses, hanging on their shoulders, braided either with pearl or ribbon, perfectly representing the figures of the Graces . . . some in conversation, some working, others drinking Coffee or sherbet . . . In short, 'tis the woman's coffee-house, where all the news of the Town is told, scandal invented, etc.[4]

Just as with the harem, hammam culture in Istanbul was not aphrodisiac fantasy but fact. As a well-bred Stamboul woman one would expect to spend four to five hours in the baths every week. Followed by servants with the day's supplies – fruit, nuts, *börek* (pastries), meatballs, towels, cakes – women would meet in these steamy pods to discuss prospective marriage alliances and to exchange the city's news (on odd occasions, through to the late nineteenth century, crowds of women would convene on the streets to protest about unpopular developments in the city, the intelligence passed on in the single-sex baths).[5] Babies who had survived their first forty days were here being ritually washed, as were brides preparing for their weddings. For these rituals a live band would often be brought in, and the festivities could go on for days. Some men just turned up for a shave, some women to have their hair plaited or their eyelashes hennaed, but this was truly where the diurnal world of Ottoman Istanbul turned.[6]

Locals and visitors alike noted that bathkeepers could afford to ride through the streets on pure-bred horses (donkeys, mules, camels and buffalo were the commoner mount). The bathkeeper was admired and despised. Although officials were meant to check for grubby towels, for fetid or cold water, there were reports of contagion (syphilis was a huge problem) in the 10,000 or so baths in Istanbul. But, however poor the services on offer, the population of the city – female and male – could not be kept away. The baths created their own ecosystems: ash from the stokeholes was sold on to be used in the preparation of ink, while the poor and orphaned would huddle next to the baths' twenty-four-hour furnaces. In winter it was reported that children ringed the stoves like a human cobweb, the sickest being allowed to lie on sheepskin rugs closest to the flames.

Legislation concerning the baths had been stringent since the establishment of the Ottoman Caliphate. Selim I had tried to prevent the ogling of both women and young boys as they left the hammams and outlawed the sharing of *peştemals* (towels) by Muslims and non-Muslims. But religions could freely mix here. When Lady Mary Wortley Montagu undressed in one bathhouse there were gasps of horror at the sight of her stays, which the Ottoman women thought to be a cage in which her husband had locked her.[7] There was a whole bathhouse culture. Nalın shoes for example kept feet clear of water djinns and raised mothers high enough to keep a close eye on their daughters. The finest of these hammam clogs were carved out of walnut, boxwood and sandalwood and were inlaid with mother of pearl.[8] Restoration work since 2006 on the splendid Kılıç Ali Paşa Hammam in Galata, built by Sinan in AD 1580 for that heroic Ottoman admiral Kiliç Ali Paşa who survived the Battle of Lepanto, has revealed the sophistication of some of the hammams in Istanbul. Peeling back 430 layers of accumulated debris, the team discovered a new secret: an insulating plaster skin that kept the rooms inside hot and steamy but allowed the walls to 'breathe' – ensuring the health of both the bathers and of those vital buildings.

And in reality there were both hammams and harems across the city that did not involve anything more exciting than a bowl of soap or a needle and thread and a drawer of medicinal herbs. Hammams were a rural as well as an urban phenomenon – the poor of Kostantiniyye expected access, recalling those hammams that had been the nucleus of female activity in the Balkan or Anatolian villages that many had left behind.

So despite commentators in the West perceiving the hammam and the harem through a mist of concupiscence, *haremliks* (private spaces) were simply protection zones, where certain behaviour was forbidden. *Odalıks* (who served the *oda*, Turkish for room) were chambermaids or old family servants, not odalisque sex-toys. Even those households that could not afford to buy in female labour had domestic quarters for men and women roughly separated by a curtain. The cotton-curtain division was to be found in most public spaces in Istanbul and continued on in the city's trams, steamers and trains well into the twentieth century. But rather than a practical bit of calico, Western observers wanted it to be a gauzy veil, a cover concealing unspeakable delights, begging to be raised.

Those who were thought to have privileged access to the harem's interior, such as piano-tuners and clockmakers, could sell on their insider knowledge. The sexually charged horror stories were told in the bedrooms and schoolrooms of Europe. Istanbul became not a fantastical city, but a projection of others' fantasies. There were widespread, excitable retellings for example of the life-story of Aimeé du Buc de Rivéry, a French convent pupil (and cousin of Empress Josephine) said to have been kidnapped on the high seas in AD 1788 by Algerian pirates, who eventually became the consort of Sultan Abdülhamid I and stepmother of Sultan Mahmud II but who died of tuberculosis aged twenty-six.[9] An anonymous English pornographer published *The Lustful Turk* in 1828, recounting the experiences of two respectable Englishwomen, Emily and Sylvia, trapped in an Ottoman harem where they are raped but then discover highly describable sexual pleasure. Benjamin Disraeli writes (in his diaries) far more excitedly about Constantinople than about Jerusalem – he brought back a hubble-bubble pipe and a divan.[10] Even Jane Austen started to sport a 'Mamluk' cap.

For men and women alike the harem had become a place to penetrate. The Warsaw-born artist Elisabeth Jerichau-Baumann in AD 1869–70 and again 1874–5 travelled to Istanbul in the hope of commissions – not just

A classic mamluk cap style, modelled in an AD 1805 fashion print

from the West but from within the Imperial City. Her account of arriving at Istanbul hints at what she imagined, indeed hoped, she would find: '[The city] lay stretched out in the morning mist, lightly veiled, gleaming pink in the early light like a made-up odalisque, with poison under her fingernails.'[11] But Jerichau-Baumann was not disappointed by the harem women either as subjects or as potential clients. An appreciation of the arts, do not forget, had long been a central part of the concubines' training. The highest-ranking women had generous allowances and were often paid by the Sultan for sex or as a gift. There was cash in that harem to spend. Ironically, many of Jerichau-Baumann's paintings, paid for by female slaves, were considered too overtly sensuous and were kept in a storeroom in Denmark for over a century.

Lady Mary Wortley Montagu, from her palace home in Pera, might have enjoyed what she described as Constantinople's pursuit of 'present pleasure', and she made her own comparisons with patriarchal enslavement: thanks to the dowry system where, 'people in my way are sold like slaves'. But the most practical lesson that she learnt as a result of her sojourn in Ottoman territory was the cure for smallpox. Inoculating her own children (Montagu's recalcitrant son Edward died a good Muslim, dressed as a Turk, speaking Turkish, and only on death relinquishing the turban he so loved in his Venetian palazzo), she revolutionised medicine in the West. She had herself been blighted by smallpox as a young woman – her brother had died of the disease – and her own face was scarred; she had extra reason perhaps to appreciate the liberation that the veil afforded Kostantiniyye's women. The veil, so they told her, allowed for secret assignations. Lady Mary followed their example and travelled through the city veiled – if only so that she could visit mosques such as the Ayasofya.

The gift of inoculation to civilisation must not be underappreciated. Another of the English women we hear of in Istanbul was Anne, Lady Glover, wife of the English ambassador Sir Thomas. Anne died in the city in AD 1608 of the plague, was interred in bran in the Embassy for almost four years and was then buried in a splendid mausoleum in what is now Taksim Square.[12]

Inevitably perhaps artists and poets did not want to memorialise the infected reality of harems and hammams in the city, the smallpox, syphillis and plague victims, the spewing TB wards, the quiet gasping deaths – the fact that contagious diseases such as TB, detected in the region as early as 7000 BC, and syphilis played their part in Istanbul's sexual politics and geopolitics.[13] They did not want to commemorate this truth.

The sultans built summer palaces along the Bosphorus and the Golden Horn partly to escape the heat, and more importantly to evade the threat of tuberculosis and other contagions. The misused and overused 'Sick Man of Europe' tag might have been a metaphorical insult, but it chimes with hard fact. Multi-ethnic, the Ottoman Empire had no natural borders with which to prevent the spread of disease. Although the Ottomans blamed Indians for bringing cholera, for example, to Mecca (via the Red Sea), the truth was that religious pronouncements from the ulema that any disease was a plague of punishment sent by God put a brake on a number of medical initiatives such as quarantine. A series of International Sanitary Conferences (from 1851 to 1938, one of which was held in Istanbul in 1866) ratified intervention in domestic affairs by international regulations.[14] On 8 July 1928 the *Pittsburgh Press* reported that there were 40,000 cases of tuberculosis in Istanbul. Even today the most exclusive hotels will warn you of this dreary danger. When we read Lady Mary's brisk account of 'Turkish women [being] the only free people in the Empire', we should also spare a thought for those women and girls – as many as 800 in the Sultan's harem alone – who had no chance to take flight, no choice but to sit and wait for infection, of many kinds.

CHAPTER 66

⊕

TULIPS AND TEXTILES

THE EIGHTEENTH CENTURY
(1111–1211 IN THE ISLAMIC CALENDAR)

Heaven in vain revolves around the world, it sees nowhere a city like Istanbul.

NABI EFENDI, *THE COUNSELS OF NABI EFENDI TO HIS SON ABOUL KHAIR*[1]

This is certainly that part of the Universe above all others, where the eye most deliciously feeds itself with a prospect every way delightful . . . For my own part, when I arriv'd there the first time, methought I was entering into an Inchanted Island.

GUILLAUME-JOSEPH GRELOT, AD 1683[2]

In 2006, Istanbul's authorities planted 3 million tulip bulbs around the city. While the airport was being dustily modernised, while immigrant workers unloaded cement and tarmac in the oily jangle of the ports and while new road systems were being scored out of the old city, red tulips were everywhere, swaying silkily despite the turmoil around them.

The mass planting was a deliberate attempt to recall and to recapture a time in Istanbul that later authors have branded the Tulip Age. From around AD 1710 onwards, a generation after the failed siege of Vienna, the sultans not only tried to rewrite the story of the city; they actively turned Istanbul into a storybook version of herself.

There was peace on the Ottomans' borders – and Sultan Ahmed III and his viziers used the opportunity to turn a private passion and a pious belief in the spiritual value of the garden into a public statement. The tulip – as happy in an urban environment as it is in the wild – became omnipresent in Istanbul. Coming from the same Central Asian plains as the Turks and taking their name from the Persian for a turban, tulips had already been exported to the West by the Ottomans, sparking the infamous 'Black Tulip' financial rush in seventeenth-century Europe. Now the tulip was imported back from Holland and Iran not as a rarity but in abundance. Visitors described 500,000 bulbs growing in the grand vizier's garden, the flowers all illuminated with jewel-coloured lamps and candles. Female as well as male tulip-growers were employed. Forty-four new varieties were propagated by the city's officials. Guests at imperial parties even had to wear clothes to complement the floral colour schemes. And ordinary citizens benefited in unexpected ways – the drive to illuminate these flowers artfully led to an increase in the lighting of public lanes and squares (typically the city's inhabitants were expected to stay indoors after the night-time prayers, which meant that Istanbul did not boast a municipal lighting scheme). Measures to prevent revolt and disturbance now required Istanbul's citizens to carry lanterns after dark. Stamboul residents of the Tulip Age talk of the delight of confidently inhabiting their, newly lucent, city by night.

On my very first visit to Istanbul aged eighteen I remember being entranced by the tales of the café-owners who described Ahmed III's tulip festivals of 250 years before as if they were happening in front of their eyes – the time when tortoises would be released with nightlights on their backs, gently rocking their way through the gardens as illumination. The topography of the city lent itself to theatrics – in the procession of guilds, confectioners would create their own tulip gardens out of sugar, while crowds were held back by lines of coloured silks. The native species of the flower might be largely extinct today, but from the eighteenth century onwards it was immortalised on tiles and textiles, a new civic brand.

Istanbul was also famous for her gorgeous embroidered textiles. As travellers and as children of the Silk Roads, the Turks had had to develop the lightest and the most transportable forms of luxury. From their very beginnings they had access to many of the most desirable raw materials in Asia. High-end textile production was their bespoke art. Two hundred textile artists worked together in the harem. Women at home too were encouraged to develop extreme embroidery skills. In addition to the cottage industry of textile production found across Anatolia and Ottoman Europe (dominated by women), fabrics were stitched or woven to represent a field of military tents, balconied houses, pleasure gardens; or

Tulip in Turkish is lale – *although the native species is extinct today the flower is memorialised on tiles and textiles*

were produced to resemble peacocks' eyes, leopard spots, sunbursts and saz leaves. Shoes were customised with snazzy contrasting velvet zigzags, pillows were stitched with pearls. Military banners were ornamented with verses from the Qur'an.

Shunning heavy, Western-style furniture – there was scarcely a chair in the city – stools and divans were draped with cloth, traders were shielded under embroidered awnings. And where Byzantium had sponsored imperial reliquary-workshops, the Ottomans supported the work of female embroiderers and male calligraphers. Masters such as Hâfiz Osman designed liquidly beautiful lines of text. Some praised Allah; others formed the documents of the Ottoman Chancery – the calligraphy could appear on vellum, paper or even on the delicacy of fallen leaves. These exquisite scripts too started to become highly prized in the West.

Monumental calligraphy had long been a feature of the Ottoman city, but now lines of the Qur'an and hadiths – realised in ceramic, bronze, marble, gold – started to appear elsewhere on the streets. Within the city in AD 1727 the first ever Ottoman-language Arabic-script printing press – the Müteferrika Press – was established (although this was a short-lived enterprise, and was mothballed within a decade). In 1746 the Tulip

Festival was revived in the Topkapı Gardens. The elevated, light Topkapı Palace library, which still entrances, filled with books printed in Arabic, would have offered a balmy retreat above the ribbons of botanical colour. The city's leaders remembered Osman's dream of Kostantiniyye and tried to recreate it. Western visitors obliged by flooding in to take notes.

As well as being motivated by trade, adventure or the opportunity for voyeurism, there was also a substantial political reason why the number of visitors to Istanbul increased in the early modern period. By the mid-seventeenth century in England, Ottoman Turks were no longer the Protestant alternative to Papists, but the royalist alternative to roundheads. Richard Flecknoe wrote excitedly of Istanbul, 'nor did I ever see truer bravery, or greater gallantry than there, every one wearing such various coloured silks, with swelling Turbans, and flowing garments, as their streets appear just like Tulipp Gardens . . .'. The tulip appeared in Robert Herrick's poetry as an allegory for the death of Stuart England.[3]

Istanbul needed her friends. After defeat at Vienna and the humiliating AD 1699 Treaty of Karlowitz, politically things had gone from bad to worse: Food was short in the city and in 1703 students, Janissaries and the people joined together, marching from Istanbul to Edirne and deposing the Sultan Mustafa II. Many were furious that the Sultans were spending much of their time in Erdine, what is now called 'Gypsy City' rather than the Queen of Cities herself. A quarter of a century on from the Siege of Vienna, the Janissaries still sang rousing songs of the sacrifices that they had made on campaign – for little thanks. Stasis threatened following this 'Edirne' incident. But when Ahmed III was installed as sultan back in Topkapı, his thanks was to turn Istanbul into a city-wide pleasure-dome. The Ottoman sultans had been reminded with gusto that in Istanbul, they needed to be seen to be believed, and to be obeyed.

Another lesson taken from the failed siege of Vienna was that the Ottomans had to learn from the West – in both military practice and culture. If Istanbul was not going to control Western European cities she could at least be edified by them. It was to France that the city's dragomans initially turned for allegiance and expertise. Envoys were sent to Paris, delivering back to the Sultan information on the French way of doing things. Mini-Versailles gardens started to appear in the city, and the number of French residents rose from a handful in the mid-seventeenth century to 175 by AD 1719. A French inventor introduced the pump-powered fire-engine to the city in 1718 (up until now fires had been fought by Janissaries with buckets). Soon French architects such as Antoine Ignace Melling, who has left us delightful images of the early eighteenth-century city, were designing palaces for Ottoman princesses along the Bosphorus. Rather than the orthodox enclosures of Turkic homes, these mansions opened out on to the water. The sultans started to favour European-style gardens – one even boasted a formal labyrinth. Parks increasingly replaced the city's wilderness. Public fountains channelled its water. Tulip gardens corralled its weeds.

And Sultan Ahmed III developed a very cross-cultural hideout for himself. Hidden in what is now a rather scrubby zone, past chicken wire and rotting pallets, is Aynalıkavak Kasrı – a little pleasure palace behind a walled garden that became this Sultan's favourite retreat. Built above the bustle of the shipyards and protected by the 10,000 cypresses planted to provide a hunting ground, the pavilion became a paragon of the collision of Eastern and Western styles. A miniature by the court painter Levni shows Ahmed III here, in front of a gilded mirror – probably one of the Murano mirrors 'as tall as poplars' that had been sent as a gift to the

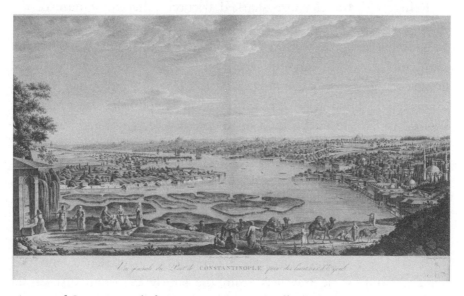

A view of Constantinople from Antoine Ignace Melling's Voyage pittoresque de Constantinople et des rives du Bosphore, *AD 1819*

Sultan – watching the water sports put on the Golden Horn to celebrate the circumcision of his four sons.

With the pull towards Westernisation there were some problems. A twenty-four-year diary kept by one of the city's inhabitants Telhisi Mustafa Efendi and discovered in the archives of the Prime Minister's Office describes officers charged with cutting off the European-style collars on the dresses worn, daringly, by some women in public. The author concurs with this policy: 'This is a strike right on target! May God allow it to continue and persist.'⁴ Riots and civil strife again in AD 1730 and 1740 (when homes and commercial properties along the Golden Horn were ransacked) reminded the city that it had a popular tradition of protest. Public cryers would alert Istanbul's population to the 'arms', ordering shops to be shut, and curfews would be imposed when it looked as though trouble was brewing. Those who were caught physically bore the signs: if they escaped execution there were amputations, floggings, foot-canings and brandings for any who were suspected of lying about their involvement (women were typically beaten on the buttocks and then exiled). Rebels were beheaded – and although Westerners described impalement as a regular hallmark of Istanbul (it wasn't), it was a prescribed punishment.

Refugees to the city also sparked friction. After the failure of the Vienna attack in AD 1683, the Sultan no longer pursued foreign campaigns, but struggles within Ottoman territory displaced many who came to Istanbul in search of salvation. In the mid-eighteenth century, 10,000–12,000 Albanian immigrants were recorded in the city. During Ramadan beggars and dervishes also regularly flooded in. These migrants seemed to have formed a kind of underclass, sleeping rough, and they were resented by the locals. There were public declarations that these 'interlopers' should travel 'back to where they came from'. Throughout the eighteenth century both organised crime and prostitution rose;⁵ tensions in the city followed and despite Ahmed III's attempt to promote peace through cultural direct action, in 1726 a mob hurled stones at the Sultan's palace over ten days and nights.

Yet the very strength of greater Istanbul had long been its mongrel nature. While some travellers from the largely Christian districts of Galata and Pera across the Golden Horn did fear for their lives when visiting Stamboul proper, there was also the chance to mingle with Kurds,

Georgians, Albanians, Arabs, Ethiopians. Many foreign visitors wrote genuinely appreciative encomia about the quality and variety of the food, wine and music available, as well as about the cleanliness of the buildings in which they were prepared and served. The water culture of Istanbul found itself compared, in this regard, extremely favourably with London, Paris and Vienna.

It is a nicely piquant fact that the most vivid evidence for the Ottoman desire to Westernise came from the 'Peintres du Bosphore' – painters in the orientalist tradition. The advent of Ottoman ambassadors in Paris in AD 1721 and 1740 spawned the fashion to dress *en sultane* (enter the mistresses of Louis XV, Madame de Pompadour and Madame du Barry). Meanwhile Alexander Pope commissioned a painting of Lady Mary Wortley Montagu in Ottoman costume which he hung in his home by the Thames. In 1750s London the portrait painter Liotard stalked the streets dressed as an Ottoman Turk. The Occidental-oriental sartorialising fetish was handed backwards and forwards like a baton in a relay race: until the official dress reforms of 1829, those at the Sultan's court would be swaddled in fur-lined robes, in traditional kaftan and turban. For the remainder of the nineteenth century the fez and the stambouline – the new button-through coat that the Sultan encouraged his citizens to wear – would be the thing.

Meanwhile, from the reign of Sultan Selim III onwards (AD 1789–1807), portraiture using Western techniques was all the rage at the Istanbul court. At home Selim III allowed his women to keep accounts, to compose music, to practise archery. The Sultan was motivated to modernise for political rather than purely aesthetic reasons. He wrote that the Ottoman Empire was 'breaking up'. On the watch of the chief eunuch Moralı Beşir Ağa, his own private army rampaged through the streets extorting bribes. Janissaries, once such a mongrel influence in the city, had made themselves enemies of change. And others from abroad were still eyeing this Caput Mundi. Napoleon Bonaparte is quoted as saying, 'If the world were one state, then Istanbul would be its capital.' In 1793 the Ottomans opened their first Embassy in London (the thirty-year-old ambassador initially based in the Royal Hotel, Pall Mall) and allied themselves with the British against Napoleon. The French took Egypt in 1798. Paris might have fetishised Eastern fashions, but Napoleon's disruptive action saw Europe flooded with the treasures of the East. The dictator's – ultimately frustrated – Egyptian campaign included teams of 'Scholars' or 'Savants' bent on a 'Scientific Expedition'. These men gathered together 5,000 or so prime historic objects, acting very much like those early art-collecting Byzantine rulers of Constantinople. But defeat meant that the great bulk of the cultural loot – such as the British Museum's Rosetta Stone – ended up in England.

Meanwhile Mecca and Medina had been sacked by the al-Saud and their fervent 'Ikhwan' soldiers in AD 1803; local, feudal rulers known as *derebeys* (lords of the valley) such as Ali Pasha in Albania and Kavalalı Mehmed Ali in Egypt maintained considerable independence from central government. The weakening and break-up of Ottoman territories still plays out in our lives today. Outside the Topkapı Palace, patrolled today by police with sunglasses and automatic weapons, is the delicate fountain ordered by Ahmed III which was designed and constructed specifically to celebrate the values of peace and international understanding. This Ottoman-Baroque wonder encapsulates the dreams of Istanbul's rulers in the years 1718–30. At the time of writing it has been cited as a target by IS fighters operating out of the ex-Ottoman territories of Egypt, Syria and Iraq.

We should not forget that Aphrodite, from her birth in the Middle East as Ishtar or Astarte, chosen as a symbol of Istanbul in all her ages, pagan, Christian and now Ottoman, had always been not just a goddess of sex, beauty and desire but a goddess of war. Although visitors of the eighteenth century might describe Istanbul as a 'Citie by destinie appointed and by nature seated for Sovereigntie',[6] in truth the Sultan and his court were struggling to keep control. On her approach to Constantinople in AD 1717 Lady Mary Wortley Montagu was shocked to find fields littered with the bones and skulls of the Ottoman dead. Istanbul might be planting tulips and garlanding her streets with artificial lighting, but she was increasingly under threat both from without and from within.

PART EIGHT

❖

CITY OF REVOLT AND OPPORTUNITY

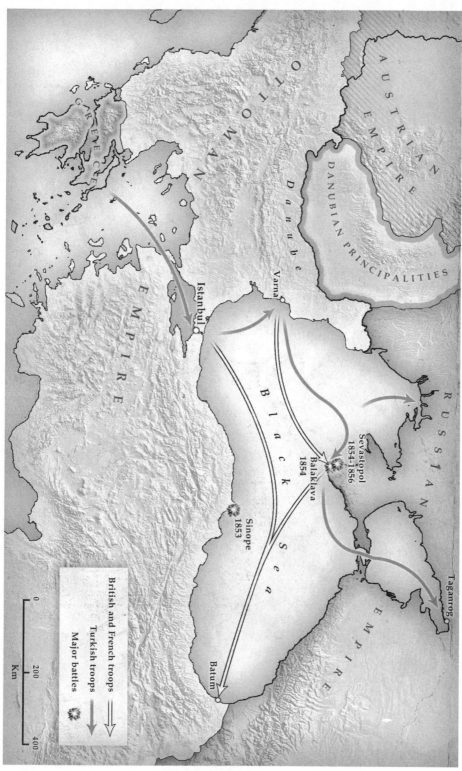

AUSTRIAN EMPIRE

DANUBIAN PRINCIPALITIES

OTTOMAN EMPIRE

G R E E C E

Danube

Varna

Istanbul

Black Sea

Sinope
1853

Balaklava
1854

Sevastopol
1854–1856

RUSSIAN

EMPIRE

Taganrog

Batum

Ottoman involvement in the Crimean War

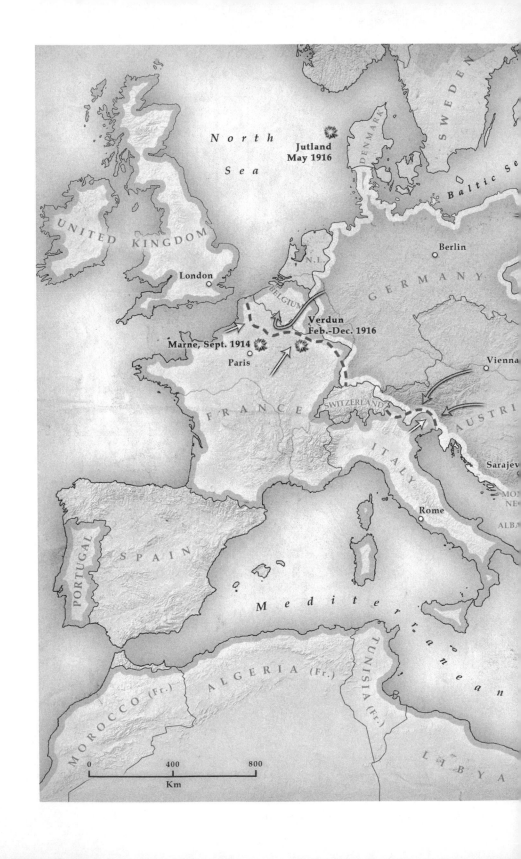

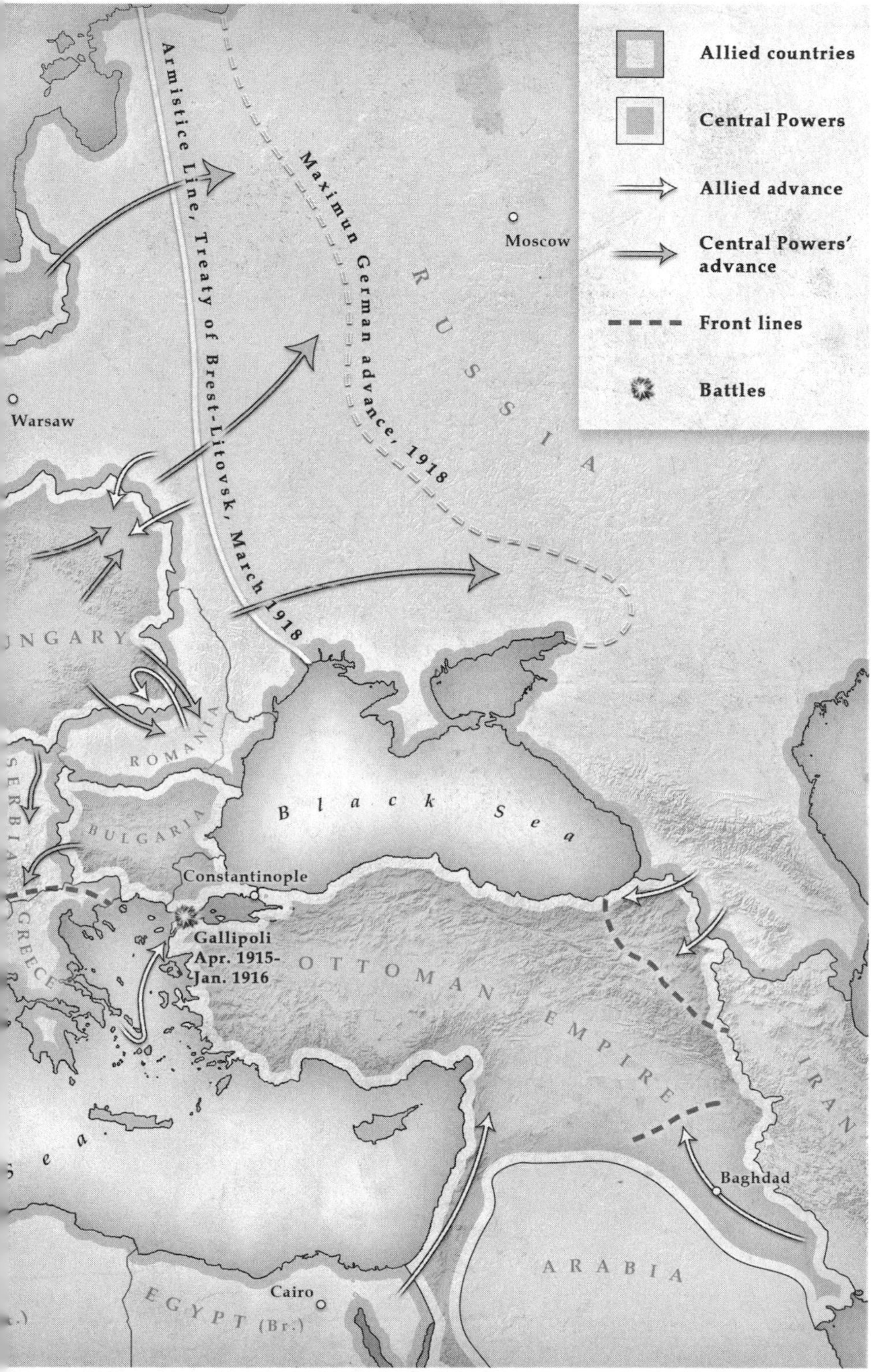

Allied countries
Central Powers
Allied advance
Central Powers' advance
Front lines
Battles
Armistice Line, Treaty of Brest-Litovsk, March 1918
Maximun German advance, 1918
Moscow
RUSSIA
Warsaw
UNGARY
ROMANIA
SERBIA
BULGARIA
GREECE
Black Sea
Constantinople
Gallipoli Apr. 1915-Jan. 1916
OTTOMAN EMPIRE
IRAN
Baghdad
ARABIA
Cairo
EGYPT (Br.)
Sea

The First World War

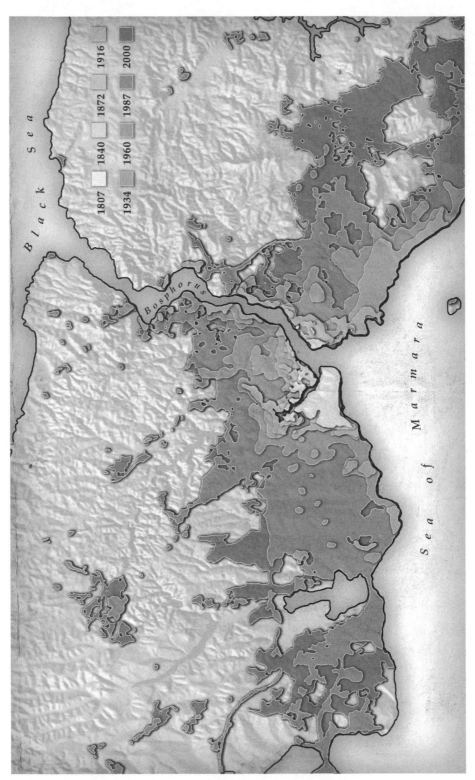

Expansion of Istanbul, AD 1807–2000

CHAPTER 67

✤

O LOVE! YOUNG LOVE!

AD 1809–1821
(1223–37 IN THE ISLAMIC CALENDAR)

And then he talk'd with him about Madrid,
Constantinople, and such distant places;
Where people always did as they were bid,
Or did what they should not with foreign graces.

LORD BYRON, *DON JUAN*[1] [2]

Opposite the Premier Inn Hotel and the defunct Ruby Blue nightclub just off Leicester Square in London, behind a bevy of immigrant workers from the old Ottoman territories of Syria and Iraq, is a handsome round building, now a Roman Catholic church. Before it was consecrated this venue had been designed specifically to show off panoramas of the greatest cities of the world: Constantinople, painted by Henry Aston Barker from a vantage point in Galata in AD 1799 and displayed in London in 1802, was three shillings' worth of curiosity. It was Henry's father who had invented the name, and indeed the concept, of the panorama – an idea which made the family rich. Aston Barker Junior's highly detailed rendition of Constantinople captures both the cosmopolitan feel of the city at the end of the eighteenth century, and the fact that this is a place often washed in a topaz light.

Where once an eager English crowd gathered to marvel at Kostantiniyye's minarets, arsenals and hammams, all painted with minute care and stretching round 360 degrees, now there are religious artworks that give an unknowing nod to human histories nourished by the ancient city. Mosaics and frescoes created by Jean Cocteau in 1960 show a rage of Roman soldiers attacking those early Christians of Asia Minor, and there is a tapestry above the altar in which a Cinderellaesque image of

Sophia – in a white frock and veil – seems very much the Near Eastern mistress of nature and knowledge, a modern-day Kybele.

As the global, political order shifted, for the inhabitants of nineteenth-century London, Paris and Berlin the forbidden fruits of Istanbul were ever more desirable – and ever more attainable.

The demographic of the streets of Istanbul was evolving. The city was attracting increasing numbers of Western visitors, arriving to enjoy a bit of orientalist tourism and sensing that change was in the air. In AD 1807 Janissaries established a puppet sultan on the throne and in 1808 they besieged Topkapı. In turn warships bombarded the rebels, starting fires that devastated buildings across the first and third hills. Idealists such as Thomas Hope and Lord Byron headed to the city. Hope – philosopher, author, art-collector – produced in Constantinople over 350 feather-fine drawings featuring not just mosques and palaces, but coffee shops and street children. For many Western visitors Istanbul would offer the first full immersion in streets thronged with people of colour (it will be why the sight of black Ottoman leaders in the Crimean War and the world's first black pilot in 1916 – Ahmed Ali Efendi – are eagerly commented on in the journals of Western visitors but pass without comment in Ottoman sources). Hope's favourite portrait shows the artist in Turkish dress in the sacred district of Eyüp, his waistcoat embroidered with Arabic.

Constantinople had been Lord Byron's primary goal on his Grand Tour of AD 1809–11, even though he was initially sidetracked to Portugal. The wandering poet arrived, having killed time by recreating the Greek hero Leander's swim across the Hellespont from Europe to Asia 'for Glory', and then spent his first night in the city, calmly, on the water, where he was mesmerised by Constantinople's deceptive peace. The following day, trying to spy on concubines in the Sultan's harem through a telescope, he instead saw a corpse being gnawed at by dogs beneath the seraglio walls; the severed heads of state enemies in those purpose-built niches outside its gate would be his next unpleasant surprise.[3]

Although he might have toyed with the idea of 'becoming a Mussulman', Byron's heart ultimately lay in Greece and his sympathies with the bandit-mountaineers he had met on the roads – a number of whom had grown rich on the Sultan's sale of regional tax rights (in many Balkan countries such as Serbia there is still a national holiday on 28 June, the day when bandits traditionally took themselves to the forests to plan attacks on their Ottoman overlords). But Byron admired Constantinople's walls, her 'battlements covered with ivy'; he enjoyed boat trips up the Bosphorus, past jauntily painted *yalıs*; and he amused himself translating Euripides' *Medea* afresh at the very rocks to which the eponymous antiheroine was said to have chased her feckless lover Jason. He appreciated the sheer beauty of Kostantiniyye's harbours, particularly when the boats sparkled at night. Byron wrote in a letter to his publisher John Murray that Constantinople boasted the best sea view in the world. And it was from Constantinople (which the poet sometimes calls Byzantium) that Byron reiterated his desire to be a citizen of the world.

But, in the city for only two months and one day, Byron chose not to write extensively about the World's Desire, thinking this had already been done well enough by Gibbon and Lady Mary Wortley Montagu.[4] Hence this sparky aside in *Don Juan*:

> Sophia's cupola with golden gleam;
> The cypress groves; Olympus high and hoar;
> The twelve isles and the more than I could dream,
> Far less describe, present the very view
> Which charmed the charming Mary Montagu.[5] [6]

After his visit seven stanzas featuring the hubbub of the city, the 'motley robe', a 'languid eye' and 'thrilling hand', did appear in *Childe Harold's Pilgrimage*. Byron's experiences in Stamboul itself were, in truth, limited – as they were for all foreigners. Allowed to visit mosques (including Ayasofya) only with the express permission of the Sultan, unable to enter the harem, chilled by the slave market and granted one audience with the Sultan, his trip generated a relatively modest degree of slavering orientalist fancy. But, paradoxically, Byron is to some degree responsible for the impression of Istanbul that many millions both then and now enjoy. The odd chance of the invention of steel-plate engraving – which meant that the poet's feelings about the city could be reimagined and made incarnate – brought Ottoman Istanbul into drawing rooms across the globe as publishers both legitimate and illegal started to reproduce attractively illustrated volumes of Byron's writings. Byron's 'Eastern' works were phenomenally successful: *The Corsair* sold 10,000 copies on its first day of publication. With the addition of such tantalising images as 'The Angel of the Harem' and 'The Boy of the Slave Market', Byron unwittingly became Istanbul's mass-market illustrator.[7] Now that the Sultan's court and his armies seemed to be losing their sting, Istanbul could become an exotic inhabitant of the respectable parlour.

But the Ottomans in Kostantiniyye were twitchy. A clandestine organisation – the Philike Hetairia, the Society of Friends – was planning trouble. Founded in Odessa in AD 1814, this secret society, which took its inspiration from Freemasonry and Italy's revolutionary Carbonarism, had quietly moved its headquarters to the capital city. Among its prominent members were Phanariot Greeks – those high-ranking families who had, since the sixteenth century, been the power-wielding dragomans of Kostantiniyye. Philike Hetairia's call was for all Greeks to rebel against their Ottoman overlords. In mid-March 1821 violence broke out in the Peloponnese and quickly spread through Ottoman-held centres. The Greek War of Independence, a conflict hijacked by external forces, had begun. All the Muslims of Corinth – women and children included – were killed, despite the fact the British had offered them safe passage. There were atrocities on both sides: the English ambassador in Istanbul, Viscount Strangford, reported cartloads of Christians' ears and noses being offered for sale in the marketplace. Even though the Greek patriarch had assured Ottoman officials that his flock were loyal to the Sultan, on Easter Sunday, 22 April, he was hanged in retribution from the Orta Kapı – the main gate of the patriarchate. The entrance-way has been painted black ever since.

Relations between the Muslims and Jews in the city had been relatively good, but the Ottomans calculatingly exploited the bad blood between Jews and Christians. In AD 1821 it was Jews who were ordered by the grand vizier Benderli Ali Pasha to take down the body of the Greek patriarch and then throw it into the sea. It turned out that a number of other high-ranking citizens had been beheaded. The Christian inhabitants took their rage to the Jewish quarters, and 5,000 Jews were said to have been injured during riots of retribution.

Erroneously suspected of involvement in the Philike Hetairia uprising, vast numbers of those Phanariot dragomans, who had stitched together Istanbul's international relations for 300 years, were executed. From ambassadors to food-buyers for the palace, all were gone in a welter of blood.

The Sultan and grand vizier admitted a few years later that they had found themselves with no one left to translate documents or to interpret messages. Meanwhile, in what would soon be the Kingdom of Greece, rebel forces continued to gather strength. Byron, now philhellene rather than philottoman, would opine, 'Why, man! If we had but 100,000 *l* sterling in hand, we should now be half-way to the city of Constantine.'[8] At a stroke, by killing those close to them, the internationalist dragomans, the Ottoman leaders and their apparatchiks had isolated themselves from a wide world, of which they had once been the centre.

CHAPTER 68

MASSACRE

AD 1822
(1237/8 IN THE ISLAMIC CALENDAR)

Greek families await slavery or death etc. See various accounts and the
newspapers of the time.

SUBTITLE OF EUGÈNE DELACROIX'S *SCÈNES DES MASSACRES DE SCIO*,

SALON EXHIBITION CATALOGUE, PARIS, AD 1824

The Turks have been here. All is bleak, in ruin.
Chios, isle of wines, is now a darkened reef.
Chios, cradled by green branches,
Chios, where curling waves mirror soft hills,
forests, palaces, and, on certain nights,
dancing choirs of young girls,
All is desert. But no, near a blackened wall
sits a Greek child, a blue-eyed boy,
alone and bending his head in shame . . .
Oh poor child . . .
What would you like? Flowers, fruits, marvellous birds?
'Friend,' replies the Greek child with the clear blue eyes,
'I want some bullets and a gun.'

VICTOR HUGO, *THE CHILD* (AD 1828)[1]

In AD 1770 the islanders of Chios, the island 300-odd miles to the south
of Kostantiniyye and a few miles from the coast of Asia Minor, which
had since early antiquity been a character in Istanbul's story, had watched
and listened as the Ottoman fleet was destroyed by the Russians on the
Turkish shoreline at the Battle of Çeşme. Catherine the Great, who had
been crowned wearing a robe decorated with the double-headed eagle of

Byzantium, was on the warpath. After travelling from the Baltic Sea for a year, her fleet was bent on slaughter. It was said in Russian sources that 90,000 Turks died in the conflict at Çeşme (the number was in fact closer to 11,000), but only thirty Russians. In 1822 it would be the Chians' turn to suffer.

When one stands on the eastern coast of wind-whipped Chios and picks out, just 5 miles across the water, the crescent moon on flags fluttering on mainland Turkey, the strategic nature of Chios is startlingly clear. The Chians had seen off Islamic invasions, described in local guidebooks as 'the raids of Mohammedan pirates', in the seventh, eighth and ninth centuries. Briefly held by Muslim forces in AD 1090–7, after the First and Second Crusades Chios had become Orthodox Christian once again – ruled by the Genoese and then, after 1566, by the Ottomans.

Chios' crowning medieval glory, declaring its umbilical connection to the mother city, is the Byzantine monastery of Nea Moni. Founded in AD 1042,[2] highly reminiscent of Constantinople's Haghia Sophia, this was one of the most important and vibrant of Byzantine religious complexes to be built beyond Constantinople. Even if Nea Moni's working dedicants are now in their twilight years and their abbess, Maria Theodora, is bedridden, in its heyday this place was considered a wonder of the Christian world. A marble refectory table with little inbuilt cutlery holders still survives, delivering a sense of the monastery's calm order. Before one's eye is drawn up to the gorgeous glitter of the mosaics here, there is first a puzzle of marble facings to get through, each block pulled in from a different outpost of Constantinople's medieval empire, the stonework a patchwork of power. Lavish colours have been used – this was Byzantium at its best.[3] In the mosaics, dressed in their distinctive jewelled tunics with their fearsome axes there are Varangians. There are Muslims too: on the walls of this Chios cloister we find one of the earliest Western representations of the Islamic crescent.

Chios' proximity to modern-day Turkey and its fertility had meant that the islanders always had some bargaining power. From the time of Plato's *Symposium* onwards, Chian wine was praised, and so was the island's workmanship: according to works attributed to the hazy, fifteenth-century figure Kodinos,[4] the famous horses of St Mark's stolen from Constantinople's hippodrome in AD 1204 were made here. And the

Chians had a trump card, in that they produced and protected a unique resource, mastic gum. Chios' name almost certainly derives from the Phoenician for mastic – a lure for pirates and invaders since antiquity. One of nature's miracles, mastic gum is a natural antibacterial; jewels of diamond-perfect sap weep, very slowly, from the *Pistacia lentiscus* var. *Chia* tree which, despite many efforts to export for commercial production, thrives only on this island.

The haunting Roman-period Fayum portraits discovered in AD 1887 by Flinders Petrie employ the gum; it was mastic that held in place the blue and gold that decorated Theodora and Justinian's chapel in Constantinople; Rubens used mastic to stabilise his paints; mastic is a foundational ingredient of authentic Turkish delight; the gum cures bacterial infections of many kinds, and we are recalling mastic each time we masticate. Throughout the history of Istanbul, those who could afford it chewed mastic gum to freshen their breath and to ward off infection.[5] In the Ottoman period, mastic made Chios one of Istanbul's most prized provinces.

Chians' special relationship with Constantinople was also apparent in Byzantine times. A number of chrysobulls – imperial decrees – codified the substantial perks that Chios enjoyed, including favourable tax arrangements and a declaration that there would not be mass enslavement of the island's children. Thanks to the desirability of their unique antibacterial resource (even in ancient times travellers wrote excited tales of the perfection of the teeth and breasts of the Chian women),[6] the Ottoman hold on the island had always felt a little light.

But in early March AD 1822 news reached Istanbul that a deputation from Samos had arrived on Chios to put steel into the sinews of Christians on the island – to ensure that they signed up to the fledgling revolutionary Hellenic cause. The first of what would within a century be 5.4 million Muslim refugees fleeing Christian persecution started to arrive on Istanbul's streets. Sultan Mahmud II – not wanting to lose the plum prize that was Chios – ordered the execution both of hostages on Chios island and of a number of Chians in Istanbul itself. As shipowners and captains, the Chians had long been valued by the capital, and they had their own quarter in the city and their Church of St John.[7] These aristocratic Chian communities provided the highly respected administrators, dragomans and businessmen frequently found in the employ of the Ottoman government. Speaking frangochiotika, their strange mix of Italian, Greek and Turkish, they were truly internationalist – and a valued and critical part of the cultural tapestry that was Istanbul.

But now they were the enemy. Kara Ali Pasha landed from Istanbul and started to purge Chios from the north.[8] Many rushed to the Nea Moni monastery for sanctuary, only for the 2,000 or so women and children hiding here to be burnt alive or cut down. Avgonyma and Anavatos, the cubist, stone villages with a Holy Land feel high in the central hills, were either occupied or eradicated. There was dreadful suffering. Ottoman forces had long had a reputation for being quick to decapitate. By the end of April some 20,000–25,000 people had been killed on the island and 40,000–45,000 had been captured, enslaved, driven to death by exhaustion or deported. Many remain unaccounted for. Before the invasion there had been over 100,000 Greeks on Chios, 5,000 Muslims and 3,000 Jews. After the Ottoman army got busy, historians recounted that just 2,000 of the Greeks were left.[9]

Across Chios today the AD 1822 massacre is remembered and there is a sense that even for a people used to fighting and to pain and to struggle, this act of brutality was simply beyond the pale. In the ossuary of Nea Moni, rows of skulls from the genocide, with their death blows gaping, are prominently displayed. And in one Chian church – built in memory of a son of Chios who died in an accident on the island – within a riot of haloed saints and just beneath the portrait of the lost twenty-year-old are Plato and Macarias, two victims of the attack whose canonisation is regularly denied to the patriarch by the Turkish authorities. The sounds of the past are all around here: there are owls in the forests above and beneath; *meltemi* winds (dry, northerly winds of the Aegean) worry at doors and latches; women chatter, as Homer once said, 'like the nymphs that haunt mountain tops'. But in the mid nineteenth century there would have been a new kind of silence. The glut in Chian slaves across Ottoman territories meant a fall in prices;[10] travellers started to notice more Chian women in the brothels of Istanbul.

At the time of writing in 2016 the island is still on the front line – handling the tens of thousands of refugees, many drowning within a few yards of the shore, who arrive daily in boatload-batches from Syria, Libya or Afghanistan.

The Massacre at Chios *by Eugène Delacroix*

The events that altered relations between Chios and Istanbul clari-
fied an emerging mood in international relations. In AD 1822 Europe
and America wanted to know and to understand the atrocity that had
happened here. The Chios massacre and the reaction to it are a potent
reminder that we are the stories we tell about ourselves. A painting – *The
Massacre at Chios* by Eugène Delacroix – was one such response. 'I am
planning to paint for the next Exhibition a picture whose subject will be
taken from the recent wars between the Turks and the Greeks – I think
that in the present circumstances this will be a way of drawing attention
to myself, as long as it is well enough painted,'[11] wrote Delacroix. Reaction
to the painting was indeed vehement. Although some were anxious about
the graphic nature of Delacroix's work – a shocking departure for a war
painting – the massacre at Chios was soon the talk of polite society. Even
if it was generated for self-serving reasons, Delacroix's horror genre – one
of the first of its kind to be displayed in a public museum – along with
Victor Hugo's fictionalised accounts of the conflict (from which I quote
at the beginning of this chapter), was key in turning the tide of feeling
against Ottoman might. And the Greeks whose families had escaped the
massacres made sure that this story was not forgotten. Their descendants

come back each summer to the 'motherland'; they visit Nea Moni; they remember why they are who they are.

For the Ottomans the slaughter on Chios was in some ways the harbinger of the end of the Ottoman Empire. It marked the moment when, in the popular consciousness, an oriental fantasy of Ottoman delights was simply no longer valid or tenable. Another popular painting now started to circulate, that of the *Başıbozuk* – irregulars in the Ottoman army who lived from plunder. And so the rocky island that we are told was Homer's birthplace – the epic bard whose tale of Troy would nourish the notion of an East–West divide – pointed to a calcification of ideas. The notion of the Muslim Ottomans firmly but justly ruling swathes of the world from Istanbul was now so brittle it could do nothing but split.[12]

CHAPTER 69

REVOLUTION

AD 1826–39

> But Istanbul is so vast a city, that if a thousand die in it, the want of them
> is not felt in such an ocean of men.
>
> EVLIYA ÇELEBI, *SEYAHATNAME* (BOOK OF TRAVELS)[1]

The men who had been the loyalist core of the Sultan's forces, the Janissaries, the phalanx which for 500 years had come to represent the reach and the spirit of the Ottoman project, revolted in AD 1826. The Sultan was attempting to reform the military – introducing European weaponry and Turkish recruits – goading his recherché, excitable, multi-ethnic warriors. Banging their cauldrons to announce their mutiny along Butchers' Row (which had once been the processional route of Byzantine emperors), where they had for centuries been given meat rations in a quasi-ritualistic offering, the Sultan's elite army was in effect declaring civil war. As Bektashis, the Janissaries could lend money more easily than other Muslims and had broken down the restrictions that once prevented them from trade – they had created their own splinter economy. Across Ottoman territories they ran tax rackets and ruled as kinglets (their descendants, the Koloğlu, still enjoy influence in Turkish affairs today).[2] These were privileged and unruly economic actors. Up until the early nineteenth century and their disbandment in 1826, Janissaries would force depositions, revolutions and executions. Many from Karl Marx to Max Weber considered them key to the degradation of despotism and sultanism – a system that validated total rule over productive slaves. In fact, as they met in their coffee houses and in the cool courtyard of the Orta Mosque – which still serves as an oasis from the commercial frenzy of the Grand Bazaar today – it seems rather that the Janissaries understood what they were due and how far they could push those demands, both for their own benefit and on behalf of other Istanbullus. The Janissaries were ordinary people with power. This was all dangerous.

The response from within the Topkapı Palace to the uprising was ruthless. As it became clear that the Sultan would retaliate with force, many Janissaries fled back to their barracks, where thousands were accommodated together. On 14 June, a combination of Ottoman cavalry, the Sipahis, and resentful locals surrounded the barrack buildings, which were then burnt to the ground. The suffering inside must have been excruciating. The gates of Istanbul were also locked and any men who escaped were rounded up and killed in the hippodrome. Stragglers were executed in Thessalonika in a prison-extermination facility by the sea that was for years called the Bloody Tower – now repainted as the more tourist-industry-friendly White Tower. The Janissary Corps, along with the Bektashi Brotherhood, was formally dissolved on 16 June, by which time at least 5,000 lay dead or dying. Their abolition was read out from Sultan Ahmed Mosque. The Janissaries were to be replaced by the Trained Triumphant Soldiers of Muhammad. In Istanbul all this was declared an 'Auspicious Incident' – in the Balkans, from where so many Janissary soldiers had come, the Incident was known as 'Unfortunate'.

So many were executed in June AD 1826 that the corpses thickened the Marmara's wash beneath the city walls. Plague broke out in July. Come the melting white heat of August and many of the city's civilian inhabitants had died. There was an attempt to eradicate the Janissary story from history. A number of the registers detailing their origins, recruitment and the day-to-day business of their lives, all held in the old Haghia Eirene, were burnt. Graves in the Janissary cemeteries – places that Byron had described as 'the loveliest on earth' – were smashed. Choosing an Armenian architect to do the work, Sultan Mahmud II rededicated what he now called Nusretiye Camii, the Mosque of Divine Victory, to commemorate their eradication.

But the Janissary presence has lingered on in odd ways. Urban legend has it that the tiny number of soldiers who did survive went underground into the stokeholes of the hammams, where they were fed by friends or family. Many composed songs which, it is whispered, are still sung in the city – the Külhan Beyler, the 'governors of the stokehole'.[3] In Istanbul

*Nusretiye Mosque, re-dedicated in AD 1826 to commemorate victory over the
Janissaries and designed by the Armenian architect Krikor Balyan, whose family
served the Sultan for five generations. Photograph taken c. 1900*

itself it is hard to track down these ballads, but on the religious holiday
of Kurban Bayramı (Eid al-Adha) I made my way to a rare, surviving
Bektashi *tekke* on the Asian side of the city. A man with a freshly ironed
check shirt and neat moustache took me up to the prayer rooms above
the equivalent of a village hall and beneath the refectory (where the poor
were offered rice and meat and the yoghurt drink *ayran* three times a
week, as they have been at *tekkes* since at least the fourteenth century),
to talk about the Bektashi religion and his pride in their Janissary ancestors. Could this Dede (a Bektashi religious leader) remember one of their
songs? Yes he could – and out came a fluid, mellifluous prayer, a song
from the religion of the road, a song of hope and of freedom, of piety and
of cosmopolitan human-heartedness.[4]

Istanbul became a city not just of revolt, but reform. The signing of the
Treaty of Constantinople in AD 1832 guaranteed Greek independence.
Rather than sulking, Istanbul chose to adapt. Four hundred years after

it had been superimposed on the Greek, Roman and Byzantine remains on the acropolis, the grand Topkapı Palace was about to be abandoned in favour of the lighter, brighter imperial alternatives that were being built along the city's waterfronts. Many of these palaces were worked on by French or Armenian architects. Although some politely pointed out that the Topkapı was a wonder of the world, Sultan Mahmud II ranted, 'None, save a rogue or a fool, could class that place [Topkapı] . . . hidden beneath high walls, amid dark trees, as though it would not brave the light of day, with these light, laughing palaces, open to the free air, and the pure sunshine of heaven. Such would I have my own; and such shall it be.'[5] Just as Mahmud II justified the Janissary massacre as a move 'to purge the garden of the Empire of its savage and useless weeds', he was now determined to 'embellish' his capital city with new 'fruits'.

What came to be called the *tanzimat* – a period of reforms announced in the Topkapı's Rose Garden in AD 1839 that would last until the introduction of the first Ottoman constitution in 1876 – was a sensible, political reordering, the Ottomans getting their 'House in Order'. Security of life and property was guaranteed, capital punishment without trial was no longer legal, and, perhaps most significantly, there was too, on paper, legal equality between Muslim and non-Muslim. This was a conscious move to make Istanbul a full member of the European club. The *tanzimat*, initiated with a document known as the 'Rescript of the Rose Chamber', prompted fallout that was cultural as well as social, political and constitutional.

From the mid-nineteenth century, had you sailed up the Bosphorus or the Golden Horn you might have glimpsed a rather extraordinary sight. From stilted bathing huts could be heard peals of women's laughter and splashes within a fenced-off area while alert guards patrolled around outside. These were the sea hammams, a go-ahead development in the city. Elsewhere, more and more European-style buildings appeared: medical and engineering schools, further-education colleges, barracks, factories, even a school for girls – all designed in a neo-classical–baroque style and sited prominently on hilltops or set off by grand public squares (it was the proposed recreation of one of these barracks as a shopping mall on Taksim Square that sparked the Gezi protests of 2013). A number of new-look mosques – such as that at Ortaköy which greets disembarking

European influence was in widespread evidence in Istanbul in the nineteenth century, including brollies on Galata Bridge. Umbrellas originally started life in the East, in ancient China, Egypt and Persia.

ferry passengers – punctuated the Bosphorus shore. British officials noted approvingly that in just one year (AD 1843–4) some 600 tons of British machinery was imported for installation in the glistening industrial buildings, often to make the stambouline out of imported British cotton or wool.[6]

Following the grant of free trade to the British in AD 1838 after a series of meetings by the Bosphorus, men in the city eagerly took to the use of British brollies as sunshades, while Ottoman goods, such as sofas, sorbets, 'Persian' cats, ottomans, divans, kiosks and sashes, started to appear in middle-class Western homes. Contact with India via the colonies had given the British a new fascination with washing (shampoo, for example, is a Hindi word). Bathtimes required sponges – cherished since antiquity, indeed mentioned in Aeschylus' *Agamemnon* – and the Ottomans, who ruled over many sponge-harvesting communities, stepped up to the mark. The tiny island of Chalki close to the Asian coast (home to that splendid, crumbling corsair castle) once supplied half of England's sponge needs. In Chalki's *kafeneion* on the harbour men deep in their cups still sing a ditty that commemorates the island's golden days: 'only when the Bank of England closes will cash stop coming to Chalki'.[7]

And one man – who immortalised the glories of the Ottoman sponge in his nonsense verse came on a trip to the land of its birth.

Arriving at dawn on 1 August AD 1848, Edward Lear was sick. Originally having set out from Corfu with a diplomatic party (the British ambassador to Istanbul quaffing champagne and reciting Byron's *Siege of Corinth* while they sailed), Lear fell ill, probably with malaria. This multi-talented, fragile man, the youngest surviving child of twenty-one, was eventually cared for on arrival by the wife of the British ambassador, Sir Stratford Canning (who had hosted Byron two decades before) at Therapeia on the European edge of the Bosphorus. Therapeia has ancient links back to the story of Jason and Medea, but by the nineteenth century it had become the place to be seen for Istanbul's *beau monde*. Unwell and peevish, Lear compared the Bosphorus unfavourably to Wapping. The wild dogs of the city troubled him – they were vicious especially at night. This artist-author described the veiled Muslim women with their 'tooth-ache' wrappings as 'ghosts'. Like Byron he saw decapitated heads that had once belonged to rebels against the Sultan. Within a month of arriving Lear had moved to the Hôtel d'Angleterre in the Galata district – the region of greater Istanbul so Occidental, so full of Europeans, it was commonly known as Frengistan.

Lear's finely observed pictures show a bosky city, lush and sprawling, those sea walls dominating all views from the water.[8] He describes cypresses reaching down to the waters and a delicious sweet made of mastic gum, sugar and attar of roses 'whose name escapes me' (Turkish delight). The artist would have appreciated the city for features that, in some rare places, still exist: apples ripening on the *elmalık* or apple-shelves above the window; *meyhanes* owned by Greeks and Armenians (Evliya Çelebi says there were more than a thousand in the city by the mid-seventeenth century) which sold both food and alcohol. Eating on the streets of Constantinople was welcomed; men and women bought snacks from public ovens and street vendors or were supplied by a mosque's soup kitchen (or, before their abolition, at a Janissary ration-point). In Istanbul only the very rich could afford private kitchens.

Fishermen's houses on the Bosphorus painted by Edward Lear, and one of the first ever daguerreotypes of a similar scene. Daguerreotypes of Istanbul were produced within a year or two of their invention.

Drama struck during Lear's visit when a raging fire took hold – with its narrow streets, wooden buildings and open braziers it was little surprise that conflagrations were so frequent. Lear recounted his horror as the night sky became as bright as day. He watched as porters bundled families and their belongings into the safety of the cemetery gardens. His sketches – which grew more affectionate as he came to understand that the spirit of this city lay not in its impression but in its detail – show us Kostantiniyye before the feel of the streets would substantially change in the second half of the nineteenth century.

Edward Lear was not the only visitor to the city in the year AD 1848. As crops failed across Europe, famine followed and the continent was rocked with revolution. But the Ottoman Empire remained plump with supplies and therefore revolt-free. While the monarchy was overturned in France, in Kostantiniyye the English diplomat Percy Smythe described the 'delightful excitement' as the Italians in the city 'hoisted caps of liberty and shouted . . . "Vive la République" to the bewilderment of the Turks'[9]. Liberals from Hungary and Poland flooded into Istanbul and the broadminded Sultan Abdülmecid I agreed to take in these political refugees. Ever since the Hunnic invasions of the fifth century AD this walled city of many names had enjoyed an almost mythic reputation as a settlement where fugitives could enjoy sanctuary. A number of international powers took a dim view of the Sultan's humanitarian generosity. Indeed, the city's engagement with the febrile politics of the age would not play out so well – because soon there would be more terror-stricken civilians running to her gates and more bodies rotting by her shores. Istanbul was about to tangle once again with one of her most invidious and persistent enemies, Russia.

CHAPTER 70

✦

TSARGRAD

AD 1768–1847
(1181–1264 IN THE ISLAMIC CALENDAR)

We have on our hands a sick man – a very sick man: it will be, I tell you
frankly, a great misfortune if, one of these days, he should slip away from
us, especially before all necessary arrangements were made.

TSAR NICHOLAS I TO THE BRITISH AMBASSADOR, SIR G. H. SEYMOUR[1]

Today, after decades of Soviet communism, the Russians are rediscovering their love of saints, icons, emperors and empresses. In Corfu, up a
side-street draped with the usual garish T-shirts and red-faced tourists is
the icon-filled cathedral of the Most Holy Theotokos Speliotissis, which
honours the ninth-century Byzantine empress St Theodora. Empress
Theodora's relics, trumpet the guidebooks, were brought here from Constantinople after the Ottoman conquest. The miraculously uncorrupted
remains are processed through Corfu Town once a year – on the first
Sunday of Lent – to the delight of eager visitors. Gaggles of Russian
women, headscarves tightly fastened, kiss Theodora's glass shroud lying
in a silver coffin while the priest says special-favour prayers over her holy
relics under a painting of the royal saint. How appropriate that one of
Constantinople's restorers of icons should be worshipped in this very
iconic way.

After the fall of Constantinople in AD 1453 it was Russia which took on
the mantle of Orthodoxy. Now the Virgin was presumed to be shrouding
Moscow, the Third Rome, with her protective veil. In the seventeenth century one of Moscow's three great city gates, behind St Basil's Cathedral,
was named Konstantino-Eleninsk after Constantine and Helen. Come
the eighteenth century it was Catherine the Great who was adored as
a blessed queen, her state clothes spangled with that Byzantine symbol

from the Palaeologian coat of arms of the double-headed eagle (the bird motif a delicious combination of the Roman single eagle and Bronze Age Anatolian sacred double-headed eagle), which had been enthusiastically adopted by Russia at the end of the fifteenth century.

The thrusting nature of Russia's ambition in the eighteenth century is still evident in the ports of Sevastopol in the Crimean peninsula and in Odessa – established by Catherine the Great as a base for her fleets and at the same time to increase Russian control of the Black Sea, to intimidate the Ottomans and to secure the requisition of lands ruled from Istanbul.[2]

Until AD 1774 the Black Sea had been an Ottoman lake, described as a 'pure and immaculate virgin',[3] but Turkish losses in the second half of the eighteenth century included the Black Sea ports of Azov[4] and Greater and Lesser Kabarda in the north Caucasus. When Cossacks pursued Polish freedom-fighters over the Ottoman border and razed and raped their way through the Ottoman city of Odessa in 1768, Sultan Mustafa III ordered the incarceration of the Russian ambassador and his entire staff in the Yedikule Fortress. Catherine II now chose to wear contemporary military attire in public, the Byzantine eagle still prominent – she had Istanbul in her sights.

Eyewitnesses reported war fever sweeping the streets of Kostantiniyye. Russia retaliated. Catherine's Baltic fleet, led by two Scottish officers, made a journey of 4,000 miles, reprovisioning at Hull and Portsmouth. Its aim was to weaken the Ottoman position by helping to foment revolt in the Peloponnese and to destroy the Sultan's maritime capabilities. In July AD 1770 this was the fleet that had arrived off the Turkish coast at Çeşme, just west of modern-day Izmir, acting upon intelligence that this was where the Ottoman navy was anchored. For the Russian ships it had been a long journey and the men on board were ready to taste blood. The Ottomans were taken entirely by surprise. Potemkin had led an attack by land, describing the Ottoman warriors as a 'torrent' and declaring that the bravest were intoxicated with opium. But in the water it was the rage of Russian fireboats that won the day. Twelve Russian ships destroyed most of the Ottoman vessels. Eleven thousand Ottomans died. It had been the Ottomans who declared war, yet it was their fleet that was all but annihilated.

Within a couple of years Moldavia, Wallachia and the Crimea (the

Khanate there, in existence as a Turkic vassal state since AD 1478, had been nominally independent, but in practice was under Ottoman control) were also lost. It was on one of these ravaging Russian campaigns – many of them conducted in the Ottomans' Caucasian territories – that the woman who would end up providing Blumenbach's Caucasian skull was captured and taken to her death in Moscow. Following the Sultan's embarrassing defeat, one of the humiliating terms agreed was that Catherine the Great would be allowed to build a Christian church in the Galata district of Istanbul. This was a symbolic concession with a very real outcome: Russia was now widely viewed as officially the protector of Orthodox Christians across what remained of the Ottoman Empire.⁵ Catherine celebrated by keeping her troops in the East to harry Syrian ports (Russian forces occupied Beirut for six months) and, at home, by developing a victory theme park, complete with commemorative lake. Cartoonists had a field day – the fantasy of a lustful Catherine goading a priapic Turk was simply too good to miss.

In Istanbul, Sultan Mustafa III's successor Abdülhamid I was broken by the Ottoman failure and died of a stroke before the war was concluded. A

Satirical cartoon by James Gillray, published in AD 1791, of Catherine the Great with one foot in Russia and the other in Constantinople

sad life, imprisoned for forty-three years before he acceded, and hailed by many as a saint (although a lusty one: in the fifteen years before he died his seven favourite harem consorts gave birth to twenty-six children), his time on the throne saw a shift in the axis of power.

The Russian presence in Istanbul escalated. The new Russian Orthodox Church became a stop-off point, or an excuse, for pilgrimage to the city that the Russians had long called Tsargrad. Now that the Russians had control of the Black Sea – and found that both Slavic and Orthodox Christian populations needed little persuading to turn their loyalty to Russia rather than to the Ottoman Sultan – the Tsarist Empire felt that there could be a forward momentum, across that Ottoman lake, no longer the Sultan's virgin, through the Bosphorus to Constantinople and then beyond the Dardanelles straits which laid bare the East and the South West alike.

The recapture of Constantinople for Christianity was a bombastic expectation that had never been allowed to subside. In the sixteenth century the *Tales of Tsargrad* by Nestor Iskander – which told of the fall of Constantinople – was a popular work of historical fiction. In AD 1779 a boy had been born to Grand Duchess Maria Fyodorovna and earmarked as the future ruler of Constantinople. He was brought up speaking Greek by a Greek nurse called Helen. The key architect of this Hellenic project was Catherine the Great's General and lover Potemkin, himself appropriately nicknamed Alcibiades.

So when the Ottomans imprisoned the Russian ambassador in Istanbul once more in AD 1787, again in the dungeons of Yedikule Fortress, all this was little less than a declaration of both cultural and sacred war.

In the summer of AD 1829 during the Greek War of Independence the Russians had made it to within a day's march of Constantinople.[6] There was no doubt that the city's reclamation would be viewed as a triumph for Orthodoxy. The Treaty of Edirne was signed in September and started to formalise the end of the Greek War, divvying up territories between the Ottoman and Russian Empires and ensuring the release of all Greek and Christian slaves who had retained their faith (although of course for many there had been no choice other than to convert to Islam). As part of the *tanzimat* reforms, in 1847, the slave market in the centre of Istanbul was closed down. But, predictably, the profitable sex industry went underground, and in some instances, as Alexandre Dumas recorded, carried on in plain sight.

'There are three hundred prime-bodied Kabardians with us at the moment travelling steerage,' the Captain said, 'Mostly women and children in the charge of two tribal chiefs and the headmen of various villages . . . They have valid passports and have paid their fare. Everything is in perfect order and they never give us any trouble. Besides, the girls do not seem to mind. They all expect to marry a pasha or join the harem of some great lord. If they complained to us we might take action. This they easily could, for twice a day they come up for fresh air and exercise, but they never say a word.'[7]

Russia had banned slave trading in Russian lands as early as AD 1805, and Russian ships patrolled the Black Sea ostensibly to prevent trafficking from their ports. But criminalisation simply increased the price of the commodities. In the 1840s Circassian girls could be sold for as much as 30,000 piastres. There was endemic bribery; slavers were given false documents with which to escape interception. A number of first-hand accounts describe those who were liberated ending up as the chattels of their so-called saviours.[8] Alexander Sergeyevich Pushkin, the Russian soldier, poet, author and essayist, scattered his work with references to the Ottoman slave trade, to the 'bloom within the harem's towers', 'daughters of delight' and in *The Moor of Peter the Great* we hear: '"He is not of humble birth," said Gavrila Afanassyevitch; "he is the son of a Moorish sultan. The pagans took him prisoner and sold him in Constantinople, and our local ambassador rescued him and presented him to the Tsar. His elder brother came to Russia with an appreciable ransom . . ."'[9]

It is not a little ironic that Pushkin – who described with wide-eyed delight the women bathing in the 'sultry waters' of the Ottoman baths in Tbilisi in modern-day Georgia, and who wrote so stereotypically of the harem's inhabitants throughout his life, was himself the product of Istanbul's trade in humans. His own great-grandfather was an Ethiopian or Cameroonian slave bought by the Russian ambassador in one of the human markets outside Istanbul's Grand Bazaar.

Pushkin's ancestry and his writings tell us how closely entwined the experience of being Ottoman and of being Russian had become. For centuries, from the moment the Rus besieged Constantinople in the eighth century AD, the World's Desire and the Land of the Rus were intimately linked in hearts, heads and history. This connection had been strengthened when the Cyrillic script spread through Russia and the Balkans from the ninth century, when Orthodox Christianity became the choice of Vladimir of Kiev in AD 988 and when Tsar Alexei had wanted to take Russian Orthodoxy back to its Byzantine roots in the seventeenth century, for instance by making the sign of the cross with three fingers, symbolising the three persons of the Trinity, the remaining digits symbolising the two natures of Christ.

And, worryingly for Istanbul, we often save our harshest punishments for those whom we have loved.

CHAPTER 71

SCUTARI

AD 1854–5
(1270–2 IN THE ISLAMIC CALENDAR)

The giaours now do Stamboul's praises sing,
but tomorrow they will crush it
With iron heel, like a sleeping serpent,
And departing will leave it thus,
Stamboul fell asleep before disaster struck

. . .

Stamboul has forgotten the sweat of battle,
And quaffs wine during hours of prayer.
There the cunning West has darkened
The wisdom of Ancient East.
Stamboul, for the sweet delights of vice,
Has forsaken prayer and sabre.

ALEXANDER PUSHKIN, *A JOURNEY TO ARZRUM*

(A JANISSARY IS DECRYING THE SOFTNESS OF

CONSTANTINOPLE IN CONTRAST WITH ARZRUM)[1]

Although Istanbul is sometimes described as a city of the night, the light of the moon here can feel unhealthy. And when a moonlit Bosphorus is broken by the glide of a boat of war, there is little that is more sinister.[2]

Ottoman territories, still spanning three continents but diminished now with Greece and parts of North Africa lost, were in danger of nurturing a proxy conflict. The nephew of Napoleon Bonaparte, having recently declared himself Emperor Napoleon III, had claimed for Catholics the right to protect holy Christian sites; in December AD 1852 the Church of the Nativity in Bethlehem was run by Latin monks, while there were fist-fights over the custodianship of the Crusader Church of the Holy

Sepulchre.[3] This was seen as an affront by the Orthodox Russian Tsar. On this point, Christendom was not united. It suited the French and the English to keep the Ottoman Sultan sweet as the head of resistance to Russian expansion and as a brake on Russian interference in the overland route to India. Furious that the French and English dragomans and ambassadors in Constantinople seemed to have the ear of the Sultan rather than their own representatives, and having had a taste of victory at Çeşme, the Russians acted. The Crimean War was the bitter result.

The charge of the Light Brigade and Florence Nightingale's lamp darting through those dark wards have given us a Pavlovian image of the Crimean War as being primarily about churned and bloodied land. It was of course primarily about access to water – and to the sweet, black, grain-bearing earth beyond.

Of the ten wars fought between Russia and the Ottomans in the years AD 1678–1917, only three were won by the Ottomans and one of these was the Crimean War. Critically, and atypically, this time Britain and France (along with the Kingdom of Sardinia) had made an alliance with Istanbul. If conversations in London, Paris and Kostantiniyye had followed a different path, the Ottoman Empire might well have been absorbed into the Russian. Wanting to protect their commercial interests in the East, London and Paris were delighted to have cause to criticise Russia for her failure to protect Christians in Ottoman territories. Russian expansionism was considered a clear and present danger. We get a glimpse of the scale of the political skulduggery in the form of a plan proposed by Britain's foreign secretary Lord Palmerston, to weaken Russia by handing back control of the Crimea and the Caucasus to Kostantiniyye.

In AD 1851 a total of 700 manufacturers and craftsmen from Istanbul had participated in the first Great Exhibition in the Crystal Palace, London. Buying rugs and glasses and tiles direct from Eastern traders in the comfort of Hyde Park helped the British middles classes to feel that the people of Kostantiniyye were a bit more 'us' than 'them'. An Ottoman orchestra would perform for Queen Victoria in the same venue. In Istanbul the Swiss Fossati brothers were busy repairing the Ayasofya. Meanwhile, from the British Embassy in Istanbul, newly rebuilt by W. J. Smith and Sir Charles Barry – the later the architect of the Houses of Parliament – the ambassador Stratford Canning fulminated against Russian hubris.

In AD 1853 the Ottomans crossed the Danube to meet Russian troops in Moldavia; in November Russia smashed an Ottoman fleet at the Black Sea port of Sinope. It was clear the Russian goal was Istanbul, and in March 1854 Britain and France declared war.

In the War Office in the Sublime Porte on Seraglio Point, preparations were under way to barrack incoming European troops around Kostantiniyye, many of whom had travelled rapidly across Europe on brand-new steam trains. The French camped outside the city walls, the British over the water at Scutari-Üsküdar – and a female freedom fighter known as Black Fatima rode into the city leading her Kurdish troops. Military hospitals were made ready for Allied soldiers in Pera, Tarabya, Fatih and Üsküdar.[4] Despite the protestations in the city of some Muslim clerics (the most hard-line were quietly evacuated on a boat to Crete) that what was being planned was an unholy alliance of Muslim and Christian forces, Ottomans and Europeans became camp-mates. Allied reports were wired back from the Crimean campaign – for the first time in military history. The embedded journalist Laurence Oliphant (a Christian mystic who grew up on a hill estate in the lush highlands of Nuwara Eliya in Sri Lanka, his family credited with bringing tea to what was then Ceylon) reported for *The Times* and then published a volume about his time in the Crimea. The accounts pulled no punches. Both copy and images could be wired. The wives of British officials and ambassadors have also obliged us by describing, in great detail, how the capital partied on during the conflict. Much, frankly, is orientalist tosh, but we do learn useful details. One Emilia Bithynia Hornby, wife of Sir Edmund Grimani Hornby – a lawyer sent to Constantinople to help administer a £5 million loan, a British–French aid package – wrote *In and Around Stamboul*,[5] describing the war-balls held in the British and French Embassies and pointing out that, for the first time, as a show of solidarity, the Ottoman Sultan had attended. British bobbies had to be imported to deal with 'Johnnies' behaving badly on the city streets.

Although Karl Marx and Friedrich Engels, writing from London and Manchester, put forward arguments from the Turkish point of view,[6] journal-writing was not favoured in Ottoman culture. To hear the Ottoman perspective on the Crimean War we often have to turn to the plays, epic poems, military marches and folk songs which proliferated after what was in reality a shallow victory.[7] On the battlefield there was little time, or cause, for contemplation or celebration.

The bulk of the Allied troops had arrived in the spring of AD 1854 at Gallipoli and Istanbul. In the city anxious Istanbullus would have seen Allied fleets slip past having left their docking points in the Dardanelles. Now deserted, plastic-bag blown, Beşik Bay had been a beaching point for warriors from the West since the Bronze Age; some argue that it witnessed the invasion that started the Trojan War (not an opinion that I share). But the conflict that the Ottomans, British, French and Russians were about to witness was as vicious as any described in Homer's *Iliad*.

As Tatars in their distinctive fur hats, smoking clay pipes, prepared the ground in the south-east of the Crimea, the Allies besieged Sevastopol and spent a year exposed to extreme weather and to the ravages of disease. A visit to the battle sites today requires one to crunch over abandoned porter bottles left by the British fighters, bottles that provided respite for those who had survived after a nine-hour day of hand-to-hand combat. The situation for soldiers on the ground had been beyond grim. Most died not of their wounds but of disease. One officer, Colonel Bell, complained that every soldier who ended up a casualty back in Scutari had been loaded 'like a donkey', half suffocated by rigid cross-belts stiffened with pipe-clay, 'that cling to his lungs like death' and by a patent-leather-covered cap that attracted rather than dispelled the early summer heat. Patriotic, bereft mothers and sisters and wives made the woolly head-warmers, often inappropriate in the glare of sites such as Balaclava, that we still call balaclavas. (The ignorance of conditions this far east would continue sixty years on when loving women knitted mittens to send out to their boys fighting at Gallipoli.) Many of the wounded were shipped back to Kostantiniyye for treatment. On the ground there were not enough medics to deal with the dying and wounded, and the proliferation of pathogens in a hygiene-free zone would have horrified those early founders of the Muslim city's hospitals. Refugees, casualties and the diseased were all brought to the centre of the city.

It is now that we meet one of Istanbul's most prominent Western protagonists, Florence Nightingale and her phalanx of thirty-eight nurses who came out to work in the converted Selimiye barracks in Scutari overlooking the urgent wash of the Bosphorus. Opinion on Nightingale ricochets between hagiography and demonology. Italian-born, determined, widely travelled, she was vigorously promoted as a national treasure at the time of the Second World War, and the press of the day certainly took up her cause. At Scutari between AD 1854 and 1856 'Nightingale Power' was said to have turned around the horror of rat-infested, blood-soaked and excrement-covered holding bays for the dead. The old Artillery Hospital, the Selimiye Barracks and hospital ships moored along the city's waterways would soon be clotted with 5,000 patients. Nightingale might indeed have been strong-willed, patrician (she complains about the lower-class doctors, describing one, John Hall, as a 'Knight of the Crimean Burial Grounds'), but she was dealing with death and abominable suffering every waking minute of her service in Istanbul. The soldiers arriving in (malarial) Scutari from the Crimea suffered from dysentery, frostbite, exhaustion, gangrene and intense psychological distress. Much of their treatment, including amputations, had to be conducted without anaesthetic and on straw.

In Scutari – the zone that had started life as the independent settlement of 'golden Chrysopolis' where Constantine had fought Licinius for control of the Roman Empire, the Lady with the Lamp might not have been solely responsible for cutting the death rate from 42 per cent (in February AD 1855) to 5.2 per cent (in May of the same year), but she played some small part. Although Nightingale was a fierce critic of the Ottoman harems, she approved of their holistic spa treatment centres to which she referred a number of her patients. Whatever the truth of her story as a Victorian heroine, in Turkey today she is remembered as a pioneer of psychiatric health[8] and of nursing.

While on service in Scutari Florence slept in a bedroom in one of the 70-foot towers that edge the Selimiye Barracks. We can imagine her looking out as the boatloads of casualties were brought across the water – some transported by the ferry services which had arrived in AD 1851. In 1890 a phonograph recording was made of Florence Nightingale's voice: 'When I am no longer even a memory, just a name, I hope my voice may perpetuate the great work of my life. God bless my dear old comrades of Balaclava and bring them safe to shore. Florence Nightingale.'

Nightingale had plenty of contemporary enemies. The British ambassador in Constantinople persuaded Queen Victoria to write to the Sultan to suggest the construction of a new Christian church as a war memorial – the first since Catherine the Great's concession – to divert

Royal Navy ratings at the signal station at the top of Galata Tower after the Crimean War

funds from Nightingale's cause. It was duly designed by George Edmund Street (architect of the Royal Courts of Justice on the Strand in London) and now stands as a little bit of neo-Gothic in the Beyoğlu district. Since the church was reopened in 1991 its basement has served as a shelter and as an education hub for those refugees in Istanbul displaced by the global conflicts of the twentieth and twenty-first centuries.

Western troops brought to Istanbul in the wake of the Crimean conflict left pedestrian traces in the city: a taste for starched shirts and for sock-suspenders; *Punch* magazine was sold on the streets of Istanbul along with Stilton, Brown Windsor soup and Tennant's Ale. (In England, men in Mayfair sported the newly fashionable beards that necessity had forced them to grow on active service in Crimea.) Handcrafted cutlery that had been traded for centuries in Istanbul's markets was replaced by mass-produced imports, and the fork – which had started off in tenth- or eleventh-century Europe as the import of a Byzantine princess who lifted

food 'to her mouth with a two-pronged gold implement' – was reintro-
duced as a Western sophistication in AD 1860. The increasing visibility
of women (for example, at the popular shadow-puppet shows) in the city
was noted – though they still had to sit in segregated areas.

With peace negotiated at the end of the Crimean War, there were celebrations in the newly built and eye-wateringly expensive Dolmabahçe
Palace (Topkapı had been all but abandoned in AD 1846). In reality there
was little to celebrate – a series of new debts and perhaps with hindsight,
in the wake of *tanzimat*, a certain loss of identity. Soon after the war,
the British and Ottoman publics both concluded that Crimea had been
a senseless and badly handled conflict. Russia's first ever feature film,
The Siege of Sevastopol, produced in 1911 by Russian film-makers, commemorated the horrors of the twelve months between 1854 and 1855. The
wonderful black and white silent movie shows a world that was moving
closer to what we feel to be modern. With the muscle-flexing in Ukraine
initiated in 2014, Putin's Russians reminded themselves that they did not
feel that they had lost the Crimean War. And we should recall what the
mid-nineteenth-century inhabitants of Istanbul knew, that Russia had no
intention of curbing her ambitions. The Ottoman Empire was a thorn in
the Russian breast.

Fighting in the Crimea and supporting the Ottomans against Russia allowed the British to continue to lobby for the abolition of the slave trade.
The Russians had already annexed much of the region: clearing out the
'troublesome' Muslim population meant that many vulnerable families
were forced out on the road – the formality of trading was broken down,
children were kidnapped. The Ottomans agreed to stop taking slaves
from Christian Georgia, but the Circassian trade was off the negotiating
table. We can perhaps appreciate the delicacy of these negotiations – British diplomats were speaking with sultans in Istanbul who were the sons
and nephews and husbands and lovers of Circassian slaves. Many, such as
William Henry Wylde, the head of the Slavery Department, found that
they had to turn not one but two blind eyes:

> We have in fact always shut our eyes to this Traffic as far as we could
> possibly do so, inasmuch as it is carried on under circumstances dif-
> fering entirely from those which characterise the African slave trade

. . . in one case the slaves are procured in the first instance by a system of murder and bloodshed which depopulates the country where slave hunting is carried on – in the other victims, if victims they can be called are voluntary ones and look forward with pleasure to the change in destiny which awaits them.

As the Russians invaded the north-west Caucasus in the AD 1860s, many hundreds of thousands of Circassians had been burnt out of their homes and forced to scrabble on to boats set for Ottoman territories. Circassian resistance to Russian encroachment would be written into the collective imagination and on to the front pages of English and American newspapers (Circassia's former capital Sochi, the location for the 2014 winter Olympics, made headlines once again when it was said that Putin's advisers had deliberately built sporting facilities over Circassian graveyards). It is estimated that by the end of 1864 around 10,000 Circassian men, women and children had died of hunger or had drowned trying to get to Istanbul. Some survived, and the ranks of Kostantiniyye's harems swelled.

In truth a harem in the city or the household of the Sultan was a better option than massacre at the hands of invading soldiers, rape by 'liberators' or the 'bride-napping' practised by locals. But the preference for Caucasian slaves in the beds of sultans and their bureaucrats represents Istanbul's own form of orientalism: a fatal feminisation of the lands to her East. So Istanbul had allowed herself to become a paradox, a city in hock to Western bank loans and Western niceties, but whose streets were filled with oriental ideas and goods and whose inhabitants still followed an Islamic calendar and clock. Her future was far from certain.

CHAPTER 72

ONE-WAY TRAFFIC

AD 1854
(1270/1 IN THE ISLAMIC CALENDAR) ONWARDS

The first view of Constantinople was beautiful, & I had no idea that the
town was of so great an extent . . . At 4 o'clock we landed at the Sultan's
Palace (in plain clothes) & was received very kindly by the Sultan in his
Palace, wh. Is very pretty, & beautifully fitted up. I had a longish audience
& rather a stiff one with him.

THE PRINCE OF WALES — THE FUTURE EDWARD VII —

IN HIS JOURNAL (AD 1862)[1]

The British ambassador to St Petersburg, Sir G. H. Seymour, in a letter
to Lord John Russell in AD 1853, reported a meeting between himself and
Tsar Nicholas I at which the latter had referred to Turkey as 'a sick man
– a very sick man' and in another as a man 'who has fallen into a state
of decrepitude'. It was an article in the *New York Times* on 12 May 1860
which coined the phrase 'the sick man of Europe' – an expression that has
stuck. Yet, when the Tsar died, men and women in Istanbul clamoured,
'Who is the sick man now! *We* are still alive!'

And certainly for a while it seemed as though the traffic between East
and West was moving good-naturedly both ways. In AD 1862 the future
Edward VII, embarked on a five-month tour of the Ottoman Empire,
explicitly to learn how a man like him might rule. Travelling on the royal
yacht *Osborne*, the Prince of Wales was in mourning for his father. There
is a poignancy to the images from the prince's adventure. Showing the
stiffest of upper lips he sits on camels, perches on rocks, gamely wears a
fez – sometimes into the photos creeps the reality of nineteenth-century
human experience: camel-boys, hawkers, traders, men and women dust-
grimed and rag-wrapped. Sale of prints of the official photographs of the

The future Edward VII (fifth from left) picnicking by the Sea of Galilee

trip brought the East in general and Istanbul in particular into many people's homes.[2]

Five years later the Sultan Abdülaziz I set out from Istanbul in a highly ornate railway carriage to visit the leaders of western Europe. The carriage itself was built in Saltley, Birmingham by the Metropolitan Carriage and Wagon Company and was a gift to the Sultan from the Ottoman Railway Company. In Britain Abdülaziz was met at Dover by the Prince of Wales, at Windsor by the Queen, and he was then invested as a Knight of the Garter on the royal yacht. The visit was commemorated with rather splendid medallions showing Londinia greeting a personification of Turkey, with Ayasofya and St Paul's as comfortable companions in the background. On the Sultan's return the city celebrated for three days, pop-up gardens appearing in the streets with orange and lemon boughs decorating buildings.

Many of the Chians who had fled the AD 1822 massacre had ended up in England. They put down roots in west London, around Bayswater and Holland Park. The Pre-Raphaelite painters were partly inspired by the Byzantine imagery that these refugees brought with them. Drawn to the East, men such as William Morris – an adviser to the Victoria & Albert Museum in London – would then arrange the purchase of both Christian and Islamic artefacts. Among them was the oldest complete carpet in the world, 'of singular perfection . . . logically and consistently beautiful', made in north-west Iran in 1539–40 probably for the shrine of the Sufi leader Shaykh Safi al-Din Ardabili and sold off to pay for earthquake damage. It looked as though the cultures of London, Paris and Kostantiniyye might productively collaborate and cross-fertilise.

But entanglement with the West brought a number of complications.[3] Istanbul had always absorbed outside influences, but now, perhaps, the diamond between two sapphires made the mistake of listening too closely to her critics. The canard about Kostantiniyye, that she was debauched and sensuous, suddenly seemed to matter: whereas Ottoman diplomats had been righteously outraged by Western condescension, now there was a niggling fear that Kostantiniyye was indeed an anomaly. At the same time, while the World's Desire had, for centuries, been the centre of disposable income, allowing her markets to boom, this was now a fact which European bankers had registered and were determined to exploit. Increasingly the city was drawn into the high capitalism of London and Paris.

The Ottomans might have been on the winning side in the Crimea, yet the treasuries in Istanbul were now almost empty. By AD 1875 the state was bankrupt. The juddering tensions of the war had helped the empire's liminal territories to split and fracture. The Caucasus was by and large in Russian hands, and the Bulgarian and Balkan 'horrors' of 1876, massacres, rape, the desecration of churches and monastaries – given the oxygen of publicity by an outraged William Gladstone – rattled the British, who assumed control of Cyprus in 1878. From the pulpit of St Paul's Cathedral, Canon Henry Liddon declared that support for the Ottomans (promoted by Disraeli as a bulwark against the Russians) was a sin. And *The Times* went on to report as fact what this cleric claimed to have seen, Turks impaling Balkan prisoners. In 1877 Russia had declared war on the Ottomans once again, capturing Edirne-Adrianopolis on 20 January the following year. Two days before, the great Ottoman palace complex from which Mehmed had progressed to conclude the endgame against Constantinople that March morning of 1453, a palace which was now in use as an arsenal, was burnt down to prevent Istanbul's enemies from gaining valuable ammunition.[4]

At the Congress of Berlin in AD 1878 the other European powers stripped Istanbul of many of her territories. New independent principalities were created – Romania, Serbia and Montenegro. Bulgaria was given nominal autonomy under Ottoman suzerainty. So the Bulgarians, whose city of Preslav had been modelled on Byzantine Constantinople with bright-eyed envy a thousand years before, now turned their backs on an empire so convinced of the value of times past that she was beginning to evince shades of Miss Havisham.

Despite all this, in Istanbul itself there were attempts to continue to pursue the dreams of the *tanzimat*. An underground railway, the Tünel funicular, was inaugurated in AD 1875, constructed by the English-owned Metropolitan Railway of Constantinople. It opened to the strains of both an Ottoman march and God Save the Queen. The steamers in the city might have run to Ottoman, Islamic time, but the train timetable followed a European clock. Smart types wore watches with two dials.[5] Publications from theatre programmes to trade union pamphlets were printed in Ottoman, French, Greek, Armenian and sometimes even Ladino.

A new museum in Istanbul was to be filled with Anatolian treasures including those from 'the eminent city of Troy from ancient times'. The idea of Troy had been a touchstone for Byzantion, Constantinople and indeed Kostantiniyye (within a decade of taking Constantinople, Mehmed the Conqueror had visited Troy, declaring that by defeating the Greeks he had avenged his Trojan ancestors).[6] It was only in AD 1870 that Homer's Troy (a day-trip south from the capital) seemed to have been rediscovered by the millionaire amateur archaeologist Heinrich Schliemann. Schliemann had made his money in indigo in St Petersburg, buying and selling gold in California and finally trading saltpetre and brimstone at the outset of the Crimean War. But this Western chancer exploited labyrinthine Ottoman bureaucracy and financial need. He first excavated illegally, then exported illegally, and next offered up a cash fine rather than return the stolen archaeological goods from his dig at Hissarlik, which he had nominated as the site of Troy. It is why, when we see Schliemann's wife draped in 'Helen's Jewels' – Early Bronze Age artefacts from what he called Priam's Treasure – they are photographed in Athens rather than in Istanbul. The ancient pieces were smuggled out of Ottoman territories in early June AD 1873 – with notes informing the Greek customs officials that as Schliemann was a philhellene – and as so many treasures had been looted from Greece – he was, as it were, returning a favour. The fine of 50,000 francs paid by Schliemann into the Ottomans' coffers was used to fund the construction of Istanbul's Archaeological Museum – whose founder, Hamdi Bey, was the son of a slaveboy captured at Chios.[7] The Troy treasures are conspicuous by their absence, but the museum still stands and protects those earliest shards of evidence of Istanbul's prehistoric foundation – the combs, the knives, even the footprints of its neolithic inhabitants.

Istanbul has always been a city of the future as well as of the past – and for the next century, more or less successfully, she would attempt to modernise. *Tanzimat* did change the tune if not the key of Ottomanism: notions of a fatherland, equality before the law, citizenship and representative government could now become part of the rhetoric. Modernisation brought change to the city at a great rate. In AD 1880, construction started on the Trans-Caspian Railway. From 1881 European powers, alternately British and French, via the Public Debt Administration, controlled all Ottoman debt and trade with the West, which accounted for three-quarters of Ottoman trading activity. In 1884 brothels were legalised. The poet C. P. Cavafy came to Constantinople as a refugee from Alexandria when his home town was being bombed by the British. In scrawling sepia ink he wrote his first poem on a postcard from the city in 1882. Cavafy's grandfather had been one of those Phanariots, a diamond-dealer in the city.[8]

In AD 1888 the first Orient Express train arrived in Istanbul (its Eastern terminus intended to be Mecca). So while high-ranking concubines, daughters and wives were being transported around the city in gilded carriages drawn by oxen, and tall-masted ships still bristled in the harbour, while men could crowd into the tiny opium dens around the Süleymaniye Mosque and seek out councils of genies in the wooded scrub of the city, new blood, new influences and new ideas were coming in via the new railways.[9] There might still have been harems across town, but the harem quarters boasted pianos, and more of their inhabitants could read and write. Sultan Abdülhamid II was a keen fan of Sherlock Holmes, honouring Conan Doyle with an award. Working together, Henry 'Harry' Pears (son of Sir Edwin Pears, who, based in Constantinople, had written of the

Bulgarian Horrors in the newspaper founded by Charles Dickens, *The Daily News*), Horace Armitage and a Mr Yani Vasilyadi helped to found the Constantinople Football Association League – the Taksim Square Barracks' parade ground being converted in 1921 to provide the city's first football stadium.

But with the loss of Balkan territories, Abdülhamid II ruled over an Eastern-weighted empire, whose influence was coming to taste like thin gruel. As national newspapers across Europe were said to foster a sense of political democracy, in Istanbul they were banned. Those with daring minds would slip across the Galata Bridge to get their contraband literature from Giaour bookshops.[10] Meanwhile Scutari – which had been a post-station for couriers, a rendezvous for caravans and the home of traders from Persia, and was now famous for the work of the Lady with the Lamp – still saw the gathering of white camels as they headed south each year on pilgrimage to Mecca. While the sultans toyed with the idea of leading a pan-Islamic movement, the Ottoman hierarchy was, on the face of it, content in the golden cage which its ancestors had spent half a millennium creating. But there is a danger in trying to maintain the dream in which you find yourself living.

Her inhabitants feared for the soul of their lovely, schizophrenic city. Poets bemoaned the fate of their ancient home town, a gorgeous, abused, confused creature that seemed determined to meet the interest of the West with a heavy, secret smile. As Tevfik Fikret wrote in his poem 'Sis' (Fog), published in 1901:

> Oh Decrepit Byzantium, Oh great bewitching dotard
> Oh widowed virgin of a thousand men
> The fresh enchantment in your beauty is still evident
> The eyes that look at you still do so with adoration.[11]

Long an inspiration for fantasies and fables, Istanbul seemed increasingly unable to write the plot of her own narrative.

CHAPTER 73

A SICK MAN IN THE ROSE GARDEN

c. AD 1880–1914
(c. 1297–1333 IN THE ISLAMIC CALENDAR)

> Truth has hit hard times, and lies prosper; the honest man falls and the hypocrite thrives; the trustworthy man weeps and the traitor laughs. The seat of the Ottoman Sultan, something that used to be a lion's lair, has now turned into a hornet's nest, with spies buzzing around in its cells.
>
> . . . [the inhabitants of Istanbul] have all been watched by a system of spies to the degree that by now anyone who has committed a crime will rush to admit their offense before informers can report it.
>
> IBRAHIM AL-MUWAYLIHI, *MA HUNALIK* (AD 1895)[1]

In April 2014 the basement of the Pera Palace Hotel was turned into an international courtroom. Wine boxes were cleared, tables dusted and a series of lawyers and clerks, representing Mauritius and Britain respectively, fought over an issue governed by the United Nations Convention on the Law of the Sea. Mauritius, legally a British colony from AD 1814 (after being ceded by Napoleon) until 1968, had objected to the UK's declaration of a Marine Protected Area around the Chagos archipelago. The Mauritians argued that this contravened international law. Of all the places in the world to fight out this symbolic dispute, Istanbul was chosen. The location was thought to be three things: internationally neutral; distant from Port Louis and London, the two capitals; and convenient, because Istanbul has long been considered a city where information can be obtained and exchanged.[2]

Perversely, one of the reasons that those lawyers could open up their dossiers and start the arbitration in the Pera Palace basement was that Istanbul had spent the last 150 years sleepwalking from one international allegiance to another. And because the city had direct access to the

Caucasus, the Middle and Near East, Central Asia, Russia, the Balkans and North Africa, almost inevitably perhaps it became an intelligence-hub where information was acquired and traded. Just as Istanbul has always been an inspiration for, and depository of, stories, it was also a critical player in the international game of truth. This was where narratives of all kinds have been traded.

As part of Sultan Abdülhamid's pervasive intelligence network, undercover agents could be found in barbers' shops, butchers, coffee houses, mosques. Secrets were traded between dragomans – or were bribed or blackmailed out of them. Death was often quick to come in Istanbul if you 'fell on the tongues of strangers'.[3] Arrests after a session at the baths tell us there were even spies in the hammam. After the disbanding of the Janissaries in AD 1826, the immediate closure of a number of the city's coffee houses – rich with tobacco smoke and the bittersweet smell of the blade from the barber-shops that often adjoined the Bektashi *tekkes* – demonstrates that these were more than just convenient caffeine-holes. Poet Janissaries had frequently met here, and as at the mosques such as Orta, there had been ample opportunity to plot and to plan: the Janissaries' victims had included Sultan Selim III, murdered as a result of his attempts at military reform.

Istanbul had become a favourite diplomatic posting from the eighteenth century onwards (ambassadors were said to live like princes, while those in Istanbul lived like kings, their summer quarters along the Bosphorus boasting fishponds, polo grounds and cricket pitches). This was a city with access to international intelligence and a training ground for intelligence agents. It was no coincidence that the British double-agent Kim Philby, who would defect to the Soviet Union during the Cold War, was MI6 head of station in Istanbul in the late 1940s – although officially the first secretary at the British Consulate in the city.

Istanbul has been called the world's spy capital. One of the earliest images from a hidden camera (stitched into a coat as a button) was taken in the Taşkızak dockyards, showing the expensive new submarines *Nordenfelt II* and *Nordenfelt III* ordered up by the Sultan in AD 1886 while tensions were mounting once again between Britain, Turkey, Russia and Greece.[4] In between the two World Wars it was said that you could stand at any hotel window in Istanbul, throw a stone, and somewhere in the street you would hit a spy. At one point the hotel manager in the Pera

Photos of submarines in Taşkızak dockyards taken by a hidden camera – the lens concealed as a button, AD 1887

Palace had to put up a sign in the lobby asking spies to relinquish their seats to paying guests.[5] As one American naval officer described it, the city was 'a dumping ground for war crooks and spies'. Here there were intelligence and counter-intelligence agents. The multilingual capabilities of many in the city, including those dragomans, proved enormously profitable. With formal military espionage a thing of the future, in the late nineteenth century men such as Frederick Gustavus Burnaby (a soldier and founder of *Vanity Fair* magazine) sent back reports of Russian encroachment in Central Asia in the 1870s through a porous Ottoman boundary. Reporting from Istanbul's territories whipped up the first recorded instance of 'jingoism'.[6] As crowds waved the Ottoman flag in Trafalgar Square they sang:

> We don't want to fight,
> But by jingo if we do,
> We've got the ships,
> We've got the men,
> We've got the money too.
> We've fought the bear before,
> And if we're Britons true,
> The Russians shall not have Constantinople![7]

There might be a healthy mixed economy of musical forms on Istanbul's streets, but spies reported back to the Sultan whenever they noticed overtly nationalist displays. Outdoor theatrical or musical performances were increasingly frowned upon in Kostantiniyye as they were deemed hard to control. The correspondence between a Greek high-school director and the Yıldız Palace (the seat of Ottoman government at the end of the nineteenth century, built in AD 1880 on former hunting grounds) in 1894 (the Greek wanted to mount a fund-raising concert to help the victims of an earthquake) reveals the swirl of anxiety.[8] Armenian demands for reform had sparked massacres, provoking some in the city to respond with terrorism. In 1896, some 6,000 Armenians were killed by a street mob, many of them clubbed to death. In 1898 Ottoman representatives could be found in Rome, alongside their European counterparts, at a clandestine conference to discuss the threat of anarchist terror on Kostantiniyye's streets. Abdülhamid II's network of spies included street vendors as well as high-ranking sheikhs – the atmosphere would perhaps have been a little like the pan- and inter-citizen surveillance, overseen by the Securitate, across Romania in the 1980s.

Over Sunday lunches in *yalıs* on the Bosphorus, which had become the diplomats' staple, the fallout from a changing city and a changing empire was discussed. Increasingly the friction points could be found not where political egos or international interests rubbed up against one another, but at the grazing of ethnic groups and religious attitudes. The British Consul General of Smyrna (1896–1908), Henry Arnold Cumberbatch (great-grandfather of actor Benedict Cumberbatch) continued the work of the military attaché Colonel Sir Herbert Chermside who had been tasked with diffusing the ongoing tensions between Armenians and the Ottoman authorities, as well as dealing – when British military commissioner on the island – with ethnic conflict in Crete where clashes between Orthodox Christians and Muslims had resulted in 53,000 Muslim refugees, homeless and propertyless, sleeping rough in Candia, soon to be renamed Heraklion.

So Istanbul was a contradiction: although the power-base she defined was crumbling, in certain ways Istanbullus had a new sense of themselves. In 1912 the Paris-educated mayor of Istanbul planned a series of improvements with the best of European influence brought into the city: twenty Italian road workers; two English engineers to build a sewerage system (along with English cement for the city's bridges); German design for a new city plan; hygiene experts from Brussels and sanitation know-how from Bucharest. The modern possibilities of the occident had been made real on the streets, while the significance of control of the Bosphorus and Dardanelles straits was being consistently recalled.

In some ways the city nourished centuries-old traditions. The illegal wine-shops – their own little theatre of subterfuge – advertised themselves with a piece of mat attached to the front door. The *nazar* (or 'evil-eye') was considered responsible for many of the citizens' woes. Men wore their fezzes resolutely, the headgear considered an essential article for official business and so kept firmly on inside and outside even during the summer heat (cheap varieties betrayed themselves by the drip of dye as their owners sweated). The poor ate couscous from North Africa on street corners. High- and low-class prostitutes alike plied their dreary trade (from contemporary descriptions it is clear that the language of the handkerchief was as eloquent as the language of the fan in seventeenth- and eighteenth-century Europe). Slave-trading, although officially outlawed in Ottoman territories in AD 1890, was reported in Istanbul up until 1916, while the Sultan's harem quarters remained untouched in the Topkapı until 1909 and the harem itself functional in the Dolmabahçe Palace until 1922.[9][10] The Sultan tried to rule, as if of old, from his 'Star' Palace, the Yıldız. But his grip on power was weak and the response was revolution.

Defeat by the Russians in AD 1878 had left the Ottomans smarting and their resources depleted. While many in Russia were aware that Kostantiniyye herself was too symbolic, too multifarious, too hydra-like to handle, some, such as Dostoevsky, indulged visions of global Russian control and of the conquest of the Queen of Cities.[11] The loss of Balkan territories meant that Istanbul was flooded with many thousands of Muslim migrants no longer welcome in their old homelands. Something had to give. It was not from Istanbul that reform would come but from Salonica (Thessaloniki), Istanbul's northern cousin, which through the centuries had shared in Istanbul's sieges, burnings, revolts, regime-changes. A number of Westward-looking constitutionalists allied themselves with a group of determined, disgruntled military officers stationed in Salonica to form the Unionists (the Committee of Union and Progress, or CUP). Popularly known as the Young Turks, their name was an anglicisation of a Westernisation; some Ottomans called these constitutionalists *Jön Türkler* – *Jeunes Turcs* in French – and gave rise to the memorable 'Young Turks' brand. Sultan Abdülhamid II was forced to accept a constitutional monarchy. Once again Istanbul's streets were filled with music and flowers. Over a long, hot summer in 1908, 60,000 gathered outside the Yıldız Palace yelling, 'Liberty, Equality, Fraternity and Justice!' On the streets of Istanbul men huzzahed and then interpreted the inch towards reform as a mile. Kids threw stones at cars, illegal traders appeared on many street corners, a counter-coup was mounted in 1909, the Society of Muhammad was established and there was a call to return to the four pillars of the empire: Islam, the House of Osman, Guardianship of Mecca and Medina, and the Possession of Kostantiniyye. But, resolute, the Young Turks sent the soldiers of the reformed government back on to the streets of Istanbul and quelled the counter-revolution.

The Sultan was deposed and replaced by the sultan Mehmed V – given the name of Kostantiniyye's AD 1453 conquering hero; many of Abdülhamid's staff, and those unfortunate enough to be perceived as enemies, were hanged from Galata Bridge. Shipyards, breweries and cement factories were built, and the Turkish Hearth, an equivalent perhaps of the Goethe Institute, or the Confucius Institute, was set up to rehabilitate the Turkish language and the Empire's reputation.

Western interests slipped in to play the situation to their own advantage. In the churn, Germany (unified in AD 1871 by Otto von Bismarck thanks to the weakening of Austria, which lost the support of Russia after failing to back Russia during the Crimean War)[12] deliberately reached out to Islamic territories. German banks sprang up in Egypt and the Sudan, and although the Ottomans declared their desire to stay out of any European war, their fate had already been written in the memos of European and Slavic war rooms.

Up at the top of the Black Sea, past Jason's legendary footprints, Russia could not fail to notice that her neighbour's sickness seemed to have become terminal. And so, as T. E. Lawrence pored over invasion maps of Gallipoli in the Cairo Mapping Office, the British aristocracy were being invited in as kings to those Balkan countries that aspired to gain their independence from the Ottomans. In the green fields of England, Rupert

Brooke thrilled to the idea that he might get a chance to see Homer's *mise-en-scène*. He wrote ecstatically to his friend Violet Asquith:

> Oh Violet it's too wonderful for belief. I had not imagined Fate could be so benign . . . I've been looking at the maps. Do you think *perhaps* the fort on the Asiatic corner will want quelling, and we'll land and come at it from behind, and they'll make a sortie and meet us on the plains of Troy . . . Will the sea be polyphloisbic and wine-dark and unvintageable . . .?[13]

Within a few weeks Rupert Brooke would die aged twenty-seven of an infected mosquito bite on his way to fight at Gallipoli.

The seas, whipped into a shape-shifting furnace of angry white by eastern Mediterranean winds, were soon to be broken by the warships of foreign nations. In the photographs of the time you see them – those tall-masted merchant ships bustling along Istanbul's waterways. Now new metal gunboats were also slipping through the water. Sometimes, watching the fretted Bosphorus and the Hellespont, it is not difficult to imagine that these waters are churned by memory and by prophecy. In 1915 there would be another battle over their control.

CHAPTER 74

GALLIPOLI: THE END OF AN EMPIRE

AD 1914–18
(1332–7 IN THE ISLAMIC CALENDAR)

And all of our trouble wasted!
All of it gone for nix!
Still . . . we kept our end up –
And some of the story sticks.
Fifty years on in Sydney
They'll talk of our first big fight,
And even in little old, blind old England,
Possibly someone might.

ARGENT, 'ANZAC' (1916)[1]

[Gallipoli] . . . the Muslim throat that gulps down every Christian nation.

DOUKAS, *HISTORIA* (C. AD 1360)[2]

On 30 May 1913 – in the dark surroundings of St James's Palace in London, built by that Henry VIII who once ate from Islamic dining services and walked on Ottoman rugs – the Sultan lost vast swathes of Ottoman territory stretching West of the Maritsa River from the Black Sea to the Aegean. Greece, Bulgaria, Montenegro and Serbia were already independent but their populations wanted more; more ethnic recognition; more clearcut nationalism. Forming the Balkan League they peeled control from Kostantiniyye's grip. Crete was ceded and the Aegean islands were put under the purview of Balkan powers. In Istanbul, the conflicts came to be known as 'the Balkan Tragedy'. The document on which all this was laid out, the London Treaty, ensured that the Ottoman Empire's boundary was now within 60 miles of Kostantiniyye. Those Western forces once despised as 'Franks', 'Latins', 'Barbarians', beyond the limits of empire, were steadily diminishing the reach of the World's Desire.

A crisis had been fomenting. In 1911 Italy had put Tripoli in Libya – Ottoman Tripolitania – under blockade and both Ottomans and Italians massacred soldiers and civilians in response. Unable to take North Africa, Italian forces then invaded Ottoman-held territory in the Mediterranean – resulting in the bizarre legacy today in Greek islands such as Chalki, where pasta is still the staple food and tavern owners remember their parents being banned from learning Greek, lessons illicitly taking place in caves and under olive trees once Italian had become the official language. A flurry of nationalism saw Ottoman territories including those in Albania and Egypt declare independence. In many cases the constitutions of these emerging nations were pushed through by those international operators who, working with the Sultan or Sublime Porte in Istanbul, had learnt their trade as dragomans or imperial counsellors. The Balkan Wars brought conflict to Kostantiniyye's front door. Just over 20 miles from Istanbul itself there was active engagement. Istanbullus recalled their windows rattling as artillery was fired; the front line was mind-sharpeningly close.[3] Protection was afforded to the west of the city by the Çatalca Lines, a series of earthworks and fortifications built against the Russians in AD 1876 – the Ottoman answer to Emperor Anastasios' Long Walls. Wounded soldiers and refugee Muslims again flooded into Istanbul itself, altering its ethnic make-up. One eyewitness reported tens of thousands of homeless families heading for shelter to Ayasofya and her gardens. Istanbul's profile was, visibly, changing. In secret communiqués some Ottoman ministers considered moving Kostantiniyye to Aleppo to ameliorate Turkish–Arab relations.

The British had been invited in to help modernise the navy, the Germans the army. The British authorities now had a thirty-year lease on the Imperial Arsenal on the Golden Horn. The Great Powers' insistence that Edirne be surrendered to Bulgaria seems to have fired the fury of constitutional rebels. And in Istanbul, the Young Turks – the political reform movement aiming to replace the absolute monarchy with a constitutional government – had first effected change and then seized power and finally splintered. Between 1913 and 1918, what was left of the empire was controlled from the Sublime Porte by the so-called Three Pashas: the grand vizier Talat Pasha, the war minister Enver Pasha and the naval minister Cemal Pasha. Their *coup d'état* took place just as the finer details of territorial appropriation in central and eastern Europe were being thrashed out in the wood-panelled rooms of London.

Talat Pasha recalled in his memoirs:

> Without considering that the majority element in a large part of Albania and Macedonia was Turkish, the 1913 London conference wielded the scalpel like a deadly surgeon and freely cut up the map of the Balkans. This operation not only did not yield the desired results, but caused the sickness to spread to other parts. Thus all of Europe was affected by an incurable illness. The Balkan War gave birth to the World War.[4]

Worse was indeed to come. On 28 June 1914 the neat bullet hole that burst into the rattling flimsiness of Archduke Franz-Ferdinand's car was just a tiny tear; the gaping rent it generated in the form of the First World War is horribly familiar. By 1914 Istanbul had already been in active conflict for two years, but she was about to become the ground of a greater quarrel.

With a new war declared on 28 July it was not immediately clear which way what was left of the Ottoman Empire would turn. The British were still demanding punitive repayments of bank loans while Germany was promising financial security and revenge.

While the Young Turks looked to an alliance with the German Kaiser (a secret agreement was signed on 1 August), the Ottoman warships *Sultan Osman I* and *Reşadiye* were still being built in British shipyards. In Newcastle, Geordie workers were riveting and securing these Dreadnoughts, the ultimate maritime weapon of the day, for their presumptive allies. In mid-August the two ships were swiftly requisitioned for the British war-effort and renamed HMS *Agincourt* and HMS *Erin* respectively. The population of Kostantiniyye was furious – these men-of-war had been paid for with public subscription. Germany offered two cruisers as replacements and Istanbul opened up the Hellespont – the Dardanelles straits – to ensure that they had safe passage to Istanbul away from the British, who were by then in hot pursuit.

Istanbul had chosen new friends and thus new enemies. On Friday 16 October, a million pounds' worth of German gold arrived by train at Sirkeci station from Berlin. Five days later, a second, matching instalment was delivered. On the streets of Istanbul posters were plastered on to

The German cruiser Breslau *(left) in the bay at Constantinople, where she was seconded to the Turkish Navy and renamed* Midilli. *On the right is the* Goeben, *also seconded and renamed* Yavuz Sultan Selim.

walls and doorways announcing a general mobilisation. Soldiers had to report for service. In German newspapers, on medallions and even on cigarette packets, a number of Turks, in particular Enver Pasha, were now portrayed as heroes. It served the Germans well to tempt the Ottomans into this conflict. The territory of this new ally of theirs was perfectly placed to pressurise Russia from the Black Sea and from the Caucasus, to attack the British in Egypt and to help foment discontent in France and Britain's Muslim territories in Asia and North Africa with a call for jihad. German pleas fell on receptive ears. The general in command of the German mission to the Ottomans, Liman von Sanders, recorded that Enver Pasha 'gave utterance to phantastic, yet noteworthy ideas. He told me that he contemplated marching through Afghanistan to India . . .'[5] In Kostantiniyye, fighting talk was back.

On 29 October 1914, German-manned Ottoman ships bombarded the Russians on the Black Sea coast at Odessa and Sevastopol: the Ottomans had entered the war. The following month, on 11 November next to relics of the Prophet in Topkapı Palace, Sultan Mehmed V declared holy war on the Allies. In the city itself, overnight, British nationals and British interests felt isolated. By December food was scarce. The blockading of access to Russia via the Dardanelles – causing shortages of cash and supplies – would help to spark the Bolshevik revolution of 1917.

London was agitated – there were many reasons why the West was interested in the East. The secession of Constantinople from an Allied embrace would send out a troubling signal to countries with large Muslim populations such as India (a handful of Indian colonial troops during the First World War did defect to the Ottomans). The red, white and black of a German flag fluttering from the walls of Topkapı was unthinkable. If anyone controlled Constantinople, 'the richest prize of the entire war',[6] the British thought it should be themselves or, failing that, the Russians. To add to this mix, in 1914 the British government had secured a 51 per cent stake in the Anglo-Persian Oil Company and had then gone on to safeguard the supply at Abadan and to occupy the city of Basra. In Mesopotamia Sir Percy Zachariah Cox, a high-ranking British soldier and strategist who had originally favoured a tactful collaboration with the Ottomans, announced to the local population, as the Union Jack was raised in Basra, that 'no remnant of the Turkish administration remains in this place. In place thereof, the British flag has been established, under which you will enjoy the benefits of liberty and justice, both in regard to your religious and secular affairs.'[7] To prevent Arabs uniting with Turks in a holy war, the British hinted at support for a religious regime-change, when 'an Arab of true race will assume the Caliphate at Mecca or Medina'.[8] By February 1915, British ships were a presence throughout Ottoman waters.

When news came of the first Allied bombardments along the Dardanelles an anxious Sultan and his household and members of the Ottoman government planned to flee Istanbul for Eskişehir – the town in which Osman had once had his vivid dream of capturing Constantinople. But in the event the number of Allied ships was depleted by assiduously laid mines. Initially it looked as though the Ottomans had fought off the assault. Although the population of Istanbul was perhaps too savvy to mount a spontaneous victory parade, the American ambassador recorded that the police were drumming up patriotism by making door-to-door visits, instructing men and women to string up celebratory bunting.[9] The diffidence of those in Istanbul was well founded. More Allied troops were heading to the Dardanelles straits – many officers with a copy of Homer's *Iliad* in their kitbags, some of them even planning a disastrous 'Trojan horse' exercise when a coal-ship, the *River Clyde*, was refitted to contain 2,100 men. This unwieldy ship of subterfuge did not storm the gates of Gallipoli but instead became a sitting target; the troops within suffered appalling casualties.

It was clear that the Allies needed not just ships in the water but boots on the ground. Back in London the Dardanelles campaign had been championed by young Winston Churchill, First Lord of the Admiralty – operations that saw the dispatch of the Constantinople Expeditionary Force, swiftly to become known as the Mediterranean Expeditionary Force. Churchill believed that the employment of his navy in the east would break the stalemate that had developed on the Western Front, that is in Belgium and France. The War Council meeting of 13 January 1915 in the Cabinet Room at 10 Downing Street[10] was described by Maurice Hankey, secretary of the council: 'Churchill suddenly revealed his well-kept secret of a naval attack on the Dardanelles! The idea caught on at once. The whole atmosphere changed. Fatigue was forgotten. The War Council turned eagerly from a dreary vista of a slogging match on the western front to brighter prospects, as they seemed, in the Mediterranean.'[11]

In early April the British 29th Division, the Royal Naval Division and a cavalry brigade along with the Anzac Corps and a newly formed French division, the Corps Expéditionnaire d'Orient, set out for the Hellespont. In official communiqués the purpose of the expedition was explicitly described as 'the conquest of Constantinople'. And so British troops found themselves travelling out to the islands of Lemnos, Imbros and Tenedos – all of which featured in Homer's tales of adventuring Greeks and which had been used so strategically as grain stores by Byzantium's emperors. The point of attack – the Gallipoli peninsula which had also seen such hectic activity 550 years before in the original Ottoman advance west, was chosen precisely because it was a totemic flashpoint. The Allied Gallipoli landings were originally planned for 23 April, St George's Day, a significantly patriotic and Christian choice – particularly given George's origins as a Christian martyr in Asia Minor. The plan was to take the straits, scrub-covered, inch by inch, and then to take Constantinople. The quiet confidence in the project is revealed by the number of ten-shilling notes overprinted in Arabic as the legal currency of the future that were found on the bodies of Allied soldiers. The plan had been for British cash to be spent liberally in this new corner of the British Empire.

Under cover of night between 24 and 25 April the Australian submarine HMAS *AE2* managed to make it through the Dardanelles, advancing towards the Sea of Marmara, and appearing and reappearing in order to give the impression that it was one of a number. Then on 27 April another submarine, HMS *E14*, sank four ships in the sea – one of them fat with troops – on their way to Gallipoli. Three days later eight battalions of reserves were dispatched from Constantinople-Istanbul; a month on and an Ottoman transport vessel, the *Stamboul*, was torpedoed in the Bosphorus, scatter-gunning panic in the city. By autumn the Allies had sealed off the eastern entrance to the Dardanelles to prevent German U-boats from making it up to the capital of their Ottoman allies. The bones of sunken cutters and battleships still appear around the coastlines here at low tide.

In Constantinople, in addition to a shortage of food there was now not enough gas for lamps. The lack of coal and the closure of the gas-works had meant that the city, described through history as lustrous, was perturbingly dark. With many farmers from Anatolia drafted in to fight, women and children in the countryside began to starve. For those in Istanbul with family members on active service through the hostilities there had already been anguish. An Ottoman mission to the Caucasus against Russia in December 1914 had proved reprehensibly disastrous. With just flatbread as their rations and lightweight uniforms, the trek through the mountains for soldiers from Istanbul was little more than a death march. Eyewitnesses described bodies ice-black and stiff in the morning, of men maddened by the snow, 10,000 dying in one day. Of the 100,000 soldiers who had set off, only 18,000 came back.[12] A Turkish attack on the Suez Canal in February 1915 also suffered heavy losses: Suez threw sandstorms where the Caucasus banked snow and was as humiliating a defeat. These were meteorological challenges but also storms of confusion, ineptitude and misfortune. And both sides had thought their victory would be easy.

In April 1915 many of the Allied troops, including Anzacs, had landed in the region of Çanakkale – British and Anzacs on the European side of the straits, and French on the Asian. The Australian prime minister

Andrew Fisher said that Australia would support Britain 'to the last man and to the last shilling'. On the sides of their ships the Anzac soldiers had scrawled, 'Constantinople or bust. On to harems. Bring on your Turkish delights.'[13] While the Turks called out to Allah, the Allies would respond with the cry, 'Eggs is cooked.' There was a ferocious propaganda campaign. Allied publications and loud-hailer announcements reminded the Turks that they had once been friends, that Germany was the real enemy, that Britain and her chums would respect the Muslims' God, Constantinople's culture and the Ottoman people.[14]

Ottoman fighters, the 'Mehmedçik' or 'Little Mehmeds' such as Mustafa Kemal – the man who would go on to shape the Turkish nation as Kemal Atatürk – were described by the Allies as 'Johnny Turk'. From all accounts – Ottoman and Allied alike – these were combatants who fought and died well.[15] On the ground there seems to have been a grudging mutual respect. In a remarkable episode, a ceasefire of nine hours was negotiated on 24 May between Mustafa Kemal and Aubrey Herbert (the half-blind half-brother of the 5th Earl of Carnarvon who seven years later discovered Tutankhamun's tomb, while Aubrey would go on to found the forerunner of the Anglo-Turkish Society). Simply too many were dead or dying, and the stench of corrupting bodies, the moans of those not yet dead, had become unbearable. Aubrey Herbert wrote that the smell of rotting flesh overwhelmed what were once thyme-filled ravines.[16] As soldiers met on no man's land while collecting the dead (by then only two soldiers were found alive) they exchanged tokens, cigarette packages and buttons from their uniforms along with shards of exploded shrapnel; they even hugged.

One man who had photographed the carnage that led to the May ceasefire, and then spoke to a number of the Turkish fighters during the few hours of peace, was known as 'Turkish Charlie'. In the Russo-Turkish wars this 'Turkish Charlie' – real name Charles Snodgrass Ryan – had worked with the Ottomans as a medical orderly; he had been decorated with Ottoman medals, and he spoke Ottoman Turkish. Snodgrass was an incarnation of the many ways the geopolitics of the late nineteenth and early twentieth centuries could have played out if fickle international allegiances had fallen a different way.

Well aware that Turkish soldiers were a formidable opponent, the War Office had summoned to the stony, snake-infested shores of Gallipoli

Anzac Beach, Gallipoli peninsula, c. June 1915. Wrecked barges can be seen in the foreground. Photograph by Charles Snodgrass Ryan.

their colonial equivalents – the Sikh 14th Regiment. These were not only formidable fighters, they did not present the complication, for the British, of using Muslim troops to fight their co-religionists. In a 100th anniversary service for Gallipoli held in 2015 in a summer-lit church on Trafalgar Square crowded with men in turbans and women in flame-coloured saris, the report of Austen Chamberlain, Secretary of State for India, to the House of Commons was read out:

> Who is there who can read without emotion of the action of the 14th Sikhs at Cape Helles . . . with a loss of 430 men out of 550 engaged? When a day or two afterwards the same ground was traversed again in a successful advance of our troops, the General who was in command has told me every Sikh had fallen facing his enemy, and most of them had one of their enemies under him.[17]

Constantinople was exerting her time-honoured magnetic pull, albeit attracting men not to her delights but to their deaths. Back in Kostantiniyye the trumpeted success of the Allies had bred fear in the city. A number of French and English nationals who had been allowed to stay on in Constantinople were peremptorily rounded up and then sent out to unfortified towns along the Dardanelles, doubling up as both hostages and human shields.

One Ottoman captain, in a letter to his 'angel of beauty', wrote:

> We are bombarded here by the English. No rest we receive and very little food and our men are dying by hundreds from disease. Discontent is also beginning to show itself among the men, and I pray God to bring this all to an end. I can see lovely Constantinople in ruins and our children put to the sword and nothing but some great favour from God can stop it . . . Oh, why did we join in this wicked war?[18]

Within a few days this captain was dead.

The campaign ended on 9 January 1916 with the Ottomans claiming the advantage. As a result of the debacle Winston Churchill was quietly sacked. Gallipoli has been judged a slim victory for Kostantiniyye, but in reality it is hard to say who emerged a winner. The campaign is remembered year in year out as pensive pilgrims, from Asia, Britain, Australia and New Zealand and beyond, shoulders hunched, walk in the heat to where so many fell. In Istanbul during prayers, the city still laments their Ottoman dead.

Of the 500,000 Allied troops sent to Gallipoli around half were casualties, with the Ottomans sustaining slightly greater losses of 90,000 dead and 165,000 wounded. During the war a total of 800,000 men from the region were lost as a result of active service or disease. In the rocky landscape around Gallipoli there are still mines, sandy boltholes and the ghosts of trenches. There are traces too of curious ragbag monuments. To mark each battle victory a monument of shell-cases, towering two men high, commemorated the triumph and the dead. These are the equivalent of the *tropaion* of antiquity – the crude trophies around which Greeks, Persians, Thracians would have circled in the ancient battles over Byzantion and her hinterland. They are a reminder of all the gore and of the quest for transient glory that this region has witnessed.

*

In the spring of 1915 Russia had attacked Ottoman land in east Anatolia – out on those wide, flat plains that had seen the establishment of Christianity in the fourth century AD and the massing of Turks at Manzikert in the eleventh. The Armenians, who had been campaigning for reforms that would have allowed for more autonomy, were said to have sided with their invaders; a number did indeed defect to the Russian army. As a result, on the Sunday before the Allied landings of 25 April – known by some as Red Sunday – a range of prominent Armenian figures in Istanbul, close on 2,500 of them (clerics, journalists, writers, lawyers, teachers, politicians, scientists) had been deported or killed. The German ambassador, Baron Hans Freiherr von Wangenheim, in response to a warning from the American ambassador Henry Morgenthau that Armenians in Anatolia would be at mortal risk as a continuation of the policy, had declared Cassandra-like in a telegram, 'So long as England does not attack Cannakaale . . . there is nothing to fear. Otherwise nothing can be guaranteed.'[19] Of those Armenians who survived the initial purge, a number were taken to Ottoman Syria. There are those who assert that the attacks on them by tribes en route were planned from within the Ottoman ministries in Istanbul.

But despite the bloodshed and the carnage, many of the Allies still believed it was a certainty that Kostantiniyye would fall and that, with their backs against the wall, the Turks were simply lashing out, destroying before they were destroyed. A disturbing perspective is supplied by the diary pages of Lewis Einstein, the 'Former Minister Plenipotentiary United States Diplomatic Service; Late Special Agent at the American Embassy at Constantinople'.[20] Initially there were lynchings; prominent Armenians were strung up outside the Kılıç Ali Pasha mosque on swiftly erected wigwam gibbets. Fearful of mob rule on the streets, the Germans acted to restore peace, and so Istanbul – the place where the Armenian hand was writ so large, in the design of the Dolmabahçe Palace and the Nusretiye Mosque, in the banking system and in the work of doctors, writers, goldsmiths – witnessed a brittle lull. Even so, hunched groups of Armenians could be seen being frog-marched to the city's police stations, and not coming home.

Scholars draw our attention to the fact that details of the Armenians who died – estimated figures range from 600,000 to 1 million – have been publicly available since 1919 in the records of the Ottoman military

tribunals which tried Ottomans charged with war crimes in both provincial cities including Trabzon – Byzantine Trebizond – and in Istanbul.[21]

Meanwhile British machinations in Arab territories saw the simmering
of Arab revolt. In 1917 the British took Baghdad and Jerusalem, in 1918
Jericho and Damascus. At Megiddo, on the site of the biblical Arma-
geddon, in 1918 the British Lieutenant General Edmund Allenby – with
the help of the irregular forces of the Arab revolt – won a conclusive
victory over Ottoman forces which had been cut off in the Judaean hills.
The following year he was created Viscount Allenby of Megiddo. The
land Allenby fought over is currently under excavation and has revealed,
among other finds, a third-century AD Christian prayer hall – the mosaic
floor decorated with fish and immortalising the fact that the altar here
was dedicated by one of those prominent early female Christian converts
as a 'memorial to the God, Jesus Christ'.

The new artery to the Middle East, the neo-Gothic Haydarpaşa railway station on the Asian edge of the Bosphorus, could have encouraged
the West to nurture sustained contact with the East. On 6 September
1917 sections of the line and the ticket hall were blown up by British
agents – the damage is still visible. The seizure of the Berlin–Baghdad
railway might have seemed a moral victory for the British but would be
long resented by many in the East.

In 1915 the last Sürre Caravan had ventured out from Üsküdar on the
Hajj to Islam's holy cities. In 1919, in order to protect 400 years' worth of
gifts to Mecca and Medina sent out from Istanbul, the golden caskets, the
jewelled swords and the cloths stitched with silver were brought back into
the city on the Bosphorus, itself a jewel within Dar al-Islam – the Abode
of Islam. Today they are popular exhibits in the Topkapı Palace.

Just two weeks before the armistice which took effect at 11 o'clock on
11 November 1918, the Ottomans had contacted Britain to seek terms for
ending hostilities with the Allied powers. Symbolically, the negotiators
met in the Aegean on the *Agamemnon* battleship. Within two days the
Bosphorus was crowded with a Western flotilla: it has been noted that
more Allied firepower was brought to Constantinople than to any other
capital city.[22] Once again there were those with cutting-edge ordnance
and great egos thrashing up and down Istanbul's waterways, the froth
of the surf changing from green to white, the urgent confidence of the

Little packs of war orphans, sleeping under old sheets and blankets, started to gather together for shelter in Istanbul's mosques as populations were displaced between 1911 and 1923.

invader in the wash. Despite the terms of the agreement that was reached on the *Agamemnon*, French and British troops had stationed themselves on either side of the Golden Horn in both Stamboul and Frengistan. One of their generals processed through the streets on a white horse, very much the chivalric conqueror. The French occupied some districts and some palaces, the British others. Istanbul was a story-book, with the Allies behaving like children, ripping out their favourite chapters to claim as their own.

The official British observer, G. Ward Price, reported on the surrender of Constantinople on 10 November 1918:

at 3 o'clock this afternoon, under a cloudy sky, but one filled with the diffused lights of the East, we rounded the point of the old Seraglio and entered the Golden Horn.

There was no demonstration of any kind. It seemed as if no one had even noticed the arrival of this herald of the British fleet. But as we drew near to the quay one saw that the houses and windows were thronged with people.

The crowd had an unusual tone of red about it, derived from all the crimson fezzes bobbing to and fro as their wearers strained for a glimpse. And a few waved handkerchiefs. A German officer stood on the quay close to where the destroyer gradually came alongside.

He was more interested than any one, but affected indifference and yawned with care from time to time. A little group of German soldiers and sailors gradually formed behind him as if for mutual moral support. For years they had been the self-ordained military gods of this place, but now their altars are overthrown and they see Turkish naval officers of high rank hurrying past them to pay respects to the representative of a nation they once thought they could despise.[23]

On 13 November 1918 an Allied fleet – forty-two vessels with HMS *Agamemnon* to the fore – sailed through the straits. Although many in the city were horrified – the Sultan at his window in the Topkapı, fishermen on the Golden Horn – the attitude of others in Istanbul created a partyish atmosphere. Biplanes added to the thrill of the moment, Christian girls threw flowers, men drank in the streets. Allied officials – inwardly jittery as a number of personal journals confess – disembarked with a swagger at the Dolmebahçe Palace. Kostantiniyye, it seemed, was now a city that belonged to the West.

There were excitable official conversations among the Allies about the spiritual and symbolic need to convert the Ayasofya back to being a church. Ottomans stood at its doors with machine guns to prevent these ideas being put into practice. Lord Curzon, the British Secretary of State for Foreign Affairs from October 1919, described the Turkish presence in Istanbul as a 'plague'. Fledgling Turkish nationalism was discouraged. In 1919 the British prime minister David Lloyd George opined: 'Stamboul in the hands of the Turks has been not only the hot bed of every sort of Eastern vice but it has been the source from which the poison of corruption and intrigue has spread far and wide into Europe itself . . . Constantinople was not Turk and the majority of the population was not Turkish.'[24] There were cogent suggestions that Turks should move out to Bursa or Konya. Non-Muslim prisoners were released from the city's prisons while Turkish nationalists were shot. In response underground resistance movements started to form. Middle-class Muslim women were forced to leave their homes for the first time in their lives and to stitch cloth in the warehouses edging the Bosphorus which are now being turned into chic art galleries. Rumours ran through the tight little lanes and were shared across balconies that 'the Turk' was indeed to be expelled from Constantinople. It was whispered that Muslim babies were being roasted; Greek women were dressing up as Turkish prostitutes. Street dogs were summoned with the call 'Come here, Mohammed.'[25] Istanbullus had dubbed their city proudly 'Dar-I Saadet ('The Abode of Happiness'), Asitane ('The Threshold'), Umm-u Dünya ('Mother of the World') – but it was no longer theirs.[26] Istanbul was the only belligerent capital city to be occupied by Allied forces beyond the Great War's 1918 declaration of peace.

All this was observed, quietly, by Mustafa Kemal as he checked into the Pera Palace the very day that the Allies began their occupation. The boy

Mustafa Kemal c. 1916

from Salonica had been decorated with French, German and Ottoman WWI medals. Respected and clearly an operator, he chose to sound out G. Ward Price. His question – how could he be involved once the British (who were preferable to the French) started to carve up the Ottoman Empire?

Ward reported Mustafa Kemal's interest back to the British authorities; they were dismissive. But Kemal would not be shunted to the sidelines of history so easily, his Great War experience would mark him, and the fate of Istanbul.

The suffering on the ground – the heat of the Arabian Desert, the thorn bushes of Gallipoli that snagged passing soldiers and the mountain passes of the Caucasus that froze men to death – was compounded by meddling of the most intrusive kind. The secretive Sykes–Picot Agreement had been scratched out in a series of handwritten letters during two rounds of discussion in November and December 1915 between the French ambassador to London Paul Cambon and the British foreign secretary Sir Edward Grey, and was then thrashed out behind closed doors with the Russian foreign minister Sergei Sazonov in Petrograd (the renamed St Petersburg). The agreement, named after the British and French diplomats who negotiated it, advocated that Ottoman territories in the Middle East, Anatolia, North Africa and Europe should be carved up after the war like a birthday cake.[27] The terms of the partition agreement were specified in a letter dated 9 May 1916, which Cambon addressed to Grey. These terms were then ratified by France and Britain in a return letter from Grey to Cambon on 16 May, and the agreement became official – albeit undeclared – in an exchange of notes among the three Allied powers on 23 May 1916.

As a result of these deliberations and the Constantinople Agreement of March 1915 it was decided that Istanbul would be handed over to Russia. The lands that had once been ruled from Kostantiniyye by the Ottomans and before them by the Byzantines, before them by the Romans – as well as many independent tracts of territory in between – were sectioned up with a series of worryingly straight lines. Sykes–Picot however was never put into effect and so is a phantom historical-driver. But many of today's divisions in the Middle East can be traced back to conversations by those who had no rightful claim over the lands that once belonged to Byzas' great city.

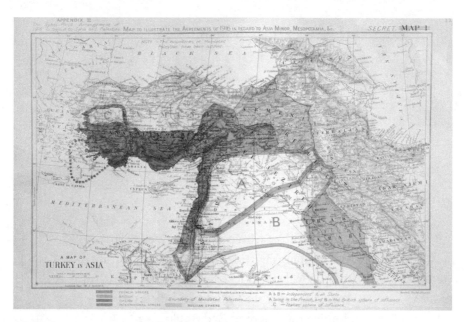

The Sykes–Picot putative agreement, drawn up in 1916

It was only the Bolshevik revolution that knocked the plan for Istanbul to become a colony of Petrograd-St Petersburg off course. Not only did the events of 1917 result in Russia's withdrawal from the conflict, but the Russian stasis also allowed for the publication of the badly worked clandestine pact. Many in the West might have neglected to remember Sykes–Picot, but it has an afterlife. It is the central feature of an IS promotional video, released in 2014, a hundred years on from the outbreak of the First World War, demanding the agreement's degradation (even though Sykes–Picot remains unimplemented) and for the unification of all Islamic territories into one state, the *ummah*. Seeking an obliteration of colonial influence, Sykes–Picot is now a web-search coupling most frequently found in the tweets of IS members and sympathisers. The group's leader, Abu Bakr al-Baghdadi, who has worked from Samarra in central Iraq – the Islamic city which had once produced those finely carved doors, repurposed for Christian monks' tombs – has used social media to radicalise and to vocalise his condemnation of this detail of a messy moment in history. IS claims to have 'smashed' Sykes–Picot. Entrance to the First World War was described, in the palaces of Istanbul, as jihad, and today it is being sold as unfinished business.

CHAPTER 75

✤

THE RED APPLE

AD 1919–22
(1337–41 IN THE ISLAMIC CALENDAR)

King, I shall arise from my enmarbled sleep,
And from my mystic tomb I shall come forth
To open wide the bricked-up Golden Gate;
And, victor over the Caliphs and the Tsars,
Hunting them beyond Red Apple Tree,
I shall rest upon my ancient bounds.

KOSTIS PALAMAS, *THE KING'S FLUTE* (1910)[1]

After the dancing in the streets to mark the end of the First World War in 1918, Britain remembered her old friends. If Constantinople was not going to become Russian, the interventionist line of thought went, it had to belong to someone. The plan was for Kostantiniyye to be reborn as Christian Constantinople once more. From the bar of the Pera Palace Hotel this might have seemed logical.

But the Allies had not counted on the grit of the Turks nor of one individual who starts to come into focus around now. That young officer Mustafa Kemal, aged thirty-eight in 1919, who had supported the Committee of Union and Progress and had made his mark on the killing fields of Gallipoli, would go on to prove himself the saviour of a unified Turkey. Born in Thessaloniki, trained in Istanbul, he was an instructor at the Military Academy of Monastir, present-day Bitola (where the guides eagerly tell you he earned the name Kemal meaning 'Excellence or Perfection'), later winning his political stripes on the coastlines of Asia and Europe. The man who would become Atatürk truly was a child of the Egnatian Way – and of the multifarious, multi-ethnic routes of communication that that highway had encouraged. When Thessaloniki was lost to Greece in the Balkan Wars, Mustafa Kemal's mother, stepfather and sister had used the Via Egnatia to make it as refugees to Istanbul. Kemal was featured in the press during the Gallipoli campaign – his image emblazoned in the newspaper *Tasvir-i Efkâr* in October 1915. Admired as a *gazi*, a holy warrior, in the newspapers and political pamphlets being furiously produced at illegal printing presses in the city, Mustafa Kemal had his own plans for The World's Desire. Because the Great War might be over, but for the inhabitants of Istanbul a new conflict was about to start. With victory in the Great War secured for the Allies, the Greek prime minister Eleutherios Venizelos had ebulliently promoted the Great Idea – proclaiming that Greece would once again sit on two continents, 'washed by five seas'.

In May 1919, Greek troops, with British support, sent by Venizelos, were back where they had started 2,600 years before, their forces landing on the coast near Smyrna (Izmir to the Turks) and heading inland. In Istanbul, Venizelos' image was triumphantly raised in Taksim Square, as were the flags of Hellas over the streets of Pera.

Meanwhile Mustafa Kemal, who had initially approached the British Authorities about advancement but had been pushed back, was then identified as a subversive and was set to be deported to Malta. The smart, ambitious, highly capable man, sent by the Sultan to oversee troops in Anatolia, saw an opportunity. Kemal catalysed the creation of the 'Association for Defence of Rights for Anatolia and Roumelia' and established his own seat of power in the East. Although there were those in Istanbul who believed him to be a rebellious traitor, elsewhere the 'hero of Gallipoli' label stuck. Postcards were produced showing an alluring, enigmatic figure slipping away from Istanbul and out to a new Anatolian dawn. Originally under instruction from the Sultan Mehmed VI but then cut loose, Kemal was, Alcibiades-like, his own man – a popular, political privateer. In the East, he turned an inspection of troops into a project to secure a resistance force. Ankara became a magnet for talented subversives. While the Sultan was unable to pay official salaries, Kemal was offering a stimulating, if risky, alternative. Weapons started to disappear mysteriously from arsenals in the capital. Frustrated by the Sultan's inactivity there was a mass rally in Sultanahmet – the high hill of the city that had been a Thracian stronghold, a Greek acropolis, a Roman provincial town, and then a Byzantine and Ottoman powerhouse. In Ankara on

Hunger map of Europe, 1918

1 May 1920, in the newly constituted Grand National Assembly, Mustafa Kemal, now recognised by many as President, called for a holy war. A document was produced demanding the rights not of the Ottomans but, for the very first time, of Türkiye – Turkey.

Meanwhile in Greece, a series of unfortunate events underlined the happenstance of history. King Constantine of Hellas, who had abdicated in 1917, returned in October 1920 under slightly unsual circumstances. In the royal estate just outside Athens, where today an empty swimming pool is defaced with graffiti and sheep turds decorate the lawns, the pet dog of his son King Alexander attacked a pet macaque and, in the subsequent commotion, the king was bitten by a second monkey. Within a month he would be dead, at the age of twenty-seven. Alexander's father Constantine was propelled back to the throne. Constantine became the Hellenic focus of quasi-eschatological fantasy. 'It is perhaps no exaggeration to remark that a quarter of a million persons died of this monkey's bite,' noted Winston Churchill. In Athens' newspapers the new King Constantine was now shown together with the dead Emperor Constantine XI – finally risen from his resting-place underneath the Golden Gate and marching in to reclaim Constantinople, slaying the Turkish dragon. The last of Pandora's curses, hope, had been released from her pernicious jar. The Greeks acted in haste but they would repent at leisure.

Meanwhile, in August 1920 in elegant Sèvres on the south-western edge of Paris, in an exhibition room of a porcelain factory, the Allies were drawing up their own papers. The Treaty of Sèvres, developed against the advice of diplomats in the field (but agreed to by the Ottoman Sultan), proposed a radical re-working of the borders within North Africa, the Middle East and the Eastern Mediterranean. The Ottoman's Arab territories were divided into new states, administered by the French and British – a continuation of colonialism in all but name. Britain acquired Iraq and Transjordan, France Lebanon; the British Mandate of Palestine and the French Mandate of Syria were established, while the coastline of Asia Minor was returned to Greece. In addition, the straits of the Dardanelles, the Bosphorus and the Sea of Marmara were to be internationalised. These waterways could no longer be subject to any blockade or act of war unless to enforce the decisions of the newly founded League of Nations. As for Istanbul herself, the old imperial city was to be run jointly by Britain, France, Bulgaria, Austro-Hungary, Italy, Japan, Greece and the US. There was a sense that Britain – whose empire by 1922 would come to hold sway over a fifth of the world's population – would have the upper hand.

In 1922 Turkish troops advanced on the city of Izmir-Smyrna; for days the city burned. As those who survived clambered on to rescue boats, while others were torn to pieces by the boats' propellers or shot, many in Istanbul thought that they would be next to suffer dreadful deaths.

Despite the rhetoric that still blazes on both sides, Greeks and Turks alike vehemently citing atrocities, the truth was that the Greco-Turkic War was chaotic and bloody. One of the Greek commanders, Prince Andrew, the father of the British Queen Elizabeth II's husband the Duke of Edinburgh, admitted to being appalled by the cruelty that he saw on the ground. Greek forces seized Edirne, then Bursa, and moved on through Anatolia. As Greek soldiers alternately advanced and fled, militias took control of the land left behind. The Istanbullu author Ismail Keskin, visibly moved, recalls the stories that he was told as a child of this desperate episode. How his great-grandmother, of mixed heritage, while trying to make it to the West with two small children – a toddler and a ten-month-old son – was hiding in a cave in the countryside. The baby boy started to cry. Petrified, the women travelling with them hissed that the mother had to leave with her child or kill him. This was Hobson's Choice: emerge and risk certain death for both children or choose – as she did – to silence her son by suffocating him with a piece of cloth.

Where the wide Maritsa River now separates Greece and Turkey, surrounded by water meadows and decorated with columns and curls of mist, many others drowned – as the Asian and African refugees of the twenty-first century have now also drowned – the snipers on the borders and armed guards on the bridges unable, or unwilling, to help. Ernest Hemingway, reporting for the *Toronto Star* in October 1922, described the scene; 'The main column crossing the Maritza River at Adrianople [Edirne] is twenty miles long. Twenty miles of carts drawn by cows, bullocks and muddy-flanked water-buffalo, with exhausted staggering men, women and children, blankets over their heads walking blindly along in the rain beside their worldly goods.'[2]

So while the British declared possession of Istanbul, threatening nationalist sympathisers with the death penalty, the city of refuge was becoming a city of refugees. First fleeing the Bolshevik Revolution, which had been in part catalysed by the fight for Istanbul and the subsequent blocking up of the Bosphorus supply-line, White Russians poured into the city; they wrapped parcels and spread their tables with sheets of uncut, unusable Russian paper currency.[3] The image on the banknotes – the double-headed eagle that had started life in Byzantium – was a symbolic bird of prey that had come back to Byzas' City but as a two-dimensional parody of itself. Many refugees slept in gutters or in the stables of the Sultan's palaces. The Flower Passage in Pera is so called because female flower-sellers found strength in numbers here when menaced by Allied soldiers. The situation was so dire that one charity fed 160,000 Russians a day.[4] Soon joining the Russians were both starving Greeks and starving Turks.

The reports of British officers in Istanbul at the time, who still held the city, ricocheted between heartfelt concern, brinkmanship, drudgery and derring-do.[5] In November 1922 when the Government of the Grand

National Assembly declared that the Sultanate was to be abolished, the British kidnapped an acquiescent Sultan Mehmed VI. The Sultan had delivered a message to General Charles Harington via his loyal bandmaster: 'Sir – Considering my life in danger in Istanbul, I take refuge with the British Government and request my transfer as soon as possible from Istanbul to another place. Mehmed Vahideddin, Caliph of the Muslims.' Pretending they were conducting an early-morning drill, British soldiers bundled the Sultan into an ambulance (with the red crosses painted out) which rushed from the Yıldız Palace to Dolmabahçe; from there the Sultan was taken by boat to the dockyards, before being transferred to a British battleship which conveyed the imperial exile to Malta and then on to Italy. Istanbul's last Sultan, Mehmed Vahdeddin, died in San Remo in 1926. General Charles Harington was left with the responsibility of looking after the Sultan's five wives. The Yıldız Palace meanwhile was turned into a casino by an Italian businessman.

On 2 October 1923, British troops finally left Kostantiniyye, their ships slipping from the quays outside the Dolmabahçe Palace. The Turkish armed forces, who, up until now, had been predominantly loyal to the Sultan – turned their faces east, the army was Mustafa Kemal's. Istanbul's last Sultan had committed the ultimate crime – effectively ceding the World's Desire, the diamond between two sapphires, The City, to her enemies. Without control of the city an old dream was broken. The revenant protagonists had woken up.

CHAPTER 76

THE CATASTROPHE

AD 1921–3
(1339–42 IN THE ISLAMIC CALENDAR)

A horrible muddle . . . a nightmare in which you can foresee all the horrible things which are going to happen and can't stretch out your hand to prevent them.

GERTRUDE BELL, DESCRIBING THE SITUATION IN THE MIDDLE EAST
AFTER THE BREAK-UP OF THE OTTOMAN EMPIRE, 1919[1]

Sancta Sophia is a sphere of light. It is the Sancta Sophia: Wisdom. It is what the world needs most and has lost.

THOMAS WHITTEMORE, THE FUTURE RESTORER OF AYASOFYA,
WRITING FROM KOSTANTINIYYE, 6 JULY 1920[2]

Just inland from Kavala in northern Greece, where Christians burnt one another's cities to the ground in the eleventh and twelfth centuries AD, there is a deserted village called Chortokopi. There is no sound here apart from larks in the trees and chickens contentedly scratching outside a nearby monastery. The neuroscientist picking his way through the rubble, the broken walls that were his schoolroom in the 1950s, remembers the poem that he was made to learn here so that he could recite it to his teacher. Originally a city boy, he recalls the thrill of hearing the jangle of goat-bells high on the hilltop. His ambition then was to become a goatherd; this would have been a loss to neuroscience. Professor Silviarides also remembers his mother weeping here in their simple kitchen at night. Silviarides' family, who came from Trebizond, were Pontic Greeks who were exchanged as a result of article 142 of the Treaty of Lausanne in 1923. In a single year 500,000 Muslims were moved from Greece to Turkey and 1.3 million Greeks from Anatolia to Greece. The Treaty recognised

Turkey's victory in the Greco-Turkic War and was also an attempt to prevent ethnic violence by keeping Christian Greeks and Muslim Turks apart. But Professor Silviarides' grandfather had just built a new house on the shores of the Black Sea where Muslims and Christians had lived together for close on 500 years; he assumed that this exchange of populations was a moment of political madness and that he would be coming back.

The deadline for families to leave was 26 December – a cruel month for such a journey. Many of the religiously cleansed refugees, travelling east or west along the Egnatian Way, had just one suitcase – you were only allowed to travel with what you could carry. Return without the express permission of their former country was illegal. The millet system had once defended minorities; now the indefensible were expelled. Soon a law was passed that ceded to the state all property left by the refugees.

Having remained undisturbed in northern Thrace for over 2,000 years, the Roman paving stones of the Via Egnatia were grubbed up as incoming families were forced to turn highway into farmland. The Treaty of Lausanne, originally written in French and signed under the cool stare of the Swiss mountains, established a dread precedent, the first of its kind in history to be sanctioned by international law, that of 'Collective Population Transfer'. Politicians were playing God with a legal concept that would continue to be abused across the twentieth century.

The exchange of populations may have generated long-term issues, but because the failing Ottoman state was all but lawless it probably prevented mass slaughter on the ground. Yet the cost to individuals' humanity was appaling. On the streets, the exchange was described by those who suffered its consequences as 'a disgraceful bartering of bodies to the detriment of modern civilisation'.[3]

There is something listless about the parts of northern Greece that watched Orthodox Christians travel in one direction and Muslims in the other: here there feels to be a melancholic impermanence. Most of those Greeks leaving Asia Minor were from the commercial classes; many only spoke Turkish; most Muslims travelling east were tobacco-growers. Across Europe, North Africa and the Middle East, smokers had puffed away for decades on Giannitsa cigarettes, the tobacco for which had been grown by European Muslims in fields around the town founded in AD 1383 by the Ottoman-Byzantine convert Evrenos Bey. Only a handful

Greek refugees trying to leave Istanbul by boat in 1922

won out from the intervention, but Asia Minor's handicap was certainly greater. Refugee camps sprang up around Istanbul, where many died.

In the city itself, although a special dispensation allowed the Greek patriarchate to remain, and a substantial number of families did stay on in the Greek district around it and in Pera, the isolation of the Orthodox Christians in the city quickly became unbearable. Around 150,000 concluded that they had no choice but to leave. In 1922 Greeks had owned 1,169 of 1,413 restaurants in the city. As with the other non-Muslim populations, they might not have held the reins, but they pumped the blood of the horse. Yet in 1932 Greek Christians were banned from participating in thirty professions from that of tailor to doctor. A decade on and their businesses were subject to a new tax. In 1955 during the 'Istanbul Pogrom' angry young Turkish men attacked Orthodox churches, businesses, schools and even cemeteries, burning and smashing property. Over a dozen people were killed, many were abused, and more just packed their bags and ran. While 240,000 Greeks had been left in the city following the Greco-Turkic War and subsequent population exchange, today there are fewer than a thousand. Fener, the quarter the Greeks had inhabited for over 2,500 years and which was one of the richest in the city, is today one of the poorest. In the collapsing wooden mansions, for centuries the homes of Istanbul's privileged Phanariot community, hand-to-mouth economic migrants now live, predominantly farm-labouring families who have come into Istanbul to find work.[4]

For those who were the victims of power-brokers seeking ethnic tidiness, it must have seemed as though their protestations were like vapour trails in the sky, a vanishing imprint on nothing.

The side effects of the Great War and the collapse of Ottoman rule might have been described by Gertrude Bell, adventurer, explorer, writer, spy and frequent visitor to the city – as 'a horrible muddle'. The Greco-Turkish War of 1920–2 and the forced expulsion of families based on their religion or history is still remembered simply as 'the Catastrophe'.

Cosmopolitan Istanbul was increasingly described by nationalists as the Byzantine Whore – a city that had surrendered herself to the tainted dabblings of foreign money and foreign love. 'The Catastrophe' – a combination of misguided do-gooding, prejudice, anti-imagination and hubris – seems to be the rotting fruits of that civilisation that had first started in that Yarımburgaz Cave.

An uncertain future awaited Istanbul. Mustafa Kemal was sincere when he declared, 'On the meeting point of two worlds, the ornament of the Turkish homeland, the treasure of Turkish history, the city cherished by the Turkish nation, Istanbul has its place in the hearts of all citizens.' But Kemal was planning a new way of being for his beloved nation, and Istanbul's place in that plan was unsure. It was said that a pocket watch had saved Kemal from death at Gallipoli. The bullet had shattered the timepiece but had not killed the man. Whether or not this is an urban myth, what is certain is that Mustafa Kemal's survival would reset the mechanical and the cultural clocks in Istanbul and across what was soon to be officially nominated the Republic of Turkey.

Remembering the other city that had welcomed him when he was a rebel, when he had been rejected by Westerners operating out of Istanbul, and acting on the convenient circumstances that Ankara had a railway line and a telegraph office, Mustafa Kemal made Ankara the centre of his revolution. The capital was formally moved to Ankara on 13 October 1923 and on the 29th of that month the Turkish Republic was founded. The proclamation of the Republic was announced, in true Ottoman style, with drumming and a volley of 101 guns firing an artillery salute. Mustafa Kemal's government was now the vessel of Turkish hopes. His portraits appeared on street walls and in cafés – a practice doggedly maintained by some to this day. Kemal was soon to be Atatürk – Father of the Turks. Nationalism ruled.[5]

Istanbul, long a destination, or a transit point, was, it seemed, yesterday's news, somewhere to abandon. The Sublime Porte had, constitutionally, become a gateway to nothing.

CHAPTER 77

✤

THE LAST CALIPH

AD 1922–44
(1340–64 IN THE ISLAMIC CALENDAR)

This mystical element cannot be eradicated from the Muslim mind without creating discord in the world of Islam.

IMAM SULTAN MUHAMMAD SHAH (THE AGA KHAN III) AND
SAYYED AMEER ALI, 'AN APPEAL TO TURKEY TO RETAIN THE
KHILAFAT', *THE TIMES*, 14 DECEMBER 1923[1]

It was an irony perhaps not lost on the last Ottoman Caliph that his own uncle[2] had built the Dolmabahçe Palace as a vision of the forward-thinking future of the city, yet the palace would come to constitute the backdrop to the end of empire, to the end of Ottoman rule and to the dissolution of the Ottoman Caliphate itself.

The setting could hardly have been more opulent. Constructed for the equivalent of around £1.5 billion sterling today, the Dolmabahçe Palace is loaded with 18 tons of gold leaf, a monstrous chandelier (donated by Queen Victoria) and swirls of porphyry and alabaster. In order to reach the upper rooms one has to travel up a crystal staircase offset with ebony and brass fittings. Empress Helena, mother of Constantine the Great, might have been the inspiration for the Cinderella story; it is fitting that an Istanbul home of Prince Charming proportions should see the end of the imperial fairy-tale.

The library of the Dolmabahçe Palace is warm, somewhat womb-like, decorated with lamps and globes. But for many this is a haunting place, because it was here that the Caliph was deposed. In 1922 (1340 in the Islamic calendar), the Sultanate and Caliphate had been separated as institutions. The Sultanate was abolished in November of that year and while the Caliphate kept its religious role, its teeth were drawn; the

Caliph was now subservient to the state. Sultan Abdülmecid II, who had succeeded his cousin Mehmed VI, had taken up the title of caliph only four months before. From the age of eight he had been confined to the Kafes, the prison for princes.

Laws had been quickly passed by the Grand National Assembly on 3 March 1924 that made the Caliphate redundant. The post was abolished and over 140 members of the Ottoman dynasty were ordered into exile. That very evening the governor of Istanbul delivered that bombshell of a message to Abdülmecid – he was to leave before dawn.[3]

But this was not going to be an easy passing. Although the Caliph himself, reading Montaigne (some accounts say the Qur'an) as the soldiers came in, initially put up little resistance, remarking that he just wanted to take his painting equipment with him, the palace was swiftly surrounded by soldiers. Telephone lines were cut. As word spread across the Muslim world, many made it clear that they considered the removal of Istanbul's Caliph to be a blow not just to the body politic but to the spiritual heart of Islam. In India the Khalifat movement had emerged as a reaction to the weakening of the Ottoman Caliph's power. Since the eighteenth century, many Muslims in India had once again acknowledged the Ottoman Sultan as the leader of the faithful. Istanbul's Sultan had been remembered in Friday prayers. The Khalifat movement aimed to stitch together the solidarity of Muslims both within and across national borders. It would be the seedbed of the India–Pakistan partition movement in the twentieth century.

Taken out from the palace by a side door before dawn, the Caliph and his family (two wives, a son and a daughter) were brought not to Sirkeci station but to Çatalca station outside the city to avoid attention and protests; accounts vary but some say they travelled at gunpoint. It was reported that the Sultan's daughter Dürrüşehvar cried that she did not want this kind of 'Western' freedom. A popular story still circulates that the stationmaster happened to be Jewish: on realising who his passengers were, he made tea and then wept when the Caliph thanked him, declaring that it was the Jews who owed the caliphs thanks for taking them in after the fall of Granada in AD 1492. Thirty-six princes, forty-eight princesses and sixty children were swiftly exiled.

So it was that on 4 March 1924 Abdülmecid, Istanbul's last Caliph, was packed on to the Orient Express with £2,000 of Turkish state money and at midnight sent to Switzerland. This was the year when there were icebergs on the Bosphorus and the city's many trees were heavy with snow. For a number of reasons, 1924 stuck in the collective memory. The King of Afghanistan, King Fuad of Egypt, King Hussein of the Hijaz and the Imam of Yemen were proposed as alternative leaders of Islam. The close link the Kurds felt to the Caliphate lowered their standing after the deposition. Kurdish tribal chiefs were resettled in western Turkey and use of the Kurdish language in public and the teaching of it were prohibited. In March 1925 it was also made illegal in Turkey to show support for the Caliphate.[4] Some suggested that in emotional, intellectual and quasi-religious terms the Turkish National Assembly should take on the Caliphate's role. The strength of character that Atatürk showed in pushing through these immense changes should not be underestimated.

There were unexpected winners in this whimpering out of a 470-year-old institution. From the second half of the nineteenth century it had been those closest to power who had enjoyed particular benefits from programmes of Westernisation and urban renewal – with the Sultan's household at the epicentre of this advance. Although the Sultan had been deposed, since they were slaves, all concubines in his harem now had the right to keep their possessions. The imperial family might be exiled but its adjuncts were not – children had to leave Istanbul, but mothers and wives did not. It was a final corrective to an entrenched slave economy that was typically heavier on the take than on the give.

The rooms behind the open courtyard of the harem, the Terrace of the Favourites at the Topkapı, remained as they had been left in 1909 – beds draped with musty covers, cobwebs stitching their own lattice from tile to tile – for the next fifty years. The last inhabitant of the sultan's household, Princess Neslişah Osmanoglu, born in 1921 and later exiled, died back in Istanbul in 2012.

In 1922 another died whose reedy, falsetto voice had been recorded in 1902. The recording is a song by one of the European eunuchs who lived while there were still eunuchs serving at the Ottoman court. This is the oldest audio evidence that we have for the presence of those castrated men who, for just short of half a millennium, enjoyed enormous power in Istanbul. We have a photograph of Ottoman eunuchs from this time too; well dressed in tweed suits and starched collars they are long-limbed, smooth-cheeked. Nineteen black men and one white sit or stand, all

Cecil Beaton's portrait of the Princess of Berar, daughter of Istanbul's last Caliph
Abdülmecid II, photographed in India in March 1944

staring thoughtfully at the camera. This was one of the final meetings
of the black eunuchs of the Sultan's harem. With the disbanding of
the Ottoman Empire in 1922 they formed a self-help group, as a way to
deal with the material and psychological shifts that they were having to
endure.

Had you walked the French Riviera from the summer of 1924 onwards, you might have seen the ex-caliph Abdülmecid quietly sketching
or walking the promenade, carrying his own sunshade. While some Jews
would be rescued by the Turkish Embassy from Nazi-occupied Paris and
smuggled back to Istanbul, Abdülmecid could not make that journey. He
finally died in August 1944 at his elegant home in the 16th Arrondisse-
ment on Boulevard Suchet, his near neighbours the Duke and Duchess
of Windsor, just two days before Paris was liberated. He had felt at home
perhaps in a city that, thanks to a fascination with 'the Orient', preserved
at least an idea of what Istanbul could be. The last Ottoman Caliph's
remains were reburied in Medina ten years later.

Byzantion, Byzantium, Constantinople, Kostantiniyye, Istanbul – The
City has tangled with or represented an 'idea' for so many, its influence
has spun so far, that her story, whether imperial, spiritual, cultural or
political, frequently ends up being played out anywhere and everywhere
other than in the city itself.

The Three Pashas all died violently in 1921–2. The locations of their deaths – Cemal assassinated in Tbilisi in Georgia, Enver killed rousing Muslims against the Bolsheviks in Central Asia, and Talat shot in Berlin by an Armenian assassin – offer a reminder of the splintering reach of Istanbul: a reach that looks set to endure.

CHAPTER 78

GLOBAL FUTURES

AD 1924
(1342/3 IN THE ISLAMIC CALENDAR) ONWARDS

> Marbles of the dancing floor
> Break bitter furies of complexity,
> Those images that yet
> Fresh images beget,
> That dolphin-torn, that gong-tormented sea.
>
> W. B. YEATS, 'BYZANTIUM'

A finely carved marble bust found in an attic in Paris, depicting a distinguished-looking gentleman with furrowed brows and traditional Constantinopolitan dress with ruched-silk buttons and topped with a fez, is the face of one of the great success stories of Istanbul. Abraham Salomon Camondo was the paterfamilias of a Jewish family that helped to stitch together the finance that would ease Istanbul's eventual transformation into modernity.

Arriving in the city in AD 1798, having left Granada in 1492 with other Sephardic Jews, the Camondos appear time and again in the records of the city, but their real turning point was the foundation in 1802 of Isaac Camondo's banking house. The business dynasty that emerged would come to be described as the 'Rothschilds of the East'. The Camondos helped to finance the Bosphorus steam ferries, and tramways, before the Crimean War diminished opportunities. In 1869 the family, who by this time had become the greatest landowners in Istanbul, moved to Paris. Here they consolidated their splendid art collections which included Marie Antoinette's ebony cabinets, Madame de Pompadour's Japanese lacquer collection and the work of early Impressionists.

The elegant Camondo steps in Galata leading to the Bankalar Caddesi, the street of banks, which the family developed, still stand. But the Camondo family, along with tens of thousands of other Jews who fled from major Ottoman cities in 1943 (such as Thessaloniki, where 54,000 were rounded up by German soldiers just a stone's throw from the location of that dreadful massacre ordered by Emperor Theodosios I more than 1,500 years before), were eradicated, entirely, in Auschwitz. As the Second World War made its ugly progression, the Turkish Embassy in Paris – hearing that Jews were being put on to trains heading for concentration camps – opened an office where Ottoman Jews were given the passports of young Muslim students so that they could escape France to travel back to Istanbul. It is estimated that in the space of two months 15,000 souls were saved in France and, by the end of the war, a further 20,000 in eastern Europe.

The day that I submitted this book to my publishers in May 2016, Istanbul hosted the first ever World Humanitarian Summit, spearheaded by the UN. It took place in the midst of the greatest refugee crisis since the Second World War, and as the dignitaries and heads of state arrived there were more international refugees in Istanbul fleeing stasis in the lands that had once been Ottoman than in any other capital city in the world. Istanbul might have been a settlement besieged since antiquity, but she fights against succumbing to a siege mentality.

Peace abroad, peace at home, was the foundation stone of the new Republic.

Today the population of the city of Istanbul is larger than those of two-thirds of the world's countries; it stretches 100 miles from end to end.[1] Yet under Kemal Atatürk's reforms, the intention was to draw political firepower away from this metropolis to Ankara, and to the wider Turkish Anatolian homeland. Atatürk pointedly rowed across the Bosphorus in a little wooden dinghy in order to distance himself from those gilded barges of the sultans, and initially conditions in Ankara were indeed pretty basic – the French Embassy started life here in a railway buffet. The desire of Atatürk and his new government was not to crush Istanbul's spirit, but to jettison the best of her influence. Foreign embassies (the British initially refused) moved from Istanbul to Ankara. Ankara had a population of only 29,000, so up to 85 per cent of civil servants and 93 per cent of Ottoman army staff officers remained in their post as the Empire moved to Republic and as the centre of administration moved a fifteen-hour car-ride east. Out in Anatolian villages a progressive education system was instituted; peasant children would be taught to play Western instruments such as the violin alongside their traditional folk songs, and to recite Shakespeare under the mulberry trees. They performed Greek tragedies in the very lands where these dramas had originally been set. The village-school experiment flourished for ten years or so. Atatürk would also insist that each morning Turkish children across the country should chant, 'I am a Turk. I am honest. I am hard working. My code is to protect those younger than me, to respect my elders, and love my homeland and my nation more than myself. My quest is to rise higher and go further. May my whole life be a gift to Turkishness.'[2]

From 1924, on postcards, for the first time there was a systematic policy to brand the diamond between two sapphires as Istanbul not Constantinople. In 1928 the Latin script replaced the Arabic. From 28 March 1930 the Turkish post office no longer delivered post addressed to Constantinople. There had been similar attempts before (during the wars with Russia in the eighteenth century, sultans had struck coins in 'Islambol' rather than Constantinople), but the Turkish Republic's endeavours were more systematic. Nations which are unaware of their history are obliged to die out, said Kemal Atatürk; his words are immortalised at Istanbul's Ottoman Military Museum.[3] All who have controlled Istanbul – Thracians, Greeks, Persians, Romans, Byzantines, Latins, Ottomans, the British, and the Turks – have come here specifically to trade goods, politics, humans or ideas, so the invisible lines of connection that have given the settlement her strength as a place and as an idea are hard to break. The city exists both as herself and beyond herself. In Kavala – that station on the Egnatian Way, burnt down by Norman Christians and taken by Ottoman Turks– a large red and yellow road sign, blazoned with the Byzantine black and white eagle, proudly points the way not to Istanbul but to Constantinople. In the Humor Monastery, in what was once Moldavia, now Romania, rebuilt in AD 1530, wondrous frescoes depict the 1453 Siege of Constantinople together with the Last Judgement and a Hymn to Theotokos – inspired by the patriarch Sergios' hymn of thanks to Mary for Constantinople's salvation in 626. There are other atavistic remains – such as the communities of monks on Mount Athos, still living the dream as articulated by the monks of the Stoudios. Greek cuisine comes in large part from Asia Minor. On the little island of Siphnos one is enthusiastically guided to the lovingly made model boat hanging in the roof of the Chrysopigi Church – itself isolated on a rocky promontory that stretches out into the sea, dedicated by a Muslim whose ship went down off the coast, but whose life was saved by Mary Theotokos. A young Greek waiter at the deserted Vitali beach taverna in the Cycladic island of Andros – accessed only via unmade-up, hairpinned tracks and hand-made signs – serves moussaka and *imam bayıldı* with the double-headed Byzantine eagle as a tattoo flexing on his shoulder. A patriotic if futile fury of spilt ink – signalling that the Greek city, Constantinople, is by rights still his.

Today the holdings of the barricaded patriarch in Istanbul, still the patriarch of a 'New Rome', might occupy a minute 1/500,000 of the Byzantine Empire at its height (during Ottoman rule the Greek Orthodox Church remained a landowner in Ottoman territories),[4] but The Fortunate City's deep history is resilient. In 2007 I sailed from Athens, past the islands of Hydra and Poros, to the southern mainland of Greece in search of a man whose business card says simply 'Nicholas Romanoff – Prince of Russia'. We talked about this putative Prince's grandmother's estate on the Black Sea and whether or not Nicholas was the last living Caesar. The old man described his uncle under house arrest in Paris, painting Orthodox icons as therapy. This living fragment of an idea of the New Roman Empire, surrounded at home by images of the double-headed eagle that started life on the Hittite plains and then came back into Byzantium via a Roman eagle standard, Prince Romanoff admitted that he would die happy knowing that the cross might replace the crescent on Ayasofya. The settlement that we now call Istanbul has always been as resonant in the landscape of the imagination as it has in real historical terms.

Istanbul's story has not yet finished, and when it comes to history there is more evidence on the horizon. Greek, Roman, Byzantine and Ottoman sites in the Levant and the Middle East still await excavation. When an electrical power station was being built at Silahtarağa on the Golden Horn in 1949 (part of the Turkish Republic's modernisation programme), an ancient Greek battle-scene between the titans and the gods in black and white marble was uncovered, the religious sculpture marking what was believed to be the site of Byzas' birth.

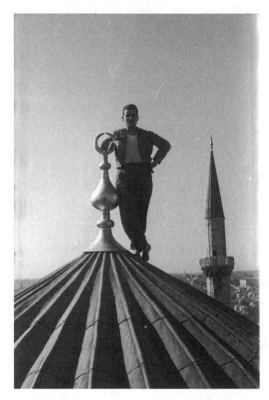

*Some of the finest black and white photographic portraits of Istanbul in the 1930s
and 1940s were taken by Nicholas V. Artamonoff, who was said to be the son of the
Russian military attaché who paid off Archduke Ferdinand's assassin. This image,
taken in 1955–60, shows a master-worker restoring the dome of the Süleymaniye
Mosque.*

In the 1960s ferocious fires on the Bosphorus, sparking because of the
transport of fossil fuels demanded by Europe and America in the new
super-tankers that ground from north to south and back again through
the straits, recalled the scene on the waterways 1,500 years before when the
Byzantines had unleashed Greek Fire. Some of the conflagrations in the
1960s burned for days. The sticky, black fumes seemed to smoke-signal an
entry to a new kind of world. A beneficiary of the Marshall Plan after the
Second World War, Istanbul started to take on the mantle of American
influence. Up until the First World War a visitor from 400 years before
would have been able to find their way around the city without too much
difficulty. After the urban developments of the early 1960s and 1970s,

they would have been lost. Istanbul's administrators harboured an ambition to become global players once again in an increasingly globalised world, from a 'modern' global city.

In the 1980s there were even rumours that the pro-market Prime Minister Turgut Özal (1983–9) wanted to move the capital back from Ankara to Istanbul; he certainly souped up his city accordingly. Many heritage groups today nostalgically yearn for the make-up of the city 'pre'-Özal. From the year 2000 the hideous pollution since the 1970s, which had left the Golden Horn a fetid, dead lagoon, was addressed and the waters cleared. The Russians invested heavily in Istanbul, particularly in her new financial district, but with both political allegiance and global finance unstable, Istanbul's great capitalist hope is, at the time of writing a white-elephant-shaped series of holes and redundant cranes above the Asian shore. Negotiations to join the European Union still shudder. Turning east, the wide skies of Anatolia and the tundra of the steppes and Central Asia seem to welcome. In autumn 2016, Turkey abandoned European Daylight Saving Time. The Shanghai Cooperation Organisation, a political, military and economic coalition of China, India, Pakistan, Russia and a number of Central Asian countries, has been described by Turkey's leaders as better, more powerful, more in tune than the European Union.[5] For at least twenty-five centuries, Istanbul has been a city that many both want and need. East and West alike still dance attendance at Turkey's court. Since her Greek foundation – as Byzantion, then as Christian Constantinople and finally under the Caliphate of Islambol – Istanbul has drawn her strength from her conviction that she was a city divinely blessed. Ayasofya, which has been both a church and a mosque, built on a pagan sanctuary, held together by belief and by time and by human endeavour, whose curves have long echoed the seven old hills of Istanbul, watches all this, her dome now cracking, and waits.

And yet, despite its profound influence, despite the fact that this has always been the first and last city of Asia and Europe, and the fastest route between North and South, that a Greco-Roman heart beat in the Byzantine body politic, despite the fact that Constantinople was the Caput Mundi throughout the medieval period and that the Ottomans drove international politics for close on 500 years, Istanbul's is still a civilisation that does not hold its own among the world's greatest hits. Its story is perhaps so complex, each chapter interwoven with the next, it does not satisfy our desire for unitary explanations for how the story of the world runs. As a city Istanbul is both 'ours' and 'other'; it is a cosmopolis that defies categorisation. In the Royal Museum of Art and History in Brussels – an institution rudely apparent in its debt to classical influences, with a rotunda and pillared colonnades, its collections adapted to celebrate the idea of a briefly united Europe – the treasures of one of the first medieval civilisations to attempt comparable unity are squashed into the basement. One gorgeous finely carved Byzantine ivory casket is boxed up next to a radiator, whereas Greece and Rome are lauded on the first floor and the culture of Islam now has its own specially designed and lavish gallery with slatted windows.[6]

Envy, fear, desire, covetousness, gossip, politicking have meant that through time the relation of the outsider with the idea of the city with three names has been charged, testy. The French say 'C'est Byzance' when they mean something is excessive, luxurious, sumptuous. The Anglo-phone world regularly describes overcomplicated administration as being Byzantine; corrupt and opaque is the implication.[7] The harem in Istanbul has been hotly imagined. What we know of the women in the city is in large part a fantasy fabricated by showmen, writers, thinkers, painters, poets, pseudo-scientists and politicians. Ottoman reality became something the West owned – a chimaera dreamt up so that we could measure ourselves up against our own creation.[8] Today giant hoardings plastered with seductively veiled dancing girls are still used to tempt in international tourists. In popular TV documentaries and dramas we hear of the leaders of Byzantium blinding their sons, burning their enemies in furnaces, of a culture that readily employed rhinotomy – nose-amputation – in AD 641 (by 705 returning emperors were commissioning solid-gold prosthetics to cover what was once flesh). After Paddy Leigh Fermor had experienced his ouzo-fuelled dreams in the Mani while on the trail of the last Byzantine Emperor, the writer-adventurer decided to walk 'to the gates of Asia'; yet he tells us that he left Istanbul with a light heart. And there is indeed something inherently mournful, melancholic about the weight of human experience that you wade through on Istanbul's streets, with the ghosts of the city's enemies who were burnt to death in the public squares or blinded in the corridors of the Great Palace, garrotted in the gardens of the Topkapı or strung up on makeshift gibbets during the First World War.

This is a city whose legends and locus might serve to stimulate fantasies, but it has also systematically nourished the hard reality of popular, political protest. Constantinople – The City, complex, variegated, ambivalent – was forged and then reworked in the heat of certain belief. Although nominally a kingdom, an empire of God, did the fast turnaround of rulers and subsequent instability serve to give voice to the people? Was that seductive topography of Byzantion, Byzantium, Constantinople, Istanbul such a character in its own right that individuals here felt a connection not just to their ruler but to the physical power of the cityscape itself? There is a scale of geography and topography in greater Istanbul that seems to demand a brio, an ideology to match. Had Constantinople truly been the inheritor of the Roman Republic – the original republic that had died on the road to Byzantion, its defeat commemorated by a collapsed triumphal arch in a maize field outside Philippi which had been raised by Mark Antony and Octavian and had once spanned the Egnatian Way? The majority of generations that have lived in the city have witnessed some form of popular protest. When President Erdoğan, a child of Istanbul and once its mayor, took to social media to try to quell

the attempted coup of summer 2016, his rallying cry was this: 'there is no power higher than the power of the people.'

'ISTANBUL – BYZANTIUM – CONSTANTINOPLE – IS OURS' Istanbullus declared on vandalised windows during the Gezi Park protest.

The graffitist's statement is a cogent one. Who does now own Istanbul? And what is her direction of travel? From those first neolithic footprints, through the adventuring work of the Greek founding fathers, Rome's empire-builders, Christendom's creators, the New Justinians and the Young Turks, this has been a settlement with precedent and purpose, a potent capital with an innate energy that refuses to run dry. Istanbul can never be listless: the topography of the city means that you always arrive at it with dynamism. Locals note sagely that the Asian and European quarters of Istanbul can simultaneously experience different weather fronts. Through history on both sides of the Bosphorus there have been earthquakes and tsunamis, storms with hailstones the size of a man's foot, and fishermen have thirty different names for the winds that pluck the waters here. The Greek poet Pindar believed that the secure foundation of cities was *eunomia*, good order, but Istanbul also encourages something which, physiologically, our minds seek – disruption. In terms of both historical fact and written histories this place reminds us why we are compelled to connect, to communicate, to exchange. But also to change. Byzantion started her historical life as a rough frontier town. Life in the city has always been demanding, even if it occasionally enjoys the odd, languid interlude. Today the Dardanelles Straits are the busiest water-ways in the world and the Bosphorus connects all the points on the compass. If Chalcedon was the city of the blind, Byzantium, Constantinople, Istanbul has long been the land of clear sight: in the very essence of the city there is photography, writing in light, before the word is invented. This foundation is one of those bright ideas, one of those lambent entities that commands the world's stare, that compels us to look. But if this was a diamond between two sapphires, it is also a gem into which we can gaze and see, as well as a multi-colour prism, our own desires reflected back.

Istanbul is not where East meets West, but where East and West look hard and longingly at one another, sometimes nettled by what they see yet interested to learn that they share dreams, stories and blood.

CODA

❖

If there were a second life
And a return one day from the other world
And every soul were set free into the universe
And could according to its pleasure find a place to settle
If fortune were to turn to me and graciously grant a star as my abode
This favour would leave me cold
I would want to return to Istanbul.

YAHYA KEMAL BEYATLI, *AZIZ ISTANBUL*[1]

Since the great geological shifts of the Pleistocene era, rivers and water-ways have shaped human history; and since the birth of the modern mind around 40,000 years ago we have understood the world by telling stories about what it is to be human. Neuroscientists now recognise that a dis-tinguishing feature of our species is not just to have ideas but to be driven to communicate them and that our minds are in their alpha state when we do what it is natural for us, as nomads, to do: when we travel. We are not forced to move from one place to another, but we do. We could have stayed in Africa; the first boat need not have crossed the Atlantic ridge. The lure of internationalism is a genetic constant. The Bosphorus, the Sea of Marmara, the Black Sea, the Golden Horn, the Hellespont and the land on either side are depositories for shared human experiences and for memories. Asia has been disconnected from Europe since the Pleistocene Ice Age, so the city that straddled the breach naturally became one of the most important and the most cherished in the world. There were many attempts to bridge the gap: Dareios and his bridge of boats, Mehmed the Conqueror's pontoon, the Ottoman Sultan Abdülmecid I commissioning an underwater tunnel project by the French engineer Simon Préault in 1860. And it was on the Bosphorus Bridge in July 2016 that some in Turkey attempted their coup.

So now that the city is connected to Asia by road bridges and by the Bosphorus tunnels, the World's Desire could have the chance to represent *ghosti* – that old word that melts together 'guest' and 'host', an etiquette of welcome that supports our determination to tangle with one another.

The Greek philosopher Aristotle in Book One of his *Politics* opined that a city works because of the civic partnerships within it. Economists tell us that cities arose as the incarnation of inequality and specialisation and that they can now survive as entities only with continued economic growth. But I think that Istanbul reminds us of another reality. Constitutionally, from that first line of prehistoric footprints, Istanbul has been a city for the Cosmopolitan, for the World Citizen. It incarnates that fine Greek word-idea, *cosmo-polis*, coined by Diogenes the Cynic, who, born in one of those early Ionian Greek colonies, Sinope on the Black Sea, was torn between Hellenic and Persian loyalty, travelled to live in Athens, slept in a clay pot in the sanctuary of the Eastern Mother of Nature Kybele and died in Corinth. It is the mood of men that makes a city, and Istanbul's mood is con-vivial.

Today the containers of international goods stacked along the Marmara shore look to be a mosaic from the sky. Tankers sit like rows of broken teeth across the horizon of the sea. Ships from north, south, east and west wait, clumped at the choke-points created by the Bosphorus' tricky currents and winds, as they have done since the beginning of history. Bektashi fishermen on the Bosphorus still brave the supertankers and the international floating hotels that clog the straits. They pray to a god that has no name but love, while Lionel Richie's music pumps from disco-lit bars. Istanbul is a settlement that, in her finest form, produces, promotes and protects the vital, hopeful notion that, wherever and whoever we end up, we understand that although humanity has many faces we share one human heart – to know Istanbul is to know what it is to be cosmopolitan – this is a city that reminds us that we are, indeed, citizens of the world.

ACKNOWLEDGEMENTS

✤

It should be clear from the length of my Bibliography the extent of the gratitude that I owe to so many. I am always inspired by other writers, thinkers, researchers and adventurers, and because the chronological reach of this book covers not centuries, but millennia, I also owe a debt of gratitude to each and every one whose name appears on the pages of this book. If for any reason I have not mentioned you or your work it is unintentional oversight and I will amend, immediately, in the next edition.

As well as works of scholarship a number of scholars have been good enough to read through chapters, parts – and in some cases – all of the text. Without exception they have saved me from infelicities – and sometimes from myself.

Munir Akdoğan, Professor Roderick Beaton, Professor Glen W. Bowersock, Professor Alan Bowman, Cafer Bozkurt Mimarlık, Professor Dame Averil Cameron, Professor Paul Cartledge, Dr Helen Castor, Professor James Clackson, Professor Kate Cooper, Professor Jim Crow, William Dalrymple, Professor Robert Dankoff, Dr Ken Dark, Professor Saul David, Dr Charalambos Dendrinos, Dr Alexander Evers, Dr Shahina Farid, Lucy Felmingham, Professor Kate Fleet, Professor Ben Fortna, Dr Peter Frankopan, Dr Annelise Freisenbruch, Dr Helen Geake, Dr David Gwynne, Professor Judith Herrin, Professor Carole Hillenbrand, Professor Robert Hoyland, Dr Timothy Hunter, Dr Richard Huscroft, Professor Judith Jesch, Agah Karliağa, Professor Bekir Karliğa, Professor Chris Kelly, Professor Martin Kemp, Professor Charles King, Professor Ufuk Kocabaş, Sinan Kuneralp, Professor Ray Laurence, Professor Noel Lenski, Dr Alexander Lingas, Professor Dr David Lordkipanidze, Lizzy

McNeill, Dr Antony Makrinos, Lucia Marchini, Professor David Mattingly, Dr Peter Meineck, Giles Milton, Dr Simon Sebag Montefiore, Caroline Montagu, Dr Alfonso Moreno, Dr Llewellyn Morgan, Dr Lucia Nixon, Professor Mehmet Özdoğan, Professor Chris Pelling, Professor Jonathan Phillips, Dr Gül Pulhan, Professor Alessandra Ricci, Andy Robertshaw, Professor Eugene Rogan, Nicholas Romanoff, Professor Charlotte Roueché, Dr Thomas Russell, Dr Lilla Russell-Smith, Professor Philippe Sands QC, William St.Clair, Dr Katherine Butler Schofield, Yasmine Seale, Professor Recep Şentürk, Professor Christopher Scull, Professor Zaza Skhirtladze, Russell Smith, Dr Victoria Solomonidis, Dr Nigel Spivey, Professor Dionysios Stathykopoulos, Dr Richard Stoneman, David Stuttard, Professor David Thomas, Lieutenant-Commander Alec Tilley and Professor Maria Vassilaki have all given time and ideas well beyond the call of duty. Thank you.

I have benefited from the hospitality and help of so many – from drivers on the Azerbaijan border to counts in their castles. Nicholas Egon and Matti have, as ever, been entirely splendid. Lord Rothschild revealed Butrint, Dr Andreas Pittas Thera, Count Flamburiari Corcyra, Professor John Camp took me to the Agora, Maritsa to Rhodes, Nick Jones to Istanbul, Damian Bamber to technological understanding.

Thank you to Shula Subramaniam, Laura Aitken-Burt, Robin Madden, Lauren Hales, Theodosia Rossi, Lydia Herridge-Ishak, Gabriella Harris, not to mention Alex Bell, Cara, Sally, Olivia, Tamara, Ioanna, Lucy M. Stephanie, Charlotte, Oliver, Rebecca, Elinor, Abigail, Marike, Eliza and Katrina.

Peter James copy-edited the book with elan worthy of any dragoman, and the rapier acuity of a Janissary. Bea Hemming edited with such grace and insight, and Holly Harley has inspired and held my hand through the final push. Julian Alexander, as ever, simply brilliant. Alan Samson – charm personified – commissioned this book after reading an article I'd written on Istanbul – thank you Alan. Thank you too to Mary Cranitch, who shared my first trip to the city of many times and the lands beyond.

The girls and Adrian, Ma and Pa, as ever, have had to put up with the curse of the looming deadline for close on a decade. Thank you – I will try to make it up to you.

TIMELINE

❖

BC

800,000 Early human remains from this era have been found in Yarımburgaz Cave above greater Istanbul.

7400–5500 Black Sea Deluge event; Bosphorus takes current form.

6000 Earliest extant evidence of human habitation in the historical centre of Istanbul.

682 First evidence of Greek colonisation along the Bosphorus.

657 BYZAS
Legend has it that Byzas from Megara founds Byzantion as a Greek colony on the west side of the Bosphorus. According to Tacitus, the settlement was founded on the orders of Apollo, who instructed Byzas to build opposite 'the city of the blind' – Chalcedon. The Chalcedonians were considered blind because their settlement on the eastern side of the Bosphorus channel was less fertile and less easy to defend.

c. 513 THE ACHAEMENID EMPIRE
Dareios I constructs a pontoon bridge across the Bosphorus (where the Fatih Sultan Mehmed Bridge now stands). The columns that were used to decorate the bridge were later brought to Byzantion where Herodotus tells us they were placed in shrines to Dionysos and Artemis.

477 THE DELIAN LEAGUE
The Delian League is formed by Athens as an alliance between Greek city-states after conflicts with Persia. Byzantion was a key location:

if the Greek allies could control the city they could prevent Persian expansion westwards, as well as securing the Bosphorus and Black Sea trade route – particularly important for the supply of grain.

477–471/470 PAUSANIAS REGENT

The Spartan commander of the Greek fleet captures Byzantion from the Persians. However, he quickly loses popularity thanks to his reported desire to create his own Persian-style satrapy in the West.

471/470 THE DELIAN LEAGUE RESTORED

After Pausanias has been expelled from Byzantion by the Athenian general Cimon and brought to trial in Sparta, the Delian League takes control of the city.

411–409 CLEARCHOS

During the final phase of the Peloponnesian War, Byzantion rebels against the Delian League in favour of Clearchos of Sparta.

409 Clearchos' methods are unpopular in Byzantion and the city returns its allegiance to Athens after Alcibiades leads a siege in 409 when Clearchos is absent from the city.

405 LYSANDER

The power struggle at Byzantion remains precarious. In 405 the Spartan general Lysander successfully takes the city after the Battle of Aegospotami. The Athenians lose control over the grain trade route.

404 The Delian League is dissolved when Athens and her allies lose the Peloponnesian War.

390 Byzantion is retaken by an Athenian fleet commanded by Thrasyboulos.

378 SECOND ATHENIAN LEAGUE/CONFEDERACY

After Sparta's former allies have grown tired of Spartan rule, many turn their allegiance to Athens in the Corinthian War against Sparta (395–387 BC). This leads to the Second Athenian League, of which Byzantion is a founder member.

359 Byzantion becomes an ally of of Philip II of Macedon.

357–355 SOCIAL WAR/WAR OF THE ALLIES

Byzantion (along with Chios, Rhodes and Cos, coordinated by King Mausolos of Caria) rebels against Athens' increasing power in the Second Athenian League.

340–339 PHILIP II OF MACEDON

Philip II of Macedon besieges Byzantion (after attempting to besiege Perinthos in 340). This leads to a breakdown in the peace established between Philip and Athens in 346 (Peace of Philocrates). The Achaemenid Empire (under Artaxerxes III) aids Byzantion and halts Philip's siege.

338 BATTLE OF CHAERONEA

Byzantion falls under Macedonian sway after Philip II defeats the Greek alliance.

334 ALEXANDER THE GREAT

Alexander begins his campaign against Dareios III and the Persian Empire – he crosses the Hellespont and is victorious at the Battle of the Granicus River. Byzantion is 'freed' from Achaemenid influence as a vast new Hellenic empire is formed.

323 With the death of Alexander the Great, Byzantion is theoretically independent.

318 ANTIGONOS MONOPHTHALMOS

Alexander the Great's general takes control of Byzantion as part of the eastern portion of Alexander's kingdom. Byzantion still remains nominally a 'free' Greek city.

270s GALATIAN INVASIONS

Byzantion suffers as Galatians (Gauls from Thrace) migrate into Asia Minor – they will eventually settle in what becomes Galatia.

220–218 RHODES DECLARES WAR ON BYZANTION

When Gauls start to move through Europe under Comontorius, they come to Byzantion and take an interest in the land. Byzantion has to pay a tribute in order to protect herself, and eventually she starts to subsidise this tribute by demanding payment of duty from ships sailing through the Bosphorus. Unhappy with this situation, Rhodes declares war on Byzantion. A peace agreement is eventually reached and such a toll is no longer imposed.

214–148 MACEDONIAN WARS
Byzantion gains privileged status under the growing Roman Empire for supporting the Romans during the four Macedonian Wars (214–205, 200–196, 172–168 and 150–148). Peace and economic recovery ensue.

c. 146 The Egnatian Way is built to facilitate military suppression of the new province of Macedonia.

129 Byzantion enters into a truce with the Romans.

AD

53 The Roman Senate remits the annual tribute imposed on the city.

73 Vespasian reconfirms the city's incorporation of the city into the Roman Empire.

193 Pescennius Niger sends an army to occupy Byzantium.
Niger sets up his headquarters in Byzantium during his competition with Septimius Severus for the title of Roman emperor. Niger and Severus clash and Niger is defeated in 194. Niger's head is sent to Byzantium to persuade the city to surrender to Severus, but they submit only in 196.

196 SEPTIMIUS SEVERUS
After Niger has been defeated, Byzantium is besieged and eventually taken by Septimius Severus. The walls of the city are destroyed as punishment for her tenacity and Byzantium becomes dependent on Perinthos.
Severus eventually repairs Byzantium and builds many monuments, appreciating the tactical value of the city. This building programme continues into the reign of Severus' son, Lucius Septimius Bassianus, nicknamed 'Caracalla' and renamed Marcus Aurelius Severus Antoninus Pius Augustus (as a result the city briefly enjoys another title: Augusta Antonina).

212 Caracalla institutes Roman citizenship for all the freeborn men in his empire and the same rights for all freeborn women as Roman women.

267 After sustained attempts the city is briefly captured by Herulians (a Gothic tribe).

269 Claudius II defeats the Herulians, erects the Column of the Goths.

284 Diocletian becomes Roman Emperor.

293 Diocletian establishes the Tetrarchy.

305 Diocletian abdicates.
Galerius is Augustus in the East, Maximin Daia his Caesar. Constantius is Augustus in the West, Severus his Caesar.

311 Galerius' Edict of Tolerance moderates persecution against Christians.

312 BATTLE OF MILVIAN BRIDGE
Constantine defeats Maxentius in Rome, and the Tetrarchy system of rule is set to be dismantled.

313 LICINIUS AND CONSTANTINE
The Edict of Milan puts a formal end to persecution of Christians in the Roman Empire. Licinius eliminates Maximin Daia and makes a triumphal entry into Nicomedia.

324 3 July: Battle of Adrianople, Constantine vs Licinius.

324–37 CONSTANTINE I
Licinius surrenders at Chrysopolis, making Constantine the sole ruler of both East and West. Constantine refounds the city of Byzantium as the capital of the Roman Empire, naming it 'New Rome' (inaugurated 330 as 'Constantinople'). The First Ecumenical Council held at Nicaea in 325.

325 20 May–19 June: First Ecumenical Council of Nicaea.

330 Byzantion is renamed Constantinople.

337–61 Constantius II rules, alongside his brothers Constantine II (337–40) and Constans I (337–50).

The empire is split between Constantine's sons – Constans I takes Macedonia and the Dacias, Constantine II takes Gaul, Britannia and Hispania and Constantius II takes Thrace including Constantinople. Constantius supervises the funeral of his father in Constantinople and buries him as the thirteenth apostle in the Church of the Holy Apostles. He elects Eusebius as bishop of Constantinople, upon whose death the supporters of the Nicene Creed riot in Constantinople. Constantius puts down the riots and cuts the city's grain dole in half. He initiates the construction of a series of aqueducts and builds the original Haghia Sophia.

361–3 JULIAN (THE APOSTATE)

Julian rejects Christianity in favour of Neoplatonic paganism.
Increases the harbour capacity of Constantinople; war with Persia continues.

363–4 JOVIAN

Declared emperor by the army. Allegedly orders the Library of Antioch to be burnt down in 363. Reinstates Christianity as the imperial religion.

364–75 VALENTINIAN I (WEST)

Becomes emperor after the death by asphyxiation of Jovian. Rules in the West.

364–78 VALENS

Brother of Valentinian I, is made Emperor of the East. Has to cope with Julian's relative Procopius attempting usurpation. Builds the Palace of Hebdomon. Killed by Goths at the Battle of Adrianople of 378.

367–83 GRATIAN (WEST)

Son of Valentinian I, journeys to the East to help Valens fight the Tervingi; however, Valens does not wait for the extra troops and dies in battle before they arrive. Gratian is executed by Magnus Maximus, a usurper from Britain.

375–92 VALENTINIAN II (WEST)

Forced to flee to Thessalonika to escape Maximus' forces. Restored to the Western throne in 388. Second Ecumenical Council held at Constantinople, 381.

378 Battle of Adrianople against Gothic forces.

378–95 THEODOSIOS I

Death of Valens leaves the Eastern Empire without a ruler. Gratian appoints a former general named Theodosios as co-ruler. After two years of campaigns, Theodosios makes peace with the Gothic invaders – he enters Constantinople in 380 and establishes his new dynasty.

Theodosios is a strict Orthodox Christian who condemns the forms of Arianism that Constantius and Valens have supported. He calls a council in 381 declaring that the bishop of Constantinople should be second in precedence to the bishop of Rome on the grounds that Constantinople is the New Rome. Founds the Church of John the Baptist to enshrine the saint's skull. Before his death, Theodosios divides the East and West Empires between his two sons with equal seniority – this is seen as a decisive split of the empire into two truly separate kingdoms.

381 COUNCIL OF CONSTANTINOPLE

395–408 ARKADIOS

Son of Theodosios I, aged eighteen when he ascends the throne. Spends most of his reign in Constantinople and is considered the first true 'Byzantine' emperor as East and West start to follow different trajectories facing different enemies.

393–423 HONORIUS (WEST)

Son of Theodosios I. Moves court from Milan to Ravenna.

406 Roman forces are withdrawn from Britain.

410 Rome sacked by Goths led by Alaric.

408–50 THEODOSIOS II

Son of Arkadios, spends most of his reign in Constantinople; the city is now firmly established as the capital of the Eastern Empire. A new forum and cisterns are built as well as the Theodosian walls, including ninety-six watchtowers extending defences a mile beyond the walls of Constantine. Largely completed by 413, these walls remain the city's principal defence for the next 1,000 years.

425 Founds a university near the Forum Tauri.

429 Vandals take North Africa.

431 and 449 Councils of Ephesus (only 431 is officially accepted; the second is termed a robber council, *latrocinium*); Mary declared Theotokos.

425–55 VALENTINIAN III (WEST)
Nephew of Honorius, ousts the usurper John.

451 COUNCIL OF CHALCEDON

455 Rome sacked by Vandals from North Africa.

450–7 MARCIAN
Marriage alliance to Theodosian dynasty via Pulcheria (daughter of Arkadios). Recognised as a saint by the Eastern Orthodox Church. Repudiates a tribute payment to Attila the Hun.

457–74 LEO I
Military figure, not part of Theodosian dynasty. Legislates in Greek as opposed to Latin.

467–72 ANTHEMIOS (WEST)
Attempts to suppress the Visigoths and the Vandals, but is unsuccessful and is killed by Ricimer, his own general of Gothic descent.

474 LEO II
Grandson of Leo I, dies of an unknown disease ten months into rule. Possibly poisoned by his mother Ariadne in order to have her husband Zeno take the throne.

474–5 JULIUS NEPOS (WEST)
Reigns from Dalmatia. Enjoys some support from Constantinople. The Roman Senate petitions Zeno (the Eastern Emperor) to appoint the non-Roman Odoacer as Patrician – an ancient Roman ruling class but an honorary title bestowed in Byzantium; this is granted but the Senate also has to acknowledge Nepos' imperial status.

475–6 Basiliskos rules in Constantinople for twenty-four months.

475–6 ROMULUS AUGUSTULUS (WEST)
Usurper who reigns from 31 October 475 until 4 September 476.

Deposed by Odoacer; seen by historians as signifying the end of the West Roman Empire and the beginning of the Middle Ages in western Europe.

474–91 ZENO

Reign plagued by religious dissension, in particular the monophysite controversy. The Henotikon letter to the church in Egypt in 482 brings a measure of order, though schism with the church in Rome ensues. As an Orthodox Christian, Zeno is not barred from the throne even though he is an Isaurian (his original name being Tarasis son of Kodissa). Appoints Theodoric as king of Italy following Odoacer's death, protecting the Eastern Empire from the Ostrogoths.

491–518 ANASTASIOS

Chosen by Ariadne (Zeno's widow) as her new husband and emperor. Has heterochromia (one eye black, one eye blue). Reforms the tax system and Byzantine coinage. Supports miaphysitism.

518–27 JUSTIN I

An illiterate swineherd by origin, Justin flees from barbarian invasion to Constantinople when a teenager. Joins the army and in 518 holds the position of commander of the palace guard. By using his influence and bribery he is elected emperor that year. In 525, Justin repeals a law that forbids a member of the senatorial class from marrying women from a lower class of society, thus enabling his nephew Justinian to marry Theodora.

527–65 JUSTINIAN I

Responsible for the *Corpus Juris Civilis*, a compilation of legal codices. Rebuilds Hagia Sophia and the Church of the Holy Apostles. His reign sees the Nika riots, which are successfully repressed.

Declares eternal peace between Byzantium and Persia, 533.

Captures Ravenna in 540 and completes conquest of Italy by 562.

Platonic Academy in Athens is closed, 529.

Marries Theodora, a performer from the hippodrome; this is much spoken about in Procopius' *Secret History*.

542 The Justinianic plague wipes out 20 per cent of the inhabitants of Constantinople.

557 Earthquake in Constantinople.

565–78 JUSTIN II
Although initially trying to reconcile the monophysites, in 571 he persecutes them and issues a creed against them which all clergy are required to sign. Chroniclers claim that the Emperor goes mad in 573 after hearing reports that Daras (a city near the modern border of Turkey and Syria) has fallen due to the negligence of the commander. Unfit to rule as emperor, he retires – or is forcibly retired – from imperial roles; however, during lucid periods he is occasionally called upon to give his permission (for example, the appointment of Tiberios as Caesar).

578–82 TIBERIOS II CONSTANTINOS
Sophia convinces her mad husband Justin II to name Tiberios as Caesar in 574 and they rule as co-regents for four years until Justin II's death, when Tiberios becomes emperor. She has hoped to marry him and have his wife Ino barred from the palace. Tiberios is said to be an affable and thoughtful man. Paul the Deacon writes that upon finding treasure under a slab he gives all of it away to the poor. He also reduces state revenue by removing taxes instituted by Justinian I on wine and bread.

582–602 MAURICE
A skilled general who has fought several successful campaigns against the Sassanid Persians. After he becomes emperor he succeeds in ending the war with Persia, causing the empire to expand to the Caucasus and ending the Roman Empire's need to pay Persians compensation to keep the peace.

602–10 PHOKAS
Usurps the throne from the Emperor Maurice. Increasingly unpopular, he is deposed by Herakleios. First Byzantine Emperor (apart from Julian the Apostate) to have a beard.

610–41 HERAKLEIOS
Introduces Greek as the official language in the Eastern Empire. Persians manage to advance along the Bosphorus in 610 but are unable to penetrate Constantinople's walls.

618 Constantinople's inhabitants lose their right to free grain as Persians block the supply from Egypt. Population decline follows.

622 Hijrah of Muhammad from Mecca to Medina.

626 Persians and Avars besiege Constantinople.

630 Herakleios returns the reliquary of the True Cross to Jerusalem.

632 Death of the Prophet Muhammad.

635 Missionaries 'from Roman lands' recorded arriving in China.

636 Battle of Yarmuk vs Muslim forces: Byzantium defeated.

641 CONSTANTINE III, HERAKLONAS
The unexpected death of Constantine III in May 641 leaves Heraklonas as the sole ruler. However, rumours abound that he and Martina have murdered Constantine, prompting a revolt led by the general Valentinos. This forces Heraklonas to recognise his young nephew Constans II as co-emperor from 641.

641–68 CONSTANS II
Son of Constantine III, aged only eleven when he ascends the throne. Large areas of the southern and eastern Byzantine provinces are lost to the Arabs during his reign. Issues Typos edict in 648 forbidding monothelete arguments (a development of the miaphysite or monophysite position, arguing that Jesus has two natures but only one will). Has brother Theodosios killed to allow succession of his son Constantine IV. Travels westward, alienating popes by aiming to make Ravenna independent, and settles in Syracuse, Sicily, until his assassination.

c. 655 The so-called Battle of the Masts.

668–85 CONSTANTINE IV POGONATOS
Son of Constans II and co-Emperor from 654. Ends the monothelete controversy with the Sixth Ecumenical Council. A large Arab fleet attacks Constantinople in 672. Fleets range along the Asia Minor coast, based at Cyzicus.

674 First Arab 'siege' of Constantinople.

680–1 Sixth Ecumenical Council convenes in the city, the Third Council of Constantinople.

685–95 JUSTINIAN II (FIRST REIGN)
Contributes to the military and administrative development of the empire. Violent persecution of Manichaeans and the suppression of popular traditions that do not have an Orthodox origin causes division within the church. In 692 the Quinisext Council at Constantinople is summoned; the outcome of the proceedings prompts Justinian to call for the arrest of Pope Sergius I, causing militias in Rome and Ravenna to rebel against him.

695–8 LEONTIOS II
Deposed in 698, has his tongue and nose slit and is imprisoned in the monastery of Psamathion in Constantinople.

698–705 TIBERIOS II
A Germanic naval officer, changes his name from Apsimaros to Tiberios and sails to a plague-stricken Constantinople in 698. Once there he gains the support of one faction as well as the backing of members of the field army and imperial guard who proclaim him emperor. His troops then pillage the city. Reorganises the administration of the military. Though a successful military campaigner, after hearing that Justinian II has recaptured the Blachernae Palace he flees. Tiberios is eventually captured, paraded through the streets and executed alongside Leontios and his commanders in the hippodrome in Constantinople.

705–11 JUSTINIAN II (SECOND REIGN)
Emerges from exile and marches on Constantinople. Unable to enter through the city gates, he gains access via an abandoned water conduit. His obsession with taking revenge on his enemies results in mass killings, alienating former supporters. He is killed by his army.

711–13 PHILIPPIKOS BARDANES
An Armenian originally called Vardanes, he is exiled by Emperor Tiberios III to Cephalonia for having pretensions to the throne. Justinian II recalls him in 711 to suppress a revolt in the Crimea (Cherson). However, the Chersons declare him emperor. He sails to

Constantinople and has Justinian and his family killed. An advocate of the monothelete heresy, he orders that a picture of the Third Council of Constantinople (also known as the Sixth Ecumenical Council) be removed from the palace and the names of those condemned by the council restored. For this, Pope Constantine refuses to recognise him as emperor. Bulgars besiege Constantinople in 712. In 713 military conspirators overthrow and blind Philippikos, installing his chief secretary Artemios on the throne as Anastasios II.

713–15 ANASTASIOS II

He is persuaded to abdicate and becomes a monk in Thessalonika. Tries to retake the throne in 720 and is executed by Leo III.

715–17 THEODOSIOS III

Lays siege to Constantinople for six months until he gains entry. With the intercession of Patriarch Germanus I of Constantinople, he gets Anastasios to agree to abdicate.

717–18 Siege of Constantinople by Arabs.

726 Eruption of Thera.

717–41 LEO III THE ISAURIAN

Carries out extensive repairs to the Theodosian walls financed by a tax levied throughout the empire. Arabs end siege of Constantinople, 718.

741-75 CONSTANTINE V KOPRONYMOS (NAME OF DUNG)

Iconoclast. Attacked by his brother-in-law Artabasdos, *strategos* or governor of the Armeniac Theme, who is barricaded inside Constantinople, Constantine has to besiege the city. He counter-attacks in 743, defeating Artabasdos. Constantine then overthrows Artabasdos' son, Niketas, and is received into Constantinople. Lombards take Ravenna in 751, ending Byzantine influence in north and central Italy. Constantine dies on campaign in the Balkans against the Bulgars.

762 Baghdad is now the centre of the power of the Caliphate.

775–80 LEO IV

Originally pursues a line of toleration with iconophiles but reverses this stance at the end of his rule. Theophanes the Confessor records that Leo dies of a fever from wearing a crown with precious stones taken from the Haghia Sophia.

780–97 CONSTANTINE VI

Iconoclast, comes to power aged ten under guardianship of his mother Eirene, who is arrested in 790 when attempting to maintain supreme power when he comes of age. However, Constantine later pardons her and, upon his marriage to his mistress Theodote, Eirene exploits dissent to depose and blind Constantine.

787 Seventh Ecumenical Council, Nicaea.

797–802 EIRENE

Regent, and tries to have herself declared as sole empress. Eirene is an iconophile and seeks to forge a closer relationship with both the Western Roman and Carolingian Empires.

Founds the monastery of St Euphrosyne. Heads the Seventh Ecumenical Council of Nicaea in 787 to re-establish the veneration of icons.

802–11 NIKEPHOROS I

Strengthens the military with income from increased taxes, but is himself killed in the Battle of Pliska with Khan Krum in July 811. Venice, Istria and Dalmatian coast in dispute between Byzantium and Charlemagne's growing empire – Nikephoros signs a non-aggression treaty with Charlemagne and regains these territories for Byzantium.

811 STAURAKIOS

Gravely wounded in the Battle of Pliska, in which his father Nikephoros is killed, and never recovers. He is emperor briefly and then retires to a monastery where he dies soon afterwards.

812 Charlemagne is recognised as *basileus*.

813 Siege by Krum of Bulgaria.

811–13 MICHAEL I

Increases state donations to monasteries and churches, and recognises Charlemagne as *basileus*. He is forced to abdicate in 813 after he is defeated by the Bulgars.

813–20 LEO V

Instates the second period of iconoclasm and is assassinated on Christmas Day, 820, in front of the high altar of Haghia Sophia by Michael (II), a man to whom he has given high military command.

820–9 MICHAEL II

Founds the Amorian dynasty after the assassination of Leo V, prompting the revolt of Thomas the Slav (820–3), which is suppressed with support from Khan Omurtag, son of Krum.

829–42 THEOPHILOS

The last iconoclast emperor, he takes steps to strengthen the empire's defences, such as building the fortress at Sarkel with the Khazars.

842–67 MICHAEL III

Overthrows his regents, Theodora (his mother) and the eunuch Theoktistos, who have reinstated the veneration of icons, in 856, and then falls under the influence of his uncle Bardas. His reign sees further strengthening of the empire's defences and the repelling of the first Rus attack on Constantinople in 860. He is assassinated.

850 Glagolitic script (which developed into Cyrillic) promoted by St Cyril.

860 Siege by the Rus.

867–86 BASIL I THE MACEDONIAN

Assassinates Michael III and reappoints Ignatios as patriarch to ease diplomacy with Rome. He defeats the Arabs in southern Italy, although Syracuse is eventually lost, along with the Dalmatian coast, the Greek coast and the Euphrates.

886–912 LEO VI THE WISE

Co-emperor from 870. A prolific writer, he makes important revisions to Justinianic law. His fourth marriage to his mistress Zoe Karbonopsina is unpopular, and leads to disagreements with the church hierarchy. Witnesses many attacks on Byzantine territory, including the loss of Sicily in 902 to the Arabs and the sacking of Thessalonika by Leo of Tripoli, and has to pay tribute to the Bulgars in the north.

907 Siege by the Rus (disputed).

912–13 ALEXANDER

Third son of Basil I. An extravagant emperor, he refuses tribute to Symeon I of Bulgaria who then prepares for war.

913–59 CONSTANTINE VII PORPHYROGENNETOS

Sole emperor at the age of eight. Marries Helena, the daughter of the admiral Romanos Lekapenos, and writes several treatises including *De Ceremoniis* ('On ceremonies') and *De Administrando Imperio* ('On governing the empire'). His reign saw the end of the war with Symeon in 927.

941 Rus attack on Constantinople fails.

920–44 ROMANOS I LEKAPENOS

Co-rules with Constantine, his son-in-law, until he is deposed. After the deposition of Romanos, Constantine rules alone.

959–63 ROMANOS II

Succeeds his father Constantine and legislates against the aristocratic *dynatoi* ('the powerful'), causing some unpopularity with the church.

963–9 NIKEPHOROS II PHOKAS

Secures numerous victories against the Arabs. He increases the minimum size of landholding soldiers can possess, but restricts the growth of church estates. He is killed in a plot involving his wife, Theophano, and his general (and nephew) John Tzimiskes.

969–76 JOHN I TZIMISKES

Exiles his co-conspirator, Theophano, to gain support from the patriarch Polyeuktos. Abolishes the limits Nikephoros II placed on church estates and acknowledges Otto I as *basileus* of the Franks.

976–1025 BASIL II, THE BULGAR-SLAYER

Tries to preserve land owned by peasants and especially the military by limiting the growth of the estates of the *dynatoi*, and orders that the wealthy pay the unpaid taxes of their impoverished neighbours. He also establishes a standing army, which definitively defeats the Bulgars in 1018, and he blinds a percentage of the defeated troops.

1025–8 CONSTANTINE VIII

Prefers chariot racing to politics. He reverses Basil II's land reforms when pressured by the *dynatoi*.

1028–34 ROMANOS III ARGYROS

Marries Constantine's daughter Zoe. Starts costly building projects and reduces the taxes of the aristocracy, throwing the finances of the state into disarray. Murdered, perhaps poisoned or drowned by Zoe.

1034–41 MICHAEL IV

Marries Zoe on the day Romanos dies. He suffers from epilepsy and largely leaves the governing of the empire to his brother, John, who was a minister under Constantine VIII and Romanos III, and who increases taxes, prompting revolts. In 1037 an important thirty-year peace treaty is signed with the Fatimid Caliphate, ending hostilities.

1041–2 MICHAEL V KALAPHATES

Reigns for only four months. He banishes his adoptive mother, Zoe, an unpopular move which leads to revolt and the arrest and blinding of Michael, who has fled to a monastery.

1042 ZOE AND THEODORA

Sisters, the daughters of Constantine VIII, they co-rule according to the Senate's wishes. They work to stop the selling of public offices and to ensure justice, but the court is divided in its support of each sister. Zoe then marries Constantine Monomachos to limit Theodora's influence.

1043 Final Viking raid on Constantinople.

1047 Siege during revolt of Leo Tornikios.

1042–55 CONSTANTINE IX MONOMACHOS

Brings his mistress, Maria Skleraina, to court, where she is second only to Zoe and Theodora, fuelling rumours that she will murder the sisters, which then leads to an uprising. He favours the *dynatoi*, granting them tax reliefs. In 1054, after a visit of papal legates to Constantinople, the Greek and Roman churches split (the Great Schism), and the patriarch Michael Keroularios is excommunicated.

1054 The so-called Great Schism between Eastern and Western Christianity.

1055–6 THEODORA

Reigns solely after the death of Zoe (1050) and Constantine (1055), even though Constantine was persuaded by his councillors to name Nikephoros Proteuon as his successor. To strengthen her control, she punishes personal enemies at court and appoints eunuchs from her household to important posts.

1056–7 MICHAEL VI

Is chosen as Theodora's successor, but as he is not related to the Macedonian dynasty, disputes over the throne ensue. Michael falls out of favour with the military after refusing to restore the property of the general Nikephoros Bryennios. He is forced to abdicate in favour of Isaac and retires to a monastery.

1057–9 ISAAC I KOMNENOS

Attempts to recover state finances. Victorious over King Andrew I of Hungary, but becomes gravely ill shortly afterwards so he abdicates and retires to a monastery.

1059–67 CONSTANTINE X DOUKAS

Makes cuts to military spending, weakening the empire's defences. He raises taxes to pay for the army, making him generally unpopular, and survives an assassination attempt in 1061.

1068–71 ROMANOS IV DIOGENES

Marries Eudokia Makrembolitissa, the wife of Constantine, to secure his position, even though she has sworn an oath not to remarry after Constantine's death. He personally leads the army in campaigns against the Turks, and reduces public spending, which means not holding any games, a cause of great unpopularity among the masses. He is captured by the Seljuq Turks at the Battle of Manzikert and then honourably released. Eudokia is forced into a monastery, and Romanos is deposed by Michael Doukas. Bari, the last Byzantine stronghold in Italy, is captured by the Normans in 1071.

1071 April: capture of Bari. August: Battle of Manzikert.

1071–8 MICHAEL VII DOUKAS

Eldest son of Constantine and Eudokia. In his reign currency is devalued. There are numerous attempts to depose Michael, and eventually he is forced to retire to a monastery.

1078–81 NIKEPHOROS BRYENNIOS

An army general, he marches upon Nicaea with the Seljuq Turks and claims the throne, with the eventual support of the aristocracy and the church. He wants to marry Eudokia to secure his position, but instead marries Maria of Alania. Nikephoros is unpopular, and the devaluation of the currency continues, prompting uprisings. He abdicates in favour of the Komnenos dynasty and withdraws to a monastery.

1081 Campaigns of Robert Guiscard in Byzantine territory.

1090 Turkic siege of Constantinople.

1095 First Crusade.

1081–1118 ALEXIOS I KOMNENOS

Wages war against the Normans and Seljuq Turks, and initiates the Komnenian restoration, a recovery of finances and territory. His reign witnesses the First Crusade, after he has requested help from Pope Urban II for his campaigns against the Seljuq Turks.

1118–43 JOHN II KOMNENOS

Reclaims some towns previously lost to the Turks and defeats the Serbs, Hungarians and Pechenegs.

1145–9 Second Crusade.

1143–80 MANUEL I KOMNENOS

Makes alliances with the pope and invades Fatimid Egypt with Kingdom of Jerusalem. His reign sees the Second Crusade take place. Arrests Venetian merchants throughout Byzantium in 1171.

1180–3 ALEXIOS II

His reign (under the governorship of regents because he is a child) sees significant defeats and the losses of Syrmia, Bosnia, Dalmatia, Cotyaeum and Sozopolis. He is strangled with a bow-string upon the order of his co-Emperor Andronikos.

1183–5 ANDRONIKOS I KOMNENOS

Marries Agnes, daughter of Louis VII of France. He seeks to limit the aristocracy's control and orders the execution of all prisoners and exiles, causing uprisings. King William of the Norman Sicilians takes advantage of the public unrest and tries to invade. Andronikos is deposed and then captured while fleeing Constantinople and ignominiously killed.

1185–95 ISAAC II ANGELOS (FIRST REIGN)

Defeats William's invasion forces. He taxes people heavily to finance the army, which leads to the Vlach–Bulgarian rebellion. Isaac then leads campaigns against Bulgaria but is suddenly overthrown by his brother Alexios, who has him blinded and imprisoned in Constantinople.

1195–1203 ALEXIOS III ANGELOS

Isaac's elder brother. He fails to defend Constantinople against the Fourth Crusade and flees the city.

1202–4 FOURTH CRUSADE

1203 ALEXIOS IV AND ISAAC II (SECOND REIGN)

Isaac II's son Alexios manages to divert the Fourth Crusade to Constantinople in order to release his imprisoned father. As he is blind and weakened by his captivity, the Crusaders insist that Isaac appoint his son as co-emperor, Alexios. Alexios and Isaac are unable to pay the Crusaders, and violence breaks out in the city. They are both deposed; Isaac dies of shock, and Alexios is later strangled (or poisoned).

1204 ALEXIOS V DOUKAS MOURTZOUPHLOS

Fails to defend Constantinople against the Crusaders of the Fourth Crusade.

LATIN EMPIRE

1204–5 BALDWIN I

Is crowned in the Haghia Sophia according to Byzantine custom. Defeated in the Battle of Adrianople by Tsar Kaloyan of Bulgaria, he is then incarcerated. During his imprisonment, his brother Henry acts as regent. Baldwin dies shortly after his incarceration, but the exact circumstances of his death are unknown. An impostor appears in Flanders several decades later.

1205–16 HENRY OF FLANDERS

Secures victories against Kaloyan and Boril of Bulgaria, and Theodore I Laskaris, Emperor of Nicaea. In 1214, he agrees a truce with Theodore.

1216–17 PETER II OF COURTENAY

Crowned in a church outside Rome, but never reaches Constantinople, as he is captured on the way by the despot of Epirus, Theodore Komnenos Doukas. He dies as a captive in 1219.

1217–19 YOLANDA OF FLANDERS (REGENT)

Peter's wife, and the sister of Baldwin and Henry of Flanders. She makes alliances with Bulgaria, and marries her daughter to Theodore I Laskaris.

1219–28 ROBERT OF COURTENAY

Loses territory to the Despotate of Epirus and the Empire of Nicaea. To make peace with John III Vatatzes, Emperor of Nicaea, he agrees to marry Theodore I Laskaris' daughter, Eudokia, but instead marries his French mistress, the Lady of Neuville, who is already betrothed. The Lady of Neuville's original intended husband drives Robert from Constantinople. He dies while fleeing to Rome to seek refuge with the pope.

1228–37 JOHN OF BRIENNE (REGENT)

Acts as regent while Baldwin, son of Peter and Yolanda, is too young to rule. He defends Constantinople against John III Vatatzes and Ivan Asen II of Bulgaria in the 1235 siege. He is also King of Jerusalem, through his marriage to Queen Maria of Jerusalem.

1260 Unsuccessful siege of Constantinople by Empire of Nicaea.

1237–61 BALDWIN II

Marries Marie of Brienne, John's daughter. He sells off relics, such as the Crown of Thorns, to raise money. The Byzantine Empire in his reign is essentially confined to the city of Constantinople, inhabited by only 35,000 people. Michael VIII Palaiologos captures the city, and Baldwin flees.

Empire of Nicaea: Theodore I Laskaris (1208–21), John III Vatatzes (1221–54), Theodore II Laskaris (1254–8), John IV Laskaris (1258–61).

RESTORED BYZANTINE EMPIRE

1259–82 MICHAEL VIII PALAIOLOGOS

Restores Byzantine customs to Constantinople when he recaptures the city in 1261, repairs churches and public buildings, and increases the city's population to 70,000. Second Council of Lyon 1274 recreates union between the Roman and Byzantine churches.

1282–1328 ANDRONIKOS II PALAIOLOGOS

Raises taxes and dismantles the navy, to recover finances. He loses much land to the Ottoman Turks, and is defeated by Theodore Svetoslav of Bulgaria. Forced to retire to a monastery by his grandson Andronikos III.

1328–41 ANDRONIKOS III

Rebuilds the navy. He fails to recover Nicaea (renamed Iznik) from the Ottoman sultan Orhan, but he does recover Epirus, Thessaly and Chios.

1331 Nicaea is taken by Ottomans.

1341 Ottomans take Chrysopolis.

1341–7 JOHN V PALAIOLOGOS (FIRST REIGN)

Succeeds his father, aged nine, but is not previously crowned his father's co-emperor or named his heir, so a civil war breaks out between his regents (his mother Empress Anna, Patriarch Kalekas and Alexios Apokaukos) and John VI Kantakouzenos, his father's aide.

1347–8 Constantinople suffers from outbreak of the Black Death.

1347–54 JOHN VI KANTAKOUZENOS

Is made co-emperor as a result of his victory in the civil war, but in effect he reigns alone, as John V is still young. He is defeated by the Genoese and makes an alliance with the Ottoman Turks. Deposed by John V, he retires to a monastery.

1354–91 JOHN V PALAIOLOGOS (SECOND REIGN)

Travels through Europe seeking aid against the Ottomans. He is deposed (for three years) by his son Andronikos IV, with help from Sultan Murad I in 1376, and by his grandson John VII (for five months) in

1390. He strengthens Constantinople's Golden Gate, but then destroys the work on the orders of Sultan Bayezid I, who holds John's son Michael captive.

1372–3 Byzantine Emperors become vassals of the Ottomans.

1376 Thirty-two-day siege of Constantinople by Andronikos IV Palaiologos with the support of the Ottoman Turks.

1376–9 ANDRONIKOS IV

1390 JOHN VII
Deposes his grandfather, but is then removed from the throne by his uncle Manuel with help from the Venetian Republic.

1396–1402 First Ottoman blockade of the city.

1422 First large-scale siege of the city by the Ottomans.

1391–1425 MANUEL II
Succeeds his father John V on his death. He defends Constantinople against the siege by Bayezid I in 1394 and then travels to European courts to request help against the Ottomans. He is the only Byzantine emperor to visit England, where he stays at Eltham Palace. He writes numerous letters, poems and treatises.

1425–48 JOHN VIII
Attends the Council of Florence, 1439, with the intention of uniting the Greek and Roman churches to gain support against the Ottomans from Pope Eugene IV.

1439 Desperate for help, the Byzantine emperor confirms papal supremacy at the Council of Florence.

1449–53 CONSTANTINE XI
Dies defending his city and loses Constantinople and what remains of her territories to Mehmed II.

OTTOMAN EMPIRE

1453–81 MEHMED II
Conquers Constantinople (now also called Kostantiniyye or Islam-bol)

aged twenty-one and the last free pockets of Byzantine rule are wiped out by 1461. Dubs himself Emperor of Rome. Construction of Topkapı Palace begins in 1459. Already Sultan in Erdine in 1444–6 and 1451–3.

1492 Fall of Granada; a number of Jews and Muslims come to Kostantiniyye from al-Andalus (Muslim Iberia).

1481–1512 BAYEZID II

Kostantiniyye devastated by an earthquake in 1509. Bayezid welcomes refugees from the Spanish Inquisition.

1512–20 SELIM I

First ruler of the city officially to call himself 'Caliph of Islam' after conquering Egypt in 1517. Inspires the Ottoman curse 'may you become a vizier of Selim's' in reference to the number of advisers he has killed.

1520–66 SÜLEYMAN I 'THE MAGNIFICENT'

Introduction of canonical law; makes changes to society, education, taxation and criminal legislation. Studies at the school of Topkapı Palace from the age of seven. Pioneers cultural development across the empire but especially within Istanbul.

1522 Ottomans attack the island of Rhodes.

1529 Failed siege of Vienna.

1537 Süleyman moves fleet to Butrint.

1544 Pierre Gilles in Istanbul to find manuscripts for the King of France.

1571 The Ottomans lose the Battle of Lepanto.

1566–74 SELIM II

Signs a treaty with the Holy Roman Emperor Maximilian II on 17 February 1568 in Istanbul in which the Holy Roman Empire agrees to pay the Ottoman Empire 30,000 ducats each year and recognises their authority in Moldavia and Wallachia.

1574–95 MURAD III

Begins reign by having his five brothers strangled. Discusses joint military operations against the Spanish with Elizabeth I. Spends entire sultanate in Kostantiniyye and never actually goes on any campaigns.

1595–1603 MEHMED III

Has nineteen of his brothers and half-brothers strangled by deaf mutes. Largely halts artistic patronage within the city and the empire as a whole. Marries a Byzantine princess from the Komnenos family.

1603–17 AHMED I

Does not commit fratricide but instead has his younger brother imprisoned in a Kafes (cage) in one of the imperial palaces. A keen poet but does not patronise the visual arts. Constructs the Sultan Ahmed Mosque (also known as the Blue Mosque), and is buried in a mausoleum outside its walls.

1617–18 MUSTAFA I (FIRST REIGN)

Until the death of Ahmed he is confined in the Kafes, which causes him to develop extreme paranoia. Deposed in 1618.

1618–22 OSMAN II

Well educated, he ascends the throne aged fourteen. Murdered by strangulation at Yedikule.

1622–3 MUSTAFA I (SECOND REIGN)

Deposed again in 1623 but is allowed to live after his mother negotiates for him to be allowed a quiet retirement.

1623–40 MURAD IV

Takes to the throne aged eleven, originally under the influence of the Valide Sultan Kösem Sultan. However, in 1632 he establishes absolute rule. Bans alcohol, tobacco and coffee in Kostantiniyye, making its consumption punishable by death. Puts revenue into architectural programmes.

1638 Baghdad surrenders to Murad, resulting in some of the divisions in the Middle East still extant today.

1640–8 IBRAHIM 'THE MAD'

Also confined in the Kafes and known for his eccentricities and for the influence of court ministers and the harem. Visits the markets in Kostantiniyye incognito and charges his grand vizier to correct any issues seen. Victim of regicide in the Topkapı Palace, 18 August 1648.

1645 Ottoman armies invade Crete and capture western region by 1646.

1648–87 MEHMED IV

Ascends the throne aged six, but gives up sultan's executive power to his grand vizier. Dies in Edirne Palace, buried near his mother's mosque in the city.

1683 Siege of Vienna.

1687–91 SÜLEYMAN II

Halts Austrian advance into Serbia. Dies at Edirne Palace.

1691–5 AHMED II

Defeated at the Battle of Slankamen, causing the Ottomans to be driven out of Hungary. Dies from illness and exhaustion at Edirne Palace.

1695–1703 MUSTAFA II

Treaty of Karlowitz in 1699 concluding the Austro-Ottoman war 1683–97 marks the beginning of major decline for the Ottoman Empire. Mustafa abdicates in 1703 and dies at the Topkapı Palace.

1703–30 AHMED III

Part of his reign – 1718–30 – becomes known as the Tulip Age: a cultural renaissance in neo-classical styles but depicted in Turkish historiography as an age of decadence and Ahmed as an unpopular lavish sultan. Patrona Halil leads a group of Janissaries and Kostantiniyye's citizens (who oppose Ahmed's social reforms) in a revolt against the palace. Ahmed agrees to have his grand vizier strangled, then voluntarily retires to the Kafes in the Topkapı Palace and dies after six years of confinement.

1727 First press in the city that prints in Arabic script.

1730–54 MAHMUD I

Recognised as sultan by mutineers and court officials, orders Halil to be strangled, effectively putting an end to the Janissary rebellion.

1730–40 Further riots in the city.

1754–7 OSMAN III

An idiosyncratic character, said to dislike music and females, banning both women and musicians from his presence. Intolerant of non-Muslims; Christians and Jews within the city are made to wear badges to denote their religion.

1757–74 MUSTAFA III

Attempts to modernise the army and the administration of the empire. Largely unsuccessful due to internal instability and lack of funds.

1774–89 ABDÜLHAMID I

Administers the fire brigade during the fire of 1782. Creates a Naval Engineering School in Kostantiniyye. An intelligent and pious man, he is dubbed Veli (Saint). Buried in Bahçekapı – a tomb he has constructed within the city.

1789–1807 SELIM III

Brings European-style army training into Istanbul. Introduces domestic reforms including increasing access to higher education. Killed in the city by assassins after being imprisoned by Janissaries.

1793 The Ottomans open their first Embassy in London.

1803 Wahhabis (Salafi) attack Mecca.

1807–8 MUSTAFA IV

Has little interest in education. His rule sees rioting in Kostantiniyye (at this point Selim III is still alive but imprisoned). Pro-reformist commander Bayraktar Mustafa Pasha marches army into the city to try and restore Selim III to the throne. Mustafa orders the assassination of Selim and his cousin Mahmud. Only Selim is killed.

1808–39 MAHMUD II

Survives assassination attempt, and is put on the throne after rebels dispose of Mustafa.

1826 Abolition of Janissary Corps.

1832 Treaty of Constantinople signifies Greek independence.

1839 The *tanzimat* reforms beginning in 1839 prove to be a catalyst for modernisation within Istanbul. Mahmud introduces the first steamships into the navy based in Kostantiniyye. Reforms continue until 1871–6.

1839–61 ABDÜLMECID I

Receives a European education. Uses laws and reform to integrate non-Muslims and Turks into Ottoman society. Fights alongside Britain and France in the Crimean War, causing the Congress of Paris to recognise the Ottoman Empire as part of the Family of Nations. One of the Sultans to hold 'reception days' every Friday so that he can listen to the public's grievances in person. Introduces paper banknotes, allows non-Muslims into the army and decriminalises homosexuality.

1854–7 Crimean War.

1859 Abdülmecid pardons those who tried to assassinate him.

1861–76 ABDÜLAZIZ I

Establishes the first rail network and Sirkeci railway station in Constantinople (terminus for the Orient Express). Sets up the Istanbul Archaeology Museum. Joins the Universal Postal Union in 1875 as a founding member. Composes classical music and helps complete the Pertevniyal Valide Sultan Mosque built under his mother's patronage.

1875 Ottoman state bankrupt.

1876 MURAD V

Deposed for alleged mental illness (probably fabricated).

1876–1909 ABDÜLHAMID II

Period of decline including government-led massacres. Abdülhamid establishes the Hijaz Railway project, population regulation and control over the press. Deposed after the Young Turk Revolution.

1909–18 MEHMED V

After the Young Turk Revolution of 1908 and then the Bab-i Ali coup of 1913, the state is controlled by the Three Pashas (Enver, Talat and Cemal) so rule is now largely symbolic. However, Mehmed formally declares jihad against the Allied powers in 1914. Buried in the ancient Eyüp district of Istanbul.

1918–22 MEHMED VI

Representatives sign the Treaty of Sèvres, 1920, which removes Ottoman control over Anatolia and recognises the Kingdom of Hejaz as a separate state. The Turkish Grand National Assembly, formed in 1920, denounces Mehmed as ruler. Escaping from Constantinople in 1922, he dies in 1926 in San Remo, Italy and is buried in the Tekkiye Mosque in Damascus.

1922–4 ABDÜLMECID II

Elected caliph by the Turkish National Assembly at Ankara. Establishes himself in Constantinople but is exiled in 1924 alongside his family. Becomes a renowned artist and dies in Paris in 1944.

REPUBLIC OF TURKEY

1923–38 MUSTAFA KEMAL ATATÜRK

The first President of the Republic of Turkey. Seeks to reform and modernise Turkey. Awarded the name Atatürk, meaning 'Father of the Turks'. During the Republic, Constantinople is formally renamed 'Istanbul'.

APPENDIX

THE OTHER ROMAN EMPIRES

Karolus serenissimus Augustus a Deo coronatus magnus pacificus imperator Romanum gubernans imperium
(Charles, most serene Augustus crowned by God, the great, peaceful emperor ruling the Roman Empire)

THE TITLE USED BY CHARLEMAGNE AFTER HE HAD

BEEN CROWNED HOLY ROMAN EMPEROR

Names matter; and in terms of international perception it mattered that Istanbul was, from the fourth century AD onwards, the New Rome. But in the ninth century, with the crowning of the Holy Roman Emperor, there was a challenger. In AD 812 in Aachen, Charlemagne was officially recognised as *basileus*. Arguably this is where we should see the start of Rome's decline and fall, not with the smash of a barbarian's axe or on the pages of Gibbon but in a pretty settlement which today is Germany's westernmost city. Pope Leo III crowned Charlemagne, and there could have been a Byzantine Holy Roman empress – Eirene from Constantinople had ruled in her own right and a marriage proposal had been sent out to Charlemagne. But Eirene was deposed and exiled before the offer could be seriously considered: that union, of the Byzantine and Frankish Empires, would have rewritten the dynamics of East and West and so too the story of Europe and of the Near East. When Charlemagne died, an anonymous monk lamented:

> From the lands where the sun rises to western shores, people are crying and wailing . . . the Franks, the Romans, all Christians, are stung with mourning and great worry . . . the young and old, glorious nobles,

all lament the loss of their Caesar . . . the world laments the death of Charles . . . O Christ, you who govern the heavenly host, grant a peaceful place to Charles in your kingdom. Alas for miserable me.

And after Charlemagne's death there were other Roman pretenders.

The reach of the idea of Byzantium is illustrated neatly in the ruined city of Preslav in Bulgaria. Symeon I (Symeon the Bulgar who ruled AD 893–927) had been educated in Constantinople from the age of thirteen or so – he became fluent in Greek and learnt the philosophy of Aristotle and the rhetoric of Demosthenes. They say imitation is the highest form of flattery and, after Symeon's return to the monastery of Preslav, the young Christian developed this capital as the 'new' Constantinople; for centuries the later village on this site was called Yeski Stambolchuk (Old Stamboul). Here there were domed churches, exquisite mosaics and gorgeous imported artefacts decorated with Greek aphorisms.

But then Symeon bit the hand that had fed him. Furious that Bulgarian goods were to be sold in Thessalonika – not in Constantinople, where their market had been before – and therefore would incur a higher rate of tax, and that Bulgars were not being given their regular tribute from Constantinople, he mounted frequent campaigns against Byzantine territory. Glowering outside the city walls while a deputation made it to the palace at Blachernae, some sources tell us that Symeon forced the patriarch to crown him. There is a crucial psychological tell here: the Bulgarian might despise his alma mater, but it was still the patriarch's blessing that he craved. Declaring himself tsar – a title of course derived from 'Caesar' – Symeon's (thwarted) lifelong ambition was to take Constantinople itself. The would-be Emperor of the Romans had to be content with expanding his territories and with declaring the Bulgarian Orthodox Church independent from the mother city.

While Islamic art at around this time focused on the power of the script (not exclusively – more and more examples are coming to light of wonderful figurative illustrations from this early period),[1] the Orthodox Church developed its own script form, now known as Cyrillic. St Cyril (c. AD 826–69), together with his brother Methodios, the two known as the 'Apostles to the Slavs', were in 1980 nominated by Pope John Paul II as co-patron saints of Europe. Cyril spent most of his life named Constantine (he lived as Cyril for only fifty days, having become a monk when he realised that his death was close) and created the Glagolitic script – which was later developed into Cyrillic – as a political move and in order to spread Christianity and Byzantine influence among Constantinople's one-time enemies, the Slavs. Bardas, brother of the Empress Theodora, supported Cyril's and Methodios' missions and initiated far-reaching educational programmes, establishing for example the University of Magnaura (with Arabic and Hebrew under his belt Cyril was able to discuss theology with the Abbasid Caliph al-Mutawakkil). Cyril attempted to prevent Khazars converting to Judaism and then became professor of philosophy in Constantinople. The lives of these men are a vivid and tangible reminder that the impact of Constantinople's culture spread far and wide.

The use of Cyrillic, which has featured on a euro note since 2013, is as politically charged now as it was then.[2] In 2015 the Bulgarian president Rosen Plevneliev gave a speech at the unveiling of a National Monument of Bulgarian (Cyrillic) in Mongolia:

> Today our alphabet brings enlightenment and knowledge to more than 50 peoples, including not just the Bulgarians and the Mongolians but also the Russians, Belorussians, Ukrainians, Serbs and many others. We Bulgarians are proud because we see as our valuable contribution the preservation of the work of the holy brothers Cyril and Methodios, and the spreading of the Cyrillic script around the world.[3]

By AD 1018 Basil II, the Macedonian ruler of Constantinople, had retaken the whole of Bulgaria from the Cometopuli dynasty which followed Symeon's descendants. It was said that in 1014, after the capture of 15,000 Bulgarian soldiers, Basil had put out the eyes of ninety-nine in every hundred, leaving the 1 per cent with one eye so that they could lead their maimed compatriots back to their Emperor, Samuel. Sitting in his castle above the royal-blue Lake Ohrid – a picture-perfect sight now, and a construction that even then had a reputation for a kind of fairy-tale perfection, as the bullfrogs croaked – a terrible sound drifted up to Emperor Samuel: the moaning and stumbling of his returning, blinded army. The shock and horror was said to have struck Samuel down with a stroke. The Emperor was dead within a few days. Four years later Bulgaria would be back in Byzantine hands.

Meanwhile, new archaeological evidence in neighbouring Hungary indicates that the conversion of the Magyars, probably as a result of missions from Constantinople, happened by stealth before St Stephen's more comprehensive missionary efforts of c. 1000.[4] The Magyars were referred to as the People of the Gog and Magog and the 'worshippers of fire', yet the number of Eastern Orthodox crosses turning up in pagan graves in the Carpathian basin suggests that someone or something – a person or an idea – was percolating through to these spirit-worshipping lands. In Ibrány for instance a young girl has been left for her journey to an afterlife with both an animal-tooth pendant and a cross around her neck. There seems to be a potent force at work here, perhaps parent power – mother or father or tribal elder wanting the next generation (because the crosses are frequently found in the graves of the young) to have better chances that, as a Christian, included an afterlife. The start of the trend was marked with a necklace and ended with a nation. So when, in a wild, Unicum- and *pálinka*-fuelled celebration of Hungary's National Day, the Budapest bridges are thick with balloons and ribbons and crosses and merry-making while St Stephen is honoured as the bringer of Christianity to his people, we should spare a moment for the nameless Magyars who, inspired almost certainly by missions from Byzantium, quietly came to the same decision by themselves long before.

When we look for the influence and the impact of Istanbul, we must travel to many lands.

NOTES

✦

EPIGRAPHS

1 Trans. Von Hammer (1878).
2 Villehardouin, trans. Shaw (1963), 58–9.
3 Lamartine (1835), 17. See also Lamartine (1861), 249.
4 Sultan Murad IV to historiographer Solák Záhdeh recorded in Efendi (1834), 103.

PROLOGUE

1 See Ahmad, *al-Musnad* 14:331:18859. al-Hakim, *al-Mustadrak* 4:421–2. al-Tabarani, *al-Muʿjam al-Kabir* 2:38:1216. al-Bukhari, *al-Tarikh al-Kabir* 2:81 and *al-Saghir* 1:306. Ibn ʿAbd al-Barr, *al-Istiʿab* 8:170.
2 Michael the Syrian, *The Syriac Chronicle*, trans. Moosa (2014).
3 Dates in the Arabic sources contradict one another; it was either AD 651–2 or 654–5.
4 A nomination, claimed the Qurʾan, awarded by Abraham 22:78: 'He has chosen you and has placed no hardship on you in practising your religion – the religion of your father Abraham. He is the one who named you "Submitters" originally.' See https://www.comp.leeds.ac.uk/nora/html/22-78.html for a comparison of translations.
5 A proverb described as Bedouin, medieval Arab and also sometimes Egyptian. Burckhardt (1972), 120.
6 Near Phoenicus or Phoenix (the modern Turkish port of Finike on the Lycian coast, now in the province of Ankara). Konstam and Dennis (2015), 58–9. Treadgold (1997), 314.
7 *Shalandī* singular – see illustrations in Konstam (2015).
8 Shia followers were originally *shiʿat Ali*, 'the party of Ali', supporters or

helpers of Ali – the Prophet's cousin and son-in-law. Sunnis were instead followers of the Prophet's *sunna*, 'model conduct'. Disputes arose as to who had the right to lead as caliph (successor). Muawiyah, a Sunni who ruled from AD 661 to 680, was the founding Caliph of the Umayyad dynasty.

9 An expedition led by Yazid, the son of the commander at Cyprus, Muawiyah.

10 See R. G. Hoyland's new translation of the lost Theophilus of Edessa in Hoyland (2011), esp. 166–8.

11 See fascinating ongoing work by Dr Marek Jankowiak.

12 With Alexandria lost to the Arabs, Sicily and Africa were the only providers of grain – and that supply line was both expensive and precarious.

13 Harris (2015), 88; see also Stathakopoulos (2004), Catalogue entry 208.

14 St Mary's Church of Blachernae, home to one of the city's great Marian icons, in its nineteenth-century iteration can still be visited in the Ayvansaray district of Istanbul. Mary's girdle, supposedly made of camel hair, was held secure here close to 'her' spring. The relic is now held on Mount Athos.

15 Hasluck (1916/18), 157–74.

16 Witness the Arab historian and philosopher Ibn Khaldun: 'the Muslims gained control over the whole Mediterranean. Their power and domination over it was vast. The Christian nations could do nothing against the Muslim fleets, anywhere in the Mediterranean. All the time, the Muslims rode its waves for conquest.' Ibn Khaldun, *The Muqaddimah: An Introduction to History*, trans. Rosenthal (1989), 210.

17 In *The Return of the King*, the third volume of the trilogy *The Lord of the Rings*: Tolkien (2012), Book Five, ch. VI.

18 Howard-Johnston (2010). See also Bosworth (1996), 157–64.

NOTE ON NAMES

1 Written Turkish has been entirely phonetic since Atatürk passed the *Law on the Adoption and Implementation of the Turkish Alphabet* in 1928. The law replaced the Arabic script that had been used for written Ottoman Turkish with a modified Latin alphabet which has 29 letters. The biggest difference between the Turkish alphabet and the Latin lies in its vowels; in addition to a, e, i, o and u, Turkish also has ı, ö and ü. The distinction between ı and i, o and ö, and u and ü is where the sound is generated. In each of the preceding pairs, the former are back vowels that are generated at the back of the mouth and the latter is a front vowel. In terms of sound, ı sounds like the e in 'open' and i sounds like the i in 'bit'. U produces a sound similar to the double o in 'foot' and ü sounds like the double o in 'food'. O sounds like the short o in 'hot' and ö sound like the ir in 'shirt', but pronounced at the front of the mouth. In addition to these vowels, Turkish

also has ş which represents a 'sh' sound, and ç which represents a 'ch' sound. The only letter with no corresponding sound in the English language is the ğ, which is a swallowed g that is almost inaudible. Perhaps most odd for the native English reader, the letter c actually makes the sound that j denotes in English – the letter j is reserved for foreign-imported words such as *plaj* (beach). Finally, the Turkish alphabet has no q, w or x. Many thanks to Robin Madden for his composition of this note.

2 See Georgacas (1947), 347–67.

3 St Jerome's Vulgate translates the Hebrew *besepharad* in Obadiah 1:20 as 'Bosforus', but other translations give it as 'Sepharad' (probably Sardis, but later identified with Spain): 'And the captivity of this host of the children of Israel, all the places of the Chanaanites even to Sarepta: and the captivity of Jerusalem that is in Bosphorus, shall possess the cities of the south' (*'et transmigratio exercitus huius filiorum Israhel omnia Chananeorum usque ad Saraptham et transmigratio Hierusalem quae in Bosforo est possidebit civitates austri'*).

4 As pointed out in Stathakopoulos (2014), Introduction.

5 Thanks to Paul Cartledge for reminding me of 'the Turk' in the *Godfather* films.

6 John Lyly, *Euphues: The Anatomy of Wyt/Wit*, f. 5, written 1578.

7 As discussed extensively in Said (1978), 59–60.

INTRODUCTION

1 Gilles, trans. J. Ball (1988), xlv.

2 Emperor Dareios' engineer Mandrocles of Samos bridged the Bosphorus: Herodotus 4.88; Xerxes also created a bridge between Sestus and Abydos on the Hellespont.

3 Thank you to Dr Ray Laurence for this information.

4 Surat al-Rum 30:1–5.

5 *Othello*, Act 2, scene 3; Act 3, scene 5; Act 5, scene 2.

6 An idea I originally came across in the writings of Orhan Pamuk – the man who first piqued my interest in Istanbul forty years ago.

7 The medieval cellars and lone Islamic shrines here hide remains of an early form of *Homo erectus* – tiny creatures, travellers out of Africa, 1.8 million years old.

CHAPTER 1: BONES, STONES AND MUD

1 Apollonius Rhodius, *Argonautica* 2.580–600, trans. Seaton (1912).

2 With many thanks to Ufuk Kocabaş, Associate Professor and Director of the Department of Conservation and Restoration at Istanbul University, for help with my frequent enquiries.

3 See e.g. http://www.cura.co.uk/turkey/the-byzantine-harbour/.

4 The 'Sweet Waters' of Asia is today an innocuous stream emerging from a respectable, well-to-do district (and around/above which some of the most expensive properties in Asia can be found). This water source was thought sacred throughout antiquity. In living memory Istanbullus could still tell you which spring their water had come from and how they preferred the taste of one to another.

5 Farrand and McMahon (1997), 537.

6 Oniz and Aslan (eds) (2011), 183.

7 Around the high promontory of Silivritepe, between the Alibey and Kağıthane creeks.

8 Oniz and Aslan (eds) (2011), 183. Dönmez (2006), 239–64.

9 Some date the Black Sea Deluge event to 7400 BC.

10 Procopius, *Buildings* 1.5.10, trans Dewing (1940).

11 Although getting fresh water to the settlement of Byzantion would be an issue throughout its long history.

CHAPTER 2: CITY OF THE BLIND

1 Herodotus, *Histories* 4.144, trans. Cartledge and Holland (2013).

2 Dönmez (2006), 239–64.

3 Euripides, *Hecuba* 492; also *Helen* 928, *Bacchae* 13, *Iphigenia in Aulis* 786. Saïd (2002), 65.

4 See the excellent discussion of these issues in West (2005), 39–64.

5 The discovery of the neolithic site of Boncuklu, the Place of Beads – where villagers had long noticed the glint of prehistoric beads after the spring rains on mounds in the Konya Plain – interestingly puts early human settlement in the region back a thousand years or so to c. 9000 BC.

6 See ongoing work by Professor Vakhtang Licheli, Director of the TSU Institute of Archaeology.

7 Tsetskhladze (ed.) (1998), 19–21.

8 Severin (1985).

CHAPTER 3: CITY OF LIGHT

1 Tacitus, *Annals* 12.63, trans. Church and Brodribb (1876).

2 Athen. 3.116b–c (Ps. – Hesiod); 7.303e (Archestratus).

3 Ancient reports also speak of vast sharks and whales the size of Moby-Dick patrolling the seething stretch of water that is the Bosphorus.

4 See Procopius, *History of the Wars* 7.29.9–21, trans. Dewing (1914). Holmes (1912), 368.

5 Although we should not think of Anatolia as simply a giant land-bridge, it did facilitate the flow of goods, ideas and beliefs into this hybrid Greco-Anatolian world. As early as 6000 BC there had been wine production and then sophisticated metalworking in the mountainous region that we now call the Caucasus. The world's oldest worked-leather shoe was found in 2008 in an Armenian cave. Mathematical and scientific advances in Babylon generated the formula for living we still employ today – that formal division of our lives into twelve hours of night and day, and of time into sixty-minute portions – which had already been in use for 2,000 years before the first Greeks arrived. Ugarit – which had an early alphabet – on the Syrian coast had a reputation as being the 'Venice' of the Bronze Age.

6 Hallof, Hermann and Prignitic (2012), 213–38, esp. 218.

7 Many thanks to Dr. Llewelyn Morgan for his close read of Part One and his interesting thought that *prounikoi* might, perhaps, be a pun on *proenoikoi*, 'former inhabitants'.

8 Herodotus, *Histories* 4.144 Cartledge and Holland (2013) trans.

CHAPTER 4: PERSIAN FIRE

1 Herodotus, *Histories* 4.88, trans. adapted from Russell (forthcoming 2016) by the author; see also trans. Holland/Cartledge (2013).

2 See work by the University of Leeds: Parsons et al. (2010), 1063–6.

3 Dionysios of Byzantium, *Anaplous Bosporou*, 109.

4 Herodotus, *Histories* 1.214.

5 Travelling here you have the sense that human booty was a secondary concern. Slaves were essential of course in these slave-driven economies. But here it is the landscape that throws down a gauntlet, man versus mountain: it is not so much the communities as the coasts that need thwarting.

6 Our source for this dark moment in ancient history is Herodotus. Following the thrilling new development of *historie* – rational enquiry – Herodotus clearly thought it was his job to observe the world to help to understand us. He asked constantly, 'Is this worthy of being recorded?' An anthropologist, ethnographer, genius storyteller and journalist, he recited his work out loud – possibly to huge crowds at, for example, the Olympic Games. He wrote so that 'human achievement' could be spared the ravages of time. Herodotus' description of the events around Byzantion touch on central themes

from ancient history. That both Athenians and Spartans considered words a cogent constituent of their armoury; that Persia was a multi-ethnic empire (Themistocles himself, ostracised from Athens in AD 471–470, became a Persian governor of the Greek city within the Persian Empire, Magnesia); that experiments in this tempestuous theatre of war – the empowering watchword democracy, the value of enquiry and an imagined fault-line between East and West – to some degree give us our ideas of ourselves today.

7 Setting out for Thermopylae, Leonidas had known this was a suicide mission – he took with him only those men who had sons to survive them.

8 The very earliest fortifications of the city seem to have been a wooden palisade built in the seventh century BC.

9 Plutarch, *Moralia* 217e.

10 Interesting that Thucydides states as fact that Pausanias asked for the hand of Xerxes' daughter while Herodotus, a historian with closer connections to the geographical area, disputes this.

11 Named after the town in Israel where one ram was found in modern excavations.

12 Pindar, fr. 64, trans. Bowra (1964).

13 Aristophanes, *The Acharnians*, lines 600–7.

14 Xenophon, *Hellenica* 1.3.14.

CHAPTER 5: CITY OF SIEGE

1 Xenophon *Anabasis* 6.6 trans. Brownson (1922), rev. Dillery (1998) [LCL].

2 Xenophon, *Hellenica* 1.3.14–16, trans. Brownson (1918).

3 'After this Alcibiades went off to the Hellespont and the Chersonese to collect money; and the rest of the generals concluded a compact with Pharnabazus . . . Now Pharnabazus thought that Alcibiades also ought to give his oath, and so waited at Chalcedon until he should come from Byzantium; but when he came, he said that he would not make oath unless Pharnabazus also should do the like to him. In the end, Alcibiades made oath at Chrysopolis to the representatives of Pharnabazus, Mitrobates and Arnapes, and Pharnabazus at Chalcedon to the representatives of Alcibiades, Euryptolemus and Diotimus, both parties not only giving the official oath but also making personal pledges to one another.' Ibid., 1.3.8–12.

4 Plutarch, *Alcibiades* 34.6.

5 Aristophanes, *Frogs* 1425, trans. Savage (2010).

6 There might have been political turmoil at home (the violent dismantling of the democracy), but this was combined with cultural florescence: Aristophanes' productions of *Birds*, *Lysistrata* and *Women at the Thesmophoria*;

Euripides' *Phoenician Women*, *Bacchae* and *Iphigenia in Aulis*, and the completion of the Erechtheion.

7 Xenophon, *Hellenica* 1.1.22.

8 In excavations in 2008 to 2014 faux-metal Athenian-style drinking cups and pots have been found here, identical to those used in the Athenian Agora at this time.

9 Moreno (2008), 655–709. Noonan (1973), 231–42. Casson (1954), 168–87.

10 In 406 BC the Athenians defeated the Spartan fleet at Arginusae. But then they lost at Aegospotami in late 405 BC, the year that the Spartans besieged the Piraeus.

11 Robertson (1980), 282–301; Bloedow (1992), 139–57; Andrewes (1953), 2–9.

12 In 405 BC Sparta was back in control in Byzantion – cutting off Athens' food supply, starving it into submission and then in 404 BC storming into Athena's city-state itself, tearing down its walls.

13 With thanks to Professor Lene Rubinstein for help with this. See Xenophon, *Hellenica* 2.2.1.

14 The younger son of Dareios II recruited an army that included many Greek mercenaries to fight against his elder brother at Cunaxa in Babylonia. The 10,000 or so survivors ended up fighting their way back through Asia to try to reach the Hellespont.

CHAPTER 6: WINE AND WITCHES

1 Menander, *The Principal Fragments*, 67K, trans. Allinson (1921). Survives through a quotation in Athenaeus (10.442d, Aelian, *Varia historia* 3.14).

2 Trans. Lucy Felmingham-Cockburn and Elizabeth McNeill, with many thanks to both. Cf. the Loeb Classical Library translation: 'Cluster, full of the juice of Dionysus, thou restest under the roof of Aphrodite's golden chamber: no longer shall the vines, thy mother, cast her lovely branch around thee, and put forth above thy head her sweet leaves.' Moero of Byzantium, 'The Dedicatory Epigrams', Number 119, trans. Paton (1916), 362 (Greek), 363 (English).

3 Described by Robin Lane Fox as a writer of slander rather than of history.

4 Theopompus of Chios, *Philippica*, Book 8, F 62. Quoted in Freely (1998), 14.

5 Aristotle, *Oeconomica* 1346b. 13–36.

6 Today the curve of Kybele's sanctuary on Chios protects Homer's Stone, 'the seat' where tourist guides assert that the bard first sat to share his epic tales. The goddess's sanctuary at Cyzicus in the Propontis is well attested, likewise Colophon in Ionia.

7 Pessinus was a city in Asia Minor, located on the Royal Road which linked

Sardis, capital of Lydia, to the Persian cities Susa and Persepolis on what is today called the Sakarya River. The legendary King Midas was traditionally thought to have ruled Phrygia from this base in the eighth century BC. Archaeological research by Ghent University (1967–73 under Pieter Lambrechts, 1987–2008 under John Devreker) suggests that the city developed c. 400 BC: see Verlinde (2012).

8 See Moreno (2008), passim.

9 *Die InSchriften von Byzantion. 1, Die InSchriften* ed. A. Lajtav (2000), IK32.

10 Berg (1974), 128–9. Marquardt (1981), 250–2. Limberis (1994), 126–7.

11 A number of the later Roman-period sources are almost certainly drawing a parallel here with the backstory of Byzantium and that of Old Rome – which was said to have been protected by the cries of geese.

12 See e.g. Diodoros Siculus, *Bibliotheca Historica,* trans. Oldfather (1989), Book 16, chs 74ff.

13 See full discussion in Moreno (2008).

14 Athen., *Deipnosophistae* 8.351c. We know that Stratonicos had visited Byzantion: Athen. 8.349f–350a.

15 The highly popular Greek *Alexander Romance*, a completely fictionalised account of Alexander's exploits, physically drew men east. Many of our Western ideas of the Caucasus were formed from this. See Stoneman, R. (1991).

16 Listed on papyrus exchanges between merchants in Alexandria and Byzantion: *P. Cair Zen.* 1. 59089.20.1, II. 20–1; *P. Cair. Zen.* 4. 59731 (257–249 BC); *P. Mich.* 18.781.10 (186–185 BC).

CHAPTER 7: ALL ROADS LEAD FROM ROME – THE EGNATIAN WAY

1 Cicero, *De Provinciis Consularibus* 2.4, trans. Gardner (1958).

2 SEG 25:711.

3 My thanks to Peter James for reminding me that *choiros* was also slang for female genitalia.

4 Pseudo-Aristotle, *On Marvellous Things Heard* 839b, trans. Hett (1936), 285.

5 See Wheeler (2011), 238; Archibald (2013), 245.

6 Pliny the Elder, *Natural History* 12.41, quoted in Lockard (2015), 172.

7 Professor Mary Beard, in conversation, April 2016.

8 Tacitus, *Annals* 12.62–3, trans. Jackson (1937).

9 Pliny the Younger, *Letters* 52–3, trans. Davis (ed.) (1913).

10 Virgil, *Georgics* 491–8, trans. Weeda (2015).

11 Vespasian makes Byzantium a province: Suetonius, *Life of Vespasian* 8.4. Source for mint: Mattingly (1921a), 216 and (1921b), 262.

12 On the aqueduct, see Crow, Bardill and Bayliss (2008) for further information, esp. 10–14, 116–17 and Fig. 2.2. (The Baths of Zeuxippos were destroyed in the Nika revolt of AD 532 but later rebuilt; they were excavated in 1928. Grig and Kelly (eds) (2012), 56).

13 Hadrian himself travels to the region but seems to prefer Nicomedia. He may not even have stayed in Byzantium, just keeping his hand in by accepting the honorary office of *hieromnemon*, priest-magistrate, for two consecutive years.

14 Cassius Dio, *Roman History* 74.14, 75.1, trans. Cary (1927), 195.

15 Herodian, *History of the Roman Empire* 3.1.5, trans. Echols (1961), 193.

16 Ibid.

17 Cassius Dio, *Roman History* 75.10–14, trans. Cary (1927), 195.

18 Herodian, *History of the Roman Empire* 3.1.5–6 and 3.6.9, trans. Echols (1961).

19 Freely (1998a), 27–8.

20 For further information, see Bomgardner (2000).

21 See A. R. Littlewood's entry on Byzantium in Wilson (2009), 136. Severus built theatre, baths, hippodrome, porticoes around the Agora.

22 A habit that continued: see Sevcenko (2002), 69–86.

23 But tellingly Severus died where Constantinople's story would start – in York.

24 Justinian I maintained one of the largest animal collections in the world. A collection still existed in AD 1453 and was maintained under the Ottomans when it was located on the western side of the southern end of the Topkapı complex. There is no zoo here now, but there is an aquarium a seven-minute walk from Topkapı.

25 Russell (2016), 42.

26 Lactantius, *De Mortibus Persecutorum*, trans. Creed (1984), 11.

27 'The ancient authors tell conflicting stories. Zosimus says that she died on the journey to Rome, before the convoy of prisoners had even crossed the straits to Byzantium'. Southern (2008), 156.

CHAPTER 8: THE ENEMY WITHIN

1 Pliny the Younger, *Letters* 96 and 97, trans. Davis (ed.) (1913), 298–300.

2 Acts 16: 11–15.

3 In the following centuries the Egnatian Way itself proved to be a robust spine along which many early churches and monasteries would be built. A number are only now emerging from the earth – dozens more than had previously been estimated.

4 Athenagoras, 'A Plea for Christians' in *Legatio and De Resurrectione*, trans. Schoedel (1972).

5 There is one ugly, gouged gap where a modern water pipe was unwittingly scored through the surface in the late 1930s, but apart from that, this mosaic is near perfect.

6 Rebuilt by Hadrian, Lydda grew to be a vital centre of dyed purple cloth – the colour which marked out emperors and kings and was traded along the Egnatian Way but which was described by one Roman author as 'the colour of congealed blood'.

7 The iconography seems to tell us that the dialogue between Jews and Christians was strong at this point. Imagery in, for example, the Dura Europos mosaics from eastern Syria, completed c. AD 244, shows two branches of the same family demonstrating that they stand on common ground, but at the same time carving up that territory – pointing out who is right to say what about which matters.

8 Zoroastrianism was promoted at Christianity's expense in Persia by the Sassanians once Ardashir I took control in AD 244. In Georgia a number of Jews converted. Mgaloblishvili and Gagoshidze (1998), 39–48. Sterk (2000), 1–39.

9 Lydda (or Lod to give it its original, biblical name) had a testing history. The entire population of the town had been sold into slavery (for failure to pay their debts) in AD 43; the town itself was then destroyed by Romans during the Jewish War of AD 66. The Jewish revolt created the Jewish diaspora, allowing Christianity to gain a foothold and for the new Judeo-Christian questions and notions of ways of being to travel around the Roman world. This, ironically, is the beginning of an *idea* of Byzantium as the heart of a faith that has not just geographical but spiritual pull.

10 There is the slimmest of chances that St George was martyred in Lydda – just at the time the mosaic was being proudly shown off as a new addition to a rich man's home. Popular sources relate that George was born in Lod, or that his mother had a house there; according to others this is where the saint was martyred for his faith and then buried – or they state that his bones were brought here from Cappadocia as relics. We are told that George, in the guard of the Roman Emperor Diocletian and unable to deny his faith, was tortured and then decapitated (the fight with the famous dragon – actually a sea-monster similar to the one that appears on the Lod mosaic – is a much later addition). From the fifth century onwards a shrine in Lydda became an international focus of pilgrimage. Byzantine rulers renamed the town Georgiopolis.

CHAPTER 9: PERSECUTION

1 Eusebius of Caesarea, *On the Martyrs of Palestine* 9.9–10, trans. Schaff and Wace (1955).

2 Quoted in Campbell (2011), 203.

3 We have to be cautious with primary sources here; the persecution was often scaled down on the ground and there were regional variations too. See Evers (2010), ch. 3 passim.

4 Lactantius, *De Mortibus Persecutorum* 12.2–5, trans. Creed (1984).

5 The ravages of a pandemic, possibly smallpox, were seen as a punishment from the gods. And who was displeasing the Olympians? Well, naturally it would be those peace-loving, unsettlingly egalitarian gods-deniers, the Christians.

6 In AD 305, the 'oriental cults' Manichaeism and Judaism, as well as Christianity, were fiercely persecuted. In 306 the Council of Illiberis ordered priests to be celibate; it was also decreed that it was undesirable to visit the homes of Jews and for Christian women to marry Jews unless they converted. Yet, when one of the most eager persecutors, Galerius, commissioned his grand triumphal arch in Thessalonika to celebrate his victory over the Sassanids – dedicated in 303 and still standing – he could not have known that he was constructing a monument that would mark the beginning of the end of the pagan Roman Empire.

7 The point has been made that Rome was perhaps lashing out as it felt fragile. Rome's tax inspectors were sent to ensure that stipulations were being met on basic foodstuffs and luxury imports, from cumin to sandals. See Frankopan (2015), 23.

8 Liebeschuetz (1979), 251–2.

CHAPTER 10: THE MEEK SHALL INHERIT THE EARTH

1 British Library Papyrus 878. There is much debate over the genuine nature of the documents quoted by Eusebius in his *Life of Constantine*.

2 Thanks to Guy de la Bédoyère for his help with this and for his original research. See de la Bédoyère (2015).

3 See discussions in e.g. Toynbee (1934).

4 Jer. Chron. 5.a.306; *Theod.* 42, Origo 2; see also Zosimus 2.8.2; Eutr. 10.2; Zon. 13.1.4; *CIL* 10:517 = *ILS* 708; *PLRE* 1 Fl Iulia Helena 3. (Lenski (ed.) (2012), 83 n. 3).

5 Barnes (1981), 73–4. NB Some believe Helena and Constantius enjoyed a common-law marriage.

6 http://www.abdn.ac.uk/geosciences/departments/archaeology/the-northern-picts-project-259.php.

7 'he made his way with all haste to his father, and arrived at length at the very time that he was lying at the point of death. As soon as Constantius saw his son thus unexpectedly in his presence, he leaped from his couch,

embraced him tenderly, and, declaring that the only anxiety which had troubled him in the prospect of death, namely, that caused by the absence of his son, was now removed, he rendered thanks to God, saying that he now thought death better than the longest life, and at once completed the arrangement of his private affairs. Then, taking a final leave of the circle of sons and daughters by whom he was surrounded, in his own palace, and on the imperial couch, he bequeathed the empire, according to the law of nature, to his eldest son, and breathed his last.' Eusebius, *Life of Constantine* 21.1–3, trans. Schaff and Wace (1955). Lenski (ed.) (2012), 61.

8 The *Panegyrici Latini* ed. Nixon and Rodgers (1994), 215–16.

9 Emergency conference held in November at Carnuntum (Petronell) on the Danube border. Lenski (ed.) (2012), 65.

10 For more information see Hartley, Hawkes, Henig and Mee (eds) (2006), 65–77.

11 For religious motivation see e.g. Socrates Scholasticus, *Ecclesiastical History* 1.2, trans. Schaff and Wace (1989).

CHAPTER 11: THE BATTLE OF MILVIAN BRIDGE

1 Eusebius, *Life of Constantine* ch. XXVIII, trans. Schaff and Wace (1955).

2 See catalogue Barbera (2013).

3 See Alföldi (1932) and Bannikov (2014).

4 Nixon and Saylor Rodgers (1994), Panegyric XII.

CHAPTER 12: CITY OF GOLD

1 Lactantius, *De Mortibus Persecutorum* 44.5, trans. Vanderspoel (1998).

2 Sozomen (d. c. 450), *Ecclesiastical History* 2.3, trans. Bohn in Davis (1913), 295–6.

3 The current thinking is that Galerius planned to be buried at his palace Felix Romuliana (named for his mother) in the east of present-day Serbia.

4 Lactantius, *De Mortibus Persecutorum* 48. Alternative translation: 'no one whatsoever should be denied the opportunity to give his heart to the observance of the Christian religion, of that religion which he should think best for himself'. See http://legacy.fordham.edu/halsall/source/edict-milan.asp.

5 On arrival in Rome Constantine did not give thanks in the Temple of Jupiter as you would expect a good pagan to do, but instead went straight to the imperial palace. He seems to have commissioned a golden victory statue for the Forum with Christian symbolism, but elsewhere he kept his options

open. Constantine's victory arch, the model for the Arc de Triomphe in Paris and the Marble Arch in London, gives thanks to a general 'Divinitas'. Following the habit of the Romans, this marked a victory; dolorous barbarian prisoners are shown; so too seasonal deities, demonstrating the eternal reach of Constantine's triumph. This showy arrival is described in contemporary sources not as a triumph but as an *adventus* – an arrival. Patched together with new work, rehashing spolia and classical carvings (possibly liberated from the warehouses of state-owned architectural salvage that archaeologists now believe to have existed in Italy), the arch celebrated two kinds of virtue: both the macho, imperial expression of sheer muscle power – the pursuit of Gloria for the benefit of SPQR, the Senatus Populusque Romanus – and a public demonstration of a new kind of worth – Virtue as an expression not just of civic or political pride, but of spiritual possibilities. A new basilica also commemorated Constantine's victory. While there seems to have been no forced scheme of destruction at this moment in Constantine's story, pagan wealth was appropriated and natural wastage was quietly encouraged – the temple of Helen of Troy's twin brothers Castor and Pollux in the Roman Forum was allowed to disintegrate.

6 Constantine first started minting coins with his image in AD 306–7 after his soldiers called him 'Augustus'. Then he began modelling himself on Augustus and Trajan on his coins. Lenski (2012), 261; see 260–2 for a general overview of Constantine's depiction on coinage.

7 Strazny (ed.) (2005), 305.

8 There is no doubt that one of the reasons travellers came here was to access the glittering products and technologies of the Asian continent. The earliest extant evidence of metalworking comes from eastern and north-eastern Turkey dating to at least 10,000 BC. Gold was worked in the fifth millennium BC – in the Carpatho-Balkan region – but the 'host rocks' of the Caucasus are so rich in diverse, complex metal resources that metal technology and trade increase here exponentially, as does a kind of mythic fascination with the region. And the gold was something else. Medea's homeland, Colchis, has yielded fabulous pieces stretching back to the third millennium BC (with the graceful production reaching a peak in the fifth century BC – just at the time Euripides et al. were penning their Hellenocentric versions of her story). The tales of metalworking Amazons here and Prometheus stealing fire from the gods to advance technology suddenly make more sense.

9 Ş. Karagöz in Pekin and Kangal (eds) (2007), 47–9.

10 Ibid., 42.

11 Ibid., 39–40 and 76 (cat. Ü11) for Kybele, 83 (Ü18) for ship motif on sherd, and 95 (Ü39) for Arabic badge; for whole Üsküdar section, 31–95.

12 See Anahit Yu. Khudaverdyan, 'Decapitations in Late Bronze Age and Iron Age sites from Sevan region (Armenia)', *Journal of Siberian Federal*

University. Humanities & Social Sciences 9 (2014), 1555–66.

13 Zosimus *New History* 2.22.7, trans. Ridley (1982).

14 Fascinatingly, Mycenaean Bronze Age burials have been found here near the docking beach of Beşik Bay. Constantine is described as planning a new capital near the Tomb of Ajax: Rykwert (1988), 202. Sozomen, *Ecclesiastical History* 2.3, trans. Hartranft (2016): 'With this intention, he repaired to a plain at the foot of Troy, near the Hellespont, above the tomb of Ajax, where, it is said, the Achaians had their naval stations and tents while besieging Troy; and here he laid the plan of a large and beautiful city, and built the gates on an elevated spot of ground, whence they are still visible from the sea to those sailing by.' The Tomb of Achilles was still intact and altars and statues still worshipped in Hector's shrine until at least AD 355, despite attempts by Christians to destroy them. The tomb is at Rhoiteion, a distance from Hisarlik. Heuck-Allen (1999), 39.

15 Sozomen, *Ecclesiastical History* 2.3, trans. Davis (1913), 295.

16 Ibid., 295–6.

CHAPTER 13: IN THE NAME OF CHRIST'S BLOOD

1 Sidonius Apollinaris, *Epistulae* 5.8.2, trans. Anderson (1989): '*Saturni aurea saecla quis requirat? / sunt haec gemmea, sed Neroniana.*'

2 The division of the land of imperial Rome into East and West and into a territory ruled by four emperors, the tetrarchs plus their assistants, in order to prevent debilitating civil wars had in some ways succeeded because of its shortcomings. With the potential for power-play forced firmly out into the open, a clever, ambitious man like Constantine could manipulate the situation to his advantage. The imperial system, developed to keep its emperors informed about precisely what was happening when and where across their vast territories – such as the numbers of troops, the level of grain in the warehouses, the whereabouts of enemies of state – must have given Constantine precisely the knowledge he needed to thwart his rivals.

3 The current building here dates back to the seventh century AD.

4 We do not yet know precisely what happened in those months when Constantine decided that Byzantium would be his new centre of operations, but the imagination of generations has been written into the record as historical fact. Edward Gibbon, in his *The History of the Decline and Fall of the Roman Empire*, tells us that Constantine was 'anxious to leave a deep impression of hope and respect on the minds of the spectators. On foot, with a lance in his hand, the emperor himself led the solemn procession, and directed the line which was traced as the boundary of the destined capital, till the growing circumference was observed with astonishment by the assistants,

who at length ventured to observe that he had already exceeded the most ample measure of a great city. "I shall advance," replied Constantine, "till HE, the invisible guide who marches before me, thinks proper to stop."' Gibbon, vol. 1, chapter 17 (1776–89).

5 '*urbis quam, aeterno nomine iubente, deo donavimus*' (the city which we have endowed with the name eternal by God's command). *Theodosian Code* 13.5.7 (AD 334), trans. Pharr (2001), 392.

CHAPTER 14: EQUAL TO THE QUEEN OF CITIES

1 Socrates Scholasticus, *Ecclesiastical History* 1.100.16, trans. Schaff and Wace (1980), vol. 2, 144.
2 Later sources tell us this was actually brought from Rome, although porphyry is often described as 'Roman stone'; either could be true. Clearly the stone originates in the Egyptian quarries.
3 Constantine's walls were *not* made with Rome's favourite building material *pozzolana* – the Bronze Age volcanic ash that, physically, cemented the empire together.
4 For notes on walls cf. Gilles (1988), Book 1, chs XIX and XXI.
5 Cf. *Chron. Pasch.* anno 330.
6 For these and other details see Bassett (2004), ch. 1.
7 For Fortuna Redux see Mango (2000), 177.

CHAPTER 15: FAITH, HOPE, CHARITY AND THE NICENE CREED

1 Eusebius, *Life of Constantine*, Book 3, trans. Richardson (1980).
2 Eusebius, *Vita Constantini* 4.10, trans. Schaff and Wace (1955).
3 See for example Pekin and Kangal (2007), 78 (cat. Ü13) and 86 (Ü25).
4 Eusebius, *Vita Constantini* III.10.3, trans. Cameron and Hall (1999).
5 Constantine says, 'You are bishops of those within the Church, but I am perhaps a bishop appointed by God over those outside.' Ibid. 4.24.
6 Many thanks to Dionysios Stathakopoulos for help with these ideas.
7 Sozomen, *Ecclesiastical History* 2.3, trans. Schaff (1994).
8 *Agrippina said*: He was not pagarch in that district.
Constantine Augustus said: But the law provides that no-one in an administrative position is to purchase anything, so that it is of no relevance whether he purchased it in his own *pagus* (district) or another's, since it is clear that he made the purchase contrary to law.

And he added: Are you aware that whatever administrators purchase, all of it is made property of the *fiscus* (the treasury)?

Agrippina said: He was not *praepositus* of that district. I made the purchase from his brother. See the deed of sale.

Constantine Augustus said: Let Codia and Agrippina recover an appropriate price from the vendor. *Codex Theodosianus* 8.15.1, trans. Pharr (2001).

9 Female visibility in the city's churches and religious institutions seems to have peaked by the seventh century, though a number of traditions did continue with some vigour in Constantinople itself up until the twelfth century.

10 Karras (2004), 272–316.

11 Hadrian built the temple of Venus at Golgotha in AD 135 (Eusebius, *Life of Constantine* 3.26).

12 With thanks to Zina Sackur for her help with this passage.

13 The Temple of Zeus at Apamea was destroyed by the zealous city's bishop by 386 (Theodoret, *Historia Ecclesiastica* 5.21).

14 Bradbury (1994), 129–30. Harl (1990), 7–27. Errington (1988), 309–18. Bowman, Garnsey and Cameron (eds) (2005), 101–2.

CHAPTER 16: HELENA

1 For further discussion of the connections between Constantine and Elagabalus in this account see Fowden (1991), 119–31.

2 Zonaras XIII. 2. 34–5; *BHG* 365 (5–6, Opitz); *Chronicle of George the Monk* (XI, 1, ii, pp. 491, 17–499, 7).

3 Thanks to Nigel Spivey for his help with these ideas.

4 Emperor Constantine's edicts of AD 326 and 333 suppressed the image of Sophia as the Embodiment of Wisdom. Just as Christ was a second Adam, so woman was a second Eve. See Jerome's worrying advice on how to raise a Virgin Daughter; following a passage where he recommends regular gentle enforced fasting ('let her meals always leave her hungry and able on the moment to begin reading or chanting') rather than near starvation, he cautions against 'abstinence turning to glutting, like that of worshippers of Isis and Kybele who gobble up pheasants and turtle-doves piping hot that their teeth may not violate the gifts of Ceres'. Jerome, Letter 107, to Laeta, AD 403, trans. Fremantle (1893).

5 Symeon the Stylite, when telling Daniel the Stylite to travel to Constantinople instead of Jerusalem, called Constantinople the Second Jerusalem – often cited as the New Jerusalem. Dawes (1948), 12–13.

CHAPTER 17: BIRTHS AND DEATHS

1 Eusebius, *Vita Constantini* 26.3, trans. Schaff and Wace (1955).
2 Socrates Scholasticus, *Ecclesiastical History* 1.38, trans. Schaff and Wace (1989), 34–5.
3 Woods (1997), 531–5. Burgess (1999), 153–61.
4 'Ita anno imperil tricesimo secundoque, cum totum orbem tredecim tenuisset, sexaginta natus atque amplius duo, in Persas tendens, aquis bellum erumpere occeperat, rure proximo Nicomediae – Achyronam vocant – excessit, cum id tetrum sidus regnis, quod crinitum vocant, portendisset.' 'Bellum versus Parthos moliens, qui iam Mesopotamiam fatigabant, uno et tricesimo anno imperii, aetatis sexto et sexagesimo, Nicomediae in villa publica obiit. Denuntiata mors eius etiam per crinitam stellam, quae inusitatae magnitudinis aliquamdiu fulsit, Graeci cometen vocant.' Eutr. *Brev.* 10.8.
'Constantinus, cum bellum pararet in Persas, in Acyrone villa publica iuxta Nicomediam moritur anno aetatis LXVI.li.' Jer. *Chron.* s.a. 337.
'Cumque bellum in Persas moliretur, in villa publica iuxta Nicomediam, dispositam bene rempublicam filiis tradens, diem obiit.' Oros. *Adv. Pag.* 7.28.30.
'cum bellum pararet in Persas, in suburbano Constantinopolitano villa publica iuxta Nicomediam'. *Origo* 35.
'cum bellum pararet in Persas, in Acyrone villa publica iuxta Nicomediam moritur'. Prosp. *Chron.* s.a. 337.
'dum bellum pararet in Persas, in Acyrone villa publica iuxta Nicomediam moritur'. Cass. *Chron.* s.a. 339.
'Obiit in Ancirone Nicomediae villa.' *Laterc. Imp. ad Justin I.* See Mai. *Chron.* 13.14.
5 My thanks to Peter Frankopan for this.
6 Stone can be a useful signifier of ambiguity. Perhaps it was his purloining of fine pagan statuary (for example, the serpentine bronze columns from Delphi, commissioned to celebrate the Greek victory of Pausanias, the Spartans et al. against the Persians, and so hubristically branded by Pausanias himself, that still twist up from Istanbul's hippodrome), perhaps it was his aggressive attitude to his co-rulers, perhaps most of all it was his troubling infatuation with a single man-god, which explains why Constantine was not honoured as you might expect with a statue during his lifetime at the sanctuary of Delphi. Once in power he passed legislation outlawing pagan sacrifice and certain kinds of sorcery; this is traditionally interpreted as a sign of his piety, but it seems more likely that this was anxiety – a legal suppression of the potentially harmful daemons that the population of the city had fervently believed in for centuries and that are still remembered to this day.

CHAPTER 18: PAGANS AND PRETENDERS

1 Julian, *The Caesars* 336B, trans. Wright (1913), 413.
2 Constantine II died in battle in AD 340; Constans ruled in the West but was assassinated in 350; Constantius II ruled in the East 337–61.
3 The Emperor Diocletian seems to have sparked a fashion for eunuchs in the imperial court when he established the East as his base.
4 Julian, *Letter to Evagrius* (362, Constantinople), trans. Wright (1913).
5 Julian, *Letter to Philip* (362, Constantinople), trans. Wright (1913) adapted. Perhaps one of Christianity's missed opportunities was that it insufficiently converted that charged pagan and animist delight in nature into a Christian rubric.
6 Ammianus Marcellinus, *Res Gestae* 20.4.
7 Zosimus, *New History* 3.75, trans. Buchanan and Davis (1967) – quoted in Freely (1998a), 51–2.
8 Building started by Constantine and finished by Julian. Murdoch (2005), 41.
9 Zosimus 3.66 tells us that Julian was in Athens 'where he lived among the philosophers and excelled all his masters in every kind of learning'. Julian did wear a beard in a clean-shaven age (see e.g. coin portraits) and wrote 'Misopogon' (Beard Hater) in Antioch in AD 363 as a satire. He seems to have liked his 'philosophy beard' and perhaps wore it as a repudiation of Christianity. See e.g. Peterkin (2001), 22.
10 Apollo is also mentioned in relation to oracles.
11 Libanios, *Oratio* 18.139, trans. in Bowersock (1978), 72.
12 As would be shown by Ambrose's control over Theodosios – there were new possibilities for those who were not from the imperial family.
13 Even in the third century Christian scholars such as Origen were arguing that scriptures needed to be interpreted allegorically rather than literally. One court orator to the Christian Emperor Jovian argued that God positively enjoyed being worshipped in a variety of ways.
14 See Scott (2014); the oracle in question could in fact originally have been Daphne rather than Delphi, but has come down to us as Delphi in the sources.
15 Ammianus Marcellinus, *Res Gestae* (The Later Roman Empire) 31.8.9, translation by Walter Hamilton adapted by the author.

CHAPTER 19: THE PROBLEM WITH GOTHS

1 Shakespeare, *Titus Andronicus*, Act I, scene I.
2 See La Vassière (2012), 144–7.

3 Frankopan (2015), 45ff.
4 Ibid.
5 Ammianus Marcellinus, *Res Gestae* (The Later Roman Empire) 31.4 translation adapted by the author.
6 Pany and Wiltschke-Schrotta (2008), 18–23.
7 The Volga pips the Danube to the post by a sturdy 500 miles.
8 Down a backstreet in Passau (Batavis to the Romans) hides the Roman Museum, recently built around the site of a Roman camp here. It houses a fine collection with many freshly dug artefacts and is not just of casual antiquarian interest. Passau is a pretty, pastel-painted place, briefly home to Hitler and Himmler, where a surprising number of the locals still seem to have a penchant for the traditional befeathered trilby hats. Roman emperors employed the men of the Batavi as international crack squads, with fighters and horses trained to keep formation while battling across raging rivers. The Batavians sailed the Channel with the Roman commander Aulus Plautius and helped to defeat native Britons at the River Battle of Medway in AD 43: Batavi muscle and nous helped to secure the Roman occupation of Britannia.
9 Murdoch and Read (2004), 157–9.
10 Themistius, *Orations* 16.206d, trans. Heather and Moncur (2001).

CHAPTER 20: A DOVE OF PEACE OR A FIST OF IRON: THEODOSIOS

1 Πάντα γὰρ τὰ κατὰ τὴν πόλιν τῶν τοιούτων πεπλήρωται, οἱ στενωποὶ, αἱ ἀγοραὶ, αἱ πλατεῖαι, τὰ ἄμφοδα· οἱ τῶν ἱματίων κάπηλοι, οἱ ταῖς τραπέζαις ἐφεστηκότες, οἱ τὰ ἐδώδιμα ἡμῖν ἀπεμπολοῦντες. Ἐὰν περὶ τῶν ὀβολῶν ἐρωτήσῃς, ὁ δέ σοι περὶ γεννητοῦ καὶ ἀγεννήτου ἐφιλοσόφησε· κἂν περὶ τιμήματος ἄρτου πύθοιο, Μείζων ὁ Πατὴρ, ἀποκρίνεται, καὶ ὁ καὶ ὁ Υἱὸς ὑποχείριος. Εἰ δὲ, Τὸ λουτρὸν ἐπιτήδειόν ἐστιν, εἴποις, ὁ δὲ ἐξ οὐκ ὄντων τὸν Υἱὸν εἶναι διωρίσατο. Οὐκ οἶδα τί χρὴ τὸ κακὸν τοῦτο ὀνομάσαι, φρενῖτιν ἢ μανίαν, ἤ τι τοιοῦτον κακὸν ἐπιδήμιον, ὃ τῶν λογισμῶν τὴν παραφορὰν ἐξεργάζεται. See forthcoming translation in Robinson (2017), 63.
2 The Nicene Creed was accepted by the Western church only in AD 1014.
3 Themistius, *Oratio XVIII*, edition of Petavius, 222.
4 Urk. IV, 586–7.
5 See Professor Jim Crow's excellent ongoing work on the waterways of the city. Crow, Bayliss and Bardill (2008), *The Water Supply of Byzantine Constantinople, Roman Society Monograph*; Bayliss, Crow and Bono (2001), 'The Water Supply of Constantinople: archaeology and hydrogeology of an early medieval city', *Environmental Geology* 40, 1325–33.
6 Onar et al. (2015), 56; Kocabaş (ed.) (2008); Sorgenfre (2013), 10.

7 Dogu, Kose, Kartal and Erdin (2010).

8 A number of alternative theological ideas were put forward in meetings – formal and informal – at this time.

9 Gregory of Nazianzus, trans. Meehan (1987), 133–5.

10 'Canons of the One Hundred and Fifty Fathers who assembled at Constantinople during the Consulate of those Illustrious Men, Flavius Eucherius and Flavius Evagrius on the VII of the Ides of July', Canon III – see https://legacy.fordham.edu/halsall/basis/const1.txt. Socrates Scholasticus wrote in the fifth century in his *Historia Ecclesiastica* 1.16 that Constantine's city in 330 was described as a Second Rome. Pelikan (1987), 75–6.

11 *Codex Theodosianus* 14.10.10, 11, 12, trans. Pharr (2001).

12 Harl (1990), 7–27; Bregman (1993), 30; Bradbury (1994), 120–39. Manichaeans were initially denied property rights and a number were then subjected to the death penalty. The Nicene debates were described by the historian Socrates as 'a battle fought at night, for neither party appeared to understand distinctly the grounds on which they calumniated one another'. Socrates, *Ecclesiastical History* trans. Walford and de Valois (1853), Book 1, Chapter 23, 499. Theodosios had already banned recalcitrant bishops such as Demophilos from the city. The exiles were then said to continue worshipping outside the walls for a number of years. The prefect of Illyricum was instructed to punish those 'insane and demented heretics' who stubbornly refused to concede. In classical Greece and the Hellenistic world all kinds of forms of supernatural god-ness and good-ness were shared, tested, discussed, defended, adapted. Depending on your point of view, Theodosian reforms meant that the possibilities for the spirit and intellectual and ethical debate alike were either intensified or cauterised.

CHAPTER 21: BATTLES IN HEAVEN AND ON EARTH: GAZA AND ALEXANDRIA

1 Mark the Deacon, *Life of Porphyry, Bishop of Gaza*, trans. Hill (1913), 66.

2 The Temple of Ilissos stood here until at least AD 1778 when it was broken up for building material by the Ottomans. It is recorded in a fine engraving now held in the John Soane Museum in London. Soon after this coin was minted Artemis' Temple of Ilissos was turned into a church.

3 See www.forumancientcoins.com/numiswiki/view.asp?key=victory

4 Caution needs to be applied here – the sources are almost certainly later (see MacMullen (1984), 86ff.) and could be introducing us to a morality tale. Further archaeology and experimental archaeology will help us to determine the truth of the literary tale.

5 Last Statues of Antiquity Database, LSA-27 (2012).

6 Mark the Deacon, *Life of Porphyry, Bishop of Gaza*, trans. Hill (1913), 66.

7 'Ancient Death Machines', programme in *Ancient Discoveries* series on the History Channel, aired 25 February 2008.

8 Perpetua's death ostensibly caused the conversion of Tertullian. He tells us that 'both sexes, every age and condition' (Brumback 2013, 23) are becoming Christian – because of course there is a delight in the idea that this kind of human sacrifice is no longer pleasing to the divinities. Author of the oldest surviving account in a woman's hand, Perpetua does interestingly say she dreams of 'becoming male' (Gold 213, 156).

9 In Alexandria, a conglomeration of pagan attitudes had been instilled into the very DNA of the city by its founder Alexander the Great. Alexander had a particular genius for taking on board the best of those around him, not least in matters of faith. In 324 BC the globe-trotting dictator's general, Ptolemy Soter, had established the Ptolemaic dynasty in North Africa, perpetuating his master's internationalist vision and plans for his namesake metropolis.

10 The Christian author Clement of Alexandria writes of 'the true Sicilian bee, gathering the spoil of the flowers of the prophetic and apostolic meadow [who] engendered in the souls of his hearers a deathless element of knowledge'. *Stromateis* I, 1 (written c. 198–c. 203), trans. Schaff (2012).

11 The language of one of his letters shows how determined he was: 'Now since I am anxious to show my gratitude to these men and to the Jews throughout the world, and to generations yet to come, I have determined that your laws shall be translated from the Hebrew tongue into the Greek language, that these books may be added to others in the library.' *The Forgotten Books of Eden* 2.2, trans. and ed. Platt (2006).

12 Hypatia died in March, according to Socrates Scholasticus, *Ecclesiastical History* 4.15.

13 A few fragments of the work of Hypatia and her father Theon would eventually be saved in the Marciana Library in Venice.

14 Palladas, fourth century AD, 'A Pagan in Alexandria considers life under Christian mobs who are destroying Antiquity' trans. Barnstone in *The Greek Poets: Homer to the Present*, ed. Constantine, Hadas, Keeley and van Dyck (2004), 281.

15 Socrates Scholasticus, *Ecclesiastical History* 7.15, trans. D. Duff (1891), *The Early Church: A History of Christianity in the First Six Centuries*, 446.

CHAPTER 22: CHRISTIAN PARTICLES IN A PAGAN ATMOSPHERE: NOVA ROMA

1 Prudentius to the Roman Senate, fifth century AD, *Contra Symmachum* 1.499–505, trans. in Alchermes (1994), 171.

2 The need for emperors from Arkadios to Justinian to re-enact the total Theodosian ban on sacrifices (Constantine's sons Constans and Constantius had already outlawed public and nocturnal sacrifice) is proof positive that these had not stopped. How could they? This was a tradition stretching back at least 10,000 years, the sacrifice itself kept the world turning and the ritual feast that followed brought large numbers of the community together. Pagan communities felt, deeply, the power of these acts – they contrived clever ways to get around the bans, individuals sacrificing on behalf of the whole community – as reported by the last 'pagan' historian Zosimus, who described the smart way a single priest had averted the effects of an earthquake in Athens by sacrificing to Achilles on behalf of the Athenian people. Correspondence between the apostate Julian and the scholarch from Constantinople Proclus makes it clear that celebration and sacrifice were thought to be the very glue that held civilisation and Greco-Romanness together. Theodosios in AD 423 actually consented to a law that encouraged Christian communities to live peacefully with their pagan and Jewish neighbours, but the monks of Syria – including Symeon the Stylite – were so vocally furious this was withdrawn in 425.

3 Interestingly, some of our best evidence for this *agalma*-mania comes from a ninth-century document, the *Parastaseis Syntomoi Chronikai*, which in essence supplies a cultural tourist guide to Constantinople. The detailed accounts herein show that the Byzantines, perhaps consciously and subconsciously, appreciated crossover between the pagan and the Christian world. Their histories start with the Creation and loyally track the exploits of the Trojans, Alexander the Great and Julius Caesar. The stories of these great pagans are as relevant as the stories of Christ or of the Bible. See Bassett (2004) and Saradi (2000).

4 See James (1996).

5 For brilliantly helpful work on this subject and catalogues of artworks cited in Constantinople see Bassett (2004).

6 Gilles (1729), 144. 'Cedrenus likewise remembereth a library in the palace of the king, at Constantinople, that contained a thousand a hundred and twenty books, amongst which there was the gut of a dragon of an hundred and twenty foot long, in which, in letters of gold, the Iliads and Odysseys of Homer were inscribed.' Chapman (1888), vol. 1, p. xciii; Cedrenus (1647), vol. 1, p. 351.

7 Statuary brought in on the orders of Emperor Justinian to his right-hand eunuch Narses.

8 *Codex Theodosianus* 16.10.8.

9 Ibid. 16.10.15.

10 For example, excavations of the early Christian layers at Apollo's sanctuary at Kato Phana.

11 See Beaumont, Archontidou-Argyri, Beames, Tsigakou and Wardle (2004).

12 From the classical period onwards pilgrims in this region had made trips to shrines of Asclepius, where they were 'miraculously' cured, and now in this Christian–pagan hybrid the tradition continued with those saints also believed to have the healing touch. It was said that emperors themselves merely had to lie on certain sacred stones and they would be cured. Stories of this and other wonders were popularly circulated through the streets of Constantinople – there must have been an invigorating sense of possibilities here.

13 Some astrologers were allowed to flourish – see later work by e.g. Rhetorius of Byzantium.

14 All listed by Vettius Valens in the second century AD.

15 Cyril I, Bishop of Jerusalem, c. AD 350, quoted in Theodossiou, Manimanis and Dimitrijevic (2012), 20.

CHAPTER 23: STATUES IN THE SKY: ASCETICS

1 Theodoret, *History of the Monks of Syria*, AD 444, ch. XXVI, Symeon (the Stylite).

2 Lucian, *De Dea Syria* 28, 29. See http://warburg.sas.ac.uk/pdf/bkg950b2390112.pdf, p. 67: 'In this entrance those phalli stand which Dionysus erected: they stand thirty fathoms high.' Often there were horns on the bases and tops of such pillars. See also references to the goddess Rhea having a pillar on her head.

3 'The Life and Works of Our Holy Father, St. Daniel the Stylite', in Dawes (1948), 10.

4 N. Baynes, 'St. Daniel the Stylite: Introduction', in Dawes (1948), 13.

5 'Now the demon of envy could not control his envy so he found an instrument worthy of his evil designs. A certain harlot, Basiane, who had lately come to Constantinople from the East, entrapped many of those who hunted after women of her sort. The sons of some heretics summoned her and made the following suggestion to her: "If you can in any way bring a scandal upon the man who stands on the pillar in Anaplus or upon any of those who are with him, we will pay you a hundred gold pieces." The shameless woman agreed and went up to the holy man with much parade and took with her a crowd of young men and prostitutes and simulated illness and remained in the suburb opposite the Saint's enclosure. And though she stayed there no little time she spent her time in vain.' Dawes (1948), 39.

6 . . . 'to serve him blamelessly and to be one body and one spirit continuing in humility and obedience. Do not neglect hospitality; never separate yourselves from your holy mother, the Church, turn away from all causes of offence and the tares of heretics'. Ibid., ch. 95.

7 Meineck (2012–13). Robertson, *History of the Christian Church* ii.41–3, 274.
8 Dawes (1948), ch. 24.

CHAPTER 24: SEX AND THE CITY: EUNUCHS

1 *Anth. Graec.* 16.33, trans. Paton (1960), 179.
2 See Shaun F. Tougher, chapter 8 in James (1997) and Tougher (2002).
3 Previously thought to be on the western side of the hippodrome.
4 Corippus, *In Laudem Iustini Augusti Minoris* 3.224–30, trans. in Cameron (ed.) (1976), 106.
5 *Life of John of Cyprus* 52.34–46, trans. Dawes (1948), 255.
6 Stevenson, *Eunuchs in Antiquity and Beyond* (2002), 123–42. Origen for example citing Matthew 19.12.
7 Of course the city as a hotbed of eunuchry was a tradition that would continue vigorously, well into the twentieth century. Once the Ottomans took control of Constantinople they constructed their own Courtyard of the Eunuchs in Topkapı Palace. With quarters on either side, the chief eunuch and his staff (of white eunuchs) controlled access to the Gate of Felicity, which represented the presence of the Sultan himself.
8 Eunapios 65.2.1–2, fourth century AD.

CHAPTER 25: THE FALL OF OLD ROME: THE PROBLEM WITH GOTHS, PART TWO

1 Zosimus, *New History* V.11.4, trans. Ridley (1982), quoted in Moorhead and Stuttard (2010), 77.
2 Quoted in Kelly (2008), 41.
3 Thank you to Chris Kelly for help with this chapter: see Kelly (2010).
4 Zosimus, *New History* V.7.5–6, trans. Ridley (1982), quoted in Moorhead and Stuttard (2010), 72.
5 St Jerome, quoting Virgil's *Aeneid* II. 361ff., trans. West (2003)
6 St Augustine, *City of God*, 1.7ff records rape and violence (see Moorhead and Stuttard (2010), 131). Jerome wrote of starvation during the siege and the sacking: 'The City which had taken the whole world was itself taken; nay more famine was beforehand with the sword and but few citizens were left to be made captives. In their frenzy the starving people had recourse to hideous food; and tore each other limb from limb that they might have flesh to eat. Even the mother did not spare the babe at her breast . . . Meantime, as was natural in a scene of such confusion, one of the bloodstained

victors found his way into Marcella's house. Now be it mine to say what I have heard to relate what holy men have seen; for there were some such present and they say that you too were with her in the hour of danger. When the soldiers entered she is said to have received them without any look of alarm; and when they asked her for gold she pointed to her coarse dress to shew them that she had no buried treasure . . . Christ softened their hard hearts and even among bloodstained swords natural affection asserted its rights. The barbarians conveyed both you and her to the basilica of the apostle Paul, that you might find there either a place of safety or, if not that, at least a tomb.' Jerome, Letter 127.12–13, trans. *Nicene and Post-Nicene Fathers: Series II* (1885).

Zosimus recorded: 'When Alaric heard that the people were trained and ready to fight, he said that thicker grass was easier to mow than thinner and laughed broadly at the ambassadors, but when they turned to discuss peace he used expressions excessive even for an arrogant barbarian: he declared that he would not give up the siege unless he got all the gold and silver in the city, as well as all movable property and the barbarian slaves. When one of the ambassadors asked what he would leave for the citizens if he took these, he replied: "Their lives."' Zosimus, *New History* 5.40, trans. Ridley (1982). Then we have Jordanes: 'When they finally entered Rome, by Alaric's express command they merely sacked it and did not set the city on fire, as wild peoples usually do, nor did they permit serious damage to be done to the holy places.' Jordanes, *The Origin and Deeds of the Goths*, 30.156, trans. Mierow (1915). And Orosius: '[Alaric] gave orders that all those who had taken refuge in sacred places, especially in the basilicas of the holy Apostles Peter and Paul, should be permitted to remain inviolate and unmolested; he allowed his men to devote themselves to plunder as much as they wished, but he gave orders that they should refrain from bloodshed . . . The third day after they had entered the City, the barbarians departed of their own accord. They have, it is true, burned a certain number of buildings, but even this fire was not so great as that which had been caused by accident in the seven hundredth year of Rome.' Orosius, *History against the Pagans* 7.39, trans. Raymond (1936). Gibbon wrote: 'In the hour of savage licence, when every passion was inflamed, and every restraint was removed, the precepts of the Gospel seldom influenced the behaviour of the Gothic Christians.' Gibbon, vol. 4, ch. 31, 662.

CHAPTER 26: VANDALS, WISDOM AND ATTILA THE HUN

1 Corippus, *In Laudem Iustini Minoris* 1.274–87, trans. Cameron.
2 During this period the Romans used dromons – a term probably applicable

to galleys from the fifth to tenth centuries AD – as they were less expensive to build and to maintain (developed from the small Roman model of galley known as the liburna or liburnian which was used for patrols or raiding). The Byzantine navy was developed by Justinian: see Pryor and Jeffreys (2006). A reconstruction of a dromon has been created based on the descriptions found within the *Tactica* of Emperor Leo VI the Wise: ibid., lxxvii, 754. For interest see models of a Knarr boat, a form possibly used by the Vandals.

3   See Merrills and Miles (2010) and Goffart (1981).
4   Callinicus, *Vita S. Hypatii*, ed. Bartelink (1971), 138.21 (Latin text with French translation). See also Goldsworthy (2009), 499 n. 1.
5   See   http://www.academia.edu/691311/Tracing_the_Language_of_the_ Vandals. Thank you to Alan Bowman for his comments.
6   Francovich Onesti (2002).
7   Wilson (1999).
8   Passage from a papyrus containing a New Kingdom didactic text (Papyrus Chester Beatty IV), as quoted in Ricardo A. Caminos, 'Peasants', in Donadoni (ed.) (1997), 16.
9   See also Numbers 5: 11–28.
10   Plato, *Phaedrus* 274e, trans. Fowler (1925).
11   Eustathios, *Commentary on the Iliad*, 2.27, trans. Stallbaum (2010).
12   For more on education see Markopoulos (2008) and (2013).
13   Later the University of the Palace Hall of Magnaura; a philosophy school was established in the great Magnaura Hall c. AD 855.
14   Constantelos (1999).
15   Markopoulos (2008).

CHAPTER 27: CITY OF THE MOTHER OF GOD

1   *Acta Concilorum Oecumenicorum*, ed. Schwartz, I, i, 2, 102.
2   Klein (2014).
3   Ferguson (1998), 505. For further information see Stephen the Deacon, *La Vie d'Etienne le Jeune par Etienne le Diacre*, trans. Auzépy (1997).
4   That later Byzantine emperors supported a quasi-compromise position of monothelitism suggests that these imperial pragmatists saw the practical – as well as the spiritual – downside of an absolute position.
5   This is noted in Janin (1953).
6   Current translation: http://www.ewtn.com/library/Doctrine/EUCHAR10. HTM, with reference: 'Ephrem the Syrian', *Inni su Santa Maria, Inno 1,* 10.14: *Monumenta Eucharistica*, I, 340.
7   See work by Professor Kate Cooper, e.g. Cooper (2013), 263–5.

8 We are told that Theodora's niece Sophia took the reins when Justin II went mad in the AD 570s; Eirene of course ruled on behalf of her son Constantine VI in the eighth century. Come the late eleventh/early twelfth century the Georgian donor and artist-monk Ioane Tokhabi develops the theme. In the Georgian monastery at Mount Sinai, an enthroned Mother of God sits in Constantinople, but is described in a Georgian inscription – unstudied until now. Skhirtladze (2015).

9 *Opp. Syr.* iii. 607, in Newman (1866), 42. Again: 'In the beginning, by the sin of our first parents, death passed upon all men; today, through Mary we are translated from death unto life. In the beginning, the serpent filled the ears of Eve, and the poison spread thence over the whole body; today, Mary from her ears received the champion of eternal happiness: what, therefore, was an instrument of death, was an instrument of life also.'

10 John Chrysostom, *In Evangelium S. Matthaei*, homily 50:3–4, pp. 58, 508–9.

11 John Chrysostom, *In Matthaeum Homiliae*, xxxiii, *Ex Capite*, xix (a), Migne, *Patrilogia Graeca*, vol. 56, p. 803.

12 From AD 569 provincial governors were to be chosen exclusively from the ranks of bishops and wealthy landowners.

13 Bishop Theodotos of Ankyra, Third Ecumenical Council, The Council of Ephesus, AD 431.

14 Justinian I refortified the city's defences. Towards the end of the sixth century Avars and Slavic tribes crossed the Danube and occupied Moesia and Scythia. Arabs, Lombards, Gepids, Goths, Cutrigurs and Antes would soon be surrounding the empire. In AD 577 and 581 Anastasios' walls held them back. See Haarer (2006), 106–9.

CHAPTER 28: THE GOLDEN AGE

1 C. P. Cavafy, 'In Church', from *Poems by C. P. Cavafy*, trans. J. C. Cavafy (2003).

2 The site was excavated by Sir Arthur Evans, also responsible for the excavation and reconstruction of Knossos on Minoan Crete.

3 Some sources give Justinian's birthplace as Baderiana. Procopius, *Buildings* 4.1.17 says that Justinian was born in Tauresium, a hamlet near the fortress Baderiana.

4 By AD 476, to all intents and purposes, Ravenna had become the capital of what was left of the old Roman Empire; seeing an opportunity, Constantinople had sent forces there – grafting a sturdy old branch on to the New Roman tree.

5 Passage quoted in Evans (2002), 108–9. Caesar Baronius lived AD 1538–1607 and his *Annales Ecclesiastici* were published 1588–1607. Evans notes

(ibid., 109) that Baronius wrote this 'before Procopius' *Secret History* was discovered in the Vatican Library and revealed Theodora's early life as a demimondaine'.

6 For a thoughtful analysis see Garland (1999) and Harvey (2011).

7 Procopius, *Secret History* 12.

8 Justinian, *Novellae* 8.1, as quoted in Evans (2002), 21.

9 Procopius, *Secret History* 10.13, trans. Williamson and Sarris (2007). The Kaldellis trans. (2010), 48 reads: 'the two of them did nothing independently of each other while they lived together'.

10 Procopius, *History of the Wars* 1.25, trans. Dewing (1914).

11 Kantorowicz (1963), 156. Featherstone (2012), 171.

12 Evans (2011), 49–50.

13 See Christophilopoulou (1956) and Constantine Porphyrogennetos, *The Book of Ceremonies*, trans. Moffat and Tall (2012), 432ff.

14 *De Ceremoniis Aulae Byzantinae* 1:39.

15 *Chronicon Paschale* 618.14–17; probably the bridge of St Callinicum.

16 Procopius refers to Theodora's predilection for long baths. He was no gentleman. *The Secret History* states that this composition was finalised in AD 550, just two years after Theodora's early death. Yet even some of Theodora's greatest fans cheerily admit that she came from a brothel; one of these was the Syrian, John, who was made bishop at Theodora's instigation.

17 Perhaps this was a private, high-stakes sparring match between them, a perverse, stimulating form of couple rivalry? Or maybe instead a pluralist strategy, a clever way of allowing both kinds of communities to feel loyal to the imperial court in general – whatever their theological leanings.

18 Garland (1999), 28–9.

19 Ibid. Evans (2011), 60–3. John of Ephesus, *Ecclesiastical History*, Book 4.

20 Bardill (2000), 6 n. 42 and Mango (1975), 392 suggest 531.

21 John of Ephesus, *Lives, Patrologia Orientalis*, 18.529, trans. Brooks (1923).

22 Garland (1999), 27.

23 Justinian, *Novellae* 5.5 (AD 535).

24 Justinian, *Codex Justinianus* 8.17 (18).12 (AD 531).

25 Procopius, *Buildings* 1.9.1–10, trans. Dewing (1940). Metanoia is supposedly underneath the Kuleli Officers' Training College, on the Asian shore of the Bosphorus, south of Vaniköy.

26 Procopius, *Secret History* 17.5, trans. Dewing (1935). Cf. also Procopius, *Buildings* 1.9.1–10.

27 Here in Constantinople we can see a partnership between *eros* and the ruling parties, not in the sexually erotic sense, but Eros as perceived in Plato's *Symposium* – a creative force that sparks sexual longing, yes, but whose transformative powers can also support a commanding ambition not just to live life but to love the living of it.

28 From Evans (2004), 21.

CHAPTER 29: EARTHQUAKES AND FIRES

1 Justinian, *Codex Justinianus* ix 47.12 ed. Krueger (1954).
2 John the Lydian, *On Offices* 3.70.
3 The chronology and detail of the Nika riots are helpfully summarised and analysed by Greatrex (1997). Other confrontations in Constantinople and elsewhere in this period include the hippodrome in Constantinople being set on fire in riots in AD 491, 498 and 507. In Antioch, after a victory in the circus by the charioteer Porphyrius in 507, riots led to the burning of a synagogue. Guttmann (1983), 16. Battle of Dara (530) against the Sassanids in the Iberian War. Haldon (2008), 27.
4 The massacre had taken place in Constantinople during the festival of Brytae in C. AD 500. Protests have always been a part of the culture of the city and they have moulded its physical condition. There had been riots and murders in 512 targeting the opponents of Chalcedon. In AD 1740 students would protest. It is interesting that in the twenty-first century the protest at Gezi Park was against the destruction of green spaces in the old city.
5 It was here that Justinian II – himself said to be capable of elaborate cruelty – would have his nose sliced through and his tongue cut out.
6 Van Millingen (1899), 28.
7 Procopius, *History of the Wars* 2.30.
8 Ibid. 1.24.33–8, trans. from Garland (1999).
9 The situation was temporarily defused when a chief court eunuch, Narses, went into the hippodrome and distributed gold coins to the Blues faction, reminding them – one imagines with a significant glint in his eye – that Justinian himself was a Blue and the chosen pretender a Green. See Bridge (1978), 73–8.
10 Although at the time of writing archaeology in the centre of the city has not revealed a mass grave.
11 John Malalas, *Chronicle* 422.14–22, trans. Jeffreys et al. (1986).

CHAPTER 30: THE PHOENIX CITY

1 Paul the Silentiary, *Description of Haghia Sophia* 617, quoted in Schibille (2014), 20.
2 Procopius, *Buildings* 1.1.27–9, trans. Dewing (1940).
3 'Jesus was born of Mary the virgin, according to the declaration in Scripture,

"The Holy Spirit will come upon you" – Sophia is the Spirit – "and the power of the Highest will overshadow you" – the Highest is the Demiurge – "wherefore that which shall be born of you shall be called holy" [Luke 1: 35]. For he has been generated not from the highest alone, as those created in the likeness of Adam have been created from the highest alone – that is, from Sophia and the Demiurge. Jesus, however, the new man, has been generated from the Holy Spirit – that is, Sophia and the Demiurge – in order that the Demiurge may complete the conformation and constitution of his body and that the Holy Spirit may supply his essence.' Hippolytus, *Refutation of all Heresies* 6.30.

4 Ousterhout (2010).
5 Themistius, fourth-century orator, *Oratio* 8, as quoted in Foltz (2014), 76.
6 Procopius, *Buildings* 1.4.4–5, trans. Dewing (1940).
7 Ibid. 1.11.1–6.
8 Constantine VII, *De Ceremoniis Aulae Byzantinae*, ed. Reisky (1829–30), vol. 1, pp. 33–4. See e.g. Harris (2007), 63–8. Bent (1887), 470: 'A short distance from this sea wall, under a little cliff, the workmen disclosed the wonderfully solid vaults of the Boukoleon palace, in which lay as if shaken by an earthquake heaps of marble pillars and capitals.'
9 The New Romans seemed to recognise that their city's enviably strong strategic and topographical position was also its weakness; there is a hobbit-like feel to the palace here – all escape tunnels and covered corridors.
10 See Mango (1997).

CHAPTER 31: SPECTACULAR, SPECTACULAR

1 From John Chrysostom's *8th Homily on the First Epistle of St Paul the Apostle to the Thessalonians*, quoted in Dalrymple (1997), 36–7.
2 In this chapter I have relied heavily on Roueché (2008).
3 Webb (2008), 102.
4 Barsanuphios and John of Gaza, Letter 837 in *Correspondence*, 3, trans. Neyt et al. (2002), 316–19.
5 Jacob of Serugh, *Homily* 5, fols 19v–20r, trans. Moss (1935), 22–3.
6 See Roueché (2008).

CHAPTER 32: LAW AND ORDER

1 Justinian's Institutes. Const. Imp. 3.

2 The *Codex* was finished in AD 529; *Digesta* 533; *Institutiones* 533; *Novellae* 534; *Syntagma* 572–7.

3 After the challenges to communism in the late 1980s and early 1990s, across central and eastern Europe remarkably it was to Justinian's *Codex* that many law-makers looked for common inspiration. As A. M. Honoré has put it, if we read those insertions that seem to be by Justinian's hand we get a sense of the man: 'forceful and persistent rather than polished; emphasizing, repeating, reformulating . . . Justinian's mind was formed, so far as we can judge, by reading of a Christian and bureaucratic sort: Church Fathers, constitutions of the Theodosian code and Novels, archives of the eastern empire in the fifth and sixth centuries, current correspondence . . . He has read the laws of the men he is determined to outshine. Procopius might have described him in speech, dress and thought as a barbarian – but a more generous assessment would be of a man determined to succeed, with unstinting energy, uninhibited by an idea of the way things should be done.' Honoré (1975), 107–23.

4 Justinian, *Novels* 8.1.

5 Humfress (2005).

6 See e.g. Silving (1959), 1327, n. 56.

7 An umbrella term for those living in the West, *Latini*, was coined around this time. There were many kinds of Latin in play in the early medieval period: demotic, biblical, political, literary, vulgate – often with many shades in between.

8 Officially banned by Pope Nicholas I: see Koven (2008), 158.

9 Agathias, *Histories* 4.1.2ff.

CHAPTER 33: THE JEWISH CITY

1 Justinian, *Digest Const. Tanta*, pr.16 (AD 533).

2 Dubnov (1968), 201.

3 For a full discussion of Byzantium's relationship with Jewish culture see Schama (2013), ch. 5.

4 The Order for Evening Prayer in the Book of Common Prayer (Church of England).

5 Whereas Julian the Apostate – in Antioch as it happened, in AD 362–3 – had offered to help with Jewish restitution to Jerusalem.

6 Evidence for this can be found in the community of the Borium of the Maghreb.

7 See e.g. Holo (2000).

8 K. N. Kanellakis, *Chiaca Analecta* (Athens, 1890) 550. Compare Hunger, *Prooimion*, 201.

CHAPTER 34: THE CLASSICAL CITY

1 Palladas, fourth century AD, trans. Willis Barnstone in *The Greek Poets: Homer to the Present,* ed. Constantine, Hadas, Keeley and van Dyck (2009).
2 John Malalas, *Chronicle* 18.47, trans. Jeffreys et al. (1986).
3 Interestingly, come the time of Charles V a game, 'The Dodecahedron of Fortune', using twelve-sided dice was still played.
4 Justinian, *Codex Justinianus* 1.11.10.
5 For further discussion see Watts (2004).
6 See Georgiou (2012) and (2013). On the streets too, what was now officially perceived as demonology stubbornly held its appeal; in AD 501 there was a revolt during the pagan festival of the Brytae – banned throughout the empire by the Emperor Anastasios, thus 'depriving the city of the most beautiful dancing'. In the 'blessed city' of Edessa, pagans still sacrificed to Zeus-Hadad deep into the sixth century. The name of Christ and Christianity was being broadcast far and wide; the works and words of the New Testament were found throughout the city – on the walls of churches, on icons, in the mouths of the faithful as part of the richly developing hymnographies. But was its original spirit being lost? No longer a pioneer, the friend of the weak? In AD 569 a decree was passed which insisted that provincial governors were to be chosen only from the ranks of bishops and wealthy landowners.
7 With the end of iconoclasm, there was also a positive revival of antique images, particularly in the scriptoria.
8 Boethius, *The Consolation of Philosophy,* Book 2, prose 6, trans. V. E. Watts (1969), 70.

CHAPTER 35: ALL IS VANITY

1 Procopius, *History of the Wars*, Book 3.XIV, trans. Dewing (1914).
2 Evagrius Scholasticus, *The Ecclesiastical History of Evagrius,* trans. Walford, 2008, 24. See also Marcellinus Comes 92.6–10 (referring to the AD 557 event).
3 For an extremely helpful account of the inscriptions and history of Lepcis see http://inslib.kcl.ac.uk/irt2009/introductions/I3_lepcismagna.html
4 Rosen (2008), 138. Lounghis (2010).
5 Procopius, *History of the Wars* 4.
6 Hachlili (1998), 312.
7 Procopius, *History of the Wars* 4.9, trans. Dewing (1914): 'And there were slaves in the triumph, among whom was Gelimer himself, wearing some sort of a purple garment upon his shoulders, and all his family, and as many of the Vandals as were very tall and fair of body. And when Gelimer

reached the hippodrome and saw the emperor sitting upon a lofty seat and the people standing on either side and realized as he looked about in what an evil plight he was, he neither wept nor cried out, but ceased not saying over in the words of the Hebrew scripture: "Vanity of vanities, all is vanity" [Ecclesiastes 1: 2].'

8   Amory (1997), 10–12.

9   The church was founded by Pope Pelagius I (556–62) and was said to be built with funds from Narses. Webb (2001), 154.

10 The Avars would go on to capture Sirmium in AD 582.

11 Excavations around the former lighthouse (fifth/sixth century) have uncovered a thin black line running around the bottom of the building. Ufuk Kocabaş suggests that it is a tsunami line: this tallies with evidence for a major earthquake around the mid-sixth century. Other evidence shows another tsunami (or at least serious 'tempest') around AD 1000. There is near-certainty that a major quake will occur in the area within approximately the next thirty years. This is unsurprisingly on the minds of archaeologists and those engineers who have constructed the sub-Bosphoran tunnel.

12 Bony, Marriner, Morhange, Kaniewski and Perinçek (2011).

13 Cf. http://www.saudiaramcoworld.com/issue/200901/uncovering.yenikapi.htm.

14 John Malalas, *Chronicle* 385, trans. Jeffreys et al. (1986).

15 John of Ephesus, *Commentary* fr. II. F p. 232 lines 18–21; cf. also Procopius, *History of the Wars* II.14.6.

16 See Kölb-Ebert (2009).

17 Stathakopoulos (2004); Little (ed.) (2008); and for interest Rosen (2008).

18 Figures for the city at the time vary – some estimate that deaths totalled 112,500 out of a population of 400,000; but certainly between 20 and 25 per cent of the population died.

19 Justinian, *Novels* 63, trans. from Freely (1998).

20 Paul the Silentiary, 'On a High House in Constantinople', trans. Paton (1917), 361.

21 Agathias Scholasticus, 'On a House situated on a Hill in Constantinople', trans. Paton (1917), 361–2.

CHAPTER 36: THE SILKWORM'S JOURNEY

1   Bishop Liutprand of Cremona, envoy of Otto I, had silks inspected by officials when leaving Constantinople. Liutprand of Cremona, *The Embassy to Constantinople and Other Writings*, trans. Wright (1993), 202–3. Harris (2007), 115–16.

2   *Chiu-t'ang-shu*, ch. 198, in Hirth (1885).

3 'Nestorian' is a pejorative term but has been used here because it appears so regularly in primary and secondary sources. My thanks to Martin Palmer for his help with this chapter – who has advised against use of the term.

4 Here and in the following six paragraphs I have relied heavily on Muthesius (1995).

5 Procopius, *History of the Wars* 1.20.9, trans. Dewing (1914).

6 *The Book of the Eparch* (AD 912) shows the way in which the guilds of Constantinople were regulated: silk production in particular was centralised and its export fiercely guarded, but still there were satellite cities – Athens, Thebes and Corinth – where the silk production became increasingly important. Initially fiercely controlled by the state, from the tenth century private guilds (five in Constantinople itself) were also allowed to produce.

7 *Jewish Encyclopedia,* ed. Jacobs, Broydé and Gottheil (1901–6)

8 From the *Chiu-t'ang-shu*, ch. 198, in Hirth (1885).

9 See Thierry and Morrisson (1994).

10 Nestorios' ideas seemed to speak clearly to those who were experiencing Christianity in a physical and intimate way – in particular the monks of the eastern deserts. Nestorios himself had been exiled to the testing climate of the Upper Egyptian desert.

11 Some missionaries seem to have travelled along a northerly route circumventing the Taklamakan desert.

12 61-folio MIK III/45. Thank you to Dr Lilla Russell Smith for her help with this.

13 Gregory of Nazianzus, *De Vita Sua*, trans. Meehan (1987), 133–5. On the 'Nestorians' – (see Palmer) Church of the East – 'The Jesus Sutras', additional and very useful treatment is to be found in Gilman and Klimkeit (1999).

14 I made a trip across distinctive Chinese landscapes to the Beilin Museum in Xian to see this extraordinary artefact. But as with much of life and much of history, I should have looked under my nose first. In west London I had often noticed the Ancient Assyrian Church of the East on the corner of Temple Road in Ealing close to my childhood dentist. A tiny fragment of the Middle East here sits next to Roddy's Bar, an Irish pub. Under a semi-permanent gazebo, damply trying to replicate the feel of the backstreets of the Middle East, men huddle and chat around faded red tablecloths and well-used ashtrays. Many speak Aramaic. Indeed our local vicar and the barber have animated Aramaic conversations. The last hereditary patriarch of the Ancient Assyrian Church, Mar Eshai, was assassinated in California in 1975, and this congregation of the Nestorian faithful, the rump of what was once the Eastern Church, now numbers no more than a few thousand, globally. The Aramaic stories of these exiles from Iraq, who still talk of the earthly humanity of Jesus, of Nestorios, the theologian exiled from

Constantinople, and of his bold, lonely decision, are a reminder that civilisations may rise and fall, but that ideas and stories have a remarkable
tenacity.

15 Thank you again to Martin Palmer for his help with this material.

16 Menander the Guardsman, fr. 19.1, trans. Blockley (1985), 173–5.

17 John of Ephesus, *Ecclesiastical History* 6.24.

18 The first mention of 'the Turks' is debated e.g. Sima Qian (Chinese historian, 163–c.90 BC): 'the Xiongnu constituted a powerful and united nation,
with the result that it was not until a hundred years later that the Chinese
were able to strengthen their position in the western region.' ref. Grousset
(1970), 20. These men are recorded in a history book, *Book of Han*, one of
twenty-four books of Chinese history in a collection called *The Records of
the Grand Historian*. For more information see Nienhause (2011).

CHAPTER 37: AL-QUSTANTINIYYA

1 Ahmad ibn-Jabir al-Baladhuri, *Kitab Futuh al-Buldha*, trans. Hitti and
Murgotten (1916 and 1924), 207–11.

2 L. Sternbach, *Analecta Avarica* 304.9–13, as quoted in Herrin (1987), 199.

3 It is interesting that Herakleios' wife, Fabia, the daughter of a North African landowner, took the name Eudokia when she became empress – Latin
was on the wane and Greek was very definitely in favour.

4 Jordanes, *The Origin and Deeds of the Goths* 35. Early references to the Slavs
can be found in the works of Procopius of Caesarea and Jordanes. Procopius' *The Wars of Justinian* contains no fewer than forty-one references to
them.

5 Herakleios built new walls around the weak point of the city at Blachernae.

6 Nikephoros, *Short History* 12, trans. Mango (1990), 55–7.

7 Sura (30) al-Rum. 'Surat al-Ram is a Meccan sura (a section of the Qur'an)
which, according to the chronological classification of Theodor Noldeke,
Geschichte des Qorans, belongs to the third Meccan period. According to
Montgomery Watt's *Muhammad's Mecca: A History in the Qur'an* (Edinburgh: Edinburgh Univ. Press, 1988), 13–14, the brevity of these initial
verses suggests that the passage may be of an even earlier date, with verses
1–5 perhaps being separate from the rest of the sara. El Cheikh (1998), 356 n.
3. The third Meccan period ends at the Hijrah (622) and Herakleios fought
the Persians between AD 622 and 628, so for it to be a 'prophecy' it would
need to be delivered in advance.

8 Sura 30: 1–5.

9 Documents in one sura of the proto-Qur'an take note of these defeats, but
Muhammad makes it clear that the defeats will be reversed – monotheism

need not fear if good Christians, Jews and the new brotherhood of Islam could live happily alongside one another. The monastery at Sinai was protected, it was declared, by a letter personally written by the Prophet Muhammad. Whether or not this was true, it shows the power both of the character and of written documents at this time. Note that the work of Ibn Rustah (a Persian explorer and geographer) becomes the basis of the canonical text for Muslims with regard to Constantinople.

10 Crowley (2008), 1–2: 'To the Ottoman Turks of the fourteenth and fifteenth centuries it was "a bone in the throat of Allah".'

CHAPTER 38: A BONE IN THE THROAT OF ALLAH

1 See Crowley (2006), 629–717.

2 'The Arab Monophysite Christian ruler, Harith b. Jabala, from the Ghassanid tribe, had been appointed by Justinian in the early sixth century to police the Byzantine border with the Bedouin Arabs in the peninsula. Around the year AD 529 Harith came to Constantinople to discuss the succession in his kingdom. He created a powerful impression on the city at large and on the emperor's nephew Justinus in particular. According to John of Ephesus, years later when Justinus had fallen into his dotage and began to rave and his chamberlains wanted to frighten him, they would simply threaten that Harith would come to attack him.' Hillenbrand (2009), 71.

3 Thank you for the following helpful explanation from Professor David Thomas of the University of Birmingham: 'Among the Sunni Hadith collections, six are given special status, al-Bukhari, Muslim ibn Hajjaj, al-Tirmidhi, Abu Dawud, al-Nasa'i and Ibn Maja, and among these the two collections of al-Bukhari and Muslim are accepted by Muslims as totally reliable because they contain only Hadiths that can indisputably be traced to Muhammad himself – needless to say, non-Muslim scholars do not accept this view, and there is general agreement that the historical reliability of any particular Hadith requires establishing before it can be accepted, if at all.'

The Arabic word *Rum* is usually translated as 'Byzantine' or 'Byzantium', and usually refers to the Eastern Romans, or to the empire, so care is needed when trying to interpret passages containing this term. al-Qustantiniyya will almost certainly be a reference to the city itself. See early Islamic authors on Constantinople in Thomas and Mallett (2010), vol. 2, 19–21.

4 E.g. John I Tzimiskes (tenth century AD) '"raised the cross-standard", prayed for divine favour at the Chalke shrine and continued to the Hagia Sophia, where he beseeched God to send an angel of victory "who would walk in front of the army and straighten its path". Then the emperor participated

in a liturgical procession to the Blachernae shrine and the final service.' McCormick (1990), 249.

5 Hillenbrand (2015), 29. Holland (2013), 333.

6 Conversation with Yusuf Islam (Cat Stevens), Royal Geographical Society, London, April 2015.

7 Words spoken by Mughira b. Shu'ba as quoted in Crone (1987), 246.

8 See Frankopan (2015), 74.

9 Detailed and extremely helpful estimates of troop format, numbers and weaponry can be found in Nicolle (1994).

10 This is an investigation that is still unfolding – newly discovered documents hint at this possibility. See e.g. Hoyland (2000), esp. 277–81.

11 See discussion of alternatives, Christians remembering Jews were to be kept out, in Frenkel (2011), 97.

12 For disussion see Kalegi (2007).

13 Greek Fire was extensively used by Byzantium at the time of the Arab attacks. See Hall (1999), xxi.

14 Translation from Olster (1995), 23–4.

15 Haldon (1990), 45–8, 59–60.

16 Quoted in Frankopan (2015), 80. Dagron and Déroche, 'Juifs et Chrétiens', 240–7.

17 Hoyland (1999), 158–9.

18 Imam Ahmad b. Hanbal, Awwal Musnad al-Kufiyyin, No. 18189. C855. See Fleming (2003).

CHAPTER 39: MONKS BY NIGHT AND LIONS BY DAY

1 Ibrahim (2013).

2 Quoted in Frankopan (2015), 84.

3 See Frankopan (2015), 88–9.

4 John Freely points out that at the Greek Apokreas and feast of St John Kynegos the Hunter, clear vestiges of these pagan rituals still remain in evidence today.

5 Flood in Evans and Ratliff (eds) (2012), 252; see also 253–4.

6 See Flood (2001), 163–83, 228–33.

7 Alain George (2009).

8 Evans and Ratliff (eds) (2012), 221–2; see 45–50 for the Grado chair.

9 Evans, Holcomb and Hallman (2001).

10 See also an early Islamic bronze ewer from Iran in the Hermitage Museum: al-Khamis (1998). And stamped jar handles from Jerusalem and Tell Qatra (excavated 2005–6): Taxel (2009).

11 Damascus is a contender for one of the oldest permanently occupied cities

in the world (another is Byblos/Gebal where several neolithic and chalcolithic burials have been discovered). It flourished from the first millennium
BC, although fringed by a series of smaller developments in the wider
Barada basin reaching back to at least 9000 BC. With the expansion of
Islam, Damascus was reinvigorated. Much of what remains of Damascus
today is based on a Roman design; up until the twelfth century sections
of the Roman wall were still standing, and streets were orientated north–
south, east–west following a Greek plan. NB See Ross Burns, who points
out that (along with the tombs of the caliphs) the Roman walls were early
targets during the Abbasid invasion of AD 750. Burns (2005), 2. Vallois, H.
V. (1937), 'Note sur les ossements humains de la nécropole énéolithique de
Byblos (avec 2 planches)', El-Cheikh (2004), 60–81.

12 Brackets that surround not a clause but an entire volume of civilisation's
history.

13 The Golden Horn is in fact the estuary of the rivers named, in modern
Turkish, Alibeyköy and Kağithane. The Golden Horn is spanned by five
bridges and houses the broken remains of the old Galata Bridge.

CHAPTER 40: BYZANTIUM AND BRITANNIA

1 Chrétien de Troyes, *Cligès*, trans. Carroll and Kibler (1991), c. AD 1176.

2 'For on the same day that this blessed man took his departure from this
life to go to his Lord, one of those who have practised the angelic way of
living and follow the monastic discipline, an admirable and virtuous man,
Sabinus by name, living in Alexandria, fell, as it were, into an ecstasy and
saw John, honoured of God, come out of his own palace with all the clergy,
bearing candles and going to the king, as, said he, a eunuch chamberlain
had summoned him.' *Life of John of Cyprus* 46, trans. Dawes and Baynes
(1948), 260.

3 See arguments in Harris (2003), passim.

4 St Just's in Cornwall could well be named for the fourth-century bishop
Justus from Lyon who continued his devotion as a hermit in the Eastern
Mediterranean.

5 Many thanks to Dr Helen Geake for her help with this chapter. For ongoing work at Rendlesham see Scull et al. (2016) and Minter et al. (2014).

6 Many thanks to Professor Christopher Scull and to Faye Minter from the
Suffolk County Council Archaeological Service for their help with the
Rendlesham material in this chapter.

7 Sutton Hoo is the name of an estate near Sutton; the burial site was named
after this estate. See *Beowulf*, 'Lay of the Last Survivor' (lines 2247–66),
which mentions the great treasures laid to rest with a great King.

8 See Bintley (2011).

9 In this chapter I have relied heavily on my own site visits to Sutton Hoo and Tintagel and on Harris (2003).

10 See Geake (1999).

11 See Marzinzik (2008). Jacoby (2004).

12 Jacoby (2004), 198–240.

13 A connection particularly strong in the west of Britain – just remember that extravagant storeroom of pottery at Tintagel.

14 Byzantine silks were sold to travellers from Britain in Rome. Liu (1996), 122; Dodwell (1982), 150–1.

15 The Collectio Avellana, after a 12th-century manuscript from the library of the Monastery of Santa Croce at Fonte Avellana, Umbria, Italy. Alexander Evers & Bernard Stolte (eds), *Religion, Power, and Politics: Bishops, Emperors, and Senators in the Collectio Avellana, 367-553 AD* (Leuven: Peeters Publishers, forthcoming).

16 As Tacitus first described Britannia in *Agricola* ch. 8.

17 Jacoby (2008). A. Muthesius, 'From Seed to Samite: Aspects of Byzantine Silk Production' and 'Constantinople and its Hinterland: Issues of Raw Silk Supply', in Muthesius (ed.) (1995), 119–34 and 315–35.

CHAPTER 41: ICONS AND ICONOCLASM

1 St. John of Damascus, *On the Divine Images* III. 12. 72, trans. Kotter (1969-88), III, 123–4.

2 *Doctor Zhivago* (1958), trans. Hayward and Harari (1958).

3 Either AD 726 or 730. Brubaker (2010), 326.

4 Some 40,000 priests and 40,000 monks and nuns also died in the Soviet terror.

5 For additional information see Cutler (2002), 565–9; Cormack (2007), ch. 2, 'How to Make an Icon'.

6 The list comes from Cormack (2007), ch. 2, on which I have relied heavily in this paragraph.

7 Theophanes, *Chronographia* 472, trans. Psellus and Sewter (1979).

8 Treadgold (1988), 224.

9 From when Justinian sent his patriarch Eutychios into exile, a great many members of the imperial court ended up on the Princes' Islands: Eirene was exiled here, to her own monastery on Prinkipo, before moving on to Lesbos, and Romanus IV was blinded and then exiled to a monastery on Proti where he later died. Brubaker and Haldon (2011), 297. Freely (1998a), 131.

10 Quoted in Silvas (2006), 23.

11   Ibid. 25.
12   Ibid. (2006).

CHAPTER 42: VIKING FOE-FRIENDS AND THE BIRTH OF RUSSIA

1   Rǫgnvaldr jarl Kali Kolsson, *Lausavísur*, 31.2 (ed. Judith Jesch) https://
    www.abdn.ac.uk/skaldic/m.php?i=3632&p=verse. See also http://www.
    abdn.ac.uk/skaldic/db.php?id=1916&if=default&table=verses&val=edition.
2   Snorri Sturluson, *Heimskringla, or The Chronicle of the Kings of Norway*,
    trans. Hollander (2010).
3   Thomov (2014).
4   Thank you to Judith Jesch, Professor of Viking Studies, Nottingham Uni-
    versity for her assiduous help with this chapter and to Gareth Williams for
    the many conversations we had about the Vikings in conjunction with the
    British Museum's *Vikings: Life and Legend* exhibition, 6 March–22 June
    2014.
5   Many of us, much of the time, could be treading in Viking footsteps. Take
    the Silverdale Hoard: 200-plus pieces of silver jewellery – finger-rings,
    arm-rings, currency, coins of the Kings Alfred the Great and Harthacnut,
    Christian symbols, Carolingian, Anglo-Saxon and Viking styles coexisting
    in one superb silver bracelet – and all discovered in 2011 by a local metal
    detectorist, after a mere twenty minutes scanning one field.
6   Jeremiah 6:22–3, ed. AV.
7   As Judith Jesch points out, the name Viking can also be simply a conven-
    ient term of reference for modern historians: see Jesch (2015), 4–8.
8   For an alternative interpretation of Beserrkers see recent work by Ruar-
    igh Dale, e.g. http://blogs.nottingham.ac.uk/wordsonwords/2014/03/11/
    the-viking-berserker/.
9   A phrase shared with me by Gareth Williams, Curator of Early Medieval
    Coinage at the British Museum.
10 See e.g. Henning (2008).
11 The trade in slaves from Scandinavia to Byzantium was thought to balance
    East–West imports and exports, 'stopping or even reversing the flow of silver
    and gold that had been leaving the western economy'. Winroth (2004), 126.
    A slave woman could be taken as a concubine and if she lived with her
    master until his death, she would be freed along with any children they had
    together. Phillips (1985), 37. As Youval Rotman has written, 'captives are not
    considered booty, and the strategos must keep them with him or take them
    to the emperor for a possible exchange of prisoners of war'. Rotman (2009),
    37 – referring to the probably eighth-century *Leges Militares*.
12 More frequently *khasi* or *majbub*.

13   Liutprand of Cremona in Henderson (1910), 440–77. Liutprand's report from Constantinople is translated in Henderson's appendix.

14   Both Scandinavian sagas and poetry speak of boats as 'chariots of the ocean' and the captain as 'the god of the ship'. Longships bear names such as *Sea Brave* and the *Sea Stallion of Glendalough*, while their movement across the sea's surface is compared to the flight of birds.

15   The ship, known as *Roskilde 6*, was probably built in Ireland in c. AD 1025, repaired in the Baltic around 1039, broken up and buried twenty years later. Ships were the engine of Viking culture, but they also served as graves, as floating battle-grounds and as a cultural touchstone. Ship-themed games of strength and skill were devised – poems describe Viking heroes balancing all the way along a single oar from port to starboard; toddlers' toys were made in the shape of miniature boats; mournful headstones memorialising the craft that went down with all hands remind us that on the ocean beds there is still waiting, undisturbed, a submerged museum of the Viking experience.

16   The Vikings wore their trading, globe-trotting hearts on their sleeves. Exotically worked metal (sporting, for example, Persian designs) was displayed prominently on neck- or arm-rings, visible proof that the successful Viking man was a cosmopolitan creature. Women (we see from their grave-goods in Finland) wore beads decorated with the Islamic silver coins known as dirhams. Arabic writers note that the Rus made neck-torques for their wives whenever they acquired a certain level of wealth.
     Viking history reminds us of the centrality of riverine and maritime travel in the story of civilisation. Even in prehistory, the sea – and the men who conquer it – are celebrated, their achievements fetishised. The Bronze Age epics from Homer's Mediterranean *Odyssey* to the Mesopotamian *Epic of Gilgamesh* are sprayed with nautical imagery. These sea-stories would have washed around village squares and the halls of great palaces alike.

17   Wren and Stults (1994), 57.

18   Raffensperger (2012), 159–61.

19   *Russian Primary Chronicle*, trans. Cross and Sherbowitz-Wetzor (1953), 86. For material here I have relied heavily on Frankopan (2015).

20   Vikings raided Muslim traders on the Caspian Sea until they were 'gorged with loot and worn out with trading'. But then the Fatimids rose to power in North Africa and the Vikings diplomatically refocused their attention on their original field of influence – the Dnieper and the Dniester Rivers (with the odd exception such as the possibility of that permanent Viking settlement on the Persian Gulf). By the second half of the eleventh century, Harold II, King of England, killed at Hastings, would be marrying his daughter Gytha to the Grand Prince of Kiev.

21   Isitt (2007).

22 Madgerau (2013), 103–4. Yotov (2008).
23 Quoted in Ciggaar (1996), 107.

CHAPTER 43: WITHIN THE WALLS

1 *Indications sur les lieux de Pèlerinage*, ed. Schefer (1881), 589.
2 Al-Jahiz, *Kitab al-Hayawan*, in *Medieval Islamic Medicine,* trans. Pormann and Savage-Smith (2007) 23.
3 With grateful thanks to Professor Camp for access to the Agora digs in Athens.
4 See Lingas (2008).
5 In AD 762 Al-Mansur, advised it was said by Nestorian monks, had started to found his circular city Baghdad on the banks of the Tigris (the encircling walls survived until they were demolished by an Ottoman reformer in 1870).
6 Greek text from J. Koder, 'Zu den Versinschriften der Limburger Staurothek', *AmrhKg* 37 (1985), trans. Featherstone (2012) 11–31.
7 See the fascinating article Pentcheva (2007).
8 Thomas and Hero (2000), vol. 1, ch. 18.
9 Anna Komnene's *Alexiad* Book VI reveals her views on astrology and contemporary astrologers. See too Niketas Choriates, *Annals.* Manuel I Komnenos (reigned 1143–80) supported the translation of occult literature in his court; he composed a 'defence of astrology' suggesting it was compatible with Christian doctrine. See George (2001a) and (2001b).
10 Al-Muqaddasi, *Best Division of Knowledge*, trans. Collins (2001).
11 While anxiety was swirling about how to deal with religious images there were decidedly stranger goings-on in the city. Just think of those occultists, magicians, alchemists, dream-diviners, interpreters of the voices of statues, bird-seers, geomancers, demonologists, masters of the apocryphal whom we know still operated vigorously. Byzantine astrology peaked in the thirteenth century; even when in decline, the reading of celestial omens was still practised.
   So Euclid, Aristotle, Euripides went from Byzantine libraries on to the desks of Arabic translators and scholars. Later al-Jazari would use the work of Archimedes, Apollonius et al. in his *Book of Contrivances* (a stark contrast with the neglect of many these ideas and inventions in the West – resonantly commented on as early as Cicero, who visited Archimedes' overgrown grave). Fashions became the thing; after experimenting with cobalt in Basra and Samarra, a distinctive blue and white fine-ware was produced that would then end up actively recognisable in China. Madrasas developed – a form of teaching and learning inspired by Buddhist monks and

their monasteries. Madrasas were vigorously promoted by the Samanids in Bukhara in Uzbekistan who also patronised research into the collection of sayings known as the hadiths. Correspondence between the patriarch of Constantinople and the Caliph indicates that lines of communication were fully open. See correspondence cited in Meyendorff (1964).

Coincidentally, the city of Athens protects another piece of evidence that speaks of the relationship between this Christian city and her Muslim neighbours at the time: in the city of Tigrit – now famous as the birthplace of Saddam Hussein – once stood a grand palace. This was the Samarra Palace, its inner rooms protected by fine doors, carved in teak and decorated with vines. The doors have ended up somewhere a little unexpected, down the backstreets of Athens, at the point in the Plaka where shops become a flea market, in a neo-classical building overlooking the ancient burial ground, the *kerameikos*. Their journey to Greece started when they were whisked away to cover coffins in a rock-cut tomb, where two bishops, Athanasios and Ignatios, lay buried. The relationship between Christians and Muslims at this time was not just suspicious, not just antagonistic, but organic.

12 al-Ya'qubi and al-Baladhuri cited by Banaji (2007), esp. 59–60.

13 Frankopan (2015), 94.

14 But it was now recognised that Byzantium provided an essential bulwark against the Arab threat. Bari became the centre of Byzantine administration in the south. The Roman Empire in the West still needed the East whether as a mediator, procurer or shield. And despite Byzantium's rage at Venetian flirtation with Arab merchants (supplying them with raw materials – iron and timber for their arms trade, the construction of ships and weapons) a document of AD 992 bears witness to a joint understanding: favourable trading conditions in return for Italian troops should the Byzantine empire need them.

CHAPTER 44: THE VARANGIAN GUARD

1 Orderic Vitalis, *The Ecclesiastical History* 4.2.172. The translation used is based on M. Chibnall's trans. *The Ecclesiastical History of Orderic Vitalis*, vol. 2, 203 and 205.

2 Nikephoros Bryennios the Younger (Anna Komnene's husband), *History*, trans. Mango (1990).

3 Dawkins (1947).

4 *The Chronicle of Matthew of Edessa*, Part 1, 39, trans. and ed. Dostourian (1993). Matthew was himself an Armenian.

5 'On the feast of the Ascension of the Saviour, when the emperor was in the usual manner taking part in a procession outside the walls . . . (where

the very beautiful church was built in honour of the Virgin), a fight broke out between some Byzantines and Armenians, in which many of the townspeople were injured by the Armenians.' *Leo the Deacon*, Book IV. The translation used is based on A. M. Maffry Talbot and D. F. Sullivan's trans. *The History of Leo the Deacon: Byzantine Military Expansion in the Tenth Century*, 113.

6 From *The Saga of Harald Sigurtharson* in Snorri Sturluson, *Heimskringla*. An alternative translation can be found in Finlay and Faulkes (2016). Another reference to Constantinople in the *Heimskringla* is:

> Fresh gales drove out gallant
> galley scurrying shoreward –
> with armored prows and poops our
> proud ships rode to harbor.
> Of Miklagarth the golden
> gables our famous prince saw.
> Many a mere-ship fair-dight
> moved toward the high-walled city.

Found in Snorri Sturluson, *Heimskringla: History of the Kings of Norway*, trans. Hollander (1964), 579.

7 Cameron (2006), 43.

8 Orderic Vitalis, *The Ecclesiastical History* 4.2.172, trans. Chibnall: 'exules igitur Anglorum favorabiliter a Grecis suscepti sunt. et Normannicus legionibus quae nimium Pelasgis adversabantur oppositi sunt'.

9 See recent fascinating academic work by Thorgunn Snædal, 'Runes from Byzantium: reconsidering the Piraeus lion', in *Byzantium and the Viking World* (2016), 187–214.

10 Constable (2008), 227.

11 Orderic Vitalis, *The Ecclesiastical History* 4.2.172, trans. Chibnall.

12 See Shepard (1973), 60–77, and Fell (1974), 192–3.

13 Robert de Clari, *La Conquête de Constantinople*, in Historiens et Chroniqueurs de Moyan Age 57.

CHAPTER 45: A GREAT SCHISM?

1 Gibbon vol. 7, ch. 60: The Fourth Crusade – Part I.

2 Plato, *Phaedrus* 275d–e, Fowler, trans. (1925).

3 I have relied here heavily on Whalen (2007) and Chadwick (2005). See also Ryder (2011) and Kolbaba (2011).

4 See Jakobsson (2008).

5 Attaleiates (2012), ch. 15, sections 91 and 92. The fourth indiction is in fact 1065 not 1066.

6   Skylitzes 8 (Emperor Alexander). 3 trans. Wortley.

CHAPTER 46: 1071, 1081 AND ALL THAT

1   Anna Komnene, *The Alexiad* 1.10, trans. Sewter (2009), 30.
2   The Pechenegs would be defeated in AD 1091 only by the wide river mouth of the Maritsa River near the modern Turkish–Greek border (and when they were, the streets of Constantinople echoed to a new popular song 'Ten thousand Pechenegs will not wake up to see the first day of May').
3   Anna Komnene, *The Alexiad* 1.10, trans. Sewter (2009), 54.
4   Kulakovskij (1908), 1–58.
5   Quoted in Hillenbrand (2007), 55.
6   Anna Komnene, *The Alexiad* 1.10, trans. Sewter (2009), 13.
7   White (2013), 2.
8   Haldon (1999), 26.
9   Twelfth-century account by al-Turtushi (d. 520/1126) in *Sirāj al-mulūk*, quoted in Hillenbrand (2007), 27–8. NB numbers are exaggerated and differ in other accounts. Ibid., 38. 'The army of Byzantium was numerous and the total of those with the sultan approached twenty thousand. As for the king of Byzantium, he had with him thirty-five thousand Franks and thirty-five thousand . . . with two hundred generals and commanders; each of them had between two thousand and five hundred horsemen. He [also] had with him fifteen thousand Ghuzz who were [living] beyond Constantinople; and one hundred thousand sappers and diggers and one hundred thousand siege engineers and four hundred carts on which were weapons, saddles, ballistas and mangonels, amongst which was a mangonel drawn by one thousand, two hundred men.' Ibn al-Jawzi (d. 597/1200) in *Al-Muntaẓam fi taʾrīkh al-mulūk waʾl-umam*.
10 Rum was 'the Arabic and Persian term for Byzantium' – Hillenbrand (2007), 17. Persian was 'the court language of the Seljuqs' – ibid., 36.
11 Hillenbrand offers a wonderfully comprehensive analysis of both Muslim and Byzantine accounts of the conflict – and of its use as the basis for myth-making. Ibid.
12 See Crowley (2005), 25–6.
13 For a useful account of these sects see http://www.iranicaonline.org/articles/cathars-albigensians-and-bogomils

CHAPTER 47: THE CITY OF CRUSADES

1 Fulcher of Chartres, *A History of the Expedition to Jerusalem, 1095–1127,* trans. F. R. Ryan (1973). Fulcher (b. 1029) was a French priest and chronicler who participated in the First Crusade.

2 Berthold of Constance, *Die Chroniken Bertholds von Reichenau und Bernolds von Konstanz,* ed. Robinson (2003).

3 Anna Komnene, *The Alexiad* 10.5, trans. Sewter (2009).

4 Ibid.

5 Frankopan (2015), 136ff.

6 R. Irwin, 'Muslim Responses to the Crusades', *History Today* 47.4, April 1997.

7 Peter Frankopan has done much to rehabilitate Anna Komnene.

8 Robert of Clari, *The Conquest of Constantinople,* 75, trans. E. R. McNeal (2005). See also Laiou and Mottahedeh (eds) (2001); Hodgson (2005). See Guibert of Nogent, 192 and Peter Tudebode, *Historia de Hierosolimitano Itinere,* trans. John Hugh Hill and Laurita L. Hill [Memoirs of the American Philosophical Society] (Philadelphia: The Americal Philosophical Society, 1974), p. 55. *Gesta Francorum et aliorum Hierosolimitanorum,* ed. and trans. Rosalind Hill (Edinburgh: Thomas Nelson and Sons, 1962).

9 E.g. Simonis Angelina Antiochina.

10 Gillespie (2011), 133.

CHAPTER 48: NEGOTIATING MONKS AND HOMICIDAL USURPERS

1 Odo of Deuil, *De Profectione Ludovici VII in Orientem* (*Journey of Louis VII to the East*) (1147), Book 4. Latin: '*in omnibus modum excedit; nam sicut divitiis urbes alias superat, sic eitam vitiis*'.

2 Researching the state of the city at this time, as ever, I found J. Harris (2015) immensely helpful, esp. ch. 8.

3 Manganeois Prodomos quoted in Harris, J. (2014), 106.

4 A. Makrinos, s.v. Eustathius, in M. Finkelberg (2010) 278–9.

5 Niketas Choniates, funerary oration viii.238, x.334.

6 Eustathios, *On the Capture of Thessaloniki,* trans. Melville Jones (1988).

7 Ibid.

8 Benjamin of Tudela, *The Itinerary of Benjamin of Tudela,* trans. Adler (1907).

9 John Tzetzes, *Antehomerica, Homerica et Posthomerica* (1793).

10 Sicily mattered. From the time of Alcibiades' ill-fated Sicilian expedition in 415 BC the island's value as food-supplier and as a stepping-stone between Africa and Europe had been held in the collective memory. Since the loss of

Egypt this island (along with other territories in Africa) was bringing in the grain.

11 The Palazzo di San Giorgio in Genoa is partly made from the sacked Venetian Embassy in Constantinople. Marco Polo was imprisoned here. See Strathern (2012), 11.

12 Phillips (2004), xxii, William of Tyre.

CHAPTER 49: VENETIAN PERIL, CHIVALRIC KINGDOMS

1 Niketas Choniates, *Historia* 301.21, trans. Magoulias (1984). (Niketas was an eyewitness to the Fourth Crusade attack on Constantinople 1204.)

2 Geoffroy de Villehardouin, 'The Conquest of Constantinople', trans. Shaw (1985), 128.

3 Robert of Clari in P. Lauer (ed.) (1924), 72–3. Quoted in Frankopan (2015), 154.

4 Nicholas Mesarites, Funeral Oration in Brand (ed.) (1969), 131–2.

5 After the sack of Constantinople in AD 1204, clearly not coincidentally, skilled silk-workers appeared in Venice. Later that century the Mongols exported silk-workers in a similar way – both to hamstring the economies of the towns they were attacking and to gain their own supply of diplomatic gifts.

6 Madden (2003), 194. Of interest e.g. Staurotheca of Henry of Flanders (now in the Treasury of St Mark, Venice), made in Constantinople by Gerard before AD 1216 and said to contain pieces of the True Cross. See Buckton et al. (1984). There is more on Pantokrator and the Latin occupation in Jacoby (2001b). Taxidis (2013), 100 n. 18.

7 Gaborit-Chopin in Buckton et al. (1984), 244–51.

8 One fragment from the fifteenth century was drawn with true perspective. Most of the frescoes at the Chora Monastery date from Theodore Metochites' restoration project between around AD 1316 and 1321. Ousterhout (1995), 65–6.

9 Pincus (1992).

10 And now Constantinople would feel the fear of another threat – Genghis Khan from the East, the man who wanted to be a 'universal ruler'. See Frankopan (2015), e.g. 154ff., 175ff.

11 The Crusading knights had come both to destroy and to heal. The vast foundations of the hospital of St John in Jerusalem – large enough to accommodate 2,000 patients at any one time – are currently being re-excavated. Founded in AD 1180, this facility had been established to treat men of all faiths. Through the remains of a stone gateway and up winding wooden stairs in the heart of London next to the Priory Church of the Order of St

John we find what is, in some ways, the business end of the Order: a beautiful silver bowl. This, it would seem at first glance, should be destined for the tables of aristocrats – but no, the bowl was made for washing the feet of the poor, of Jews and Muslims as well as Christians. An inscription reminds us: 'The Lord, who does not want anyone to perish, mercifully admits men of the pagan [Muslim] faith and Jews . . . because Christ prayed for those afflicting him saying: "Father forgive them, they know not what they do." In this blessed house is powerfully fulfilled the heavenly doctrine . . . "Love your enemies and do good to those who hate you."' It is a strange fact that these men were theologically persuaded that their fighting too was an act of love. On paper it might have been possible (if a convoluted exercise in theological logic) to prove that this was a way to love God, but for the populations of the Middle East crusading aggression must have been very hard to appreciate as an incarnation of Christ's teaching that you should love your neighbour.

12 Georgius Pachymeres 4.529 in Kyriakidis (2011), 124.
13 Tacitus, *Agricola* 30 ('atque, ubi solitudinem faciunt, pacem appellant').
14 Sailing conditions were so favourable here and natural harbours so abundant that Rhodes evolved a sea law still used as precedent in international maritime negotiations.
15 Nicolle (2007).
16 Fric, Portolous, Manolopoulos and Kastritis (2012), 151.
17 See Frankopan (2015), 157ff.
18 Ramon Muntaner, *The Catalan Expedition to the East: From the Chronicle of Ramon Muntaner*, trans. Hughes (2006), 46, 49.

CHAPTER 50: YILDIRIM: THE THUNDERBOLT

1 Creasy (1854), 10–11.
2 Osman's name originally may have been Atman (also given as Otman) Ghazi.
3 There are interesting parallels here with the dream that William the Conqueror's mother was said to have had when she carried him.
4 'Aşıkpaşazade, *Chronik*, bab 18, p. 23. Quoted in Boyar and Fleet (2010), 20.
5 Recent studies have shown that the prevalence of the plague gerbil could have been escalated by 50 per cent with just a 1 per cent rise in temperature. See Stenseth et al. (2006).
6 Doukas, *Historia*, p. 34; Doukas, *Decline*, p. 73. Quoted in Boyar and Fleet (2010), 21.
7 Ibid.
8 Hilsdale (2014), 1–2. Also see Cavafy trans. Sachperoglou (2009), 153.

9 Doukas, *Historia* and *Decline*. Quoted in Boyar and Fleet (2010), 21.

10 See discussions of date in e.g. Zachariadou (1970), 211–17.

11 Words of Çandarli Kara Halil.

12 In vast numbers since the collapse of the Mongol Empire; within a century and a half 120 metric tonnes of silk would be passing through the town.

13 Forthcoming. Ongoing analysis.

14 Bogdanovićc (2012), 187–202. Ganchou (2010), 277–359.

15 Inalcik and Oğuz (eds.) (1978), *Gazavât-i Sultân Murâd b. Mehemmed Hân Izaldi ve Varna Savaslari* (1443–4), *Üzerine Anonim Gazavâtnâme*, 15a.

16 Thessalonika had already welcomed the Ottomans in once before in AD 1387.

17 With thanks to Professor Barbara Graziosi for help with this enquiry; see e.g. Graziosi (2013).

18 The ambition that would become the façade of Santa Maria Novella – to be realised by Leon Battista Alberti – was discussed here; and the San Marco Altarpiece by Fra Angelico was designed here. The *Journey of the Magi* fresco in the Magi Chapel (by Benozzo Gozzoli, AD 1459–61), which was said to depict the arrival of dignitaries in Florence for the Council, shows Balthazar as resembling the Byzantine Emperor John VIII Palaiologos. Cardini (2001), 31. For a different opinion see Acidini Luchinat (ed.) (1993), 126.

19 At the Council of Ferrara in AD 1438 (the convention was moved to Florence in 1439 because of a plague scare), which effected a brief union of Western and Eastern churches, papal supremacy was reconfirmed: 'We likewise define that the holy Apostolic See, and the Roman Pontiff, hold the primacy throughout the entire world; and that the Roman Pontiff himself is the successor of blessed Peter, the chief of the Apostles, and the true vicar of Christ, and that he is the head of the entire Church, and the father and teacher of all Christians; and that full power was given to him in blessed Peter by our Lord Jesus Christ, to feed, rule, and govern the universal Church.' Quoted in Brandmüller (2009), 36. Those who decried the union back in Constantinople sparked rioting on the streets. Bowls of wine were carried from home to home in religious-themed protest. Byzantine delegates who visited Venice at this time of course recognised all that loot from their city, which had been much mourned when it was snatched and dragged away in 1204. On the Bull of Union of 1439 the signature of the Emperor John VIII Palaiologos is clearly visible in a distinctive red ink – the black counter-signatures of bishops and papal staff crowd around like spiders. The British Library were kind enough to show me this manuscript – Bull of Union, Florence, 6 July 1439. Cotton MS Cleopatra E. iii, ff. 80v–81r. in British Library Programme 'Two thousand years of Greek Manuscripts', 10 June 2014.

20 Tursun Bey (1978), *History* f. 35b. Quoted in Boyar and Fleet (2010), 13.

CHAPTER 51: NO COUNTRY FOR OLD MEN

1 Doukas, *Fragmenta Historicorum Graecorum*, quoted in Crowley (2005), 97.
2 There has been much conjecture over the source of this poem and whether Mehmed II repeats the verse word for word (the line taken by Gibbon and others) or extemporises (the line taken by Cantemir and Tursun). The original seems to be Ferdowsi's account of the night attack on Afrasiyab by Rustam (*Shah-Nama* x.18) Ferdowsi (2016), 18. However, there is no word for 'spider' in the main concordance for this work. This is probably why the poem is also attributed to Saadi and even Rumi, both of whom mention spiders in other works.
3 Experienced by the author May 2013.
4 See: Crowley (2005).
5 A phrase popular in accounts of the siege from the sixteenth to twentieth centuries.
6 'Aşıkpaşazade, *Chronik, bab* 123, 132. Quoted in Boyar and Fleet (2010), 11.
7 Boyar and Fleet (2010), 18.
8 Kritoboulos, *History of Mehmed the conqueror*, Hans. Riggs (1954).
9 Grant by Mehmed II to the Genoese of Galata, Constantinople, 1 June 1453. Egerton MS 2817, see British Library Programme 'Two thousand years of Greek Manuscripts', 10 June, 2014.
10 Embassies were established here – the Swedish Palace (now the Consulate but originally the Embassy) opened in AD 1757 is Sweden's oldest state-owned property abroad. This is a district that would, for the next 500 years, be a centre of international intelligence.
11 Steffano Infessura, *Diario della Città di Roma* (1890). See also Stetton (1978).
12 Melvile Jones (ed. and trans.) (1972), 54.
13 Bisaha (2004b), in Housley (ed.), 39–52; Bisaha (2004); Meserve (2006), 440–80.

CHAPTER 52: TWILIGHT CITY

1 *Gesta Francorum et Aliorum Hierosolimitanorum*, (ed. and trans.) R. Hill (1962) 3, 21.
2 Demanded by Bayezid at the end of the fourteenth century. Reported by Doukas. Cited in Necipoğlu (2009), 138–9.
3 Sphrantezes, *Chronicles* 16 (VII.3).

4 See work by Dr Ionna Sitaridou (2011–16), *The Romeyka Project*. For more information on this and other exceptional projects see, Cambridge Group for Endangered Languages and Cultures, Cambridge University.
5 George of Trebizond. Quoted in Goodwin (1999).
6 Niketas, trans. Magoulias (1984).

CHAPTER 53: THE ABODE OF FELICITY

1 Necipoğlu (1992), 163, 8.
2 See e.g. M. Canard, 'Les Expéditions des Arabes contre Constantinople dans l'histoire et dans les légendes', *Journal Asiatique* (1926), 61–121.
3 Tursun Bey, *Tarih*, 41. Quoted in Boyar and Fleet (2010), 12.
4 Called after a palace with the same name, meaning 'Cannon Gate', a structure long since gone, destroyed in a fire during Mahmud I's reign.
5 List from Taylor (2010), a delightful companion guide for time spent in Istanbul.
6 See Necipoğlu (1993), passim.
7 Freely (1998a) is plump with diverting details such as this.
8 Inalcik (2012).

CHAPTER 54: ONE GOD IN HEAVEN, ONE EMPIRE ON EARTH

1 Setton (1984), vol. 3, 172. Quoted in Frankopan (2015).
2 Allen (1938), 254 and Tracy (2002), 27.
3 See Inalcik (1990), 1–23 passim.
4 Doukas, *Historia*, 306; Doukas, *Decline*, 235. Quoted in Boyar and Fleet (2010), 10.
5 Kritoboulos, *History*, trans. Rigg (1954), 105.
6 As discussed, many assert that the name Istanbul in fact derives from *eis ten polin* – the Greek for into the city.
7 See e.g. Alexander (2006).
8 Quoted in Wasti (2005).
9 Gibb (1882), 'Ottoman Poems', 33.
10 Although a change of faith did result, the first official recognition of the Sultan as Caliph would have to wait a further 250 years when, as the Ottomans were losing territory to the Russians, the caliphate claim was thought to buttress their spiritual heft.
11 Here I have relied heavily on Kuban (2010).
12 Boyar and Fleet (2016), 14.

13 Gamm, *Hurriyet Daily News*.

14 Haghia Eirene had been a depot for military equipment from AD 1703. In 1730 during the reign of Sultan Ahmed III it was converted into a weapons museum, with antiquities being formally collected from 1846.

15 An extant stone building from the fifteenth century on the edge of the hippodrome reminds us that a sign of status at this time was how far the harem could be situated from the general quarters – ideally beyond three courtyards, each of them guarded. This was a distance, it now seems, that allowed the early female inhabitants of Istanbul time and space to shape the city without. Many domestic buildings in the city centre were now constructed by the Ottoman inhabitants using mudbrick or cement and rubble. The single surviving example of architecture from the sixteenth century, facing on to the hippodrome, is now a museum; it has lasted only because it was, unusually, built in stone.

16 Hamidullah (1973), 36.

CHAPTER 55: RENAISSANCE CITY

1 Tursun Bey (1978), f. 63a. Quoted in Boyar and Fleet (2010), 27.

2 Translation from the Turkish by Ilker Evrim Binbaş of Royal Holloway, University of London. With thanks to Professor Martin Kemp for his help with this chapter.

3 The destruction of a few of the remaining trees in 2013 sparked the protests in Gezi Park and Taksim Square. Collective memory perhaps of this city as a place of wood and water?

4 Examples all discussed at some length in Brotton (2002).

5 Boyar and Fleet (2010), 48ff. I have relied heavily on this work here.

6 See e.g. d'Ohsson (1824); Pakalin (1971).

7 Düzbakar (2006), 14.

8 Baer (2004), 159–81.

9 Necipoğlu (1992), 163.

10 Grivna (2013), 130.

CHAPTER 56: A GARDEN OF MIXED FRUIT

1 Montagu (2013), 163.

2 Başaran and Kocabaş (2008).

3 İnalcık (1990), 12.

4 At the end of the fifteenth century, Arnold von Haff wrote that the Jewish

population of Istanbul was 36,000 (not just incoming Jews). Lewis (1985), 122.

5 Aboab, *Nomologia, o Discursos legales compuestos* (1629), 125, and D. Altabé, *Spanish and Portuguese Jewry before and after 1492* (1983), quoted in Frankopan (2015), 200.

6 Hattenhauer and Bake (eds) (2012). Quoted in Bell (2008), 60. See also Rozen (1998); Heyd (1953); Zarinebaf (2012); Baer (2004).

7 The printing press was invented in AD 1439–40 by Johannes Gutenberg.

8 For a full and fascinating discussion of the interplay of silk production at this time see Jacoby (2004), 197–240.

9 Charlemagne was buried in the finest cloth – made in Constantinople itself and decorated with elephants. Roger II of Sicily – whose gorgeous silk cape was later used as a coronation mantle for the Holy Roman Emperors – besieged Byzantine Corinth and Thebes and then transported many of their silk-workers to Palermo, forcing them to share their knowledge with locals. Even patches of Byzantine silk were considered so valuable they were reused. St Thomas Becket's chasuble contained high-end scraps including one section from Almería in Spain.

10 Silk production finally stopped on a large scale in Bursa in 1922 with the expulsion of Greek families. It had been vigorous since the fourteenth century, with the flourishing locals famously dressed head to toe in silks and velvets. One Greek silk producer Taki Terliktsoglou remembered that when the silk was being balled up in the streets it was impossible for pedestrians to pass.

11 Vlami (2015), 268.

12 Shaw (1991), 114.

13 Soulis (1961), 141, 143–65.

14 Mansel (1997), 102.

CHAPTER 57: A DIAMOND BETWEEN TWO SAPPHIRES

1 Evliya Çelebi as quoted in Lewis (1963), 110–11.

2 The Greek Kritovoulos, quoted in J. Taylor (2007), 125. Bayezid II.

3 Butrint was romantically tempting for a cosmopolitan crew of visitors – Benedict of Peterborough in AD 1191, the Arab travel-writer al-Idrisi, Byron, Cavafy and Vlach shepherds who made the remains their home; it was also said to be the resting place of Medea and a stopping-off point for Aeneas on his way home from Troy to found Rome – the reason Mussolini supported the excavation of the site in the mid-1920s.

4 New treasures are discovered each and every excavating season; in 2005 an entire Roman forum, stretches of the aqueduct in 2007, most recently a

Hellenistic tower – all protected by massive sixth-century AD walls. Wells magical in their day, bringing life-giving powers, yield delights for archaeologists. The Great Basilica is built on top of the synagogue here. The Baptistry promises the benefits of Christianity – peacocks symbolise paradise. Of comfort perhaps to martyrs thrown to the beasts here AD c. 249–51 and those slaves who do not appear in the lists of the freed on the stones of the theatre.

5 Necipoğlu (2007), 141–83 ; Kuban (2010), 288–312 (chapters 24 and 25).
6 See e.g. Suvari (2010), 412.
7 Here I have relied heavily on Ergin (2008).
8 In Lyon in AD 1561 Pierre Gilles published *Three Books on the Thracian Bosphorus* and *Four Books on the Topography of Constantinople and its Antiquities*.

CHAPTER 58: THE MUSLIM MILLENNIUM

1 Matteo Zane, *Alberi* III, 442–3. quoted in Kármán and Kunčević, trans. Lucia Marchini (2013), 81.
2 Păun (2013), 263.
3 al-Suyuti, Jalal al-Din. N.d. al. Hawi li-l-fatawa, 2 vols. Beirut: Dar al-Fikr, 2:86–9 in C. Wessinger (2016), 271.
4 If this 'blessed' handkerchief was worn by the man they desired for forty days it was thought that their prospective beau would find the owner irresistible.
5 Hasluck (1916/17-1917//18), 171.
6 See e.g. Topinka 8 (2009), 114–30; Welch et al., Jenkins and Kane (1983–4), 4–8.
7 G. K. Chesterton, *Lepanto* (1915). The American Chesterton Society: http://www.chesterton.org/lepanto/
8 J. Brotton has recently written illuminatingly and extensively on these subjects. See Brotton (2016).
9 Miguel de Cervantes Saavedra (1825), trans. Charles Jarvis, 109. ch. 'Wherein the captive relates his life and adventures'.
10 Norwich (2007), 325.
11 'The sultan rushed from his summer palace in Edirne to the capital to oversee the construction of a new fleet'. White (2011), 15. See also Imber (1996), 85–101.

CHAPTER **59**: GUNPOWDER EMPIRES AND GUNNING PERSON-
ALITIES: DRAGOMANS AND EUNUCHS

 1 Gelibolulu Mustafa Ali, *Sûr*, p. 124. Boyar and Fleet (2010), 52.
 2 Sujan Rai, *Khulasat al-Tawarikh* f. as quoted in Blake (2002), 193.
 3 Khan (1990), Begley and Desai, eds, 28.
 4 The holy cities of Mecca and Medina represented a source not just of
    emotional and spiritual, but of material riches. The Ottomans perpetuated
    the Byzantines' passion for relic collection. Relics and treasures were both
    taken as offerings to Mecca (many have ended up on display in the Topkapı
    Palace following the attempt by European powers to extend influence in the
    Middle East at the beginning of the twentieth century), since gathered back
    to Istanbul for safe-keeping. Selim I, recall, had declared that Shia was not
    a true form of Islam.
 5 Grateful thanks to Katherine Schofield for her advice on Ottoman and
    Mughal musical styles.
 6 The splendour of the ritual of the Ottoman Sultan's procession to Friday
    prayers – with cavalry mounted on white horses, white sea-sand carpeting
    the route, men at arms gathering in front of the palace to walk respectfully
    behind their leader – was still commented on with awe by visitors from
    India and Japan in the nineteenth century.
 7 Quoted in Farooqi (1989).
 8 See Rothman (2009), 771–800.
 9 See Philliou (2008), 661–75.
10 Tolan et al. (2013), 148.
11 See Marana (1687), *Lettters Writ by a Turkish Spy, Who Lived Five and Forty
    Years Undiscovered at Paris.*
12 Lad (2010).
13 See Skilliter (1965), 148.

CHAPTER **60**: THE SULTANATE OF WOMEN

 1 Philip Massinger, *The Renegado*, Act 1, scene 3.
 2 Ostovik *et al.* (2008), 66.
 3 Bicknell (2001), 72.
 4 Dallam (1893).
 5 Arbel (1992), 241–59.
 6 See Peirce (1993) *passim.*
 7 Ibid., 147.
 8 Ibid., 226.

9   Ibid., 208. The mosque was described as a 'mountain of light' by Evliya
    Çelebi. See ibid., 186.
10 In this chapter I have relied heavily on Pierce. See Ibid., 209.
11 Although Safiye too procured concubines for her bedmate.
12 Quoted in Peirce (1993), 202.
13 Boyar and Fleet (2016), 233.
14 Skilliter (1965), 132–3.
15 Quoted in Peirce (1993), 228.
16 Skilliter (1965), 43.
17 Ottaviano Bon, *The Sultan's Seraglio*, ed. Goodwin (1996), 46.
18 From 'A Form to be used in common prayer . . . to excite all godly people
    to pray unto God for the delivery of those Christians that are now invaded
    by the Turk', reprinted in Keatinge Clay (ed.) (1847), 519–23, esp. 519.
19 I have relied heavily here on research in Vitkus (1997), 519–23, esp. 519.
20 Montefiore (2016), 239.
21 MacLean (2004), 165.
22 Bernard Yeazell (2000), passim.

CHAPTER 61: THE JANISSARIES

1   Quoted in Wheatcroft (2008), 163.
2   Robert Walsh, *Narrative of a Residence at Constantinople* (1828), as quoted in
    Wheatcroft (1993), 86.
3   Adolphus Slade, *Record of Travels in Turkey, Greece etc. and of a Cruise in the
    Black Sea with the Captain Pasha in the Years 1828, 1829, 1830, 1831* (1833), as
    quoted in Wheatcroft (1993), 92.
4   In general terms the rise of the West, with patterns of trade disrupted by
    the successful voyages of Christopher Columbus and Vasco da Gama, is the
    one reason that strategists in the Sublime Porte and the harem had to be
    apprised of not just regional but international opportunities and loyalties.
    Murad IV organised a theatrical week of grandstanding. A procession of
    guilds marched through the city. We might question the motivation. What
    did this prove? That this was a society held together by a faith? By an idea?
    By gaudy traded things? On 25 December AD 1638 Baghdad surrendered to
    Murad IV; boundaries were drawn in the Middle East whose ghosts still
    survive today. In 1645 Ottoman armies landed on Crete and in 1683 the
    grand vizier's eyes were turned north – to the natural, tenacious boundary
    of the great Danube River. None of this would have been possible without
    the Janissaries.
5   But as a rule Jews, Romans, Kurds, Persians and Turks were not as welcome
    as Janissaries.

6 Using court registers and probate registers excellent work has been done by Gulay Yılmaz – see her dissertation Yılmaz (2011).

7 Askan (1998), 116–25. Kafadar (1991), 273–80. Wheatcroft (1993), 84–137.

8 Or 160–90 grams in metric measurement.

CHAPTER 62: THE GREAT SIEGE OF VIENNA

1 Mehmed IV, *The Great Turks Declaration of war against the Emperor of Germany (At his Pallace at Adrinople, Feb 20, 1683)*, printed by G.C. for John Mumford (1683).

2 From Sobieski's letter to Innocent XI sent together with the 'Standard of the Prophet' taken from the Ottomans. Sobieski was leader of the cavalry charge against the Ottoman forces.
Taken from the Exorcism rite against Satan and the Apostate Angels known as 'St Anthony's brief' which St Anthony gave to a Portuguese woman about to take her own life in the twelfth century cf Apocalypse 5.5, 'Weep not: behold the lion of the tribe of Juda, the root of David, hath prevailed to open the book and to loose the seven seals thereof').

3 Archaeological and restoration work on the walls is ongoing.

4 *Nähere Untersuchung der Pestansteckung*, 42, Pascal Joseph von Ferro, Joseph Edler von Kurzbek k.k. Hofbuchdrucker, Wien, AD 1787.

5 Cf. the 'Armada of candles', on the eve of the Battle of Mohàcs in AD 1526: 'It seemed as if all the stars of the seven skies were gathered. Everywhere was illuminated and the valley was turned into a rose garden,' wrote Solak-zâde, the chronicler of the Sultan. 'The echo of kös [big drums], davuls and horns caused hubbub in the horizons and a clamour eveywhere from the ground up to the skies.' Solak-zâde, *Tarihi*, trans. 1999, 40. See also Jezernik (ed.) (2009), 38–9, and Ware Allen (2015), 155.

6 Georgievitz (1661), 46.

7 Murphey (1999), 152. Baer (2008), 216; Baer discusses Ahmed Agha, *The Events or Calamities of Vienna* (*Vekayi-i Beç*) at 213ff.

8 'Before noon [on 25 August] the Grand Vizir entered the trenches and summoned to his headquarters Hussein pasha, Bekir pasha, the Aga of the Janissaries . . . as well as other commanders. He gave solemn warnings to them all and ordered each one of them to do his utmost to bring the enterprise to a successful conclusion, expending life and property for the true faith . . . It seemed as if the struggle would never end and the fighting continued with incredible bitterness.' See Stoye (2012), ch. 8.II.

9 Sources vary on the exact number involved but this was said to be the largest cavalry charge in history: 20,000 cavalry following 3,000 heavy Polish lancers/hussars led by Sobieski; 47,000 Germans/Austrians with 37,000

Poles/Lithuanians; 20,000 Janissaries; 100,000 infantry; 40,000 Tatar auxiliaries. Overy (2014), 58. See also Varvounis (2012), 152; Jenkins (2000), 205.

10 'After 8 hours of fighting, darkness forced them to retreat. Next morning, Turks had fled leaving 10,000 dead on battlefield after Sobieski's charge. 3,000 Christian dead on the battlefield.' Jenkins (2000), 205.

11 From *A True and Exact Relation of the Raising of the Siege of Vienna and the Victory obtained over the Ottoman Army, the 12th of September 1683*.

12 Jenkins (2000), 206.

13 See Goodwin (2006), 176–7.

14 See recent excellent work by Dankoff and Kim (2010).

15 Dankoff (2004), 117.

16 Ibid., 105–6. With many thanks to Professor Dankoff for his help with this.

17 Frankopan (2015), 261–2.

CHAPTER 63: THE WHITE SLAVE TRADE AND THE WHITE PLAGUE

1 Wagner (1856).

2 Mansel (2011).

3 The connection between the two settlements is still memorialised. The main cathedral in Poti – built in 1907 – was modelled on Haghia Sophia in Constantinople.

4 Augustine of Hippo, *Letters* 10.6, trans. Eno (1989).

5 Mansel (1997), 131.

6 Shakespeare, *Henry IV, Part 2*, Act 5, scene 2. Malieckal (2008), 58–73. Magdalino and Mavroudi (2006).

7 Hathaway (2011), 182.

8 Baris and Hillerdal (2009), 171.

9 See ibid., 170–3, and Ersoy, Gungor and Akpinar (2011), 53.

10 Brookes (2008).

CHAPTER 64: WHITE CAUCASIANS

1 Quoted in Baum (2008), 84.

2 Thackeray (1846), 'The Paris sketch book'. 'Memoirs of Mr. Charles J. Yellowplush'. 'The Irish sketch book'. 'Notes of a Journey from Cornhill to Grand Cairo, by way of Lisbon, Athens, Constantinople, and Jerusalem: Performed in the Steamers of the Peninsular and Oriental Company',

Volume 2 of *Miscellanies*, (Fields, Osgood & Company, 1869), original from Harvard University, 534.

3 Blumenback (2000), 31.

4 Leo Tolstoy, *The Wood Felling*, trans. Maude and Cooper (2001).

5 King (2008), 134.

6 Alberi, *Relazioni*, 2, p. 97; also *Queen Elizabeth and the Levant Company*, 23 (a report for the English ambassador in Rosedale).

7 Barnum to Greenwood, 14 May 1864, in Saxon (ed.) (1983), 115–27.

8 See King (2011), 35ff.

9 Interview with Nell Irvin Painter, *Caucasian Roots*, BBC Radio 3, first broadcast in March 2015. See also Painter (2011), 83–4.

10 Painter (2003).

CHAPTER 65: SOAP AND SMALLPOX

1 Crooke (1637), 69.

2 Byron (1837), 107.

3 Brown (1909).

4 Montagu (2013), 101–2.

5 See, Boyar and Fleet (2016), 238.

6 For a more detailed study of Turkish bathing culture in Istanbul, see Cichocki (2005), 254–8.

7 Montagu (2013).

8 See Boyar and Fleet (2010), 254, 258.

9 For those who did have access inside the harem itself, descriptions seemed to prove good copy rather than a basis for campaign; in the *Englishwoman's Review* of AD 1877 we hear that 'to him [the male Muslim] she is a mere animal'.

10 Cf. 'Cigar Divan' George Cruikshank, *Scraps and Sketches* (1832).

11 Jerichau-Baumann, *Brogede Rejsebilleder* (*Motley Images of Travel*) (Copenhagen, 1881.

12 MacLean (2004)

13 Hershkovitz et al. (2008).

14 See Ersoy, Güngör and Akpinar (2011).

CHAPTER 66: TULIPS AND TEXTILES

1 Nabi Efendi (1901), 182–5, trans. de Courteille and Arnot.

2 Grelot (1683), 58, trans. J. Phillips.

3 Robinson (2009).
4 Kafadar (1989), 129.
5 See Zarinebaf (2010), 176.
6 Quoted in Mather (2009), 113.

CHAPTER 67: O LOVE! YOUNG LOVE!

1 Lord Byron, *Don Juan*, Canto XIII, stanza xxiii.
2 Byron (1837), 594.
3 See Marchand (1973).
4 Lady Mary Wortley Montagu's letters to her friend Alexander Pope were rich in incidental detail, describing the intimidating sight of the Sultan's soldiers leaving the city to fight in Austria and Hungary.
5 Byron, *Don Juan*, Canto V, stanza iii.
6 Byron (1837), 136.
7 With thanks to William St Clair for his kind help with these ideas. Thank you too for his work – and for the tea.
8 Quoted in Beaton (2013), 203.

CHAPTER 68: MASSACRE

1 Kevin Smith, trans. (2007) originally published in *The Redwood Coast Review*, 9 (3), Summer 2007.
2 At a time when, in England the last King from the house of Wessex ascended the throne while in Armenia, the last Bagratid King, the young Gagik II, tried to defend his capital Ani against troops from Byzantium and the Emirat of Dvin. See Chahin (2001), 231.
3 The rash of establishment in the tenth century had been so florid that Nikephoros II Phokas had banned the foundation and endowment of new monasteries. It all seemed too brash; a number of enterprises no longer motivated by piety and charity.
4 Credited as the author (though he must be the editor) of a number of works describing Constantinople's history and monuments.
5 With each tree producing only around 9 ounces a year (250 grams) there is an inbuilt sense of proportion and preservation. In the gated town of Meste, for centuries citizens were not allowed in or out after sunset.
6 Today elderly women in the Bridget Rileyesque grey, black and white village of Pyrgi still flash picture-perfect smiles – either the effects of mastika-use or of its sale. All income from mastika is shared within a cooperative.

7   Kitromilides (2010), 227.
8   See e.g. Brewer (2011).
9   Figures vary according to sources. According to Miller (2013), 80: 'it was calculated that of the 113,000 Christians [in Chios] . . . in April, only 1,800 remained there in August . . . 23,000 had been slain, 47,000 sold into slavery'. See also Rodogno (2011), 69; Fraze (1969), 51; Phillips, W. A. (1897), 94.
10 Schiffer (1999), 188.
11 Eugène Delacroix, *Correspondance générale*, ed. Joubin (Paris: Plon, 1935), 18.
12 For a chronology of the history of Chios see e.g. www.christopherlong. co.uk/pub/chiosinfo.html

CHAPTER 69: REVOLUTION

1   Quoted in King (2014), xv.
2   Stone (2010), ch. 6.
3   Freely (1998), 263–5.
4   In AD 1827, within a year of the Auspicious Incident, the British, French and Russians – the British culturally setting themselves perhaps against the Napoleonic French who were fascinated by Ancient Roman culture, and anxious that the Russians should not support Greece and enrich themselves at Ottoman expense – destroyed an Ottoman fleet at Navarino Bay (modern-day Pylos) in order to nourish the Greeks' bid for autonomy. In 1832 the small independent kingdom of Greece, with a German king, started to rule tentatively from the seaside resort of Nafplion.
5   Pardoe (1838), 19.
6   Wharton (2015), 114.
7   Boatmen from neighbouring islands such as Symi were judged the best the Mediterranean could offer and were employed by the Ottomans to operate their empire-wide water-borne postal service, running from Iraq to the Danube.
8   For a delightful account of Edward Lear's travels see Hyman (1988).
9   De Foblanque (1877), 262.

CHAPTER 70: TSARGRAD

1   Parliamentary Papers. Accounts and Papers: Thirty-Six Volumes: Eastern Papers, V. Session 31 January–12 August 1854, Vol. LXXI (London: Harrison & Son, 1854), doc. 1. Temperley (1936), 272 (page 2).

2 Both still function as naval bases, with Sevastopol closed to Russian tourists until 1997 and Balaklava (which is now part of Sevastopol) remaining unmarked on Soviet maps to protect the submarines stationed there.

3 Montefiore (2011) 215–23. See also Montefiore (2000).

4 De Madariaga (1990), 48.

5 Article 14 of the Treaty of Küçük Kaynarca in AD 1774, which was signed after the defeat of the Ottoman forces by the Russians, states that the Russians had the right to build a church in Galata. See Davidson (1979), 46–52.

6 Wren and Stults (1994), 325.

7 Bullough (2010) has this as Dumas' own observation when he is travelling through the port of Poti in the 1850s.

8 King (2008), 63.

9 Pushkin (2008), 33.

CHAPTER 71: SCUTARI

1 Pushkin, *A Journey to Arzrum*. Notes written by Pushkin while on the AD 1829 campaign. The Janissary is Amin-Oglu; Arzrum is the eastern Anatolian town renamed when it was taken by Seljuk Turks after the Battle of Manzikert in 1071.

2 The slow, subdued journey of a Russian warship from the Sea of Marmara to the Black Sea in advance of Russia's annexation of Crimea rang warning bells in early 2014.

3 See Stone (2010), 105.

4 Gul (2009), 41.

5 Published in London in AD 1858.

6 Marx (1897).

7 For a detailed account of all extant sources for the Crimean War see Badem (2010).

8 Terakye and Oflaz (2007), 73–83.

CHAPTER 72: ONE-WAY TRAFFIC

1 The Prince of Wales's journal. See Cairo to Constantinople (2014).

2 See some of these in Gordon (2013).

3 In Istanbul itself there were problems. When Empress Eugénie, the wife of Napoleon III, went to the harem (in the new Dolmebahçe Palace) with Abdülaziz, the Valide Sultan was purportedly so offended by her presence that she slapped her. Back in Paris, Mark Twain had written a very

unfavourable comparison of Abdülaziz and Napoleon. Freely (2000), 273.

4 Yildirim and Karakaş (2006), 89.

5 Mansel (1997), 295.

6 See Rose (1998), 386–403.

7 With thanks to Professor Charlotte Roueché for drawing this detail to my attention.

8 See also 'Leaving Therapeia', at 2.30 p.m. on 16 July AD 1882. Thank you to Dr Victoria Solomonides for sharing with me the first postcard that Cavafy sent from Constantinople.

9 In AD 1899 Kaiser Wilhelm II built his strange Byzantine-Ottoman mash-up fountain in the hippodrome, representative of a neo-Ottoman architectural style that was now favoured across German territories.

10 See e.g. Sadri Sema (2000), *Hatıraları*, 12.

11 Fikret (2007), 370, 371.

CHAPTER 73: A SICK MAN IN THE ROSE GARDEN

1 Allen (2008), 77–83.

2 Thank you to Philippe Sands.

3 Quoted in Boyar and Fleet (2010), 46, n. 110.

4 Zhukov and Vitol (2001).

5 I have relied heavily in this chapter on King (2014), passim.

6 Thank you to Philip Mansel for drawing my attention to this. Mansel (1997), 307.

7 Chorus of the AD 1878 song by G. H. MacDermott and George William Hunt.

8 See Erol (2013), 706–5.

9 The Ottoman slave trade was formally outlawed in the Brussels Conference Act (Convention Relative to the Slave Trade and Importation into Africa of Firearms, Ammunition and Spiritous Liquors) – signed by sixteen countries. Passionate supporters of the Circassian cause started to become vocal in Western circles, men such as the orientalist diplomat David Urquhart, who went on to found a chain of steam-bath establishments across Europe (the last in London, the Jermyn Street Hammam, survived until it was bombed in the Blitz of 1941). Urquhart designed the Circassian national flag, and it was said that his son, an Oxford don, was offered the presidency of the North Caucasus Mountain Republic in 1919.

10 See the delightful descriptions in King (2007), 238–55.

11 For fascinating discussion of Russian interest in the city see e.g. Lieven (2015), 73.

12 Ibid., 26.

13 Keynes (ed.) (1968), 662. Brooke was writing in February 1915, one of his last letters home.

CHAPTER 74: GALLIPOLI: THE END OF AN EMPIRE

1   Published in the *Mayorough and Dunolly Advertiser*, 12 April 1916.
2   Doukas, *Historia* 155; Doukas, *Decline* 144, quoted in Boyar and Fleet (2010), 21.
3   See King (2014), 34.
4   *Talat Paşa'nin Anilari* [Memoirs of Talat Pasha] (1994), trans. from Wasti (2004), 71 n. 4.
5   Liman von Sanders (1927), trans. Reichmann.
6   See Rogan (2015), 133.
7   Moberly (1923), 130–1, quoted in Frankopan (2015), 334.
8   Cheetham to Foreign Office, 13 December 1914, PRO FO 371/1973/87396, quoted in Frankopan (2015), 335.
9   Rogan (2015), 140.
10 FitzSimons (2015). Lecane (2015).
11 Gilbert (2004), 27.
12 Rogan (2015), 110ff.
13 Quoted in FitzSimons (2015), 246.
14 The campaign was reported by the father of Rupert Murdoch, the Melbourne correspondent Keith Murdoch.
15 The humble, man-at-arms mindset of Istanbul's post-conquest native inhabitants was often commented upon. On the way back from Friday prayers the Sultan would drive himself in a normal chariot – a theatrical memory of his Turkic-warrior origins. One Muslim traveller-writer at the end of the nineteenth century, Shibli Nu'mani, although stating that no other city could vie with Constantinople, praised the relatively modest size of houses and households to India's detriment, opining that the inhabitants of Istanbul had not compromised their warrior honesty.
16 Thank you to the Countess of Carnarvon, who examines the story of Aubrey Herbert in Carnarvon (2011), for drawing my attention to this detail.
17 Cited in National Memorial Service 1914 Sikhs Order of Service Monday 8 June 2015. Quoted in Srivastava (1973), 66.
18 King (2014), 36.
19 Ross (2006), 189.
20 Published in 1918 as *Inside Constantinople – A Diplomatist's Diary during the Dardanelles Expedition April–September 1915*.
21 Rogan (2015), 338.
22 King (2014), 42.

23 Horne (ed.) (1923), 344.
24 Quoted in Mansel (2011).
25 Ibid., 65, 66.
26 Data from Ilber Ortayli in *Istanbul' dan Sayflar* cited by Professor Nur Bilge Criss in Serim (2015).
27 See McMeekin (2015) for an interesting analysis of Sykes–Picot.

CHAPTER 75: THE RED APPLE

1 Quoted in Mansel (2011).
2 Quoted in Lecouras (2001).
3 Ibid., 99.
4 Here I have relied heavily on Mansel (1995), 396–7.
5 Charles King drew my attention to one loving rendition of the tale of a Caucasian bear which, after being plied with port by British soldiers at Christmas, toppled into the Bosphorus and was hooked out by fishermen.

CHAPTER 76: THE CATASTROPHE

1 Cited by Fitzherbert (1985), 219.
2 Haghia Sophia was finally turned into a museum in 1934 following an agreement between Greece and Turkey, but today you will hear the call to prayer from its minarets – a political statement in contravention of this agreement. In 1939 Goebbels visited both the Pera Palace and the Haghia Sophia – he found the church inspiring.
3 Mazower (2004), 344.
4 Although during the writing of this book the area has been gradually gen-trified and has recently become a fashionable destination for artists and independent travellers.
5 Turkey was the only country in the Middle East to emerge from the First World War as an independent nation-state.

CHAPTER 77: THE LAST CALIPH

1 Quoted in Boivin (2003).
2 Finkel (2006), 545 (Abdülmecid II succeeded his cousin Mehmed VI, who was a son of Abdülmecid I).
3 Ibid., 546.

4 'In March 1924, determined to strike at the heart of the old order, he had
   the Caliphate and the office of the *Sheikh-ul-Islam* abolished . . . In September 1925, following a revolt among the Kurdish tribes, inspired in part by
   supporters of the Caliphate, he had the numerous dervish orders, brother-
   hoods and sects operating in Turkey dissolved, and the wearing of religious
   vestments or insignia not holding a recognized religious office banned. In
   November he had the famous Hat Law enacted, forbidding the wearing of
   the fez, the primary outward manifestation of religious affiliation.' MacFie
   (2013), 136.

   The Islamist group Hizb ut-Tahrir is banned in Turkey and nearly 200
   members were arrested in 2009. http://news.bbc.co.uk/1/hi/world/
   europe/8166972.stm. Yet Hizb ut-Tahrir held a pro-caliph conference in
   Istanbul in 2015 (see http://www.khilafah.com/hizb-ut-tahrir-wilayah-
   turkey-held-a-khilafah-conference-on-the-anniversary-of-khilafahs-
   abolition-in-istanbul/) and arranged rallies in 2014 and 2015 (https://www.
   youtube.com/watch?v=DUgERpmTuK0). See also http://www.voanews.
   com/content/critics-even-supporters-say-erdogan-is-the-man-who-would-
   be-caliph/3024375.html.

   Fuat Özgür Çalapkulu (of Turkey's ruling party, the AKP) tweeted on
   17 March 2015: 'The caliph is coming, get ready.' The tweet caused an
   outcry and he 'released a written statement on March 19, saying he has
   a different "perception" of the word "caliph". "I use this word to refer
   to a leader who has command of all the problems, institutions and administration of his country; a leader who is the independent and powerful voice of the world's downtrodden; the protector of the oppressed;
   a good, successful, pioneering and visionary leader."' http://www.
   hurriyetdailynews.com/get-ready-for-erdogans-caliphate-turkeys-ruling-
   party-official-says.aspx?pageID=238&nID=79883&NewsCatID=338. And
   see https://www.washingtonpost.com/news/worldviews/wp/2015/03/19/
   the-caliph-is-coming-get-ready-pro-erdogan-turkish-politician-tweets/.

CHAPTER 78: GLOBAL FUTURES

1 King (2014), 9.
2 Student Oath recited across Turkey, with some alterations 1933–2013.
3 And indeed old habits do die hard. Many in the city, Muslim and Christian
   alike, prefer to celebrate the old feast of the Assumption in mid-August.
   St Helena's name was painted on to anti-aircraft guns during the siege of
   Sarajevo – the reanimation of a Muslim–Christian tension that the city had
   wearily watched for 1,500 years.
4 Thanks to Alexander Bell for this calculation.

5 'Erdogan's Shanghai Organization remarks lead to confusion, concern', *Today's Zaman*, 28 January 2013.
6 Situation at the time of author's visit in 2011.
7 Mentions can be checked in Hansard online and open access. Thank you to Dr Peter Frankopan for this suggestion.
8 We do occasionally hear authentic voices. Murad V's concubine Filizten wrote from the Baroque marble cage of the Çırağan Palace – where she lived for twenty-eight years. See Brookes (ed.) (2008).

CODA

1 Yahya Kemal Beyatlı, *Aziz Istanbul*, 67. Quoted in Boyar and Fleet (2010), 328.

APPENDIX: THE OTHER ROMAN EMPIRES

1 Blair and Bloom (eds) (2012).
2 Dikov (2015) and http://www.euractiv.com/euro-finance/cyrillic-alphabet-appearance-eur-news-516974.
3 Dikov (2015).
4 See discussions in Salamon, Wołoszyn, Musin and Špehar (2012), esp. Bollók at 131–44.

BIBLIOGRAPHY

✣

PRIMARY SOURCES

AGATHIAS, *Histories*
AGATHIAS SCHOLASTICUS, 'On a House Situated on a Hill in Constantinople'
　W. R. Paton, trans. (1917 updated 1960) *The Greek Anthology*, Epigram 654. Loeb Classical Library. Cambridge, MA: Harvard University Press.
AHMAD IBN-JABIR AL-BALADHURI, *Kitab Futuh al-Buldha*
　P. K. Hitti, trans.; F. C. Murgotten, trans. (1916 and 1924) '*Al-Baladhuri: The Battle of the Yarmuk (636) and After' in The Origins of the Islamic State, being a translation from the Arabic of the Kitab Futuh al-Buldha of Ahmad ibn-Jabir al-Baladhuri*. Studies in History, Economics and Public Law, LXVIII. New York: Columbia University Press.
AL-HAKIM, *al-Mustadrak'*
AL-MUQADDASI, *Aḥsanu-t-taqāsīm fī ma rifati-l-aqālīm*
　B. Collins, trans. (2001) In 'Best Division of Knowledge'. Reading: Ithaca Press.
AMMIANUS MARCELLINUS, *The Later Roman Empire (AD 354–378)*
　W. Hamilton, trans. (1986). London: Penguin.
ANNA KOMNENE, *The Alexiad*
ANONYMOUS, *Gesta Francorum et Aliorum Hierosolimitanorum*
　R. Hill, trans. (1962). Oxford: Clarendon Press
　E. R. A. Sewter, trans., with introduction and notes by P. Frankopan (2009). London: Penguin.
APOLLONIUS RHODIUS, *Argonautica*
　R. C. Seaton, trans. (1912). Loeb Classical Library. Cambridge, MA: Harvard University Press.
ARISTOPHANES, *Frogs*
　J. Savage, trans. (2010). MA: Hardpress Publishing.
ARISTOTLE, *Minor Works*
　Hett, trans. (1936). Loeb Classical Library. Cambridge and London: Harvard University Press.

ATHENAGORAS, *Legatio and De Resurrectione*
W. R. Schoedel, trans. and ed. (1972). Oxford: Clarendon Press.
AUGUSTINE OF HIPPO, *Letters*
R. Eno, trans. (1989). Washington, DC: Catholic University of America Press.
BARSANUPHIOS AND JOHN OF GAZA, *Correspondence*
F. Neyt et al., eds and trans. (2002) Paris: Editions du Cerf.
BERNOLD OF CONSTANCE, *Die Chroniken Bertholds von Reichenau und Bernolds von Konstanz*
I. Robinson, ed. (2003). Bournemouth: Hanover.
BOETHIUS, *The Consolation of Philosophy*
V. E. Watts, trans. (1969). Book 2, prose 6. London: Penguin
CALLINICUS, *Vita S. Hypatii*
G. Bartelink, ed., *Vie d'Hypatios* (1971). Paris: Editions du Cerf.
CASSIUS DIO, *Roman History*
E. Cary, trans. (1927). Loeb Classical Library. Cambridge, MA: Harvard University Press.
CAVAFY C. P., 'In Church' from *The Canon*, trans. Cavafy
CEDRENUS, *Compendium Historiarum*
J. Scylitzes, trans. (1647). Parisiis: e Typographia regia.
CICERO, *De Provinciis Consularibus*
R. Gardner, trans. (1958). Loeb Classical Library. Cambridge, MA: Harvard University Press.
CLEMENT OF ALEXANDRIA, *The Sacred Writings of Clement of Alexandria*
P. Schaff, trans. (2012)
CONSTANTINE VII PORPHYROGENITOS, *De Ceremoniis Aulae Byzantinae*
J. Reisky, ed. (1829–30). Bonn.
CONSTANTINE PORPHYROGENNETOS, *The Book of Ceremonies*
Moffat and M. Tall, trans. (2012). Canberra: Australian Association for Byzantine Studies.
CORIPPUS, *In Laudem Iustini Augusti Minoris*
Cameron, trans. and ed. (1976). London: The Athlone Press.
DIODOROS SICULUS, *Bibliotheca Historica*
C. H. Oldfather, trans. (1989). Vols. 4–8. Cambridge, MA: Harvard University Press; London: William Heinemann.
DIONYSIUS OF BYZANTIUM, *Anaplus Bospori: Anaplous Bosporou*
R. Güngerich (1958). Berlin: Weidmann.
DOUKAS
I. Bekker, ed. (1843). *Historia Byzantina*. Bonn: Weber
H.J Magoulias, trans. (1979). *Decline and Fall of the Ottoman Turks*. Detroit: Wayne State University Press.

EUSEBIUS

A. Cameron and S. G. Hall, trans. (1999) *Eusebius' Life of Constantine* with introduction and commentary. Oxford: Oxford University Press, 1999. Vol. 1

P. Halsall, trans. (1990). *Library of Nicene and Post Nicene Fathers,* Second Series, Vol. 1. New York: Christian Literature Co.

E. C. Richardson, trans. (1980). *Life of Constantine,* from *Nicene and Post-Nicene Fathers,* Second Series, Vol. 1. P. Schaff and H. Wace, ed. Buffalo, NY: Christian Literature Publishing Co.

P. Schaff and H. Wace, eds (1955) in *A Select Library of Nicene and Post-Nicene Fathers of the Christian Church.* Edinburgh: T&T Clark.

EUSTATHIOS, *The Capture of Thessaloniki*

J. R. Melville Jones, trans. (1988). Canberra: Byzantina Australiensia.

EVAGRIUS SCHOLASTICUS

E. Walford, trans. (1846). *The Ecclesiastical History of Evagrius: A History of the Church from AD 431 to AD 594.* London: Samuel Bagster and Son.

GREEK POETS, THE: HOMER TO THE PRESENT

P. Constantine, R. Hadas, E. Keeley, K. van Dyck, eds with introduction by R. Hass (2009). New York, London: W. W. Norton & Company.

GREGORY OF NAZIANUS, *De Vita Sua*

D. Meehan, trans. (1987) *Saint Gregory of Nazianzus: Three Poems.* Washington, DC: Catholic University of America Press.

HERODIAN, *History of the Roman Empire*

E. C. Echols, trans. (1961) *Herodian of Antioch's History of the Roman Empire.* Berkeley and Los Angeles: University of California Press.

HERODOTUS, *The Histories*

T. Holland, trans. (2013) in *Herodotus, The Histories*, ed. and with introduction by P. Cartledge. London: Penguin.

HIPPOLYTUS, *Refutation of All Heresies*

HOMER, *The Iliad of Homer*

G. Chapman, trans., with introduction by R. Hooper (1888). London: John Russell Smith.

HOMER, *Odyssey*

JACOB OF SERUGH, *Homily 5*

C. Moss trans. (1935).

W. S. Davis, ed. (1913) *Readings in Ancient History: Illustrative Extracts from the Sources*, Vol. 2: *Rome and the West.* Boston: Allyn & Bacon.

JEROME, *Letters*

W. H. Fremantle, trans. (1885). *Nicene and Post-Nicene Fathers of the Christian Church: Series II.* Edited by P. Schaff and H. Wace. New York: The Christian Literature Company, 1893, VI: 248–9.

JOHN CHRYSOSTOM, *In Mattheum Homiliae*

ST JOHN OF DAMASCUS, *On the Divine Images*
B. Kotter, ed. (1969–88). Berlin and New York: Walter de Gruyter.
JOHN OF EPHESUS, *Commentary*
JOHN OF EPHESUS, *Ecclesiastical History*
JOHN OF EPHESUS
E. W. Brooks, ed. (1923). *Patrologia Orientalis, Lives of the Eastern Saints I.*
Paris: Firmin-Didot
JOHN MALALAS
E. Jeffreys et al., trans. (1986) *The Chronicle of John Malalas: A Translation*,
Byzantina Australiensia 4. Melbourne: Australian Association for Byzantine
Studies.
JORDANES, *The Origin and Deeds of the Goths*
C. C. Mierow, trans. (1915) Princeton: Princeton University Press.
JULIAN, *The Caesars*
W. C. Wright, trans. (1913). Loeb Classical Library. Cambridge, MA: Harvard University Press.
JUSTINIAN, *Codex Justinianus, Corpus Iuris Civilis*
P. Krueger, ed. (1929). Berlin: Weidmann.
JUSTINIAN, *Novels*
R. Schoell and W. Kroll, eds. (1954). *Novellae, in Corpus Juris Civilis*. Vol.3.
6th edition. Berlin: Weidmann.
S. P. Scott, trans. (1932). Cincinnati, OH: The Central Trust Company. See
also J. Freely, (1998) *Istanbul: The Imperial City*. London: Penguin.
JUSTINIAN, *Institutes*
P. Birks and G. McLeod, trans. with the Latin of P. Krueger (1987). *Justinian's Institutes*, London: Duckworth.
W. H. JONES (1906). 'Anzac', *Maryborough and Dunolly Advertiser*, 1.
KRITOBOULOS, *History of Mehmed the Conqueror*
C. T. Riggs, trans. (1954). New Jersey: Princeton University Press.
LACTANTIUS, *De Mortibus Persecutorum*
J. Creed, ed. and trans. (1984). Oxford: Clarendon Press.
J. Vanderspoel, ed. (1998). Alberta: University of Calgary.
LIUTPRAND OF CREMONA, *The Embassy to Constantinople and Other Writings.*
F. A. Wright, trans. (1993). London: J. M. Dent.
MARK THE DEACON, *Life of Porphyry, Bishop of Gaza*
G. F. Hill, trans. (1913). Oxford: Clarendon Press.
MATTHEW OF EDESSA, *Chronicle*
A. E. Dostourian, trans. and ed. (1993). *Armenia and the Crusades: Tenth to
Twelfth Centuries – The Chronicle of Matthew of Edessa* Maryland: University
Press of America.
MEHMED, SULTAN OF THE TURKS, *The Great Turks declaration of war*

against the Emperour of Germany, at his pallace at Adrinople, February 20. *1683.* (1683) London: printed by G. C. for John Mumford

MENANDER, *The Principal Fragments*
F. G. Allinson, trans. (1921). Loeb Classical Library. Cambridge, MA: Harvard University Press.

MENANDER THE GUARDSMAN, Fragment 19.1
R. C. Blockley, trans. (1985) *The History of Menander the Guardsman.* Liverpool: Francis Cairns.

MICHAEL THE SYRIAN,
M. Moosa, trans. (2014) *The Syriac Chronicle of Michael Rabo (The Great): A Universal History from the Creation.* Syriac Orthodox Church of Antioch, Archdiocese for the Eastern United States. Teaneck, NJ: Beth Antioch Press.

MOERO OF BYZANTIUM, 'The Dedicatory Epigrams'
W. R. Paton, trans. (1917) *The Greek Anthology,* Vol. 1. Loeb Classical Library. Cambridge, MA: Harvard University Press.

MUNTANER
R. Muntaner (2006) *The Catalan Expedition to the East: From the Chronicle of Ramon Muntaner,* trans. R. D. Hughes. Woodbridge and Barcelona: Barcino Tamesis.

NIKEPHOROS, *Short History*
C. A. Mango, trans. (1990) *Saint Nicephorus (Patriarch of Constantinople).* Washington, DC: Dumbarton Oaks Research Library and Collection.

NIKETAS CHONIATES, *Annals*
H. J. Magoulias, trans. (1984) *O City of Byzantium: Annals of Niketas Choniates.* Detroit, MI: Wayne State University Press.

OROSIUS, *History Against the Pagans*
I. W. Raymond, trans. (1936). *Seven Books Against the Pagans.* New York: Columbia University Press.

PASTERNAK, B., *Dr Zhivago*
M. Hayward and M. Harari, trans. (1958). Glasgow: Collins and Harvill Press.

PAUL THE SILENTIARY, 'On a High House in Constantinople'
W. R. Paton, trans. (1917) *The Greek Anthology* 9, Epigram 651. Loeb Classical Library. Cambridge, MA: Harvard University Press.

PINDAR, *Pindar*
C. M. Bowra (1964). Oxford: Oxford Scholarly Classics.

PLATO, *Phaedrus*
H. N. Fowler, trans. (1925). Cambridge, MA: Harvard University Press.

PLINY THE YOUNGER, *Letters*
Davis, trans. and ed. (1913)

PLUTARCH, *Lives volumes 1 and 2*
B. Perrin, trans. (1914 and 1948). London: W. Heinemann.

PLUTARCH, *Moralia*

PRISCUS, fr. 8 in *Fragmenta Historicorum Graecorum*
'Priscus at the court of Attila' J. B. Bury, trans. http://faculty.georgetown.edu/jod/texts/priscus.html.

PROCOPIUS, *History of the Wars*
H. B. Dewing, trans. (1914). Loeb Classical Library. Cambridge, MA: Harvard University Press.

PROCOPIUS, *Buildings*
H. B. Dewing, trans. (1940). Loeb Classical Library. Cambridge, MA: Harvard University Press.

PROCOPIUS, *The Secret History*
H. B. Dewing, trans. (1935). Loeb Classical Library. Cambridge, MA: Harvard University Press.
P. Sarris, ed. and G. Williamson, trans. (2007) London: Penguin.
A. Kaldellis, ed. and trans. (2010) *The Secret History: with related texts*. Indianapolis: Hackett Publishing Company.

SIDONIUS APOLLINARIS, *Epistulae,* W. B. Anderson, trans. (1989). Cambridge, MA: Harvard University Press.

SNORRI STURLUSON, *Heimskringla: History of the Kings of Norway*
L. Hollander, trans. (1964). Austin, TX: University of Texas Press.

SOCRATES SCHOLASTICUS, *Ecclesiastical History*
P. Schaff and H. Wace (eds) (reprinted 1989) *A Select Library of Nicene and Post-Nicene Fathers of the Christian Church*, Vol. 2: *Socrates and Sozomenus: Church Histories.* Edinburgh: T&T Clark.
D. Duff, trans. (1891) *The Early Church: A History of Christianity in the First Six Centuries.*
E. Walford and H. de Valois (1853), *Ecclesiastical History.* London: Bohn.

SOZOMEN, *Historia Ecclesiastica*
W. S. Davis (ed.) (1913) *Readings in Ancient History: Illustrative Extracts from the Sources*, Vol. 2: *Rome and the West.* Boston: Allyn & Bacon.
Hartranft, trans. (2016). *The Ecclesiastical History of Sozmenus.* London: Aeterna Press.

SPHRANTZES, G. *Chronicles. 16* (VII.3)
W. S. Davis (ed.) (1913) *Readings in Ancient History: Illustrative Extracts from the Sources*, vol. 2: *Rome and the West.* Boston: Allyn & Bacon.

STEPHEN THE DEACON, *La Vie d'Etienne le Jeune par Etienne le Diacre*
M.-F. Auzépy, trans. (1997). Aldershot: Variorum.

STRABO, *Geography*
H. L. Jones, trans. (1917–32). Loeb Classical Library. Cambridge, MA: Harvard University Press.

TACITUS, *Agricola*
M. Hutton and W. Peterson, trans. (1914). Loeb Classical Library. Cambridge, MA: Harvard University Press.

TACITUS, *Annals*
    J. Jackson, trans. (1937). Loeb Classical Library. Cambridge, MA: Harvard University Press.
    A. J. Church and W. J. Brodribb, trans. (1876). London, New York: Macmillan.
THEMISTIUS, *Orations*
    H. Schenkl, G. Downey and A. Norman, ed. (1965-74), 3 vols, Leipzig, P. Heather and D. Moncur, trans. (2001). *The Goths in the Fourth Century.* Liverpool: Liverpool University Press.
    Petavius (1684), Paris: Aldine Press.
THEODORET, *History of the Monks of Syria*
    R. M. Price, trans. and ed. (1985). Cistercian Publications.
THEODOSIAN, *The Theodosian Code and Novels and the Sirmondian Constitutions*
    C. Pharr, trans. (2001) *The Theodosian Code and Novels and the Sirmondian Constitutions.* Union, NJ: The Lawbook Exchange.
THEOPHANES, *Chronographia*
    M. Psellus and E. R. A. Sewter, trans. (1979). London: Penguin.
THEOPHILUS OF EDESSA
    R. G. Hoyland, trans. (2011) in *Theophilus of Edessa's Chronicle and the Circulation of Historical Knowledge in Late Antiquity and Early Islam.* Liverpool: Liverpool University Press.
THEOPOMPUS OF CHIOS, *Philippica*
THUCYDIDES, *History of the Peloponnesian War*
    R. Warner, trans. (1972). Harmondsworth: Penguin.
TROYES, *Arthurian Romances*
    C. Carroll and W. Kibler, trans. (1991). Harmondsworth: Penguin.
IOANNIS TZETZES, *Antehomerica, Homerica et Posthomerica*
    Tzetzes, I. (1793). Montana: Kessinga Publishing Co.
VILLEHARDOUIN, G. de, *The Conquest of Constantinople*
    Jean de Joinville and Geoffrey de Villehardouin, *Chronicles of the Crusades,* trans. M. R. B. Shaw (1963). London: Penguin.
VIRGIL, *The Aeneid*
    D. West, trans. (2003). Harmondsworth: Penguin.
XENOPHON, *Anabasis*
    C. L. Brownson, trans. (1922) rev. J. Dillery (1998). Loeb Classical Library. Cambridge, MA: Harvard University Press.
XENOPHON, *Hellenica*
    C. L. Brownson, trans. (1918). Loeb Classical Library. Cambridge, MA: Harvard University Press.
ZOSIMUS, *New History*
    J. J. Buchanan and H. T. Davis, trans. (1967). San Antonio, TX: Trinity University Press.

R. T. Ridley, trans. (1982). Canberra: Australian Association for Byzantine Studies, University of Sydney.

MISCELLANEOUS

Begley, W. and Desai, Z. (eds and trans.) (1990) *The Shah Jahan Nama of 'Inayat Khan*. Oxford: Oxford University Press.

Bon, O., *The Sultan's Seraglio: An Intimate Portrait of Life at the Ottoman Court (From the Seventeenth-Century Edition of John Withers)*, ed. G. Goodwin (1996). London: Saqi.

Dankoff, R. and Kim, S. (eds and trans.) (2010), *An Ottoman Traveller: Selections from the Books of Travels of Evliya Çelebi*. London: Eland.

Georgievitz, B. (1661) *The Rarities of Turkey Gathered by One that was Sold Seven Times as Slave in the Turkish Empire* ... London.

Ibn Khaldun, *The Muqaddimah: An Introduction to History*, ed. N. J. Dawood, trans. F. Rosenthal (1989). Princeton: Princeton University Press.

Marana, G. P. (1687) *Lettters Writ by a Turkish Spy, Who Lived Five and Forty Years Undiscovered at Paris*. London.

Oberhelman, S. M. (2008), *Dreambooks in Byzantium: Six 'Oneirocritica' in Translation, with Commentary and Introduction*. Aldershot: Ashgate.

Rutherford H. Platt, Jr. (1926), *The Forgotten Books of Eden*. Apocryphal Press.

A True and Exact Relation of the Raising of the Siege of Vienna and the Victory obtained over the Ottoman Army, the 12th of September 1683, pamphlet 'Printed for Samuel Crouch at the Corner of Popes-Head Alley next Cornhill, 1683' in *German History in Documents and Images*, vol. 2: *From Absolutism to Napoleon, 1648–1815*. http://germanhistorydocs.ghi-dc.org/sub_document.cfm?document_id=3580 [accessed 19.01.2016].

SECONDARY SOURCES

Abulafia, D. (2011) *The Great Sea*. Oxford: Oxford University Press.

Acidini Luchinat, C. (ed.) (1993) *The Chapel of the Magi: Benozzo Gozzoli's Frescoes in the Palazzo Medici-Riccardi Florence*, trans. E. Daunt (1994). London: Thames & Hudson.

Ackerman, G. M. (1997) *Jean-Léon Gérôme: His Life, his Work*. Paris: ACR Edition.

Adam, J. P. (2001) *Roman Building: Materials and Techniques*. London: Routledge.

Adam, R. (1764) *Ruins of the Palace of the Emperor Diocletian at Spalatro in Dalmatia*. London.

Adler, M. N. (1907) *The Itinerary of Benjamin of Tudela*. NY: Philipp Feldham.

Ágoston, G. (2008) 'The Image of the Ottomans in Hungarian Historiography',

Acta Orientalia Academiae Scientiarum Hungaricae 61.1/2: 15–26.

Ahmed, A. (2007) *Journey into Islam: The Crisis of Globalization*. Washington, DC: Brookings Institution Press.

Ahunbay, M. and Ahunbay, Z. (2000) 'Recent Work on the Land Walls of Istanbul: Tower 2 to Tower 5', *Dumbarton Oaks Papers* 54: 227–39.

Akçam, T. (2006) *A Shameful Act: The Armenian Genocide and the Question of Turkish Responsibility*. London: Picador.

Akçam, T. (2012) *The Young Turks' Crime against Humanity: The Armenian Genocide and Ethnic Cleansing in the Ottoman Empire*. Princeton and Oxford: Princeton University Press.

Akgündüz, A. and Öztürk, S. (2011) *Ottoman History: Misperceptions and Truths*. Rotterdam: IUR Press.

Aksan, V. H. (1998), 'Mutiny and the Eighteenth Century Ottoman Army', *Turkish Studies Association*, 22(1), 116–25.

Alchermes, J. (1994) '*Spolia* in Roman Cities of the Late Empire: Legislative Rationales and Architectural Reuse', *Dumbarton Oaks Papers* 48: 167–78.

Alexander, D. (2006), 'Swords from Ottoman and Mamluk Treasuries', in Komaroff, L. (ed.), *Pearls from Water, Rubies from Stone: Studies in Islamic Art in Honour of Priscilla Soucek*, Part 1. *Artibus Asiae* (special volume) 66.2: 13–34.

Alföldi, A. (1932) 'The Helmet of Constantine with the Christian Monogram', *Journal of Roman Studies* 22.1: 9–23.

Alföldi, A. (1947) 'On the Foundation of Constantinople: A Few Notes', *Journal of Roman Studies* 37: 10–16.

Algan, O., Yılmaz, Y., Yalçın, M. N., Özdoğan, M., Sarı, E., Kırcı-Elmas, E., Yılmaz, I., Bulkan-Yeşiladalı, O., Ongan, D., and Gazioglu, C. (2010) 'Geo-archaeology of the Ancient Theodosius Harbour (Yenikapi-Istanbul): Implications to Holocene Sea Level and Coastal Changes', paper given at Geological Society of America Denver Annual Meeting, 31 October–3 November. Geological Society of America, *Abstracts with Programs* 42.5: 29.

Allen, P. S., Allen, H. M. and Garrod, H. W. (1938) *Opus Epistolarum Desedirii Erasmi Roterodami*, vol. 9: *1530–1532*. Oxford: Oxford University Press.

Allen, R. (2008) *Spies, Scandals, & Sultans: Istanbul in the Twilight of the Ottoman Empire*. First English Translation of Egyptian Ibrahim al-Muwaylihi's *Ma Hunalik*. Lanham, MD: Rowman & Littlefield Publishers.

Altabé, D. F. (1983). *Spanish and Portuguese Jewry before and after 1492*. New York: Sepher-Hermon Press, Inc.

Alwis, A. P. (2006) 'Review of Shaun Tougher, *Eunuchs in Antiquity and Beyond*', *Classical Review* 56.1: 185–7.

Amory, P. (1997) *People and Identity in Ostrogothic Italy, 489–554*. Cambridge: Cambridge University Press.

Anderson, F. M. and Hershey, A. S. (1918) *Handbook for the Diplomatic History of Europe, Asia, and Africa 1870–1914*. Prepared for the National Board for

Historical Service. Washington, DC: Government Printing Office.

Anderson, S. (2013) *Lawrence in Arabia: War, Deceit, Imperial Folly and the Making of the Modern Middle East*. London: Atlantic Books.

Andrewes, A. (1953) 'The Generals in the Hellespont, 410–407 B.C.', *Journal of Hellenic Studies* 73: 2–9.

Andrews, W. E. (ed.) (1814) *The Orthodox Journal and Catholic Monthly Intelligencer*, vol. 2. London.

Androshchuk, F., Shepard, J. and White, M. (eds) (2016) *Byzantium and the Viking World*. Uppsala: Acta Universitatis Upsaliensis.

Angelova, D. (2004) 'The Ivories of Ariadne and Ideas about Female Imperial Authority in Rome and Early Byzantium', *Gesta* 43.1: 1–15.

Arbel, B. (1992) 'Nur Banu (c. 1530–1583): A Venetian Sultana?', *Turcica* 24: 241–59.

Archibald, Z. H. (2013) *Ancient Economies of the Northern Aegean: Fifth to First Centuries BC*. Oxford: Oxford University Press.

Argenti, P. P. (1970) *The Religious Minorities of Chios: Jews and Catholics*. Cambridge: Cambridge University Press.

Armstrong, G. T. (1974) 'Constantine's Churches: Symbol and Structure', *Journal of the Society of Architectural Historians* 33.1: 5–16.

Arsebük, G. (1996) 'The Cave of Yarimurgaz (the Oldest Stratified Site Yet Known in Turkey)', in U. Magen and M. Rashad (eds) *Vom Halys zum Euphrat*. Munster: Ugarit-Verlag. 1–13.

Ashley, S. (2013) 'How Icelanders Experienced Byzantium, Real and Imagined', in C. Nesbitt, and M. Jackson (eds) *Experience Byzantium*. Farnham: Ashgate.

Askan, V. H. (1998) 'Mutiny and the Eighteenth Century Ottoman Army', *Turkish Studies Association Bulletin* 22.1: 116–25.

Attaleiates, M. (2012) *The History*, trans. A. Kaldellis and D. Krallis. Cambridge, MA: Harvard University Press.

Aydingün, S. (2009) 'Early Neolithic Discoveries at Istanbul', *Antiquity* 83.320, June *passim* http://antiquity.ac.uk/projgall/aydingun320/.

Aydingün, S. and Güldoğan, E. (2011) 'ITA (Istanbul Prehistoric Survey) Researches in 2008', in H. Oniz and E. Aslan (eds) *SOMA 2009: Proceedings of the XIII Symposium on Mediterranean Archaeology, Selcuk University of Konya, Turkey, 23–24 April 2009*. Oxford: Archaeopress.

Aydingün, S. and Oniz, H., *RAPOR. Istanbul Congress 2011: Istanbul Küçükçekmece Lake Basin Excavations. Eastern Mediterranean University, Underwater Research and Imaging Center Kocaeli University, Department of Archaeology*.

Bachhuber, C. (2009) 'The Treasure Deposits of Troy: Rethinking Crisis and Agency on the Early Bronze Age Citadel', *Anatolian Studies* 59: 118.

Badem, C. (2010) *The Ottoman Crimean War (1853–1856)*. Leiden: Brill.

Baer, M. (2004) 'The Great Fire of 1600 and the Islamization of Christian and

Jewish Space in Istanbul', *International Journal of Middle East Studies* 36.2: 159–81.

Baer, M. (2008) *Honored by the Glory of Islam: Conversion and Conquest in Ottoman Europe*. Oxford: Oxford University Press.

Bagnall, R. S. (2007) *Egypt in the Byzantine World*. Cambridge: Cambridge University Press.

Banaji, J. (2007) 'Islam, the Mediterranean and the Rise of Capitalism', *Historical Materialism* 15: 47–74.

Bannikov, A. V. (2014) 'Late Roman Auxilia and Constantine's "Vision"', *World Applied Sciences Journal* 30.11: 1656–9.

Barber, C. (2001) 'Mimesis and Memory in the Narthex Mosaics at the Nea Moni, Chios', *Art History* 24.3: 323–37.

Barbera, M. (ed.) (2013) *Costantino 313 d.C.* Milan: Electa.

Bardill, J. (1997) 'The Palace of Lausus and Nearby Monuments in Constantinople: A Topographical Study', *American Journal of Archaeology* 101.1: 67–95.

Bardill, J. (2000) 'The Church of Sts. Sergius and Bacchus in Constantinople and the Monophysite Refugees', *Dumbarton Oaks Papers* 54: 1–11.

Baris, Y. I. and Hillerdal, G. (2009) 'Tuberculosis in the Ottoman Harem in the 19th Century', *Journal of Medical Biography* 17: 170–3.

Barnes, D. (1981) *Constantine and Eusebius*. Cambridge, MA: Harvard University Press.

Barnes, T. (2011) *Constantine: Dynasty, Religion and Power in the Later Roman Empire*. Chichester: Wiley-Blackwell.

Baron, B. and Keddie, N. R. (eds) (1977) *Women in Middle Eastern History: Shifting Boundaries in Sex and Gender*. New Haven: Yale University Press.

Baskins, C. (2012) 'The Bride of Trebizond: Turks and Turkmens on a Florentine Wedding Chest, circa 1460', in *Muqarnas* 29: 83–100.

Başaran, S. and Kocabaş, U. (2008) 'From the Theodosian Harbour to Yenikapi Shipwrecks', *Colloquium Anatolicum* 7: 1-22

Bassett, S. G. (2000) '"Excellent Offerings": The Lausos Collection in Constantinople', *Art Bulletin* 82.1: 6–25.

Bassett, S. G. (2004) *The Urban Image of Late Antique Constantinople*. Cambridge: Cambridge University Press.

Battiscombe, C. F. (1956) *The Relics of St Cuthbert*. Oxford: Oxford University Press.

Baum, B. (2008) *The Rise and Fall of the Caucasian Race: A Political History of Racial Identity*. New York: New York University Press.

Bayliss, R. (2003) 'Archaeological Survey and Visualisation: The View from Byzantium', in L. Lavan and W. Bowden (eds), *Theory and Practice in Late Antique Archaeology*. Leiden and Boston: Brill, 288–313.

Beard, M. (2007) *The Roman Triumph*. Cambridge, MA and London: The Belknap Press of Harvard University Press.

Beaton, R. (2013) *Byron's War: Romantic Rebellion, Greek Revolution*. Cambridge: Cambridge University Press.

Beaumont, L., Archontidou-Argyri, A., Bearnes, H., Tsigkou, A. and Wardle, N. (2004) 'Excavations at Kato Phana, Chios: 1999, 2000, and 2001', *Annual of the British School at Athens* 99: 201–55.

Bell, A. (2004) *Spectacular Power in the Greek and Roman City*. Oxford: Oxford University Press.

Bell, D. P. (2008) *Jews in the Early Modern World*. Lanham, MD: Rowman & Littlefield.

Bent, T. (1887), 'Byzantine Palaces', *English Historical Review*, 2.1: 466–81.

Berg, W. (1974) 'Hecate: Greek or "Anatolian"?', *Numen* 21.2: 128–9.

Bernard Yeazell, R. (2000) *Harems of the Mind*. New Haven and London: Yale University Press.

Bicknell, S. (2001) *The History of the English Organ*. Cambridge: Cambridge University Press.

Bintley, M. D. J. (2011) 'The Byzantine Silver Bowls in the Sutton Hoo Ship Burial and Tree-Worship in Anglo-Saxon England', *Papers from the Institute of Archaeology* 21: 34–45.

Birely, A. R. (2013) *Hadrian: The Restless Emperor*. London: Routledge.

Bisaha, N. (2004a) *Creating East and West: Renaissance Humanists and the Ottoman Turks*. Philadelphia: University of Pennsylvania Press.

Bisaha, N. (2004b) 'Pope Pius II and the Crusade', in N. Housley (ed.) *Crusading in the Fifteenth Century: Message and Impact*. Basingstoke: Palgrave, 39–52.

Blackhurst, A. (2004) 'The House of Nubel: Rebels or Players?', in A. H. Merrills (ed.), *Vandals, Romans and Berbers: New Perspectives on Late Antique North Africa*. Aldershot: Ashgate.

Blackman, D. (2001–2) 'Archaeology in Greece 2001–2002', *Archaeological Reports* 48: 1–115.

Blair, S. and J. Bloom (eds) (2012) *God Is Beautiful and Loves Beauty: The Object in Islamic Art and Culture*. New Haven and London: Yale University Press.

Blake, S. P. (2002) *Shahjahanabad: The Sovereign City in Mughal India 1639–1739*. Cambridge: Cambridge University Press.

Blanch, L. (1954, 1982) *The Wilder Shores of Love*. New York: Simon & Schuster.

Blodgett, M. D. (2007) *Attila, flagellum Dei? Huns and Romans, Conflict and Cooperation in the Late Antique World*. Santa Barbara, CA: University of California Press.

Bloedow, E. F. (1992) 'Alcibiades "Brilliant" or "Intelligent"?', *Historia: Zeitschrift für Alte Geschichte* 41.2: 139–57.

Blumenbach, J. F. (2000). 'On the Natural Variety of Mankind', in Bernasconi, R. (ed.) *The Idea of Race*. Indianapolis: Hackett Publishing.

Boatwright, M. T. (2003) *Hadrian and the Cities of the Roman Empire*. Princeton: Princeton University Press.

Bobokhyan, A. (2009) 'Trading Implements in Early Troy: In memoriam Professor Manfred Korfmann', *Anatolian Studies* 59: 19–51.

Bogdanović, J. (2008) 'Tetrapylon', in *Encyclopaedia of the Hellenic World, Constantinople*. constantinople.ehw.gr/forms/fLemmaBodyExtended.aspx?-lemmaID=12429 [accessed: 20.06.2013].

Bogdanović, J. (2012) 'Life in a Late Byzantine Tower: Examples from Northern Greece', in M. J. Johnson, R. Ousterhout and A. Papalexandrou (eds) *Approaches to Byzantine Architecture and its Decoration: Studies in Honor of Slobodan Ćurčić*. Farnham: Ashgate. 187–202.

Boivin, M. (2003) *La Rénovation du Shî'isme Ismaélien en Inde et au Pakistan d'après les écrits et les discours de Sultan Muhammad Shah Aga Khan (1902–1954)*. London and New York: Routledge Curzon.

Bolgar, R. R. (1954) *The Classical Heritage and its Beneficiaries*. Cambridge: Cambridge University Press.

Bollók, A. (2012) 'Byzantine Missions among the Magyars during the Later 10th Century?', in M. Salamon, M. Wołoszyn, A. Musin and P. Špehar (eds) *Rome, Constantinople and Newly-Converted Europe: Archaeological and Historical Evidence*, vol. 2. Crakow, Leipzig, Rzeszów and Warsaw: Instytut Archeologii i Etnologii Polskiej akademii nauk. 131–44.

Bomgardner, D. L. (2000) *The Story of the Roman Amphitheatre*. London: Routledge.

Bon, O., and Goodwin, G. (eds) (1996) *The Sultan's Seraglio: An Intimate Portrait of Life at the Ottoman Court*, trans. R. Withers. London: Saqi Books.

Bonner, G., Rollason, D. and Stancliffe, C. (eds) (1989) *St Cuthbert, his Cult and Community*. Woodbridge: Boydell & Brewer.

Bono, P., Crow, J. and Bayliss, R. (2001) 'The Water Supply of Constantinople: Archaeology and Hydrogeology of an Early Medieval City', *Environmental Geology* 40.11: 1325–33.

Bony, G., Marriner, N., Morhange, C., Kaniewski, D. and Perinçek, D. (2011) 'A High-Energy Deposit in the Byzantine Harbour of Yenikapi, Istanbul (Turkey)', *Quaternary International* 30: 1–14.

Borsook, E. (2000) 'Rhetoric or Reality: Mosaics as Expressions of a Metaphysical Idea', *Mitteilungen des Kunsthistorischen Institutes in Florenz* 44.1: 2–18.

Bosworth, C. E. (1996) 'Arab Attacks on Rhodes in the Pre-Ottoman Period', *Journal of the Royal Asiatic Society*, 6.2: 157–64.

Bouras, C. (2002) 'Aspects of the Byzantine City, Eighth–Fifteenth Centuries', in A. E. Laiou (ed.) *The Economic History of Byzantium: From the Seventh through the Fifteenth Century*. Washington, DC: Dumbarton Oaks Research Library and Collection.

Bowersock, G. W. (1978) *Julian the Apostate*. Cambridge, MA: Harvard University Press.

Bowersock, G. W. (2012) *Empires in Collision in Late Antiquity*. Waltham, MA: Brandeis University Press.

Bowes, K. (2008), *Private Worship, Public Values, and Religious Change in Late Antiquity*. Cambridge: Cambridge University Press.

Bowman, A., Garnsey, P. and Cameron, A. (eds) (2005) *The Cambridge Ancient History*, vol. 12: *The Crisis of Empire, AD 193–337*. Cambridge: Cambridge University Press.

Boyar, E. and Fleet, K. (2010) *A Social History of Ottoman Istanbul*. Cambridge: Cambridge University Press.

Boyar. E. and Fleet. K. (2016) *Ottoman Women in Public Space*, Leiden and Boston: Brill.

Bradbury, S. (1994) 'Constantine and the Problem of Anti-Pagan Legislation in the Fourth Century', *Classical Philology* 89:2. 120–39.

Bradford, E. (1969, 2009) *The Sultan's Admiral: Barbarossa – Pirate and Empire-Builder*. London and New York: I. B. Tauris (2009); first published by Hodder & Stoughton (1969).

Brand, C. M. (ed.) (1969) *Icon and Minaret: Sources of Byzantine and Islamic Civilization*. Englewood Cliffs, NJ: Prentice-Hall.

Brandmüller, W. (2009) *Light and Shadows: Church History amid Faith, Fact and Legend*. San Francisco: Ignatius Press.

Bregman, J. A. (1993) 'Synesius of Cyrene', in A. Cameron (ed.) *Barbarians and Politics at the Court of Arcadius*. Berkeley and Los Angeles: University of California Press. 1360.

Brewer, D. (2011) *The Greek War of Independence: The Struggle for Freedom and from Ottoman Oppression*. New York: The Overlook Press.

Bridge, A. (1978) *Theodora: Portrait in a Byzantine Landscape*. London: Cassell.

Brookes, D. S. (trans. & ed.) (2008) *The Concubine, the Princess, and the Teacher: Voices from the Ottoman Harem*. Austin, TX: University of Texas Press.

Brooks, E. W. (1899) 'The Campaign of 716–718 from Arabic Sources', *Journal of Hellenic Studies* 19: 19–31.

Brotton, J. (2002) *The Renaissance Bazaar: From the Silk Road to Michelangelo*. Oxford: Oxford University Press.

Brotton, J. (2016) *This Orient Isle: Elizabethan England and the Islamic World*. London: Allen Lane.

Brown, V. (1909) *Haremlik*. Boston; New York: Houghton & Mifflin Co.

Browning, R. (1962) 'The Patriarchal School at Constantinople in the Twelfth Century', *Byzantion* 32: 186–93.

Brubaker, L. (2010) 'Icons and Iconography', in L. James (ed.) *A Companion to Byzantium*. Oxford: Blackwell, 326.

Brubaker, L. and Haldon, J. (2011) *Byzantium in the Iconoclast Era, c. 680–850: A History*. Cambridge: Cambridge University Press.

Brumback, R. H. (2007) *History of the Church through the Ages: From the Apostolic Age, through the Apostasies, the Dark Ages, the Reformation and the Restoration*. Oregon: Wipf and Stock.

Brummett, P. (2015) *Mapping the Ottoman's Sovereignty, Territory, and Identity in the Early Modern Mediterranean*. Cambridge: Cambridge University Press.

Bruns, G. (1935) *Der Obelisk und seine Basis auf dem Hippodrom zu Konstantinopel*. Istanbul: Archäologische Institut des deutschen Reiches, Abteilung Istanbul.

Buenger Robbert, L. (1995) 'Rialto Businessmen and Constantinople, 1204–61', in *Dumbarton Oaks Papers* 49: 43–58.

Bulliet, R. W. (2009) *Cotton, Climate, and Camels In Early Islamic Iran: A Moment in World History*. New York: Columbia University Press.

Bullough, O. (2010). *Let Our Fame Be Great: Journeys among the defiant people of the Caucasus*. London: Penguin.

Burckhardt, J. L. (1972) *Arabic Proverbs*. London: Curzon Press.

Burgess, R. W. (1999) Ἀχυρών or Προάστειον? The Location and Circumstances of Constantine's Death', *Journal of Theological Studies* 50: 151–61.

Burns, R. (2005) *Damascus: A History*. London: Routledge.

Byron (1837) *The Complete Works of Lord Byron,* A. and W. Galignani and Company.

Cameron, A. (1970) *Agathias*. Oxford: Oxford University Press.

Cameron, A. (2000) 'Vandal and Byzantine Africa', in A. Cameron, B. Ward-Perkins and M. Whitby (eds) *The Cambridge Ancient History*, vol. 14: *Late Antiquity: Empire and Successors*. Cambridge: Cambridge University Press, 552–69.

Cameron, A. (2006), *The Byzantines*. Oxford: Blackwell.

Cameron, A. (ed.) (2013) *Late Antiquity on the Eve of Islam*. The Formation of the Classical Islamic World 1. Farnham: Ashgate.

Campbell, B. (2011) *The Romans and their World: A Short Introduction*. London and New Haven: Yale University Press.

Canav-Özgümüş, Ü. (2012) 'Recent Glass Finds in Istanbul', in D. Ignatiadu and A. Antonaras (eds) *Annales du 18e Congrès de l'Association Internationale pour l'Histoire du Verre*. Thessaloniki: Ziti, 326–32.

Cardini, F. (2001) *The Chapel of the Magi in Palazzo Medici*. Florence: Mandragora.

Carnarvon, F. (8th Countess of Carnarvon) (2011) *Lady Almina and the Real Downton Abbey: The Lost Legacy of Highclere Castle*. London: Hodder & Stoughton.

Carr, M. (2013) 'The Hospitallers of Rhodes and their Alliances against the Turks', in S. Phillips and E. Buttigieg (eds) *Islands and Military Orders, c. 1291–1798*. Farnham: Ashgate, 167–76.

Cartledge, P. (2002) *The Spartans*. London: Channel Four Books.

Cartledge, P. (2004) *Alexander the Great: The Hunt for a New Past*. Basingstoke and Oxford: Macmillan.

Cartledge, P. (2011) *Ancient Greece: A Very Short Introduction*. Oxford and New York: Oxford University Press.

Casson, L. (1954) 'The Grain Trade in the Hellenistic World', *Transactions and Proceedings of the American Philological Association* 85: 168–87.

Cavafy, C. P. (2003) *Poems by C.P Cavafy*, trans. J. C. Cavafy. Athens: Ikaros.

Cavaliero, R. (2010) *Ottomania: The Romantics and the Myth of the Islamic Orient*. London: I. B. Tauris.

Cecota, B. (2012) 'Islam, the Arabs and Umayyad Rulers According to Theophanes the Confessor's Chronography'. Translations by Konrad Figat in *Studia Ceranea* 2: 97–111.

Ceka, N. (1999) *Butrint: A Guide to the City and its Monuments* [trans. Sally Martin]. London: Butrint Foundation.

Cervantes Saavedra, M. (1825) *The Life and Exploits of the Ingenious Gentleman Don Quixote De La Mancha*, trans. C. Jarvis. New York: Evert Duyckinck.

Chadwick, H. (2005) *East and West: The Making of a Rift in the Church from Apostolic Times until the Council of Florence*. Oxford: Oxford University Press.

Chahin, M. (2001) *The Kingdom of Armenia: A History*. Richmond: Curzon Press.

Chibnall, M. (trans.) (1990) 'The Ecclesiastical History of Orderic Vitalis', Vol. 2, Oxford: Clarendon Press, 203 and 205.

Christophilopoulou, A. (1956) Εκλογή, αναγόρευσις και στέψις του βυζαντινού αυτοκράτορος [Πραγματείαι της Ακαδημίας Αθηνών, τ. 22/2]. Athens (reissued 2003).

Cichocki, N. (2005) 'Continuity and Change in Turkish Bathing Culture in Istanbul: A Life Story of the Çemberlitaş Hamam', *Turkish Studies* 6.1: 93–112.

Ciggaar, K. N. (1996) *Western Travellers to Constantinople: The West and Byzantium 962–1204*. Netherlands: Brill.

Cilliers, L. and Retief, F. P. (2004) 'The Eunuchs of Early Byzantium', *Scholia* 13: 108–17.

Clark, J. (2004) *Christianity and Roman Society*. Cambridge: Cambridge University Press.

Connor, C. L. (2004) *Women of Byzantium*. New Haven and London: Yale University Press.

Conrad, L. I. (1996) 'The Arabs and the Colossus', *Journal of the Royal Asiatic Society* 6.2: 165–87.

Constable, G. (2008) *Crusaders and Crusading in the Twelfth Century*. Aldershot: Ashgate.

Constantelos, D. (1999) 'The Formation of the Hellenic Christian Mind', in D. Constantelos, *Christian Hellenism: Essays and Studies in Continuity and Change*. New Rochelle, New York and Athens: Aristide D. Caratzas, *passim*.

Cooper, K. (2013) *Band of Angels: The Forgotten World of Early Christian Women*. London: Atlantic Books.

Cormack, R. (2007) *Icons*. Cambridge, MA: Harvard University Press.

Cormack, R. and Vassilaki, M. (eds) (2008) *Byzantium: 330–1453*. London: Royal Academy of Arts.

Creasy, E. S. (1854). *History of the Ottoman Turks: From the beginning of their Empire to the Present Time.* London: R. Bentley.

Critobulus, M. (1954). *History of Mehmet the Conqueror,* trans. Charles T. Riggs. Princeton: Princeton University Press.

Croke, B. (1983) 'The Context and Date of Priscus Fragment 6', *Classical Philology* 78.4: 297–308.

Crone, P. (1987) *Meccan Trade and the Rise of Islam.* Oxford: Blackwell.

Crooke, A. (1637). *A Relation of a Journey Begun An Dom: 1610: Fovre Bookes.* Library of the Ohio State University, Digitised 2014.

Cross S. H. and Sherbowitz-Wetzor, O. P. (1953) *Russian Primary Chronicles.* Cambridge, MA.

Crow, J., Bardill, J. and Bayliss, R. (2008) *The Water Supply of Byzantine Constantinople,* Journal of Roman Studies Monograph 11. London: Society for the Promotion of Roman Studies. http://www.academia.edu/3165827/The_water_supply_of_Byzantine_Constantinople.

Crowley, R. (2005). *Constantinople: The Last Great Siege, 1453.* London: Faber & Faber.

Crowley, R. (2006), *1453: The Holy War for Constantinople and the Clash of Islam and the West.* New York: Hyperion Books.

Crowley, R. (2008) *Empires of the Sea: The Final Battle for the Mediterranean, 1521–1580.* London: Faber & Faber.

Crowson, A. (2007) *Venetian Butrint.* London and Tirana: Butrint Foundation.

Cruikshank, G. (1832) *Scraps and Sketches.* Publisher unknown.

Cui, Y. et al. (2012) 'Historical Variations in Mutation Rate in an Epidemic Pathogen, *Yersinia pestis*', *Proceedings of the National Academy of Sciences of the United States of America* 110.2: 577–82.

Cunliffe, B. (2008) *Europe between the Oceans 9000 BC–AD 1000.* New Haven and London: Yale University Press.

Curta, F. (2001) *The Making of the Slavs: History and Archaeology of the Lower Danube Region c. 500–700.* Cambridge: Cambridge University Press.

Cutler, A. (2002) 'The Industries of Art', in A. E. Laiou (ed.), *The Economic History of Byzantium: From the Seventh through the Fifteenth Century.* Washington DC: Dumbarton Oaks Research Library and Collection, 555–87.

Dagron, G. (2003) *Emperor and Priest: The Imperial Office in Byzantium,* trans. J. Birrell. Cambridge: Cambridge University Press.

Dagron, G. and Déroche, V. (2010) 'Juifs et Chrétiens'. Paris: Amis du Centre d'Histoire et Civilisation de Byzance, 240–7.

Dalby, A. (2003, 2010) *Tastes of Byzantium: The Cuisine of a Legendary Empire.* London: I. B. Tauris.

Dallam, T. (1893). The Diary of Master Thomas Dallam, 1599–1600. *Early Voyages and Travels in the Levant,* 2.

Dalrymple, W. (1997) *From the Holy Mountain: A Journey in the Shadow of Byzantium.* London: HarperCollins.

Dalrymple, W. (2005) *Re-Orienting the Renaissance: Cultural Exchanges with the East*, New York and Basingstoke: Palgrave Macmillan.

D'Amato, R. (2010) *The Varangian Guard 988–1453*. Oxford: Osprey Publishing.

Dankoff, R. (2004) *An Ottoman Mentality*. Leiden: Brill.

Darwin, J. (2007) *After Tamerlane: The Rise & Fall of Global Empires, 1400–2000*. London: Allen Lane.

Davidson, R. H. (1979) 'The "Dosografa" Church in the Treaty of Küçük Kaynara', *Bulletin of the School of Oriental and African Studies*, 42.1: 46–52.

Davis, N. Z. (2007) *Trickster Travels in Search of Leo Africanus: A Sixteenth-Century Muslim between Worlds*. London: Faber & Faber.

Davis, W. S. (ed.) (1912–13) *Readings in Ancient History: Illustrative Extracts from the Sources*. 2 vols. Boston: Allyn & Bacon.

Dawes, E. (1948) *Three Byzantine Saints: Contemporary Biographies of St. Daniel the Stylite, St. Theodore of Sykeon and St. John the Almsgiver*, with introductions and notes by N. H. Baynes. Oxford: Blackwell.

Dawkins, R. M. (1947) 'The Later History of the Varangian Guard: Some Notes', *Journal of Roman Studies* 37.1–2: 39–46.

Dawood, N. (ed. and trans.) (2014) *The Koran: With a Parallel Translation of the Arabic Text*. London: Penguin.

Deakin, M. A. B. (2007) *Hypatia of Alexandria: Mathematician and Martyr*. Amherst, NY: Prometheus Books.

De Amicis, E. (2010) *Constantinople*, trans. S. Parkin. London: One World Classics.

de Busbecq, O. G. (2001/2005) *Turkish Letters*, trans. E. S. Forster. London: Eland. First published by Oxford and The Clarendon Press in 1927.

de Fonblanque, E. B. (1877). *Lives of the Lords Strangford: With Their Ancestors and Contemporaries Through Ten Generations*. London: Cassell, Petter & Galpin.

de la Bédoyère, G. (2015) *The Real Lives of Roman Britain*. New Haven and London: Yale University Press.

de Madariaga, I. (1990) *Catherine the Great: A Short History*. New Haven and London: Yale University Press.

de Polignac, F. and Jacob, C. (eds) (2000) *Alexandria, Third Century BC: The Knowledge of the World in a Single City*. Alexandria: Harpocrates Publishing.

Dendrinos, C. and Antonopoulos, P. (2001) 'The Eastern Roman Empire at the time of the first millennium', in *Europe around the year 1000*, ed. P. Urbanczyk. Warsaw: Institute of Archaeology and Ehenology, Polish Academey of Sciences, 167–203.

Despina, L. (2008) 'Walls of Constantine', in *Encyclopaedia of the Hellenic World, Constantinople* http://www.ehw.gr/l.aspx?id=11742 [date accessed 20.06.2013].

De Waal, T. (2010) *The Caucasus: An Introduction*. Oxford: Oxford University Press.

Dikov, I. (2015) 'Bulgaria Unveils Monument of Cyrillic (Bulgarian) Alphabet in Mongolia's Capital Ulan Bator', *Archaeology in Bulgaria*. http://archaeologyinbulgaria.com/2015/05/11/bulgaria-unveils-monument-of-cyrillic-bulgarian-alphabet-in-mongolias-capital-ulan-bator/.

Dillery, J. (2015) *Clio's Other Sons: Berossus & Manetho*. Ann Arbor: University of Michigan Press.

Dixon, S. (2009) *Catherine the Great*. London: Profile Books.

Dodwell, C. (1982) *Anglo-Saxon Art: A New Perspective*. Manchester: Manchester University Press.

Dogu, D., Kose, C., Kartal, N. S. and Erdin, N. (2011) 'Wood Identification of Wooden Marine Piles from the Ancient Byzantine Port of Eleutherius/ Theodosius', *BioResources* 6.2: 987–1018.

d'Ohsson, M. (1788–1824) *Tableau général de l'Empire Othoman*. 7 vols. Paris: Firmin Didot.

Donadoni, S. (ed.) (1997) *The Egyptians*. Chicago: University of Chicago Press.

Dönmez, S. (2006) 'The Prehistory of the Istanbul Region: A Survey', *Ancient Near East Studies* 43: 239–64.

Downey, G. (1957) 'Nikolaos Mesarites: Description of the Church of the Holy Apostles at Constantinople', *Transactions of the American Philosophical Society* 47.6: 855–924.

Downing, B. (2004) 'The Sideways Medusa', *Journal of Literature and Art* 40: 70.

Dubnov, S. (1968) *History of the Jews: From the Roman Empire to the Early Medieval Period*, trans. M. Spiegel. South Brunswick, NJ: Yoseloff.

Düring, B. S. (2008) 'The Early Holocene Occupation of North-Central Anatolia between 10,000 and 6,000 BC Cal: Investigating an Archaeological Terra Incognita', *Anatolian Studies* 58: 15–46.

Düzbakar, O. (2006) 'Charitable Women and their Pious Foundations in the Ottoman Empire: The Hospital of the Senior Mother, Nurbanu Valide Sultan', *Journal of the International Society for the History of Islamic Medicine* 5: 11–20.

Eames, A. (2009/2010) *Blue River, Black Sea: A Journey along the Danube into the Heart of the New Europe*. London: Transworld Publishers.

Edwards, J. (2005) *Ferdinand and Isabella: Profiles in Power*. Harlow: Pearson Education.

Efendi, E. (1834) *Narrative of Travels in Europe Asia and Africa in the Seventeenth Century*, trans. J. von Hammer. London: Printed for the Oriental Translation Fund.

Einstein, L. (1917/2012) *Inside Constantinople: A Diplomatist's Diary during the Dardanelles Expedition, April–September, 1915*. London: Forgotten Books (originally London: John Murray).

El Cheikh, N. M. (1998) 'Sūrat Al-Rūm: A Study of the Exegetical Literature', *Journal of the American Oriental Society* 118.3 (July–Sept.): 356–64.

El Cheikh, N. M. (2004) *Byzantium Viewed by the Arabs*. Cambridge, MA: Harvard University Press.

Elsner, J. (1998) *Imperial Rome and Christian Triumph*. Oxford: Oxford University Press.

Eraly, A. (1997, 2007) *The Mughal World: India's Tainted Paradise*. London: Weidenfeld & Nicolson.

Ergin, N. (2008) 'The Soundscape of Sixteenth-Century Istanbul Mosques: Architecture and Qur'an Recital', *Journal of the Society of Architectural Historians* 67.2: 204–21.

Erol, M. (2013) 'Surveillance, Urban Governance and Legitimacy in Late Ottoman Istanbul: Spying on Music and Entertainment during the Hamidian Regime (1876–1909)', *Urban History* 40: 706–25.

Errington, R. M. (1988) 'Constantine and the Pagans', *Greek, Roman and Byzantine Studies* 29: 309–18.

Ersoy, N., Gungor, Y. and Akpinar, A. (2011) 'International Sanitary Conferences from the Ottoman Perspective (1851–1938)', *Hygiea Internationalis* 10.1: 53.

Evans, H. C., Holcomb, M. and Hallman, R. (2001) 'The Arts of Byzantium', *Metropolitan Museum of Art Bulletin* 58.4: 1, 4–68.

Evans, H. C. and Ratliff, B. (2012) *Byzantium and Islam: Age of Transition 7th–9th Century*. New Haven and London: Yale University Press.

Evans, J. A. (2002) *The Empress Theodora: Partner of Justinian*. Austin, TX: University of Texas Press.

Evans, J. A. (2011) *The Power Game in Byzantium: Antonina and the Empress Theodora*. London: Continuum.

Evers, A. (2010) *Church, Cities, and People: A Study of the Plebs in the Church and Cities of Roman Africa in Late Antiquity*. Leuven: Peeters.

Facaros, D. and Pauls, M. (2007) *Venice, Venetia & the Dolomites*. London: Cadogan Guides.

Farah, C. (2003) 'Anglo-Ottoman Confrontation in the Persian Gulf in the Late 19th and Early 20th Centuries', *Proceedings of the Seminar for Arabian Studies* 33: 117–32. Oxford: Archaeopress.

Farooqi, N. R. (1989) *A Study of Political and Diplomatic Relations between Mughal India and the Ottoman Empire, 1556–1748*. Delhi: Idarah-i Adabiyat-i Delli.

Faroqui, S. (2005) *Subjects of the Sultan: Culture and Daily Life in the Ottoman Empire*. London: I. B. Tauris.

Farrand, W. R. and McMahon, J. P. (1997) 'History of the Sedimentary Infilling of Yarimburgaz Cave, Turkey', *Geological Sciences* 12.6: 537–65.

Featherstone, J. (1990) 'Olga's Visit to Constantinople', *Harvard Ukrainian Studies* 14: 293–312.

Featherstone, J. M. (2012) '*De cerimoniis* and the Great Palace', in P. Stephenson (ed.) *The Byzantine World*. New York: Routledge, 162–74.

Featherstone, M. (2003) 'Olga's Visit to Constantinople in *De Cerimoniis*', *Revue des Etudes Byzantines* 61: 241–51.

Ferdowsi, A. (2016) *Shahnameh*, trans. Dick Davis. New York: Viking.

Ferguson, E. (1998) *Encyclopedia of Early Christianity*, vol. 1. London: Taylor & Francis.

Fell, C. (1974) 'The Icelandic Saga of Edward the Confessor: Its Version of the Anglo-Saxon Emigration to Byzantium', *Anglo-Saxon England,* 3: 179–96.

Fields, N. (2004) *Troy c. 1700–1250 BC*. Oxford: Osprey Publishing.

Fikret, T. (2007) *Rübab-ı Şikeste*, Kemal Bek (ed.). Istanbul: Bordo Siyah Yayınları.

Finkel, C. (2006) *Osman's Dream: The Story of the Ottoman Empire 1300–1923*. London: John Murray.

Finkelberg, M. (2011) *The Homer Encyclopedia*. Hoboken, NJ: Wiley-Blackwell.

Finlay, A. and Faulkes, A. (2016) *Heimskringla*, vol. 3. London: The Viking Society.

Fishman-Duker, R. (2011) 'Images of Jews in Byzantine Chronicles: A General Survey', in R. Bonfil, O. Irshai, G. G. Stroumsa and R. Talgam (eds), *Jews in Byzantium: Dialectics of Minority and Majority Cultures*. Leiden: Brill, 777–98.

Fitzherbert, M. (1985) *The Man Who Was Greenmantle: A Biography of Aubrey Herbert*. London: Oxford University Press (originally London: John Murray, 1983).

FitzRoy, C. (2013) *The Sultan's Istanbul: On Five Kurush a Day*. London: Thames & Hudson.

FitzSimons, P. (2015) *Gallipoli*. London: Bantam Press.

Fleet, K. (2001) 'Early Turkish Naval Activities', *Oriente Moderno* 20.1: 129–38.

Fleming, K. E. (2003) 'Constantinople: From Christianity to Islam', *Classical World* 97.1: 69.

Fletcher, R. (1992) *Moorish Spain*. London: Phoenix.

Flood, F. B. (2001) *The Great Mosque of Damascus: Studies on the Makings of an Umayyad Visual Culture*. Leiden: Brill.

Flower, M. A. (1997) *Theopompus of Chios: History and Rhetoric in the Fourth Century BC*. Oxford: Clarendon Press.

Foltz, B. V. (2014) *The Noetics of Nature: Environmental Philosophy and the Holy Beauty of the Visible*. New York: Fordham University Press.

Foot, S. and Robinson, C. F. (eds) (2012) *The Oxford History of Historical Writing*, vol. 2: *400–1400*. Oxford: Oxford University Press.

Foss, C. and Winfield, D. (1986) *Byzantine Fortifications: An Introduction*. Pretoria: University of South Africa Press.

Fouracre, P. and McKittrick, R. (2015) *The New Cambridge Medieval History*, vol. 1: *C. 500–c. 700*. Cambridge: Cambridge University Press.

Fowden, G. (1991) 'Constantine's Porphyry Column: The Earliest Literary Allusion', *Journal of Roman Studies* 81: 119–31.

Francovich Onesti, N. (2002) *I Vandali: Lingua e storia*. Rome: Carocci.

Frankopan, P. (2011) *The First Crusade: The Call from the East*. London: The Bodley Head.

Frankopan, P. (2015) *The Silk Roads: A New History of the World*. London: Bloomsbury.

Fraze, C. A. (1969) *The Orthodox Church and Independent Greece 1821–1852*. Cambridge: CUP Archive.

Freely, J. (1993) *The Bosphorus*. Istanbul: Redhouse Press.

Freely, J. (1998a) *Istanbul: The Imperial City*. London: Penguin.

Freely, J. (1998b) *Turkey around the Marmara*. Turkey: Matbaacılık ve Yayıncılık.

Freely, J. (2000) *Inside the Seraglio: Private Lives of the Sultans in Istanbul*. London: Penguin.

Freely, J. (2004) *The Western Shores of Turkey: Discovering the Aegean and Mediterranean Coasts*. London: I. B. Tauris.

Freely, J. (2005) *Jem Sultan: The Adventures of a Captive Turkish Prince in Renaissance Europe*. London: Harper Perennial.

Freely, J. and Çakmak, A. (2004) *Byzantine Monuments of Istanbul*. Cambridge: Cambridge University Press.

Freely, J. and Sumner-Boyd, H. (1972) *Strolling through Istanbul: A Guide to the City*. Istanbul: Redhouse Press.

Freeman, C. (2008) *AD 381: Heretics, Pagans and the Christian State*. London: Pimlico.

Frend, W. H. C. (2004) 'From Donatist Opposition to Byzantine Loyalism: The Cult of Martyrs in North Africa 350–650', in A. H. Merrills (ed.) *Vandals, Romans and Berbers: New Perspectives on Late Antique North Africa*. Aldershot: Ashgate, 259–69.

Frenkel, Y. (2011) 'The Use of Islamic Materials by Non-Islamic Writers', in Michael M. Laskier and Yaacov Lev (eds) (2011) *The Convergence of Judaism and Islam: Religious, Scientific and Cultural Dimensions*. Gainesville: University of Florida Press, 89–108.

Fric, J., Portolous, D., Manolopoulos, A. and Kastritis, T. (2012) *Important Areas for Seabirds in Greece*. Athens: Hellenic Ornithological Society.

Fry, M. G. et al. (eds) (2002) 'The Eastern Question, 1814–1923', in *Guide to International Relations and Diplomacy*. London: Continuum, 130–47.

Fryde, E. (2000) *The Early Palaeologan Renaissance*. Leiden: Brill.

Fulcher of Chartres, F. R. Ryan, trans. (1973) *A History of the Expedition to Jerusalem*, 1095–1127. NY: W. W. Norton and Company, 79.

Funu, S. (1902) *Tevcihat ve Havadis Kismi*, no. 577, 6 Sefer 1320: 34.

Ganchou, T. (2010) 'L'Ultime Testament de Géôrgios Goudélès, homme d'affaires, *mésazôn* de Jean V et *ktètôr* (Constantinople, 4 mars 1421)', in *Mélanges Cécile Morrisson*. Travaux et Mémoires 16. Paris. 277–359.

Garipzanov, I. and Tolochko, O. (2011) *Early Christianity on the Way from the*

Varangians to the Greeks. Kiev: Institute of Ukrainian History.

Garland, L. (1999) *Byzantine Empresses: Women and Power in Byzantium AD 527–1204.* London: Routledge.

Garland, L. (ed.) (2006) *Byzantine Women: Varieties of Experience AD 800–1200.* Aldershot: Ashgate.

Geake, H. (1999) 'Invisible Kingdoms: The Use of Grave-Goods in Seventh-Century England', in T. Dickinson and D. Griffiths (eds) *The Making of Kingdoms.* Anglo-Saxon Studies in Archaeology and History 10. Oxford: Oxford University School of Archaeology, 203–15.

Georgacas, D. J. (1947) 'The Names of Constantinople', *Transactions and Proceedings of the American Philological Association* 78: 347–67.

George, A. (2009) 'Calligraphy, Colour and Light in the Blue Qur'an' *Journal of Qur'anic Studies* 11.1: 75–125.

George, D. (2001a) 'Manuel I Komnenos and Michael Glykas: A Twelfth-Century Defence and Refutation of Astrology', *Culture and Cosmos: A Journal of the History of Astrology and Cultural Astronomy* 5.1: 3–48.

George, D. (2001b) 'Manuel I Komnenos and Michael Glykas: A Twelfth-Century Defence and Refutation of Astrology', *Culture and Cosmos: A Journal of the History of Astrology and Cultural Astronomy* 5.2: 23–51.

Georgiou, A. (2012) 'The Cult of Flavia Iulia Helena in Byzantium. An Analysis of Authority and Perception through the Study of Textual and Visual Sources from the Fourth to the Fifteenth Century'. Doctoral thesis, University of Birmingham.

Georgiou, A. (2013) 'Helena: The Subversive Persona of an Ideal Christian Empress in Early Byzantium', *Journal of Early Christian Studies* 21.4: 597–624.

Georgopoulou, M. (1995) 'Late Medieval Crete and Venice: An Appropriation of Byzantine Heritage', *Art Bulletin* 77.3: 479–96.

Georgopoulou, M. (2004) 'The Artistic World of the Crusaders and Oriental Christians in the Twelfth and Thirteenth Centuries', *Gesta* 43.2: 115–28.

Gerelyes, I. (2005) *Turkish Flowers: Studies on Ottoman Art in Hungary.* Budapest: Hungarian National Museum.

Gero, S. (1973) *Byzantine Iconoclasm during the Reign of Leo III, with Particular Attention to the Oriental Sources.* Louvain: Secrétariat du Corpus SCO.

Gerstel, S. E. J. (1998) 'Painted Sources for Female Piety in Medieval Byzantium', *Dumbarton Oaks Papers* 52: 89–111.

Gerstel, S. E. J. (2015) *Rural Lives and Landscapes in Late Byzantium: Art, Archaeology, and Ethnography.* Cambridge: Cambridge University Press.

Gibb, A. R. (1958) 'Arab–Byzantine Relations under the Umayyad Caliphate', *Dumbarton Oaks Papers* 12: 219, 221–33.

Gibb, E. J. W. (trans. and ed.) (1882) 'Ottoman Poems'. MA: Harvard University.

Gibbon, E. (1988) *The History of the Decline and Fall of the Roman Empire.* Abridged A. Lentin and B. Norman. Ware, Herts: Wordsworth Editions.

Gilbert, M. (2004), 'Churchill and Gallipoli' in MacLeod, J. (ed.) *Gallipolli: Making History*. London: Frank Cass.

Gilles, P. (1729) *The Antiquities of Constantinople*, trans. and ed. J. Ball. London.

Gilles, P., Musto, R. G. (ed.) (1988) *The Antiquities of Constantinople*, trans. J. Ball. New York: Italica Press.

Gillespie, A. (2011) *A History of the Laws of War*, vol. 2: *The Customs and Laws of War with Regards to Civilians in Times of Conflict*. Oxford and Portland, OR: Hart Publishing.

Gilman, I. and Klimkeit, H.-J. (1999) *Christians in Asia before 1500*. Richmond: Curzon Press.

Goffart, W. (1981) 'Rome, Constantinople, and the Barbarians', *American Historical Review* 86.2: 275–306.

Gold, B. K. (2013) 'Gender Fluidity and Closure in Perpetua's Prison Diary' in J. Hallett, D. Lateiner, B. Gold and J. Perkins (eds.), *Roman Literature, Gender and Reception*. London: Routledge.

Goldsworthy, A. (2009) *The Fall of the West: The Death of the Roman Superpower*. London: Weidenfeld & Nicolson.

Goodwin, G. (2006) *The Janissaries*. London: Saqi Publishing.

Goodwin, J. (1999) *Lord of the Horizons: A History of the Ottoman Empire*. New York: Vintage Publishing.

Gordon, S. (with contributions from El Hage, B. and Nasini, A.) (2013) *Cairo to Constantinople: Francis Bedford's Photographs of the Middle East*. London: Royal Collection Trust.

Grabar, O. (1973, 1987) *The Formation of Islamic Art*. New Haven and London: Yale University Press.

Gracanin, H. (2003) 'The Western Roman Embassy to the Court of Attila in AD 449', *Byzantinoslavica* 61: 53–74.

Grafton, A., Most, G. and Settis, S. (eds) (2010) *The Classical Tradition*. Cambridge, MA and London: Harvard University Press.

Grave, P. et al. (2013) 'Cultural Dynamics and Ceramic Resource Use at Late Bronze Age/Early Iron Age Troy, North-western Turkey', *Journal of Archaeological Science* 40.4: 1760–77.

Graves, R. (1955) *The Greek Myths*. London: Penguin.

Graziosi, B. (2013) *The Gods of Olympus: A History*. London: Profile Books.

Greatrex, G. (1997) 'The Nika Riot: A Reappraisal', *Journal of Hellenic Studies* 117: 60–86.

Green, M. H. (ed.) (2014) *The Medieval Globe*, vol. 1: *Pandemic Disease in the Medieval World: Rethinking the Black Death*. Michigan: Arc Medieval Press.

Greene, M. (2015) *The Edinburgh History of the Greeks, 1453 to 1768: The Ottoman Empire*. Edinburgh: Edinburgh University Press.

Gregory, T. (2011) *A History of Byzantium*. Chichester: Wiley & Sons.

Grelot, G. H. (1683) *A late voyage to Constantinople*. London: John Playford

Grierson, P. (1999) *Byzantine Coinage*. Washington, DC: Dumbarton Oaks Byzantine Collection Publications.

Grig, L. and Kelly, G. (eds) (2012) *Two Romes: Rome and Constantinople in Late Antiquity*. Oxford: Oxford University Press.

Grivna, B. (2013) *My Father's Father*. Xlibris Self-Publishing Corporation.

Grousset, R. (1970) *The Empire of the Steppes: A History of Central Asia*. New Jersey: Rutgers University Press.

Guibert of Nogent, 192 and Peter Tudebode, 'Historia de Hierosolimitano Itinere', trans. John Hugh Hill and Laurita L. Hill, *Memoirs of the American Philosophical Society*. Philadelphia: The American Philosophical Society, 1974, 55.

Gul, M. (2009) 'Istanbul between the Crimean War and the First World War', in M. Gul, *Emergence of Modern Istanbul: Transformation and Modernisation of a City*. London: Tauris Academic Studies.

Guttmann, A. (1983) 'Roman Sports Violence', in J. H. Goldstein (ed.) *Sports Violence*. New York: Springer-Verlag, 7–19.

Gwynn, D. (2014) 'The Christological Controversies', in D. Gwynn *Christianity in the Later Roman Empire: A Sourcebook*. London: Bloomsbury, 247–62.

Gwynn, D. (2015) 'Christian Controversy and the Transformation of Fourth-Century Constantinople', in A. Busine (ed.) *Religious Practices and Christianization of the Late Antique City (4th–7th cent.)*. Leiden: Brill, 206–20.

Haag, M. (2012) *The Tragedy of the Templars: The Rise and Fall of the Crusader States*. London: Profile Books.

Haarer, F. K. (2006) *Anastasius I: Politics and Empire in the Late Roman World*. Cambridge: Francis Cairns.

Habachi, L. (1984) *The Obelisks of Egypt: Skyscrapers of the Past*. Cairo: American University in Cairo Press.

Hachlili, R. (1998) *Ancient Jewish Art and Archaeology in the Diaspora*. Leiden: Brill.

Haldon, J. (1990) *Constantine Porphyrogenitus: Three treatises on imperial military expeditions*. Vienna: Verlag der Österreichischen Akademie der Wissenschaften (Austrian Academy of Sciences).

Haldon, J. (1995) *Byzantium in the Seventh Century: The Transformation of a Culture*. Revised edn. Cambridge: Cambridge University Press.

Haldon, J. (1999) *Warfare, State and Society in the Byzantine World, 565–1204*. London and New York: Taylor & Francis.

Haldon, J. (2008) *The Byzantine Wars*. Stroud: The History Press.

Haldon, J. (ed.) (2009) *A Social History of Byzantium*. Chichester: Wiley-Blackwell.

Hall, B. S. (1999) 'Introduction', in J. R. Partington *A History of Greek Fire and Gunpowder*. Baltimore and London: Johns Hopkins University Press.

Hallof, K., Hermann, K. and Prignitic, S. (2012) 'Alte und neue Inschriften aus Olympia I', *Chiron* 42: 213–38.

Halsall, P. (1999) 'Women's Bodies, Men's Souls: Sanctity and Gender in Byzantium'. Doctoral thesis, Fordham University.

Hamidullah, M. (1973). 'The Muslim Conduct of State'. Kuala Lumpur: Islamic Book Trust.

Hansen, I. L. (2009) *Hellenistic and Roman Butrint*. London and Tirana: Butrint Foundation.

Harl, K. W. (1990) 'Sacrifice and Pagan Belief in Fifth- and Sixth-Century Byzantium', *Past & Present* 128: 7–27.

Harris, A. (2003) *Byzantium, Britain and the West: The Archaeology of Cultural Identity, AD 400–650*. Stroud and Charleston, SC: Tempus.

Harris, J. (2003, 2009, 2011, 2012, 2013) *Byzantium and the Crusades*. London and New York: Bloomsbury Academic.

Harris, J. (2007) *Constantinople: Capital of Byzantium*. London: Continuum.

Harris, J. (2015) *The Lost World of Byzantium*. New Haven and London: Yale University Press.

Hartley, E., Hawkes, J., Henig, M. and Mee, F. (eds) (2006) *Constantine the Great: York's Roman Emperor*. York and Aldershot: York Museums and Gallery Trust, with Lund Humphries.

Hartlie, P. (2007) *The Monks and Monasteries of Constantinople, ca. 350–850*. Cambridge: Cambridge University Press.

Harvey, S. A. (2011) *Theodora, The Believing Queen*. New England, Brown University Press

Hasluck, F. W. (1916/18) 'The Mosques of the Arabs in Constantinople', *Annual of the British School of Athens* 22: 157–74.

Hathaway, J. (2009) 'Eunuch Households in Istanbul, Medina, and Cairo during the Ottoman Era', *Turcica* 41: 291–303.

Hathaway, J. (2011) 'Habeşi Mehmed Ağa: The First Chief Harem Eunuch', in A. Ahmed and B. Sadeghi (eds) *The Islamic Scholarly Tradition: Studies in History, Law, and Thought in Honor of Professor Michael Allan Cook*. Leiden: Brill, 179–98.

Hattenhauer, H. and Bake, U. (eds) (2012) *Ein Fugger-Kaufmann im Osmanischen Reich: Berricht von einer Reise nach Konstantinople und Kleinasien 1553–1555*. Frankfurt: Peter Lang.

Haythornthwaite, P. J. (1991) *Gallipoli 1915: Frontal Assault on Turkey*. Oxford: Osprey Publishing.

Heilo, O. (2015) 'Empire of Clay and Iron: Divisions in the Byzantine State Ideology and Christian Apocalyptic Expectations from the Reigns of Heraclius to Leo III (610–718)', *Scandinavian Journal of Byzantine and Modern Greek Studies* 1: 49–64.

Hellenic Ministry of Culture, Directorate of Byzantine and Post Byzantine

Monuments (2000) *On Water in Byzantium*. Athens: Hellenic Ministry of Culture.

Henderson, E. F. (1910) *Select Historical Documents of the Middle Ages*. London: George Bell.

Henning, J. (2008) 'Strong Rulers – Weak Economy? Rome, the Carolingians and the Archaeology of Slavery in the First Millennium AD', in J. Davis and M. McCormick (eds) *The Long Morning of Medieval Europe: New Directions in Early Medieval Studies*. Aldershot: Ashgate, 33–53.

Herrin, J. (1987) *The Formation of Christendom*. Princeton: Princeton University Press.

Herrin, J. (2000) 'The Imperial Feminine in Byzantium', *Past & Present* 169: 3–35.

Herrin, J. (2002) *Women in Purple: Rulers of Medieval Byzantium*. London: Phoenix Press.

Herrin, J. (2007) *Byzantium: The Surprising Life of a Medieval Empire*. London: Penguin.

Herrin, J. (2013a) *Margins and Metropolis*. Princeton: Princeton University Press.

Herrin, J. (2013b) *Unrivalled Influence: Women and Empire in Byzantium*. Princeton: Princeton University Press.

Hershkovitz, I. et al. (2008) 'Detection and Molecular Characterization of 9000-Year-Old Mycobacterium Tuberculosis from a Neolithic Settlement in the Eastern Mediterranean', in PLoS ONE 3(10): dx.doi.org/10.1371/journal.pone.0003426.

Hetherington, P. and Forman, W. (1983) *Byzantium: City of Gold, City of Faith*. London: Orbis Publishing.

Heuck-Allen, S. (1999) *Finding the Walls of Troy: Frank Calvert and Heinrich Schliemann at Hisarlik*. Berkeley: University of California Press.

Heyd, U. (1953) 'The Jewish Communities of Istanbul in the Seventeenth Century', *Oriens* 6.2: 299–314.

Hieromonk Nicephore of Mikra Agia Anna (2003) *The Holy Mountain: Athos*, trans. P. Heers. Thessaloniki.

Hill, A. (1733) *A full and just account of the present state of the Ottoman Empire in all its branches . . . faithfully related from a serious observation taken in many years travels thro' those countries*. London: G. Parker.

Hill, R., (ed. and trans.) (1962) *Gesta Francorum et aliorum Hierosolimitanorum*, Edinburgh: Thomas Nelson and Sons.

Hillenbrand, C. (1999, 2006, 2009, 2010) *The Crusades: Islamic Perspectives*. Edinburgh: Edinburgh University Press.

Hillenbrand, C. (2007) *Turkish Myth and Muslim Symbol: The Battle of Manzikert*. Edinburgh: Edinburgh University Press.

Hillenbrand, C. (2009) 'Some Medieval Muslim Views of Constantinople', in S. R. Goodwin (ed.) *World Christianity in Muslim Encounter: Essays in Memory of David A. Kerr*, vol. 2. London: Continuum.

Hillenbrand, C. (2015) *Islam: A New Historical Introduction*. London: Thames & Hudson.

Hilsdale, C. J. (2014) *Byzantine Art and Diplomacy in an Age of Decline*. Cambridge: Cambridge University Press.

Hirth, F. (1885) *China and the Roman Orient: Researches into their Ancient and Mediaeval Relations as Represented in Old Chinese Records*. Shanghai and Hong Kong: G. Hirth.

Hodges, R. (2008) *The Rise and Fall of Byzantine Butrint*. London and Tirana: Butrint Foundation.

Hodgson, N. R. (2005) 'Nobility, Women and Historical Narratives of the Crusades and the Latin East', *Al-Masaq: Journal of the Medieval Mediterranean* 17.1: 61–85.

Hodgson, N. R. (2007) *Women, Crusading and the Holy Land in Historical Narrative*. Woodbridge: The Boydell Press.

Holland, T. (2013) *In the Shadow of the Sword*. London: Abacus.

Hollis, E. (2009) *The Secret Lives of Buildings: From the Parthenon to the Vegas Strip in Thirteen Stories*. London: Portobello Books.

Holmes, W. G. (1912) *The Age of Justinian and Theodora: A History of the Sixth Century A.D.* London: G. Bell & Sons.

Holo, J. (2000) 'A Genizah Letter from Rhodes Evidently Concerning the Byzantine Reconquest of Crete', *Journal of Near Eastern Studies* 59.1: 1–12.

Bible, The Holy, New Living Translation, copyright 1996. Used by permission of Tyndale House Publishers, Wheaton, I.

Honoré, A. M. (1975) 'Some Constitutions Composed by Justinian', *Journal of Roman Studies* 65: 107–23.

Hopkirk, P. (1980) *Foreign Devils on the Silk Road: The Search for the Lost Treasures of Central Asia*. London: John Murray.

Hopkirk, P. (1994) *On Secret Service East of Constantinople: The Plot to Bring Down the British Empire*. London: John Murray.

Horden, P. (2005) 'The Earliest Hospitals in Byzantium, Western Europe, and Islam', *Journal of Interdisciplinary History* 35.3: 361–89.

Hornblower, S. and Spawforth A. (eds) (2005) *The Oxford Classical Dictionary*. Oxford: Oxford University Press.

Horne, C. F. (ed.) (1923) *Source Records of the Great War*, vol. 6. New York: National Alumni.

Howard-Johnston, J. (2010) *Witnesses to a World Crisis: Historians and Histories of the Middle East in the Seventh Century*. Oxford: Oxford University Press.

Hoyland, R. G. (1997) *Seeing Islam as Others Saw It: A Survey and Evaluation of Christian, Jewish and Zoroastrian Writings on Early Islam*. Princeton: Darwin Press.

Hoyland, R. G. (1999) 'Jacob of Edessa on Islam', in G. Reinink and A. Cornelis Klugkist (eds) *After Bardasian: Studies on Continuity and Change in Syriac Christianity*. Leuven: Peeters. 158–9.

Hoyland, R. G. (2000) 'The Earliest Christian Writings on Muhammad: An Appraisal', in H. Motzki (ed.) *The Biography of Muhammad: The Issue of the Sources*. Leiden: Brill. 276–97.

Hughes, P. (1961) *The Church in Crisis: A History of the General Councils 325–1870*. Garden City, NY: Hanover House.

Humfress, C. (2005) 'Law and Legal Practice in the Age of Justinian', in M. Maas (ed.) *The Cambridge Companion to the Age of Justinian*. Cambridge: Cambridge University Press.

Hyman, S. (1988) *Edward Lear in the Levant: Travels in Albania, Greece and Turkey in Europe 1848–1849*. London: John Murray.

Ibrahim, R. (2013) 'The Siege of Byzantium', in *National Review*. NY.

Imber, C. (1996) 'The Reconstruction of the Ottoman Fleet after the Battle of Lepanto', in C. Imber (ed.) *Studies in Ottoman History and Law*. Istanbul: Gorgias Press, 85–101.

İnalcık, H. (1971) 'Istanbul', in P. Bearman, T. Bianquis, C. E. Bosworth, E. van Donzel and W. P. Heinrichs (eds) *Encyclopaedia of Islam*, 2nd edn, vol. 4. Leiden and New York: Brill. 2016. Oxford University libraries. 30 January 2016 http://ezproxy-prd.bodleian.ox.ac.uk:2134/entries/encyclopaedia-of-islam-2/istanbul-COM_0393.

İnalcık, H. (1990) 'Istanbul: An Islamic City', *Journal of Islamic Studies* 1: 1–23.

İnalcık, H. (2006) *Turkey and Europe in History*. Istanbul: Eren.

İnalcık, H. (2012) 'Istanbul', in P. Bearman, Th. Bianquis, C. E. Bosworth, E. van Donzel and W. P. Heinrichs (eds) *Encyclopaedia of Islam*. 2nd edn. Brill Online.

Inayat Khan (1990) *The Shah Jahan Nama*. Begley, W. and Desai, Z. (eds and trans). Oxford: OUP India.

Infessura, S. (1890) *Diario della città di Roma*. Rome: Roma Forzani.

Irshai, O. (2011a) 'Confronting a Christian Empire: Jewish Life and Culture in the World of Early Byzantium', in R. Bonfil, O. Irshai, G. G. Stroumsa and R. Talgam (eds) *Jews in Byzantium: Dialectics of Minority and Majority Cultures*. Leiden: Brill, 15–64.

Irshai, O. (2011b) 'Jews and Judaism in Early Church Historiography: The Case of Eusebius of Caesarea (Preliminary Observations and Examples)', in R. Bonfil, O. Irshai, G. G. Stroumsa and R. Talgam (eds) *Jews in Byzantium: Dialectics of Minority and Majority Cultures*. Leiden: Brill. 799–828.

Irwin, R. (2004, 2005) *The Alhambra*. London: Profile Books.

Irwin, R. (2007) *For Lust of Knowing: The Orientalists and their Enemies*. London: Penguin.

Isitt, G. (2007) 'Vikings in the Persian Gulf', *Journal of the Royal Asiatic Society* 17.4: 389–406.

Jablonka, P., Pernicka, E. and Aslan, R. (2011) 'Preliminary Report on Work in Troia 2009 and 2010', *Studia Troica* 19: 7–43.

Jacobs, J., Broydé, I., Gottheil, R. (1901–1906). 'Jewish Encyclopedia'.

Jacoby, D. (2001a) 'The Jews and the Silk Industry of Constantinople', in D. Jacoby, *Byzantium, Latin Romania and the Mediterranean*. Aldershot: Ashgate, 1–20.

Jacoby, D. (2001b) 'The Urban Evolution of Latin Constantinople (1204–1261)' in N. Necipoğlu (ed.) *Byzantine Constantinople: Monuments, Topography and Everyday Life*. Leiden, Boston and Cologne: Brill, 277–98.

Jacoby, D. (2004) 'Silk Economics and Cross-Cultural Artistic Interaction: Byzantium, the Muslim World, and the Christian West', *Dumbarton Oaks Papers* 58: 197–240.

Jacoby, D. (2008) 'Silk Production', in E. Jeffreys, J. Haldon and R. Cormack (eds) *The Oxford Handbook of Byzantine Studies*. Oxford: Oxford University Press, 421–8.

Jakobsson, S. (2008) 'The Schism that Never Was: Old Norse Views on Byzantium and Russia', *Byzantinoslavica* 1/2: 173–88.

James, L. (1996) '"Pray Not to Fall into Temptation and Be on Your Guard": Pagan Statues in Christian Constantinople', *Gesta* 35.1: 12–20.

James, L. (ed.) (1997) *Women, Men and Eunuchs: Gender in Byzantium*. London and New York: Routledge.

James, L. (ed.) (2010) *A Companion to Byzantium*. Chichester: Wiley-Blackwell.

Janin, R. (1953) *La Géographie ecclésiastique de l'Empire Byzantin*, vol. 1.3: *Les Eglises et les monastères*. Paris: Institut Français d'Etudes Byzantines.

Janin, R. (1964) *Constantinople byzantine. Développement urbaine et répertoire topographique*. Paris: Institut Français d'Etudes Byzantines.

Jankowiak, M. (2013) 'The First Arab Siege of Constantinople', in C. Zuckerman (ed.) *Constructing the Seventh Century*. Paris: Association des Amis du Centre d'Histoire et Civilisation de Byzance. 237–320.

Jeffreys, E., Haldon, J. and Cormack, R. (eds) (2008) *The Oxford Handbook of Byzantine Studies*. Oxford: Oxford University Press.

Jenkins Jr, E. (2000) *Muslim Diaspora: A Comprehensive Chronology of the Spread of Islam in Asia, Africa, Europe and the Americas*, vol. 2: *1500–1799*. Jefferson, NC: McFarland.

Jesch, J. (2015) *The Viking Diaspora*. London: Routledge.

Jesch, Judith (ed.) (2009) 'Rǫgnvaldr jarl Kali Kolsson, Lausavísur 31' in Kari Ellen Gade (ed.), *Poetry from the Kings' Sagas 2: From c. 1035 to c. 1300. Skaldic Poetry of the Scandinavian Middle Ages*. Brepols: Turnhout, 607–8.

Jezernik, B. (ed.) (2009) *Imagining the 'Turk'*. Newcastle: Cambridge Scholars Publishing.

Jilek, S. (with Breeze, D. and Thiel, A.) (2009) *Frontiers of the Roman Empire: The Danube Limes – A Roman River Frontier*. Warsaw: Warsaw University.

Jones, A. H. M. (1928) *Preliminary Report upon the Excavations Carried Out in the Hippodrome of Constantinople in 1927*. Oxford: Oxford University Press.

Jones, M. W. (2000) 'Genesis and Mimesis: The Design of the Arch of Constantine in Rome', *Journal of the Society of Architectural Historians* 59.1: 50–70.

Jowett, P. S. (2015) *Armies of the Greek–Turkish War 1919–22*. Oxford: Osprey Publishing.

Kaegi, W. E. (1992) *Byzantium and the Early Islamic Conquests*. Cambridge: Cambridge University Press.

Kaegi, W. E. (2007) *Heraclius, Emperor of Byzantium*. Cambridge: Cambridge University Press.

Kafadar, C. (1989) 'Self and Others: The Diary of a Dervish in Seventeenth Century Istanbul and First-Person Narratives in Ottoman Literature', *Studica Islamica* 69: 121–50.

Kafadar, C. (1991) 'On the Purity and Corruption of the Janissaries', *Turkish Studies Association Bulletin* 15.2: 273–80.

Kafescioglu, C. (2009) *Constantinopolis/Istanbul: Cultural Encounter, Imperial Vision, and the Construction of the Ottoman Capital*. University Park, PA: Pennsylvania State University Press.

Kaldellis, A. (2003) 'Things Are Not What They Are: Agathias Mythistoricus and the Last Laugh of Classical Culture', *Classical Quarterly* 53.1: 295–300.

Kaldellis, A. (2007) *Hellenism in Byzantium*. Cambridge: Cambridge University Press.

Kanellakis, K. (1890) *Χιακ αναλεκτα: Χυλλογ ηθώ κα εθίμω* (Chiaka Analekta. Collection on Mores and Customs). Athens: privately published.

Kantorowicz, E. H. (1963) 'Oriens Augusti. Lever du Roi', *Dumbarton Oaks Papers* 17: 117–77.

Karaiskaj, G. (2009) *The Fortifications of Butrint*, ed. and trans. A. Crowson. London and Tirana: Butrint Foundation.

Karliga, B. *The Horizon of Katip Celebi's Thought*. Bahcesehir University Civilisation Studies Center access online via muslimheritage.com

Kármán, G. and Kunčević, L. (2013) *The European Tributary States of the Ottoman Empire in the Sixteenth and Seventeenth Centuries*, trans. L. Marchini. Leiden and Boston: Brill.

Karras, V. A. (2004) 'Female Deacons in the Byzantine Church', *Church History* 73.2: 272–316.

Karras, V. A. (2005) 'The Liturgical Functions of Consecrated Women in the Byzantine Church', *Theological Studies* 66.1: 96–116.

Kazhdan, A. P. (ed.) (1991) *The Oxford Dictionary of Byzantium*. Oxford: Oxford University Press.

Keatinge Clay, W. (ed.) (1847) *Liturgical Services of the Reign of Queen Elizabeth: Liturgies and Occasional Forms of Prayer Set Forth in the Reign of Queen Elizabeth*. Cambridge: Cambridge University Press.

Kelly, C. (2008) *Attila the Hun, Barbarian Terror and the Fall of the Roman Empire*. London: Bodley Head.

Kelly, C. (2010) *The End of Empire: Attila the Hun and the Fall of Rome.* New York: W. W. Norton.

Kelly, C. (ed.) (2013) *Theodosius II: Rethinking the Roman Empire in Late Antiquity.* Cambridge: Cambridge University Press.

Kemal, Y. (1964) *Aziz Istanbul.* Istanbul: Istanbul Fetih Cemiyeti Yayinlar

Kennedy, H. (1986) *The Prophet and the Age of the Caliphates.* London: Pearson.

Kennell, N. M. (2011) *Spartans: A New History.* Chichester: Wiley-Blackwell.

Kessler, H. L. (2011) 'Judaisim and the Development of Byzantine Art', in R. Bonfil, O. Irshai, G. G. Stroumsa and R. Talgam (eds) *Jews in Byzantium: Dialectics of Minority and Majority Cultures.* Leiden: Brill, 455–99.

Keynes, G. (ed.) (1968) *The Letters of Rupert Brooke.* London: Faber & Faber.

Khalek, N. (2011) 'Dreams of Hagia Sophia: The Muslim Siege of Constantinople in 674 CE, Abu Ayyub Al-Ansari, and the Medieval Islamic Imagination', in A. Q. Ahmed, B. Sadeghi and M. Bonner (eds) *The Islamic Scholarly Tradition: Studies in History, Law, and Thought in Honor of Professor Michael Allan Cook.* Leiden: Brill.

al-Khamis, U. (1998) 'An Early Islamic Bronze Ewer Reexamined', *Muqarnas* 15: 9–19.

Kia, M. (2011) *Daily Life in the Ottoman Empire.* Santa Barbara, CA: Greenwood.

Kiliçkaya, A. (2010) *Hagia Sophia and Chora.* Istanbul: Silk Road Publications.

King, C. (2004) *The Black Sea: A History.* Oxford: Oxford University Press.

King, C. (2007) 'Imagining Circassia: David Urquhart and the Making of North Caucasus Nationalism', *Russian Review* 66.2: 238–55.

King, C. (2008) *The Ghost of Freedom: A History of the Caucasus.* Oxford: Oxford University Press.

King. C. (2011) *Odessa: Genius and Death in the City of Dreams.* New York and London: W. W. Norton.

King, C. (2014) *Midnight at the Pera Palace: The Birth of Modern Istanbul.* New York and London: W. W. Norton.

Kinross, P. (1979) *The Ottoman centuries: The rise and fall of the Turkish Empire.* New York: Morrow.

Kirli, C. (2009) 'Surveillance and Constituting the Public in the Ottoman Empire', in S. Shami (ed.) *Publics, Politics and Participation: Locating the Public Sphere in the Middle East and North Africa.* New York: Social Science Research Council, 177–204.

Kitromilides, P. M. (2010) 'The Ecumenical Patriarchate', in L. Leustean (ed.) *Eastern Christianity and the Cold War, 1945–91.* Abingdon: Routledge, 221–39.

Kitzinger, E. (1966) 'The Byzantine Contribution to Western Art of the Twelfth and Thirteenth Centuries', *Dumbarton Oaks Papers* 20: 25–47.

Klein, H. A. (2004) 'Eastern Objects and Western Desires: Relics and Reliquaries between Byzantium and the West', *Dumbarton Oaks Papers* 58: 283–314.

Klein, M. K. (2014) 'Holy Haulage: Shipping Hagia Sophia to Palestine', presentation given at King's College London, 11 February.

Kocabaş, U. (ed.) (2008) *The Old Ships of the New Gate / Yenikapı'nın Eski Gemileri*. Istanbul: Ege Yayınları.

Kölb-Ebert, M. (ed.) (2009) *Geology and Religion: A History of Harmony and Hostility*. London: Geological Society.

Kolbaba, T. (2011) '1054 Revisited: Response to Ryder', *Byzantine and Modern Greek Studies* 35.1: 38–44.

Kolluoğlu, B. and Toksöz, M. (eds) (2010, 2014) *Cities of the Mediterranean: From the Ottomans to the Present Day*. London and New York: I. B. Tauris.

Konstam, A. (2003) *Lepanto 1571: The Greatest Naval Battle of the Renaissance*. Oxford and New York: Osprey Publishing.

Konstam, A. and Dennis, P. (2015) *Byzantine Warship vs. Arab Warship: 7th–11th Centuries*. Oxford: Osprey Publishing.

Kotsis, K. (2012) 'Defending Female Authority in Eighth-Century Byzantium: The Numismatic Images of the Empress Irene (797–802)', *Journal of Late Antiquity* 5.1: 185–215.

Kourkoutidou-Nikolaidou, E. and Tourta, A. (1997) *Wandering in Byzantine Thessaloniki*. Athens: Kapon Editions.

Koven, S. G. (2008) *Responsible Governance: A Case Study Approach*. Armonk, NY: M. E. Sharpe.

Kraemer, R. S. (1992) *Her Share of the Blessings: Women's Religions among Pagans, Jews, and Christians in the Greco-Roman World*. Oxford: Oxford University Press.

Kraemer, R. S. (ed.) (2004) *Women's Religions in the Greco-Roman World: A Sourcebook*. Oxford: Oxford University Press.

Krallis, D. (2009) '"Democratic" Action in Eleventh-Century Byzantium: Michael Attaleiates's "Republicanism" in Context'. *Viator* 40.2: 35–53.

Krotscheck, U. (2006) *Going with the Grain: Athenian State Formation and the Question of Subsistence in the 5th and 4th Centuries BCE*. Princeton/Stanford Working Papers in Classics, http://www.princeton.edu/~pswpc/pdfs/krotscheck/010603.pdf.

Kruft, H.-W. (1996) *A History of Architectural Theory: From Vitruvius to the Present*. New York: Princeton Architectural Press.

Kuban, D. (1996) *Istanbul: An Urban History: Byzantion, Constantinopolis, Istanbul*. Istanbul: Türkiye İş Bankasi Kültür yayınları.

Kuhrt, A. (1997) *The Ancient Near East c. 3000–330 BC*, Vols 1 and 2. London: Routledge.

Kulakovskij, J. A. (1908) *Mémoires de l'Académie Impériale des sciences de St. Pétersbourg*, 8th ser., no. 9, *Classe historico-philologique*. St Petersburg, 1–58.

Kyriakidis, S. (2009) 'The Employment of Large Groups of Mercenaries in Byzantium in the Period ca. 1290–1305 as Viewed by the Sources', *Byzantion* 79: 208–30.

Kyriakidis, S. (2011) *Warfare in Late Byzantium, 1204–1453*. Leiden: Brill.

Lad, J. (2010) 'Panoptic Bodies: Black Eunuchs as Guardians of the Topkapı Harem', in M. Booth (ed.) *Harem Histories: Envisioning Places and Living Spaces*. Durham, NC: Duke University Press, 136–76.

Ladner, G. B. (1975) 'Justinian's Theory of Law and the Renewal Ideology of the *Leges Barbarorum*', *Proceedings of the American Philosophical Society* 119.3: 191–200.

Lafontaine-Dosogne, J. (1995) *L'Art Byzantin et chrétien d'orient. Aux Musées Royaux d'art et d'histoire*. Brussels: Les Musées.

Laiou, A. E. (2002) 'Exchange and Trade, Seventh–Twelfth Centuries', in A. E. Laiou (ed.) *The Economic History of Byzantium: From the Seventh through the Fifteenth Century*. Washington, DC: Dumbarton Oaks Research Library and Collection.

Laiou, A. E. (ed.) (2002) *The Economic History of Byzantium: From the Seventh through the Fifteenth Century*, Washington DC: Dumbarton Oaks Research Library and Collection.

Laiou, A. E. (2005) 'The Byzantine Village (5th–14th Century)', in J. Lefort, C. Morrisson, and J.-P. Sodini (eds) *Les Villages dans l'Empire byzantine (IVe–XVe siècle)*. Paris: Lethielleux, 31–53.

Laiou, A. E. (2011) *Women, Family and Society in Byzantium*. Aldershot: Ashgate.

Laiou, A. E. and Mottahedeh, R. P. (eds) (2001) *The Crusades from the Perspective of Byzantium and the Muslim World*. Washington, DC: Dumbarton Oaks Research Library and Collection.

Lamartine, A. de (1835) *A pilgrimage to the Holy Land; comprising recollections, sketches, and reflections, made during a tour in the East in 1832–1833*. Philadelphia: Carey, Lea & Blanchard.

Lamartine, A. de (1861) *Souvenirs, impressions, pensées, et paysages pendant un voyage en Orient, 1832–1833*. Leipzig.

Lane Fox, R. (1973) *Alexander the Great*. London: Penguin.

Lane Fox, R. (1986) *Pagans and Christians in the Mediterranian World from the Second Century A.D. to the Conversion of Constantine*. London: Viking.

Lane Fox, R. (2015) *Augustine, Conversions and Confessions*. London: Allen Lane.

Lansford, T. (2009) *The Latin Inscriptions of Rome: A Walking Guide*. Baltimore: Johns Hopkins University Press.

Lapidge, M. (2013) 'Byzantium', in M. Lapidge et al. (eds) *The Wiley-Blackwell Encyclopedia of Anglo-Saxon England*. Chichester: Wiley-Blackwell.

Lau, M. (2012) 'The Integration of Conquered Territory in the 10th and 12th Centuries – A Continuation of Imperial Policy by Other Means?', paper delivered at the Society of the Promotion of Byzantine Studies Symposium 2012.

La Vassière, E. de (2012) 'Central Asia and the Silk Road', in S. F. Johnson (ed.)

The Oxford Handbook of Late Antiquity. Oxford: Oxford University Press, 142–69.

Lear, E. (1851) *Journals of a Landscape Painter in Albania &c.* London: R. Bentley.

Lecane, P. (2015) *Beneath a Turkish Sky: The Royal Dublin Fusiliers and the Assault on Gallipoli.* Dublin: The History Press.

Lecaque, T. (2010) 'An Englishman in Byzantium: Political Motivations for Ethnic Change in the Varangian Guard', *Apprentice Historian* 16: 46–62.

Lecky, W. H. (1869) *A History of European Morals from Augustus to Charlemagne.* 2 vols. London.

LeClerq, A. S. W. (ed.) (2006) *Elizabeth Sinkler Coxe's Tales from the Grand Tour, 1890–1910.* Columbia, SC: University of South Carolina Press.

Lecouras, P. (2001) 'Hemingway in Constantinople', *Midwest Quarterly* 43: 29–41.

Lenski, N. (ed.) (2012) *The Cambridge Companion to the Age of Constantine.* Revised edn. New York: Cambridge University Press.

Leone, L. (2003) 'Topographies of Production in North African Cities during the Vandal and Byzantine Periods', in L. Lavan and W. Bowden (eds) *Theory and Practice in Late Antique Archaeology.* Leiden and Boston: Brill. 257–87.

Leonhardt, J. (2013) *Latin: Story of a World Language,* trans. K. Kronenberg. Cambridge, MA: The Belknap Press of Harvard University Press.

Leustean, L. (ed.) (2010) *Eastern Christianity and the Cold War, 1945–91.* Abingdon: Routledge.

Levey, M. (1975) *The World of Ottoman Art.* London: Thames & Hudson.

Levi, M. (2012) *Istanbul Was a Fairy Tale,* trans. Ender Gürol. Champaign, IL: Dalkey Archive Press.

Lewis, B. (1963) *Istanbul and the Civilization of the Ottoman Empire.* Norman, OK: University of Oklahoma Press.

Lewis, B. (1985) *The Jews of Islam.* Princeton: Princeton University Press.

Lewis, B. (2002) *What Went Wrong? Western Impact and Middle Eastern Response.* London: Phoenix.

Lewis, B. (2004) *From Babel to Dragomans: Interpreting the Middle East.* London: Weidenfeld & Nicolson.

Lewis, D. (2008) *God's Crucible: Islam and the Making of Europe, 570–1215.* London: W. W. Norton.

Lewis, G. (2001) *Domenico's Istanbul,* trans. with commentary by M. J. L. Austin. Warminster: Aris & Phillips (for the E. J. W. Gibb Memorial Trust).

Lewis, R. (2004) *Rethinking Orientalism: Women, Travel and the Ottoman Harem.* London: I. B. Tauris.

Lichter, C. (ed.) (2005) *How Did Farming Reach Europe? Anatolian–European Relations from the Second Half of the 7th through the First Half of the 6th Millennium cal BC.* Proceedings of the International Workshop, Istanbul, 20–22 May 2004; Byzas 2. Istanbul: Deutsches Archäologisches Institut.

Liebeschuetz, J. H. W. G. (1979) *Continuity and Change in Roman Religion.* Oxford: Oxford University Press.

Lieu, S. N. C. and Montserrat, D. (eds) (1996) *From Constantine to Julian: Pagan and Byzantine Views: A Source History.* London and New York: Routledge.

Lieu, S. N. C. and Montserrat, D. (eds) (1998) *Constantine: History, Historiography and Legend.* London and New York: Routledge.

Lieven, D. (2015) *Towards the Flame: Empire, War and the End of Tsarist Russia.* London: Allen Lane.

Limberis, V. (1994) *Divine Heiress: The Virgin Mary and the Creation of Christian Constantinople.* Abingdon: Routledge.

Lingas, A. (2008) 'Music', in E. Jeffreys, J. Haldon and R. Cormack (eds) *The Oxford Handbook of Byzantine Studies.* Oxford: Oxford University Press. 915–35.

Little, L. K. (ed.) (2008) *Plague and the End of Antiquity: The Pandemic of 541–750.* Cambridge: Cambridge University Press.

Littlewood, A., Maguire, H. and Wolschke-Bulman, J. (eds) (2002) *Byzantine Garden Culture.* Washington, DC: Dumbarton Oaks Research Library and Collection.

Liu, X. (1996) *Silk and Religion.* Oxford: Oxford University Press.

Lockard, C. A. (2015) *Societies, Networks, and Transitions: A Global History,* vol. 1: *To 1500.* Stamford, CT: Cengage Learning.

Lounghis, T. C. (2010) *Byzantium in the Eastern Mediterranean: Safeguarding East Roman Identity, 407–1204.* Nicosia: Cyprus Research Centre.

Lovén, L. L. and Strömberg, A. (eds) (2003) *Gender, Cult, and Culture in the Ancient World from Mycenae to Byzantium: Proceedings of the Second Nordic Symposium on Gender and Women's History in Antiquity. Helsinki 20–22 October 2000.* Sävedalen: Paul Åströms Förlag.

Lowry, H. W. (2012) *In the Footsteps of Evliyâ Çelebi: The Seyahatnâme as Guidebook.* Istanbul: Bahçeşehir University Press.

Lyly, J. (1916) *Euphues:The Anatomy of Wyt/ Wit.* London: G. Routledge & Sons, Ltd; New York: E. P. Dutton & Co.

Maalouf, A. (1988) *Leo the African,* trans. Peter Sluglett. London: Abacus.

Maas, M. (2000) *Readings in Late Antiquity: A Sourcebook.* Abingdon and New York: Routledge.

Maas, M. (ed.) (2005) *The Cambridge Companion to the Age of Justinian.* Cambridge: Cambridge University Press.

Maas, M. (ed.) (2015) *The Cambridge Companion to the Age of Attila.* Cambridge: Cambridge University Press.

MacCormack, S. G. (1981) *Art and Ceremony In Late Antiquity.* Berkeley, Los Angeles and London: University of California Press.

McCormick, M. (1990) *Eternal Victory: Triumphal Rulership in Late Antiquity, Byzantium and the Early Medieval West.* Cambridge: Cambridge University Press.

MacCulloch, D. (2011) 'What if the Arians Had Won? A Reformation Historian Reconsiders the Medieval Western Church', lecture given at Yale University, Thursday 6 October.

MacFie, A. L. (2013) *Atatürk*. London and New York: Routledge.

MacLean, G. (2004) *The Rise of Oriental Travel: English Visitors to the Ottoman Empire, 1580–1720*. Basingstoke and New York: Palgrave Macmillan.

McMeekin, S. (2015) *The Ottoman Endgame: War, Revolution and the Making of the Modern Middle East, 1908–1923*. London: Allen Lane.

MacMullen, R. (1969, 1987) *Constantine*. London, New York and Sydney: Croom Helm.

MacMullen, R. (1984) *Christianizing the Roman Empire: A.D. 100–400*. New Haven and London: Yale University Press.

Madden, T. F. (2003) *Enrico Dandolo and the Rise of Venice*. Baltimore: Johns Hopkins University Press.

Madgerau, A. (2013) *Byzantine Military Organization on the Danube, 10th–12th Centuries*. Leiden: Brill.

Magdalino, P. (2000) 'The Maritime Neighborhoods of Constantinople: Commercial and Residential Functions, Sixth to Twelfth Centuries', *Dumbarton Oaks Papers* 54: 210–26.

Magdalino, P. and Mavroudi, M. (2006) *The Occult Sciences in Byzantium*. Geneva: La Pomme d'Or.

Magdalino, P. and Nelson, R. (Symposiarchs) (2006) 'The Old Testament in Byzantium', delivered at the Dumbarton Oaks Symposium, 1–3 December. Washington, DC: Dumbarton Oaks Research Library and Collection.

Mak, G. (2009) *The Bridge: A Journey between Orient and Occident*, trans. S. Garrett. London: Vintage Books.

Malatras, C. (2009) 'The Perception of the Roman Heritage in 12th Century Byzantium', *Rosetta* 7.5: 1–8.

Malcolm, N. (2015) *Agents of Empire: Knights, Corsairs, Jesuits and Spies in the Sixteenth-Century Mediterranean World*. London: Allen Lane.

Malcomson, Scott L. (2000) 'Safe as Houses', *Transition* 85.10.1: 30–46.

Malieckal, B. (2008) 'Slavery, Sex and the Seraglio: "Turkish" Women and Early Modern Texts', in H. Ostovich, M. V. Silcox and G. Roebuck (eds) *The Mysterious and the Foreign in Early Modern England*. Newark, DE: University of Delaware Press. 58–73.

Mango, C. (1975), 'The Church of Sts. Sergius and Bacchus Once Again', *Byzantinische Zeitschrift* 67: 385–92.

Mango, C. (1997) 'The Palace of the Boukoleon', *Cahiers Archéologiques* 45: 41–50.

Mango, C. (2000) 'The Triumphal Way of Constantinople and the Golden Gate', *Dumbarton Oaks Papers* 54: 173–88.

Maniatis, George C. (2000) 'The Organizational Setup and Functioning of the

Fish Market in Tenth-Century Constantinople', *Dumbarton Oaks Papers* 54: 13–42.

Mansel, P. (1997) *Constantinople: City of the World's Desire, 1453–1924*. London: Penguin.

Mantran, R (1973) 'L'Echo de la Bataille de Lépante à Constantinople', *Annales. Histoire, Sciences Sociales* 28.2: 396–405.

Marchand, L. A. (ed.) (1973a) *Byron's Letters and Journals*, vol. 1: *'In my Hot Youth'*. London: John Murray.

Marchand, L. A. (ed.) (1973b) *Byron's Letters and Journals*, vol. 2: *'Famous in my Time'*. London: John Murray.

Marenbon, J. (ed.) (2009) *The Cambridge Companion to Boethius*. Cambridge: Cambridge University Press.

Markopoulos, A. (2008) 'Education', in E. Jeffreys, J. Haldon and R. Cormack (eds) *The Oxford Handbook of Byzantine Studies*. Oxford: Oxford University Press. 785–95.

Markopoulos, A. (2013) 'In Search for "Higher Education" in Byzantium', *Recueil des Travaux de l'Institut d'Etudes Byzantines* 50: 29–44.

Marozzi, J. (2014) *Baghdad: City of Peace, City of Blood*. London: Allen Lane.

Marquardt, P. A. (1981) 'A Portrait of Hecate', *American Journal of Philology* 102.3: 250–2.

Marx, K. (1897) *The Eastern Question. A Reprint of Letters Written 1853–1856 Dealing with the Events of the Crimean War*, ed. E. Marx Aveling and E. Aveling. New York: B. Franklin, 1968. London: Frank Cass, 1969.

Marzinzik, S. (2008) 'Expressions of Power – Luxury Textiles from Early Medieval Northern Europe', *Textile Society of America Symposium Proceedings* 1, Lincoln: Textile Society of America, University of Nebraska.

Masters, B. (2013) *The Arabs of the Ottoman Empire 1516–1918: A Social and Cultural History*. Cambridge: Cambridge University Press.

Mather, J. (2009) *Pashas: Traders and Travellers in the Islamic World*. New Haven and London: Yale University Press.

Matossian, J. (2009) *Silent Partners: The Armenians and Cyprus, 578–1878*. Nicosia: Lusignan Press.

Mattingly, H. (1921a) 'The Mints of Vespasian', *Numismatic Chronicle and Journal of the Royal Numismatic Society* 1.3/4: 187–225.

Mattingly, H. (1921b) 'The Mints of the Empire: Vespasian to Diocletian', *Journal of Roman Studies* 11: 254–64.

Mayer, W. (1999) 'Constantinopolitan Women in Chrysostom's Circle', *Virgiliae Christianae* 53.3: 265–88.

Mazower, M. (2004) *Salonica: City of Ghosts: Christians, Muslims and Jews 1430–1950*. London: Harper Perennial.

Meinardus, O. F. A. (2002) *Two Thousand Years of Coptic Christianity*. Cairo: American University in Cairo Press.

Meineck, P. (2013) 'Dionysos, Divine Space and Dopamine: A Cognitive Approach to the Greek Theatre', *CHS Research Bulletin* 1.2, delivered at a research symposium at Center of Hellenic Studies, Washington, DC, 26 April 2013. http://wp.chs.harvard.edu/chs-fellows/author/pmeineck/.

Mernissi, F. (1994) *The Harem Within: Tales of a Moroccan Girlhood*. London: Doubleday.

Merrills, A. and Miles, R. (2010) *The Vandals*. Chichester: Wiley-Blackwell.

Meserve, M. (2006) 'News from the Negroponte: Politics, Popular Opinion, and Information Exchange in the First Decade of the Italian Press', *Renaissance Quarterly* 59: 440–80.

Metzger, B. M. (1977) *The Early Versions of the New Testament: Their Origin, Transmission, and Limitations*. Oxford: Oxford University Press.

Meyendorff, J. (1964) 'Byzantine Views of Islam', *Dumbarton Oaks Papers* 18: 113–32.

Meyer, K. E. and Brysac, S. B. (2008) *Kingmakers: The Invention of the Modern Middle East*. New York and London: W. W. Norton.

Meyer, M. (2011) 'Refracting Christian Truths through the Prism of the Biblical Female in Byzantine Illuminated Manuscripts', in R. Bonfil, O. Irshai, G. G. Stroumsa and R. Talgam (eds) *Jews in Byzantium: Dialectics of Minority and Majority Cultures*. Leiden: Brill, 969–98.

Mgaloblishvili, T. and Gagoshidze, I. (1998) 'The Jewish Diaspora and Early Christianity in Georgia', in T. Mgaloblishvili (ed.) *Ancient Christianity in the Caucasus*. Richmond: Curzon Press, 39–48.

Miller, S. (2008) *Vienna 1683: Christian Europe Repels the Ottomans*. Oxford and New York: Osprey Publishing.

Miller, W. (2013) *The Ottoman Empire and its Successors 1801–1927: With an Appendix 1927–1936*, 4th edn. Cambridge: Cambridge University Press.

Milton, G. (2008) *Paradise Lost: Smyrna, 1922. The Destruction of Islam's City of Tolerance*. London: Sceptre.

Miraj, L. F. (2013) *Dyrrachium in the Early Christian and Byzantine Period*. Tirana: n.p.

Mitchell, J. (2008) *The Butrint Baptistery and its Mosaics*. London and Tirana: Butrint Foundation.

Mitchell, P. (2011) 'Post-Medieval Archaeology in Vienna', in *Proceedings of Workshop 15, International Conference on Cultural Heritage and New Technologies*, 15–17 November 2010, Vienna, 20–31.

Mitchell, P. (2013) 'The Architecture of Absolutism', in N. Mehler (ed.) *Historical Archaeology in Central Europe*, Society for Historical Archaeology Special Publication 10. Rockville, MD, 365–78.

Moberly, F. (1923) *History of the Great War Based on Official Documents: The Campaign in Mesopotamia 1914–1918*, vol. 1. London: HMSO, 130–1.

Montagu, Lady Mary Wortley (2013) *The Turkish Embassy Letters*, ed. T. Heffernan and D. O'Quinn. Ontario: Broadview Press.

Montefiore, S. S. (2011a) *Jerusalem: The Biography*. London: Weidenfeld & Nicolson.

Montefiore, S. S. (2011b) *Catherine the Great & Potemkin: The Imperial Love Affair*. London: Weidenfeld & Nicolson.

Montefiore, S. S. (2016) *The Romanovs: 1613–1918*. London: Weidenfeld & Nicolson.

Moorhead, J. (1978) 'Boethius and Romans in Ostrogothic Service', *Historia: Zeitschrift für Alte Geschichte* 27.4: 604–12.

Moorhead, S. and Stuttard, D. (2010) *AD 410: The Year that Shook Rome*. London: The British Museum Press.

Moreno, A. (2008) 'Hieron: The Ancient Sanctuary at the Mouth of the Black Sea', *Hesperia: The Journal of the American School of Classical Studies at Athens* 77.4: 655–709.

Morrisson, C. and Sodini, J.-P. (2002) 'The Sixth-Century Economy', in A. E. Laiou (ed.) *The Economic History of Byzantium: From the Seventh through the Fifteenth Century*. Washington, DC: Dumbarton Oaks Research Library and Collection.

Mourad, K. (1994), *Living in Istanbul*, with photographs by J. Darbly. Paris: Flammarion.

Mowafi, R. (1981) *Slavery, Slave Trade and Abolition Attempts in Egypt and the Sudan 1820–1882*. Lund Studies in International History 14. Lund: Scandinavian University Books.

Mundell Mango, M. (2000) 'The Commercial Map of Constantinople', *Dumbarton Oaks Papers* 54: 189–207.

Murdoch, A. (2005) *The Last Pagan: Julian the Apostate and the Death of the Ancient World*. Stroud: Sutton Publishing.

Murdoch, B. and Read, M. (eds) (2004) *Early Germanic Literature and Culture*. Rochester, NY: Camden House.

Murphey, R. (1999) *Ottoman Warfare: 1500–1700*. London: UCL Press.

Muthesius, A. (1995) *Studies in Byzantine and Islamic Silk Weaving*. London: Pindar Press.

Muwayhili, Ibrahim al- (2008) *Spies, Scandals, & Sultans: Istanbul in the Twilight of the Ottoman Empire*, trans. R. Allen. Rowman & Littlefield Publishers, Inc.

Nabi Efendi (1901) 'Eulogy of Istanbul' in de A. P. Courteille and R. Arnot (eds and trans.) *The Counsels of Nabi Efendi to his Son Aboul Khair*. New York: The Colonial Press.

Necipoğlu, G. (1992) *Architecture, Ceremonial and Power: The Topkapı Palace in the Fifteenth and Sixteenth Centuries*. Cambridge, MA: MIT Press.

Necipoğlu, G. (1993) 'Framing the Gaze in Ottoman, Safavid and Mughal Palaces', Pre-Modern Islamic Palaces special issue, *Ars Orientalis* 23: 303–42.

Necipoğlu, G. (2005) *The Age of Sinan: Architectural Culture in the Ottoman Empire*. London: Reaktion Books.

Necipoğlu, G. (2007) 'Creation of a National Genius: Sinan and the Historiography of "Classical" Ottoman Architecture', *Muqarnas* 24: 141–83.

Necipoğlu, N. (2009) *Byzantium between the Ottomans and the Latins: Politics and Society in the Late Empire*. Cambridge: Cambridge University Press.

Nelson, R. S. and Krueger, D. (2013) 'The New Testament in Byzantium', *Byzantine Studies Symposium, April 26–28,* University of North Carolina at Greensboro.

Der Nersessian, S. (1987) 'Two Miracles of the Virgin in the Poems of Gautier de Coincy', in *Dumbarton Oaks Papers* 41: 157–63.

Neuhäusler, J. (1960) *What Was It Like in the Concentration Camp at Dachau? An Attempt to Come Closer to the Truth*. Munich and Dillingen: Manz A.G.

Newman, J. H. (1866) *A letter to the Rev. E.B. Pusey, D.D. on his recent Eirenicon*. London: Longmans, Green, Reader, and Dyer.

Nicol, D. M. (1988) *Byzantium and Venice: A Study in Diplomatic and Cultural Relations*. Cambridge: Cambridge University Press.

Nicolle, D. (1994) *Yarmuk AD 636: The Muslim Conquest of Syria*. Oxford: Osprey Publishing.

Nicolle, D. (2007) *Crusader Castles in Cyprus, Greece and the Aegean 1191–1571*. Oxford: Osprey Publishing.

Nienhause, W. (2011) 'Sima Qian and the Shiji', in Andrew Feldherr and Grant Hardy (eds) *The Oxford History of Historical Writing*, vol. 1: *Beginnings to AD 600*. Oxford: Oxford University Press. 463–84.

Nixon, C. E. V. and Saylor Rodgers, B. (1994) *In Praise of Later Roman Emperors: The Panegyrici Latini*. Berkeley: University of California Press.

Nixon, P. (2012) *St Cuthbert of Durham*. Stroud: Amberley.

Noldeke, T. (1909) *Geschichte des Qorans*. Leipzig: Dietrich.

Noonan, T. (1973) 'The Grain Trade of the Northern Balkan Sea in Antiquity', *American Journal of Philology* 93.3: 231–42.

Noppen, R. K. (2015) *Ottoman Navy Warships 1914–18*. Oxford: Osprey Publishing.

Norwich, J. J. (2007) *The Middle Sea: A History of the Mediterranean*. London: Vintage Books.

Oikonomides, N. (1986) 'Silk Trade and Production in Byzantium from the Sixth to the Ninth Century: The Seals of the Kommerkiarioi', *Dumbarton Oaks Papers* 40: 49–51.

Oikonomides, N. (1999) 'L'"Unilinguisme" officiel de Constantinople byzantine (VIIe–XIIe s.)', *Byzantina Symmeikta* 13: 9–22.

Olson, R. W. (1977) 'Jews, Janissaries, Esnaf and the Revolt of 1740 in Istanbul: Social Upheaval and Political Realignment in the Ottoman Empire', *Journal of the Economic and Social History of the Orient* 20.2: 185–207.

Olster, D. (1995) 'Theodore Grammaticus and the Arab Siege of 674–8', *Byzantinoslavica* 56: 23–8.

Onar, V., Pazvant, G., Gezer Ince, N., Alpak, H., Janeczek, M. and Kiziltan, Z. (2013) 'Morphometric Analysis of the Foramen Magnum of Byzantine Dogs Excavated in Istanbul Yenikapi at the Site of Theodosius Harbour', *Mediterranean Archaeology and Archaeometry* 13.1: 135–42.

Onar, V. et al. (2015) 'Estimating the Body Weight of Byzantine Dogs from the Theodosius Harbour at Yenikapi, Istanbul', *Kafkas Universitesi Veteriner Fakultesi Dergisi* 21: 55–9.

Onesti, N. F. (2013) *Tracing the Language of the Vandals*. University of Siena.

Oniz, H. and Aslan, E. (eds) (2011) *SOMA 2009: Proceedings of the XIII Symposium on Mediterranean Archaeology, Selcuk University of Konya, Turkey 23–24 April 2009*. Oxford: Archaeopress.

Orga, A. (ed.) (2007) *Istanbul: A Collection of the Poetry of Place*. London: Eland.

Orga, I. (2002) *The Caravan Moves On: Three Weeks among Turkish Nomads*. Reprint. London: Eland.

Orga, I. (2004) *Portrait of a Turkish Family*. Reprint. London: Eland.

Ostovik, H., Silcox, M. V. and Roebuck, G. (2008) *The Mysterious and the Foreign in Early Modern England*. Associated University Presses.

Ousterhout, R. (1995) 'Temporal Structuring in the Chora Parekklesion', *Gesta* 34.1: 63–76.

Ousterhout, R. (2010) 'New Temples and New Solomons: The Rhetoric in Byzantine Architecture', in P. Magdalino and R. Nelson (eds) *The Old Testament in Byzantium*. Washington, DC: Harvard University Press, 223–54.

Overy, R. (2014) *History of War in 100 Battles*. Oxford: Oxford University Press.

Özdogan, M., Miyake, Y. and Dede, N. (1991) 'An Interim Report on Excavations at Yarimburgaz and Toptepe in Eastern Thrace', *Anatolica* 12: 59–121.

Paine, L. (2013) *The Sea and Civilisation*. London: Knopf.

Painter, N. I. (2003) 'Why White People Are Called Caucasian?', *Proceedings of the Fifth Annual Gilder Lehrman Center International Conference, Yale University, 7–8 November 2003*, http://glc.yale.edu/sites/default/files/files/events/race/Painter.pdf.

Painter, N. I. (2011) *The History of White People*. New York and London: W. W. Norton.

Pakalin, M. Z. (1971) *Osmanlı tarih deyimleri ve terimleri sözlüğü*. Istanbul: Milli Eğitim Basımevi.

Palmer, M. (2001) *The Jesus Sutras: Rediscovering the Lost Scrolls of Taoist Christianity*. Wellspring/Ballantine.

Pamuk, O. (2005) *Istanbul*. London: Faber & Faber.

Pamuk, O. (2006) *The Black Book*, trans. M. Freely. London: Faber & Faber.

Pamuk, O. (2010) *The Museum of Innocence: A Novel*. London: Faber & Faber.

Pany, D. and Wiltschke-Schrotta, K. (2008) 'Artificial Cranial Deformation in a Migration Period Burial of Schwarzenbach, Central Austria', *VIAVIAS* 2: 18–23.

Papp, A. (2011) 'Building and Builder: Constructions under Sokollu Mustafa Pasha's Reign in Medieval Buda', in B. Biedronska-Slota, M. Ginter-Frolow and J. K. Malinowsku (eds) *The Art of the Islamic World and the Artistic Relationships between Poland and Islamic Countries*. Budapest: History Museum, 75–83.

Pardoe, J. (1838) *The Beauties of the Bosphorus*. London: George Virtue, 26, Ivy Lane.

Parker, P. (2014) *The Northmen's Fury: A History of the Viking World*. London: Jonathan Cape.

Parsons, R. et al. (2010) 'Gravity-Driven Flow in a Submarine Channel Bend: Direct Field Evidence of Helical Flow Reversal', *Geology* 38: 1063–6.

Patricios, N. N. (2014) *The Sacred Architecture of Byzantium: Art, Liturgy and Symbolism in Early Christian Churches*. London: I. B. Tauris.

Păun, R. G. (2013) 'Enemies Within: Networks of Influence and the Military Revolts against the Ottoman Power (Moldavia and Wallachia, Sixteenth–Seventeenth Centuries)', in G. Kármán and L. Kunčević (eds) *The European Tributary States of the Ottoman Empire in the Sixteenth and Seventeenth Centuries*. Leiden and Boston: Brill, 209–49.

Payne, C. (ed.) (2003) *Butrinti, 1993–2003: Ten Years of Research*. London: Butrint Foundation.

Peirce, L. P. (1993) *The Imperial Harem: Women and Sovereignty in the Ottoman Empire*. New York and Oxford: Oxford University Press.

Pekin, A. K. and Kangal, S. (2007) *Istanbul: 8000 Years Brought to Daylight: Marmaray, Metro, Sultanahmet Excavations*. Istanbul: Vehbi Koç Foundation.

Pelikan, J. (1987) *The Excellent Empire: The Fall of Rome and the Triumph of the Church*. Eugene, OR: Wipf & Stock.

Pennanen, R. P. (2004) 'The Nationalization of Ottoman Popular Music in Greece', *Ethnomusicology* 48.1: 1–25.

Pentcheva, B. V. (2007) 'Containers of Power: Eunuchs and Reliquaries in Byzantium', *RES: Anthropology and Aesthetics* 51: 108–20.

Perra, P. (2013) 'Aspects of the Relations between the Hospitaller Knights of Rhodes and the Republic of Venice: Contacts and Collaboration during the Second Venetian–Ottoman War (1499–1502/03)', in S. Phillips and E. Buttigieg (eds) *Islands and Military Orders, c. 1291–1798*. Farnham: Ashgate.

Peterkin, A. (2001) *One Thousand Beards: A Cultural History of Facial Hair*. Vancouver: Arsenal Pulp Press.

Philliou, C. (2008) 'The Paradox of Perceptions: Interpreting the Ottoman Past through the National Present', *Middle Eastern Studies* 44.5: 661–75.

Phillips, J. (2004) *The Fourth Crusade and the Sack of Constantinople*. London: Jonathan Cape.

Phillips, J. (2010) *Holy Warriors: A Modern History of the Crusades*. London: Vintage Books.

Phillips, W. A. (1897) *The War of Greek Independence 1821–1833*. London: Smith, Elder.

Phillips, W. D. (1985) *Slavery from Roman Times to the Early Transatlantic Trade*. Manchester: Manchester University Press.

Phillips Cohen, J. (2014) *Becoming Ottomans: Sephardi Jews and Imperial Citizenship in the Modern Era*. Oxford: Oxford University Press.

Pickles, T. (1998) *Malta 1565: Last Battle of the Crusades*. Oxford and New York: Osprey Publishing.

Pierce, L. (1993) *The Imperial Harem: Women and Sovereignty in the Imperial Harem*. New York; Oxford: Oxford University Press.

Pincus, D. (1992) 'Venice and the Two Romes: Byzantium and Rome as a Double Heritage in Venetian Cultural Politics', *Artibus et Historiae* 13.26: 101–14.

Pingree, D. (2001) 'From Alexandria to Baghdad to Byzantium: The Transmission of Astrology', *International Journal of the Classical Tradition* 8.1: 3–37.

Pohl, W. (2004) 'The Vandals: Fragments of a Narrative', in A. H. Merrills (ed.) *Vandals, Romans and Berbers: New Perspectives on Late Antique North Africa*. Farnham: Ashgate, 31–48.

Pormann, P. E. and Savage-Smith, E. (2007) *Medieval Islamic Medicine*. Washington, DC: Georgetown University Press.

Proud, L. (2000) *Icons: A Sacred Art*. Norwich: Pitkin Guides.

Pryor, J. (2008) 'Shipping and Seafaring', in E. Jeffreys, J. Haldon and R. Cormack (eds) *The Oxford Handbook of Byzantine Studies*. Oxford: Oxford University Press, 482–91.

Pryor, J. and Jeffreys, E. M. (2006) *The Age of the ΔΡΟΜΩΝ: The Byzantine Navy ca 500–1204*. Leiden: Brill.

Pushkin, A. S. (2008) *Complete Prose Tales: The Moor of Peter the Great* trans. G. Aitken. London: Random House.

Quataert, D. (2000, 2005) *The Ottoman Empire 1700–1922*. New York: Cambridge University Press.

Raffensperger, C. (2012) *Reimagining Europe: Kievan Rus' in the Medieval World*. Cambridge, MA: Harvard University Press.

Re'em, A., Seligman, J., 'Adawi, Z. and Abu Raya, R. (2001) 'Crusader Remains in the Muristan, Old City of Jerusalem: A Decade of Archaeological Gleanings', *'Attiqot* 66: 137–54.

Retief, F. P. and Cilliers, L. (2006) 'The Epidemic of Justinian (AD 542): A Prelude to the Middle Ages', *Acra Theologica* 26.2: 117–27.

Reynolds, L. D. and Wilson, N. G. (1991) *Scribes and Scholars: A Guide to the Transmission of Greek and Latin Literature*. Oxford: Clarendon Press.

Rives, J. B. (1999) 'The Decree of Decius and the Religion of Empire', *Journal of Roman Studies* 89: 135–54.

Robert of Clari (1924) *La Conquête de Constantinople*, P. Lauer (ed.). Paris:

Robert of Clari (2005) *The Conquest of Constantinople*, trans. E. R. McNeal NY: Columbia University Press. 57–75.

Roberts, M. (2007) *Intimate Outsiders: The Harem in Ottoman and Orientalist Art and Travel Literature*. Durham, NC, and London: Duke University Press.

Robertson, J. C. (1858) *History of the Christian Church*. London: J. Murray.

Robertson, N. (1980) 'The Sequence of Events in the Aegean in 408 and 407 B.C.', *Historia: Zeitschrift für Alte Geschichte* 29.3: 282–301.

Robinson, B. S. (2009) 'Green Seraglios: Tulips, Turbans and the Global Market', *Journal for Early Modern Cultural Studies* 9.4: 107–8.

Robinson, T. A. (2017) *Who Were the First Christians? Dismantling the Urban Thesis*. Oxford: Oxford University Press.

Rodogno, D. (2011) *Against Massacre: Humanitarian Interventions in the Ottoman Empire 1815–1924*. Princeton: Princeton University Press.

Rogan, E. (2015) *The Fall of the Ottomans: The Great War in the Middle East, 1914–1920*. London: Allen Lane.

Rogerson, B. (2010) *The Last Crusaders: The Hundred-Year Battle for the Center of the World*. New York: The Overlook Press.

Romane, J. (2015) *Byzantium Triumphant: The Military History of the Byzantines 959–1025*. Barnsley: Pen & Sword.

Rose, C. B. (1998) 'Troy and the Historical Imagination', *Classical World* 91.5: 386–403.

Rosen, W. (2008) *Justinian's Flea: Plague, Empire and the Birth of Europe*. London: Pimlico.

Ross, S. H. (2006) *How Roosevelt Failed America in World War II*. Jefferson, NC: McFarland.

Rothman, N. E. (2009) 'Interpreting Dragomans: Boundaries and Crossings in the Early Modern Mediterranean', *Comparative Studies in Society and History* 51.4: 771–800.

Rotman, Y. (2009) *Byzantine Slavery and the Mediterranean*, trans. Jane Marie Todd. Cambridge, MA: Harvard University Press.

Roueché, C. (2008) 'Entertainments, Theatre, and Hippodrome', in E. Jeffreys, J. Haldon and R. Cormack (eds) *The Oxford Handbook of Byzantine Studies*. Oxford: Oxford University Press, 677–84.

Roy, T. (2012) *India in the World Economy: From Antiquity to the Present*. Cambridge: Cambridge University Press.

Rozen, M. (1998) 'Public Space and Private Space among the Jews of Istanbul in the Sixteenth and Seventeenth Centuries', *Turcica* 30: 331–46.

Russell, G. (2014) *Heirs to Forgotten Kingdoms: Journeys into the Disappearing Religions of the Middle East*. New York: Simon & Schuster.

Russell, T. (2016) *Byzantium and the Bosporus: A Historical Study, from the Seventh Century BC until the Foundation of Constantinople*. Oxford Classical Monographs. Oxford: Oxford University Press.

Ryder, J. R. (2011) 'Changing Perspectives on 1054', *Byzantine and Modern Greek Studies* 35.1: 20–37.

Rykwert, J. (1988) *The Idea of a Town: The Anthropology of Urban Form in Rome, Italy and the Ancient World.* Cambridge, MA: MIT Press.

Şahin, M. and Mert, H. (eds) (2011) *The Proceedings of the International Workshop: Localisation of the 1st Council Palace in Nicaea.* Bursa: Uludağ Üniversitesi.

Said, E. (1978) *Orientalism.* London: Penguin.

Saïd, S. (2002) 'Greeks and Barbarians in Euripides' Tragedies: The End of Differences?', trans. A. Nevill, in T. Harrison (ed.) *Greeks and Barbarians.* New York: Routledge, 62–100.

Salamon, M., Wołoszyn, M., Musin, A. and Špehar, P. (eds) (2012) *Rome, Constantinople and Newly-Converted Europe: Archaeological and Historical Evidence*, vol. 2. Crakow, Leipzig, Rzeszów and Warsaw: Instytut Archeologii i Etnologii Polskiej akademii nauk.

Saradi, H. (2000) 'Perceptions and Literary Interpretations of Statues and the Image of Constantinople', *Byzantiaka* 20: 3–41.

Saradi-Mendelovici, H. (1990) 'Christian Attitudes toward Pagan Monuments in Late Antiquity and their Legacy in Later Byzantine Centuries', *Dumbarton Oaks Papers* 44: 47–61.

Saxon, A. H. (ed.) (1983) *Selected Letters of P. T. Barnum.* New York: Columbia University Press.

Schama, S. (2014) *The Story of the Jews: Finding the Words (1000 BCE–1492).* London: Vintage.

Schefer, C. (1881) 'Indications sur les lieux de Pèlerinage' in *Archives de l'Orient latin, 1.* Paris.

Schibille, N. (2014) *Hagia Sophia and the Byzantine Aesthetic Experience.* Farnham: Ashgate.

Schiffer, R. (1999) *Oriental Panorama: British Travellers in 19th Century Turkey.* Amsterdam: Rodopi.

Schrunk, I. and Studer-Karlen, M. (2012), 'Spalatum (Split, Spalato): Diocletian's Palace', in *The Encyclopedia of Ancient History.* http://onlinelibrary. wiley.com/doi/10.1002/9781444338386.wbeah16139/abstract.

Scott, A. (2014) *Turkish Awakening: A Personal Discovery of Modern Turkey.* London: Faber & Faber.

Scott, M. (2014) *Delphi: A History of the Centre of the Ancient World.* Oxford and Princeton: Princeton University Press.

Seal, J. (2012) *Meander: East to West along a Turkish River.* London: Chatto & Windus.

Serim, A. (2015) *Konstantiniyye 1918.* Istanbul: Denizler Kitabevi.

Sethe, K., Helck, W. and Steindorff, G. (1909) *Urkunden des ägyptischen Altertums.* Leipzig: Hinrichs. Setton, K. (1984) *The Papacy and the Levant, 1204–1571.* Philadelphia: American Philological Society.

Sevcenko, N. (2002) 'Wild Animal in the Byzantine Park', in A. Littlewood, H. Maguire and J. Wolschke-Bulmahn (eds) *Byzantine Garden Culture*. Washington, DC: Dumbarton Oaks Research Library and Collection, 69–86.

Severin, T. (1985) *The Jason Voyage: The Quest for the Golden Fleece*. London: Hutchinson.

Shahid, I. (2010) *Byzantium and the Arabs*. Washington, DC: Dumbarton Oaks Research Library and Collection.

Shaw, S. (1991) *The Jews of the Ottoman Empire and the Turkish Republic*. New York: New York University Press.

Shepard, J. (1973) 'The English and Byzantium: A Study of their Role in the Byzantine Army in the Later Eleventh Century', *Traditio* 29: 53–92.

Shepard, J. (2008) 'The Viking Rus and Byzantium', in S. Brink (ed.) *The Viking World*. London and New York: Routledge, 496–516.

Shipley, G. (2006) 'Landscapes of the Ancient Peloponnese: A Human-Geographical Approach', *Leidschrift* 21.1: 27–43.

Shores, T. (2013) *Varangian: Norse Influences within the Elite Guard of Byzantium*. http://www.academia.edu/3628861/Varangian_Norse_Influences_Within_the_Elite_Guard_of_Byzantium

Silvas, A. M. (2006) 'Kassia the Nun c. 810–c. 865: An Appreciation', in L. Garland (ed.) *Byzantine Women: Varieties of Experience AD 800–1200*. Aldershot: Ashgate, 17–39.

Silving, H. (1959) 'The Oath: I', *Yale Law Journal* 68.7: 1329–90.

Sizgorich, T. (2009) *Violence and Belief in Late Antiquity: Militant Devotion in Christianity and Islam*. Philadelphia: University of Pennsylvania Press.

Skhirtladze, Z. (2015) 'The Image of the Virgin on the Sinai Hexaptych and the Apse Mosaic of Hagia Sophia', *Dumbarton Oaks Papers* 68: 369–86.

Skilliter, S. (1965) 'Three Letters from the Ottoman "Sultana" Safiye to Queen Elizabeth I', in S. M. Stern (ed.) *Documents from Islamic Chanceries*. Cambridge, MA: Harvard University Press, 129–57.

Skylitzes, J. (2010) 'A Synopsis of Byzantine History, 811–1057' Cambridge: Cambridge University Press.

Snaedal, T. (2016) 'Runes from Byzantium: reconsidering the Piraeus lion', in F. Androshchuk, J. Shepard, M. White (eds) *Byzantium and the Viking World*. Stockholm: Uppsala University, 198–214.

Soldani, M. E. and Duran i Duelt, D. (2012) 'Religion, Warfare and Business in Fifteenth-Century Rhodes', in *Religion and Religious Institutions in the European Economy 1000–1800*. Florence: Firenze University Press, 257–70.

A Solemn Commemoration of the Contribution of the Sikh Regiment at the Battle of Gallipoli & throughout the Great War, held at St Martin-in-the-Fields, London, 8 June 2015. https://sikhchic.com/current_events/order_of_service_gallipoli_the_sikhs_national_memorial_service_part_iii.

Sorgenfre, J. (2013) *Port Business*. Self-published.

Soulis, G. C. (1961) 'The Gypsies in the Byzantine Empire and the Balkans in the Late Middle Ages', *Dumbarton Oaks Papers* 15: 141, 143–65.

Southern, P. (2008) *Empress Zenobia: Palmyra's Rebel Queen*. London: Bloomsbury.

Spatharakis, I. (1976) *The Portrait in Byzantine Illuminated Manuscripts*. Byzantina Neerlandica 6. Leiden: Brill.

Srivastava, Nagendra M. P. (1973). *Growth of Nationalism in India: Effects of International Events*. Meerut: Meenakshi Prakashan.

Stacton, D. (1965) *The World on the Last Day*. London: Faber & Faber.

Starr, J. (1970) *Jews in the Byzantine Empire, 641–1204*. New York: Burt Franklin.

Stathakopoulos, D. (2004) *Famine and Pestilence*. Farnham: Ashgate.

Stathakopoulos, D. (2014) *A Short History of the Byzantine Empire*. London: I. B. Tauris.

Stathopoulou, C. (2006) 'Exploring Informal Mathematics of Craftsmen in the Designing Tradition of "Xysta" at Pyrgi of Chios', *For the Learning of Mathematics* 26.3: 9–14.

Stenseth, N. et al. (2006) 'Plague Dynamics Are Driven by Climate Variation', *Proceedings of the National Academy of Sciences of the United States of America* 103: 13110–15.

Stephenson, P. (2009) *Constantine: Unconquered Emperor, Christian Victor*. London: Quercus.

Stephenson, P. (ed.) (2012) *The Byzantine World*. New York: Routledge.

Sterk, A. (2000) 'Mission from Below: Captive Women and Conversion on the East Roman Frontiers', *Church History* 79.1: 1–39.

Stevens, R. (1962, 1965) *The Land of the Great Sophy*. London: Methuen.

Stevenson, S. W. (1889) 'Barba', in C. R. Smith and F. W. Madden, *A Dictionary of Roman Coins: Republican and Imperial*. London: George Bell.

Stevenson, W. (2002) 'Eunuchs and Early Christianity', in Shaun Tougher (ed.) *Eunuchs in Antiquity and Beyond*. Swansea: The Classical Press of Wales, London: Duckworth.

Stone, N. (2010) *Turkey: A Short History*. London: Thames & Hudson.

Stoneman, R. (2008) *Alexander the Great: A Life in Legend*. New Haven and London: Yale University Press.

Stoneman, R. (2010) *Across the Hellespont: A Literary Guide to Turkey*. London: Tauris Parke Paperbacks.

Stoneman, R. (2015) *Xerxes: Persian Life*. New Haven and London: Yale University Press.

Stoye, J. (2012) *The Siege of Vienna*. Edinburgh: Birlinn.

Strathern, P. (2012) *The Spirit of Venice: From Marco Polo to Casanova*. London: Jonathan Cape.

Strazny, P. (ed.) (2005) *Encyclopedia of Linguistics*. New York: Fitzroy Dearborn.

Stroumsa, G. G. (2011) 'Barbarians or Heretics? Jews and Arabs in the Mind of Byzantium (Fourth to Eighth Centuries)', in R. Bonfil, O. Irshai, G. G. Stroumsa and R. Talgam (eds) *Jews in Byzantium: Dialectics of Minority and Majority Cultures.* Leiden: Brill, 761–76.

Sudár, B. (2008) 'Bektasi Monasteries in Ottoman Hungary (16th–17th Centuries)', *Acta Orientalia Academiae Scientiarum Hungaricae* 61.1: 229–32.

Suny, R. G. (2015) *'They Can Live in the Desert but Nowhere Else': A History of the Armenian Genocide.* Princeton and Oxford: Princeton University Press.

Suvari, Ç. C. (2010) 'A Brief Review of Ethnicity Studies in Turkey', *Iran & the Caucasus* 14.2: 407–17.

Sweetman, J. (1987) *The Oriental Obsession: Islamic Inspiration in British and American Art and Architecture 1500–1920.* Cambridge: Cambridge University Press.

Talbot, A. M. (1983) 'Bluestocking Nuns: Intellectual Life in the Convents of Late Byzantium', *Harvard Ukrainian Studies* 7: 604–18.

Talbot, A. M. (ed.) (1996) *Holy Women of Byzantium: Ten Saints' Lives in English Translation.* Washington, DC: Dumbarton Oaks Research Library and Collection.

Talbot, A. M. (2001) *Women and Religious Life in Byzantium.* Farnham: Ashgate.

Tawfick, R. (2010) 'Sultans' Jewels: The Lasting Legacies of Qalawun and Barquq', *Horus* February/March: 24–8.

Taxel, I. (2009) 'Late Byzantine/Early Islamic Stamped Jar Handles from Jerusalem and Tell Qatra', *Israel Exploration Journal* 59.2: 185–93.

Taxidis, I. (2013) 'The Monastery of Pantokrator in the Narratives of Western Travellers', in S. Kotzabassi (ed.) *The Pantokrator Monastery in Constantinople.* Boston and Berlin: De Gruyter.

Taylor, J. (2010) *Imperial Istanbul: A Traveller's Guide (includes Iznik, Bursa and Edirne).* London: Tauris Parke Paperbacks.

Temperley, H. (1936) *England and the Near East.* London: Longmans, Green.

Tepper Y. and Di Segni, L. (2006) *A Christian Prayer Hall of the Third Century CE at Kefar 'Othnay (Legio). Excavations at the Megiddo Prison 2005.* Jerusalem: Israel Antiquities Authority.

Terakye, G. and Oflaz, F. (2007) 'A Historical Overview of Psychiatric Mental Health Nursing in Turkey', *International Journal of Mental Health*, 36.3: 73–83.

Theodossiou, E., Manimanis, V. and Dimitrijevic, M. S. (2012) 'Astrology in the Early Byzantine Empire and the Anti-Astrology Stance of the Church Fathers', *European Journal of Science and Theology* 8.2: 7–24.

Thierry, F. and Morrisson, C. (1994) 'Sur les monnaies byzantines trouvées en Chine', *Revue Numismatique*, 6th series, 36: 109–45.

Thomas, D. and Mallett, A. (2010) *Christian–Muslim Relations: A Bibliographical History*, vol. 2: *900–1050.* Leiden: Brill.

Thomas, J. P. and Hero, A. C. (2000) *Byzantine Monastic Foundation*

Documents, 5 vols. Washington, DC: Dumbarton Oaks Research Library and Collection.

Thomov, T. (2014) 'Four Scandinavian Ship Graffiti from Hagia Sophia', *Byzantine and Modern Greek Studies* 38.2: 168–84.

Timbs, J. (1839) (ed.) *The Literary World: A Journal of Popular Information and Entertainment*, vol. 1. London: G. Berger.

Tolan, J., Veinstein, G. and Laurens, H. (2013) *Europe and the Islamic World: A History*. Princeton: Princeton University Press.

Tolkien, J. R. R. (2012), *The Lord of the Rings: The Return of the King*. London: HarperCollins.

Tolstoy, L. (2001). 'The Wood-Felling' in *Collected Shorter Fiction*, vol. 1., trans. A. Maude, L. Maude and N. Cooper. New York and Toronto: Alfred A. Knopf.

Toner, J. (2013) *Homer's Turk: How Classics Shaped Ideas of the East*. Cambridge, MA and London: Harvard University Press.

Topinka, R. J. (2009) 'Islam, England, and Identity in the Early Modern Period: A Review of Recent Scholarship', *Mediterranean Studies* 18: 114–30.

Tougher, S. (ed.) (2002) *Eunuchs in Antiquity and Beyond*. London: The Classical Press of Wales and Duckworth.

Toynbee, J. M. C. (1934) *The Hadrianic School: A Chapter in the History of Greek Art*. Cambridge: Cambridge University Press.

Tracy, J. D. (2002) *Emperor Charles V: Impresario of War, Campaign Strategy, International Finance, and Domestic Politics*. Cambridge: Cambridge University Press.

Treadgold, W. (1988) *The Byzantine Revival, 780–842*. Stanford: Stanford University Press.

Treadgold, W. (1997) *A History of the Byzantine State and Society*. Stanford: Stanford University Press.

Troianos, S. N. (2011) 'Christians and Jews in Byzantium: A Love–Hate Relationship', in R. Bonfil, O. Irshai, G. G. Stroumsa and R. Talgam (eds) *Jews in Byzantium: Dialectics of Minority and Majority Cultures*. Leiden: Brill, 133–48.

Tsetskhladze, G. R. (ed.) (1998) *The Greek Colonisation of the Black Sea Area*. Stuttgart: Franz Steiner Verlag.

Turchini, A. (1992) *Rimini Medievale. Contributi per la storia della città*. Rimini: Bruno Chigi Editore.

Turnbull, S. (2004) *The Walls of Constantinople AD 324–1453*. Oxford: Osprey Publishing.

Tursun Bey (1978) *The History of Mehmet the Conqueror*, trans. H. İnalcık and R. Murphey. Minneapolis: Bibliotheca Islamica.

Turton, G. (1974) *The Syrian Princesses: The Women Who Ruled Rome A.D. 193–235*. London: Cassell.

Twain, M. (1867) *From Innocents Abroad, written on the occasion of the Exposition Universelle*. Access online via Project Gutenburg.

Tyerman, C. (2006) *God's War: A New History of the Crusades*. London: Allen Lane.

Uslu, G. (2009) 'Ottoman Appreciation of Trojan Heritage 1870–1875', in *Tijdschrift voor Mediterrane Archeologie* 21.41: 4–10.

Vallois, H. V. (1937) *Note sur les ossements humains de la nécropole énéolithique de Byblos (avec 2 planches)*. Vol. 1. Bulletin of the Museum of Beirut.

Van Millingen, A. (1899) *Byzantine Constantinople: The Walls of the City and Adjoining Historical Sites*. London: John Murray.

Van Millingen, A. (1912) *Byzantine Churches in Constantinople: Their History and Architecture*. London: Hesperides Press.

Varvounis, M. (2012) *Jan Sobieski: The King Who Saved Europe*. Bloomington, IN: Xlibris.

Vasiliev, A. A. (1984) *History of the Byzantine Empire 324–1453*, vol. 1. Madison, WI: University of Wisconsin Press.

Vassilaki, M. (ed.) (2005) *Images of the Mother of God: Perceptions of the Theotokos in Byzantium*. Farnham: Ashgate.

Verlinde, A. (2012) 'The Temple Complex of Pessinus: Archaeological Research on the Function, Morphology and Chronology of a Sanctuary in Asia Minor', doctoral thesis, Ghent University.

Via Egnatia Foundation (2010) *Via Egnatia Revisited: Common Past, Common Future: Proceedings VEF Conference, Bitola, February 2009*. Driebergen: Via Egnatia Foundation.

Villehardouin, G. de (1963), 'The Conquest of Constantinople', in Jean de Joinville and Geoffrey de Villehardouin, *The Chronicles of the Crusades*, trans. M. R. B. Shaw. London: Penguin.

Vitkus, D. J. (1997) 'Turning Turk in *Othello*: The Conversion and Damnation of the Moor', *Shakespeare Quarterly* 48.2: 145–76.

Vlami, D. (2015) *Trading with the Ottomans: The Levant Company in the Middle East*. London: I. B. Tauris.

Von Hammer (1878) *History of the Ottoman Turks*, ed. E. S. Creasy. London: Richard Bentley.

von Sanders, O. L. (1927) *Five Years in Turkey*, trans. C. Reichmann. Annapolis: United States Naval Institute.

Wade Labarge, M. (2001) *Women in Medieval Life*. London: Penguin.

Wagner, M. (1856). *Travels in Persia, Georgia and Koordistan with sketches of the Cossacks and the Caucasus*. London: Hurst and Blackett Publishers. Digitised by Google.

Waksman, Y. (2008-9) 'Istanbul Ceramic Workshops Project: First Laboratory Study of a Constantinopolitan Production of Byzantine Ceramics', *Dumbarton Oaks Project Grants Reports*. http://www.doaks.org/research/byzantine/project-grant-reports/2008-2009/waksman [date accessed: 19/01/2016].

Walker, P. (2002) *Exploring an Islamic Empire: Fatimad and Islamic and its Sources*. London: I. B Tauris.

Walmsley, A. (2007) *Early Islamic Syria: An Archaeological Assessment*. London: Duckworth.

Ware Allen, B. (2015) *The Great Siege of Malta: Battle between the Ottomans and the Knights of St John*. Lebanon, NH: University Press of New England.

Wasti, S. T. (2004) 'The 1912–13 Balkan Wars and the Siege of Edirne', *Middle Eastern Studies* 40.4: 59–78.

Wasti, S. T. (2005) 'The Ottoman Ceremony of the Royal Purse', *Middle Eastern Studies* 41.2: 193–200.

Watt, M. (1982) *The Influence of Islam on Medieval Europe*. Edinburgh: Edinburgh University Press.

Watt, M. (1988) *Muhammad's Mecca: A History in the Qur'an*. Edinburgh: Edinburgh University Press.

Watts, E. (2004) 'Justinian, Malalas, and the End of Athenian Philosophical Teaching in A.D. 529', *Journal of Roman Studies* 94: 168–82.

Webb, M. (2001) *The Churches and Catacombs of Early Christian Rome: A Comprehensive Guide*. Brighton: Sussex Academic Press.

Webb, R. (2008) *Demons and Dancers: Performance in Late Antiquity*. Cambridge, MA: Harvard University Press.

Weeda, L. (2015) *Virgil's Political Commentary: In the Eclogues, Georgics and Aeneid*. Berlin: De Gruyter.

Weitzmann, K. (1960) 'The Survival of Mythological Representations in Early Christian and Byzantine Art and their Impact on Christian Iconography', *Dumbarton Oaks Papers* 14: 43–45–68.

Welch, S. C., Jenkins, M. and Kane, C. (1984) 'Islamic Art', *Notable Acquisitions 1983–1984*. New York: Metropolitan Museum of Art, 4–8.

Wellesz, E. (ed.) (1957) *The New Oxford History of Music*, vol. 1: *Ancient and Oriental Music*. Oxford: Oxford University Press.

Wells, C. (2007) *Sailing from Byzantium: How a Lost Empire Shaped the World*. New York: Delta Trade.

Wells, P. S. (2009) *Barbarians to Angels: The Dark Ages Reconsidered*. New York and London: W. W. Norton.

West, M. L. (2005) '"Odyssey" and "Argonautica"', *Classical Quarterly* 55.1: 39–64.

Whalen, B. (2007) 'Rethinking the Schism of 1054: Authority, Heresy, and the Latin Rite', *Traditio* 62: 1–24.

Wharton, A. (2015) *The Architects of Ottoman Constantinople: The Baylan Family and the History of Ottoman Architecture*. London: I. B. Tauris.

Wheatcroft, A. (1993) *The Ottomans*. London: Viking.

Wheatcroft, A. (2008) *The Enemy at the Gate: Habsburgs, Ottomans and the Battle for Europe*. London: Random House.

Wheeler, E. L. (2011) 'The Army and the Limes in the East', in P. Erdkamp (ed.) *A Companion to the Roman Army*. Chichester: Wiley-Blackwell, 235–66.

White, M. (2013) *Military Saints in Byzantium and Rus, 900–1200*. Cambridge: Cambridge University Press.

White, S. (2011) *The Climate of Rebellion in the Early Modern Ottoman Empire*. Cambridge: Cambridge University Press.

Whitley, J. et al. (2007) 'Archaeology in Greece 2006–2007', *Archaeological Reports* 53: 1–121.

Wickham, C. (2005) 'The Development of Villages in the West, 300–900', in J. Lefort, C. Morrisson and J.-P. Sodini (eds) *Les Villages dans l'Empire byzantin (IVe–XVe siècle)*. Paris: Lethielleux, 54–70.

Wickham, C. (2009) *The Inheritance of Rome: A History of Europe from 400 to 1000*. London: Allen Lane.

Wiechmann, I. and Grupe, G. (2005) 'Detection of *Yersinia pestis* DNA in Two Early Medieval Skeletal Finds from Aschheim (Upper Bavaria, 6th Century AD)', *American Journal of Physical Anthropology* 126: 48–55.

Wilson, A. I. (1999) 'Commerce and Industry in Roman Sabratha', *Libstud* 30: 29–52.

Wilson, M. (2012) *Biblical Turkey: A Guide to the Jewish and Christian Sites of Asia Minor*. Istanbul: Ege Yayınları.

Wilson, N. (ed.) (2009) *Encyclopaedia of Ancient Greece*. London: Routledge.

Wilson, N. G. (1967) 'The Libraries of the Byzantine World', *Greek, Roman and Byzantine Studies* 8: 53–80.

Wilson, N. G. (1992) *From Byzantium to Italy: Greek Studies in the Italian Renaissance*. London: Duckworth.

Wilson, P. H. (2016) *The Holy Roman Empire: A Thousand Years of Europe's History*. London: Penguin.

Winroth, A. (2004) *The Age of the Vikings*. Princeton: Princeton University Press.

Wood, I. (2003) 'Before and after the Migration to Britain', in J. Hines (ed.) *The Anglo-Saxons from the Migration Period to the Eighth Century: An Ethnographic Perspective*. Woodbridge: The Boydell Press, 41–64.

Woods, D. (1997) 'Where Did Constantine I Die?', *Journal of Theological Studies* 48.2: 531–5.

Woods, D. (1998) 'On the Death of the Empress Fausta', *Greece and Rome* 45.1: 70–86.

Woolf, L. (1917) *The Future of Constantinople*. London: Allen & Unwin.

Worthington, I. (2008) *Philip II of Macedonia*. New Haven and London: Yale University Press.

Wren, M. C. and Stults, T. (1994) *The Course of Russian History*. Eugene, OR: Wipf & Stock.

Wright, D. H. (1987) 'The True Face of Constantine the Great', *Dumbarton Oaks Papers* 41: 493–507.

Wright, G. R. H. (1968) 'Simeon's Ancestors (or the Skeleton on the Column)', *Australian Journal of Biblical Archaeology* 1.1: 41–9.

Wright, L. (2006) *The Looming Tower: Al Qaeda's Road to 9/11*. London: Allen Lane.

Yeats, W. B. (1933) 'Byzantium' from Finneran, R. J. (ed.) *The Poems of W. B. Yeats: A New Edition*. London: Macmillan.

Yildirim, O. (2007) 'The Battle of Lepanto and its Impact on Ottoman History and Historiography', in R. Cancila (ed.) *Mediterraneo in Armi*. Palermo: Quaderni di Mediterranea.

Yildirim, Ş. and Karakaş, G. (2006) *Edirne Museums and Sites*. Istanbul: Yapı Kredi Yayınları.

Yilmaz, F. (2015) *A Former Ottoman Officer among the ANZACs: Dr. Charles Snodgrass Ryan*. Istanbul: Bahçeşehir University Press.

Yılmaz, G. (2011) 'The Economic and Social Roles of Janissaries in a 17th Century Ottoman City: The Case of Istanbul', doctoral thesis, McGill University, Montreal. digitool.library.mcgill.ca/thesisfile104500.pdf [date accessed 28.01.16].

Yotov, V. (2008) 'The Vikings on the Balkans (10th–11th Centuries): Strategic and Tactical Changes: New Archaeological Data on the Weaponry', *Archaeologia Baltica* 8: 321–7.

Yücel, E. (2010) *Great Palace Mosaic Museum*, trans. A. Sheridan and M. D. Sheridan. Istanbul: Bilkent Kultur Girisimi Publications.

Zachariadou, E. (1970) 'The Conquest of Adrianople by the Turks', *Studii Veneziani* 12: 211–17.

Zampaki, T. (2012) 'The Mediterranean Muslim Navy and the Expeditions Dispatched against Constantinople', *ICHSS 2012 Proceedings* 8: 9–17.

Zarinebaf, F. (2010) *Crime and Punishment in Istanbul 1700–1800*. Berkeley and Los Angeles: University of California Press.

Zarinebaf, F. (2012) 'Intercommunal Life in Istanbul during the Eighteenth Century', *Review of Middle East Studies* 46.1: 79–85.

Zens, R. (2015) 'Some Approaches to the Ottoman Empire as Part of a World History Curriculum', *World History Connected* 10.3. http://worldhistoryconnected.press.illinois.edu/10.3/zens.html

Zhukov, K. and Vitol, A. (2001) 'The Origins of the Ottoman Submarine Fleet', *Oriente Moderno* 20(81).1: 221–32.

Zim, R. (2009) 'Writing Behind Bars: Literary Contexts and the Authority of Carceral Experience', *Huntington Library Quarterly* 72.2: 291–311.

Zuckerman, C. (2005) 'Learning from the Enemy and More: Studies in "Dark Centuries" Byzantium', *Millennium* 2: 79–135.

CATALOGUES AND GUIDES

Portraits from the Empire: The Ottoman World and the Ottomans from the 18th to the 20th Century with Selected Works of Art from the Suna and Inan Kiraç Foundation Collection (2005), exhibition catalogue. Istanbul: Pera Museum Publication 1.

Nea Moni on Chios, educational programme. Ministry of Culture, Department of Byzantine and Post-Byzantine Monuments, Byzantine Museums Section, 3rd Ephorate of Byzantine Antiquities, UNESCO.

Buckton, D. et al. (1984) *The Treasury of San Marco*, catalogue of the exhibition at the Metropolitan Museum of Art, New York. Milan: Olivetti.

Buckton, D. (ed.) (1994) *Byzantium: Treasures of Byzantine Art and Culture from British Collections*, exhibition catalogue. London: British Museum Press.

Drandaki, A., Papanikola-Bakirtzi, D. and Tourta, A. (eds) (2013) *Heaven & Earth: Art of Byzantium from Greek Collections*, exhibition catalogue. Athens: Hellenic Ministry of Culture and Sports and the Benaki Museum.

Evans, H. C. and Ratliff, B. (eds) (2012) *Byzantium and Islam: Age of Transition*, exhibition catalogue. New Haven and London: Yale University Press.

Hartley, E., Hawkes, J., Henig, M. and Mee, F. (eds) (2006) *Constantine the Great: York's Roman Emperor*, exhibition catalogue. York and Aldershot: York Museums and Gallery Trust, with Lund Humphries.

Makariou, S. (ed.) (2012) *Islamic Art at the Musée du Louvre*, exhibition catalogue. Paris: Hazan.

Moysidou, J. (ed.) (2010) *Byzantine Museum: The Permanent Exhibition*, exhibition catalogue. Athens: Byzantine and Christian Museum, Ministry of Culture and Tourism.

Istanbul: 8000 Years Brought to Daylight: Marmaray, Metro, Sultanahmet Excavations (2007), excavation catalogue. Istanbul: Vehbi Koç Foundation.

Institut du Monde Arabe (2012) *Les Mille et Une Nuits*, exhibition catalogue, ed. E. Bouffard and A.-A. Joyard. Paris: Hazan.

Constantino 313 D.C (2013), exhibition catalogue. Ministero per i Beni e le Attività Culturali, Soprintendenza Speciale per i Beni Archaeologici di Roma. Milano: Mondadori Electa S.p.A.

Baker, E. M. and Finkel, A. (n.d.) *A History of the Sultanahmet Prison*, catalogue. Istanbul: The Four Seasons Hotel.

Ballain, A. (ed.) (2011) *Relics of the Past: Treasures of the Greek Orthodox Church and the Population Exchange: The Benaki Museum Collections*, exhibition catalogue. Milan: 5 Continent Editions.

Bursa City Guide (2012). Bursa: Bursa Special Provincial Administration.

Ortalli, J. (2007) *The Surgeon's House and the Piazza Ferrari Excavations*, excavation catalogue, trans. John Denton. Rimini: Comune di Rimini.

Sacred, exhibition guide, British Library, London, 27 April–23 September 2007. London: British Library Publishing.

Byzantium 330–1453, Royal Academy of Arts, London, 25 October 2008–22 March 2009. ed. R Cormack and M. Vassilaki. London: Royal Academy of Arts.

Karliga, B. (n.d.) MEDAM: Bahcesehir University Civilisation Studies Center, institution guide.

Kourkoutidou-Nikolaïdou, E. and Nalpandis, D. (2000) *Museum of Byzantine Culture, Thessaloniki*, gallery guide, trans. D. Hardy. Athens: Hellenic Ministry of Culture.

Paissidou, M. (n.d.) *Ephoreia of Byzantine Antiquities of Thessaloniki: Byzantine Churches of Thessaloniki*, gallery guide, trans. D. Whitehouse and J. Lillie. Athens: Hellenic Ministry of Culture.

Paissidou, M. (n.d.) *Monuments of the Ottoman Period of Thessaloniki*, gallery guide, trans. D. Whitehouse and J. Lillie. Athens: Hellenic Ministry of Culture.

Ballain, A. (ed.) (2006) *Benaki Museum: A Guide to the Museum of Islamic Art*, trans. J. Avgherinos. Athens: Benaki Museum.

Delivorrias, A. (2000) *A Guide to the Benaki Museum*, trans. A. Doumas. Athens: Benaki Museum.

Konstantios, D. (gen. ed.) (2010) *Byzantine and Christian Museum: Byzantine Collections: The Permanent Exhibition*, exhibition guide. Athens: Hellenic Ministry of Culture.

The Piri Reis World Map of 1513 (14 June 2013, University of Greenwich), conference brochure.

York Minster: A Short Guide (2012). York: York Minster and Jigsaw Design and Publishing.

Walking with the Romans: Daily Life in Eboracum: A Walking Trail (2012). York: York Museums Trust, History Works.

Experiencing the Great War: York in World War One: A Walking Trail (2012). York: York Museum Trust, History Works.

Suleyman the Magnificent: An Exhibition at the British Museum, exhibition guide, 18 January–30 May 1988, British Museum, London

Parliamentary Papers *Accounts and Papers: Thirty-Six Volumes: Eastern Papers* (1854), Session 31 January–12 August 1854, vol. 71. London: Harrison & Son.

NEWSPAPERS, MAGAZINE ARTICLES AND WEBSITES

AFP, 'UNESCO to display ancient artifacts recovered from thieves', 19.06.2012. http://www.rawstory.com/2012/06/unesco-to-display-ancient-artifacts-recovered-from-thieves/

Birand, M. A. 'The shame of Sept. 6–7 is always with us', *Hurriyet: Turkish Daily News* 09.07.2015.

Bolton, M. 'Tales of Sarajevo', *Lonely Planet* June 2010.

Campbell, M. 'What Now for the Young Turks?', *Sunday Times* 09.06.2013.

Campbell, M. 'Knights of the Radar Sally Forth in Search of Cervantes's Bones', *Sunday Times* 16.03.2014.

Covington, R. 'Uncovering Yenikapi', *Saudi Aramco World* 60.1 January/February 2009. www.saudiaramcoworld.com/issue/200901/uncovering.yenikapi.htm [accessed 20.06.2013].

Curry, A. 'The First Vikings', *Archaeology* 10.06.2013. http://www.archaeology.org/issues/95-1307/features/941-vikings-saaremaa-estonia-salme-vendel-oseberg [accessed 29.01.2014].

Dalrymple, W. 'England's Mustaphas', *Guardian* 20.03.1999.

Dalrymple, W. 'Art Treasures of the Mughal Empire', *Guardian* 30.11.2012.

Darwent, C. 'Swept Away by an Old Greek Perspective', *Independent on Sunday* 13.05.2012.

de Bellaigue, C. 'Turkey's Hidden Past', *New York Review* 08.03.2001.

de Bellaigue, C. 'Turkish Epitaph', *Saturday Guardian* 26.10.2013.

de Lange, N., Panayotov, A. and Rees, G. (2013) 'Mapping the Jewish Communities of the Byzantine Empire'. www.byzantinejewry.net [accessed 18.01.2016].

'Democrat or Sultan?', *Economist* 08.06.2013.

Emin, E. 'Someone to Watch Over Me', *Guardian* 08.11.2013 (photographer).

Furtado, P. 'York's Roman Emperor', *History Today* 56.3, March 2006.

Gamm, N. 'Women in Ottoman Society', *Hurriyet Daily News* 10.03.2012. http://www.hurriyetdailynews.com/women-in-ottoman-society-.aspx?pageID=238&nID=15651&NewsCatID=438 [accessed 19.01.2016].

Gordon, R. 'Battle of Chalons: Attila the Hun Versus Flavius Aetius', *Military History* December 2013.

Holland, C. 'Jihad by Sea' 10.08.2010. http://www.historynet.com/jihad-by-sea.htm [accessed 07.10.2014].

Irwin, R. 'Muslim Responses to the Crusades', *History Today* 47.4, April 1997.

Jégo, M. 'Sainte-Sophie menacée', *Le Monde* 22.08.2015.

Judah, T. Numerous reports for *The Times* 1992–3.

Kelly, C. 'Barbarians at the gate', *Omnibus* 63: 30–2. http://www.theclassicslibrary.com/JACT/O63%20Kelly.pdf

Kelly, C. 'Constantine: Britain's Roman Emperor', *History Today* 56.7, July 2006.

Kennedy, F. 'Dig uncovers Vandal fleet', *Independent* 11.02.2001. http://www.independent.co.uk/news/world/europe/dig-uncovers-vandal-fleet-5365629.html.

Last Statues of Antiquity Database, LSA-27 (2012) University of Oxford. http://laststatues.classics.ox.ac.uk/database/discussion.php?id=399

McCall, C. 'The Great Palace of Constantinople: Discovering the Mosaic Magic of Early Byzantine Rulers', *Current World Archaeology* 67, October 2014.

Pascal, J. 'A People Killed Twice', *Guardian* 27.01.2001.

Rule, V. 'Arabian Nights', *Guardian* 09.12.2000.

Sayfa, A. 'The shame of Sept. 6–7 is always with us', *Hurriyet Daily News* 13.06.2013.

Shafak, E. 'Someone to Watch Over Me', *Guardian* 08.11.2013.

Stone, N. 'The Last Crusades: The Hundred Year Battle for the Centre of the World', *Guardian* 22.08.2009.

Stone, N. 'What's eating Turkey', *Spectator* 08.06.2013.

Stone, N. 'Dancing to a New Dawn in Turkey's Velvet Revolution', *Daily Telegraph* 08.06.2013.

Stone, N. 'Erdogan's dreams of empire are perilous for his country', *Guardian* 07.12.2015.

Turgut, P. 'Constantinople's Gypsies Not Welcome in Istanbul', *Time* 09.06.2008. http://content.time.com/time/world/article/0,8599,1812905,00.html.

'Turkey Debates Making Museum into a Mosque', *The Times* 18.11.2013.

UNESCO World Heritage (2005) *Diocletian's Palace and the Historical Nucleus of Split*. http://whc.unesco.org/en/list/97

UNESCO World Heritage *Ancient City of Damascus*. http://whc.unesco.org/en/list/20

Whitehouse, D. 'Space impact "saved Christianity"', *BBC News Online* 23.06.2003. http://news.bbc.co.uk/1/hi/sci/tech/3013146.stm [accessed 21.06.2013].

INDEX

✤

Aachen, Germany, 634

Abadan, Iran, 563

Abbasid Caliphate, 288, 290, 310, 322, 636

Abbott, Bartholomew Edward, 427

Abd al-Malik, Umayyad Caliph, 287

Abd-ar-Rahman III, Umayyad Caliph, 319

Abdülaziz I, Ottoman Sultan, 547, 632

Abdülhamid I, Ottoman Sultan, 496, 534–5, 631

Abdülhamid II, Ottoman Sultan, 487, 550–51, 553, 555–7, 632

Abdülmecid I, Ottoman Sultan, 471, 487, 531, 601–2, 632

Abdülmecid II, Ottoman Caliph, 587–90, 633

Abraham (biblical figure), 166

Abu Ayyub al-Ansari, 407

Abu Bakr (companion of Muhammad), 281

Abu Bakr al-Baghdadi (jihadist), 575

Abu Sufyan ibn Harb, 442

Achaemenid Empire, 30, 31–6, 40, 42–3, 57

Achilles (mythological figure), 27

Ad Quintum, 64, 423

Adam (biblical figure), 353, 655n4

'Adi b. Zayd (Bedouin poet), 279–80

Adrianople, 101–2, 381; *see also* Edirne

Adrianople, Battle of (378), 144–5, 147

Adrianople, Battle of (1205), 624

Aeetes, King (mythological figure), 53

Aegeae, 121

Aegospotami, Battle of (405 BC), 45, 645n10

Aeneas (mythological figure), 104, 112, 697n3

Aeschylus, 187, 528

Afghanistan, 56, 285

Afqa, Lebanon, 121

Afrosiyab, 266; *see also* Samarkand

Afyonkarahisar, 378

Aga Khan III, 587

Agamemnon (mythological figure), 27, 103

Agamemnon, HMS, 570, 572

Agathias Scholasticus, 237–8, 255

Agincourt, HMS, 561

Agnes of France, Byzantine Empress, 355, 356

Agra, 456, 457

Ahmed I, Ottoman Sultan, 229, 629

Ahmed II, Ottoman Sultan, 630

Ahmed III, Ottoman Sultan, 476, 499–500, 502, 503–4, 506, 630, 695n15

Ahmediye Mosque, 470

Ahmet Ali Effendi, 514

Aigistos (mythological figure), 103

Ajax (mythological figure), 104, 652*n*14

Ajmer, 455

Akathistos (prayer), 274

Akbar the Great, Mughal Emperor, 455–7

Alaric, King of the Visigoths, 178–81, 665*n*6

Albania, 57, 60, 61, 64, 78, 436, 560; Christianity in, 116–17

Albano, 121

Alberti, Leon Battista, 692*n*17

Alcibiades, 41–6, 244

alcohol consumption, 49–50, 556, 629

Aleppo, 168, 560

Alexander the Great, 55–7, 60, 104, 158, 205, 417, 607, 660*n*9

Alexander, Byzantine Emperor, 620

Alexander, King of Greece, 578

Alexander, Patriarch of Alexandria, 118

Alexander Romance, 417, 646*n*15

Alexandria: foundation and classical era, 56, 57, 66, 157–9; Christianity in, 117–18, 159–61; Arab conquest, xxii, xxiii, 284, 285; 19th century, 550

Alexandria (buildings and landmarks): Caesareum, 160; Komm El Dikka, 159; Library, 56, 158, 160, 186; Temple of Serapis, 151, 159

Alexandropoulis, 55

Alexei, Russian Tsar, 537

Alexios I Komnenos, Byzantine Emperor, 325, 326, 339–42, 345, 352, 354–5, 623; and First Crusade, 346–8

Alexios II, Byzantine Emperor, 355, 356, 623

Alexios III Angelos, Byzantine Emperor, 359, 362, 624

Alexios IV, Byzantine Emperor, 337, 350, 624

Alexios V Doukas Mourtzouphlos, Byzantine Emperor, 362–3, 624

Ali Pasha, Benderlı, 516

Ali Pasha, Kara, 521

Ali Pasha, Kılıç, 466

Ali Pasha, Müezzinzade, 445–6

Ali Pasha, Muhammad, 506

'Ali Sher Nava'i, 456

Ali Ufki, 458

Allan, Sir William, *The Slave Market*, 485

Allectus (Roman usurper), 81

Allenby, Edmund, 1st Viscount, 570

Alopen (missionary), 271

alphabet, Turkish, 641*n*1

Altai Mountains, 346, 378

Amantios (eunuch), 156, 173

Amazons (mythological figures), 22, 245, *289*, 652*n*8

Ambrose, Bishop of Milan, 82, 126, 152, 657*n*12

Amcazade Pavilion, 480

Ammianus Marcellinus, 69, 135, 140

Ammonios (pagan), 157

Anadolu Hisarı (fortress/prison), 384, 386, 404

Anaplous (Arnavutköy), 169

Anastasios I, Byzantine Emperor, 203, 206, 219, 248, 294, 613, 673*n*6

Anastasios II, Byzantine Emperor, 617

Andalus, al- (Muslim Iberia), 143, 290, 308, 319, 357, 392, 403, 425–6

Andrew I, King of Hungary, 622

Andrew, Prince of Greece and Denmark, 579

Andrew, St, 72, 119, 125

Andronikos I Komnenos, Byzantine Emperor, 355–6, 623–4

Andronikos II Palaiologos, Byzantine Emperor, 428, 626
Andronikos III, Byzantine Emperor, 626
Andronikos IV, Byzantine Emperor, 627
Andros, 435, 595
Anemas, Prison of, 345
Angelico, Fra, 693*n*17
Anglo-Persian Oil Company, 563
Anglo-Saxons, 294–7
Anglo-Turkish Society, 566
animal shows, 66, 230; *see also* zoos and animal collections
Ankara, 577, 586, 593; Battle of (1402), 384, 456
Anna of France, Byzantine Empress, 355, 356
Anna Komnena, 350, 686*n*2; *Alexiad*, 339, 342, 347, 350, 685*n*9
Anna Porphyrogenita, Grand Princess of Kiev, 312
Antalya, 433
Anthemios, Western Roman Emperor, 612
Anthemios of Tralles, 222–3
Anthony the Great, St, 137
Antigonos Monophthalmos, 607
Antioch, 69, 99, 240, 252, 285, 349, 670*n*3; Golden Octagon church, 121
Antiochos (eunuch), 77
Antonina (wife of Belisarios), 249, 250
Antonine Wall, 83
Anzac Corps (First World War), 564, 565–6, 568
Apamea, Syria, 121
Aphrodisias, 230
Aphrodite (goddess), 51, 102, 114, 121, 163, 304, 493, 506
Apocalypse of Pseudo-Daniel, 57
Apocrypha (religious texts), 225

Apollo (god), 27, 36, 51, 77, 82, 97, 109, 114
Apollonius Rhodius, *Argonautica*, 15
Appia, Via, 61
Aqua Viva, Pannonia, 85
aqueducts, 64, 139–40
Arab Revolt (1916), 570
Arap Mosque, 426
Ararat, Mount, 50, 108, 342, 489
Arasta Bazaar, 229
Archaeology Museum, Istanbul, 103, 549–50
Archimedes, 685*n*11
Ardashir I, King of Persia, 648*n*8
Ardashir II, King of Persia, *138*
Areni Cave, Armenia, 50
Ares (god), 77
Aretino, Pietro, 417
Argent (pseud.), 'Anzac', 559
Argonauts (mythological figures), 15, 21–2, 68, 483
Arianism, 118, 127, 129, 144, 152, 182
Aristarchos of Samos, 158
Aristophanes, 42
Aristotle, 51, 120, 246, 635, 685*n*11; *Natural History*, 266; *Politics*, 602
Arius, 117–18, 127; death, 129–30
Arkadios, Byzantine Emperor, 153, 154–5, 165, 177–8, 611
Arles, 85
Armenia: pre-history, 22, 50, 103; Christianity in, 108; Persian invasions, 251; Arab rule, 284, 322; Romani population, 428; independence, 555, 569
Armenian massacres: (1896), 555; (1915), 569
Armenians in Constantinople, 24, 322, 399, 427, 428, 429, 430, 529, 555, 569
Armitage, Horace, 551
Arnavutköy, 169

Arras medallion, *82*
Arsenal, Imperial, 433, 446, 560
Arslan, Alp, 343
Artabasdos, Byzantine Emperor, 617
Artemis (goddess), 51, 102, 103, 163,
    209
Artemisia I, Queen of Halicarnassus,
    34, 463
Artemisia II, Queen of Caria, 463
Artemisium, Battle of (480 BC), 33–4
Arthur, King (legendary figure), 291,
    292
asceticism, 129, 137, 167–71, 198, 214
Asclepius (god), 662*n*12
Asoka, Indian Emperor, 56, 107
Aspar, Cistern of, 402
Asquith, Violet, Baroness Asquith of
    Yarnbury, 557
Asterios of Amaseia, 76
astrology, 56, 165–6, 685*n*9–11
astronomy, 117, 158, 165–6, 337
Astyanax (mythological figure), 245
Atatürk, Mustafa Kemal, 21, 566,
    573–4, *573*, 576–8, 585–6, 589,
    593–4, 633
Atatürk Airport, 3, 499
Athanasios of Alexandria, 129
Athanatoi (Immortals; military unit),
    323
Athena (goddess), 51, 68, 112, 163, 184
Athenagoras, 'A Plea for Christians',
    73
Athens: Persian Wars, 36; Golden
    Age, 38–40; Peloponnesian War,
    40, 42–6; under Macedon, 55;
    sacked by Visigoths, 178; closing of
    Platonic Academy, 243–4, 245
Athens (buildings and landmarks):
    Acropolis, 34, 200; Agora, 45,
    50, 52, 315–16; Areopagus, 244;
    Byzantine Museum, 154; city
    walls, 36; Epigraphical Museum,

39; Painted Stoa, 315; Parthenon,
    39, 45, 200; Plaka, 686*n*11; Pnyx,
    45; Temple of Ilissos, 154, 660*n*2
Athos, Mount, 173, 594
Athyra, 185; *see also* Büyükçekmece
Atik Valide Mosque, 420, 463
Atmeydanı *see* hippodrome,
    Ottoman
Attaleiates, Michael, 337; poorhouse,
    318
Attikos, Patriarch of Constantinople,
    23
Attila the Hun, 183–5, 220
Attis (mythological figure), 173
Augusteion, 115, 226
Augustine of Canterbury, St, 296–7
Augustine of Hippo, St, 152, 183, 202,
    483; *City of God*, 665*n*6
Augustus (Octavian), Roman
    Emperor, 54, 62, 63, 113, 114, 120,
    160, 599
Aulus Plautius, 658*n*8
Aurangzeb, Mughal Emperor, 480
Aurelian, Roman Emperor, 69, 81
Aurispa, Giovanni, 385
'Auspicious Incident' (1826), 525, 527
Austen, Jane, 496, *497*
Australia, Anzac Corps, 564, 565–6,
    568
Austria, 480, 557; Austro-Ottoman
    War (1683–97), 473, 475–80, 502,
    630; *see also* Vienna
Autun, France, 85
Avars, 142, 251, 272–3, 276, 280
Axum, Kingdom of, 251
Ayasofya *see* Haghia Sophia
Aynalıkavak Palace, 503–4
Ayşe, Ottoman Princess, 487
Azov, 533
Azov, Sea of, 325

Baalbek (Heliopolis), xxii, 121

Babylon, 31, 32, 56, 203, 235, 642*n*5
Bacchos, St, 213
Badr, Battle of (624), 281
Baedeker (guide-book), 467
Baffo, Violante, 462
Baghdad, 290, 317, 319, 322, 378, 457, 471, 570, 685*n*5
Bahira (monk), 279
Balaclava, 541, 542, 707*n*2
Balat, 426
Baldwin I, Latin Emperor, 362, 624
Baldwin II, Latin Emperor, 625
Balearic Islands, 324
Balkan League (military alliance), 559
Balkan Wars (1912–13), 559–61, 577
Banu Hashim (clan), 280
Barbarossa Hayreddin Pasha, 435–7, 462
Barbary pirates, 466
Bardas (Byzantine noble), 619, 636
Bari, 340, 686*n*14
Barker, Henry Aston, panorama of Constantinople, 513
Barnum, Phineas T., 491
Baronius, Caesar, 207
Barry, Sir Charles, 539
Barry, Madame du, 505
Barsanuphios (hermit), 233
Barton, Sir Edward, 460, 481
Başıbozuk (Ottoman army irregulars), 523
Basil I the Macedonian, Byzantine Emperor, 174, 619, 620
Basil II the Bulgar-Slayer, Byzantine Emperor, 312, 323, 620, 636
Basil, St, 166
Basil Lekapenos (eunuch), 318
Basil the Physician, 344–5
Basilica Cistern (reservoir), 211
Basiliskos, Byzantine Emperor, 189, 248, 612
Basra, Iraq, 563, 685*n*11

Batavians, 658*n*8
bathhouses, 64, 212, 227, 424, 463; *see also* hammams
Bathildis, St, Frankish Queen, 296
Baths of Zeuxippos, 65, 109, 139, 165, 225, 647*n*12
Battersea Shield, 142
Batumi, Georgia, 22, 251, 483
Bayeux Tapestry, 337
Bayezid I, Ottoman Sultan, 384, 456, 627
Bayezid II, Ottoman Sultan, 408, 416, 426, 432–3, 628
Bayraktar Mustafa Pasha, 631
bazaars, 111, 229, 412–13, 484
Beaton, Sir Cecil, *590*
Beauvais, France, 85
Bedesten (Old Bazaar), 412–13, 484
Bedouins, 279–80
Beethoven, Ludwig van, 472
Beirut, 188, 534
Bektashism, 382–3, 442, 472, 524, 525, 526, 553
Belgrade, 479
Belgrade Forest, 64, 139
Belisarios (Byzantine general), 206, 217, 218, 220, 249–50, 293
Bell, Gertrude, 582, 584
Bellini, Gentile, *Sultan Mehmed II*, 389, 400
Bellona (goddess), 135
Bendis (goddess), 52
Benedict Biscop, 296
Benedict of Peterborough, 697*n*3
Benjamin of Tudela, 268
Bennu (deity), 147
Berlin, Congress of (1878), 549
Bertrandon de la Broquière, 381–2
Beşik Bay, 105, 541, 652*n*14
Beşiktaş, 420, 436
Bethlehem, 121, 124; Church of the Nativity, 538

Beyoğlu *see* Pera
Bible, translations of, 144, 158, 240
Bismarck, Otto von, 557
Bitola, Macedonia, 576
Blachernae: shrine to Virgin Mary, 199–200, 274, 390; St Mary's Church, 640*n*14
Blachernae Palace, 225, 345, 352, 359, 390, 635
Black Death (1347–48), 380, 482
Black Fatima (Kurdish military leader), 540
Blue Mosque (Sultan Ahmed Mosque), 36, 227, 229, 409, 525, 629
Blumenbach, Johann Friedrich, 488–90, 491–2, 534
boats *see* sea-faring
Boccaccio, Giovanni, 386
Bodrum, 34, 366, 436
Boethius, 245–6
Boğazkesen Castle *see* Rumeli Hisarı
Boğdan Sarayı (St Nicholas' Church), 321–2
Bogomilism, 344–5
Bohemond I, Prince of Antioch, 341, 349
Bolli Bollason, 314
Bolsheviks, 563, 574–5, 580, 591
Bolverk Arnorsson, 323
Bon, Ottaviano, *The Sultan's Seraglio*, 465–6
Boncuklu (neolithic site), 642*n*5
Boril, Tsar of Bulgaria, 624
Bosnia, 384, 469
Bosphorus: formation (c.5500 BC), 17–18; name, xxx, 19–20; flow and currents, 31; bridging of, 3, 601–2, 605, 638*n*2
Bosporia (festival), 53
Bosra, Syria, 279
Bostancı (Ottoman imperial guard), 434, 486

Boudicca, 117
Boulogne, 84
Brindisi, 60, 61
Britain: Roman province, 70, 80–81, 83–4, 108, 142, 177, 180, 658*n*8; Byzantine trading, 291–6, 297–8, 326; Anglo-Saxons, 294–7; Christianity in, 296–7; Viking incursions, 308, 309, 324; Norman conquest, 322, 324; medieval, 325–6, 384; Crusades, 328; 16th–18th centuries, 246, 437, 443–4, 446–7, 502, 505; 19th century, 527–9, 539, 546–8; Crimean War, 539–44; Treaty of London (1913), 559–60, 561; First World War, 557–8, 561–74, 576; partitioning of Ottoman Empire, 574–5, 579, 580–81; *see also* London
British Empire, 447, 480, 528, 579
Bronze Age, 20–24, 103, 199, 266, 458
Brooke, Rupert, 557–8
Brusa *see* Bursa
Brown, Demetra Vaka, *Haremlik*, 493
Brussels, Royal Museum of Art and History, 597–8
Brussels Conference Act (1890), 708*n*9
Brutus, 54, 63, 72
Bryas Palace, 319
Brytae (festival), massacre (c.500), 232, 670*n*4, 673*n*6
Bucoleon Palace, 214, 219, 227–9, 363, 671*n*8
Buda, Siege of (1541), 440
Budapest, 142, 476, 477, 637
Buddhism, 28, 56, 107, 202, 266, 304, 310, 685*n*11
Bukhara, Uzbekistan, 685*n*11
Bulgaria, 143, 312, 357, 548, 549, 559, 560, 624, 635–6

Bulgars, xxiv, 617, 618, 619, 620

bullfighting, 230

Burnaby, Frederick Gustavus, 554

Bursa (Prousa, Brusa), 212, 254, 378–9, 380, 383, 386, 427, 579, 697*n*10

Burton, Richard, 435

Busbecq, Ogier Ghiselin de, 411

Butrint, 436, 697*n*3–4

Butrint, Bay of, naval battle (1084), 341

Büyükçekmece, 185; Caravanserai, 423–4

Byron, George, 6th Baron, 493, 513, 514–16, 517, 525, 529, 697*n*3

Byzantine Empire: Constantine selects Byzantium as site of capital, 104–5, 653*n*4; under Constantine, 106–132; spread of Christianity, 108–9, 119–22, 137–8; under Constantinian dynasty after Constantine, 133–9, 173; attempted de-Christianisation of Julian the Apostate, 136–9; Christianity reinstated by Jovian, 139; under Valentinian dynasty, 139–45; Gothic War (376–82), 140, 141–5; under Theodosios I, 145, 146–53, 239; under Arkadios and Theodosios II, 154–5, 177–8, 183–6, 188–9; threatened by Goths and Vandals, 177–86, 189; under Justinian I and Theodora, 205–255, 267, 272, 293; Nika riots (532), 216–21, 232, 233, 248; Justinian's military campaigns, 217, 248–51; plague (541–42), 253–4, 613; under Justin II and Maurice, 272–3, 275, 614; usurpation of Phokas, 275, 614; under Heraclian dynasty, 275–88, 614; threatened by Slavs and Avars, 251, 272–3, 274–6,

280; defeat of Sassanid Persia, 272, 275–7, 278, 280; defeated by Muslim forces at Yarmuk (636), xxii, 274, 282–3; territorial losses to Muslim Arabs, 284–8; dispute over iconoclasm, 299–305, 319; besieged by Rus (860), 290, 307–8, 323, 536; establishment of Varangian Guard, 323–6; Great Schism (1054), 335–7; under Komnenos dynasty, 339–56; attacked by Normans and Turks, 339–47; defeated at Battle of Manzikert (1071), 343–4; besieged by Pecheneg Turks (1090), 346–7; 12th-century Crusades, 347–51; attacked by Normans of Sicily, 353–6, 356; threat from Venetians, 354–5, 358–9; Fourth Crusade and siege of 1204, 290, 324, 358, 358–62, 365; disintegration and reconquest, 362–7, 626–7; wars with Ottomans, 379–82, 383–5; fall of (1453), 387–92, 393–5

Byzas (mythological figure), 20, 68, 595, 605

Cadiz, Battle of (1596), 444

Caesarea, 275, 284

Cairo, 241, 408, 409, 413, 481

Çalapkulu, Fuat Özgür, 712*n*4

calendars: Greek, 29, 53; Islamic, 281; Roman, 297

calligraphy, 501

Callinicus, *Life of St Hypatius*, 185

Cambon, Paul, 574

camel skeleton, excavation of, 474–5

Camondo family, 592–3

Çanakkale, 565, 569

Candavia Road, 60

Candia (Heraklion), Crete, 555

Canning, Stratford, 1st Viscount Stratford de Redcliffe, 529, 539

cannons, 386, 388, *389*, 419, 436
Cape Bon, Battle of (468), 189
Capitolum, 110, 113
Capua, 121
Caracalla, Roman Emperor, 65–6, 68, 109, 120, 608–9
Carausius (Roman military commander), 80–81
caravanserais (roadside inns), 279, 413, 423–4
Caria, 41, 53
Carnarvon, George Herbert, 5th Earl of, 566
Carneia (religious festival), 29, 52
carpets and textiles, Ottoman, 446, 500–501
Carthage, 183, 249, 276
cartography, 126, 434
Cassius, 54, 63, 72
Cassius Dio, *Roman History*, 64, 65, 117
Castor and Pollux (mythological figures), 182, 652*n5*
castration, 134, 172–3, 174, 309; *see also* eunuchs
Çatalca Lines (Ottoman fortifications), 560
Çatalca railway station, 588
Çatalhöyük, 15, 52
Catherine II the Great, Russian Empress, 491–2, 518–19, 532–4, *534*
Cavafy, C.P., 550, 697*n3*; 'In Church', 205
Caxton, William, 246
Cedrenus, 662*n6*
Celts, 309
Cemal Pasha, 560–61, 591
Cervantes, Miguel de, 445
Çeşme, Battle of (1770), 518–19, 533, 539
Ceylon, 540
Chaeronea, Battle of (338), 607

Chagos archipelago, 552
Chalcedon: Greek settlement, 19, 23–5, 33, 43–4, 47; Roman era, 62, 76, 77, 117, 137, 139; medieval, xxiii, 276, 359; present day Kadıköy, 24
Chalcedon, Council of (451), 77, 198, 209, 212–13, 270
Chaldiran, Battle of (1514), 408
Chalke Gate, 228, 300
Chalki, 366, 528–9, 560
Chalkoprateia, 239
Châlons, France, 85
Chamberlain, Sir Austen, 567
chamberlains (Byzantine), 173
Chardin, Sir John, 488, 489
chariot-racing, 66, 151–2, 184, 208, 217–18
Charisios Gate (Edirnekapı), 136, 321, 391, 420
charity and philanthropy, 419–20
Charlemagne, Holy Roman Emperor, 305, 319, 322, 618, 634–5, 697*n9*
Charles II, King of England, 466
Charles V, Holy Roman Emperor, 435
Charles Martel, 289
Chaucer, Geoffrey, 246
Chelles Abbey, France, 296
Chermside, Sir Herbert, 555
Chersonesus, 184
Chesterton, G.K., *Lepanto*, 443
Chi Rho (Christian symbol), 96, 97, 131, 296
childlessness, legislation on, 120
China, 47–8, 141, 253, 277, 285, 480, 597; silk trade, 266; relations with Byzantine Constantinople, 265, 268–9; Christianity in, 270–72
Chios, 32, 50, 55, 60, 164, 200, 390, 433, 518–20; Nea Moni Monastery, 519, 521, 523; massacre (1822), 518, 520–22, 547–8

cholera, 487, 498
Chora Monastery, 322, 364, 365, 391,
    691*n*8
Chortokopi, 582
Chrétien de Troyes, 291
Christianity: arrival in Byzantium,
    70, 71–3; Great Persecution, 74–5,
    76–9, 100, 123, 155; Constantine
    as follower, 96–7, 100, 105, 107–9,
    116–17, 123–4; Edicts of Toleration
    (311, 313), 99, 100; First Council of
    Nicaea (325), 116, 117–19, 150, 198,
    336; spreads through Constantine's
    empire, 108–9, 119–22; co-
    existence with paganism, 122, 132,
    134–5, 155–67, 244–6; reprisals
    against Christians following
    Constantine's death, 130–31;
    attempted de-Christianisation of
    empire under Julian the Apostate,
    136–9; reinstated as state religion
    by Jovian, 139; First Council
    of Constantinople (381), 146,
    150–51, 198, 611; Theodosian Edicts
    (391–2), 151–3, 155, 164; Councils of
    Ephesus and Chalcedon (431, 449,
    451), 77, 198, 203, 209, 212–13, 270,
    612; Chalcedonian Definition,
    212–13; Henotikon (Decree of
    Unity, 482), 270, 613; Quinisext
    Council (692), 288, 616; Second
    Council of Nicaea (787), 301;
    Great Schism (1054), 335–7; in
    Ottoman Empire, 395–7, 413–15,
    480; *Regnans in Excelsis* papal bull
    (1570), 444; in Republic of Turkey,
    584; *see also* Arianism; asceticism;
    Gnosticism; icons; Marianism;
    missionaries; monasticism;
    Nestorians; relic-collecting
Christodoulos (architect), 395
Chryseis (mythological figure), 103
Chrysopolis, 32, 43, 44, 45, 46, 47, 50,
    62, 103, 117, 379; Battle of (324),
    102–4; *see also* Scutari; Üsküdar
Chrysos (mythological figure), 103
Church of the East *see* Nestorians
Churchill, Sir Winston, 564, 568, 578
Cicero, 59, 685*n*11
Cid, El, 357
Çinili Köşk (pavilion), 400
Circassians, 484, 490–92, *492*, 536,
    544–5, 709*n*9
Circe (mythological figure), 22
circumcision, 407, 410, 417–19, 459
Civitot, 325
Clarke, Edward Daniel, 490–91
Claudius II, Roman Emperor, 68, 85,
    105, 609
Clearchos (Spartan general), 40, 44,
    46, 606
Clement of Alexandria, 661*n*10
Cleopatra, 158, 160
Cleopatra (film), 435–6
Clermont, Council of (1095), 347
Clibinarii *see* Kataphraktoi
clothes and fashions, 296, 318,
    410–411, 429, 446, 485–6, 505, 556
Clovis II, Frankish King, 296
Clytemnestra (mythological figure),
    103
Cnut, Viking King, 310
Cocteau, Jean, 513
Codex Argenteus, 144
Codex Theodsianus, 189
coffee houses, 553
coffin, world's oldest wooden, 15–16,
    17
Colchis, Kingdom of, 22, 237–8, 392,
    652*n*8
Cologne, 85
Columbus, Christopher, 434, 701*n*4
Column of Constantine, 111–12, 226,
    361

Column of the Goths, 68, 609
Column of Justinian, 225–6, *226*
comets, 253, 337–8, *444*
Committee of Union and Progress *see* Young Turks movement
Commodus, Roman Emperor, 64
Comontorius, King of Thrace, 607
Confucius, 28
Constans I, Byzantine Emperor, 133, 609–610
Constans II, Byzantine Emperor, xxi–xxiii, xxv, 265, 285, 615
Constantia (wife of Emperor Licinius), 101
Constantine the Great, Roman Emperor: birth, 82; early life, education and training, 79, 80, 82–4, 123; declared emperor, 84–5; early reign as co-emperor, 85–6, 95–6; divine vision, 86, 95, 96–7; becomes follower of Christianity, 96–7, 100, 105, 107–9, 116–17, 123–4; defeats Maxentius at Milvian Bridge, 95–8; established in Rome, 100–101; issues Edict of Milan, 100; defeats Licinius at Chrysopolis, 101–4; becomes sole emperor, 104, 107; selects Byzantium as site of capital, 104–5, 653n4; execution of wife and son, 106–7; foundation of Constantinople, 107–110; development of the city, 110, 111–15, 119–20, 129, 163, 222; at First Council of Nicaea, 116, 117–19, 336; spread of Christianity through empire, 119–22, 240; later reign, 127, 128–30; death, 119, 130–32, 392; succession, 133–4
Constantine I, King of Greece, 578–9
Constantine II, Byzantine Emperor, 133, 609–610

Constantine III, Byzantine Emperor, 615
Constantine III, Western Roman Emperor, 180
Constantine IV Pogonatos, Byzantine Emperor, 615
Constantine V Kopronymos, Byzantine Emperor, 300, 617
Constantine VI, Byzantine Emperor, 302, 618, 667n8
Constantine VII Porphyrogennetos, 320, 359, 620; *De Ceremoniis*, 320, 671n8
Constantine VIII, Byzantine Emperor, 620–21
Constantine IX Monomachos, Byzantine Emperor, 241–2, 245, 428, 621–2
Constantine X Doukas, Byzantine Emperor, 622
Constantine XI, Byzantine Emperor, 300, 389–90, 391–2, 394, 579, 627
Constantine, Pope, 617
Constantinople, First Council of (381), 146, 150–51, 198, 611
Constantinople, Third Council of (680–81), 615, 616, 617
Constantinople, Treaty of (1832), 526
Constantinus, Flavius (Praetorian prefect), 184
Constantius I, Roman Emperor: as Caesar, 69–70, 81–3, *82*, 101, 123; as Augustus, 82, 83–4, 609; death, 84
Constantius II, Byzantine Emperor, 133–4, 135–6, 139, 163, 609
constitution, Ottoman (1876), 527
consular games, 231, *232*
Contarini, Bartolomeo, 434
Copernicus, 117, 417
copper-working, 199, 239
Corbusier, Le, 404
Córdoba, 317, 319

Corfu, 60, 165, 200, 355, 436; Theotokos Speliotissis Cathedral, 532

Corinth, 172, 178, 516

Corinthians, First Epistle to the, 197

Corippus, *In Laudem Iustini Augusti Minoris*, 174–5, 182

Cornuti (Roman army unit), 96, *97*

Cornwall, 291–3, 681*n*4

Cosmas, St, 407

councils, ecumenical *see* ecumenical councils

Cox, Sir Percy, 563

Cravarites (pirates), 61

Crete, xxi, 241, 266, 284, 364, 483, 555, 559

Crimea, 103, 325, 380, 533–4

Crimea Memorial Church, 542–3

Crimean War (1853–56), 471, 476, 514, 538–44, 548, 557

Crispus (son of Constantine the Great), 102, 233; death, 106–7

Critobulus, Michael, 398

Crusades, 347–51, 357, 366, 384, 385; Fourth Crusade, 117, 163, 326, 350, 351, 359–62, 365

Ctesiphon, 276

Çukurbostan (Sunken Garden), 402

Cumberbatch, Benedict, 555

Cumberbatch, Henry Arnold, 555

Cunaxa, Battle of (401 BC), 645*n*14

Curzon, George, 1st Marquess Curzon of Kedleston, 572

Cuthbert, St, 297–8

Cyprus, xxi, 36, 284, 357, 444, 458, 483, 548; Kolossi castle, 366

Cyril, St, 635–6

Cyril of Alexandria, St, 159–60, 197, 198

Cyrillic script, 537, 619, 635–6

Cyrus the Great, King of Persia, 33

Cyzicus, xxiii, 284, 615, 645*n*6; Battle of (410 BC), 43; Siege of (73 BC), 63

Da Gama, Vasco, 701*n*4

Dagestan, 408

Dagon (god), 155

Dajnan (mountain), 281

Dallam, Robert, 461

Dallam, Thomas, 461–2, 473, 481

Damascus, 268, 275, 317, 570, 680*n*11; Arab conquest, 285, 288

Damian, St, 407

Dandolo, Enrico, Doge of Venice, 361

Danelis (Peloponnesian woman), 174

Daniel the Stylite, St, 169–71, 655*n*5

Danube, River, 142–3, 183, 476–7, 478

Dareios I, King of Persia, 30, 31–3, 53, 98, 323, 601, 605, 638*n*2

Dareios II, King of Persia, 645*n*14

Dareios III, King of Persia, 57, 607

Dascylium, 30

de Busbecq, Ogier Ghiselin, 411

deaconesses, 121

Decius, Roman Emperor, 77, 124

Delacroix, Eugène, *Scenes of the Massacres at Chios*, 518, 522, *522*

Delhi, 456, 457

Delian League, 39, 240, 605–6

Delos, 39, 240

Delphi, 366; oracle, 27, 36, 138–9; Serpent Column, 36, 110, 127, 229, 362, 656*n*6; Temple of Apollo, 127, 151

Demetrios Palaiologos, Despot of Morea, 394

Demetrios of Thessaloniki, St, 100, 354

Demophilos (bishop), 660*n*12

Demosthenes, 635

Dernschwam, Hans, 426

Dickens, Charles, 551

Didascalia (treatise), 158

Didyma, oracle of Apollo, 77
Didymoteichon, 380
Diocletian, Roman Emperor, 69, 83, 105, 173, 216, 609; persecution of Christians, 77–9, 123, 155
Diodoros Siculus, 44
Diogenes the Cynic, 602
Dionysios of Byzantium, 68
Dionysos (god), 50, 51, 53, 73, 245, 288, 605
Disraeli, Benjamin, 1st Earl of Beaconsfield, 496, 548
Divan-ı Hümâyûn (Ottoman Imperial Council), 400, 404
Divanyolu Street, 66, 114, 400
Dmanisi, Georgia, 6
Dolmabahçe Palace, 544, 569, 581, 587
dolphins, 27
Domenico Hierosolimitano, Rabbi, 42
Dominicans, 363, 426
Donation of Constantine (forgery), 336
Donne, John, 'A Valediction of the Book', 177
Dormition, Feast of the, 200
Dostoevsky, Fyodor, 556
Doukas (historian), 380, 387, 559
Doyle, Sir Arthur Conan, 550
dragomans, 458–9, 516–17
Drepanum, 124
dromons (boats), xxii, 666n2
du Buc de Rivéry, Aimée, 496
Dublin, 309
Dumas, Alexandre, 536
Dura Europos, 648n7
Dürer, Albrecht, 417
Durham Cathedral, 297–8
Durrës see Dyrrachium
Dürrüşehvar, Princess of Berar, 588, 590

dye production, 72, 239, 266, 267, 310, 648n6
Dyrrachium (Durrës), 57, 60, 116–17, 253–4, 362; Battle of (1081), 340–41, 342

eagle (symbol), 229, 435, 518–19, 532–3, 580, 594, 595
earthquakes, 252–3, 674n11; (447), 184, 252; (557, 558), 252; (1509), 408; (1766), 413
Easter, date of, 118, 297
Eboracum (York), 80, 83–4, 85
Ebru (marbled paper), 446
ecumenical councils: First (Nicaea, 325), 116, 117–19, 150, 198, 336; Second (Constantinople, 381), 146, 150–51, 611; Third (Ephesus, 431), 198, 203, 209, 612; Fourth (Chalcedon, 451), 77, 198, 209, 212–13, 270; Sixth (Constantinople, 680–81), 615, 616, 617; Seventh (Nicaea, 787), 301
Edessa, 59, 285, 673n6
Edinburgh, Prince Philip, Duke of, 579
Edirne, 144, 381–2, 391, 400, 429, 502, 548–9, 560, 579; Selimiye Mosque, 438; see also Adrianople
Edirne, Treaty of (1829), 535
Edirnekapı (Charisios Gate), 136, 321, 391, 420
Edmund, King of Wessex, 297
education see schooling; universities
Edward VII, King, 546–7, 547
Egnatian Way, 57–8, 58, 59–64, 66, 71–2, 126, 128–9, 340, 353, 383, 583; bathhouses and inns, 64, 423–4
Einstein, Lewis, 569
Eirene, Byzantine Empress, 301, 302, 618, 634, 667n8, 682n9
Elagabalus, Roman Emperor, 123

Eleanor of Aquitaine, 350
Eleusinian Mysteries, 111–12, 135
Elizabeth I, Queen, 246, 444–5, 461, 464–5
Elizabeth II, Queen, 579
Eltham Palace, England, 384
embassies: Ankara, 593; Istanbul, 459, 539, 553, 690n11, 694n7
Eminönü, 427; Gülhane Park, 51, 68, 400; Yeni Mosque, 420, 427
Enderun (Janissary school), 472, 485
Engels, Friedrich, 540
Enver Pasha, 560–61, 562, 591
Ephesus, 209, 223
Ephesus, Councils of (431, 449), 198, 203, 209, 612
Ephrem Syrus, St, 201
Epirus, Depostate of, 625
Equality of Religion, Edict of (362), 137
Eratosthenes, 158
Erdoğan, Recep Tayyip, 3, 219, 599
Erin, HMS, 561
Eris (goddess), 304
Eros (god), 117, 669n27
Ertuğrul (Ottoman frigate), 433
eschatology, xxiv, 252–3, 277, 349, 423, 441–3
Eski Saray (Old Palace), 398, 421
Eskişehir, 378, 563
espionage, 366, 552, 553–5
Euclid, 322, 685n11
Eudaemon (prefect), 218
Eudokia, Byzantine Empress (wife of Herakleios), 677n3
Eudokia Makrembolitissa, Byzantine Empress, 622, 623
Eudoxia, Aelia, Byzantine Empress, 155–6, 156, 157, 173, 177, 179, 239; statue, 155–6, 202, 229, 362
Eugene IV, Pope, 627

Eugénie, Empress of the French, 708n3
eunuchs, 133–4, 137, 172–6, 309, 317–18, 335, 364, 483, 664n5–6; black African, 459–60, 589–90
Euphemia, St, 76–7, 276, 300
Eupolis, 42
Euripides, 45, 223, 644n6, 652n8, 685n11; *Iphigenia in Tauris*, 103; *Medea*, 515
Eusebius (eunuch), 133–4, 137
Eusebius of Caesarea, 36; *Life of Constantine*, 95, 97, 116, 128, 650n7; *On the Martyrs of Palestine*, 76
Eusebius of Nicomedia, 118, 130, 610
Eustathios of Thessalonika, 353–4, 385
Eutropios (eunuch), 177–80
Eutychios, Patriarch of Constantinople, 682n9
Eve (biblical figure), 126, 201, 202, 206, 655n4, 667n9
Evergetis Monastery, 318
Evliya Çelebi, 432, 479–80, 524, 529
Evrenos, Gazi (Ottoman military commander), 383, 583
executions, public, 66, 230–31, 232, 473
Eyüp, 514; Eyüp Sultan Mosque, 407
Ezidis (religious group), 138

Fabia Eudokia, Byzantine Empress, 677n3
'False Mustafa' (Ottoman pretender), 385, 393
Famagusta, Siege of (1571), 444
famines and food shortages, xxiv, 141, 253, 531, 563, 565, 578, 580
Fatih, 540; Mosque 396, 413
Fatih Sultan Mehmed Bridge, 3, 605
Fausta, Roman Empress, 95, 125; death, 106–7
Fayum portraits, 520

Felicitas, St, 157

Fener, 387, 584; St George's Church, 77, 125, 396

Fenerbahçe Yacht Harbour, archaeological explorations, 20, 21

Ferdinand II, Holy Roman Emperor, 477

Ferdinand II, King of Spain, expulsion of Muslims and Jews, 426, 435

Ferrara, Council of (1438), 693n18

fertility symbols, 52, 155, 168, 298, 418

festivals, 29, 52, 53, 231, 387–8, 413, 418–19, 430, 500, 501

Fethiye Carnii (mosque), 364–5, 395

fez (hat), 505, 556; outlawed, 711n4

Fikirtepe, 24

Fikret, Tevfik, 551

Filarete (Renaissance artist), 417

Filizten (concubine), 712n7

fires, 470, 502–3, 529–30, 596; (475), 164, 169–70, 189; (532), 216, 218, 219, 221; (1204), 363, 365; (1660), 404, 427; (1740), 427; (1808), 514; (1870), 322

fireworks, 418, 475

First World War, 557–8, 561–74; Gallipoli Campaign, 22, 45, 380–81, 541, 564–8, 567, 577

Fisher, Andrew, 565–6

fishing, 27–8, 39

flag, Turkish, 54

Flaminia, Via, 85, 96, 98

Flecknoe, Richard, 502

Florence, 386, 394, 692n17–18

Florence, Council of (1439), 627

food and drink, 49–50, 316, 379, 399, 424, 471–2, 543, 556; see also grain supplies

football, 200, 551

forks (cutlery), 5, 543

Fortuna (goddess), 113, 114

Forum of Constantine, 110, 111, 113, 129, 163, 226–7

Forum Tauri, 146, 245, 397, 398

Forum of Theodosios, 146, 398

Fossati brothers (architects), 539

Fourth Crusade (1202–4), 117, 163, 326, 350, 351, 359–62, 365

Francis, St, 363

Franks, 289, 296, 326, 352, 360, 385

Franz-Ferdinand, Archduke of Austria, 561, 596

fratricide, 486–7

Frome, Somerset, 81

Fulcher of Chartres, History of the Expedition to Jerusalem, 346

Gaddafi, Muammar, 67–8

Gagik II, King of Armenia, 705n2

Gainas (Gothic leader), 178, 179–80

Galata, 211, 253, 391, 427, 430, 433, 459, 472, 529; Arap Mosque, 426; Camondo steps, 592–3; Galata Tower, 379–80, 543; Megalos Pyrgos, 290, 361

Galata Bridge, 528, 557; 16th-century proposed structure, 416–17, 418

Galatians, 607

Galen of Pergamon, 158

Galerius, Roman Emperor, 69–70, 83, 84, 173, 609, 649n6; persecution of Christians, 77, 99, 100; death, 85, 99, 101

Gallipoli, 380, 433, 540, 557, 559

Gallipoli Campaign (1915–16), 22, 45, 380–81, 541, 564–8, 567, 577

Gallus, Constantius, 137

gardens, Ottoman, 402–5, 417, 423, 434, 499–500, 502

Garga Samhita (astrological treatise), 56

Gaul (Roman province), 70, 81, 84, 85, 135

Gauls, 57, 607
Gaza, 283; Christianisation, 155–7
Gelimer, King of the Vandals, 250
Genevan Psalter, 458
Genghis Khan, 366, 691n10
Gennadios II, Patriarch of
    Constantinople, 395, *396*, 413–14
Genoa and Genoese, 355, 366,
    379–80, 385, 390, 462, 482, 519,
    690n11
George I, King of England, 478
George, St, 383, 564, 648n10
George of Trebizond, 395
Georgievitz, Bartholomaeus, 442
Gepids, 251
Gerlach, Stephen, 417
Germany: unification, 557; First
    World War, 561–3, 565; Second
    World War, 590
Gesta Francorum (chronicle), 393
Gezi Park, riots (2013), 6, 131, 216, 219,
    527, 599, 670n4, 696n3
Ghassanids, 213, 283–4, 678n2
Ghaznavids, 343, 428
Ghiberti, Lorenzo, 417
ghosti (Proto-Indo-European
    concept), 4, 602
Giannitsa (Yiannitsa), 383, 583
Gibbon, Edward, *Decline and Fall of
    the Roman Empire*, 335, 515, 634,
    653n4, 666n6, 693n2
Gibraltar, xxiii
Gilles, Pierre, 1, 413, 423, 438–9
Gladiator (film), 73
gladiator shows, 74, 107
Gladstone, William Ewart, 548
Glagolitic script, 635–6
Glover, Anne, Lady, 497–8
Glover, Sir Thomas, 497
Gnosticism *see* Bogomilism;
    Manichaeism; Paulicianism
Goebbels, Joseph, 711n2

Goffe, Thomas, *The Raging*, 465
Golan Heights, 283
Golden Gate, 147, 206, 391, 392, 439
Golden Horn: formation (c.5500 BC),
    17–18; name, 20, 27
Golden Horn chain (defences), 290,
    324, 361, 388
Gonio fortress, Georgia, 251
Goths, 57, 68, 113, 151–2, 177–81,
    214, 293; Gothic War (376–82),
    140, 141–5; sack of Rome (410),
    177, 180–81, 665n6; Gothic War
    (535–554), 250; *see also* Herulians;
    Ostrogoths; Visigoths
Goths, Column of the, 68, 609
Göttingen University, 488, 489
Gozo, 436
'Grado' chair (ivory), 288
grain supplies, 43, 55, 158, 179, 211,
    285, 289, 293, 690n10
Granada, 403, 426, 588
Grand Bazaar, 111, 239, 484
Gratian, Western Roman Emperor,
    145, 610
Great Exhibition (London, 1851),
    539
Great Palace, Imperial, 131, 139, 140,
    164, 189, 220, 225, 227–9, 250
Great Schism (1054), 335–7
Great Turkish War (1683–99), 314
Greco, El, 364
Greece (modern): War of
    Independence (1821–32), 516–17,
    526, 535; Chios massacre, 518–23;
    Treaty of Constantinople (1832),
    526; Balkan Wars (1912–13),
    559–60, 576–7; restoration of
    King Constantine, 578–9; Greco-
    Turkish War (1920–22), 577,
    579–80, 584; population exchange
    with Turkey (1923), 154–5, 582–4;
    Colonels' Junta (1967–74), 26, 200

Greek Fire (weapon), xxiii, 284, 311, 385, 679*n*13

Gregoras, Nikephoros, 68

Gregory I the Great, Pope, 296–7

Gregory III, Pope, 300

Gregory the Illuminator, St, 108, 117

Gregory of Nazianus, St, 201

Greville, Fulke, 1st Baron Brooke, *The Tragedy of Mustapha*, 465

Grey, Edward, 1st Viscount Grey of Fallodon, 574

Gripsholm runestone, Sweden, 304

Guiscard, Robert, 339–42, 349

Gül Mosque, 300

Gülhane Park, 51, 68, 400

gunpowder, 385, 418

gypsies *see* Romani

Gytheion, 47

Hadrian, Roman Emperor, 64, 121, 155, 647*n*13, 648*n*6

Hadrian's Wall, 83, 142

Haemos, 223

Hafez Shirazi (poet), 456

Haghia Eirene (Church of Peace), 114, 119, 131, 150, 198, 300; use by Janissaries, 413, 470, 525, 695*n*15

Haghia Sophia (Ayasofya): first structures, 121, 202, 218, 222; Justinian's reconstruction, 222–5, *224*; dome, 222, 287, 379; altar cloths, 267; lamps, 276; mosaic of the Virgin, 303, 307–8; Viking graffiti, 306–7, 314; burial of Dandolo, Doge of Venice, 361; as Ottoman mosque, 406, 412, 415, 572; 19th-century repairs, 539; conversion to museum, 711*n*2

Hajj (pilgrimage), 409, 570

Halicarnassus, 34, 366, 436

Halil, Patrona, 630

Hall, Sir John, 542

Halley's comet, 337–8

Hamdi Bey, 550

Hamitsri, Solomon, 268

hammams, 212, 493, 494–5; sea hammams, 527

Hankey, Maurice, 1st Baron, 564

Harald Hardrada, King of Norway, 323–4

Harawi, Hasan Ali al-, 315, 406

harbours, Theodosian, 148–50, *149*, 252, 426

harems, 420–21, 434, 460, 462–5, 467, 485–7, 494–6, 550; Western accounts of, 488, 490–91, 493

Harington, Sir Charles, 581

Harold Godwinson, King of England, 324, 684*n*20

Harrogate, Yorkshire, 307

Harun al-Rashid, 319

Harun ibn Yahya, 317

Haryreddin Pasha *see* Barbarossa

Hasköy, 426

Hassan Ağa (eunuch), 466

Hat Law (1925), 711*n*4

Hattusa, 199

Haydarpaşa railway station, 24, 570

Haydn, Joseph, 472

Hebron, 121

Hecate (goddess), 53–4, 55, 73

Hecebolios (Christian teacher), 134

Hejaz, Kingdom of, 632

Helbert, Antoine, *226*

Helen of Troy, 22, 47, 73, 163, 182, 208, 223, 304, 353

Helena (mother of Constantine the Great), 82, 100, 101, 106–7, 114, 123–6, *126*, 134, 587

Helenopolis, 124

Helgö, Sweden, 310

Heliopolis (Baalbek), xxii, 121

Helladios (pagan), 157

Hellenic League, 35–9

Hemingway, Ernest, 580
Henotikon (Decree of Unity, 482), 270, 613
Henry of Flanders, Latin Emperor, 624–5, 691n6
Henry II, King of England, 326
Henry IV, King of England, 384
Henry V, King of England, 351
Henry VIII, King of England, 446, 559
Hephaistion of Thebes, 166
Hera (goddess), 19, 31, 51, 163, 174
Herakleios, Byzantine Emperor, 241, 274–8, 280, 282–4, 614, 677n3
Herakles (mythological figure), 21, 278
Heraklion, Crete, 555
Heraklonas, Byzantine Emperor, 615
Herbert, Aubrey, 566
Hermaphroditos (mythogical figure), 163
Hermione (port), 36
hermits, 137, 167–71
Herodian, History of the Roman Empire, 64
Herodotus, 3, 19, 31, 33, 34, 172–3, 412, 643n6
Herrick, Robert, 502
Herulians (tribe), 609
Hieron see To Hieron
Hijrah of Muhammad (622), 280–81, 407, 441
Hilarianus (Roman governor of Africa), 157
Hill, Aaron, 499
Himyarite Kingdom, 251
Hinton St Mary, Dorset, 137
Hipparchos, 117
Hippo Regius, 183, 483
hippodrome: foundation, 66, 109; Byzantine, 110, 114, 165, 208, 217, 227, 231, 232, 361, 363, 670n3;

Ottoman (Atmeydanı), 401, 439, 439, 708n9
Hippolytus (mythological figure), 106
Hippolytus of Rome, Refutation of All Heresies, 671n3
Hissarlik archaeological site, 549
Hittites, 199, 458
Holy Apostles, Church of the, 119, 131, 136, 187, 413
Holy League: formation, 444; victory at Battle of Lepanto, 444–6, 466
Holy Roman Empire, 305, 308, 322, 435, 618, 634–5; see also Vienna, Siege of
Homer, 22, 224, 244, 353, 361, 394, 523; snakeskin-bound works of, 164, 170; Iliad, xxix, 137, 187, 188, 245, 353, 386, 417, 564; Odyssey, 188, 353, 521
homosexuality, 152, 238, 632
Honorius, Western Roman Emperor, 154, 611
Hope, Thomas, 514
Horace, 63
Hormisdas, Palace of see Bucoleon Palace
Hornby, Sir Edmund, 540
Hornby, Emilia, Lady, In and Around Stamboul, 540
horses, 47–8, 150, 277, 346, 400
Horus (god), 199
hospitals, 119–20, 267, 352, 356, 420, 439, 471, 541–2
Hoxha, Enver, 116
Hugo, Victor, The Child, 518, 522
Humayma, al-, Jordan, 288
Humayun, Mughal Emperor, 457
Humbert of Silva Candida, Cardinal, 335
Humor Monastery, Romania, 594
Hungary, 385, 441, 531, 622, 636–7; see also Budapest

Huns, 141–3, 183–5, 214, 244; *see also* Kotrigurs

Hürrem (concubine), 421–2

Husayni, Al-, *Akhbār al-Dawla al-Saljūqiyya*, 342

Hyacinthia (religious festival), 29, 52

Hypatia of Alexandria, 159–61, 198

Hypatios (Byzantine noble), 218, 219, 220

Ibn al-Fakih, *Kitab al-Buldan*, 319

Ibn al-Jawzi, 688n9

Ibn Khaldun, 640n16

Ibrahim 'the Mad', Ottoman Sultan, 480, 629

Ibrány, Hungary, 637

Ibret Taşlari (Example Stones), 473

Iceland, 309, 337

icons, Christian, 164, 287, 299–300, 301–2, 303, 305, 364; iconoclasm, 299–305, 319

Idrisi, al-, 697n3

Ikhwan (Arabic militia), 506

Illiberis, Council of (306), 649

Imbros, 22, 564

Immortals *see* Athanatoi; Ten Thousand

Imru' al-Qais (Bedouin poet), 280

Indus Valley, 285

Ingelheim, Germany, 308

Ingiliz Mustafa, 466

Ingres, Jean-Auguste-Dominique, 490–91

Innocent III, Pope, 351

Innocent XI, Pope, 474

International Byzantine Plan, 114

International Sanitary Conferences, 498

Io (mythological figure), 19–20

Ioane Tokhabi (monk), 667n8

Ionian revolt (499–493 BC), 35, 173

Ios, 435

Iphigenia (mythological figure), 103

Iran, 138, 343, 408, 457, 483, 500; *see also* Persia

Iraq, 104, 138, 563, 575; *see also* Baghdad; Mesopotamia

Iron Age, 20, 22–3

Isaac I Komnenos, Byzantine Emperor, 622

Isaac II Angelos, Byzantine Emperor, 359, 624

Isabella I, Queen of Spain, expulsion of Muslims and Jews, 426, 435

Isaiah, Book of, 172

Ischia, 435–6

Isfahan, 457

Isidorus of Miletus, 222–3

ISIL/ISIS *see* Islamic State

Isis (goddess), 52, 126, 164, 199

Islam: birth of, 279–82; early expansion, 284–90, 320; Sunni–Shia split, xxiii, 640n8; in Ottoman Empire, 406–413, 417–18, 425, 557

Islamic State (ISIL/ISIS; militant group), 69, 138, 506, 575

Ismail I, Shah of Persia, 408

Isocrates, 26

'Istanbul Pogrom' (1955), 584

Ivan Asen II, Tsar of Bulgaria, 625

ivory carving, 288

Izmir (Smyrna), 471, 577, 632; fire (1922), 579

Izmit, 117; *see also* Nicomedia

Iznik, 117; *see also* Nicaea

Jabala, King of the Ghassanids, 283–4, 678n2

Jacob of Serugh, 233

Jahiz, Al-, *Kitab al-Hayawan*, 315

James, St, 166

James VI, King of Scotland, 466

Janissaries, 382–3, 428, 442, 468–73, *471*, 480, 485; revolts, 408, 473, 505, 514, 524–5, 630; disbanding, 525–6, 527, 553

Jason (mythological figure), 15, 21–2, 23, 43, 53, 68, 392, 483

Jazari, Isamail al-, 685*n*11

Jerichau-Baumann, Elisabeth, 496

Jericho, 203, 570

Jerome, St, 655*n*4, 665*n*6

Jerusalem: Arab conquest, 284, 285–6; First Crusade, 347, 349; captured by Saladin, 350, 356–7; Ottoman rule, 456, 459; British rule, 570

Jerusalem (buildings and landmarks): Church of the Holy Sepulchre, 121, 124, 131, 277, 285–6, 538; Dome of the Rock, 288, 350; Mount of Olives, 124; Nea Church, 200; Solomon's Temple, 200; Temple Mount, 284

Jevad Pasha, 468

Jewish population: Byzantine city, 24, 238, 239–42, 268, 284, 309; Ottoman city, 425–8, 430, 516, 592; Turkish city, 241, 593

Joachim III, Patriarch of Constantinople, *414*

Jodhpur, 171

John, King of England, 326

John I Tzimiskes, Byzantine Emperor, 323, 620, 679*n*4

John II Komnenos, Byzantine Emperor, 623

John III Vatatzes, Emperor of Nicaea, 625

John IV Laskaris, Emperor of Nicaea, 364, 625

John V Palaiologos, Byzantine Emperor, 380, 626–7; conversion to Roman Catholicism, 381

John VI Kantakouzenos, Byzantine Emperor, 380, 626

John VII Palaiologos, Byzantine Emperor, 626–7

John VIII Palaiologos, Byzantine Emperor, 627, 693*n*18

John the Almsgiver, St, 175, 292–3

John the Apostle, St, 110, 240

John of Austria, Don, 445

John the Baptist, St, 72, 202, 360, 611

John of Brienne, Latin Emperor, 625

John the Cappadocian, 218

John Chrysostom, St, 56, 201–2, 230, 232–3, 240

John of Damascus, St, 299

John of Ephesus, 163, 210, 213, 669*n*16, 678*n*2

John of Gaza, 233

John Italos, 344

John the Lydian, *On Offices*, 216

John Malalas, 243, 248

John Paul II, Pope, 635

Jordanes, *The Origin and Deeds of the Goths*, 665*n*6, 677*n*4

Josephine, Empress of the French, 496

jousting, 382

Jovian, Byzantine Emperor, 139, 610

Judaism, 24, 240–41

Julian the Apostate, Byzantine Emperor, 133, 134–9, *138*, 610, 662*n*2

Julius Caesar, 63, 160, 163

Julius Nepos, Western Roman Emperor, 612

July 26 (Constantine's accession day), 127

July 2016 coup attempt, 3, 6, 602

Juno (goddess), 113

Jupiter (god), 113

justice and law: Byzantine, 234–8, 239–40, 255, 672n3; Ottoman, 400, 412, 419–20, 425, 486, 495, 527, 550
Justin I, Byzantine Emperor, 205, 206, 613
Justin II, Byzantine Emperor, 173, 200, 273–4, 614, 667n8
Justinian I, Byzantine Emperor: early life and marriage, 200, 205–215, 207, 254; social, legal and religious reforms, 214–15, 218, 233–8, 239–40, 241, 242–7, 255, 267, 672n3; supression of Nika riots, 216–21, 232, 248; reconstruction of the city, 222–9, 255, 267, 301; diplomatic and military campaigns, 217, 248–51, 293; reaction to natural disasters, 251–4; death, 250, 254, 272
Justinian II, Byzantine Emperor, 287, 288, 616
Justinian plague (541–42), 253–4, 613
Justus of Lyon, St, 681n4

Kadıköy, 24
Kalenderhane Mosque, 301, 363
Kaloyan, Tsar of Bulgaria, 624
Kanlı Kilise see St Mary of the Mongols, Church of
Kant, Immanuel, 491
Karbada, 533
Karlowitz, Treaty of (1699), 480, 502, 630
Karnak, 147
Karpos, St, 124
Kasımpaşa shipyards, 433
Kaskin, Ismael, 579–80
Kassia, St, 303–4
Kataphraktoi (Byzantine military unit), 340–41
Kavala, Greece, 353, 582, 594

Kemal, Mustafa see Atatürk, Mustafa Kemal
Keroessa (mythological figure), 20
Khadija (wife of Muhammad), 280
Khala'iq, al-, Saudi Arabia, 281
Khalid ibn al-Walid, 283
Khazars, 312, 619, 636
Khor Virap, Armenia, 108
Khusraw II, King of Persia, 276, 277
Kiev, 232, 311, 312–13
Kievan Rus see Rus (tribes)
Kılıç Ali Pasha Mosque, 569
Knidos, 50, 163, 174
Knights Hospitaller, 356, 366, 436, 691n11
Kodinos, George, 519
Kolmodin, Johannes, 458
Koloğlu people, 524
Kolossi, Cyprus, 366
Kommos, Crete, 266
kontakia (sacred poems), 221
Kontoskalion, Harbour of, 136–7
Konya, 344, 462, 572
Kos, xxi, 266, 284
Kosmidion, 407; see also Eyüp
Kosovo, Battle of (1389), 384
Kotrigurs, 244, 252
Krakatoa, 253
Kritoboulos, History of Mehmed the Conqueror, 398
Krum, Khan of Bulgaria, 618
Küçük Kaynarca, Treaty of (1774), 707n5
Küçükçekmece Gölü (lagoon), 16, 17
Kumkapı, 136–7
Kurds, 317, 540, 589
Kurşunlu Mahzen Mosque, 442
Kuruçeşme, 144, 169
Kuşadası, 436–7
Kybele (goddess), 52, 53, 73, 102, 109, 112, 113, 137, 151, 168, 173, 378, 514

Kyd, Thomas, *The Tragedie of Solimon and Perseda*, 465

Kynegion (arena), 66, 230–31

Laclos, Pierre Choderlos de, 490

Laconia *see* Lakonia

Lactantius, 107; *De Mortibus Persecutorum*, 78, 99

Lahore, 455, 457

Lakica *see* Colchis

Lakonia, 46–7, 223, 355

Lamartine, Alphonse de, *A Pilgrimage to the Holy Land*, xiii

Lampedusa, 435

Lampridius, Aelius, *The Life of Elagabalus*, 123

Latin Empire (1204–61), 362–3, 624–5

Latin, use in Byzantine Empire, 237, 677n3

Lausanne, Treaty of (1923), 582–3

Lausos (eunuch), 164, 169–70, 174

law *see* justice and law

Lawrence, T.E., 557

Lawrence, Sir William, 489

Lazica, 134, 251

League of Nations, 579

Leander (mythological figure),

Leander's Tower, 43

Lear, Edward, 529–31, *530*

Leda (mythological figure), 116–17, 208

Leighton, Sir Frederic, 491

Lemnos, 385, 564

Leo I the Thracian, Byzantine Emperor, 612

Leo II, Byzantine Emperor, 612

Leo III the Isaurian, Byzantine Emperor, xxv, 199, 290, 300, 617

Leo III, Pope, 322, 634

Leo IV, Byzantine Emperor, 617–18

Leo V, Byzantine Emperor, 302–3, 618–19

Leo VI the Wise, Byzantine Emperor, 164, 619, 666n2

Leo the Mathematician, 319

Leo of Ohrid, 335–6

Leo of Tripoli, 619

Leonardo da Vinci, 416–17, *418*

Leonidas I, King of Sparta, 35, 178

Leontios II, Byzantine Emperor, 616

Leontios Pilatos, 386

Leontios Scholastikos, 172

Leopold I, Holy Roman Emperor, 474, 477

Lepanto (Naupactus), 362

Lepanto, Battle of (1571), 443–6, 466

Lepcis Magna, Libya, 67–8, 185, 249

Lesbos, 32, 60, 682n9; Mytilene, 437

Levant Company, 427

Levni, Abdulcelil, 501, 503

Lewis Maximilian Mahomet, 478

Li Xian (Chinese general), 269

Libanios (Greek teacher), 233, 240

libraries, 137, 164, 186–7, 365, 385, 417, 463, 501

Libya, 67–8, 164, 223, 560

Licinius, Roman Emperor, 84, 85, 100; defeat at Battle of Chrysopolis, 101–4; death, 109

Liddon, Henry, 548

Liman von Sanders, Otto, 562

Limes Germanicus (frontier fortifications), 142–3, 183

'lingua franca', 5, 424

Liotard, Jean-Étienne, 505

Liqf, Saudi Arabia, 281

Little Haghia Sophia *see* St Sergios and St Bacchos, Church of

Liutprand, Bishop of Cremona, 265, 675n1

Liutprand (diplomat), 174

Lloyd George, David, 1st Earl Lloyd-George of Dwyfor, 572

Lod *see* Lydda

Lombards, 251, 289

Londinium, 81

London: churches, 183, 274, 513–14, 676n14; shipbuilding, 443–4; Great Exhibition (1851), 539; Chian refugees, 547–8; Victoria & Albert Museum, 548; St James's Palace, 559; Jermyn Street Hammam, 709n9

London, Treaty of (1913), 559–60, 561

Long Walls (Byzantine fortifications), 203, 229, 560

Longo, Giovanni Justiniani, 390

Louis the Pious, Holy Roman Emperor, 308

Louis XV, King of France, 505

Lucian, *De Dea Syria*, 168

Lucillian, St, 76

Lucullus (Roman consul), 63

Luke, St, 72, 119, 200, 299

Lullingstone, Kent, 108

Luoyang, China, 47–8, 272

Lutetia (Paris), 135

Lydda (Lod), 73–5, 122, 648n6, 9, 10

Lydia of Thyateira, 72, 73

Lykos River, 28, 166

Lyon, Second Council of (1274), 626

Lysander (Spartan admiral), 45, 606

Macar Bay, 53

Macedonia, 54–8, 60, 63, 205

Macedonia (spy), 210

Machiavelli, Niccolò, 5

madrasas (schools), 404, 412, 685n11

Maedi, 55

Magnaura (palace/university building), 309, 636, 667n13

Magnus Maximus, Roman usurper, 178, 610

Magyars, 636–7

Mahmud, Emir of Ghazni, 428

Mahmud I, Ottoman Sultan, 630

Mahmud II, Ottoman Sultan, 487, 496, 520, 524, 525, 527, 631

Maine (US state), 310

malaria, 141, 484, 542

Malchi, Esperanza, 465

Malta, 436, 466, 581

Mamluks, 408, 409, 413, 460

Mandaeism, 138

Mandrocles of Samos (engineer), 31, 32, 638n2

Manichaeism, 244, 345, 616, 649n6, 659n12

Manisa, 463

Mansur, Al-, Abbasid Caliph, 685n5

Manuel I Komnenos, Byzantine Emperor, 326, 355, 361, 623, 685n9

Manuel II, Byzantine Emperor, 384, 393, 627

Manzikert, Battle of (1071), 343–4, 569

Mar Eshai Shimun XXIII, Patriarch, 676n14

Marathon, Battle of (490 BC), 33, 34

Marcian, Byzantine Emperor, 612

Marco Polo, 50, 489, 690n11

Marcus Aurelius, Roman Emperor, 64, 73

Mardin, 344

Mardonios (eunuch), 135

Margaret of Beverley, 350

Maria of Antioch, Byzantine Empress, 355, 356

Maria Fyodorovna, Russian Empress, 535

Maria Palaiologina, 396

Marianism, 5, 197–203, 209–210, 274–5

Marie Antoinette, Queen of France, 592

Mariefred, Sweden, 305

Maritsa River, 102, 381, 580

Mark Antony, 54, 63, 72, 160, 599

Mark the Deacon, *Life of Porphyry, Bishop of Gaza*, 154, 156
Martyrion of SS Karpos and Papylos, 124
Marx, Karl, 524, 540
Mary, Virgin *see* Marianism
Maslama (Umayyad general), xxiv, 287
Mason, John, *The Turke*, 465
Massinger, Philip, *The Renegado*, 461
mastic gum, Chian, 519–20
Masts, Battle of the (c.655), xxi–xxii, 284
Matala, Crete, 266
mathematics, 159, 166, 642*n*5
Matrona (fifth-century woman), 197
Matthew, Gospel of, 172, 664*n*5
Maurice, Byzantine Emperor, 275, 614
Mauritius, 552
Mauropous, John, 245
mausoleum, Byzantine imperial, 113, 119, 254
Mausolus, King of Caria, 41, 53, 436, 463
Maxentius, Roman Emperor, 85, 101; defeated at Milvian Bridge, 95–8
Maximian, Roman Emperor, 69, 78, 85, 101
Maximinus Daia, Roman Emperor, 77, 83, 85, 609
Maximus Byzantius, 166, 167
May 11 (dedication day), 113, 114
May 29 (conquest celebrations), 387–8
Meat Square, 470
Mecca, 281, 408–9, 456, 459, 498, 506, 570
Medea (mythological figure), 22, 23, 53, 483, 515, 529, 652*n*8, 697*n*3
Medici family, 386, 417, 427; Catherine de' Medici, 419, 462–3
Medina, 280, 281–2, 408, 409, 456, 459, 506, 570, 590

Medway, Battle of the (43), 658*n*8
Megabazus (Persian general), 19, 30
Megalos Pyrgos (Great Tower), Galata, 290, 361
Megara and Megarians, 25, 26–30, 46, 139, 359
Megiddo, Israel, 570
Mehmed I, Ottoman Sultan, 393, 402
Mehmed II the Conqueror, Ottoman Sultan, 396; early life and first reign, 388, 391, 393, 486; besieges Constantinople, 386, 387–91; enters city, 136, 387, 391, 406; repopulation and governance of city, 395, 398, 400–401, 407, 413–14, 417, 424–6, 432; reconstruction of city, 397, 398, 400, 403, 407, 412; death, 408, 430
Mehmed III, Ottoman Sultan, 418, 458, 461, 464, 629
Mehmed IV, Ottoman Sultan, 474, 475–6, 477, 479, 630
Mehmed V, Ottoman Sultan, 557, 562–3, 563, 572, 632
Mehmed VI, Ottoman Sultan, 487, 577, 579, 581, 588, 632–3
Melania (fifth-century woman), 198
Melling, Antoine Ignace, *401*, 503, *503*
Memphis, 31
Menander, 49, 245, 288
Mermer Kule (Marble Tower), 385
Mese (Middle Road), 66, 114, 206, 400
Mesopotamia, 56, 67, 408, 563; *see also* Iraq
Metanoia Convent, 214–15
Methodios, St, 635–6
Metochites, Theodore, 691*n*8
Mevlevihane Gate, 184
Mhrimah Sultan Mosque, 420
Michael I, Byzantine Emperor, 616

Michael II, Byzantine Emperor, 302, 619

Michael III, Byzantine Emperor, 619

Michael IV, Byzantine Emperor, 621

Michael V Kalaphates, Byzantine Emperor, 325, 621

Michael VI, Byzantine Emperor, 622

Michael VII Doukas, Byzantine Emperor, 340, 622–3

Michael VIII Palaiologos, Byzantine Emperor, 364, 396, 625, 626

Michael Keroularios, Patriarch of Constantinople, 335, 621

Michael the Syrian, *The Syriac Chronicle*, xxi

Michelozzo (Renaissance artist), 417

Midas, King, 52, 645*n*7

Midilli (cruiser), 562

Midnight Express (film), 28

Milan, 69, 85, 101, 153

Milan, Edict of (313), 100

Milion (monument), 66–7, *67*, 68, 114–15

Militaris, Via, 102, 391

millenarianism, 349, 423, 441–3

millet system, 425, 429, 583

Milošević, Slobodan, 384

Milvian Bridge, Battle of (312), 95–8

Mindaros (Spartan naval commander), 40

Minerva (goddess), 113

missionaries, Christian, 270–72

Mithridates VI, King of Pontus, 62, 63

Mocius, St, 74

Moero of Byzantium, 49

Moldavia, 459, 533, 539

Molière, 5

monasticism, 202–3, 317, 318, 363, 519, 705*n*5

Monastir, Macedonia, 576

Monemvasia, xxiii

Mongols, 142, 366, 378, 384, 396, 456

Montagu, Edward Wortley, 497

Montagu, Lady Mary Wortley, 423, 438, 494, 495, 497, 498, 505, 506, 515

Montecristo, 435

Montenegro, 549, 559

Montesquieu, Charles-Louis de Secondat, Baron de, 490

Morali Besir Ağa (eunuch), 505

Morgenthau, Henry, 569

Morosini, Francesco, 313

Morris, William, 548

Moscow, 532

Moses (biblical figure), 278

Moshe Agura (Jewish citizen), 241

Mother of God of Pharos, Church of the, 313

Mouchliotissa, Panagia *see* St Mary of the Mongols, Church of

Moundos (Byzantine general), 220

Mozart, Wolfgang Amadeus, 472

Mtskheta, Georgia, 108

Muawiyah I, Umayyad Caliph, xxv, 265, 640*n*8–9

Mughal Empire, 422, 455–7, 480

Muhammad (prophet), 279–82, 283, 284, 285, 286, 287, 392, 406; Hijrah (622), 280–81, 407, 441

Muntaner, Ramon, 366–7

Murad I, Ottoman Sultan, 381, 384, 626

Murad II, Ottoman Sultan, 382, 385

Murad III, Ottoman Sultan, 418–19, 420, 421, 427, 428, 462, 463, 628

Murad IV, Ottoman Sultan, 460, 629, 701*n*4

Murad V, Ottoman Sultan, 632, 712*n*7

Murray, John, 515

Muscovy, Grand Duchy of, 414–15

music, 317, 403, 429, 456, 458, 472, 526–7

Mussolini, Benito, 697n3
Mustafa I, Ottoman Sultan, 629
Mustafa II, Ottoman Sultan, 502,
630
Mustafa III, Ottoman Sultan, 533–4,
631
Mustafa IV, Ottoman Sultan, 514,
631
Mustafa Ali, 455
Mustafa Pasha, Kara, 477, 479
Mu'ta, Battle of (629), 283
Mutawakkil, al-, Abbasid Caliph, 636
Müteferrika Press, 501
Muwaylihi, Ibrahim al-, 552
Mystras, 393–4
mythology: Egyptian, 52, 126, 147,
164, 199; Greek, 19–20, 21–2, 23,
27, 51–2, 53, 103, 116–17, 155, 163–5,
173, 208, 245, 304, 483; Hittite, 199;
Roman, 52, 97, 100, 101, 104, 112,
113, 122, 151, 163–5
Mytilene, 437

Nabi Efendi, 499
Nadir Shah of Persia, 457
Naissus (Niš), 82
names for Istanbul, xxviii–xxx, 2,
392, 430, 535, 594
Naples, 121
Napoleon I, Emperor, 85, 505, 538, 552
Napoleon III, Emperor, 538, 708n3
Narni, 181
Narses (eunuch), 173, 174–5, 250,
662n7, 670n9
natural disasters: Christianity and,
253, 299–300; see also earthquakes;
plagues; volcanic eruptions
Naupactus see Lepanto
Navarino, Battle of (1827), 706n4
navy: Byzantine, 255, 291–2, 666n2;
Ottoman, 432–7, 446, 553, 560,
561, 562, 706n4

Nea Moni Monastery, Chios, 519, 521,
523
Neapolis, 165
Nebuchadnezzar III, King of
Babylon, 32
Nero, Roman Emperor, 77, 390
Nestor, King (mythological figure), 21
Nestor Iskander, Tales of Tsargrad,
535
Nestorians, 266, 270–71, 322, 675n3,
676n14; Nestorian stele (China),
271, 271
Nestorios, Patriarch of
Constantinople, 198, 270, 676n10,
14
New Order (Ottoman army), 471
New Zealand, Anzac Corps, 564,
565–6, 568
Newcastle-upon-Tyne, 561
Nicaea, 65, 117, 349, 356, 362, 379;
Church of Haghia Sophia, 301
Nicaea, Empire of, 625
Nicaea, First Council of (325), 116,
117–19, 150, 198, 336
Nicaea, Second Council of (787), 301
Nicagoras, 111–12
Nicene Creed, 5, 116, 117–19, 150, 151,
152
Nicholas I, Russian Tsar, 532, 546
Nicholas of Myra, St, 118
Nicocles (Spartan pagan), 134
Nicomedia, 69, 76, 82–3, 99, 105, 117,
121, 130, 379
Nicomedia, Edict of (303), 78
Nicopolis, 61, 384; Battle of (1396),
384
Niger, Pescennius, Roman Emperor,
64–5, 117, 608
Nightingale, Florence, 471, 539, 541–3
Nika riots (532), 216–21, 232, 233, 248
Nikephoros I, Byzantine Emperor,
618

Nikephoros II Phokas, Byzantine
  Emperor, 341, 343, 620, 705n3
Nikephoros Proteuon, 622
Niketas Choniates, 358, 397
Nikophoros Bryennios the Elder, 622,
  623
Nikophoros Bryennios the Younger,
  History, 321
Nineveh, 277
Noah (biblical figure), 50, 112, 222,
  342, 489
Nonnos, *Dionysiaka*, 245
Nores, Giacomo, 458
Norfolk, 296
Normans, 324, 339–42, 353–6
Northumbria, 296, 297
nose-amputation (rhinotomy), xxiii,
  598
Notitia Urbis Constantinopolitanae
  (regionary), 186
Novgorod, Russia, 309
Nubians, 309
Nufăru, Romania, 314
Nu'mani, Shibil, 710n14
Numidia, 183
Nurbanu Valide Sultan, 420, 462–3,
  464, 491
Nusretiye Mosque, 525, *526*, 569
Nymphaeum, 113

Obelisk of Theodosios, 112, 145,
  146–7, 163
occultism, 165–7, 337–8, 442,
  685n9–11
Ochrid, Macedonia, 175
Octavian *see* Augustus (Octavian),
  Roman Emperor
Odessa, 514, 533
Odo of Deuil, 318–19, 352
Odoacer, 189, 612–13
Oedipus, 61
Ohrid, Lake, 636

oil production, 563
Old Bazaar, 412–13, 484
Olga of Kiev, St, 312
Oliphant, Laurence, 540
Olympia, 29, 151, 163
Olympic Games: ancient, 29, 643n6;
  modern, 545
Olympius (eunuch), 180
Olympus, Mount (Uludağ), 379
Omurtag, Khan of Bulgaria, 619
One Thousand and One Nights (folk-
  tales), 286, 319
Opium (Afyonkarahisar), 378
Optatianus Porphyrius, Publilius,
  670
Orderic Vitalis, *Ecclesiastical History*,
  321, 324
Orhan Gazi, Ottoman Sultan, 378,
  379, 380, 382, 407
Orient Express (train), 550, 588, 632
orientalism, 490–91, 493–8, 505, 514,
  523
Origen, 175, 658n13, 664n5
Origo Constantini (chronicle), 82
Orléans, France, 185
Orosius, *History Against the Pagans*,
  665–6n6
orphanages, 119–20
Orpheus (mythological figure), 21
Orsippus, 29
Orta Gate, 516
Orta Mosque, 470, 524, 553
Ortaköy, 169, 427, 527
Oseberg Viking ship, 310, 324
Oslo, 417
Osman I, Ottoman Sultan, 378, 379,
  393; Osman's Dream, xiii, 377, 378,
  382, 386, 440, 502, 563
Osman II, Ottoman Sultan, 471, 629
Osman III, Ottoman Sultan, 630–31
Osrhoene (Roman province), 165
Ostia, 100, 121, 435

Ostrogoths, 144, 246, 250
Ottomans, origins, 378
Ottoman Empire: rise and early
    expansion, 377–86, 393; capture
    of Constantinople, 386, 387–92;
    reconstruction of city, 398–400,
    402–5, 416–21; early governance
    and rule of city, 398, 401–2, 407,
    411–15, 424–5; expansion under
    Selim I, 408–411, 456; development
    under Süleyman the Magnificent,
    421–2, 435–41, 456; defeat at Battle
    of Lepanto (1571), 443–6, 466;
    failed siege of Vienna (1683), 473,
    475–80, 502; Treaty of Karlowitz
    (1699), 480, 502, 630; Tulip
    Age, 411, 476, 499–506; Greek
    War of Independence (1821–32),
    516–17, 535; Chios massacre (1822),
    518–23; Treaty of Constantinople
    (1832), 526; *tanzimat* reforms,
    526–8, 535–6, 544, 549–50, 631;
    Crimean War (1853–56), 471, 476,
    514, 538–44, 548; Congress of
    Berlin (1878), 549; Young Turks
    movement, 556–7, 560–61, 576,
    632; Balkan Wars and Treaty of
    London (1912–13), 559–61, 576–7;
    First World War, 557–8, 561–74;
    Sykes–Picot Agreement proposals,
    574–5, *575*; Treaty of Sèvres (1920),
    579, 632; Greco-Turkish War
    (1920–22), 577, 579–80, 583, 584;
    dissolution of empire, 579–81,
    587–91
Ovid, 52
Oxford, New College, 461
Ozal, Turgut, 597

paganism: and Christianity, 122,
    132, 134–5, 155–67, 199, 244–6;
    outlawed, 151, 152–3, 155, 242–4,
288; massacres and destruction
    of temples, 155–7, 160, 165; *see also*
    mythology; statuary, pagan
Pakistan, 285, 588, 597
Palamas, Kostis, *The King's Flute*, 576
Palea Kameni *see* Thera
Palestine, British Mandate, 579
Palladas (poet), 160, 243
Palmyra, 69
Pammakaristos, Church of, 364–5,
    395
Pamuk, Orhan, 638n6
Pan (god), 165
Pandidakterion (university), 188
Pantokrator Monastery, 352, 360, 362
Papylos, St, 124
Paris, 135, 385, 502, 505, 548, 590, 593
Paris, Congress of (1856), 632
Paris (mythological figure), 47, 223,
    304
Paros, 435; Church of a Hundred
    Doors, 124, 200
Partito Terrarum Imperii Romaniae
    (treaty, 1204), 362
Passau, Germany, 143, 658n8
Pasternak, Boris, *Doctor Zhivago*, 299
Paul, St, 54, 97, 153, 317
Paul of Aegina, 174
Paul the Silentiary, 255
Paulicianism, 345
Pausanias, 34–9, *35*, 110, 606, 656n6
Pavia (Ticinum), 100
pax Romana, 109, 119, 181, 365
Peace, Church of *see* Haghia Eirene
Pears, Sir Edwin, 550–51
Pears, Henry 'Harry', 550–51
Pechenegs (tribe), 310, 312, 339;
    besiege Constantinople (1090),
    346–7, 688n2
'Peintre du Bosphore' (art
    movement), 505
Peleus (mythological figure), 304

Pella, Macedonia, 60

Peloponnesian War (431–404 BC), 40, 42–6

Pera (Beyoğlu), 322, 395, 497, 540, 577, 580; Crimea Memorial Church, 542–3

Pera Palace Hotel, 552, 553–4, 573

perfume trade, 316

Pergamon, 186, 223

Perinthos, 65, 607, 608

Perpetua, St, 157, 660n8

Persepolis, 31, 645n7

Perseus (mythological figure), 278

Persia: Achaemenid Empire, 30, 31–6, 40, 42–3, 57; Sassanid Empire, 69, 116, 130, 138, 141, 217, 251, 648n8; defeated by Byzantines, 272, 275–7, 278, 280; Muslim conquest, 284, 285; Timurid Empire, 384, 456; Safavid dynasty, 408, 422, 457; see also Iran

Pertevniyal Valide Sultan Mosque, 632

Pessinus, 52, 645n7

Pest, Siege of (1542), 440

Peter II of Courtenay, Latin Emperor, 625

Peter, St, 72, 153, 336

Peter the Hermit, 348

Petrarch, 386

Petrie, Sir Flinders, 520

Petrion (Plateia), Church of St Laurentius, 217

Petulantes (Roman army unit), 135

Peutinger Map, 126–7, 163

Phaedra (mythological figure), 106

Phanar see Fener

Pharnabazus, 644n3

Phidaleia (mythological figure), 20

Phidias, statue of Zeus, 163–4, 174

Philby, Kim, 553

Philiki Hetairia (secret society), 516

Philip II of Macedon, 54–5, 60, 606–7

Philip the Good, Duke of Burgundy, 392

Philippi, 54, 71–2, 599; Battle of (42 BC), 54, 63, 72

Philippikos Bardanes, Byzantine Emperor, 616–17

Philo Mechanicus, 47

Phoenicians, 24, 35

Phokas, Byzantine Emperor, 275, 614

Photios, Patriarch of Constantinople, 307, 311, 336

Phrixos (mythological figure), 53

Phrygia and Phrygians, 28

Picts, 83

Pindar, 22, 187, 600

Piraeus, 45, 200; lion sculpture, 313, 314, 325

Piri Reis (Ahmed Hacı Muhiddin Piri), 434

Piron, Giovanni, 458

Pisa, 355, 385, 462

Pius V, Pope, 444

plagues, 433, 477, 497–8, 525, 692n5; (541–42), 253–4, 613; Black Death (1347–48), 380, 482

Plataea, Battle of (479 BC), 34, 35

Plato, 135, 187, 245, 246, 335, 386, 669n27; Timaeus, 137

Platonic Academy, Athens, 222, 243–4

Platonic Academy, Florence, 386, 394

Plethon, 386, 394

Plevneliev, Rosen, 636

Pliny the Elder, 62

Pliny the Younger, 63, 71

Pliska, Battle of (811), 618

Plovdiv, 380

Plutarch, 243, 245

Poitiers, Battle of (732), 289

polo (sport), 382, 400

Pompadour, Madame de, 505, 592
Pompey (Byzantine noble), 218, 219, 220
Pompey (Roman commander), 63; campaign against the pirates, 62
Ponticas, Via, 61
poorhouses, 120, 318, 463
Pope, Alexander, 505, 705n4
population exchange between Greece and Turkey (1923), 154–5, 582–4
population totals (of Istanbul), 5, 29, 120, 179, 316, 408, 430, 593, 675n18
Porphyrius (charioteer), 670n3
Porphyry of Gaza, St, 154, 155–7, 164
Portland Bay, Dorset, 308
Poseidon (god), 20, 51
Potemkin, Grigory, 492, 533, 535
Poti, Georgia, 482–3, 484
Praetorian Guard, 322
Praetorium, 113, 218, 235
Praxiteles, Aphrodite of Knidos, 163–4, 174
Pre-Raphaelites (artistic movement), 547–8
Préault, Simon, 602
Preslav, Bulgaria, 549, 635
Priam's Treasure (archaeological artifacts), 549–50
Princes' Islands (Sea of Marmara), 302, 480, 682n9
printing, 392, 427, 501, 549
Priscian (grammarian), 237
Priscilla (biblical figure), 197, 201
Proclos (prefect), 147
Proclus (scholar), 662n2
Procopius (Roman usurper), 139
Procopius of Caesarea, 207, 218, 248, 249, 250, 266, 293; on Empress Theodora, 210, 215, 219–20, 251, 254, 669n16; on reconstruction of Constantinople, 222, 223–4, 227

Procrustes (mythological figure), 61
prostitution, 209, 214–15, 303, 535–6, 550, 556
Prousa, 212, 254, 378; see also Bursa
Prudentius, 162
Psellos, Michael, 316, 344
Pseudo-Aristotle, 60
Ptolemaic dynasty, 57, 158, 661n9
Public Debt Administration, Ottoman, 550
Pulcheria, Byzantine Empress, 239, 244, 612
purple dye production, 72, 239, 266, 267, 648n6
Pushkin, Alexander, 536, 538
Pythagoras, 135
Pythion, 212; see also Yalova

Qudayd valley, 281
Quinisext Council (692), 288, 616
Qur'an, 288, 409, 677n7–9
Quraysh tribe, 280, 281

racial theory, 488–90
Racine, Jean, 490
Ragazzoni, Jacopo, 491
railways, 24, 549, 550, 570, 632
Rajab Khan, Governor of Surat, 456
Rajasthan, 428
Ramses VI, Pharaoh, 111
rape and sexual violence, 214, 309, 351, 354
Ratiaria, 184
Ravenna, 144; mosaics, 206, 207, 254
Red Apple, prophesy of, 442–3
Regensburg, Germany, 143
Reggio, Italy, 267
Regnans in Excelsis (papal bull, 1570), 444
relic-collecting, 124–5, 198, 199–200, 296, 317–18, 699n4

religion *see* Bektashism; Buddhism;
Christianity; Islam; Judaism;
mythology; paganism
Renaissance, 385–6, 394, 416–19, 434
Rendlesham, Suffolk, 293–4
'Rescript of the Rose Chamber'
(1839), 527
Revolutions of 1848, 531
Rhea (mythological figure), 51, 113,
114
rhinotomy (nose-amputation), xxiii,
598
Rhodes: Hellenic age, 50, 55, 57, 163,
223, 607–8; Byzantine period, 163,
223; Arab occupation, xxi, xxv–
xxvi, 241, 284; taken by Knights
Hospitaller, 366; Ottoman control,
436
Rhodes, Colossus of, xxv–xxvi
Richard I the Lionheart, King of
England, 357, 476
Richard II, King of England, 351
Rimini, Piazza Ferrari excavations,
143–4
River Clyde, SS, 564
Robert of Clari, *The Conquest of
Constantinople*, 326, 350
Robert of Courtenay, Latin Emperor,
625
Roger II, King of Sicily, 355, 697*n*9
Rognvaldr jarl Kali Kolsson, 306
Roman Empire: early relations
with Byzantium, 62–3, 608;
construction of Egnatian Way,
57–8, *58*, 59–62; incorporation
of Byzantium, 64, 608; rule of
Septimius Severus and Caracalla,
64–8, 607–8; institution of
universal Roman citizenship, 68,
120; early barbarian invasions,
68; establishment of Tetrarchy,
69–70, 77–9, 653*n*2; persecution
of Christians, 74–5, 76–9, 100;
early reign of Constantine
the Great, 84–6, 95, 100–101;
Constantine's victories at Milvian
Bridge and Chrysopolis, 95–8,
101–4; Constantine becomes sole
emperor, 104, 107; Western Roman
emperors, 139, 145, 154, 178, 180,
189, 610–613; Germanic invasions,
170, 177, 180–81, 185, 189; end of
empire, 181, 189; *see also* Byzantine
Empire
Romani (gypsies), 124, 428–9
Romania, 469, 549; Securitate, 555
Romaniotes (Greek-speaking Jews),
268, 426
Romanoff, Prince Nicholas, 595
Romanos I Lekapenos, Byzantine
Emperor, 241, 318, 620
Romanos II, Byzantine Emperor, 620
Romanos III Argyros, Byzantine
Emperor, 621
Romanos IV Diogenes, Byzantine
Emperor, 342, 343, 622, 682*n*9
Romanos (poet), 'On Earthquakes
and Fires', 221, 252
Rome: sack of 410, 177, 180–81,
665*n*6; sack of 455, 185, 248; fall
of 476, 170, 181, 189; Gothic and
Byzantine rule, 250; alliance with
Normans, 339; reaction to fall of
Constantinople, 392
Rome (buildings and landmarks):
Arch of Constantine, 100, 651*n*5;
Colosseum, 100; Kybele shrine,
52; St John Lateran, 100; Santa
Costanza, 136; Santa Dodici
Apostoli, 250; Trevi Fountain, 185;
Vatican, 100; Villa Malborghetto,
95, 98
Romulus Augustulus, Western
Roman Emperor, 189, 612–13

Romulus and Remus (mythological figures), 163
Rosetta Stone, 506
Roskilde, Denmark, 324
Rowlandson, Thomas, *Harem*, 490
Rowlie, Samson, 466
Rubens, Sir Peter Paul, 520
Rufinus (consul), 177, 178, 179
Rumeli Hisarı (Boğazkesen Castle), 386, 388, 404, 470
Rus (tribes), 312–14, 323, 336; siege of 860, 290, 307–8, 536; *see also* Varangian Guard
Russell, John, 1st Earl, 546
Russia, 414–15, 532–7, 544–5, 556; Russo-Ottoman wars, 479, 480, 518–19, 533–6, 539, 548–9; Crimean War, 471, 476, 514, 538–44, 548, 557; First World War, 562–3, 565, 568–9; Revolution (1917), 563, 574–5, 580; post-Soviet, 597; *see also* Soviet Union
Russian Orthodox Church, 385, 532, 535, 536
Ryan, Sir Charles Snodgrass, 566

sacrifice: animal, 52, 54, 59, 77, 657*n*6, 661*n*2; human, 103, 309
Safi al-Din ardabili, Sufi Shaykh, 548
Safiye Sultan, 420, 427, 463–5
St George, Church of, 77, 125, 396
St John, Church of, 520, 611
St John, Knights of *see* Knights Hospitaller
St John of Stoudios (monastery), 187, 246, 304, 317, 594
St Just's, Cornwall, 681*n*4
St Laurentius, Church of, 217
St Mary of Blachernae, Church of, 640*n*14
St Mary of the Mongols, Church of, 396–7

St Nicholas, Church of, 321–2
St Paul, Church of, 426
St Peter and St Paul, Church of, 227
St Petersburg (Petrograd), 574
St Sergios and St Bacchos, Church of (Little Haghia Sophia), 213, 227
Sakarya, River, 378
Saladin, 350, 356–7
Salamis, Battle of (480 BC), 34
Salome (biblical figure), 202
Salonica *see* Thessaloniki
salt production, 26
Samarkand, 266, 307, 456
Samarra, Iraq, 575, 685–6*n*11
Samatya, 304; St John of Stoudios, 187, 246, 304, 317, 594
Samos, 32, 39–40, 42, 163, 520
Samuel, Emperor of Bulgaria, 636
Sand, Vebjørn, 417
Sanderson, John, 464
Sandys, George, 493
Santorini *see* Thera
Sarajevo, 477, 712*n*3
Sarayburnu (Seraglio Point), 20, 424, 540
Sardinia, 324; Kingdom of, 539
Sassanid Empire, 69, 116, 130, 138, 141, 217, 251, 648*n*8; defeated by Byzantines, 272, 275–7, 278, 280
Saud, House of, 506
Sayyed Ameer Ali, 587
Sazonov, Sergei, 574
Schliemann, Heinrich, 549–50
schooling, 187–8, 244, 304, 353, 417, 527, 594; *see also* madrasas
Schweigger, Solomon, 412
scriptoria, 186–7, 188, 365
Scutari, 62, 102–3, 551; Semiye Barracks, 471, 540, 541–2; *see also* Chrysopolis; Üsküdar
Scythia and Scythians, 32, 33, 53

sea-faring: ancient Greek, 23, 32, 38–9; Roman, 666n2; Vandals, 183, 666n2; Byzantine, 255, 291–2; Arabic, xxii, xxiii; Vikings, 310, 683n15; Ottoman, 432–7, 446, 553; British, 437, 443–4; *see also* navy

Second World War, 241, 541, 590, 593

Selden Map, 480

Seleucid Empire, 56

Selim I, Ottoman Sultan, 400, 408–411, 423, 495, 628, 699n4

Selim II, Ottoman Sultan, 418, 438, 444–5, 446, 462, 463, 628

Selim III, Ottoman Sultan, 505, 553, 631

Seljuk Turks, 342–4, 349, 378, 428, 707n1

Selymbria (Silivri), 19, 44

Semestra (nymph), 20

Senate House, 110, 113, 155, 163, 226

Seraglio Point (Sarayburnu), 20, 424, 540

Serapis (god), 52, 53

Serbia, 82, 380, 383–4, 514, 549, 559

Sergios, St, 213

Sergius I, Pope, 616

Serifos, 435

Serpent Column, 36–8, 37, 110, 127, 229, 362, 656n6

Sevastopol, 533, 541

Severus, Septimius, Roman Emperor, 64–8, 107, 109, 117, 608

Sèvres, Treaty of (1920), 579, 632

sewerage system, 555–6

Seymour, Sir George Hamilton, 532, 546

shadow-puppet shows, 544

Shajar al-Durr, 350

Shakespeare, William: *Henry IV, Part 2*, 486; *Henry V*, 465; *The Merchant of Venice*, 444; *Othello*, 5, 465; *Timon of Athens*, 465; *Titus Andronicus*, 141

Shanghai Cooperation Organisation, 597

Shapur II, King of Persia, 116, 130, 131

shipping *see* navy; sea-faring

Sichelgaita (wife of Robert Guiscard), 341

Sicily, xxii, xxiii, 250, 285, 289; Sicilian Expedition (415 BC), 42, 690n10

Sidon, 283

Sidonius Apollinaris, *Epistulae*, 106

Siege of Sevastopol, The (film), 544

siege warfare, art of, 47, 65, 388–9

sieges: (478 BC), 36, 244; (408 BC), 44–5, 244; (515), 244, 248; (559), 244, 252; (674–8), xxv, 284–5, 407; (717–18), xxi, xxiii–xxv, 287, 288, 290; (860), 290, 307–8, 536; (1090), 346–7, 688n2; (1204), 290, 324, 358–62, 365; (1394–1401), 384; (1422), 385; (1453), 386, 387–91

Silahtarağa Power Station, 595

Silchester, Hampshire, 81

Silistra, Bulgaria, 143

silk production and trade, 265–72, 310–311, 363, 377–8, 383, 427, 691n5, 697n10; *see also* carpets and textiles

Silk Roads, 6, 48, 61, 269–70, 272, 277, 310

Silko, King of the Nobatai, 213

Silverdale Hoard, 683n5

Silviarides family, 582–3

Silivri (Selymbria), 19, 44

Sima Qian, 677n18

Sinai, Mount, 200, 211, 286, 667n8

Sinan, Mimar, 420, 423, 436, 437

Sinope, 50, 540, 602

Sipahi (Ottoman cavalry corps), 525

Siphnos, 200, 595

Sirat al-Zabir, 349

Sirente crater, Italy, 96

Sirkeci, 50, 426; railway station, 66, 561, 588, 632

Sirmio, 85

Sirmium, 69, 674*n*10

Sis, Armenia, 469

Skleraina, Maria (mistress of Constantine IX), 245, 621

Skopje, 205

Skylitzes, John, 325

Slade, Sir Addolphus, *Record of Travels in Turkey*, 468

Slankamen, Battle of (1691), 630

slavery, 120, 174, 309, 430, 435, 481; white slave trade, 309, 481, 482–7, 488, 536, 544–5, 556, 708*n*9

Slavs, 251, 275, 309, 636

Sleepless Monks, Office of the, 317

smallpox, 497–8, 649*n*5

Smith, W.J., 539

Smyrna (Izmir), 471, 577, 632; fire (1922), 579

Smythe, Percy, 6th Viscount Strangford, 516, 531

Snorri Sturluson, *Heimskringla*, 306, 687*n*6

Sobieski, Jan, 474, 701*n*2

Sochi, 545

Society of Muhammad, 557

Socrates, 28, 40, 42, 46–7, 154, 315

Socrates Scholasticus, 157, 161; *Ecclesiastical History*, 111, 127, 129, 659*n*10, 661*n*12

Sogdiana, 266

Söğüt, 378

Sol Invictus (sun god), 97, 100, 101, 109, 112

solidi (Roman coins), 100–101, 269

Sophia (Holy Wisdom), 224–5, 246, 671*n*3

Sophia, Byzantine Empress (wife of Justin II), 614, 667*n*8

Sophocles, 187

Souda (encyclopaedia), 353

Soviet Union, 301, 532

Sozomen, *Ecclesiastical History*, 99, 652*n*14

Sparta and Spartans, 34–40, 46–7, 178, 244, 394; Peloponnesian War, 40, 42–6

Spencer, Edmund, *Travels in Circassia*, 490

Split (Spalatum), Diocletian's palace, 78–9

sponges, 528–9

sport, 29, 231, 382, 400, 545, 551

spying *see* espionage

Sremska Mitrovica, Serbia, 69; *see also* Sirmium

Sri Lanka, 540

Stamboul (transport ship), 565

Stamford Bridge, Battle of (1066), 324

statuary, pagan, 162–5, 174, 656*n*6, 662*n*3

Staurakios, Byzantine Emperor, 618

Stefan Uroš IV Dušan, Emperor of the Serbs, 380

Stephen of Hungary, St, 637

Stilicho (Roman general), 178–80

Stoics, 119, 315

Stone Age, 15–17, 24, 50, 550, 642*n*5, 680*n*11

Strangford, Percy Smythe, 6th Viscount, 516, 531

Stratation (military training ground), 55, 65–6, 127

Stratford de Redcliffe, Stratford Canning, 1st Viscount, 529, 539

Stratonicos, 56

Street, George Edmund, Crimea Memorial Church, 542–3

Stylites, 168–71, *170*, 655*n*5, 662*n*2

Sublime Porte (Ottoman
government), 400, 560

submarines, 553, *554*, 565

Suetonius, 104

Suez Canal, 565

Sujan Rai, 455

Süleyman, Umayyad Caliph, xxiv,
287

Süleyman I the Magnificent,
Ottoman Sultan, 399, 401, 414,
417, 421–2, 434–41, *439*, 456, 628

Süleyman II, Ottoman Sultan, 480,
630

Süleyman Pasha Han (slave market),
484–5, *485*

Süleymaniye Mosque, 432, 437–8, 550

Sulla (Roman general), 63

Sultan Ahmed Mosque *see* Blue
Mosque

Sultanahmet, 66, 220, 228, 577

Sulukule, 429

Surat Castle, India, 456

Sürre caravans, 409–410, *410*, 570

Susa, 31, 645*n*7

Sutton Hoo ship burial site, 293–6,
295, 341

Suyuti, Jalal al-Din al-, 441–2

Svyatoslav I, Grand Prince of Kiev,
312

Sybilline oracles, 96

Sykai, 211; *see also* Galata

Sykes–Picot Agreement, 574–5, *575*

Sylvester I, Pope, 123, 336

Symeon I, King of Bulgaria, 620, 635,
636

Symeon the Sanctified (eunuch), 173

Symeon the Stylite, St, 168–9, *170*,
655*n*5, 662*n*2

synagogues, 24, 239–40, 241, 284,
426, 427

syphilis, 495, 498

Syracuse, xxiii, 285

Syrian Civil War (2011–), 69, 168,
214, 521

Szigetvár, Battle of (1566), 441

Tabriz, 457

Tacitus, 26, 27, 62–3, 365

T'ai-tsung, Emperor of China, 265,
271–2

Taj Mahal, 456

Taksim Square, 3, 498, 551, 577; riots
(2013), 6, 131, 216, 219, 527, 599,
670*n*4, 696*n*3

Talaat Pasha, 560–61, 591

talismanic shirts (Islamic), 410–411

Tamar, Queen of Georgia, 362

Tamerlane, 384, 456, 457

tanzimat reforms (1839), 526–8, 535–6,
544, 549–50, 631

Tarabya (Therapeia), 23, 529, 540

Taşkızak dockyards, 553, *554*

Tatars, 541

Tauresium, 205

Tauris, 103; *see also* Crimea

Taygetus, Mount, 394

Taylor, Elizabeth, 435

Tbilisi, 362, 536, 591

Telhisi Mustafa Efendi, 504

Ten Thousand (Greek mercenaries),
46–7, 323

Tenedos, 52, 211, 293, 564

Teotihuacán, Mexico, 253

Teresa, Mother, 205

Terliktosglou, Taki, 697*n*10

Tertullian, 660*n*8

Tetrarchy (Roman Empire), 69–70,
77–9, 653*n*2; ending of, 104, 107,
609

Tetrastoon (Byzantium), 109–110, 115;
see also Augusteion

textiles, Ottoman *see* carpets and
textiles

Thackeray, William Makepeace, 488

Thassos, 50, 60

Thawr (mountain), 281

Theagenes of Megara, 29

theatres: Roman era, 66; Byzantine, 213, 221, 230–33; Ottoman, 555

Thebes, 122, 166, 676n6, 697n9

Themistius, *Orations*, 145, 146, 147, 227

Themistocles, 34, 643n6

Theodora, Roman Empress, 101

Theodora, Byzantine Empress (wife of Justinian I), 206–215, *207*, 219–20, 234, 235–6, 251, 254, 463, 532, 669n16

Theodora, Byzantine Empress (wife of Theophilos), 303, 619

Theodora, Byzantine Empress (wife of Constantine IX), 621, 622

Theodora Kantakouzene (wife of Orhan Gazi), 380

Theodore (Byzantine general), 283

Theodore I Laskaris, Emperor of Nicaea, 624–5

Theodore II Laskaris, Emperor of Nicaea, 625

Theodore, St, 276

Theodore Grammaticus, 284–5

Theodore Komnenos Doukas, Despot of Epirus, 625

Theodore Svetoslav, Tsar of Bulgaria, 626

Theodore of Tarsus, Archbishop of Canterbury, 297

Theodoret, *History of the Monks of Syria*, 168

Theodoric the Great, King of the Ostrogoths, 144, 613

Theodosia of Constantinople, St, 300

Theodosios I, Byzantine Emperor, 145, 146–53, 165, 239, 611

Theodosios II, Byzantine Emperor, 147, 165, 183–5, 188–9, 244, 611

Theodosios III, Byzantine Emperor, 617

Theophilos, Byzantine Emperor, 304, 308, 319, 619

Theopompus of Chios, 49

Thera (Santorini), volcanic eruptions, 21, 299–300

Therapia (Tarabya), 23, 529, 540

Thermopylae, 178; Battle of (480 BC), 33–4, 35

Theseus (mythological figure), 61

Thessaloniki (Salonica), 57, 101, 173, 385, 427, 556, 576–7, 593; Arch of Galerius and Rotunda, 99–100, 101, 121, 649n6; Egnatian Way excavations, 128–9; Gothic garrison, 151–2; St Demetrios' Church, 100, 354; White Tower, 525

Thessaloniki, Massacre of (390), 151–2, 178

Thessaloniki, Sack of (1185), 353–4, 356, 385

Thetis (mythological figure), 304

Thjodolf (Norwegian skald), 324

Thomas Becket, St, 697n9

Thomas Palaiologos, Despot of Morea, 394

Thomas the Slav, 619

Thrace and Thracians, 20, 27, 29, 52, 55, 178; pottery, 20, *21*

Thrasyllos, 44

Three Pashas, 560–61, 591, 632

Thucydides, 36, 644n10

Thyateira, 72

Tiberios II Constantinos, Byzantine Emperor, 614

Ticinum (Pavia), 100

Tigrit, Iraq, 686n11

Timothy, St, 119

tin production, 292–3
Tinos, 200
Tintagel, Cornwall, excavations, 291–2, 293
Tiridates III, King of Armenia, 108
Tissaphernes, 42
Titus, Roman Emperor, 250
To Hieron (shrine), 32, 52–3, 384, 386
tobacco, 583, 629
Tobias, Bishop of Rochester, 296
Toleration, Edicts of (311, 313), 99, 100
Tolkien, J.R.R., *The Lord of the Rings*, xxv
Tolstoy, Leo, 490
Topkapı Palace, 20, 398–400, *401*, 413, 438, 461, 473, 485, 501–2, 526, 544; grounds and gardens, 114, 403, 501, 506; *see also* Enderun
Torcello, 359
Trabzon *see* Trebizond
Trajan, Roman Emperor, 63, 71, 652*n*6
Trans-Caspian Railway, 550
Trebizond (Trabzon), 362, 393, 394, 395, 408, 484, 569
Tribonian (jurist), 218, 236–7, 253
Trier, Germany, 70, 84–5, 126, 139
Tripoli, xxii, 560
Trojan War, 27, 112, 115, 163, 211, 244, 245, 541
troubadours, 342, 349, 392
Troy, 22, 24, 73, 104–5, 112, 203, 549; fall of, 163, 269, 392
True Cross, relics of, 114–15, 124–5, 276, 277, 317, 318, 691*n*6
tsunamis, 252, 674*n*11
tuberculosis, 487, 498
tulips, 411, 476, 499–500, *501*, 502
Tulln-on-Danube, Austria, 474–5
tuna fish, 27, 39
tunnels, sub-Bosphoran, 3, 17, 148, 602, 675*n*11

Turfan oasis, China, 270
Turhan Hatice Sultan, 420
Turin, 95
Turkey, Republic of, 585–600
Turkish delight (confectionery), 520, 529
Turkish Hearth (institute), 557
Turks: origins and early expansion, 272; early relations with Constantinople, 142, 272, 277; slaves, 309; expansion into Byzantine Empire, 342–4; besiege Constantinople (1090), 346–7, 688*n*2; and First Crusade, 348, 349; *see also* Ottomans; Pechenegs; Seljuk Turks
Turks (London boat-building family), 443–4
Tursun Bey, *History of Mehmet the Conqueror*, 407, 416
Turtushi, al-, 688*n*9
Tuthmosis III, Pharaoh, 147, 163
Twain, Mark, 708*n*3
Tyche (goddess), 112, 113, 114, 158
Typos Edict (648), 615
Tyre, 283
Tzetzes, John, 355

Ugarit, 642*n*5
Uldin, King of the Huns, 179–80
Ulfilas, Bishop, 144
Um er-Rasas, Jordan, 165
'Umr ibn al-Khattab (caliph), 283, 284
underground railway, 549
'Unfortunate Incident' (1826), 525, 527
United Nations: Convention on the Law of the Sea, 552; World Humanitarian Summit, 593
Universal Postal Union, 632
universities, 188, 417, 631, 636
Uppsala, Sweden, 144, 458

Urartu, Kingdom of, 342
Urban (Hungarian engineer), 385, 388
Urban II, Pope, 347, 348, 623
Urquhart, David, 709n9
Üsküdar, 32, 62, 102–3, 409, 420, 427, 457; see also Chrysopolis; Scutari
Uthina, 185

vakif (religious endowment), 419–20
Vale of York Viking hoard, 307
Valens, Byzantine Emperor, 139, 143, 144–5, 610, 611
Valentinian I, Western Roman Emperor, 139, 145, 610
Valentinian II, Western Roman Emperor, 610
Valentinian III, Western Roman Emperor, 612
Valerian, Roman Emperor, 69, 77
Vandals, 143, 178, 181–6, 189, 214, 248–50
Varanasi, 455
Varangian Guard, 314, 322–6, 325, 340, 341, 342, 519
Varna, Battle of (1444), 385
Venetians in Constantinople, 354, 366, 379–80, 462, 465; bailo, 458, 459
Venice, Republic of, 355, 358–9, 363–4, 385, 446; Fourth Crusade and siege of 1204, 290, 324, 359–62, 365; slave trade, 309, 482, 483
Venice (buildings and landmarks): Chios Horses, St Mark's, 164–5, 361, 519; Lion of Venice, St Mark's, 365; Piraeus Lion, Arsenale, 313, 314, 325; Santa Maria Assunta, Torcello, 359
Venier, Nicolò, Lord of Paros, 462
Venizelos, Eleutherios, 577
Verona, 95

Vespasian, Roman Emperor, 64, 608
Vestal Virgins, 151
Via Egnatia see Egnatian Way
Victoria, Queen, 539, 542, 547, 587
Vienna, 435, 440, 474–5; Siege of (1683), 473, 475–80, 502
Vienne, France, 85
Vikings, 305, 306–314, 324; see also Varangian Guard
Villehardouin, Geoffrey de, 'The Conquest of Constantinople', xiii, 358
Virgil, 163, 245; Eclogues, 81; Georgics, 63
Visigoths, 143, 178–81
Vitalian (Byzantine general), 248
Vladimir the Great, Grand Prince of Kiev, 312–14, 323, 537
Vladimir, Prince of Novgorod, 324
Vlanga, 423, 426
volcanic eruptions, 21, 299–300

Wagner, Moritz, Travels in Persia, 482
Wallachia, 459, 533
walls, city: Byzantium, 36, 38, 57, 64, 65, 105; Constantinople, xxiv, 110, 113, 184, 185, 385; Istanbul, 439
Walsh, Robert, Narrative of a Residence at Constantinople, 468
Wangenheim, Baron Hans von, 569
waqf (religious endowment), 419–20
Ward Price, George, 571–2, 573
water supplies, 64, 139–40, 147–8, 211, 225, 417, 639n4
Webbe, Edward, 418
Weber, Max, 524
Weymouth, Dorset, 309
Whitby, Synod of (664), 297
white slave trade, 309, 481, 482–7, 488, 536, 544–5, 556, 708n9
Whittemore, Thomas, 582
Wilhelm II, German Kaiser, 708n9

William I the Conqueror, King of
England, 324, 692n3
William II, King of Sicily, 624
William of Malmesbury, *De Gesta
Regum Anglorum*, 325
Windsor, Edward, Duke of, 590
Windsor, Wallis, Duchess of, 590
wine, 49–50, 519, 556
Wolf, Hieronymus, xxviii
Woolf, Leonard, 590–91
Wylde, William Henry, 544–5

xenia (concept of hospitality), 4, 73,
361
Xenophon, 41, 43, 44; Ten Thousand,
46–7
Xeropholos, 124
Xerxes I, King of Persia, 30, 33–4, 38,
104, 173, 323, 638n2, 644n10
Xian, China, 277; Nestorian stele,
271, *271*
Xinjiang, China, 270

Yahya Kemal Beyatlı, 601
Yalova, 57, 124, 212
Yang-ti, Emperor of China, 265
Yarımburgaz Cave, 16, 584
Yarmuk, Battle of (636), xxii, 274,
282–3
Yaroslav, Grand Prince of Kiev, 324
Yathrib *see* Medina
Yavuz Sultan Selim (cruiser), *562*
Yazid I, Umayyad Caliph, xxv,
x640n9
Yeats, W.B., 'Byzantium', 1–2, 26,
389, 592
Yedikule Fortress, 388, 439, 471, 472,
473, 535
Yeni Mosque, 420, 426

Yenikapı archaeological excavations,
15–17, 66, 113, 148, 252, 463
Yenişehir, 378
Yeraltı Mosque, 442
Yiannitsa (Giannitsa), 383, 583
Yıldız Palace, 555, 556, 557, 581
Yolanda of Flanders, Latin Empress,
625
York (Eboracum), 80, 83–4, 85
Yoros Tepesi, 53, 384
Young Turks movement, 556–7,
560–61, 576, 632
Yugoslav wars (1990s), 384, 712n3
Yusuf, Mimar, 456

Zaganos Pasha, 391
Zane, Matteo, 441
Zara, Dalmatia, 359
Zealand, Denmark, 310, 324
Zeno, Byzantine Emperor, 189, 612,
613
Zenobia, Queen of Palmyra, 69
Zeus (god), 19, 32, 116–17, 137, 163,
165, 208, 245
Zeus Marna (god), 155
Zeuxippos (mythological figure), 52
Zeuxippos, Baths of, 65, 109, 139, 165,
225, 647n12
Zoe, Byzantine Empress (daughter of
Constantine VIII), 316, 621, 622
Zoe Karbonopsina, Byzantine
Empress, 619
Zoodochos Pege, 200
zoos and animal collections, 66, 68,
428, 647n24
Zoroastrianism, 138, 648n8
Zosimus, *New History*, 107, 179,
647n27, 657n9, 661n2, 665n6
Zurnacı, Faris, 42